Media Effects
Advances in Theory and Research

Edited by
Jennings Bryant
Dolf Zillmann
University of Alabama

LEA LAWRENCE ERLBAUM ASSOCIATES, PUBLISHERS
1994   Hillsdale, New Jersey   Hove, UK

Lawrence Erlbaum Associates, Inc., Publishers
365 Broadway
Hillsdale, New Jersey 07642

Library of Congress Cataloging-in-Publication Data

Media effects : advances in theory and research / edited by Jennings
  Bryant, Dolf Zillmann.
       p.   cm.
    Includes bibliographical references and index.
    ISBN 0-8058-0917-1 (cloth : alk. paper). — ISBN 0-8058-0918-X
(pbk. : alk. paper)
    1. Mass media—United States—Psychological aspects. 2. Mass
media—Social aspects—United States. 3. Mass media—Political
aspects—United States. 4. Mass media—United States—Influence.
I. Bryant, Jennings. II. Zillmann, Dolf.
HN90.M3M415   1993
302.23—dc20   93-8614
                                                   CIP

Books published by Lawrence Erlbaum Associates are printed on acid-free paper, and their
bindings are chosen for strength and durability.

Printed in the United States of America
10 9 8 7 6 5 4 3 2

Contents

Preface

The intellectual ancestor of this volume is *Perspectives on Media Effects*, which we were privileged to edit. Published in 1986 and reprinted several times, *Perspectives* not only met our goal of serving as a reference volume for scholars interested in the topic, it also received unanticipated widespread adoption as a textbook for classes in media effects. Certainly we are most grateful for this unanticipated "bonus"; however, when a book begins to be used as a course text, subtle changes in ownership occur. The book evolves from being "ours" (the editors' and contributors') to being "theirs" (the teachers' and students').

To a certain extent, that is what happened with *Perspectives on Media Effects*. We first noticed this a couple of years ago, when instructors began to engage us in conversations at conferences and ask, "Don't you think *we* should update the *Perspectives* book soon?" Or one of us would get a letter asking, "When is the new edition of *Perspectives on Media Effects* coming out? My students and I are going to need a new edition soon." Moreover, several correspondents felt that they had enough vested interest in the volume to suggest "improvements" like, "When you redo the media effects book, I hope you include a chapter on advertising effects" (or on political communication effects, or on the impact of public communication campaigns), or "When you come out with a new edition of *Media Effects*, I'd hope you won't include that chapter on X, Y, or Z."

We listened. In preparing this new volume on media effects, we carefully reviewed the correspondence file on *Perspectives on Media Effects*, reviewed our notes from conference conversations, re-read several published reviews of the volume, and systematically surveyed a sample of adopters of the previous volume—both those who had used the book as a text for their classes and those who had relied on *Perspectives* primarily for their own intellectual edification and scholarship.

This "new and improved" volume on media effects retains six "tried and true" chapters from *Perspectives*, all extensively updated and revised by the original authors, some with new collaborators. We also retained three other topics from *Perspectives on Media Effects* authored by scholars whose work is mainstream in the area. And we added, both by popular demand and because we personally see the field moving in new directions, seven new topics, with each chapter written by leading "lights" in that research arena.

What resulted is a book so dramatically different from *Perspectives on Media Effects* that we thought it would be dishonest to call this a "Second Edition." Nonetheless, *Media Effects: Advances in Theory and Research*, was built on the foundation of the earlier volume.

In the nearly 8 years since our last edited media effects volume was published, research into the social and psychological impacts of mediated communication has changed substantially. Nowadays, a key descriptor for media effects research appears to be *maturity*. Programmatic research on several critical topics in media effects abounds and is represented at almost every annual communication conference as well as in the pages of each new issue of our major communication journals. Innovative new research initiatives have emerged and matured in the interim as well. Moreover, the media effects area now features several meta-analyses, many of which seem to be stabilizing as well as shedding new light on old topics.

Despite increasing maturity, no one who seriously ponders the media effects environment could possibly see things as staid or calm. New research methods, fresh theories, and eager new researchers staking out new territory constantly foster changes from within. Not all change is internally generated, however. Media effects research regularly is re-shaped by critics from the outside, whose provocative critiques cause us to re-think our assumptions, re-examine our findings, and re-cast our theories. No one ever said that being "an adult" would be easy. Even mature areas of inquiry have their "passages."

The contributors to the present volume represent some of the finest scholars in the media effects tradition. They have weathered the private storms from within and the public storms from the outside and have emerged as respected scholars and valued educators in the media effects tradition. Each truly has made, in the words of our subtitle: *Advances in Theory and Research*.

The first chapter of *Media Effects* sees the return of Maxwell McCombs for a retrospective on "News Influence on Our Pictures of the World." The agenda-setting and agenda-building research presented in this chapter spans three decades. Nonetheless, fresh research in this area graces many of the most recent volumes of our journals, attesting to the topic's importance and "staying power."

George Gerbner, Larry Gross, Michael Morgan, and NancySignorielli provide a major update to cultivation research in "Growing Up with Television: The Cultivation Perspective." In *Perspectives on Media Effects*, cultivation research was positioned as "a complement to traditional approaches to media effects research." The present chapter offers a bolder, more expansive view of the role of cultivation theory in explaining the place of television in our lives.

In "A Priming Effect Analysis of Media Influences," Eunkyung Jo and Leonard Berkowitz offer "An Update" to *Perspectives'* influential treatment of priming. The earlier version of this chapter caused many scholars to radically re-think the meaning of their media effects research. The present chapter further hones the theoretical and empirical dimensions of this important re-interpretation of media influences.

Although long a stalwart to media effects research, Albert Bandura is a newcomer to this series. His "Social Cognitive Theory of Mass Communication" thoughtfully incorporates the cognitive and meta-cognitive turns in communication research that have so influenced our thinking of late. Those whose images of "observational learning" or "social learning" have not been updated since the 1960s and 1970s will be surprised to see just how far research in this area has come.

Clearly one of the communication research topics that received the most radical re-structuring during the past decade is attitude change. Two major contributors to this revolution, Richard Petty and Joseph Priester, explain and interpret the most influential new view of attitude change in "Mass Media Attitude Change: Implications of the Elaboration Likelihood Model of Persuasion."

Another imortant new contribution to this volume is Jack McLeod, Gerald Kosicki, and Douglas McLeod's in-depth treatment of political communication. Their chapter title is indicative of the scope of their analysis, as they explore "The Expanding Boundaries of Political Communication Effects."

The topic of media violence has become "hot" once again. Its history is so rich and its theoretical lineage so complex and convoluted that a major treatment is obligatory. Barrie Gunter ably meets these challenges in "The Question of Media Violence."

A relatively new but extremely important research area that in certain ways offers a different "spin" on media violence research is that of "Fright Reactions to Mass Media." This chapter is authored by the fright reaction area's senior investigator, Joanne Cantor.

Continuing to create much heat and occasional light is the issue of the effects of sexually oriented media fare. Richard Harris guides readers through these troubled waters in "Impact of Sexually Explicit Media."

Bradley Greenberg and Jeffrey Brand provide a major update to the issue of gender and race stereotyping, both in terms of portrayals in media and their resultant effects. Their "Minorities and the Mass Media: 1970s to 1990s" is as accessible as it is instructive.

One major omission to *Perspective on Media Effects* was a chapter on advertising impact. Quite frankly, we had thought that it would be impossible to synthesize this massive research tradition in a single chapter. David Stewart and Scott Ward proved us wrong, however, and provide both manageability and integrity to their chapter, "Media Effects on Advertising."

Another arena in which *Perspectives* was remiss was in not chronicling research on the effects of communication and information campaigns. Ronald Rice and Charles Atkin rectify that previous oversight in "Principles of Successful Public Communication Campaigns."

One genre of communication campaign research that has been particularly prominent during the past decade is that of public health campaigns. In "Effects of Media on Personal and Public Health," Jane Brown and Kim Walsh-Childers consider more than cases in which health educators and communication specialists have combined their areas of expertise to affect health-related behaviors; they also examine unintended, potentially harmful effects of media on health.

Often considered a complement to media effects is uses-and-gratifications research. Like media effects research, uses and gratifications has come of age during recent years. Alan Rubin updates his earlier watershed chapter and integrates these research traditions in "Media Uses and Effects: A Uses-and-Gratifications Perspective."

Another update is provided by the editors, who re-examine "Entertainment as Media Effect." This, too, is an area that has matured substantially during the most recent era and has now moved from the "fringes" into the mainstream of communication research.

Many of the contributors to *Media Effects: Advances in Theory and Research* have discussed several significant changes brought to their research traditions by rapid advances in media technologies. Frederick

Williams, Sharon Strover, and August Grant focus directly on this "hot" topic in conceptualizing and reviewing research on "Social Impacts of New Media Technologies."

We are most grateful to our contributors for making this volume possible, and we are forever in debt to our spouses for their tolerance of our latest foray into editing a volume on media effects. Nearly a decade ago we dedicated *Perspectives on Media Effects* to our mutual best friends, Jennings Bryant, Sr., and Elvira Bryant. Just as the study of media effects has matured, so too have the bonds of friendship and affection we have for these two special people. We dedicate *Media Effects: Advances in Theory and Research* to our two best friends.

—*Jennings Bryant*
—*Dolf Zillmann*

1

News Influence on Our Pictures of the World

MAXWELL McCOMBS
University of Texas at Austin

News impacts many facets of our daily lives! How we dress for work, sometimes the route we take to work, what we plan to do this weekend, our generel feelings of well-being or insecurity, the focus of our attention toward the world beyond immediate experience, and our concerns about the issues of the day all are influenced by the daily news.

Occasionally, our total behavior is instantly and completely dictated by the news. Everyone old enough to remember at all remembers where they first heard the news of John F. Kennedy's assassination and how so much of the next 3 or 4 days was spent absorbing and discussing the news. Even on less traumatic occasions, millions of Americans follow the national political conventions, watch the presidential candidates debate, or follow the tabulation and projection of the nation's vote on election night. And daily, millions of citizens dutifully glean their knowledge of politics and public affairs from the pages of their local newspaper.

For the vast majority of Americans, this use of the mass media, coupled with brief visits to the voting booth on election day, represents their total participation in politics. This is one of the reasons why the most enduring and sustained line of scholarly research on mass communication traces the influence of the news media on voter behavior. Beginning with the classic study of Erie County, Ohio, by Columbia

1

University sociologists Lazarsfeld, Berelson, and Gaudet (1944) during the 1940 U.S. presidential election, there has been an ever-widening array of studies exploring the impact of news media on voter behavior. But as sociologists Lang and Lang (1959) noted, the influence of the news media extends far beyond the political campaigns:

> All news that bears on political activity and beliefs—and not only campaign speeches and campaign propaganda—is somehow relevant to the vote. Not only during the campaign, *but also in the periods between*, the mass media provide perspectives, shape images of candidates and parties, help highlight issues around which a campaign will develop, and define the unique atmosphere and areas of sensitivity which mark any particular campaign. (p. 226)

Over a half century ago, Lippmann (1922) also noted this role of the news media in defining our world, not just the world of politics during and between elections, but almost all of our world beyond immediate personal and family concerns. The issues, personalities, and situations toward which we hold feelings of endorsement or rejection, those points of attention about which pollsters seek the public pulse, are things about which we depend on the media to inform us.

Lippmann made an important distinction between the *environment* (i.e., the world that is really out there) and the *pseudo-environment* (i.e., our private perceptions of that world.) Recall that the opening chapter of his book, *Public Opinion,* is entitled "The World Outside and the Pictures in Our Heads." And, as Lippmann eloquently argued, it is the news media that sketch so many of those pictures in our heads. This view of the impact of news was congruent with both scholarly and popular assessment in Lippmann's day of the power of mass communication, views that grew out of experiences with mass communication and propaganda during World War I. But subsequent scholarly investigations, such as the Erie County study, led scholars down another path in later decades.

Focused squarely on the ability of the news media and mass communication to persuade and change voters' attitudes, early empirical studies of mass communication instead discovered the strength of the individual, secure in his or her personal values and social setting and inured from change. The result was the law of minimal consequences, a scientific statement of a limited-effects model for mass communication. Although this law may have been the proper palliative for the sometimes near-hysterical ascription of super persuasive powers to mass communication, such a constrained view of mass communication overlooks many effects that are plausibly ascribed to the mass media, especially to the news media.

After all, it is not the goal of professional journalists to persuade anybody about anything. The canons of objectivity, which have dominated professional journalistic practice and thought for generations, explicitly disavow any effort at persuasion. This is not to say that the news stories of the day are not exactly that, news *stories*. They are indeed! And like all stories, they structure experience for us, filtering out many of the complexities of the environment and offering a polished, perhaps even literary, version in which a few objects and selected attributes are highlighted. Many scholars have shifted their attention to the audience's experience with these stories.

CHANGING PERSPECTIVES

Explorations of audience attention and awareness signal a shift to research on the cognitive, long-term implications of daily journalism, research that begins to test empirically the ideas put forward by Lippmann in the 1920s. Rather than addressing mass communication from the perspective of a model of limited effects, research in the 1960s began to consider a variety of limited models of effects.

As the history of science repeatedly demonstrates, just changing the perspective—or dominant paradigm, as Kuhn (1970) termed it—changes the picture sketched by the empirical evidence. Consider, for example, the large body of evidence on knowledge of public affairs. From the perspective of a model of limited effects, Hyman and Sheatsley's (1947) portrait of low levels of knowledge about public affairs and the existence of a sizable group of "chronic know-nothings" is hardly surprising.

But shifting the perspective to limited models of media effects focuses attention on those situations in which the transfer of functional information of some sort from the mass media to individuals in the audience does take place. Part of the scientific puzzle, of course, is to identify exactly what is transferred—the denotative message and its "facts," the cultural and individual connotations associated with those facts and the style of their presentation, or some other attribute of the message.

Part of this new look at mass communication has been the discovery that the audience not only learns some facts from exposure to the news media, but that it also learns about the importance of topics in the news from the emphasis placed on them by the news media. Considerable evidence has accumulated that journalists play a key role in shaping our pictures of the world as they go about their daily task of selecting and reporting the news.

Here may lie the most important effect of the mass media: their ability to structure and organize our world for us. As Cohen (1963) remarked, the press may not be very successful in telling us what to think, but it is stunningly successful in telling us what to think about! This ability of the mass media to structure audience cognitions and to effect change among existing cognitions has been labeled the agenda-setting function of mass communication.

AGENDA-SETTING ROLE OF NEWS

Initially studied in the traditional context of mass communication and voter behavior, the concept of agenda setting took its metaphorical name from the idea that the mass media have the ability to transfer the salience of items on their news agendas to the public agenda. Through their routine structuring of social and political reality, the news media influence the agenda of public issues around which political campaigns and voter decisions are organized.

Each day journalists deal with the news in several important ways. First, they decide which news to cover and report and which to ignore. Next, all these available reports must be assessed. On the typical daily newspaper, over 75% of the potential news of the day is rejected out of hand and never transmitted to the audience. There is not enough space in the newspapers to print everything that is available. Choices must be made. These are the first steps in the gatekeeping routine. But the items that pass through the gate do not receive equal treatment when presented to the audience. Some are used at length and prominently displayed. Others receive only brief attention. Newspapers, for example, clearly state the journalistic salience of an item through its page placement, headline, and length.

Agenda setting asserts that audiences acquire these saliences from the news media, incorporating similar sets of weights into their own agendas. Even though the communication of these saliences is an incidental and inevitable byproduct of journalistic practice and tradition, these saliences are one of the attributes of the messages transmitted to the audience. Agenda setting singles out the transmission of these saliences as one of the most important aspects of mass communication. Not only do the news media largely determine our awareness of the world at large, supplying the major elements for our pictures of the world, they also influence the prominence of those elements in the picture!

The basic idea of an agenda-setting role of the news media can be traced at least as far back as Lippmann, and a variety of empirical evidence about mass communication influence on voting can be interpreted—post hoc, of course—in agenda-setting terms. But the concept of an agenda-setting role for the news media was put to direct empirical test in the 1968 presidential election when McCombs and Shaw (1972) simultaneously collected data on the agenda of the news media and the agenda of the public. Reasoning that any impact of the news media was most likely to be measurable among undecided voters, their study surveyed undecided voters in Chapel Hill, North Carolina, and content analyzed the local and national news media, both print and broadcasting, regularly used by these voters. The high degree of correspondence between these two agendas of political and social issues established a central link in what has become a substantial chain of evidence for an agenda-setting role of the press.

This early study also firmly established the viability of the concept of agenda setting, a limited model of media effects, vis-à-vis the concept of selective perception, a key explanatory element in the then-prevailing model of limited effects. Although still undecided about their presidential ballot, some of these Chapel Hill voters were leaning toward the Republican or Democratic candidate. Using this preference, comparisons were made between these voters' agendas and two different press agendas (viz., the total agenda of issues reported in the news *or* only the agenda of issues attributed to the preferred party and its candidates). If the correlation between voters' agenda and the total news agenda is the highest, this is evidence of agenda setting. If the correlation with the preferred party's agenda is higher, there is evidence of selective perception. Out of 24 comparisons, 18 favored an agenda-setting interpretation.

Correlations alone do not establish the causal assertion that the news media influence the public agenda. These correlations might even be spurious, an artifact resulting from a common source for both the news and public agendas. However, the rebuttal to this argument as well as new evidence buttressing the concept of an agenda-setting role for the news media was reported by Funkhouser (1973) from an intensive study of public opinion trends in the 1960s. His creative secondary analysis brought together three key elements: (a) public opinion, assessed by the Gallup Poll's question about the most important problem facing the nation; (b) news coverage, determined by a content analysis of *Time*, *Newsweek*, and *U.S. News and World Report*; and (c) statistical indicators of "reality" for these key concerns of the 1960s. Replicating the findings from the Chapel Hill voter study, Funkhouser found substantial correspondence between public opinion and news coverage. But most important, he found little correspondence between either of these and his statistical indicators of reality. For example, press coverage and public concern about Vietnam, campus unrest, and urban riots during the 1960s peaked considerably before the actual trends measured by such indicators as the number of troops committed to Vietnam, number of campus demonstrations, and number of civil disturbances.

More recently, the agenda-setting power of the news media has been established experimentally in the laboratory. In a series of controlled experiments conducted by Iyengar and Kinder (1987), participants viewed television news programs that had been edited to highlight certain issues, such as national defense or pollution of the environment. When the participants' ratings of the importance of these experimentally manipulated issues were compared to the salience for them of other issues of the day, clear agenda-setting effects emerged. The issues emphasized in the experimental versions of the newscasts were perceived as more important. In some experiments, exposure to a single television news program created agenda-setting effects. Usually, agenda-setting effects were found only after viewing a number of newscasts.

In what may be the ultimate field study of the agenda-setting influence of the news media, Brosius and Kepplinger (1990) replicated the design of the original McCombs and Shaw study by comparing a content analysis of the major West German television news programs for an entire year with weekly public opinion polls on the issues considered most important by West Germans. Strong agenda-setting effects were found for five issues: energy, East–West relations, defense, the environment, and European Community politics. For other issues, news coverage trailed public opinion, or there simply was no correlation between the two. This pattern of findings makes the important point that the news media are not a monolithic "Big Brother" totally dictating public attention.

Agenda setting is a theory of limited media effects. One goal of contemporary research is to identify the conditions under which this agenda-setting influence of the news media does and does not occur. But the existence of an agenda-setting phenomenon is clear. Findings generated by two kinds of fieldwork methodologies, content analysis and survey research, provide evidence of its external validity, and experiments provide evidence of its internal validity. Additionally, the fact that much of this recent evidence, for example, the Iyengar and Kinder experiments and the Brosius and Kepplinger fieldwork, is based on television news further strengthens support for the basic hypothesis because other evidence in the literature (e.g., Shaw & McCombs, 1977) suggests that television news has weaker agenda-setting effects than newspapers.

Other major support for the basic idea of agenda-setting is found in Mackuen's (1981) comparison of national public opinion on eight issues from 1960 to 1977 with coverage in *Time, Newsweek,* and *U.S. News & World Report*; Smith's (1987) examination of 19 local issues and *Louisville*

Times coverage over a period of 8 years; and Eaton's (1989) comparison of national concern about 11 major issues between 1983 and 1986 with news coverage of these issues on network television, in news magazines, and five major newspapers.

CONTINGENT CONDITIONS

Because the agenda-setting perspective is a model of limited media effects—unlike earlier views of powerful mass communication effects—Shaw and McCombs (1977) turned their attention in 1972 to simultaneous examination of the basic hypothesis and the contingent conditions that limited that hypothesis. Unlike the small-scale Chapel Hill study, which sought agenda-setting effects among undecided voters during the 1968 presidential election, their study during the next presidential election was a three-wave longitudinal study among the general population of voters in Charlotte, North Carolina. Its search for the contingent conditions limiting agenda setting established a theoretical goal that has prompted researchers to venture in many directions. Some scholars sought to identify the personal characteristics of voters or the content characteristics of news stories that limited or enhanced their influence (Winter, 1981). But the most fruitful examinations have examined not isolated properties of people, issues, or news content, but rather the interaction of issues and individual situations. Whereas broad descriptors, such as the income or level of education for an individual or the emotional content of an issue, are surrogates for this interaction, more explicit conceptualizations of this interaction have been the most valuable. Two examples are considered here in some detail.

Issues can be arrayed along a continuum ranging from obtrusive to unobtrusive. As the term implies, some issues literally obtrude in our daily lives. In 1990, the rapidly rising price of gasoline following Iraq's invasion of Kuwait was such an obtrusive issue. No one depended on television or newspapers to inform them about the existence of this inflation. Daily experience put this issue in conversations and on the national agenda. In contrast, our knowledge of other issues, as Lippmann pointed out in *Public Opinion*, is virtually dependent on the news media. What most Americans knew about the situation in the Middle East and U.S. foreign and military policy came entirely from the news media.

For a great many issues there is considerable similarity in where they fall on the obtrusive/unobtrusive continuum for most Americans. This is true for the two examples just presented, inflated gasoline prices and the Middle East crisis. But there are issues where considerable variation exists among individuals. Unemployment is a good example. For tenured college professors and even for most college students, employment is an unobtrusive issue. The salience of unemployment in our minds is essentially the product of our exposure to the issue in the news media (Shaw & Slater, 1988). But for many industrial workers in declining or cyclical industries, such as steel and automobiles, unemployment is a highly obtrusive issue. Even if it has not been experienced firsthand, these workers are aware of the trends in their industry and most likely have friends or family members who have been unemployed in recent years.

Broad brush portraits of the agenda-setting role of the media reveal strong effects for unobtrusive issues and no effects at all on obtrusive issues (Weaver, Graber, McCombs, & Eyal, 1981; Winter & Eyal, 1981; Zucker, 1978). More finely etched portraits, which require knowing where an issue falls on the continuum for each individual, show similar results (Blood, 1981).

The concept of need for orientation is the psychological equivalent of the physical axiom that nature abhors a vacuum. Based on the idea of cognitive mapping, this concept recognizes that individuals who are in an unfamiliar setting will strive to orient themselves. For the voter confronted with the issues of a political campaign, there are two important criteria defining his or her level of need for orientation: the individual's level of interest in the election and the degree of uncertainty in that individual's mind about what the important issues are. Voters characterized by high interest in the election and a high degree of uncertainty about the issues, that is, those voters with a high need for orientation, are open to considerable agenda-setting influence. These individuals are exposed to more news about the campaign and its issues and—in line with the basic agenda-setting hypothesis—have personal agendas that more closely reflect the agenda of the news media. In contrast, voters with a low need for orientation are exposed less to news of the political campaign and show less agreement with the agenda of issues advanced by the news media. For example, among Charlotte voters with a high need for orientation, the correlation between their agenda and the coverage of issues in the local newspapers was +.68 in October of 1972; among voters with a low need for orientation, the correlation was +.29 in October of 1972.

The concept of need for orientation provides a general psychological explanation for the agenda-setting process and subsumes a number of lower order variables and more limited explanations. For example, research findings based on the distinction between obtrusive and unobtrusive issues can be explained in the more general terms of need for orientation. In most cases, persons should have less uncertainty about obtrusive issues and, hence, a lower need for orientation. Of course, it might be counterargued that individuals sometimes have less interest in more distant, unobtrusive issues, thus lowering their need for orientation. In most cases, persons should have less uncertainty about obtrusive issues and hence, a lower need for orientation. But remember that the role of the news media as defined by its professional traditions and values is, at least in part, to stimulate our interest and involvement in such issues. In any event, the concept of need for orientation provides more specific descriptions and predictions than does the concept of obtrusive/unobtrusive issues.

SHAPING THE NEWS AGENDA

Initially, the focus in agenda setting was on the influence of the news agenda on the public agenda. For many persons, the term *agenda setting* is synonymous with the role of mass communication in shaping public opinion and public perceptions of what the most important issues of the day are. But in recent years there has been a broader look at the public opinion process. Early agenda-setting scholars asked who set the public agenda. The empirical answer was that to a considerable degree the news media set the public agenda. More recently, scholars have asked who sets the news agenda. The empirical answer to this question is not quite as parsimonious. In part, as common sense would dictate, the news agenda is set by external sources and events not under the control of journalists. But the news agenda also is set, in part, by the traditions, practices, and values of journalism as a profession. Whereas this newer facet of agenda setting may lack the parsimony of the original hypothesis, it has integrated a substantial sociology of news literature with the agenda-setting literature.

Looking first at external influences on the news agenda, the president of the United States is the nation's number one news maker. Even a president's dog can become better known than most government officials. Who are Feller, Checkers, and Millie? Many people can identify each of these dogs with a president. Can you name a secretary of state for each of those same presidents? Presidents enjoy tremendous access to the mass media. Teddy Roosevelt essentially invented the presidential press conference as the operational definition of the presidency's bully pulpit. Woodrow Wilson turned a dull report mandated by the Constitution, the State of the Union report, into a major public event (Juergens, 1981). Does this central role played by the president on the media stage allow the president to be the nation's number one agenda-setter?

Like so many questions about contemporary history, the answer is "Yes, sometimes" (Gilberg, Eyal, McCombs, & Nicholas, 1980; Wanta, Stephenson, Turk, & McCombs, 1989). The State of the Union address provides a particularly useful vantage point for observing the president's agenda-setting influence because it is the sole occasion when the president's agenda is laid out in a single document. Richard Nixon's 1970 State of the Union address did influence the subsequent coverage of NBC, *The New York Times,* and, ironically, the *Washington Post.* There also is weak evidence of similar effects following Ronald Reagan's 1982 State of the Union address. Furthermore, these correlations between the president's agenda and subsequent news coverage are not spurious relationships resulting from the influence of earlier news coverage on both the president and the press. But in contrast, comparisons of the president's agenda and news coverage reveal that the news media influenced both President Carter's 1978 State of the Union and Reagan's 1985 State of the Union address.

A broader look at the president's role as an agenda-setter is provided by Wanta's (1989) detailed examination of four recent administrations. Of course, as just noted, the news media can influence the president's agenda rather than the converse; or, the overall relationship between the president's agenda and the news agenda can be reciprocal. Across the administrations of Nixon, Ford, Carter, and Reagan, there are numerous examples of all three relationships. On balance, the relationships are reciprocal. Of course, the comparisons here are between the overall presidential agenda, eight or more issues, and the news coverage of this entire set of issues. The president may well prevail as the agenda-setter on individual issues. Wanta provided specific evidence, for example, that President Carter was an agenda-setter for the energy issue and President Reagan for foreign affairs during their administrations.

SOURCES OF NEWS

In any event, because the president is the nation's number one news maker, the media spend considerable energy, time, and money on this coverage. In contrast, much of the daily news report is prepared from materials not just provided, but initiated, by the public information officers and public relations staffs of government agencies, corporations, and interest groups. At the beginning of this century, the president read all his own mail, the Washington press corps literally could gather around his desk to find out what the entire federal establishment was up to, and Ivy Lee was just inventing public relations. In today's corporate and government world, public relations is a key component. Despite professional myths to the contrary, public relations also is necessary to today's news media. As Lippmann (1922) observed, all the reporters in the world could not keep an eye on all the events in the world because there are not that many reporters. Even the largest and best national newspapers with their huge staffs of reporters and editors, newspapers such as *The New York Times* and *Washington Post*, obtain over half their daily material from press releases, press conferences, and other routine channels created by government agencies, corporations, and interest groups. Only a small proportion of the daily news results from the initiative and innovation of the news organizations (Sigal, 1973).

But to contradict another myth, this one especially popular along one stretch of the political continuum, public relations pronouncements on behalf of the establishment do not control the news agenda. Judy Turk (1985, 1986) examined the success of public information officers in six Louisiana state government agencies in placing their press releases in the major newspapers of the state. Their batting average was about .500. What the readers of Louisiana's major dailies knew about their state government was not limited to what the government passed out in press releases nor to those issues emphasized in those press releases.

Because the daily news obviously is rooted in the events and trends of the day, it is hardly surprising that those who are major players in these events and those who can enhance access to many of these events have some impact on the news agenda. But news media are not mirrors that simply reflect the deeds of the president or the pronouncements of public information offices. Journalism is a long-established profession with its own entrenched traditions, practices, and values. These are the filters through which the day's happenings are filtered and refracted for presentation in the newspaper or on television. The news is not a reflection of the day; it is a set of stories constructed by journalists about the events of the day.

Like Moliere's gentleman who learned that he had been speaking prose all his life, it sometimes is difficult to assess a situation in which we are immersed as producers and consumers of the news. To better highlight the situation here in the United States, two studies based on European observations are cited as examples of the power that these journalistic traditions, practices, and values have on the daily set of news stories. The first example comes from Sweden, where political parties often have direct connections with, including outright owner- ship of, daily newspapers. But as journalism increasingly has become professionalized, there is little benefit to the political parties from these affiliations. Although one might regard a party newspaper as a captive mouthpiece for the party line, Asp (1983) found this hardly to be the case when he compared party agendas, as reflected in the acceptance speeches of party leaders, with the news coverage of the major campaign issues. Party leaders fared little better in their own newspaper's coverage than in the coverage afforded by the commercial newspapers and newspapers of other parties. The dominant filters on the political news of the day were journalistic values, not partisan values.

The strength of news values over partisan values also is reflected in *The Formation of Campaign Agendas,* a comparative study of American and British press coverage of national elections (Semetko, Blumler, Gurevitch, & Weaver, 1991). Whereas there obviously is variation among the behavior of each nation's news corps, the modal pattern among British journalists during the 1983 general election was to follow the lead of the parties. Television, especially, placed heavy emphasis on the substantive daily events of the campaign trail, reporting more of the material directly provided by the politicians in their morning press conferences, afternoon walkabouts, and evening rallies. The result is a substantial correlation between the party agendas and the agendas of the news media. In contrast, American journalists covering the 1984 U.S. presidential election followed the lead of the parties far less in determining the issue emphasis in their coverage. The correlations between the two agendas are very weak. In comparison to British journalists, U.S. journalists exercised considerably more professional discretion in the framing of the campaign agenda in the news. This discretionary power of the professional journalist seems to lie largely in the freedom to go beyond the issues and to report other aspects of the campaign, especially its strategic and tactical machinations.

Whereas this freedom is exercised more frequently by American journalists than by British journalists, one might ask just how well served the public is by this discretionary power. Numerous critics have decried the excessive reporting of campaign trail hoopla in recent U.S. elections (Buchanan, 1991). Be that as it may, both of these European examples underscore the strength of news values and ideology — whatever they may be — on the shaping of the daily news.

Detailed examination of how these values, traditions, and practices of journalists shape the news agenda has produced a vast library of books and articles over the past 25 years (e.g., Epstein, 1973; Gans, 1979; Golding & Elliot, 1979). This literature, collectively called the sociology of news, recently has been integrated by Shoemaker and Reese (1991) in *Mediating the Message: Theories of Influences on Mass Media Content.*

The strength of these internal professional influences on the shape of the news agenda is further revealed by the gatekeeping tradition in journalism research. Usually, such studies focused on the wire editors of daily newspapers and their decisions about which stories to select and which to reject for the daily news report. A reanalysis of the classic Mr. Gates studies by Don Shaw revealed substantial correlations between the agendas of the wire services and Mr. Gates (McCombs & Shaw, 1976). An early study of news selection patterns among Iowa dailies also revealed that the pattern of topics reported by those newspapers closely resembled the pattern of topics offered by the Associated Press even though each newspaper used only a tiny proportion of the available wire report (Gold & Simmons, 1965).

In another facet of gatekeeping, the substantial agenda-setting role of *The New York Times* is also well known. Going beyond the usual anecdotal evidence of this influence, Reese and Danielian (1989) documented the agenda-setting role of *The Times* for the drug issue during 1986. Once *The Times* had assigned a reporter full time to drugs and led off with a front page story on crack, other major media quickly followed suit. Extensive coverage of the drug issue began to appear in the *Washington Post* and *Los Angeles Times*. One Sunday in May of 1986, all three New York City newspapers had extensive articles on drugs. It also is particularly obvious, according to Reese and Danielian, that *The New York Times* set the agenda on this issue for the television networks in 1986.

In summary, the question of who sets the news agenda is best pursued through that venerable metaphor of peeling the onion. The core of the onion, the daily news report, is surrounded and shaped by several layers of influence. At the outer layer are the news makers and events, including the pseudo-events arranged for news coverage, that provide much of the grist for the daily news. But all of this is shaped in turn by the values, practices, and traditions of journalism as a profession. And these professional decisions are reaffirmed by the behavior of the news leaders, especially *The New York Times*, who on occasion can set the agenda as firmly as any president or dictator.

SUMMING UP

Fifty million or more persons read a newspaper each day of the week. About the same number watch the news on television each day. Many Americans do both. One significant result of the audience's experience with these news stories is that over time the public comes to perceive that the important issues of the day are those emphasized in the news. Grounded in ideas first put forward by Lippman in the 1920s, this phenomenon has come to be called the agenda-setting role of the news media. Contrasting this view with earlier expectations of massive media effects on attitudes and opinions, Cohen (1963) noted that the press may not be very successful in telling us what to think, but it is stunningly successful in telling us what to think about!

Initial empirical investigations of this agenda-setting influence of the news media were field studies employing survey research and content analysis to ascertain the degree of correspondence between the news agenda and the public agenda. This approach to observing the agenda-setting phenomenon may well have reached its apex in Brosius and Kepplinger's (1990) extensive investigation of agenda setting in West Germany, a study based on a year-long content analysis of television news and weekly public opinion polls indentifying the most important problem facing the country. Other tests of the basic hypothesis have taken agenda setting into the laboratory and verified this phenomenon experimentally (Iyengar & Kinder, 1987).

Almost simultaneously with the initial empirical tests of the agenda-setting hypothesis, scholars began to explore the contingent conditions for this phenomenon. No one contends that the news media influence the salience of all issues for all people. Whereas many different characteristics of people and many characteristics of the news have been identified as contingent conditions affecting the strength of the agenda-setting relationship, two conceptualizations of the interaction between issues and individual situations have proved especially valuable. These are the concepts of need for orientation and obtrusiveness/unobtrusiveness.

Need for orientation is based on the psychological assumption that individuals who are in an unfamiliar situation will be uncomfortable until they orient themselves. Elections, with their previously unknown or only vaguely known candidates or with their complex issues and the uncertainties of how to resolve them, frequently create situations where many voters feel a need for orientation. Under these circumstances they may turn to the news media for orientation and adopt its agenda. The agenda-setting influence of the news media increases with the degree of need for orientation among the audience. But this influence is largely limited to unobtrusive issues, those issues remote from personal ken. Some issues, such as inflation in general or the price of gasoline, obtrude into our daily lives. We experience them directly and do not depend on the news media for our knowledge of their significance. Both personal experience and a need for orientation are contingent conditions that provide important explanations for how the agenda-setting process works.

Consonant with the effects tradition in mass communication research, the early agenda-setting studies explored the impact of the news agenda on the public agenda. More recently, the news agenda has shifted from being an independent variable to a dependent variable. The central research question has changed from who sets the public agenda to who sets the news agenda. Answers to this new question are best presented in terms of that venerable metaphor, peeling the layers of an onion.

At the outer layer, of course, are those events and activities that make up the stuff of the daily news. But only a small proportion of the day's events and activities ever make the news, and even fewer are directly observed by journalists. The observations of news sources, especially those organized in the form of press conferences and press releases, are key elements in the construction of the news agenda each day. But even the most powerful of these news sources, the president of the United States, plays a very limited part in setting the news agenda. Journalists' professional values, traditions, and practices shape their judgments about the use of this material. The strength of these internal professional influences is underscored by the concept of gatekeeping. Wire services influence the play of stories in local news media, and national newspapers, especially *The New York Times*, influence all the news media.

Who sets the public agenda? For many issues, it is the news media who exert considerable, albeit far from complete, influence on the public agenda. Who sets the news agenda? Of necessity, this is a shared responsibility, but the news media themselves are the dominant influence on the shape of the news agenda for most public issues.

REFERENCES

Asp, K. (1983). The struggle for the agenda: Party agenda, media agenda, and voter agenda in the 1979 Swedish election campaign. *Communication Research, 10,* 333–355.

Blood, R. W. (1981). *Unobtrusive issues in the agenda-setting role of the press.* Unpublished doctoral dissertation, Syracuse University, Syracuse, NY.

Brosius, H. B., & Kepplinger, H. M. (1990). The agenda-setting function of television news: Static and dynamic views. *Communication Research, 17,* 183–211.

Buchanan, B.(1991). *Election a president.* Austin: University of Texas Press.

Cohen, B. C. (1963). *The press and foreign policy.* Princeton, NJ: Princeton University Press.

Eaton, H., Jr. (1989). Agenda-setting with bi-weekly data on content of three national media. *Journalism Quarterly, 66,* 942–948, 959.

Epstein, E. J. (1973). *News from nowhere: Television and the news.* New York: Random House.

Funkhouser, G. R. (1973). The issues of the sixties: An exploratory study in the dynamics of public opinion. *Public Opinion Quarterly, 37,* 62–75.

Gans, H. J. (1979). *Deciding what's news: A study of CBS evening news, NBC Nightly News, Newsweek and Time.* New York: Pantheon Books.

Gilberg, S., Eyal, C. H., McCombs, M. E., & Nicholas, D. (1980). The state of the union address and the press agenda. *Journalism Quarterly, 57,* 584–588.

Gold, D., & Simmons, J. L. (1965). News selection patterns among Iowa dailies. *Public Opinion Quarterly, 29,* 425–430.

Golding, P., & Elliot, P. (1979). *Making the news.* London and New York: Longman.

Hyman, H. H., & Sheatsley, P. B. (1947). Some reasons why information campaigns fail. *Public Opinion Quarterly, 11,* 412–423.

Iyengar, S., & Kinder, D. R. (1987) *News that matters: Agenda-setting and priming in a television age.* Chicago: University of Chicago Press.

Juergens, G. (1981). *News from the White House: The presidential–press relationship in the progressive era.* Chicago: University of Chicago Press.

Kuhn, T. S. (1970). *The structure of scientific revolutions* (2nd ed.). Chicago: University of Chicago Press.

Lang, K., & Lang, G. E. (1959). The mass media and voting. In E. Burdick (Ed.), *American voting behavior* (pp. 217–235). Glencoe, IL: Free Press.

Lazarsfeld, P., Berelson, B., & Gaudet, H. (1944). *The people's choice: How the voter makes up his mind in a presidential campaign* (3rd ed.). New York and London: Columbia University Press.

Lippmann, W. (1922). *Public opinion.* New York: MacMillan.

MacKuen, M. B. (1981). *More than news: Media power in public affairs.* Beverly Hills, CA: Sage.

McCombs, M. E., & Shaw, D. L. (1972). The agenda-setting function of mass media. *Public Opinion Quarterly, 36,* 176–187.

McCombs, M. E., & Shaw, D. L. (1976). Structuring the 'unseen environment.' *Journal of Communication, 26*(2), 18–22.

Reese, S., & Danielian, L. (1989). Intermedia influence and the drug issue: Converging on cocaine. In P. Shoemaker (Ed.), *Communication campaigns about drugs* (pp. 29–46). Hillsdale, NJ: Lawrence Erlbaum Associates.

Semetko, H. A., Blumler, J. G., Gurevitch, M., & Weaver, D. H. (1991). *The formation of campaign agendas.* Hillsdale, NJ: Lawrence Erlbaum Associates.

Shaw, D. L., & McCombs, M. E. (1977). *The emergence of American political issues: The agenda-setting function of the press.* St. Paul, MN: West Publishing.

Shaw, D. L., & Slater, J. W. (1988). Press puts unemployment on agenda: Richmond community opinion, 1981–1984. *Journalism Quarterly, 65,* 407–411.

Shoemaker, P. J., & Reese, S. D. (1991). *Mediating the message: Theories of influence on mass media content.* New York: Longman.

Sigal, L. V. (1973). *Reporters and officials: The organization and politics of newsmaking.* Lexington, MA: D. C. Heath.

Smith, K. (1987). Newspaper coverage and public concern about community issues. *Journalism Monographs,* No. 101.

Turk, J. V. (1985). Information subsidies and influence. *Public Relations Review, 11*(3), 10–25.

Turk, J. V. (1986). Public relation's influence on the news. *Newspaper Research Journal, 7,* 15–27.

Wanta, W. (1989). *The president, press and public opinion: An examination of the dynamics of agenda-building.* Unpublished doctoral dissertation, University of Texas, Austin.

Wanta, W., Stephenson, M. A., Turk, J. V., & McCombs, M. E. (1989). How president's state of the union talk influenced news media agendas. *Journalism Quarterly, 66,* 537–541.

Weaver, D., Graber, D. A., McCombs, M. E., & Eyal, C. H. (1981). *Media agenda-setting in a presidential election: Issues, images, and interests.* New York: Praeger.

Winter, J. P. (1981). Contingent conditions in the agenda-setting process. *Mass communication review yearbook 2.* Beverly Hills, CA: Sage.

Winter, J. P., & Eyal, C. H. (1981). Agenda-setting for the civil rights issue. *Public Opinion Quarterly, 45,* 376–383.

Zucker, H. G. (1978). The variable nature of news media influence. In B. D. Ruben (Ed.), *Communication yearbook 2* (pp. 225–240). New Brunswick, NJ: Transaction Books.

2

Growing Up with Television: The Cultivation Perspective

GEORGE GERBNER
LARRY GROSS
University of Pennsylvania

MICHAEL MORGAN
University of Massachusetts-Amherst

NANCY SIGNORIELLI
University of Delaware

Television is the source of the most broadly shared images and messages in history. It is the mainstream of the common symbolic environment into which our children are born and in which we all live out our lives. Its mass ritual shows no signs of weakening and its consequences are increasingly felt around the globe. For most viewers, new types of delivery systems such as cable, satellite, and VCRs signal even deeper penetration and integration of the dominant patterns of images and messages into everyday life.

Our research project, Cultural Indicators, has tracked the central streams of television's dramatic content since 1967 and has explored the consequences of growing up and living with television since 1974. The project has accumulated a large database that we have used to develop and refine the theoretical approach and the research strategy we call cultivation analysis (see Gerbner, Gross, Morgan, & Signorielli, 1980a; Signorielli & Morgan, 1990). In this chapter we summarize and illustrate our theory of the dynamics of the cultivation process, both in the United States and around the world. This chapter updates and expands the one prepared for *Perspectives on Media Effects* (Gerbner, Gross, Morgan, & Signorielli, 1986).

TELEVISION IN SOCIETY

Television is a centralized system of storytelling. Its drama, commercials, news, and other programs bring a relatively coherent system of images and messages into every home. That system cultivates from infancy the predispositions and preferences that used to be acquired from other "primary" sources and that are so important in research on other media.

Transcending historic barriers of literacy and mobility, television has become the primary common source of socialization and everyday information (mostly in the form of entertainment) of otherwise heterogeneous populations. Many of those who now live with television have never before been part of a shared national culture. Television provides, perhaps for the first time since preindustrial religion, a daily ritual that elites share with many other publics. The heart of the analogy of television and religion, and the similarity of their social functions, lies in the continual repetition of patterns (myths, ideologies, "facts," relationships, etc.) that serve to define the world and legitimize the social order.

Television is different from other media also in its centralized mass production of a coherent set of images and messages produced for total populations, and in its relatively nonselective, almost ritualistic use by most viewers. Exposure to the total pattern rather than only to specific genres or programs is what accounts for the historically new and distinct consequences of living with television: the cultivation of shared conceptions of reality among otherwise diverse publics.

We do not minimize the importance of specific programs, selective attention and perception, specifically targeted communications, individual and group differences, and research on individual attitude and behavior change. But primary concentration on those aspects and terms of traditional media effects research risks losing sight of what is most distinctive and significant about television as the common storyteller of our age.

Compared to other media, television provides a relatively restricted set of choices for a virtually unrestricted variety of interests and publics. Most of its programs are by commercial necessity designed to be watched by large and heterogeneous audiences in a relatively nonselective fashion. Surveys show that the general amount of viewing follows the style of life of the viewer. The audience is always the group available at a certain time of the day, the week, and the season. Viewing decisions depend more on the clock than on the program. The number and variety of choices available to view when most viewers are available to watch is also limited by the fact that many programs designed for the same broad audience tend to be similar in their basic makeup and appeal (Signorielli, 1986).

In the typical U.S. home the television set is in use for almost 7 hours a day. Actual viewing by persons over 2 years old averages more than 3 hours a day. And the more people watch, the less selective they can be (Sun, 1989).

The most frequently recurring features of television cut across all types of programming and are inescapable for the regular viewer (Signorielli, 1986). Researchers who attribute findings to news viewing or preference for action programs, and so forth overlook the fact that most of those who watch more news or action programs watch more of all types of programs, and that, in any case, many different types of programs, including news, share similar important features of story-telling.

Various technological developments such as cable and VCRs have contributed to a significant erosion in audience share (and revenue) of the three major broadcasting networks and have altered the marketing and distribution of movies. However, there is no evidence that prolif-eration of channels has led to substantially greater diversity of content. On the contrary, rapid concentration and vertical integration in the media industries, the absorption of most publishing houses by elec-tronic conglomerates, the growing practice of producing the same material for several media markets, and the habit of time-shifting by VCR users (recording favorite network programs to play back more often and at more convenient times) suggest that the diversity of what is actually viewed may even have decreased.

Viewers may feel a new sense of power and control derived from the ability to freeze a frame, review a scene, and zip through commercials (or zap them entirely). The availability of prerecorded cassettes and films may also give viewers an unprecedented range of potential choices. But again there is no evidence that such a sense of power and choice has changed viewing habits or that the content that regular VCR users and heavy television viewers watch presents world views, values, and stereotypes fundamentally different from most network-type pro-grams (Morgan, Shanahan, & Harris, 1990).

Given the tight links among the various industries involved in the production and distribution of electronic media content, and the fact that most of them are trying to attract the largest and most heteroge-neous audience, the most popular program materials present consistent and complementary messages, often reproducing what has already proven to be profitable. For example, Waterman and Grant (1991) examined network and cable programming and Nielsen ratings and found that "broad-appeal programming" already aired accounts for "a major proportion of cable television menus, and a still higher proportion of cable viewing" (p. 138). Most of the variety we observe comes from novelty effects of styles, stars, and plots rather than from changes in program structure and perspective.

What is most popular naturally tends to reflect—and cultivate— dominant cultural ideologies. Certainly, the VCR allows selective (mostly light) viewers to seek out specialized, often "fringe" material (Dobrow, 1990). But most regular viewers use VCRs and cable to watch more of the most popular fare, which enhances rather than undermines established effects of television (Morgan, Alexander, & Shanahan, 1990; Morgan, Shanahan, & Harris, 1990).

What is most likely to cultivate stable and common conceptions of reality is, therefore, the overall pattern of programming to which total communities are regularly exposed over long periods of time. That is the pattern of settings, casting, social typing, actions, and related outcomes that cuts across program types and viewing modes and defines the world of television. Viewers are born into that symbolic world and cannot avoid exposure to its recurrent patterns, usually many times a day.

THE SHIFT FROM "EFFECTS"
TO "CULTIVATION" RESEARCH

The bulk of scientific inquiry about television's social impact follows theoretical models and methodological procedures of marketing and persuasion research. Much time, energy, and money have been invested in efforts to change people's attitudes and behaviors. By and large, however, the conceptualization of effect as short-run individual change has not produced research that helps us understand the distinctive features of television we have just noted above. These features include massive, long-term and common exposure of large and heterogeneous publics to centrally produced, mass-distributed, and repetitive systems of stories. But research traditions and ideological inhibitions both tend to produce resistance to the "cultivation perspective."

Traditional effects research is based on evaluating specific informational, educational, political, or marketing efforts in terms of selective exposure and measurable differences between those exposed and others. Scholars steeped in those traditions find it difficult to accept the emphasis of cultivation analysis on total immersion rather than selective viewing and on the spread of stable similarities of outlook rather than on the remaining sources of cultural differentiation and change.

Similarly, we are still imbued with the ideology of print culture and its ideals of freedom, diversity, and an active electorate. This ideal also assumes the production and selection of information and entertainment from the point of view of a variety of competing and conflicting interests. That is why many also resist what they assume to be the emphasis of cultivation analysis on the "passive" viewer and the dissolution of authentic publics that this emphasis implies. It seems logical to argue that other circumstances do intervene and can affect and in some cases even neutralize the cultivation process, that many, even if not most, viewers do watch selectively, and that program selections should make a difference.

We do not dispute these contentions. In fact, we account for them in our analytical strategies. But we believe, again, that concentrating on individual differences and immediate change misses the profound historical challenge television poses not only for research strategies but also for traditional theories of democratic government. That challenge is the absorption of diverse conceptions and attitudes into a stable and common mainstream. Cultivation theory is based on the results of research finding a persistent and pervasive pull of the television mainstream on a great variety of conceptual currents and countercurrents. The focus on broad commonalities of perspective among heavy viewers of otherwise varied backgrounds requires a theoretical and methodological approach different from traditional media effects research and appropriate to the distinct dynamics of television. Such an approach has been developed through the Cultural Indicators project.

CULTURAL INDICATORS

The project we call Cultural Indicators is historically grounded, theoretically guided, and empirically supported (Gerbner, 1969, 1970, 1972a). Although most early efforts focused primarily on the nature and functions of television violence, the Cultural Indicators project was broadly conceived from the outset. Even violence was found to be primarily a demonstration of power in the world of television, with serious implications for social control and for the confirmation and perpetuation of minority status as well as for disruption (Gerbner, Gross, Signorielli, Morgan, & Jackson-Beeck, 1979; Morgan, 1983). As it developed, the project continued to take into account a wider range of topics, issues, and concerns (Gerbner & Gross, 1976). We have investigated the extent to which television viewing contributes to audience conceptions and actions in areas such as gender, minority and age-role stereotypes, health, science, the family, educational achievement and aspirations, politics, religion, and other topics, all of which are increasingly also being examined in cross-cultural comparative contexts.[1]

The Cultural Indicators approach involves a three-pronged research strategy. (For a more detailed description see Gerbner, 1973.) The first prong, called institutional process analysis, is designed to investigate the formation of policies directing the massive flow of media messages. (For some examples see Gerbner, 1972b, 1988.) More directly relevant to our present focus are the other two prongs we call message system analysis and cultivation analysis. Both relate to—and help develop—theories about the most subtle and widespread impacts of television.

In the second prong, we have since 1967 recorded annual week-long samples of U.S. network television drama (and samples in other cooperating countries, whenever possible) and subjected these systems of messages to content analysis in order to reliably delineate selected features and trends in the world that television presents to its viewers.[2] We believe that the most pervasive patterns common to many different types of programs but characteristic of the system of programming hold the potential lessons television cultivates. We use these overarching patterns of content as a source of questions for the third prong, cultivation analysis.

In the third prong, we examine the responses given to questions about social reality among those with varying amounts of exposure to the world of television. (Nonviewers are too few and demographically too scattered for serious research purposes; Jackson-Beeck, 1977.) We want to determine whether those who spend more time with television are more likely to answer these questions in ways that reflect the potential lessons of the television world (give the "television answer") than are those who watch less television but are otherwise

---

[1]The Cultural Indicators project began in 1967-1968 with a study for the National Commission on the Causes and Prevention of Violence. It continued under the sponsorships of the U.S. Surgeon General's Scientific Advisory Committee on Television and Social Behavior, the National Institute of Mental Health, The White House Office of Telecommunications Policy, the American Medical Association, the U.S. Administration on Aging, and the National Science Foundation. Cross-cultural comparative extensions of this work, involving long-planned international research coordination and cooperation, began in 1987 under a grant by the W. Alton Jones Foundation, and has continued with the support of the International Research and Exchanges Board (IREX), the Carter Center of Emory University, the Hoso Bunka Foundation of Japan, the Finnish Broadcasting Company, the Hungarian Institute for Public Opinion Research, Moscow State University, the National Center for Public Opinion Research of the USSR, and the Universities of Pennsylvania, Massachusetts, and Delaware.

[2]The message system database accumulated detailed coded observations of over 26,000 characters and over 2,200 programs during the first two decades of its existence.

comparable (in terms of important demographic characteristics) to the heavy viewers.

We have used the concept of "cultivation" to describe the independent contributions television viewing makes to viewer conceptions of social reality. The "cultivation differential" is the margin of difference in conceptions of reality between light and heavy viewers in the same demographic subgroups.

MULTIDIRECTIONAL PROCESS

Our use of the term *cultivation* for television's contribution to conceptions of social reality is not just another word for "effects." Nor does it necessarily imply a one-way, monolithic process. The influences of a pervasive medium on the composition and structure of the symbolic environment are subtle, complex, and intermingled with other influences. This perspective, therefore, assumes an interaction between the medium and its publics.

The elements of cultivation do not originate with television or appear out of a void. Layers of social, personal, and cultural contexts also determine the shape, scope, and degree of the contribution television is likely to make. Yet, the "meanings" of those contexts and factors are in themselves aspects of the cultivation process. That is, although a viewer's gender, or age, or class makes a difference in perspective, television viewing can make a similar and interacting difference. Viewing may help define what it means, for example, to be an adolescent female member of a given social class. The interaction is a continuous process (as is cultivation) beginning with infancy and going on from cradle to grave.

Thus, television neither simply "creates" nor "reflects" images, opinions, and beliefs. Rather, it is an integral aspect of a dynamic process. Institutional needs and objectives influence the creation and distribution of mass-produced messages that create, fit into, exploit, and sustain the needs, values, and ideologies of mass publics. These publics, in turn, acquire distinct identities as publics partly through exposure to the ongoing flow of messages.

The question of "which comes first" is misleading and irrelevant. People are born into a symbolic environment with television as its mainstream. Children begin viewing several years before they begin reading, and well before they can even talk. Television viewing both shapes and is a stable part of lifestyles and outlooks. It links the individual to a larger if synthetic world, a world of television's own making.

Many of those with certain social and psychological characteristics, dispositions, and world views, and fewer alternatives as attractive and compelling, use television as their major vehicle of cultural participation. To the extent that television dominates their sources of entertainment and information, continued exposure to its messages is likely to reiterate, confirm, and nourish—that is, cultivate—its own values and perspectives (see Gerbner, 1990; Morgan & Signorielli, 1990).

Cultivation should not be confused with simple reinforcement (although, to be sure, reaffirmation and stability in the face of pressures for change is not a trivial influence). Nor should it suggest that television viewing is merely symptomatic of other dispositions and outlooks. Finally, it should not be taken as saying that we do not think any change is involved. We have certainly found change with the first "television generation" (Gerbner & Gross, 1976), and in studies that have followed viewers over time (Morgan, 1982; Morgan, Alexander, Shanahan, & Harris, 1990; Morgan & Rothschild, 1983). Change is also apparent as television spreads to various areas of the country (Morgan, 1986), and the world (Morgan, 1990).

When we talk about the "independent contribution" of television viewing, we mean that the development (in some) and maintenance (in others) of some set of outlooks or beliefs can be traced to steady, cumulative exposure to the world of television. Our longitudinal studies of adolescents (Gerbner et al., 1980a; Morgan, 1982, 1987; Morgan, Alexander, et al., 1990) show that television can exert an independent influence on attitudes and behaviors over time, but that belief structures and concrete practices of daily life can also influence subsequent viewing.

The point is that cultivation is not conceived as a unidirectional but rather more like a gravitational process. The angle and direction of the "pull" depends on where groups of viewers and their styles of life are with reference to the line of gravity, the "mainstream" of the world of television. Each group may strain in a different direction, but all groups are affected by the same central current. Cultivation is thus part of a continual, dynamic, ongoing process of interaction among messages and contexts. This holds even though (and in a sense because) the hallmark of the process, once television is established as the main cultural arm of a stable society, is either relative stability or only slow change. A radical change of social relations may, of course, lead to a change in the system of messages and consequently to the cultivation of new and different perspectives.

When studies of media campaigns advocating change found little or no change, conventional effects-research wisdom concluded that media had no or only limited effects. In fact, however, cultivation analysis may lead to the opposite conclusion: "No change" often reflects the strength of the everyday cultivation process. In a relatively stable social structure, cultivation implies a commonality of outlooks and resistance to change.

As successive generations grow up with television's version of the world, the former and more traditional distinctions established before the coming of television—and still maintained to some extent among light viewers—become blurred. Cultivation implies the steady entrenchment of mainstream orientations for most viewers. That process of apparent convergence of outlooks we call *mainstreaming*.

METHODS OF CULTIVATION ANALYSIS

Cultivation analysis begins with message system analysis identifying the most recurrent, stable, and overarching patterns of television content. These are the consistent images, portrayals, and values that cut across most types of programs and are virtually inescapable for the regular (and especially the heavy) viewers. They are the aggregate messages embedded in television as a system rather than in specific programs, types, or genres.

We must emphasize again that testing "cultivation" on the basis of program preferences, short run exposures, or claims of program changes or diversity (all of which have been tried as "replications") may illuminate some media effects but does not address fundamental assumptions of cultivation theory. That is that only repetitive, long-range, and consistent exposure to patterns common to most programming, such as casting, social typing, and the "fate" of different social types, can be expected to cultivate stable and widely shared images of life and society.

There are many critical discrepancies between the world and the "world as portrayed on television." Findings from systematic analyses of television's message systems are used to formulate questions about the potential "lessons" of viewing concerning people's conceptions of social reality. Some of the questions are semiprojective, some use a forced-error format, and others simply measure beliefs, opinions, attitudes, or behaviors. (None asks respondents' views about television itself.)

Using standard techniques of survey methodology, the questions are posed to samples (national probability, regional, convenience) of adults, adolescents, or children. Secondary analyses of large-scale national surveys (e.g., the National Opinion Research Center's General Social Surveys) have often been used when they include questions that relate to potential "lessons" of the television world and viewing data are available for the respondents.

Television viewing is usually assessed by multiple indicators of the amount of time respondents watch television on an "average day." Because the amount of viewing is used in relative terms, the determination of what constitutes "light," "medium," and "heavy" viewing is made on a sample-by-sample basis, using as close to an even three-way split of hours of daily television viewing as possible. What is important is that there should be significant relative differences in viewing levels, not the actual or specific amount of viewing. The heaviest viewers of any sample of respondents form the population on which cultivation can be tested.[3]

The questions posed to respondents do not mention television, and the respondents' awareness of or beliefs in the sources of their information are seen as irrelevant. The resulting relationships, if any, between amount of viewing and the tendency to respond to these questions in the terms of the dominant and repetitive facts, values, and ideologies of the world of television (again, other things held constant) reflect television's contribution to viewers' conceptions of social reality.

The observable evidence of cultivation is likely to be modest in terms of absolute size. Even light viewers may be watching several hours of television a day and of course live in the same general culture as heavy viewers. Therefore, the discovery of a systematic pattern of even small but pervasive differences between light and heavy viewers may be of far-reaching consequence. It takes but a few degrees shift in the average temperature to have an ice age or global warming. A range of 3% to 15% margins (typical of our "cultivation differentials") in a large and otherwise stable field often signals a landslide, a market takeover, or an epidemic, and it certainly tips the scale of any closely balanced choice, vote, or other decision. A slight but pervasive (e.g., generational) shift in the cultivation of common perspectives may alter the cultural climate and upset the balance of social and political decision making without necessarily changing observable behavior. A single percentage point ratings difference in a large market is worth many millions of dollars in advertising revenue—as the networks know only too well.

---

[3]In all analyses we use a number of demographic variables as controls. These are applied both separately and simultaneously. Included are gender, age, race, education, income, and political self-designation (liberal, moderate, conservative). Where applicable, other controls, such as urban-rural residence, newspaper reading, and party affiliation are also used.

VARIATIONS IN CULTIVATION

We have noted cultivation is not a unidirectional flow of influence from television to audience, but part of a continual, dynamic, ongoing process of interaction among messages and contexts. In many cases, those who watch more television (the heavy viewers) are more likely — in all or most subgroups — to give the "television answers." But often the patterns are more complex.

Cultivation is both dependent on and a manifestation of the extent to which television's imagery dominates viewers' sources of information. For example, personal interaction makes a difference. Parental co-viewing patterns and orientations toward television can either increase (Gross & Morgan, 1985) or decrease (Rothschild & Morgan, 1987) cultivation among adolescents. Also, children who are more integrated into cohesive peer or family groups are more resistant to cultivation (Rothschild, 1984).

Direct experience also plays a role. The relationship between amount of viewing and fear of crime is strongest among those who live in high crime urban areas. This is a phenomenon we have called *resonance*, in which everyday reality and television provide a "double dose" of messages that "resonate" and amplify cultivation. The relationships between amount of viewing and the tendency to hold exaggerated perceptions of violence are also more pronounced within those real-world demographic subgroups (e.g., minorities) whose fictional counterparts are relatively more frequently victimized on television (Morgan, 1983).

Television viewing usually relates in different but consistent ways to different groups' life situations and world views. A major theoretical and analytical thrust of many cultivation analyses has been directed toward the determination of the conditional processes that enhance, diminish, or otherwise mediate cultivation.

There are many factors and processes that produce systematic and theoretically meaningful variations in cultivation patterns. One process, however, stands out, both as an indicator of differential vulnerability and as a general, consistent pattern representing one of the most profound consequences of living with television. That is the process of mainstreaming.

MAINSTREAMING

Most cultures consist of many diverse currents. But there is typically a dominant set of attitudes, beliefs, values, and practices. This dominant current is not simply the sum total of all the cross-currents and subcurrents. Rather, it is the most general, functional, and stable mainstream, representing the broadest dimensions of shared meanings and assumptions. It is that which ultimately defines all the other cross-currents and subcurrents, including what Williams (1977) called "residual and emergent strains." Television's central role in our society makes it the primary channel of the mainstream of our culture.

This mainstream can be thought of as a relative commonality of outlooks and values that heavy exposure to the television world tends to cultivate. "Mainstreaming" means that heavy viewing may absorb or override differences in perspectives and behavior that ordinarily stem from other factors and influences. In other words, differences found in the responses of different groups of viewers, differences that usually are associated with the varied cultural, social, and political characteristics of these groups, are diminished in the responses of heavy viewers in these same groups. For example, regional differences, political ideology, and socioeconomic differences are much less influential on the attitudes and beliefs of heavy viewers.

As a process, mainstreaming represents the theoretical elaboration and empirical verification of television's cultivation of common perspectives. It represents a relative homogenization, an absorption of divergent views, and an apparent convergence of disparate outlooks upon the overarching patterns of the television world.

Former and traditional distinctions (which flourished, in part, through the relative diversity provided by print) become blurred as successive generations and groups are enculturated into television's version of the world. Through the process of mainstreaming, television may have become the true 20th century "melting pot" of the American people—and increasingly of other countries around the globe.

Figure 2.1 illustrates some of the different models of the cultivation process that emerge when subgroups are compared. In Graph a, the subgroups show different baselines, but the associations are equivalent, and there is no interaction. Graphs b, c, and d show typical instances of mainstreaming, and imply that the light–heavy viewer differences need not point in the same direction or involve all subgroups. The pattern in Graph e depicts the kind of interaction we call resonance, and in Graph f there are no relationships within any subgroup. Except for Graph f, all these models reflect the cultivation process and relate to its center of gravity, the television mainstream.

THE FINDINGS OF CULTIVATION ANALYSIS

Clear-cut divergences between symbolic reality and independently observable ("objective") reality provide convenient tests of the extent to which television's versions of "the facts" are incorporated or absorbed

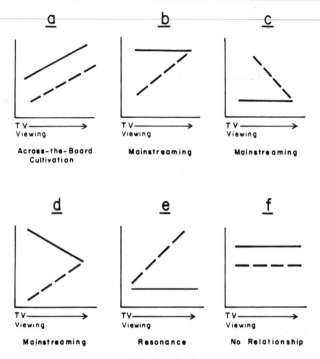

FIG. 2.1. Models of cultivation.

into what heavy viewers take for granted about the world. For example, we found that television drama tends to sharply underrepresent older people. Although those over 65 constitute the fastest growing segment of the real-world population in the United States, heavy viewers were more likely to feel that the elderly are a "vanishing breed"—that compared to 20 years ago there are fewer of them, that they are in worse health, and that they don't live as long—all contrary to fact (Gerbner, Gross, Morgan, & Signorielli, 1980b).

As another example, consider how likely television characters are to encounter violence compared to the rest of us. Well over half of all major characters on television are involved each week in some kind of violent action. Although FBI statistics have clear limitations, they indicate that in any 1 year less than 1% of people in the United States are victims of criminal violence. We have found considerable support for the proposition that heavy exposure to the world of television cultivates exaggerated perceptions of the number of people involved in violence in any given week (Gerbner et al., 1979; Gerbner et al., 1980a), as well as numerous other inaccurate beliefs about crime and law enforcement.

To repeat what we have emphasized earlier, cultivation analysis centers on overarching patterns of casting and other characteristics that are common to most types of programming and that are long enduring. But the investigation is not limited to the lessons of television "facts" compared to real-world (or even imaginary but different) statistics. Some of the most interesting and important issues for cultivation analysis involve the symbolic transformation of message system data into hypotheses about more general issues and assumptions.

The "facts" of the television world are evidently learned quite well, whether or not viewers profess a belief in what they see on television or claim to be able to distinguish between factual and fictional presentations. (In fact, most of what we know, or think we know, is a mixture of all the stories we have absorbed. "Factual," which may be highly selective, and "fictional," which may be highly realistic, are more questions of style than function within a total framework of knowledge.) The repetitive "lessons" we learn from television, beginning with infancy, are likely to become the basis for a broader world view, making television a significant source of general values, ideologies, and perspectives as well as specific assumptions, beliefs, and images. Hawkins and Pingree (1982) called this the cultivation of "value systems." (See also Hawkins & Pingree, 1990.)

One example of this is what we have called the "mean world" syndrome. Our message data say little directly about either the selfishness or altruism of people, and there are certainly no real-world statistics about the extent to which people can be trusted. Yet, we have found that long-term exposure to television, in which frequent violence is virtually inescapable, tends to cultivate the image of a relatively mean and dangerous world. Responses of heavier compared to matching groups of lighter viewers suggest the conception of reality in which greater protection is needed, most people "cannot be trusted," and most people are "just looking out for themselves" (Gerbner et al., 1980a; Signorielli, 1990a).

The Mean World Index, composed of violence-related items, also illustrates the mainstreaming implications of viewing (Signorielli, 1990a). For example, combining data from the 1980, 1983, and 1986 General Social Surveys, heavy and light viewers who have not been to college are equally likely to score high on the Mean World Index: 53% of both the heavy and light viewers agree with two or three of the items. However, among those who have had some college education, television viewing makes a considerable difference: 28% of the light viewers compared to 43% of the heavy viewers in this subgroup have a high score on the Mean World Index. There is thus a 25-percentage point difference between the two subgroups of light viewers but only a 10-point spread between the two subgroups of heavy viewers. The heavy viewers of otherwise different groups are both in the "television mainstream."

Another example of extrapolated assumptions relates to the image of women. The dominant majority status of men on television does not mean that heavy viewers ignore daily experience and underestimate the number of women in society. But underrepresentation in the world of television means a relatively narrow (and thus more stereotyped) range of roles and activities. Most groups of heavy viewers—with other characteristics held constant—score higher on a "sexism scale" using data from the NORC General Social Surveys (Signorielli, 1989).

Several other studies have examined assumptions relating to gender roles in samples of children and adolescents. Morgan (1982) found that television cultivated such notions as "women are happiest at home raising children" and "men are born with more ambition than women." Rothschild (1984) found that 3rd- and 5th-grade children who watched more television were more likely to stereotype both gender-related activities (e.g., cooking, playing sports) and gender-related qualities (e.g., warmth, independence), along traditional gender-role lines. Although viewing seems to cultivate adolescents' and children's attitudes about gender-related chores, viewing was not related to actually doing these chores (Morgan, 1987; Signorielli & Lears, 1991).

Other studies have dealt with assumptions about marriage and work. Signorielli (1990b, in press) found that television seems to cultivate rather realistic views about marriage but seemingly contradictory views about work. Heavy viewing adolescents were more likely to want high-status jobs that would give them a chance to earn a lot of money but also wanted to have their jobs be relatively easy with long vacations and time to do other things.

Other extrapolations from content patterns involve political views. For example, we have argued that as television seeks large and heterogeneous audiences, its messages are designed to disturb as few as possible. Therefore they tend to "balance" opposing perspectives, and to steer a "middle course" along the supposedly nonideological mainstream. We have found that heavy viewers are substantially more likely to label themselves as being "moderate" rather than either "liberal" or "conservative" (see Gerbner, Gross, Morgan, & Signorielli 1982, 1984).

We have observed this finding in many years of the General Social Survey (GSS) data. GSS data from 1990 reveal this pattern once again, as shown in Table 2.1. Heavy viewers in all subgroups tend to see themselves as "moderate" and avoid saying they are either "liberal" or "conservative." Figure 2.2 shows the patterns for Democrats, Independents, and Republicans. The percentage choosing the "moderate" label is again substantially higher among heavy viewers, regardless of party, and heavy viewing Democrats are less likely to say they are "liberal," whereas heavy viewing Republicans are less likely to call themselves

TABLE 2.1
Television Viewing and Political Self-Designation, in the 1990 General Social Survey
(N = 885)

		Liberal				Moderate				Conservative		
TV viewing:	L	M	H	Gamma	L	M	H	Gamma	L	M	H	Gamma
Overall	28	29	25	−.04	33	35	45	.17	40	36	30	−.14
Males	24	31	23	−.03	32	32	43	.12#	42	37	34	−.09
Females	30	27	27	−.05	32	38	47	.20	38	35	27	−.17
Young	38	27	21	−.26	30	38	47	.23	32	35	32	−.00
Middle	26	34	28	.05	32	34	42	.11#	42	32	30	−.16
Older	18	15	25	.21#	39	33	49	.19#	43	52	26	−.32
Lo Educ.	19	29	22	−.00	42	39	49	.12#	39	32	29	−.13#
Hi Educ.	33	30	31	−.04	27	31	38	.15	40	39	31	−.11#
Lo Income	27	26	22	−.08	34	35	49	.21	39	39	29	−.16
Hi Income	31	31	28	−.04	30	34	40	.13#	39	35	33	−.09
Democrat	42	36	33	−.11	33	38	45	.15	25	26	22	−.06
Indep.	25	31	22	−.04	44	42	58	.18	32	28	20	−.19
Repub.	18	20	17	−.00	24	25	32	.13	59	55	51	−.10

# p < .10. *p < .05. **p < .01.

Note. TV Viewing: Light = 1 hour or less daily (N = 224); Medium = 2 or 3 hours daily (N = 418); Heavy = 4 or more hours daily (N = 243). Gender: Males (N = 394); Females (N = 491). Age: Younger = 18 to 30 years old (N = 203); Middle = 31 to 64 years old. (N = 515); Older = 65 years or older (N = 167). Education: Low = 12 or fewer years (No college; N = 449); High = 13 years or more years (at least some college; N = 435). Income: Low = less than $25,000 yearly (N = 368); High = $25,000 or more yearly (N = 433). Party: Democrats (N = 320); Independents (N = 268); Republicans (N = 287)

"conservative." The general pattern shown in these data has appeared every year since 1975.

Yet, looking at the actual positions taken on a number of political issues shows that the mainstream does not mean the "middle of the road." When we analyzed responses to questions in the NORC General Social Surveys about attitudes and opinions on such topics as racial segregation, homosexuality, abortion, minority rights, and other issues that have traditionally divided liberals and conservatives, we found such division mostly among those who watch little television. Overall, self-styled moderates are much closer to conservatives than they are to liberals. Among heavy viewers, liberals and conservatives are closer to each other than among light viewers. We have also noted (Gerbner et al., 1982, 1984) that although mainstreaming bends toward the right on political issues, it leans towards a populist stance on economic issues (e.g., demanding more social services but lower taxes), reflecting the influence of a marketing orientation and setting up potential conflicts of demands and expectations.

Implications of cultivation for foreign policy were reflected in a study

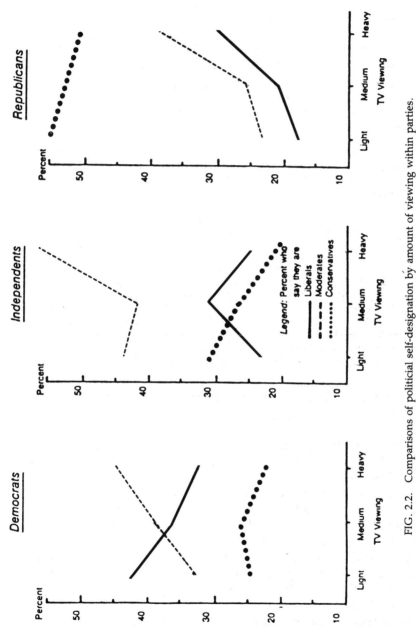

FIG. 2.2. Comparisons of politicial self-designation by amount of viewing within parties.

33

of attitudes toward the war in the Persian Gulf (Lewis, Jhally, & Morgan, 1991). Heavy television viewers were more familiar with the military terminology used and more supportive of the war but less informed about issues and the Middle East in general. Overall amount of viewing was far more important than specific exposure to news.

INTERNATIONAL CULTIVATION ANALYSIS

Cultivation analysis is well suited to multinational and cross-cultural comparative study (Gerbner, 1977, 1989; Morgan, 1990). In fact, such study is the best test of system-wide similarities and differences across national boundaries, and of the actual significance of national cultural policies.

Every country's television system reflects the historical, political, social, economic, and cultural contexts within which it has developed (Gerbner, 1958, 1969). Although U.S. films and television are a significant presence on the screens of most countries (Varis, 1984), they combine with local and other productions to compose synthetic "worlds" that are culture specific. Other media systems and policies may or may not project images and portrayals that are as stable, coherent, and homogeneous as those of U.S. media (as, for example, we have found, surprisingly, in the former Soviet Union, as we note later). Therefore, they may or may not lend themselves to the type of cultivation and mainstreaming we find in the United States (see Gerbner, 1990; Morgan, 1990; Tamborini & Choi, 1990).

International work in cultivation analysis attempts to answer the question of whether the medium or the system is the message. It reveals the extent to which, and the ways in which, each message system contributes to conceptions of social reality congruent with its most stable and recurrent messages and images. Of course, given the range of variations in susceptibility to cultivation even within the United States, there is no reason to assume that cultivation patterns will be identical or invariant across cultures.

Pingree and Hawkins (1981) found that exposure to U.S. programs (especially crime and adventure) was significantly related to Australian students' scores on "Mean World" and "Violence in Society" indices concerning Australia, but not the United States. Viewing Australian programs was unrelated to these conceptions, but those who watched more U.S. programs were more likely to see Australia as dangerous and mean. Weimann's (1984) study of high school and college students in Israel found that heavy viewers had an idealized, "rosier" image of the standard of living in the United States.

In England, Wober (1978) found little support for cultivation in terms of images of violence. (See also Gunter, 1987; Gunter & Furnham, 1984; Wober, 1984, 1990; Wober & Gunter, 1988.) But there was little violence in British programs, and U.S. programs only made up about 15% of British screen time. Piepe, Charlton, and Morey (1990) found evidence of political "homogenization" (mainstreaming) in Britain that was highly congruent with U.S. findings (Gerbner et al., 1982), as did Morgan and Shanahan (1991) in Argentina.

In the Netherlands, Bouwman (1984) found weak associations between amount of viewing and perceptions of violence, victimization, and mistrust. But the findings reveal the importance of cultural context in comparative cultivation research. Content analyses showed a good deal of similarity between U.S. and Dutch television (Bouwman & Signorielli, 1985; Bouwman & Stappers, 1984) and much programming was imported from the United States. Yet, it was found that both light and heavy viewers see about equal amounts of fictional entertainment, but heavy viewers see more "informational" programs, a situation quite different from that of the United States. (See also Bouwman, 1982, 1983, 1987; Bouwman, Nelissen, & Meier, 1987; Stappers, 1984.)

Cultivation analyses about conceptions of violence, sex roles, political orientations, "traditional" values, social stereotypes, and other topics have been conducted in numerous other countries, including Sweden (Hedinsson & Windahl, 1984; Reimer & Rosengren, 1990), Argentina (Morgan & Shanahan, 1991), the Philippines (Tan, Tan, & Tan, 1987), Taiwan and Mexico (Tan, Li, & Simpson, 1986), Japan (Saito, 1991), and Thailand (Tan & Suarchavarat, 1988). These studies show the complex ways in which the viewing of local or imported programming can interact with distinct cultural contexts. For example, in Korea, Kang and Morgan (1988) found that exposure to U.S. television was associated with more "liberal" perspectives about gender roles and family values among females. At the same time, more viewing of U.S. television among Korean male students correlated with greater hostility towards the United States and protectiveness toward Korean culture, suggesting a "backlash" of nationalism among the more politicized college students.

Most of these studies examined single countries. Comparative cross-cultural research typically requires complex joint development and collaboration. It takes longer, costs more, and is more difficult to fund. Nevertheless, recent research has begun to emphasize the comparative aspects of cultivation analysis. Morgan and Shanahan (1992) analyzed adolescents in Taiwan and Argentina. In Argentina, where television is supported by commercials and features many U.S. programs, heavy viewing cultivates traditional gender roles and authoritarianism. In Taiwan, where media are more state controlled, with fewer U.S.

imports, and where overall viewing is much lighter, cultivation was much less apparent. Also, Morgan (1990) compared the cultivation of sex-role stereotypes in five different countries.

Large-scale comparative cultivation analyses involving many countries were underway or planned in the early 1990s. One of the first to be concluded, a study of U.S. and (what was then) Soviet television conducted in 1989 and 1990, found that television plays a different role in the two countries. In the United States, but not in the former Soviet Union, television heightens anxieties about neighborhood safety (including comparisons of light and heavy viewers in the same types of neighborhoods), perhaps as a result of the much lower frequency of violence on Soviet television. In both countries, but especially in the former Soviet Union, the more people watch television the more they are likely to say that housework is primarily the responsibility of the woman. General satisfaction with life is consistently lower among heavy than among light television viewers in the United States but not in the former Soviet Union (where it is relatively low for everyone).

In both places, greater viewing tends to reduce social and economic differences in attitudes, but this is especially so in the United States, where such differences are greater. Lacking regular prime-time dramatic series and relying more on movies, theater, documentaries, and the classics, Soviet television did, in fact, present more diversified dramatic fare than U.S. television. At any rate, television viewing seems to have greater mainstreaming consequences in the United States than was the case in the Soviet Union. The availability of different cultural and language programming in the different former Soviet republics may also have contributed to the relative diversity of their television—and to the centrifugal forces that tore the Union apart.

In summary, in countries in which television's portrayals are less repetitive and homogeneous than in the United States, the results of cultivation analysis also tend to be less predictable and consistent. The extent to which cultivation will occur in a given country will also depend on various structural factors, such as the number of channels available, overall amount of broadcasting time, and amount of time audiences spend viewing. But it will especially depend on the amount of diversity in the available content, which is not necessarily related to the number of channels. A single channel with a diverse and balanced program structure can foster (and, in fact, compel) more diversified viewing than many channels competing for the same audience, using similar appeals, and lending themselves to viewer selection of the same "preferences" most of the time.

Different media systems differ along all these dimensions, and complex interactions among these elements may account for substantial cross-cultural variations in cultivation. Imported U.S. programs can augment, diminish or be irrelevant to these dynamics. The key questions are: (a) how important is television in the culture, and (b) how consistent and coherent is the total system of its messages? The more important, consistent, and coherent, the more cultivation can be expected.

CONCLUSIONS

Television pervades the symbolic environment. Cultivation analysis focuses on the consequences of exposure to its recurrent patterns of stories, images, and messages. Our theories of the cultivation process attempt to understand and explain the dynamics of television as the distinctive and dominant cultural force of our age.

Our explorations and formulations have been challenged, enriched, confirmed, and extended by studies of numerous independent investigators in the United States and abroad, and are still evolving especially as they are being applied in more and more countries.

Cultivation analysis is not a substitute for but a complement to traditional approaches to media effects. Traditional research is concerned with change rather than stability and with processes more applicable to media that enter a person's life at later stages (with mobility, literacy, etc.) and more selectively.

Neither the "before and after exposure" model, nor the notion of "predispositions" as intervening variables, so important in traditional effects studies, apply in the context of cultivation analysis. Television enters life in infancy; there is no "before exposure" condition. Television plays a role in the formation of those very "predispositions" that later intervene (and often resist) other influences and attempts at persuasion.

Cultivation analysis concentrates on the enduring and common consequences of growing up and living with television. Those are the stable, resistant, and widely shared assumptions, images, and conceptions expressing the institutional characteristics and interests of the medium itself.

Television has become the common symbolic environment that interacts with most of the things we think and do. Exploring its dynamics can help develop an understanding of the forces of social cohesion, cultural dependence and resistance to change, as well as the requirements of developing alternatives and independence essential for self-direction and self-government in the television age.

REFERENCES

Bouwman, H. (1982). "Cultural Indicators": Die Gerbnersche Konzeption der "message system analysis" und erste empirische Befunde aus den Niederlanden [Gerbner's conception of message system analyses and first empirical findings from The Netherlands]. *Rundfunk und Fernsehen, 30*(1), 341-355.

Bouwman, H. (1983). Een antwoord vanuit het cultural indicator perspectief. *Massacommunicatie, XI*(2), 68-74.

Bouwman, H. (1984). Cultivation analysis: The Dutch case. In G. Melischek, K. E. Rosengren, & J. Stappers (Eds.), *Cultural indicators: An International Symposium* (pp. 407-422). Vienna: Verlag der Osterreichischen Akademie der Wissenschaften.

Bouwman, H. (1987). *Televisie als cultuur-schepper.* Amsterdam: VU Uitgeverij.

Bouwman, H., Nelissen, P., & Meier, U. (1987). Culturele indicatoren 1980-1985. *Massacommunicatie, XV*(1), 18-35.

Bouwman, H., & Signorielli, N. (1985). A comparison of American and Dutch programming. *Gazette, 35,* 93-108.

Bouwman, H., & Stappers, J. (1984). The Dutch violence profile: A replication of Gerbner's message system analysis. In G. Melischek, K. E. Rosengren, & J. Stappers (Eds.), *Cultural indicators: An International Symposium* (pp. 113-128). Vienna: Verlag der Osterreichischen Akademie der Wissenschaften.

Dobrow, J. R. (1990). Patterns of viewing and VCR use: Implications for cultivation analysis. In N. Signorielli & M. Morgan (Eds.), *Cultivation analysis: New directions in media effects research* (pp. 71-84). Newbury Park, CA: Sage.

Gerbner, G. (1958). On content analysis and critical research in mass communication. *AV Communication Review, 6*(2), 85-108.

Gerbner, G. (1969). Toward "Cultural Indicators": The analysis of mass mediated message systems. *AV Communication Review, 17*(2), 137-148.

Gerbner, G. (1970). Cultural indicators: The case of violence in television drama. *The Annals of the American Academy of Political and Social Science, 388,* 69-81.

Gerbner, G. (1972a). Communication and social environment. *Scientific American, 227*(3), 152-160.

Gerbner, G. (1972b). The structure and process of television program content regulation in the U.S. In G.A. Comstock & E. Rubinstein (Eds.), *Television and social behavior, Vol. 1: Content and control* (pp. 386-414). Washington, DC: U.S. Government Printing Office.

Gerbner, G. (1973). Cultural indicators: The third voice. In G. Gerbner, L. Gross, & W.H. Melody (Eds.), *Communications technology and social policy* (pp. 555-573). New York: Wiley.

Gerbner, G. (1977). Comparative cultural indicators. In G. Gerbner (Ed.), *Mass Media Policies in Changing Cultures* (pp. 199-205). New York: Wiley.

Gerbner, G. (1988). Violence and terror in the mass media. In *Reports and papers in mass communication* (No. 102). Paris: Unesco.

Gerbner, G. (1989). Cross-cultural communications research in the age of telecommunications. In The Christian Academy (Eds.), *Continuity and change in communications in post-industrial society* (Vol. 2) Seoul, Korea: Wooseok.

Gerbner, G. (1990). Epilogue: Advancing on the path of righteousness (maybe). In N. Signorielli & M. Morgan (Eds.), *Cultivation analysis: New directions in media effects research* (pp. 249-262). Newbury Park, CA: Sage.

Gerbner, G., & Gross, L. (1976). Living with television: The violence profile. *Journal of Communication, 26*(2), 173-199.

Gerbner, G., Gross, L., Morgan, M., & Signorielli, N. (1980a). The "Mainstreaming" of America: Violence profile no. 11. *Journal of Communication, 30*(3), 10–29.

Gerbner, G., Gross, L., Morgan, M., & Signorielli, N. (1980b). Aging with television: Images on television drama and conceptions of social reality. *Journal of Communication, 30*(1), 37–47.

Gerbner, G., Gross, L., Morgan, M., & Signorielli, N. (1982). Charting the mainstream: Television's contributions to political orientations. *Journal of Communication, 32*(2), 100–127.

Gerbner, G., Gross, L., Morgan, M., & Signorielli, N. (1984). Political correlates of television viewing. *Public Opinion Quarterly, 48*(1), 283–300.

Gerbner, G., Gross, L., Morgan, M., & Signorielli, N. (1986). Living with television: The dynamics of the cultivation process. In J. Bryant & D. Zillmann (Eds.), *Perspectives on media effects* (pp. 17–48). Hillsdale, NJ: Lawrence Erlbaum Associates.

Gerbner, G., Gross, L., Signorielli, N., Morgan, M., & Jackson-Beeck, M. (1979). The demonstration of power: Violence profile no. 10. *Journal of Communication, 29*(3), 177–196.

Gross, L., & Morgan, M. (1985). Television and enculturation. In J. R. Dominick & J. E. Fletcher (Eds.), *Broadcasting research methods* (pp. 221–234). Boston: Allyn & Bacon.

Gunter, B. (1987). *Television and the fear of crime.* London: Libbey.

Gunter, B., & Furnham, A. (1984). Perceptions of television violence: Effects of programme genre and type of violence on viewers' judgements of violent portrayals. *British Journal of Social Psychology, 23*(2), 155–164.

Hawkins, R. P., & Pingree, S. (1982). Television's influence on social reality. In D. Pearl, L. Bouthilet, & J. Lazar (Eds.), *Television and behavior: Ten years of scientific progress and implications for the 80's, Vol. II, Technical reviews* (pp. 224–247). Rockville, MD: National Institute of Mental Health.

Hawkins, R. P., & Pingree, S. (1990). Divergent psychological processes in constructing social reality from mass media content. In N. Signorielli & M. Morgan (Eds.), *Cultivation analysis: New directions in media effects research* (pp. 35–50). Newbury Park, CA: Sage.

Hedinsson, E., & Windahl, S. (1984). Cultivation analysis: A Swedish illustration. In G. Melischek, K. E. Rosengren, & J. Stappers (Eds.), *Cultural indications: An International Symposium* (pp. 389–406). Vienna: Verlag der Osterreichischen Akademie der Wissenschaften.

Jackson-Beeck, M. (1977). The non-viewers: Who are they? *Journal of Communication, 27*(3), 65–72.

Kang, J. G., & Morgan, M. (1988). Culture clash: U.S. television programs in Korea. *Journalism Quarterly, 65*(2), 431–438.

Lewis, J., Jhally, S., & Morgan, M. (1991). *The Gulf War: A study of the media, public opinion, and public knowledge* (Research Report). The Center for the Study of Communication, Department of Communication, University of Masschusetts/Amherst.

Morgan, M. (1982). Television and adolescents' sex-role stereotypes: A longitudinal study. *Journal of Personality and Social Psychology, 43*(5), 947–955.

Morgan, M. (1983). Symbolic victimization and real-world fear. *Human Communication Research, 9*(2), 146–157.

Morgan, M. (1986). Television and the erosion of regional diversity. *Journal of Broadcasting and Electronic Media, 30*(2), 123–139.

Morgan, M. (1987). Television, sex-role attitudes, and sex-role behavior. *Journal of Early Adolescence, 7*(3), 269–282.

Morgan, M. (1990). International cultivation analysis. In N. Signorielli & M. Morgan

(Eds.), *Cultivation analysis: New directions in media effects research* (pp. 225–248). Newbury Park, CA: Sage.

Morgan, M., Alexander, A., Shanahan, J., & Harris, C. (1990). Adolescents, VCRs, and the family environment. *Communication Research, 17*(1), 83–106.

Morgan, M., & Rothschild, N. (1983). Impact of the new television technology: Cable TV, peers, and sex-role cultivation in the electronic environment. *Youth and Society, 15*(1), 33–50.

Morgan, M., & Shanahan, J. (1991). Television and the cultivation of political attitudes in Argentina. *Journal of Communication, 41*(1), 88–103.

Morgan, M., & Shanahan, J. (1992). Comparative cultivation analysis: Television and adolescents in Argentina and Taiwan. In F. Korzenny & S. Ting-Toomey (Eds.), *Mass media effects across cultures: International and intercultural communication annual* (Vol. 16, pp. 173–197). Newbury Park, CA: Sage.

Morgan, M., Shanahan, J., & Harris, C. (1990). VCRs and the effects of television: New diversity or more of the same? In J. Dobrow (Ed.), *Social and cultural aspects of VCR use* (pp. 107–123). Hillsdale, NJ: Lawrence Erlbaum Associates.

Morgan, M., & Signorielli, N. (1990). Cultivation analysis: Conceptualization and methodology. In N. Signorielli & M. Morgan (Eds.), *Cultivation analysis: New directions in media effects research* (pp. 13–34). Newbury Park, CA: Sage.

Piepe, A., Charlton, P., & Morey, J. (1990). Politics and television viewing in England: Hegemony or pluralism? *Journal of Communication, 40*(1), 24–35.

Pingree, S., & Hawkins, R. P. (1981). U.S. programs on Australian television: The cultivation effect. *Journal of Communication, 31*(1), 97–105.

Reimer, B., & Rosengren, K. E. (1990). Cultivated viewers and readers: A life-style perspective. In N. Signorielli & M. Morgan (Eds.) *Cultivation analysis: New directions in media effects research* (pp. 181–206). Newbury Park, CA: Sage.

Rothschild, N. (1984). Small group affiliation as a mediating factor in the cultivation process. In G. Melischek, K. E. Rosengren, & J. Stappers (Eds.), *Cultural indicators: An International Symposium* (pp. 377–387). Vienna: Verlag der Osterreichischen Akademie der Wissenschaften.

Rothschild, N., & Morgan, M. (1987). Cohesion and control: Relationships with parents as mediators of television. *Journal of Early Adolescence, 7*(3), 299–314.

Saito, S. (1991). *Does cultivation occur in Japan?: Testing the applicability of the cultivation hypothesis on Japanese television viewers.* Unpublished master's thesis, the Annenberg School for Communication, University of Pennsylvania, Philadelphia.

Signorielli, N. (1986). Selective television viewing: A limited possibility. *Journal of Communication, 36*(3), 64–75.

Signorielli, N., (1989). Television and conceptions about sex roles: Maintaining conventionality and the status quo. *Sex Roles, 21*(5/6), 337–356.

Signorielli, N. (1990a). Television's mean and dangerous world: A continuation of the cultural indicators perspective. In N. Signorielli & M. Morgan (Eds.), *Cultivation analysis: New directions in media effects research* (pp. 85–106). Newbury Park, CA: Sage.

Signorielli, N. (1990b, November). *Television's contribution to adolescents' perceptions about work.* Paper presented at annual conference of the Speech Communication Association, Chicago.

Signorielli, N. (in press). Adolescents and ambivalence towards marriage: A cultivation analysis. *Youth and Society.*

Signorielli, N., & Lears, M. (1991). *Children, television and conceptions about chores: Attitudes and behaviors.* Unpublished manuscript, University of Delaware, Newark.

Signorielli, N., & Morgan, M. (Eds.). (1990). *Cultivation analysis: New directions in media effects research.* Newbury Park, CA: Sage.

Stappers, J. G. (1984). De eigen aard van televisie; tien stellingen over cultivatie en culturele indicatoren. *Massacommunicatie, XII*(5/6), 249–258.

Sun, L. (1989). *Limits of selective viewing: An analysis of "diversity" in dramatic programming.* Unpublished master's thesis, The Annenberg School for Communication, University of Pennsylvania, Philadelphia

Tamborini, R., & Choi, J. (1990). The role of cultural diversity in cultivation research. In N. Signorielli & M. Morgan (Eds.), *Cultivation analysis: New directions in media effects research* (pp. 157–180). Newbury Park, CA: Sage.

Tan, A. S., Li, S., & Simpson, C. (1986). American television and social stereotypes of Americans in Taiwan and Mexico. *Journalism Quarterly, 63,* 809–814.

Tan, A. S., & Suarchavarat, K. (1988). American TV and social stereotypes of Americans in Thailand. *Journalism Quarterly, 65*(4), 648–654.

Tan, A. S., Tan, G. K., & Tan, A. S. (1987). American TV in the Philippines: A test of cultural impact. *Journalism Quarterly, 64*(1), 65–72.

Varis, T. (1984). The international flow of television programs. *Journal of Communication, 34*(1), 143–152.

Waterman, D., & Grant, A. (1991). Cable television as an aftermarket. *Journal of Broadcasting & Electronic Media, 35*(2), 179–188.

Weimann, G. (1984). Images of life in America: The impact of American TV in Israel. *International Journal of Intercultural Relations, 8*(2), 185–197.

Williams, R. (1977). *Marxism and literature.* Oxford: Oxford University Press.

Wober, J. M. (1978). Televised violence and paranoid perception: The view from Great Britain. *Public Opinion Quarterly, 42*(3), 315–321.

Wober, J. M. (1984). Prophecy and prophylaxis: Predicted harms and their absence in a regulated television system. In G. Melischek, K. E. Rosengren, & J. Stappers (Eds.), *Cultural indicators: An International Symposium* (pp. 423–440). Vienna: Verlag der Osterreichischen Akademie der Wissenschaften.

Wober, J. M. (1990). Does television cultivate the British? Late 80s evidence. In N. Signorielli & M. Morgan (Eds.), *Cultivation analysis: New directions in media effects research* (pp. 207–224). Newbury Park, CA: Sage.

Wober, J. M., & Gunter, B. (1988). *Television and social control.* New York: St. Martin's Press.

3

A Priming Effect Analysis of Media Influences: An Update

EUNKYUNG JO
LEONARD BERKOWITZ
University of Wisconsin-Madison

> The producers of "New Jack City" state they are "totally unconvinced by the idea that a movie can have a significant effect on the behavior of moviegoers." What do they need to convince them?
>
> Remember "Walk Proud" and "Boulevard Nights," violence-filled films about teen-age gangs? Five people were shot and three stabbed at two theaters on the opening night of "Boulevard Nights." As for "Walk Proud," there were four shootings and one stabbing at a screening of that film in San Francisco, and a 15-year-old boy was shot and two other teen-agers stabbed at a screening of the same film in Ontario, Calif. The film was hurriedly withdrawn from both theaters. Why, if the violence in the film had nothing to do with the violence in the audience?
>
> —From a letter to *The New York Times* (April 7, 1991)

The letter writer just quoted could have added many more anecdotal reports of violent outbreaks following the showing of violent movies. He certainly could have pointed to the aftereffects of *New Jack City*, the film that prompted his letter. This movie evidently has led to so much aggression that several theaters have decided not to exhibit it. According to one newspaper, "in Las Vegas, a fight in a theater lobby led to 15 arrests. In Brooklyn, a teenager was killed during a shootout outside a theater. In Sayreville, six were arrested, four injured. In Chicago, two groups exchanged 15 to 20 gunshots outside a theater" (*USA Today,* March 12, 1991). If the people who had made the movie did not believe that a film could influence the viewers' actions, Warner Brothers, the studio funding the production, apparently did not share this conviction and promised to reimburse theater owners for whatever extra security costs they had to incur when they exhibited *New Jack City* (*USA Today,* March 18, 1991).

But however dramatic these anecdotal observations might be, they obviously do not provide adequate evidence as to whether violent movies do indeed foster aggressive behavior by people in the audience. Much better evidence can be found in the scores and scores of controlled investigations examining the behavioral consequences of these films. Although some critics (e.g., Cook, Kendzierski, & Thomas, 1983; Freedman, 1984; McGuire, 1986; Messner, 1986) believe that media depictions of violence have, at best, only a very small effect on the viewers, statistical analyses of the total pattern of findings suggest the influence can be somewhat more substantial than the critics suppose. Andison (1977) carried out a meta-analysis of 31 of these laboratory experiments and concluded that, over all of the studies, witnessed violence led to a significantly greater level of aggression than did the control films. More convincingly perhaps, Wood, Wong, and Chachere (1991) restricted their meta-analysis to 28 separate experiments in which the participants were free to display "natural" aggression (rather than, say, press a button on a Buss aggression machine). They concluded from their results not only that observed violence tended to heighten the likelihood of aggressive behavior by the viewers but that "the mean effect of exposure to violent media on unconstrained aggression is in the small to moderate range, typical of social psychological predictors" (p. 379). This "small to moderate" influence is not trivial, the reviewers noted, if one considers the very large size of the media audiences.

For the present writers as well as other researchers, then, there is no longer a question as to whether the portrayal of violence in the mass media can increase the chances that some people in the audience will act aggressively themselves. Such an effect can occur and often does. We believe it is now time to go further and identify the conditions under which this influence does or does not arise. Accomplishing this obviously requires a specification of the psychological processes governing media effects and, more generally, a theory of how people are affected by the events they see on the television or movie screen and/or hear about on the radio and/or read about on the printed page.

Berkowitz offered a beginning version of such a theory some years ago (Berkowitz, 1984; Berkowitz & Rogers, 1986), emphasizing the media's short-run, relatively transient influences on the thoughts and actions of audience members. Without minimizing the long-term consequences of repeated exposure to scenes of violence on the television and movie screens, Berkowitz noted that the events depicted in the mass media can also have temporary effects on the adults as well as children in the audience so that, for a short time afterwards, their thoughts and actions are colored by what they have just seen, heard, and/or read (cf. Berkowitz, 1986, for a further discussion of these relatively short-lived effects). Still concentrating on the media's transient influences, the present paper attempts to update this formulation by incorporating more recent research into the analysis. It does not provide a comprehensive survey of all of the ways in which the mass media can affect people in the audience and is not even as far-ranging as Berkowitz's earlier discussions of his cognitive-neoassociationistic framework. Instead, this chapter summarizes the findings of a relatively few investigations in order to spell out the formulation's major implications.

THE THEORETICAL FORMULATION

Priming Effects, Associative Networks, and Spreading Activation

Although a number of psychological processes undoubtedly contribute to the mass media's influence, the present model concentrates on just a few of the processes that involve the audience's thoughts. It essentially holds that when people witness, read, or hear of an event via the mass media, ideas having a similar meaning are activated in them for a short time afterwards, and that these thoughts in turn can activate other semantically related ideas and action tendencies.

This analysis derives from a cognitive-neoassociationistic perspective (Anderson & Bower, 1973; Landman & Manis, 1983) that regards memory as a collection of networks, with each network consisting of units or nodes that represent substantive elements of thought, feelings, and so forth, linked through associative pathways. The strength of these associative connections is presumably determined by a variety of factors, including contiguity, similarity, and semantic relatedness.

Although we cannot here go into the intricacies of this conceptual scheme or discuss the technical controversies regarding a number of details (cf. Fiske & Taylor, 1991; Klatzky, 1980; Landman & Manis, 1983; Reed, 1988; Wyer & Srull, 1981, for a more comprehensive discussion), the present analysis goes beyond the memory-structural notions to emphasize the operation of priming effects. In accord with a considerable body of research and theorizing (cf. Fiske & Taylor, 1991, for a convenient summary), it maintains that the presentation of a certain stimulus having a particular meaning "primes" other semantically related concepts, thus heightening the likelihood that thoughts with much the same meaning as the presentation stimulus will come to mind. It is as if the activation of the primed ideas has spread along the associative pathways (Collins & Loftus, 1975) to other semantically related thoughts.

Feelings and motor tendencies can also be activated. Along with network formulations of emotion (e.g., Berkowitz, 1990; Bower, 1981; Lang, 1979; Leventhal, 1984), the theoretical model offered here proposes that ideas having emotional significance are also linked associatively to particular feelings and motor programs. The activation of these emotion-related ideas therefore tends to arouse the feelings and action tendencies that are associated with them. Depressive thoughts frequently generate depressive feelings (Velten, 1968), whereas ideas having an aggressive meaning can, under the right conditions, evoke angry feelings and even aggressive action tendencies (Berkowitz & Heimer, 1989).

Taking all of this together, the present analysis suggests what could well be the result of depictions of violence in the mass media: Under certain circumstances and for a short period of time, there is an increased chance that the viewers will (a) have hostile thoughts that can color their interpretation of other people, (b) believe other forms of aggressive conduct are justified and/or will bring them benefits, and (c) be aggressively inclined.

Evidence of Priming Effects in Social Interactions

A rapidly increasing body of research testifies to the influence priming effects can have on people's thoughts and actions. Several of the best known studies in this area have demonstrated, for example, that the ideas brought to mind by a verbal task can shape the participants' later impression of others. To mention only one of the many experiments that could be cited here, Wyer and Srull (1981) required their participants to construct sentences in a series of trials using three of the four words shown to them each time. Some of these word sets contained words with aggressive connotations, whereas other sets contained only neutral words. Some time after the participants finished this initial priming task (immediately afterward, 1 hour later, or on the next day), they were given a brief description of a target person and asked to indicate their impression of this individual. As the investigators had predicted, the greater the proportion of aggression-related sentences the participants had constructed, the less favorable was their evaluation of the target person. This effect decreased with the passage of time but was still noticeable after 24 hours. The use of aggression-related words in the sentence construction task apparently activated other aggressive and hostile thoughts, and these ideas colored the participants' judgments of the target person for some time afterward.

Bargh and Pietromonaco (1982) showed that this priming process can occur automatically and even without awareness. In their experiment, participants were unknowingly exposed to single words, some of which were semantically related to hostility. Then, after reading a brief description of a target person, the participants had to evaluate him. Even though the participants had not been consciously aware of the priming words, the more hostility-related words to which they had been exposed, the more negative was their evaluation of the target person.

This type of effect is not restricted to written impressions. Wilson and Capitman (1982), along with other investigators, reported that the primed ideas can also affect social interactions. In their study, male participants read a story describing either a "boy-meets-girl" encounter or a control story. Those who read the boy-meets-girl story later smiled more, talked more, leaned forward more, and gazed at the female confederate more than did those who read the control story. Similarly, Herr (1986) also found that the activated social thoughts could increase behavior consistent with these thoughts. In his experiment, participants were exposed to the names of people having varying degrees of association with the notion of hostility. Thus, the prize fighter Joe Frazier had a moderately strong association with this concept, whereas the tennis player Billie Jean King was typically associated with non-hostility. When the participants were then given a chance to evaluate an ambiguously described person, those who were primed with the names linked to moderate hostility subsequently rated this target individual as more hostile than did those who had previously been exposed to nonhostile peoples' names. But more important for us now, the participants who had been given the moderately hostile primes subsequently behaved in a more hostile and competitive fashion toward their partner in a prisoner's dilemma game than did those who were exposed to the nonhostile names.

Carver, Ganellan, Fromming, and Chambers (1983) reported similar findings. In one of their experiments, male undergraduates primed to have aggressive thoughts by means of a sentence construction task subsequently delivered the most intense electric shocks to a fellow student whenever that person made a mistake.

Also in accord with our formulation, still other research indicates that even the thought of carrying out a particular action increases the probability that this behavior will be performed soon afterward. In a study by Anderson (1983), the participants who imagined themselves engaging in a particular type of behavior reported a greater inclination to perform that action than did others who imagined someone else carrying out the behavior. It is as if the thought of the particular action had, to some degree, activated the motor program linked to this idea.

APPLICATION OF THE ANALYSIS
TO MEDIA RESEARCH FINDINGS

Priming of Aggression-Related Ideas

There is both direct and indirect evidence that the observation of aggression evokes aggression-related ideas in viewers. Where we can only infer such an influence from the previously cited research by Wyer and Srull (1981) and Bargh and Pietromonaco (1982), another priming study has more direct evidence. Carver, Ganellan, Froming, and Chambers (1983) showed that people who watched a brief film depicting a hostile interaction between a businessman and his secretary subsequently perceived more hostility in another, ambiguous stimulus person.

More directly still, Berkowitz, Parker, and West (cited in Berkowitz, 1973, pp. 125–126) demonstrated that aggression portrayed in comic books activates specifically aggression-related thoughts. When they asked school children to read either a war comic book (*Adventures of the Green Berets*) or a neutral comic book (*Gidget*) and then complete sentences by choosing one of two words presented, they found that the youngsters given the war comics were more likely to select words with aggressive connotations than were youngsters who read the neutral book.

An investigation of the consequences of aggressive humor (Berkowitz, 1970) is conceptually similar to these studies. In this experiment, young women were asked to listen to a tape recording of either a hostile (Don Rickles) or nonaggressive (George Carlin) comic routine and then rate a job applicant. The results showed that exposure to the hostile comedy led to harsher evaluations of the applicant, even when the participants had not been provoked by the person they were judging.

More recently, Bushman and Geen (1990) directly tested the assumptions of the cognitive-neoassociationistic model. In their study, participants watched either a highly violent videotaped movie (e.g., *48 Hours*), a mildly violent movie (e.g., *Soylent Green*), or an equally long nonviolent tape (e.g., "Dallas"). When all of the respondents were asked to list the thoughts that occurred to them at the end of the movie, those who saw a highly violent videotape produced more aggressive ideas than did those who watched a less violent film. Also in accord with the model, participants who reported feeling more hostile after viewing the videotape than before tended to list a greater number of aggressive thoughts after viewing the film.

Priming Effects Arising From Radio, Video Games, and Sports

Although the great preponderance of studies examining the social consequences of media violence has dealt with television and movie effects, there is good reason to believe that portrayals of aggression in the print and aural media can also influence members of the audience adversely. The Berkowitz, Parker, and West experiment mentioned earlier presented violent scenes to the participants on printed pages, whereas a number of priming experiments required their participants to read and think about printed lists of words. In all of these cases the people seeing the aggressive words and/or symbols were relatively harsh towards another person.

Radio programs and music videos can conceivably also bring aggressive ideas and inclinations to mind. Many of them contain as much violent content as violent television programs and they could also have significant effects on the audiences' thought processes and behavior. Employing current television content analysis techniques, Boemer (1984) compared the violent content of both adult and children's popular thriller radio dramas, such as the adult programs "The Shadow" and "Suspense" and "The Lone Ranger" program for children, with the content of television programs that were popular in the years from 1967 through 1978. Boemer reported that the adult radio thriller dramas were quite similar in violent content to prime-time action television programs. However, the children's radio thrillers had somewhat less violent content than the weekend morning action programs and cartoons on television, probably because the children's radio dramas were shorter than the television programs.

Although we could not locate any investigations of the possible aggressive consequences of radio-reported violence, it certainly is reasonable to suggest that the radio depictions are capable of activating associated thoughts and actions. Indeed, because the radio portrayals typically allow the listeners' imagination relatively free rein, those hearing these programs conceivably might have ideas that are especially stimulating for them.

There is somewhat better evidence of the influence of video games. Video games, including arcade games and home video games such as Nintendo, are not only exceedingly popular with children and many adults these days, but many of them also have a lot of violent content, and it is not surprising that some researchers have sought to determine what effects they might have on youngsters.

In one of these studies, Mehrabian and Wixen (1986) measured the emotional responses to 22 common arcade video games and found that the predominant reaction to the games was aggression and hostility. Anderson and Ford (1987) focused more specifically on the content of these games, investigating the short-term effects of highly or mildly aggressive video games. Participants were assigned to play either a highly aggressive video game, a mildly aggressive game, or no-game control condition, and their hostility, anxiety, and depression were assessed afterwards. Anderson and Ford reported that hostility was increased in both aggressive game conditions relative to the control group. The high-aggression game led to higher hostility than the mild-aggression game, although the difference did not attain the conventional level of significance. However, indicating one possible adverse consequence of exposure to aggressive content, those who had played the high-aggression game were significantly more anxious than the participants who played the mild-aggression game or those who played no game.

Even sporting events can prime aggressive thoughts and inclinations—if these games are viewed as being aggressive in nature. Goldstein and Arms (1971, cited in Goldstein, 1986) compared the emotional reactions of spectators at an aggressive sport (football) and those at a relatively nonaggressive event (a gymnasium competition), and found that the former reported a greater increase in feelings of hostility whether their preferred team had won or lost the contest.

Football is so widely regarded as an aggressive sport that even the thought of this game can at times activate aggression-related ideas. Wann and Branscombe (1990) asked their participants to work on a scrambled sentences task, with some of the sentences containing the names of aggressive contact sports (e.g., boxing) and others having the names of sports usually taken as nonaggressive in nature (e.g., golf). When the participants then rated an ambiguous target person, those who were primed with aggressive-sports names rated the target as significantly more hostile and as more likely to prefer aggressive activities than did the participants exposed to sentences containing references to nonaggressive sports.

CONDITIONS FACILITATING
THE DISPLAY OF OVERT AGGRESSION

In spite of all this evidence, there are also exceptions. We noted at the start of this paper that media-depicted violence does not always have aggression-enhancing consequences. And contact sports certainly do not always generate aggression and hostility. It is also clear that even when the aggressive events do activate ideas, feelings, and action tendencies associated with aggression, these internal responses do not necessarily lead to the open display of violent behavior. Various intervening variables may influence the chances that people viewing the media violence will be overtly assaultive themselves.

The Communication's Meaning

A very important factor affecting the relationship between the media-reported events and the viewers' subsequent behavior is the communication's meaning for the audience. Aggression-related thoughts will not be activated unless the depicted scenes are considered aggressive by the viewers.

This point is particularly important in understanding the effects of contact sports. Although football is commonly taken to be an aggressive game, as was indicated earlier, many fans do not actually think of the players as being aggressive toward their opponents. For these viewers, aggression is a deliberate attempt to hurt another person, and they think of the players primarily as athletes engaged in a contest of skill and determination. Not viewing the game as aggression, then, these people may not be aggressively stimulated by what they see (unless they are psychologically very involved in the contest and their team loses).

Berkowitz and Alioto (1973) examined this possibility in an experiment inquiring into the aggression-enhancing influence of contact sports. Assuming that most people think of aggression as the intentional injury of another person, these researchers hypothesized that contact sports are most likely to stimulate aggressive inclinations in the on-lookers when they believe the players are trying to hurt each other. The male university student participants in their experiment were angered and then exposed to a brief film, either of a prizefight or a football game. Participants were also led to interpret the observed contest either as aggressive in nature (the opponents were supposedly trying to injure each other) or as nonaggressive (the contestants were said to be professionals unemotionally engaged in their business). At the end of the movie, when they were given a chance to shock the person who had angered them earlier, the men who had been led to think of the contest as an aggressive encounter were more punitive to the provocateur. They had to define the witnessed event as "aggression" if it was to activate strong aggression-related thoughts and inclinations in them. Consistent with this proposition, Donnerstein and Berkowitz (1983) reported that the intensity of their male participants' punishment of a woman who had provoked them earlier was significantly correlated with the rated aggressiveness of the movies they had seen before they could deliver the shocks.

Interpreting the Witnessed Aggression
as Worthwhile and/or Justified

Other thoughts besides the aggressive meaning of the witnessed event can also determine how the communication will affect people in the audience. The portrayed occurrence might activate aggressive thoughts and inclinations but these could be restrained if the viewers also think at this time that the observed aggression is unjustified and/or is risky behavior that is very likely to have negative consequences. Conversely, their interpretation of the portrayed aggression as morally proper and/or as likely to benefit the aggressor might well reduce their inhibitions against aggression for a short time afterward and conceivably could even intensify the activated aggressive tendencies. Probably because of a spreading activation to related concepts, these meanings often generalize, providing a context within which observers interpret their own aggressive actions.

The viewers' willingness to attack someone after seeing the depicted violence can be influenced to a substantial extent by the observed aggressor's outcomes, as studies have now demonstrated (Bandura, 1965, 1971). The viewers appear to draw a lesson from what they see: What happens on the screen (or is reported in the media) might also happen to them if they exhibit the same behavior (Bandura, 1971; Comstock, 1980; Comstock, Chaffee, Katzman, McCombs, & Roberts, 1978; Huesmann, 1982). Perhaps when observers witness the consequence of the aggressor's action, other occasions in which there was the same type of outcome are recalled. With this kind of outcome in mind, as the availability heuristic suggests, the viewers might then overestimate the frequency and probability of the same type of consequence, thus increasing their willingness to perform that kind of behavior themselves.

On the other side of the proverbial coin, seeing or learning of an aggressor suffering as a result of his or her behavior could well make the viewers reluctant to follow suit. Their inhibitions against aggression could also be strengthened if they are reminded that violence could have serious negative consequences for the victims. In an experiment by Goranson (1969), angry participants had an opportunity to attack their tormentor after they watched a filmed prize fight in which the loser received a bad beating. Those people led to believe the loser then died from the injuries he received in the fight were much less punitive to the provocateur than were the other participants not given this information.

The possibility that violence might have unfortunate consequences apparently dominated the former participants' thoughts, and these ideas evidently led them to restrain their aggression. However, we must recognize that the participants in this experiment neither held ill feelings toward the victim in the movie nor associated that character with someone whom they might have wanted to hurt. Their film-activated aggressive ideas and inclinations might not have been inhibited as strongly if, in their minds, they did connect the movie victim with their own antagonist. In such a case they might not have regarded the witnessed aggression as unjustified or wrong and, thus, might not have held themselves back. And then too, Goranson's participants also might not have restrained themselves if the fight victim had only suffered somewhat, rather than died. Because angry people typically wish to hurt someone, the victim's pain might actually have been gratifying for the angry participants (Baron, 1977). The observed aggression could then have been seen as successfully leading to a desired consequence (i.e., revenge), and the end result might have been a heightened assault on the participants' tormentor (Berkowitz, 1974; Donnerstein & Berkowitz, 1981).

Identification With The Characters

Several authors (e.g., Dorr, 1981; Tannenbaum & Gaer, 1965) suggested that the observers' identification with the media characters influences the extent to which they are affected by the witnessed occurrence. As was mentioned earlier, Anderson (1983) showed that the college students who had previously imagined themselves carrying out a certain kind of behavior expressed the strongest intentions of later engaging in the action. The viewers who identify with the actors they watch might vividly imagine themselves as these characters and think of themselves as carrying out the depicted actions. As a consequence, the ideas and action tendencies associated with this witnessed behavior should be activated relatively strongly, and they should then be especially likely to carry out the same kind of behavior themselves. In accord with this possibility, Singer and Singer (1981) found that children whose play was guided by a prosocial theme displayed little aggression afterward. The prosocial thoughts brought to mind in the course of their play could have activated ideas and feelings that were incompatible with aggression, thereby lessening their aggressive tendencies.

An experiment by Turner and Berkowitz (1972) provides fairly direct support for the present reasoning. Male college students were first provoked and then watched a movie of a prize fight. Most of the participants were asked to think of themselves either as the winner of the fight or as the referee. The others simply watched the movie without any specific instructions. Additionally, half of the participants in each condition were asked to think "hit" each time the victor landed a blow and were thus induced to have aggressive ideas. And then later, all participants were given the opportunity to shock the person who had previously tormented them. The men attacked their tormentor most severely if they had imagined themselves as the winner and had thought "hit" with each punch they saw on the screen.

The "hit" ideas could have served as aggression-retrieval cues, especially for those who had thought of themselves as the fight victor. When participants said the word "hit" and at the same time imagined themselves punching their opponents, memories of past experiences with fighting may have come to mind. Thoughts, feelings, and expressive movements related to the aggression they had exhibited at these times might have been activated by the word "hit" so that their present aggression was intensified. Leyens and Picus (1973) have also reported findings consistent with this analysis. In their study, the angry men who had been asked to imagine themselves as the person who then won the filmed fight shown to them were later the most aggressive of all the participants toward the person who had insulted them.

It could be that the viewers who identify with (or think of themselves as) the movie aggressor are especially apt to have aggression-related thoughts as they watch the violent events. In their minds they strike at the film victim along with the movie aggressor so that these aggression-related thoughts then prime their aggression-associated mental networks relatively strongly.

The Reality of the Media Depiction

This interpretation of the part played by the viewers' identification with the movie aggressors implies that the media depiction's influence increases with the audience's involvement in the observed scene. There is reason to believe that the perceived reality of the media-reported occurrence can determine how involved the viewers will be psychologically in the events they witness or read about.

Berkowitz and Alioto (1973) found that participants who had been angered by another person gave that person electric shocks of longer duration after watching a war film described as actual combat than after seeing the same film described as a Hollywood reenactment. In line with this finding, Atkin (1983) reported more recently that fifth- and sixth-grade boys and girls who watched a realistic news portrayal of a fight scored higher on an aggression index than other youngsters who had seen the same story in a fantasy entertainment condition or than the control group shown an ordinary product commercial. Moreover, within the realistic news condition, those children who regarded the fight scene as "very real" scored significantly higher on the aggression measure than those rating the action as moderate or low in realism.

Reactivating Previously Acquired Associative Networks

Although the present analysis emphasizes the influence of the immediate situation on people's thought and actions, it is also important to recognize that these effects arise because of prior learning. The words and/or scenes the viewers encounter activate previously acquired associative networks. They are essentially reminded of other occasions in which they had semantically similar thoughts and inclinations, and this reminder basically sets the related network of ideas and motor programs into operation, so to speak.

However, not all presentation stimuli are equally effective in activating the previously developed associative networks. Memory research has demonstrated that stimuli linked to visual images are better recalled than stimuli that are entirely verbal in nature (cf. Reed, 1988, pp. 138–140). If a person has acquired a network of ideas and action tendencies associated with aggression, then, a visual stimulus mentally connected to this network might well be a better activator of the network than a purely verbal stimulus.

Turner and Layton (1976) extended this reasoning to the priming effects of words. Generalizing from the findings in memory research, they suggested that words having aggressive connotations would be powerful activators of aggressive inclinations to the degree that they could easily evoke images in the viewers' minds. The high imagery-aggressive words would presumably serve as good retrieval cues for prior aggressive episodes stored in memory and, thus, should strongly activate other aggression-related thoughts and behavioral inclinations.

Turner and Layton asked their participants to learn lists of words that were either high or low in imagery value and representative of either aggressive or neutral ideas. When this learning was completed, the respondents were physiologically aroused by exposing them to white noise and then were given an opportunity to shock a partner. The researchers obtained the results they had expected: The participants were most punitive if they had previously encountered the high imagery-aggressive words.

These findings are obviously highly relevant to mass media influences. In particular, they indicate that the nature of an aggressive communication can be an important determinant of how strongly it will activate previously learned aggressive ideas and action tendencies. Holding the communication's meaning constant, visual portrayals on a movie or television screen presumably will have a more powerful effect than a verbal description. But even verbal reports can prime aggression-related thoughts and inclinations, especially to the degree that these reports are rich in imagery rather than being entirely abstract in nature.

Memory phenomena are also important in considering how long the influence of any particular media-transmitted communication will last. Although the present analysis emphasizes relatively transient effects, there are occasions when a report in the mass media seems to have a fairly long-lasting impact. Thus, Berkowitz and Macaulay (1971) found that news stories of spectacular murders, such as President Kennedy's assassination, were followed by a rise in violent crimes a month or more afterward.

At least two different processes could contribute to these more durable priming effects. For one, the audience members might continue to think about the reported events, and even act on them, for a fairly long period of time. These news-prompted continued thoughts and behaviors could keep the related memory networks active where otherwise they would have subsided and become dormant. And then too, the people in the audience might encounter other stimuli that remind them of the reported occurrence, reactivating the associated memories, ideas, and action tendencies.

In accord with this last mentioned possibility, an experiment by Josephson (1987) illustrates how external cues connected with an aggressive movie can prolong the film's aggressive influence. In her experiment, second-and third-grade school boys played a game of floor hockey some minutes after they had watched a short television program that was either violent or nonviolent in nature. Just before the game, some of the boys were interviewed by an adult observer who carried a walkie-talkie (supposedly because he was playing the part of a television sports reporter). This instrument was important because walkie-talkies were prominently featured in the violent program used in the experiment.

Josephson found that boys shown the violent video and who then later saw a walkie-talkie were more aggressive in their floor hockey game than any of the other youngsters, including those who watched the violent movie but did not encounter the walkie-talkie. This instrument, which had been associated with violence in the video, apparently had reactivated the aggression-related ideas and motor programs that had been primed by the violent movie.

CONCLUSIONS

There has been widespread concern for many years about the high level of violence portrayed on the movie and televisions screens or reported in the press. (A considerable body of research indicates that the actions of aggression in the mass media can influence the thinking and actions of people in the audience and that the concern about these media effects is warranted.) This chapter attempts to account for some of this influence by focusing on one set of psychological processes that could be set into operation by the portrayed or described violence.

(Emphasizing the possibility of media-generated priming effects, we proposed that the violent media can activate aggressive ideas and inclinations that promote antisocial behavior.) This heightened likelihood of aggression can come about because of thoughts justifying assaults on others and/or beliefs that the aggression will be rewarded, and/or because the direct instigation of aggression-related ideas and action tendencies. These effects are not limited to the visual media, such as television and movies, but can also occur as a result of the depiction or report of aggression by radio, video games, comic books, and contact sports, although realistic portrayals of media violence seem to produce stronger effects than less realistic portrayals. The present analysis also notes that the thoughts and inclinations primed by the media communications are usually active only for a relatively short time but some other stimulus associated with the witnessed or described violence can reactivate the aggressive thoughts and action tendencies. (Repeated exposure to media violence presumably leads to a greater probability that the aggressive ideas and inclinations will be activated.)

This chapter, unlike its predecessors, does not discuss the effects of prosocial media content, in part because we wanted to concentrate the discussion on the more controversial question of the adverse consequences of media violence but also because there is not much recent research dealing with the prosocial effects of the mass media. However, the present formulation proposes that the media can promote prosocial behavior as well as increase the chances of antisocial conduct by reporting and/or portraying instances of socially desirable forms of behavior. Depictions of prosocial actions on movie and television screens or over the radio or on the printed page can activate thoughts and memories that foster helpfulness, kindness, and other socially constructive behaviors.

(All in all, it must be recognized that the mass media do more than entertain their audiences or transmit news. They can also influence the thoughts and behavior of people receiving the media communications.) Of course, not everyone in the audience is so affected. As this chapter also emphasizes, there are many intervening variables that can moderate the likelihood that the media-activated thoughts will be translated into actual behavior. One of the strengths of the present analysis is that it can help account for both the relatively short-term consequences of observed aggression and the exceptions.

REFERENCES

Anderson, C. A. (1983). Imagination and expectation: The effect of imagining behavioral scripts on personal intentions. *Journal of Personality and Social Psychology, 45*, 293–305.

Anderson, J., & Bower, G. (1973). *Human associative memory.* Washington, DC: Winston.

Anderson, C., & Ford, C. M. (1987). Affect of the game player: Short-term effects of highly and mildly aggressive video games. *Personality and Social Psychology Bulletin, 12*, 390–402.

Andison, F. (1977). TV violence and viewer aggression: A cumulation of study results 1956–1976. *Public Opinion Quarterly, 41*, 314–331.

Atkin, C. (1983). Effects of realistic TV violence vs. fictional violence on aggression. *Journalism Quarterly, 60*, 615–621.

Bandura, A. (1965). Vicarious processes: A case of no-trial learning. In L. Berkowitz (Ed.), *Advances in experimental social psychology* (Vol. 2, pp. 1–55). New York: Academic Press.

Bandura, A. (1971). *Social learning theory.* New York: General Learning Press.

Bargh, J., & Pietromonaco, P. (1982). Automatic information processing and social perception: The influence of trait information presented outside of conscious awareness on impression formation. *Journal of Personality and Social Psychology, 43*, 437–449.

Baron, R. A. (1977). *Human aggression.* New York: Plenum.

Berkowitz, L. (1970). Aggressive humors as a stimulus to aggressive responses. *Journal of Personality and Social Psychology, 16*, 710–717.

Berkowitz, L. (1973). Words and symbols as stimuli to aggressive responses. In J. Knutson (Ed.), *Control of aggression: Implications from basic research* (pp. 113–143). Chicago: Aldine-Atherton.

Berkowitz, L. (1974). Some determinants of impulsive aggression: Role of mediated associations with reinforcements for aggression. *Psychological Review, 81*, 165–176.

Berkowitz, L. (1984). Some effects of thoughts on anti- and prosocial influences of media events: A cognitive-neoassociation analysis. *Psychological Bulletin, 95*, 410–427.

Berkowitz, L. (1986). Situational influences on reactions to observed violence. *Journal of Social Issues, 42*(3), 93–106.

Berkowitz, L. (1990). On the formation and regulation of anger and aggression: A cognitive-neoassociationistic analysis. *American Psychologist, 45*, 494–503.

Berkowitz, L., & Alioto, J. (1973). The meaning of an observed event as a determinant of its aggressive consequences. *Journal of Personality and Social Psychology, 28*, 206–217.

Berkowitz, L., & Heimer, K. (1989). On the construction of the anger experience: Aversive events and negative priming in the formation of feelings. In L. Berkowitz (Ed.), *Advances in experimental social psychology* (Vol. 22, pp. 1–37). New York: Academic Press.

Berkowitz, L., & Macaulay, J. (1971). The contagion of criminal violence. *Sociometry, 34*, 238–260.

Berkowitz, L., & Rogers, K. H. (1986). A priming effect analysis of media influence. In J. Bryant & D. Zillmann (Eds.), *Perspectives on media effects* (pp. 57–81). Hillsdale, NJ: Lawrence Erlbaum Associates.

Boemer, M. L. (1984). An analysis of the violent content of the radio vs. TV. *Journal of Broadcasting, 28*, 341–353.

Bower, G. (1981). Mood and memory. *American Psychologist, 36*, 129–148.

Bushman, B., & Geen, R. (1990). Role of cognitive-emotional mediators and individual differences in the effects of media violence on aggression. *Journal of Personality and Social Psychology, 58*, 156–163.

Carver, C., Ganellen, R., Fromming, W., & Chambers, W. (1983). Modeling: An analysis in terms of category accessibility. *Journal of Experimental Social Psychology, 19*, 403–421.

Collins, A., & Loftus, E. (1975). A spreading-activation theory of semantic memory. *Psychological Review, 82,* 407–428.

Comstock, G. (1980). New emphasis in research on the effects of television and film violence. In E. Palmer & A. Dorr (Eds.), *Children and the faces of television* (pp. 129–148). New York: Academic Press.

Comstock, G., Chaffee, S., Katzman, N., McCombs, M., & Roberts, D. (1978). *Television and human behavior.* New York: Columbia University Press.

Cook, T. D., Kendzierski, D. A., & Thomas, S. V. (1983). The implicit assumptions of television research: An analysis of the 1982 NIMH report on *Television and behavior. Public Opinion Quarterly, 47,* 161–201.

Donnerstein, E., & Berkowitz, L. (1981). Victim reactions in aggressive erotic films as a factor in violence against women. *Journal of Personality and Social Psychology, 41,* 710–724.

Donnerstein, E., & Berkowitz, L. (1983). *Effects of film content and victim association on aggression behavior and attitudes.* Unpublished study, University of Wisconsin, Madison.

Dorr, A. (1981). Television and affective development and functioning: Maybe this decade. *Journal of Broadcasting, 25,* 335–345.

Fiske, S. T., & Taylor, S. E. (1991). *Social cognition.* New York: McGraw-Hill.

Freedman, J. L. (1984). Effect of television violence on aggressiveness. *Psychological Bulletin, 96,* 227–246.

Goldstein, J. H. (1986). *Aggression and crimes of violence.* New York, Oxford: Oxford University Press.

Goranson, R. (1969). *Observed violence and aggressive behavior: The effects of negative outcomes to the observed violence.* Unpublished doctoral dissertation, University of Wisconsin, Madison.

Herr, P. (1986). Consequences of priming: Judgment and behavior. *Journal of Personality and Social Psychology, 51,* 1106–1115.

Huesmann, L. (1982). Violence and aggression. In National Institute of Mental Health, *Television and behavior: Ten years of scientific progress* (Vol. 1, pp. 36–44). Washington, DC: U.S. Government Printing Office.

Josephson, W. (1987). Television violence and children's aggression: Testing the priming, social script, and disinhibition predictions. *Journal of Personality and Social Psychology, 53,* 882–890.

Klatzky, R. (1980). *Human memory* (2nd ed.). San Francisco: Freeman.

Landman, J., & Manis, M. (1983). Social cognition: Some historical and theoretical perspectives. In L. Berkowitz (Ed.), *Advances in experimental social psychology* (Vol. 16, pp. 49–123). New York: Academic Press.

Lang, P. J. (1979). A bio-informational theory of emotional imagery. *Psychophysiology, 16,* 495–512.

Leventhal, H. (1984). A perceptual-motor theory of emotion. In L. Berkowitz (Ed.), *Advances in experimental social psychology* (Vol. 17, pp. 117–182). New York: Academic Press.

Leyens, J.-P., & Picus, R. (1973). Identification with the winner of a fight and name mediation: Their differential effects upon subsequent aggressive behavior. *British Journal of Clinical Psychology, 12,* 374–377.

McGuire, W. J. (1986). The myth of massive media impact: Savaging and salvaging. In G. Comstock (Ed.), *Public communication and behavior* (Vol. 1, pp. 173–257). Orlando, FL: Academic Press.

Mehrabian, A., & Wixen, W. J. (1986). Preferences for individual video games as a function of their emotional effects on players. *Journal of Applied Social Psychology, 16,* 3–15.

Messner, S. F. (1986). Television violence and violent crime: An aggregate analysis. *Social Problems, 33,* 218–235.

Reed, S. K. (1988). *Cognition: Theory and applications*. Belmont, CA: Brooks/Cole.

Singer, J., & Singer, D. (1981). *Television, imagination and aggression*. Hillsdale, NJ: Lawrence Earlbaum Associates.

Tannenbaum, P., & Gaer, E. P. (1965). Mood changes as a function of stress of protagonist and degree of identification in film-viewing situation. *Journal of Personality and Social Psychology, 2*, 612–616.

Turner, C., & Berkowitz, L. (1972). Identification with film aggressor (covert role taking) and reactions to film violence. *Journal of Personality and Social Psychology, 21*, 256–264.

Turner, C., & Layton, J. (1976). Verbal imagery and connotation as memory induced mediators of aggressive behavior. *Journal of Personality and Social Psychology, 33*, 755–763.

Velten, E. (1968). A laboratory task for the induction of mood states. *Behavior Research and Therapy, 6*, 473–482.

Wann, D., & Branscombe, N. (1990). Person perception when aggressive or nonaggressive sports are primed. *Aggressive Behavior, 16*, 27–32.

Wilson, T., & Capitman, J. (1982). Effects of script availability on social behavior. *Personality and Social Psychology Bulletin, 8*, 11–19.

Wood, W., Wong, F. Y., & Chachere, G. (1991). Effects of media violence on viewers' aggression in unconstrained social interaction. *Psychological Bulletin, 109*, 371–383.

Wyer, R., Jr., & Srull, T. (1981). Category accessibility: Some theoretical and empirical issues concerning the processing of information. In E. Higgins, C. Herman, & M. Zanna (Eds.), *Social cognition* (Vol. 1, pp. 161–197). Hillsdale, NJ: Lawrence Erlbaum Associates.

Social Cognitive Theory of Mass Communication

ALBERT BANDURA
Stanford University

Because of the influential role the mass media play in society, understanding the psychosocial mechanisms through which symbolic communication influences human thought, affect, and action is of considerable import. Social cognitive theory provides a conceptual framework within which to examine the determinants and mechanisms of such effects. Human behavior has often been explained in terms of one-sided determinism. In such modes of unidirectional causation, behavior is depicted as being shaped and controlled either by environmental influences or by internal dispositions. Social cognitive theory explains psychosocial functioning in terms of triadic reciprocal causation (Bandura, 1986). In this model of reciprocal determinism, behavior; cognitive, biological, and other personal factors; and environmental events all operate as interacting determinants that influence each other bidirectionally (see Fig. 4.1). Reciprocality does not mean that the different sources of influences are of equal strength. Some may be stronger than others. Nor do the reciprocal influences all occur simultaneously. It takes time for a causal factor to exert its influence and activate reciprocal influences. Reciprocal causation provides people with opportunities to exercise some control over events in their lives, as well as set limits of self-direction. Because of the bidirectionality of influence, people are both products and producers of their environment.

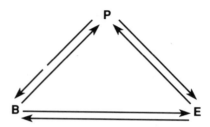

FIG. 4.1.   Schematization of triadic reciprocal determinism. *B* signifies behavior; *P* the cognitive, biological, and other internal events that can affect perceptions and actions; and *E* the external environment.

Seen from the sociocognitive perspective, human nature is characterized by a vast potentiality that can be fashioned by direct and observational experience into a variety of forms within biological limits. To say that a major distinguishing mark of humans is their endowed plasticity is not to say that they have no nature or that they come structureless (Midgley, 1978). The plasticity, which is intrinsic to the nature of humans, depends on neurophysiological mechanisms and structures that have evolved over time. These advanced neural systems for processing, retaining, and using coded information provide the capacity for the very characteristics that are distinctly human—generative symbolization, forethought, evaluative self-regulation, reflective self-consciousness, and symbolic communication.

SYMBOLIZING CAPABILITY

In analyzing the personal determinants of psychosocial functioning, social cognitive theory accords a central role to cognitive, vicarious, self-regulatory, and self-reflective processes. A remarkable capacity for symbolization provides humans with a powerful tool for comprehending their environment and for creating and regulating environmental events that touch virtually every aspect of their lives. Most external influences affect behavior through cognitive processes. Cognitive factors partly determine which environmental events will be observed, what meaning will be conferred on them, whether they leave any lasting effects, what emotional impact and motivating power they will have, and how the information they convey will be organized for future use. It is with symbols that people process and transform transient experiences into cognitive models that serve as guides for judgment and action. Through symbols, people give meaning, form, and continuity to the experiences they have had.

People gain understanding of causal relationships and expand their knowledge by symbolically manipulating the information derived from personal and vicarious experiences. The remarkable flexibility of symbolization enables them to create ideas that transcend their sensory experiences. Through the medium of symbols they can communicate with others at any distance in time and space. However, in keeping with the interactional perspective, social cognitive theory devotes much attention to the social origins of thought and the mechanisms through which social factors exert their influence on cognitive functioning.

SELF-REGULATORY CAPABILITY

People are not only knowers and performers. They are also self-reactors with a capacity for self-direction. The self-regulation of motivation, affect, and action operates partly through internal standards and evaluative reactions to one's own behavior (Bandura, 1989b). The anticipated self-satisfaction gained from fulfilling valued standards provides one source of incentive motivation for personal accomplishments. Perceived negative discrepancies between performance and the standard individuals seek to attain creates self-dissatisfaction that serves as another incentive motivator for enhanced effort. The motivational effects do not stem from the standards themselves but rather from the fact that people respond evaluatively to their own behavior.

Most theories of self-regulation are founded on a negative feedback model. This system functions as a motivator and regulator of action and cognitive change through a discrepancy reduction mechanism. Discrepancy between one's perceived performance and reference standard motivates action to reduce the incongruity. Discrepancy reduction clearly plays a central role in any system of self-regulation. However, in the negative feedback control system, if performance matches the standard, the person does nothing. Such a feedback control system would produce circular action that leads nowhere.

Self-regulation by negative discrepancy tells only half the story and not necessarily the more interesting half. In fact, people are proactive, aspiring organisms. Human self-regulation relies on *discrepancy production* as well as *discrepancy reduction*. People motivate and guide their actions through proactive control by setting themselves valued goals that create a state of disequilibrium and then mobilizing their abilities and effort based on anticipatory estimation of what is required to reach the goals. Reactive feedback control comes into play in subsequent adjustments of strategies and effort to attain desired results. After people attain the goal they have been pursuing, those with a strong sense of efficacy set higher goals for themselves. Adopting further challenges creates new motivating discrepancies to be mastered. Self-regulation of motivation and action thus involves a dual control process of disequilibrating discrepancy production (proactive control) followed by equilibrating discrepancy reduction (reactive control).

In areas of functioning involving achievement strivings and cultivation of competencies, the internal standards that are selected as a mark of adequacy are progressively altered as knowledge and skills are acquired and challenges are met. In many areas of social and moral behavior the internal standards that serve as the basis for regulating one's conduct have greater stability. That is, people do not change from week to week what they regard as right or wrong or good or bad. After they adopt a standard of morality, their self-sanctions for actions that match or violate their personal standards serve as the regulatory influencers (Bandura, 1991).

The capability of forethought adds another dimension to the process of self-regulation. Most human behavior is directed toward events and outcomes projected into the future. The future time perspective manifests itself in many different ways. People anticipate the likely consequences of their prospective actions, they set goals for themselves, and they otherwise plan courses of action that are likely to produce desired outcomes. Because future events have no actual existence they cannot be causes of current motivation and action. However, by being represented cognitively in the present, conceived futures can have causal impact on current behavior. Through the exercise of forethought, people motivate themselves and guide their actions anticipatorily.

SELF-REFLECTIVE CAPABILITY

The capability for self-reflection concerning one's own thinking and personal efficacy is another dimension of self-influence that receives prominent attention in social cognitive theory. Effective cognitive functioning requires ways of distinguishing between accurate and faulty thinking. In verifying thought by self-reflective means, people monitor their ideas, act on them or predict occurrences from them, then they judge from the results the adequacy of their thoughts and change them accordingly. Judgments concerning the validity and functional value of one's thoughts are formed by comparing how well thoughts match some indicant of reality. Four different modes of thought verification can be distinguished. They include *enactive, vicarious, persuasory,* and *logical* forms.

Enactive verification relies on the adequacy of the fit between thought and the results of one's actions. Good matches corroborate thoughts; mismatches tend to refute them. In the vicarious mode of thought verification, observing other people's transactions with the environment and the effects they produce serves as a way of checking the correctness of one's own thinking. Vicarious thought verification is not simply a supplement to enactive experience. Symbolic modeling greatly expands the range of verification experiences that cannot otherwise be attained by personal action. A related mode of thought verification relies on comparing one's thoughts to the judgments of others. When experiential verification is either difficult or impossible, people evaluate the soundness of their beliefs by comparing them to the judgments of others. Thoughts are also verified by inferential means. In the course of development, people acquire rules of inference. By reasoning from what is already known, they can derive knowledge about things that extend beyond their experience and check the validity of their reasoning.

Such metacognitive activities usually foster veridical thought, but they can produce faulty thought patterns as well. Forceful actions arising from erroneous beliefs often create social environments that confirm the misbeliefs (Snyder, 1980). We are all acquainted with problem-prone individuals who, through their aversive behavior, predictively breed negative social climates wherever they go. Verification of thought by comparison with distorted televised versions of social reality can foster shared misconceptions of people, places, or things (Hawkins & Pingree, 1982). Social verification can foster bizarre views of reality if the shared beliefs of the reference group with which one affiliates are peculiar and the group is encapsulated from outside social ties and influences (Bandura, 1982a; Hall, 1987). Deductive reasoning will be flawed if the propositional knowledge on which it is based is faulty or if biases intrude on reasoning processes (Falmagne, 1975).

Among the self-referent thoughts that influence human motivation, affect, and action, none is more central or pervasive than people's judgments of their efficacy to exert control over their level of functioning and events that affect their lives. The self-efficacy mechanism plays a central role in human agency (Bandura, 1986, 1989a). People's beliefs in their personal efficacy influence what courses of action they choose to pursue, how much effort they will invest in activities, how long they will persevere in the face of obstacles and failure experiences, and their resiliency following setbacks. People's judgments of their capabilities additionally influence whether their thought patterns are self-hindering or self-enhancing, and how much stress and despondency they experience during anticipatory and actual transaction with the environment. A high sense of self-efficacy thus pays off in performance accomplishments and personal well-being. In collective endeavors, the stronger the perceived collective efficacy, the greater and more perseverant is the group effort to effect social changes.

VICARIOUS CAPABILITY

Psychological theories have traditionally emphasized learning through the effects of one's actions. If knowledge and skills could be acquired only by direct experience, the process of human development would be greatly retarded, not to mention exceedingly tedious and hazardous. A culture could never transmit its language, mores, social practices, and requisite competencies if they had to be shaped tediously in each new member by response consequences without the benefit of models to exemplify the cultural patterns. The abbreviation of the acquisition process is vital for survival as well as for human development because natural endowment provides few inborn skills and errors can be perilous. Moreover, the constraints of time, resources, and mobility impose severe limits on the situations and activities that can be directly explored for the acquisition of new knowledge and competencies.

Humans have evolved an advanced capacity for observational learning that enables them to expand their knowledge and skills on the basis of information conveyed by modeling influences. Indeed, virtually all learning phenomena resulting from direct experience can occur vicariously by observing people's behavior and its consequences for them (Bandura, 1986; Rosenthal & Zimmerman, 1978). Much social learning occurs either deliberately or inadvertently by observing the actual behavior of others and the consequences for them. However, a great deal of information about human values, thinking patterns, and behavior is gained from models portrayed symbolically through verbal or pictorial means.

A major significance of symbolic modeling lies in its tremendous multiplicative power. Unlike learning by doing, which requires altering the actions of each individual through repeated trial-and-error experiences, in observational learning a single model can transmit new ways of thinking and behaving simultaneously to many people in widely dispersed locales. There is another aspect of symbolic modeling that magnifies its psychological and social impact. During the course of their daily lives, people have direct contact with only a small sector of the physical and social environment. They generally travel the same routes, visit the same places, and see the same group of associates. Consequently, their conceptions of social reality are greatly influenced by vicarious experiences—by what they see and hear—without direct experiential correctives. To a large extent, people act on their images of reality. The more people's images of reality depend on the media's symbolic environment, the greater is its social impact (Ball-Rokeach & DeFleur, 1976).

Most psychological theories were cast long before the advent of enormous advances in the technology of communication. As a result, they give insufficient attention to the increasingly powerful role that the symbolic environment plays in present-day human lives. Whereas previously modeling influences were largely confined to the behavior patterns exhibited in one's immediate environment, the accelerated growth of video delivery technologies has vastly expanded the range of models to which members of society are exposed day in and day out. By drawing on these modeled patterns of thought and behavior, observers can transcend the bounds of their immediate environment. New ideas and social practices are now being rapidly diffused by symbolic modeling within a society and from one society to another (Bandura, 1986; Pearl, Bouthilet, & Lazar, 1982). Because television occupies a large part of people's lives, the study of acculturation in the present electronic age must be broadened to include electronic acculturation.

MECHANISMS GOVERNING OBSERVATIONAL LEARNING

Because symbolic modeling is central to full understanding of the effects of mass communication, the modeling aspect of social cognitive theory is discussed in somewhat greater detail. Observational learning is governed by four subfunctions, which are summarized in Fig. 4.2.

Attentional processes determine what is selectively observed in the

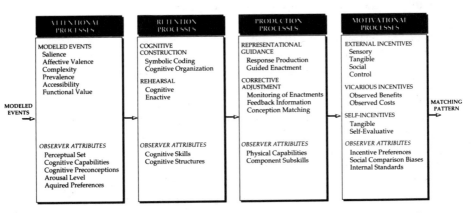

FIG. 4.2. The four major subfunctions governing observational learning and the influential factors operating within each subfunction.

profusion of modeling influences and what information is extracted from ongoing modeled events. A number of factors influence the exploration and construal of what is modeled in the social and symbolic environment. Some of these determinants concern the cognitive skills, preconceptions, and value preferences of the observers. Others are related to the salience, attractiveness, and functional value of the modeled activities themselves. Still other factors pertain to the structural arrangements of human interactions and associational networks, which largely determine the types of models to which people have ready access.

People cannot be much influenced by observed events if they do not remember them. A second major subfunction governing observational learning concerns cognitive *representational processes*. Retention involves an active process of transforming and restructuring information about events for memory representation in the form of rules and conceptions. Retention is greatly aided by symbolic transformations of modeled information into memory codes and cognitive rehearsal of the coded information. Preconceptions and affective states exert biasing influences on these representational activities. Similarly, recall involves a process of reconstruction rather than simply retrieval of registered events.

In the third subfunction in modeling—the *behavioral production process*—symbolic conceptions are translated into appropriate courses of action. This is achieved through a conception-matching process in which conceptions guide the construction and execution of behavior patterns and the adequacy of the action is compared against the conceptual model. The behavior is then modified on the basis of the comparative information to achieve close correspondence between conception and action. The mechanism for translating cognition into action involves both transformational and generative operations. Execution of a skill must be constantly varied to suit changing circumstances. Adaptive performance, therefore, requires a generative conception rather than a one-to-one mapping between cognitive representation and action. By applying an abstract specification of the activity, people can produce many variations on the skill. Conceptions are rarely transformed into masterful performance on the first attempt. Monitored enactments serve as the vehicle for transforming knowledge into skilled action. Performances are perfected by corrective adjustments during behavior production. The more extensive the subskills that people possess, the easier it is to integrate them to produce new behavior patterns. When deficits exist, the subskills required for complex performances must first be developed by modeling and guided enactment.

The fourth subfunction in modeling concerns *motivational processes*. Social cognitive theory distinguishes between acquisition and performance because people do not perform everything they learn. Performance of observationally learned behavior is influenced by three major types of incentive motivators: *direct, vicarious,* and *self-produced.* People are more likely to exhibit modeled behavior if it results in valued outcomes than if it has unrewarding or punishing effects. The observed detriments and benefits experienced by others influence the performance of modeled patterns in much the same way as do directly experienced consequences. People are motivated by the successes of others who are similar to themselves, but are discouraged from pursuing courses of behavior that they have seen often result in adverse consequences. Personal standards of conduct provide a further source of incentive motivation. The evaluative reactions people generate to their own behavior regulate which observationally learned activities they are most likely to pursue. They pursue activities they find self-satisfying and give them a sense of worth but reject those they personally disapprove.

The different sources of consequences may operate as complimentary or opposing influences on behavior (Bandura, 1986). Patterns of behavior are most firmly established when social and self-sanctions are compatible. Under such conditions, socially approvable behavior is a source of self-pride and socially disapprovable behavior is self-censured. Behavior is especially susceptible to external influences in the absence of countervailing self-sanctions. People who are not much committed to personal standards adopt a pragmatic orientation, tailoring their behavior to fit whatever the situation seems to call for (Snyder & Campbell, 1982). They become adept at reading social situations and guiding their actions by expediency.

One type of conflict between social and self-produced sanctions arises when individuals are socially punished for behavior they highly value. Principled dissenters and nonconformists often find themselves in this predicament. Here, the relative strength of self-approval and social censure determine whether the behavior will be restrained or expressed. Should the threatened social consequences be severe, people hold in check self-praiseworthy acts in risky situations but perform them readily in relatively safe settings. These are individuals, however, whose sense of self-worth is so strongly invested in certain convictions that they will submit to prolonged maltreatment, rather than accede to what they regard as unjust or immoral.

People commonly experience conflicts in which they are socially pressured to engage in behavior that violates their moral standards. When self-devaluative consequences outweigh the benefits for socially accommodating behavior, the social influences do not have much sway. However, the self-regulation of conduct operates through conditional application of moral standards. We shall see shortly that self-sanctions can be weakened or nullified by selective disengagement of internal control.

ABSTRACT MODELING

Modeling is not merely a process of behavioral mimicry. Highly functional patterns of behavior, which constitute the proven skills and established customs of a culture, may be adopted in essentially the same form as they are exemplified. However, in many activities, subskills must be improvised to suit varying circumstances. Modeling influences convey rules for generative and innovative behavior as well. This higher level learning is achieved through abstract modeling. Rule-governed judgments and actions differ in specific content and other details but they embody the same underlying rule. For example, a model may confront moral conflicts that differ widely in content but apply the same moral standard to them. In abstract modeling, observers extract the rule governing the specific judgments or actions exhibited by others. Once they learn the rule, they can use it to judge or generate new instances of behavior that go beyond what they have seen or heard. Much human learning is aimed at developing cognitive skills on how to gain and use knowledge for future use. Observational learning of thinking skills is greatly facilitated by having models verbalize their thoughts aloud as they engage in problem-solving activities (Meichenbaum, 1984). The thoughts guiding their decisions and action strategies are thus made observable.

Acquiring generative rules from modeled information involves at least three processes: extracting the determining features from various social exemplars: integrating the extracted information into composite rules; and using the rules to produce new instances of behavior. Through abstract modeling, people acquire, among other things, standards for categorizing and judging events, linguistic rules of communication, thinking skills on how to gain and use knowledge, and personal standards for regulating one's motivation and conduct (Bandura, 1986; Rosenthal & Zimmerman, 1978). Evidence that generative rules of thought and conduct can be created through abstract modeling attests to the broad scope of observational learning.

INHIBITORY AND DISINHIBITORY EFFECTS

The discussion thus far has centered on the acquisition of knowledge, cognitive skills, and new styles of behavior through observational learning. Social cognitive theory distinguishes among several modeling functions, each governed by different determinants and underlying mechanisms. In addition to cultivating new competencies, modeling influences can strengthen or weaken restraints over behavior that has been previously learned. The effects of modeling on restraints rely heavily on the information conveyed about the performability and probable consequences of modeled courses of action. The impact of such information on personal restraint depends on several factors. These include observers' judgments of their ability to accomplish the modeled behavior, their perception of the modeled actions as producing favorable or adverse consequences, and their inferences that similar or unlike consequences would result if they, themselves, were to engage in similar activities. Inhibitory and disinhibitory effects of modeling have been studied most extensively in relation to transgressive, aggressive, and sexual behavior (Berkowitz, 1984; Liebert, Sprafkin, & Davidson, 1982; Malamuth & Donnerstein, 1984; Zillmann & Bryant, 1984).

Transgressive behavior is regulated by two major sources of sanctions: social sanctions and internalized self-sanctions. Both control mechanisms operate anticipatorily. In motivators arising from social sanctions, people refrain from transgressing because they anticipate that such conduct will bring them social censure and other adverse consequences. In motivators rooted in self-reactive control, people refrain from transgressing because such conduct will give rise to self-reproach. Media portrayals can alter perceived social sanctions by the way in which the consequences of different styles of conduct are portrayed. For example, televised aggression is often exemplified in ways that tend to weaken restraints over aggressive conduct (Goranson, 1970; Halloran & Croll, 1972; Larsen, 1968). In televised representations of human discord, physical aggression is a preferred solution to interpersonal conflicts; it is acceptable and relatively successful; and it is socially sanctioned by superheroes triumphing over evil by violent means.

Inhibitory and disinhibitory effects stemming from self-sanctions are mediated largely through self-regulatory mechanisms. After standards have been internalized, they serve as guides and deterrents to conduct by the self-approving and self-reprimanding consequences people produce for themselves. However, moral standards do not function as fixed internal regulators of conduct. Self-regulatory mechanisms do not operate unless they are activated, and there are many processes by which moral reactions can be disengaged from inhumane conduct (Bandura, 1986, 1991). Selective activation and disengagement of internal control permits different types of conduct with the same moral standards. Figure 4.3 shows the points in the self-regulatory process at which moral control can be disengaged from censurable conduct.

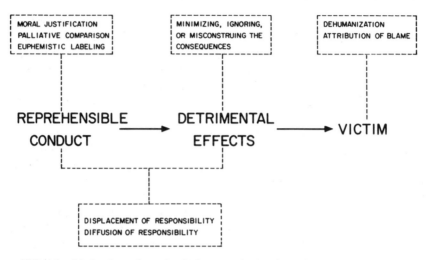

FIG. 4.3. Mechanisms through which internal control is selectively activated and disengaged from detrimental conduct at different points in the self-regulatory process.

One set of disengagement practices operates on the construal of the behavior itself by *moral justification*. People do not ordinarily engage in reprehensible conduct until they have justified to themselves the morality of their actions. What is culpable is made personally and socially acceptable by portraying it in the service of moral purposes. Moral justification is widely used to support self-serving and otherwise culpable conduct. Moral judgments of conduct are also partly influenced by what it is compared against. Self-deplored acts can be made righteous by contrasting them with more flagrant transgressions. Because examples of human culpability abound, they lend themselves readily to cognitive restructuring of transgressive conduct by *advantageous comparison*. Activities can take on a very different appearance depending on what they are called. *Euphemistic labeling* provides another convenient device for masking reprehensible activities or even conferring a respectable status upon them. Through convoluted verbiage, reprehensible conduct is made benign and those who engage in it are relieved of a sense of personal agency.

Cognitive restructuring of behavior through moral justifications and palliative characterizations is the most effective psychological mechanism for promoting transgressive conduct. This is because moral restructuring not only eliminates self-deterrents but engages self-approval in the service of transgressive exploits. What was once morally condemnable becomes a source of self-valuation.

Ball-Rokeach (1972) attached special significance to evaluative reactions and social justifications presented in the media, particularly in conflicts of power. This is because relatively few viewers experience sufficient inducement to use the aggressive strategies they have seen, but the transmitted justifications and evaluations can help to mobilize public support for policy actions favoring either social control or social change. The justificatory changes can have widespread social and political ramifications.

The mass media, especially television, provide the best access to the public through its strong drawing power. For this reason, television is increasingly used as the principle vehicle of justification. Struggles to legitimize and gain support for one's values and causes and to discredit those of one's opponents are now waged more and more through the electronic media (Ball-Rokeach, 1972; Bandura, 1990; Bassiouni, 1981). Because of its potential influence, the communication system itself is subject to constant pressures from different factions within society seeking to sway it to their ideology. Research on the role of the mass media in the social construction of reality carries important social implications.

Self-sanctions are activated most strongly when personal causation of detrimental effects is apparent. Another set of disengagement practices operates by obscuring or distorting the relationship between actions and the effects they cause. People will behave in ways they normally repudiate if a legitimate authority sanctions their conduct and accepts responsibility for its consequences (Diener, Dineen, Endresen, Beaman, & Fraser, 1975; Milgram, 1974). Under conditions of *displacement of responsibility*, people view their actions as springing from the dictates of others rather than their being personally responsible for them. Because they are not the actual agent of their actions, they are spared self-prohibiting reactions. The deterrent power of self-sanctions is also weakened when the link between conduct and its consequences is obscured by *diffusion of responsibility* for culpable behavior. Through division of labor, diffusion of decision making, and group action, people can behave detrimentally without any one person feeling personally responsible (Kelman & Hamilton, 1989). People behave more injuriously under diffused responsibility than when they hold themselves personally accountable for what they do (Bandura, Underwood, & Fromson, 1975; Diener, 1977).

Additional ways of weakening self-deterring reactions operate through *disregard or distortion of the consequences of action*. When people pursue detrimental activities for personal gain or because of social inducements, they avoid facing the harm they cause or they minimize it. They readily recall the possible benefits of the behavior but are less able to remember its harmful effects (Brock & Buss, 1962, 1964). In addition to selective inattention and cognitive distortion of effects, the misrepresentation may involve active efforts to discredit evidence of the harm they cause. As long as the detrimental results of one's conduct are ignored, minimized, distorted, or disbelieved there is little reason for self-censure to be activated.

The final set of disengagement practices operates at the point of recipients of detrimental acts. The strength of self-evaluative reactions to detrimental conduct partly depends on how the perpetrators view the people toward whom the behavior is directed. To perceive another as human enhances empathetic or vicarious reactions through perceived similarity (Bandura, 1992b). As a result, it is difficult to mistreat humanized persons without risking self-condemnation. Self-sanctions against cruel conduct can be disengaged or blunted by *dehumanization*, which divests people of human qualities or invests them with bestial qualities. Whereas dehumanization weakens self-restraints against cruel conduct (Diener, 1977; Zimbardo, 1969), humanization fosters considerate, compassionate behavior (Bandura, Underwood, & Fromson, 1975).

Attribution of blame to one's antagonists is still another expedient that can serve self-exonerative purposes. Deleterious interactions usually involve a series of reciprocally escalative actions, in which the antagonists are rarely faultless. One can always select from the chain of events an instance of the adversary's defensive behavior and view it as the original instigation. Injurious conduct thus becomes a justifiable defensive reaction to belligerent provocations. Others can, therefore, be blamed for bringing suffering on themselves. Self-exoneration is similarly achievable by viewing one's detrimental conduct as forced by circumstances rather than as a personal decision. By blaming others or circumstances, not only are one's own actions excusable but one can even feel self-righteous in the process.

Because internalized controls can be selectively activated and disengaged, marked changes in moral conduct can be achieved without changing people's personality structures, moral principles, or self-evaluative systems. It is self-exonerative processes rather than character flaws that account for most inhumanities. The massive threats to human welfare stem mainly from deliberate acts of principle rather than from unrestrained acts of impulse.

Research in which the different disengagement factors are systematically varied in media portrayals of inhumanities attests to the disinhibitory power of mass media influences (Berkowitz & Geen, 1967; Donnerstein, 1984; Meyer, 1972). Viewers' punitiveness is enhanced by exposure to media productions that morally justify injurious conduct, blame and dehumanize victims, displace or diffuse personal responsibility, and sanitize destructive consequences. Research assessing self-reactive control provides evidence that sanctioning social conditions are linked to self-regulatory influences that in turn, are linked to injurious conduct (Bandura, Underwood, & Fromson, 1975). The same disengagement mechanisms are enlisted heavily by members of the television industry in the production of programs that exploit human brutality for commercial purposes (Baldwin & Lewis, 1972; Bandura, 1973).

ACQUISITION AND MODIFICATION
OF AFFECTIVE DISPOSITIONS

People are easily aroused by the emotional expressions of others. Vicarious arousal operates mainly through an intervening self-arousal process (Bandura, 1992b). That is, seeing others react emotionally to instigating conditions activates emotion-arousing thoughts and imagery in observers. As people develop their capacity for cognitive self-arousal, they can generate emotional reactions to cues that are only suggestive of a model's emotional experiences (Wilson & Cantor, 1985). Conversely, they can neutralize or attenuate the emotional impact of modeled distress by thoughts that transform threatening situations into non-threatening ones (Bandura, 1986; Cantor & Wilson, 1988; Dysinger & Ruckmick, 1933).

If the affective reactions of models only aroused observers fleetingly, it would be of some interest as far as momentary communication is concerned, but of limited psychological import. What gives significance to vicarious influence is that observers can acquire lasting attitudes, emotional reactions, and behavioral proclivities toward persons, places, or things that have been associated with modeled emotional experiences. They learn to fear the things that frightened models, to dislike what repulsed them, and to like what gratified them (Bandura, 1986; Duncker, 1938). Fears and intractable phobias are ameliorated by modeling influences that convey information about coping strategies for exercising control over the things that are feared. The stronger the instilled sense of coping self-efficacy, the bolder the behavior (Bandura, 1982b). Values can similarly be developed and altered vicariously by repeated exposure to modeled preferences.

SOCIAL CONSTRUCTION OF REALITY

Televised representations of social realities reflect ideological bents in their portrayal of human nature, social relations, and the norms and structure of society (Adoni & Mane, 1984; Gerbner, 1972). Heavy exposure to this symbolic world may eventually make the televised images appear to be the authentic state of human affairs. Some disputes about the vicarious cultivation of beliefs have arisen over findings from correlational studies using global indices based on amount of television viewing (Gerbner, Gross, Morgan, & Signorielli, 1981; Hirsch, 1980). Televised influence is best defined in terms of the contents people watch rather than the sheer amount of television viewing. More particularized measures of exposure to the televised fare show that heavy television viewing shapes viewers' beliefs and conceptions of reality (Hawkins & Pingree, 1972). The relationship remains when other possible contributing factors are simultaneously controlled.

Vicarious cultivation of social conceptions is most clearly revealed in studies verifying the direction of causality by varying experimentally the nature and amount of exposure to media influences. Controlled laboratory studies provide converging evidence that television portrayals shape viewer's beliefs (Flerx, Fidler, & Rogers, 1976; O'Bryant & Corder-Bolz, 1978). Portrayals in the print media similarly shape conceptions of social reality (Heath, 1984; Siegel, 1958). To see the world as the televized messages portray it is to harbor some misconceptions. Indeed, many of the shared misconceptions about occupational pursuits, ethnic groups, minorities, the elderly, social and gender roles, and other aspects of life are at least partly cultivated through symbolic modeling of stereotypes (Buerkel-Rothfuss & Mayes, 1981; McGhee & Frueh, 1980; Tan, 1979). Verification of personal conceptions against televised versions of social reality can thus foster some collective illusions.

SOCIAL PROMPTING OF HUMAN BEHAVIOR

The actions of others can also serve as social prompts for previously learned behavior that observers can perform but have not done so because of insufficient inducements, rather than because of restraints. Social prompting effects are distinguished from observational learning and disinhibition because no new behavior has been acquired, and disinhibitory processes are not involved because the elicited behavior is socially acceptable and not encumbered by restraints.

The influence of models in activating, channeling, and supporting the behavior of others is abundantly documented in both laboratory and field studies (Bandura, 1986). By exemplification one can get people to behave altruistically, to volunteer their services, to delay or seek gratification, to show affection, to select certain foods and drinks, to choose certain kinds of apparel, to converse on particular topics, to be inquisitive or passive, to think creatively or conventionally, or to engage in other permissible courses of action. Thus, the types of models that prevail within a social milieu partly determine which human qualities, from among many alternatives, are selectively activated. The actions of models acquire the power to activate and channel behavior when they are good predictors for observers that positive results can be gained by similar conduct.

The fashion and taste industries rely heavily on the social prompting power of modeling. Since the potency of vicarious influences can be enhanced by showing modeled acts bringing rewards, vicarious outcomes figure prominently in advertising campaigns. Thus, drinking a certain brand of wine or using a particular shampoo wins the loving admiration of beautiful people, enhances job performance, masculinizes self-conception, actualizes individualism and authenticity, tranquilizes irritable nerves, invites social recognition and amicable reactions from total strangers, and arouses affectionate overtures from spouses.

The types of vicarious outcomes, model characteristics, and modeling formats that are selected vary depending on what happens to be in vogue at the time. Model characteristics are varied to boost the persuasiveness of commercial messages. Prestigeful models are often enlisted to capitalize on the high regard in which they are held. The best social sellers depend on what happens to be popular at the moment. Drawing on evidence that similarity to the model enhances modeling, some advertisements portray common folk achieving wonders with the wares advertised. Because vicarious influence increases with multiplicity of modeling, the beers, soft drinks, and snacks are being consumed with gusto in the advertised world by groups of wholesome, handsome, fun-loving models. Eroticism is another stimulant that never goes out of style. Therefore, erotic modeling does heavy duty in efforts to command attention and to make advertised products more attractive to potential buyers (Kanungo & Pang, 1973; Peterson & Kerin, 1979).

In sum, modeling influences serve diverse functions—as tutors, inhibitors, disinhibitors, social prompters, emotion arousers, and shapers of values and conceptions of reality. Although the different modeling functions can operate separately, in nature they often work concurrently. Thus, for example, in the spread of new styles of aggression, models serve as both teachers and disinhibitors. When novel conduct is punished, observers learn the conduct that was punished as well as the restraints. A novel example can both teach and prompt similar acts.

DUAL-LINK VERSUS MULTIPATTERN
FLOW OF INFLUENCE

It has been commonly assumed in theories of mass communication that modeling influences operate through a two-step diffusion process. Influential persons pick up new ideas from the media and pass them on to their followers through personal influence. Some communication researchers have claimed that the media can only reinforce change but cannot initiate it (Klapper, 1960). Such a view is at variance with a substantial body of evidence. Media influences create personal attributes as well as alter preexisting ones (Bandura, 1986; Liebert, Sprafkin, & Davidson, 1982).

The different modes of human influence are too diverse in nature to have fixed relative strengths. Most behavior is the product of multiple determinants operating in concert. Hence, the relative contribution of any given factor in a pattern of influences can change depending on the nature and strength of coexisting determinants. Even the same determinant operating within the same causal structure of factors can change in its causal contribution with further experience (Wood & Bandura, 1989). In the case of atypical behavior, it is usually produced by a unique constellation of the determinants, such that if any one of them were absent the behavior would not have occurred. Depending on their quality and coexistence of other determinants, media influences may be subordinate to, equal to, or outweigh nonmedia influences. Given the dynamic nature of multifaceted causal structures, efforts to affix an average strength to a given mode of influence calls to mind the nonswimming analyst who drowned while trying to cross a river that averaged three feet in depth.

The view that the path of media influence is exclusively a filter-down process is disputed by a wealth of knowledge regarding modeling influences. Human judgment, values, and conduct can be altered by televised modeling without having to wait for an influential intermediary to adopt what has been shown and then to serve as the diffuser. Watt and van den Berg (1978) tested several alternative theories about how media communications relate to public attitudes and behavior. The explanatory contenders included the views that media influence people directly; media influence opinion leaders who then affect others; media have no independent effects; media set the public agenda for discussions by designating what is important but do not otherwise influence the public; and finally, media simply reflect public attitudes and behavior rather than shape them. The direct-flow model from media to the public received the best empirical support. In this study, the behavior was highly publicized and could bring benefits without risks.

When the activities being advocated require the investment of time and resources, and failures can be costly, people are inclined to seek verification of functional value from other sources as well before they act.

Chaffee (1982) reviewed substantial evidence that calls into question the prevailing view that interpersonal sources of information are necessarily more persuasive than media sources. People seek information that may be potentially useful to them from different sources. Neither informativeness, credibility, nor persuasiveness are uniquely tied to interpersonal sources or to media sources. How extensively different sources are used depends, in large part, on their accessibility and the likelihood that they will provide the kinds of information sought.

Modeling affects the adoption of new practices and behavior patterns in several ways. It instructs people about new ways of thinking and behaving by informative demonstration or description. Learning about new things does not rely on a fixed hierarchy of sources. Efficacious modeling not only cultivates competencies but also enhances the sense of personal efficacy needed to transform knowledge and skills into successful courses of action. The relative importance of interpersonal and media sources of information in initiating the adoption process varies for different activities and for the same activity at different stages in the adoption process (Pelz, 1983). Models motivate as well as inform and empower. People are initially reluctant to adopt new practices that involve costs and risks until they see the advantages that have been gained by early adopters. Modeled benefits accelerate social diffusion by weakening the restraints of the more cautious potential adopters. As acceptance spreads, the new ways gain further social support. Models also display preferences and evaluative reactions, which can alter observers' values and standards. Changes in evaluative standards affect receptivity to the activities being modeled. Models not only exemplify and legitimate new practices, they also serve as advocates for them by directly encouraging others to adopt them.

In short, there is no single pattern of social influence. The media can implant ideas either directly or through adopters. Analyses of the role of mass media in social diffusion must distinguish between their effect on learning modeled activities and on their adoptive use, and examine how media and interpersonal influences affect these separable processes. In some instances the media both teach new forms of behavior and create motivators for action by altering people's value preferences, self-beliefs of efficacy, and outcome expectations. In other instances, the media teach but other adopters provide the incentive motivation to perform what has been learned observationally. In still other instances, the effect of the media may be entirely socially mediated. That is, people who have had no exposure to the media are influenced by adopters who have had the exposure and then, themselves, become the transmitters of the new ways. The hierarchical pattern is more likely to obtain for the print media, which has a more limited audience, than for the ubiquitous video media. Within these different patterns of social influence, the media can serve as originating, as well as reinforcing, influences.

SOCIAL DIFFUSION
THROUGH SYMBOLIC MODELING

Much of the preceding discussion has been concerned mainly with modeling at the individual level. As previously noted, a unique property of modeling is that it can transmit information of virtually limitless variety to vast numbers of people simultaneously through the medium of symbolic modeling. Extraordinary advances in the technology of communication, which increase the range and speed of social influence immensely, have transformed the social-diffusion process. The video system feeding off telecommunications satellites has become the dominant vehicle for disseminating symbolic environments. Social practices are not only being widely diffused within societies, but ideas, values, and styles of conduct are being modeled worldwide. The electronic media are coming to play an increasingly influential role in transcultural change. Televised modeling is now being used to effect social change at community and society-wide levels (Bandura, 1986; Sabido, 1981; Singhal & Rogers, 1989; Winett, Leckliter, Chinn, Stahl, & Love, 1985).

Social cognitive theory analyzes social diffusion of new behavior patterns in terms of three constituent processes and the psychosocial factors that govern them. These include the acquisition of knowledge about innovative behaviors, the adoption of these behaviors in practice, and the social networks through which they spread and are supported. Diffusion of innovation follows a common pattern (Robertson, 1971; Rogers, 1983). New ideas or practices are introduced by notable example. Initially, the rate of adoption is slow because new ways are unfamiliar, customs resist change, and results are uncertain. As early adopters convey more information about how to apply the new practices and their potential benefits, the innovation is adopted at an accelerating rate. After a period in which the new practices spread rapidly, the rate of diffusion slows down. The use of the innovation then either stabilizes or declines, depending on its relative functional value.

MODELING DETERMINANTS OF DIFFUSION

Symbolic modeling usually functions as the principal conveyer of innovations to widely dispersed areas. This is especially true in the early stages of diffusion. Newspapers, magazines, radio, and television inform people about new practices and their likely risks or benefits. Early adopters, therefore, come from among those who have had greater access to media sources of information about innovations (Robertson, 1971). The psychosocial determinants and mechanisms of observational learning, which were reviewed earlier, govern the rate with which innovations are acquired.

Differences in the knowledge, skills, and resources particular innovations require produce variations in rate of acquisition. Innovations that are difficult to understand and use receive more reluctant consideration than simpler ones (Tornatzky & Klein, 1982). When television models new practices on the screens in virtually every household, people in widely dispersed locales can learn them. However, not all innovations are promoted through the mass media. Some rely on informal personal channels. In such instances, physical proximity determines which innovations will be repeatedly observed and thoroughly learned.

It is one thing to acquire skills, it is another thing to use them effectively under difficult circumstances. Human competency requires not only skills, but also self-belief in one's capabilities to use those skills well. Modeling influences must, therefore, be designed to build self-efficacy as well as convey knowledge and rules of behavior. Perceived self-efficacy affects every phase of personal change (Bandura, 1992a). It determines whether people even consider changing their behavior, whether they can enlist the motivation and perseverance needed to succeed should they choose to do so, and how well they maintain the changes they have achieved.

The influential role of people's beliefs in their personal efficacy in social diffusion is shown in their response to health communications aimed at altering health-impairing habits. Meyerowitz and Chaiken (1987) examined four alternative mechanisms through which health communications could alter health habits: by transmission of factual information, fear arousal, change in risk perception, and enhancement of perceived self-efficacy. They found that health communications fostered adoption of preventive health practices primarily by their effects on perceived self-efficacy. Beck and Lund (1981) similarly showed that preventive health practices are better promoted by heightening self-efficacy than by elevating fear. Analyses of how community-wide media campaigns produce changes reveal that both the preexisting and induced level of perceived self-efficacy play an influential role in the adoption and social diffusion of health practices (Maibach, Flora, & Nass, 1991; Slater, 1989). The stronger the preexisting perceived self-efficacy, and the more the media campaigns enhance people's beliefs in their self-regulative efficacy, the more likely they are to adopt the recommended practices. The findings reviewed above underscore the need to shift the emphasis from trying to scare people into healthy behavior to empowering them with the tools and self-beliefs for exercising personal control over their health habits. People must also experience sufficient success using what they have learned to become convinced of their efficacy and the functional value of what they have adopted. This is best achieved by combining modeling with guided mastery, in which newly acquired skills are first tried under conditions likely to produce good results, and then extended to more unpredictable and difficult circumstances (Bandura, 1986).

ADOPTION DETERMINANTS

The acquisition of knowledge and skills regarding innovations is necessary but not sufficient for their adoption in practice. A number of factors determine whether people will act on what they have learned. Environmental inducements serve as one set of regulators. Adoptive behavior is also highly susceptible to incentive influences, which may take the form of material, social, or self-evaluative outcomes. Some of the motivating incentives derive from the utility of the adoptive behavior. The greater the relative benefits provided by an innovation, the higher the incentive is to adopt it (Ostlund, 1974; Rogers & Shoemaker, 1971). However, benefits cannot be experienced until the new practices are tried. Promoters, therefore, strive to get people to adopt new practices by altering their preferences and beliefs about likely outcomes, mainly by enlisting vicarious incentives. Advocates of new technologies and ideologies create expectations that they offer better solutions than do established ways. Modeled benefits increase adoptive decisions. Modeling influences can, of course, impede as well as promote the diffusion process (Midgley, 1976). Modeling negative reactions to a particular innovation, as a result of having had disappointing experiences with it, dissuades others from trying it. Even modeled indifference to an innovation, in the absence of any personal experience with it, will dampen the interests of others.

Many innovations serve as a means of gaining social recognition and status. Indeed, status incentives are often the main motivators for adopting new styles and tastes. In many instances, the variant styles do not provide different natural benefits or, if anything, the most innovative styles are the most costly. Status is thus gained at a price. People who strive to distinguish themselves from the common and the ordinary adopt new styles in clothing, grooming, recreational activities, and conduct, thereby achieving distinctive status. As the popularity of the new behavior grows, it loses its status-conferring value until eventually it, too, becomes commonplace. It is then discarded for a new form.

Adoptive behavior is also partly governed by self-evaluative reactions to one's own behavior. People adopt what they value, but they resist innovations that violate their social and moral standards or that conflict with their self-conception. The more compatible an innovation is with prevailing social norms and value systems, the greater its adoptability (Rogers & Shoemaker, 1971). However, we saw earlier that self-evaluative sanctions do not operate in isolation from the pressures of social influence. People are often led to behave in otherwise personally devalued ways by strategies that circumvent negative self-reactions. This is done by changing appearances and meanings of new practices to make them look compatible with people's values.

The amenability of an innovation to brief trial is another relevant characteristic that can affect the ease of adoption. Innovations that can be tried on a limited basis are more readily adoptable than those that have to be tried on a large scale with substantial effort and costs. The more weight given to potential risks and the costs of getting rid of new practices should they fail to live up to expectations, the weaker the incentive to innovate. And finally, people will not adopt innovations even though they are favorably disposed toward them if they lack the money, the skills, or the accessory resources that may be needed. The more resources innovations require, the lower their adoptability.

Analysis of the determinants and mechanisms of social diffusion should not becloud the fact that not all innovations are useful, nor is resistance to them necessarily dysfunctional (Zaltman & Wallendorf, 1979). In the continuous flow of innovations, the number of disadvantageous ones far exceeds those with truly beneficial possibilities. Both personal and societal well-being are well served by initial wariness to new practices promoted by unsubstantiated or exaggerated claims. The designations "venturesome" for early adopters and "laggards" for later adopters are fitting in the case of innovations that hold promise. However, when people are mesmerized by alluring appeals into trying disadvantageous innovations, the more suitable designation is gullibility for early adopters and astuteness for resisters. Rogers (1983) criticized the prevalent tendency to conceptualize the diffusion process from the perspective of the promoters. This tends to bias the search for explanations of nonadoptive behavior in negative attributes of nonadopters.

SOCIAL NETWORKS AND FLOW OF DIFFUSION

The third major factor that affects the diffusion process concerns social network structures. People are enmeshed in networks of relationships that include occupational colleagues, organizational members, kinships, and friendships, just to mention a few. They are linked not only directly by personal relationships. Because acquaintanceships overlap different network clusters, many people become linked to each other indirectly by interconnected ties. Social structures comprise clustered networks of people with various ties among them, as well as persons who provide connections to other clusters through joint membership or a liaison role. Clusters vary in their internal structure, ranging from loosely knit ones to those that are densely interconnected. Networks also differ in the number and pattern of structural linkages between clusters. They may have many common ties or function with a high degree of separateness. In addition to their degree of interconnectedness, people vary in the positions and status they occupy in particular social networks, which can affect their impact on what spreads through their network. One is more apt to learn about new ideas and practices from brief contacts with causal acquaintances than from intensive contact in the same circle of close associates. This path of influence creates the seemingly paradoxical effect that innovations are extensively diffused to cohesive groups through weak social ties (Granovetter, 1983).

Information regarding new ideas and practices is often conveyed through multilinked relationships (Rogers & Kincaid, 1981). Traditionally, the communication process has been conceptualized as one of unidirectional persuasion flowing from a source to a recipient. Rogers emphasized the mutuality of influence in interpersonal communication. People share information, give meaning by mutual feedback to the information they exchange, gain understanding of each other's views, and influence each other. Specifying the channels of influence through which innovations are dispersed provides greater understanding of the diffusion process than simply plotting the rate of adoptions over time.

There is no single social network in a community that serves all purposes. Different innovations engage different networks. For example, birth control practices and agricultural innovations diffuse through quite different networks within the same community (Marshall, 1971). To complicate matters further, the social networks that come into play in initial phases of diffusion may differ from those that spread the innovation in subsequent phases (Coleman, Katz, & Menzel, 1966). Adoption rates are better predicted from the network that subserves a particular innovation than from a general communication network. This is not to say that there is no generality to the diffusion function of network structures. If a particular social structure subserves varied activities, it can help to spread the adoption of innovations in each of those activities.

People with many social ties are more apt to adopt innovations than those who have few ties to others (Rogers & Kincaid, 1981). Adoption rates increase as more and more people in one's personal network adopt an innovation. The effects of social connectedness on adoptive behavior may be mediated through several processes. Multilinked relations can foster adoption of innovations because they convey more factual information, they mobilize stronger social influences, or it may be that people with close ties are more receptive to new ideas than those who are socially estranged. Moreover, in social transactions, people see their associates adopt innovations as well as talk about them. Multiple modeling alone can increase adoptive behavior (Bandura, 1986).

If innovations are highly conspicuous, they can be adopted directly without requiring interaction among adopters. Television is being increasingly used to forge large single-link structures, in which many people are linked directly to the media source, but they may have little or no direct relations with each other. For example, television evangelists attract loyal followers who adopt the transmitted precepts as guides for how to behave in situations involving moral, social, and political issues. Although they share a common bond to the media source, most members of an electronic community may never see each other. Political power structures are similarly being transformed by the creation of new constituencies tied to a single media source, but with little interconnectedness. Mass marketing techniques, using computer identification and mass mailings, create special-interest constituencies that by-pass traditional political organizations in the exercise of political influence.

Advances in communications and computer technologies provide the means for creating new social structures that link people together in widely dispersed locales. Computer records of the patterns of communications among individuals over time provide data for assessing the nature and contribution of network structures to adoptive behavior (Rogers, 1987). Interactive computer networking interconnects numerous people in ways that transcend the barriers of time and space (Hiltz & Turoff, 1978). In computerized network systems, participants communicate with each other by sending and receiving information at the place and time of their own convenience. Through this electronic interactive format people exchange information, share new ideas, and transact any number of pursuits. Computerized networking provides a ready vehicle for creating diffusion structures, expanding their membership, extending them geographically, and disbanding them when they have outlived their usefulness.

Although structural interconnectedness provides potential diffusion paths, psychosocial factors largely determine the fate of what diffuses through those paths. In other words, it is the transactions that occur within social relationships rather than the ties themselves that explain adoptive behavior. The course of diffusion is best understood by considering the interactions among psychosocial determinants of adoptive behavior, the properties of innovations that facilitate or impede adoption, and the network structures that provide the social pathways of influence. Structural and psychological determinants of adoptive behavior should, therefore, be included as complementary factors in a comprehensive theory of social diffusion, rather than be cast as rival theories of diffusion.

ACKNOWLEDGMENTS

Major sections of this chapter include revised and expanded material from the book, *Social Foundations of Thought and Action: A Social Cognitive Theory*, 1986, Prentice-Hall, and from a volume by J. Groebel and P. Winteroff-Spurk (Eds.), *Empirische Medien Psychologie*, München: Psychologie Verlags Union, 1989.

REFERENCES

✻ Adoni, H., & Mane, S. (1984). Media and the social construction of reality: Toward an integration of theory and research. *Communication Research 11*, 323–340.
Baldwin, T. F., & Lewis, C. (1972). Violence in television: The industry looks at itself. In G. A. Comstock & E. A. Rubinstein (Eds.), *Television and social behavior: Vol. 1. Media content and control* (pp. 290–373). Washington, DC: U.S. Government Printing Office.
✻ Ball-Rokeach, S., & DeFleur, M. (1976). A dependency model of mass media effects. *Communication Research, 3*, 3–21.
Ball-Rokeach, S. J. (1972). The legitimation of violence. In J. F. Short, Jr. & M. E. Wolfgang (Eds.), *Collective violence* (pp. 100–111). Chicago: Aldine-Atherton.
Bandura, A. (1973). *Aggression: A social learning analysis*. Englewood Cliffs, NJ: Prentice-Hall.
Bandura, A. (1982a). The psychology of chance encounters and life paths. *American Psychologist, 37*, 747–755.
Bandura, A. (1982b). Self-efficacy mechanism in human agency. *American Psychologist, 37*, 122–147.
Bandura, A. (1986). *Social foundations of thought and action: A social cognitive theory*. Englewood Cliffs, NJ: Prentice-Hall.
Bandura, A. (1989a). Perceived self-efficacy in the exercise of personal agency. *The Psychologist: Bulletin of the British Psychological Society, 2*, 411–424.
Bandura, A. (1989b). Self-regulation of motivation and action through internal standards and goal systems. In L. A. Pervin (Ed.), *Goal concepts in personality and social psychology* (pp. 19–85). Hillsdale, NJ: Lawrence Erlbaum Associates.
Bandura, A. (1990). Mechanisms of moral disengagement. In W. Reich (Ed.), *Origins of terrorism: Psychologies, ideologies, states of mind* (pp. 162–191). Cambridge: Cambridge University Press.
Bandura, A. (1992a). Self-efficacy mechanism in psychobiological functioning. In R. Schwarzer (Ed.), *Self-efficacy: Thought control of action* (pp. 355–394). Washington, DC: Hemisphere.
Bandura, A. (1992b). Social cognitive theory and social referencing. In S. Feinman (Ed.), *Social referencing and social construction of reality in infancy* (pp. 175–208). New York: Plenum.
Bandura, A. (1991). Social cognitive theory of moral thought and action. In W. M. Kurtines & J. L. Gerwirtz (Eds.), *Handbook of moral behavior and development* (Vol. 1, pp. 45–103). Hillsdale, NJ: Lawrence Erlbaum Associates.

Bandura, A., Underwood, B., & Fromson, M. E. (1975). Disinhibition of aggression through diffusion of responsibility and dehumanization of victims. *Journal of Research in Personality, 9,* 253–269.

Bassiouni, M. C. (1981). Terrorism, law enforcement, and the mass media: Perspectives, problems, proposals. *The Journal of Criminal Law & Criminology, 72,* 1–51.

Beck, K. H., & Lund, A. K. (1981). The effects of health threat seriousness and personal efficacy upon intentions and behavior. *Journal of Applied Social Psychology, 11,* 401–415.

Berkowitz, L. (1984). Some effects of thoughts on anti- and prosocial influences of media events: A cognitive-neoassociation analysis. *Psychological Bulletin, 95,* 410–427.

Berkowitz, L., & Geen, R. G. (1967). Stimulus qualities of the target of aggression: A further study. *Journal of Personality and Social Psychology, 5,* 364–368.

Brock, T. C., & Buss, A. H. (1962). Dissonance, aggression, and evaluation of pain. *Journal of Abnormal and Social Psychology, 65,* 197–202.

Brock, T. C., & Buss, A. H. (1964). Effects of justification for aggression and communication with the victim on postaggression dissonance. *Journal of Abnormal and Social Psychology, 68,* 403–412.

Buerkel-Rothfuss, N. L., & Mayes, S. (1981). Soap opera viewing: The cultivation effect. *Journal of Communication, 31,* 108–115.

Cantor, J., & Wilson, B. J. (1988). Helping children cope with frightening media presentations. *Current Psychological Research and Reviews, 7,* 58–75.

Chaffee, S. H. (1982). Mass media and interpersonal channels: Competitive, convergent, or complementary? In G. Gumpert & R. Cathcart (Eds.), *Inter/Media: Interpersonal communication in a media world* (pp. 57–77). New York: Oxford University Press.

Coleman, J. S., Katz, E., & Menzel, H. (1966). *Medical innovation: A diffusion study.* New York: Bobbs-Merrill.

Diener, E. (1977). Deindividuation: Causes and consequences. *Social Behavior and Personality, 5,* 143–156.

Diener, E., Dineen, J., Endresen, K., Beaman, A. L., & Fraser, S. C. (1975). Effects of altered responsibility, cognitive set, and modeling on physical aggression and deindividuation. *Journal of Personality and Social Psychology, 31,* 328–337.

Donnerstein, E. (1984). Pornography: Its effect on violence against women. In N. M. Malamuth & E. Donnerstein (Eds.), *Pornography and sexual aggression* (pp. 53–81). New York: Academic Press.

Duncker, K. (1938). Experimental modification of children's food preferences through social suggestion. *Journal of Abnormal Social Psychology, 33,* 489–507.

Dysinger, W. S., & Ruckmick, C. A. (1933). *The emotional responses of children to the motion-picture situation.* New York: Macmillan.

Falmagne, R. J. (1975). *Reasoning: Representation and process in children and adults.* Hillsdale, NJ: Lawrence Erlbaum Associates.

Flerx, V. C., Fidler, D. S., & Rogers, R. W. (1976). Sex role stereotypes: Developmental aspects and early intervention. *Child Development, 47,* 998–1007.

Gerbner, G. (1972). Communication and social environment. *Scientific American, 227,* 153–160.

Gerbner, G., Gross, L., Morgan M., & Signorielli, N. (1981). A curious journey into the scary world of Paul Hirsch. *Communication Research, 8,* 39–72.

Goranson, R. E. (1970). Media violence and aggressive behavior. A review of experimental research. In L. Berkowitz (Ed.), *Advances in experimental social psychology* (Vol. 5, pp. 2–31). New York: Academic Press.

Granovetter, M. (1983). The strength of weak ties—A network theory revisited. In R. Collins (Ed.), *Sociological theory 1983* (pp. 201–233). San Francisco: Jossey-Bass.

Hall, J. R. (1987) *Gone from the promised land: Jonestown in American cultural history.* New Brunswick, NJ: Transaction Books.

Halloran, J. D., & Croll, P. (1972). Television programs in Great Britain: Content and control. In G. A. Comstock & E. A. Rubinstein (Eds.), *Television and social behavior: Vol. 1. Media content and control* (pp. 415–492). Washington, DC: U.S. Government Printing Office.

Hawkins, R. P., & Pingree, S. (1982). Television's influence on social reality. In D. Pearl, L. Bouthilet, & J. Lazar (Eds.), *Television and behavior: Ten years of scientific progress and implications for the eighties* (Vol. II, pp. 224–247). Rockville, MD: National Institute of Mental Health.

Heath, L. (1984). Impact of newspaper crime reports on fear of crime: Multimethodological investigation. *Journal of Personality and Social Psychology, 47,* 263–276.

Hiltz, S. R., & Turoff, M. (1978). *The network nation: Human communication via computer.* Reading, MA: Addison-Wesley.

Hirsch, P. M. (1980). The "scary world of the nonviewer" and other anomalies: A reanalysis of Gerbner et al.'s findings on cultivation analysis. Part I. *Communication Research, 7,* 403–456.

Kanungo, R. N., & Pang, S. (1973). Effects of human models on perceived product quality. *Journal of Applied Psychology, 57,* 172–178.

Kelman, H. C., & Hamilton, V. L. (1989). *Crimes of obedience: Toward a social psychology of authority and responsibility.* New Haven, CT: Yale University Press.

Klapper, J. T. (1960). *The effects of mass communication.* New York: Free Press.

Larsen, O. N. (Ed.). (1968). *Violence and the mass media.* New York: Harper & Row.

Liebert, R. M., Sprafkin, J. N., & Davidson, E. S. (1982). *The early window: Effects of television on children and youth* (2nd ed.). Elmsford, NY: Pergamon.

Maibach, E. W., Flora, J., & Nass, C. (1991). Changes in self-efficacy and health behavior in response to a minimal contact community health campaign. *Health Communication, 3,* 1–15.

Malamuth, N. M., & Donnerstein, E. (Eds.). (1984). *Pornography and sexual aggression.* New York: Academic Press.

Marshall, J. F. (1971). Topics and networks in intravillage communication. In S. Polgar (Ed.), *Culture and population: A collection of current studies* (pp. 160–166). Cambridge, MA: Schenkman Publishing Company.

McGhee, P. E., & Frueh, T. (1980). Television viewing and the learning of sex-role stereotypes. *Sex Roles, 6,* 179–188.

Meichenbaum, D. (1984). Teaching thinking: A cognitive-behavioral perspective. In R. Glaser, S. Chipman, & J. Segal (Eds.), *Thinking and learning skills* (Vol. 2): *Research and Open Questions* (pp. 407–426). Hillsdale, NJ: Lawrence Erlbaum Associates.

Meyer, T. P. (1972). Effects of viewing justified and unjustified real film violence on aggressive behavior. *Journal of Personality and Social Psychology, 23,* 21–29.

Meyerowitz, B. E., & Chaiken, S. (1987). The effect of message framing on breast self-examination attitudes, intentions, and behavior. *Journal of Personality and Social Psychology, 52,* 500–510.

Midgley, D. F. (1976). A simple mathematical theory of innovative behavior. *Journal of Consumer Research, 3,* 31–41.

Midgley, M. (1978). *Beast and man: The roots of human nature.* Ithaca, NY: Cornell University Press.

Milgram, S. (1974). *Obedience to authority: An experimental view.* New York: Harper & Row.

O'Bryant, S. L., & Corder-Bolz, C. R. (1978). The effects of television on children's stereotyping of women's work roles. *Journal of Vocational Behavior, 12,* 233–244.

Ostlund, L. E. (1974). Perceived innovation attributes as predictors of innovativeness. *Journal of Consumer Research, 1,* 23–29.

Pearl, D., Bouthilet, L., & Lazar, J. (Eds.). (1982). *Television and behavior: Ten years of scientific progress and implications for the eighties.* Rockville, MD: National Institute of Mental Health.

Pelz, D. C. (1983). Use of information channels in urban innovations. *Knowledge, 5,* 3–25.

Peterson, R. A., & Kerin, R. A. (1979). The female role in advertisements: Some experimental evidence. *Journal of Marketing, 41,* 59–63.

Robertson, T. S. (1971). *Innovative behavior and communication.* New York: Holt, Rinehart & Winston.

Rogers, E. M. (1983). *Diffusion of innovations* (3rd ed.). New York: Free Press.

Rogers, E. M. (1987). Progress, problems and prospects for network research: Investigating relationships in the age of electronic communication technologies. *Social Networks, 9,* 285–310.

Rogers, E. M., & Kincaid, D. L. (1981). *Communication networks: Toward a new paradigm for research.* New York: Free Press.

Rogers, E. M., & Shoemaker, F. (1971). *Communication of innovations: A cross-cultural approach* (2nd ed.). New York: Free Press.

Rosenthal, T. L., & Zimmerman, B. J. (1978). *Social learning and cognition.* New York: Academic Press.

Sabido, M. (1981). *Towards the social use of soap operas.* Mexico City, Mexico: Institute for Communication Research.

Siegel, A. E., (1958). The influence of violence in the mass media upon children's role expectation. *Child Development, 29,* 35–56.

Singhal, A., & Rogers, E. M. (1989). Pro-social television for development in India. In R. E. Rice & C. K. Atkin (Eds.), *Public communication campaigns* (2nd ed., pp. 331–350). Newbury Park, CA: Sage.

Slater, M. D. (1989). Social influences and cognitive control as predictors of self-efficacy and eating behavior. *Cognitive Therapy and Research, 13,* 231–245.

Snyder, M. (1980). Seek, and ye shall find: Testing hypotheses about other people. In E. T. Higgins, C. P. Herman, & M. P. Zanna (Eds.), *Social cognition: The Ontario Symposium on Personality and Social Psychology* (Vol. 1, pp. 105–130). Hillsdale, NJ: Lawrence Erlbaum Associates.

Snyder, M., & Campbell, B. H. (1982). Self-monitoring: The self in action. In J. Suls (Ed.), *Psychological perspectives on the self* (pp. 185–207). Hillsdale, NJ: Lawrence Erlbaum Associates.

Tan, A. S. (1979). TV beauty ads and role expectations of adolescent female viewers. *Journalism Quarterly, 56,* 283–288.

Tornatzky, L. G., & Klein, K. J. (1982). Innovation characteristics and innovation adoption-implementation: A meta-analysis of findings. *IEEE Transactions of Engineering and Management, EM-29,* 28–45.

Watt, J. G., Jr., & van den Berg, S. A. (1978). Time series analysis of alternative media effects theories. In R. D. Ruben (Ed.), *Communication Yearbook 2* (pp. 215–224). New Brunswick, NJ: Transaction Books.

Wilson, B. J., & Cantor, J. (1985). Developmental differences in empathy with a television protagonist's fear. *Journal of Experimental Child Psychology, 39,* 284–299.

Winett, R. A., Leckliter, I. N., Chinn, D. E., Stahl, B. N., & Love, S. Q. (1985). The effects of television modeling on residential energy conservation. *Journal of Applied Behavior Analysis, 18,* 33–44.

Wood, R. E., & Bandura, A. (1989). Social cognitive theory of organizational management. *Academy of Management Review, 14,* 361–384.

Zaltman, G., & Wallendorf, M. (1979). *Consumer behavior: Basic findings and management implications.* New York: Wiley.

Zillmann, D., & Bryant, J. (1984). Effects of massive exposure to pornography. In N. M. Malamuth & E. Donnerstein (Eds.), *Pornography and sexual aggression* (pp. 115–138). New York: Academic Press.

Zimbardo, P. G. (1969). The human choice: Individuation, reason, and order versus deindividuation, impulse, and chaos. In W. J. Arnold & D. Levine (Eds.), *Nebraska Symposium on Motivation, 1969* (pp. 237–309). Lincoln: University of Nebraska Press.

5

Mass Media Attitude Change: Implications of the Elaboration Likelihood Model of Persuasion

RICHARD E. PETTY AND JOSEPH R. PRIESTER
The Ohio State University

> *It is conceivable that one persuasive person could, through the use of mass media, bend the world's population to his will.*
>
> —Cartwright (1949, p. 253,
> in summarizing earlier views on the power of the media)

Undoubtedly, few social scientists today think that the mass media have the power to sway huge audiences to the extent once believed likely. Nevertheless, the technological advances of the 1900s have made it possible for individual communicators to have access to unprecedented numbers of potential message recipients. At present, millions of dollars are spent each year in attempts to change peoples' attitudes about political candidates, consumer products, health and safety practices, and charitable causes. In most of these instances, the ultimate goal is to influence peoples' behavior so that they will vote for certain politicians or referenda, purchase specific goods, engage in safer driving, eating, and sexual activities, and donate money to various religious, environmental, and educational organizations and institutions. To what extent are media persuasion attempts effective?

The success of media campaigns depends in part on (a) whether the transmitted communications are effective in changing the attitudes of the recipients in the desired direction, and (b) whether these modified attitudes in turn influence peoples' behaviors. Our goal in this chapter is to present a brief overview of current psychological approaches to mass media influence, and to outline in more detail a general framework that can be used to understand the processes responsible for mass media attitude change. This framework is called the Elaboration Likelihood Model of persuasion (ELM; Petty & Cacioppo, 1981, 1986b). Before addressing the contemporary approaches, we provide a very brief historical overview of perspectives on mass media influence.

EARLY EXPLORATIONS
OF MASS MEDIA PERSUASION

Direct Effects Model

The initial assumption about the effects of the mass media by social scientists in the 1920s and 1930s was that mass communication techniques were quite potent. For example, in an analysis of mass communication during World War I, Lasswell (1927) concluded that "propaganda is one of the most powerful instrumentalities in the modern world" (p. 220). During this period, there were several salient examples of seemingly effective mass communication effects. These included the panic following the 1929 stock market crash; the well-publicized mass hysteria following the radio broadcast of Orson Wells' *War of the Worlds* in 1938; and the rise in popularity of individuals such as Adolf Hitler in Germany, and the right wing Catholic Priest, Father Coughlin, and Louisiana Senator Huey Long in the United States. The assumption of Lasswell and others was that transmission of information via mass communication produced direct effects on attitudes and behavior (e.g., Doob, 1935; Lippmann, 1922). In detailing the views about mass communication during this period, Sears and colleagues noted that it was assumed that "the audience was captive, attentive, and gullible . . . the citizenry sat glued to the radio, helpless victims" (Sears & Kosterman, in press), and that "propaganda could be made almost irresistible" (Sears & Whitney, 1973, p. 2).

Many analysts of the period based their startling assessments of the power of the media on informal and anecdotal evidence rather than careful empirical research. For example, few attempts were made to actually measure the attitudes of message recipients prior to and following propaganda efforts. Thus, although it could be that the great propagandists of the time were changing the attitudes of their audience, it was also possible that the communicators were mostly attracting an audience that already agreed with them, or some combination of the two. Of course, not all analysts of the period were so optimistic about the prospects for the mass media to produce dramatic changes in opinion, but it was the dominant view (Wartella & Middlestadt, 1991).[1]

Indirect Effects Model

mention in conclusion ↓

The direct effects model was tempered considerably in the next two decades largely as a result of the subsequent empirical research conducted. For example, in analyzing survey information gathered by the National Opinion Research Center, Hyman and Sheatsley (1947) concluded that the effectiveness of mass communication campaigns could not be increased simply by increasing the flow of messages. Rather, the specific psychological barriers to effective information dissemination must be considered and overcome (see also, Cartwright, 1949). For example, they noted that people often distort incoming information to be consistent with prior attitudes, making change less likely. A similar conclusion was reached by Lazarsfeld, Berelson, and Gaudet (1948) in their influential study of the impact of the media in the 1940 presidential campaign. A major result from this study was that the media appeared to reinforce people's already existing attitudes rather than producing new ones (see also Klapper, 1960). Some researchers argued that when public attitude change was produced, it was only indirectly attributable to the media. That is, the media were more effective in influencing various opinion leaders than the average person, and these opinion leaders were responsible for changes in the mass public (i.e., a "two-step" flow of communication; Katz & Lazarsfeld, 1955).

Studies conducted during World War II reinforced the "limited effects" view of the media. Most notably, the wartime studies by Carl Hovland and his colleagues showed that although various military training films had an impact on the knowledge of the soldier recipients, the films were relatively ineffective in producing mass changes in attitudes and behavior. Instead, the persuasive power of the films depended on a large number of moderating variables (Hovland, Lumsdaine, & Sheffield, 1949; see also, Shils & Janowitz, 1948). When World War II ended, Hovland returned to Yale University and the systematic examination of these moderating variables was begun in earnest.

---

[1]In one of the relatively rare empirical efforts of the period, Peterson and Thurstone (1933) examined the power of movies such as D. W. Griffith's *Birth of a Nation*, controversial because of its depiction of Blacks, to modify the racial attitudes of adolescents. The conclusions of this research foreshadowed the modern period in that various moderators of effective influence were uncovered (e.g., greater influence for those with low knowledge, message repetition, etc.; see Wartella & Reeves, 1985).

CONTEMPORARY APPROACHES
TO MASS MEDIA PERSUASION

The Attitude Construct

Contemporary social psychologists concerned with the study of media influence, like their predecessors (e.g., Peterson & Thurstone, 1933), have focused on the concept of "attitudes," or peoples' general predispositions to evaluate other people, objects, and issues favorably or unfavorably. The attitude construct achieved its preeminent position in research on social influence because of the assumption that a person's attitude is an important mediating variable between the acquisition of new information, on the one hand, and behavioral change, on the other. For example, a television commercial might be based on the idea that giving people information about a candidate's issue positions will lead to favorable attitudes toward the candidate and ultimately to contributing money to and voting for the candidate.

Over the past 50 years, numerous theories of attitude change and models of knowledge–attitude–behavior relationships have been developed (see reviews by Eagly & Chaiken, 1993; McGuire, 1985; Petty, Priester, & Wegener, in press; Petty, Unnava, & Strathman, 1991). Contemporary analyses of mass media persuasion have focused on the variables that determine when the media will be effective versus ineffective and what the underlying processes are by which the media induce change. Perhaps the most well known psychological framework for categorizing and understanding mass media persuasion effects was popularized by Hovland and his colleagues (e.g., Hovland, 1954, 1959; Hovland, Janis, & Kelley, 1953) and elaborated considerably by William McGuire (1985, 1989).

The Communication/Persuasion Matrix Model
of Media Effects

One of the earliest assumptions of theories of attitude change (e.g., Kitson, 1922) that is also evident in contemporary approaches (e.g., McGuire, 1985) was that effective influence required a sequence of steps (Petty & Cacioppo, 1984b). For example, Fig. 5.1 presents McGuire's (1985, 1989) communication/persuasion matrix model of influence. This model outlines the inputs (or independent variables) to the persuasion process that media persuaders can control along with the outputs (or dependent variables) that can be measured to see if any influence attempt is successful.

Outputs:	Communication Inputs:				
	SOURCE	MESSAGE	RECIPIENT	CHANNEL	CONTEXT
EXPOSURE					
ATTENTION					
INTEREST					
COMPREHENSION					
ACQUISITION					
YIELDING					
MEMORY					
RETRIEVAL					
DECISION					
ACTION					
REINFORCEMENT					
CONSOLIDATION					

FIG. 5.1. The communication/persuasion process as an input/output matrix. The figure depicts the primary independent and dependent variables in mass media persuasion research (adapted from McGuire, 1989).

Matrix Inputs. The inputs to the persuasion process in Fig. 5.1 are based in part on Lasswell's (1964) classic question: Who says what to whom, when, and how? First, a communication typically has some *source*. The source can be expert or not, attractive or not, male or female, an individual or group, and so on. This source provides some information, the *message*, and this message can be emotional or logical, long or short, organized or not, directed at a specific or a general belief, and so forth. The message is presented to a particular *recipient*, who may be high or low in intelligence, knowledge, experience, and so on. The message is presented via some *channel* of communication. Different media allow different types of input such as audio only (e.g., radio), audio plus visual (television), print only, or print plus visual (e.g., magazines). Some media allow presentation of the message at the recipient's own pace, whereas other media control the pace externally. Finally, the message is presented to the recipient in some *context*. The persuasion context may be pleasant or unpleasant, noisy or quiet, and so forth.

Matrix Outputs. Each of the inputs to the persuasion process can have an impact on one of the outputs depicted in Fig. 5.1. The communication/persuasion matrix model contends that in order for effective influence to occur, a person first needs to be *exposed* to some new information. Media are often selected by potential persuaders after estimating the number and type of people the message is likely to reach. Secondly, the person must *attend* to the information presented. Just because a person is sitting in front of the television doesn't mean that he or she knows what is going on. Even if the person does notice the information, this doesn't mean that the person's *interest* will be engaged. The next two stages involve *comprehension* and *acquisition*, or the question of what part of the information presented the person actually understands and learns. It is only at step 6 that attitude change or *yielding* occurs. Once the person accepts the information in the message, the next step in the sequence involves *memory* or storage of the new information and the attitude that it supports. The next three steps detail the processes involved in translating the new attitude into a behavioral response. That is, at some subsequent behavioral opportunity, the person must *retrieve* the new attitude from memory, *decide* to act on it, and perform the appropriate *action*. Finally, the model notes that if the attitude-congruent behavior is not *reinforced*, the new attitude might be undermined. If the behavior is rewarding, however, the attitude-consistent behavior might lead to attitudinal *consolidation*, making the new attitude more likely to persist over time.

Variants of this general information processing model were often interpreted in theory and in practice as suggesting that a change early in the sequence (e.g., attention) would inevitably lead to a change later in the sequence (e.g., yielding). McGuire (1989) noted, however, that the likelihood that a message will evoke each of the steps in the sequence should be viewed as a conditional probability. Thus, even if the likelihood of achieving each of the first six steps in a mass media campaign was 60%, the maximum probability of achieving all six steps (exposure, attention, interest, comprehension, learning, and yielding), would be 0.6^6 or only 5%.

In addition, it is important to consider the fact that any one input variable can have different effects on the different output steps. For example, Hyman and Sheatsley (1947) noted that in the political domain, the knowledge and interest of a message recipient was positively related to exposure to political messages (i.e., the "chronic know-nothings" are more difficult to reach in a political campaign), but negatively related to attitude change (i.e., high interest and knowledge tends to produce assimilation of messages to one's original point of view). In a cogent analysis of this point, McGuire (1968) noted that several variables might have opposite effects on the steps involving *reception* of information (e.g., exposure, attention, comprehension, acquisition, memory) versus *acceptance* of (yielding to) the information. For example, recipient intelligence is related positively to reception processes, but negatively related to yielding. The joint action of reception and yielding processes implies that people of moderate intelligence should be easier to persuade than people of low or high intelligence (see also Rholes & Wood, 1992).

Additional Issues for the Communication/Persuasion Matrix Model.
Although McGuire's input/output matrix model serves as a very useful
way to think about the steps involved in producing attitude and
behavior change via the mass media or other means, it is important to
appreciate a number of things that the model does not address. First, it
is now clear that some of the steps in the postulated information
processing sequence may be completely independent of each other,
rather than sequential. For example, although a person's ability to learn
and recall new information (e.g., facts about a political candidate) was
often thought to be an important causal determinant of and prerequisite
to attitude and behavior change (e.g., favoring and voting for the
candidate), little empirical evidence has accumulated to support the
view that message learning is a necessary step (Greenwald, 1968;
McGuire, 1985; Petty & Cacioppo, 1981). Rather, the existing evidence
shows that message comprehension and learning can occur in the
absence of attitude change, and that a person's attitudes can change
without learning the specific information in the communication. That is,
a person might be able to comprehend all of the intended information
perfectly, but not be persuaded either because the information is
counterargued or seen as personally irrelevant. On the other hand, a
person might get the information all wrong (scoring zero on a knowledge test) but think about it in a manner that produces the intended
change. This analysis helps to explain why previous research on mass
media effects has sometimes found that message learning and changes
in knowledge occur in the absence of attitude change and vice-versa
(Petty, Baker, & Gleicher, 1991).

Second, the model tells us little about the factors that produce
yielding. Even though the initial steps in the information processing
sequence are viewed as prerequisites to acceptance, McGuire did not
mean to imply that people would invariably yield to all information they
comprehended and learned. That is, the earlier steps were thought to be
necessary but not sufficient for yielding. Rather, just as source and other
variables determine the extent of attention, they also determine the
extent of acceptance. As implied by the communication/persuasion
matrix, current psychological research on influence focuses on how and
why various features of a persuasion situation (i.e., aspects of the
source, message, channel, recipient and context) affect each of the steps
in the communication sequence (e.g., how does the credibility of the
source affect attention to the message?). The most research by far,
however, focuses on how variables affect the processes responsible for
yielding to or resisting the communication.

Cognitive response theory (Greenwald, 1968; Petty, Ostrom, &

Brock, 1981) was developed explicitly to address the two issues unaddressed by the communication/persuasion matrix. That is, cognitive response analysis attempted to account for the low correlation between message learning and persuasion observed in many studies, and for the processes responsible for yielding. This theory holds that the extent of yielding is related to the idiosyncratic cognitive responses (pro and counterarguments) generated to the message rather than learning of the message, and persistence of persuasion is related to memory for these cognitive responses rather than the message content per se. Although the cognitive response approach provided some important insights into the persuasion process, it overemphasized the extent to which people were active processors of the information provided to them. The theory did not account very well for persuasion in situations where people were not actively thinking about the message content (e.g., Petty, Cacioppo, & Goldman, 1981).

THE ELABORATION LIKELIHOOD MODEL
OF PERSUASION

The elaboration likelihood model of persuasion (ELM) is a theory about the processes responsible for yielding to a persuasive communication (Petty & Cacioppo, 1981, 1986a, 1986b) and is an outgrowth of the cognitive response approach (Petty, Wegener, Fabrigar, Priester, & Cacioppo, in press).[2] The model holds that the processes that occur during the yielding stage can be thought of as emphasizing one of two relatively distinct "routes to persuasion." These routes are depicted in Fig. 5.2.

Central and Peripheral Routes to Persuasion

Central Route. The first, or "central route," to persuasion involves effortful cognitive activity whereby the person draws upon prior experience and knowledge in order to carefully scrutinize all of the information relevant to determining the central merits of the position advocated

---

[2]Although the ELM has implications for the other stages in the information processing sequence, it does not attempt to provide a *general* theory of information exposure, memory, and so on. For example, even though the ELM would expect people to seek out and attend to messages of high personal relevance more so than messages of low personal relevance, the ELM provides an incomplete account of exposure because variables unrelated to yielding processes could also determine message exposure. (e.g., see Zillmann & Bryant, chapter 15, this volume).

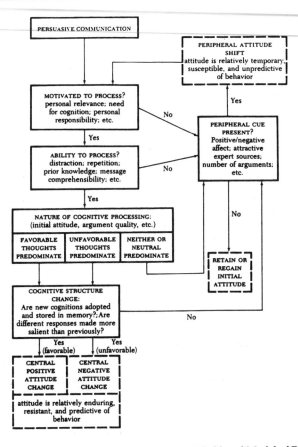

FIG. 5.2. Schematic depiction of The Elaboration Likelihood Model of Persuasion. The figure shows the possible endpoints after exposure to a persuasive communication for people following central and peripheral routes to attitude change (from Petty & Cacioppo, 1986a).

(Petty, in press; Petty & Cacioppo, 1986a). Consistent with the cognitive response approach to persuasion, the message recipient under the central route is actively generating favorable and/or unfavorable thoughts in response to the persuasive communication. The goal of this cognitive effort is to determine if the position advocated by the source has any merit. Not every message received from the media is sufficiently interesting or important to think about, and not every situation provides the time and opportunity for careful reflection. When people are motivated and able to take the central route, they carefully appraise the extent to which the communication provides information that is fundamental or central to the perceived merits of the position advocated.

Of course, the particular kind of information that is perceived central to the merits of any particular issue can vary from person to person and from situation to situation. For example, recent research has shown that when some people think about social issues (e.g, capital punishment), religious considerations and arguments are particularly persuasive, but for others, legalistic arguments carry the most weight (Cacioppo, Petty, & Sidera, 1982). Likewise, research has shown that when some people evaluate ads for consumer products, they are primarily concerned about how usage of the product will affect the image that they project; for other people, this dimension is unimportant (DeBono & Packer, 1991; Snyder & DeBono, 1989). Research suggests that an important function of the media in the political domain is to make certain political and social issues more salient than others (see Iyengar & Kinder, 1987; McCombs, chapter 1, this volume). For example, a recent study of magazine stories showed that over the past 30 years, stories about drug abuse and nutrition increased dramatically, stories about communism and desegregation declined, and stories on pollution remained about the same (Paisley, 1989). If people come to believe that certain issues are more important due to extensive media coverage, it is reasonable that these dimensions of judgment will become more central in evaluating the merits of political candidates.[3]

The end result of the effortful information processing involved in the central route is an attitude that is well articulated and integrated into the person's belief structure. Just because the attitude change process involves considerable cognitive work does not mean that the attitude formed will be a rational or "accurate" one, however. The important point is that sometimes attitudes are changed by a rather thoughtful process in which people attend carefully to the issue-relevant information presented, examine this information in light of their relevant experiences and knowledge, and evaluate the information along the dimensions they perceive central to the merits of the issue. People engaged in this effortful cognitive activity have been characterized as engaging in "systematic" (Chaiken, Liberman, & Eagly, 1989), "mindful" (Palmerino, Langer, & McGillis, 1984), and "piecemeal" (Fiske & Pavelchak, 1986) processing. Attitudes changed by the central route have been shown to have a number of distinguishing characteristics. In particular, these attitudes have been found to be relatively accessible, persistent over time, predictive of behavior, and

---

[3]Of course, much of the correlation between media coverage and ratings of issue importance is due to the fact that the media cover issues people already think are important. Nevertheless, some research shows that the media coverage can precede public perceptions (e.g., MacKuen, 1981).

resistant to change until they are challenged by cogent contrary information (e.g., Haugtvedt & Petty, 1992; see Petty & Krosnick, in press, for an extensive discussion of the determinants of attitude strength).

Peripheral Route. In stark contrast to the central route to persuasion, the ELM holds that attitude change does not always require effortful evaluation of the persuasive communication. Instead, when a person's motivation or ability to process the issue-relevant information is low, persuasion can occur by a "peripheral route" in which simple cues in the persuasion context influence attitudes. The peripheral route to persuasion recognizes that it is neither adaptive nor possible for people to exert considerable mental effort in thinking about all of the media communications to which they are exposed. In order to function in contemporary society, people must sometimes act as "lazy organisms" (McGuire, 1969) or "cognitive misers" (Taylor, 1981), and employ simpler means of evaluation (see also, Bem, 1972). For example, various features of a communication (e.g., pleasant scenery in a TV commercial) can elicit an affective state (e.g., a good mood) that becomes associated with the advocated position (as in classical conditioning, Staats & Staats, 1958). Or, the source of a message can trigger a relatively simple inference or heuristic such as "experts are correct" (Chaiken 1987) that a person can use to judge the message. Similarly, the responses of other people who are exposed to the message can serve as a validity cue (e.g., "if so many agree, it must be true"; Axsom, Yates, & Chaiken, 1987). The Institute for Propaganda Analysis, in an early report on propaganda techniques, listed a number of "tricks" that speakers of the time used to persuade their audiences that relied on peripheral cues (e.g., the "bandwagon" effect was giving the sense that most other people already supported the speaker; see Lee & Lee, 1939).

We do not mean to suggest that peripheral approaches are necessarily ineffective. In fact, they can be quite effective in the short term. The problem is that over time, moods dissipate, peoples' feelings about sources can change, and the cues can become dissociated from the message. These factors would then undermine the basis of the attitude. Laboratory research has shown that attitude changes based on peripheral cues tend to be less accessible, less enduring, and less resistant to subsequent attacking messages than attitudes based on careful processing of message arguments (Petty & Cacioppo 1986a). In sum, attitudes changed via the central route tend to be based on active thought processes resulting in a well-integrated cognitive structure, but attitudes changed via the peripheral route are based on more passive acceptance or rejection of simple cues and have a less well-articulated foundation.[4]

Persuasion Processes
in the Elaboration Likelihood Model

Variables Affecting the Amount of Thinking. Our discussion of the central and peripheral routes to persuasion has highlighted two basic processes of attitude change, but the depiction of the ELM in Fig. 5.2 outlines more specific roles that variables can play in persuasion situations. That is, some variables affect a person's general *motivation* to think about a message. Mendelsohn (1973) noted that placing potential media recipients "along a continuum ranging from those whose initial interest in a given subject area may be high to those who literally have no interest in what may be communicated becomes an essential step in developing effective public information campaigns" (p. 51). Several variables enhance interest in media messages. Perhaps the most important determinant of interest and motivation to process the message is the perceived personal relevance of the communication. In one study (Petty & Cacioppo 1979b), for example, undergraduates were told that their own university (high personal involvement) or a distant university (low personal involvement) was considering implementing a policy requiring all seniors to pass an exam in their major as a prerequisite to graduation. The students then listened to a radio editorial that presented either strong or weak arguments in favor of the exam policy. As predicted by the ELM, when the speaker advocated that the exams should be instituted at the students' own campus, the quality of the arguments in the message had a greater impact on attitudes than when the speaker advocated that the exams should be instituted at a distant institution. That is, as the personal relevance of the message increased, strong arguments were more persuasive, but weak arguments were less persuasive than in the low relevance conditions (see left panel of Fig. 5.3). In addition, an analysis of the thoughts that the students listed after the message suggested that the more extreme attitudes were accompanied by more extreme thoughts. When the arguments were strong, students exposed to the high relevance message produced more than twice as many favorable thoughts as low relevance subjects, and when the arguments were weak, high relevance respondents generated

---

[4]For expository purposes we have emphasized the distinction between the central and the peripheral routes to persuasion. That is, we have focused on the prototypical processes at the end points of the elaboration likelihood continuum. In most persuasion situations (which fall somewhere along this continuum), some combination of central and peripheral processes is likely.

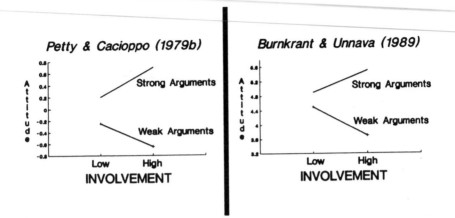

FIG. 5.3. Self-relevance increases message processing. In each panel, as self-relevance (involvement) increases, argument quality becomes a more important determinant of the attitudes expressed after exposure to a persuasive message. Data in the left panel are from an experiment by Petty and Cacioppo (1979b). Data in the right panel are from an experiment by Burnkrant and Unnava (1989). In each panel, higher numbers indicate more favorable attitudes toward the position taken in the persuasive message.

almost twice as many unfavorable thoughts as students exposed to the low relevance version. In an interesting extension of this work, Burnkrant and Unnava (1989) found that simply changing the pronouns in a message from the third person (e.g., "one" or "he and she") to the second person (i.e., "you") was sufficient to increase personal involvement and processing of the message arguments (see right panel of Fig. 5.3). That is, when the messages contained the self-relevant pronouns, strong arguments were more persuasive and weak arguments were less persuasive than when third person pronouns were used.

Although increasing the perceived personal relevance of a message is an important way to increase thinking (e.g., Brickner, Harkins, & Ostrom, 1986; Leippe & Elkin 1987; see Petty, Cacioppo, & Haugtvedt, 1992, for a review), it is not the only one. For example, several studies have shown that when a person is not normally motivated to think about the message arguments, more thinking can be provoked by summarizing the major arguments as *questions* rather than as *assertions* (Howard 1990; Petty, Cacioppo, & Heesacker, 1981; Swasy & Munch 1985). Thus, if an argument in a radio commercial was followed by a question (Isn't this candidate the best one?) rather than by an assertion (This candidate is the best one), greater processing of the arguments would result. Greater thinking about a message can also be induced by having the individual arguments presented by multiple sources rather than just one (Harkins & Petty, 1981; Moore & Reardon, 1987). The multiple source effect is attenuated if people suspect that the multiple sources are not providing independent analyses of the issue (Harkins & Petty, 1987; Wilder, 1990). In a recent study, unexpected headlines in newspaper stories were found to increase message processing (Baker & Petty, in press). For example, if a headline implied that many people favored something that the message recipient disliked or that few people favored something the recipient liked, message scrutiny was increased over cases in which the headline implied that few favored what the recipient disliked or many favored what the recipient liked. Of course, the enhanced thinking evoked by rhetorical questions, multiple sources, or surprising headlines will aid persuasion only if the arguments in the communication are subjectively cogent. The enhanced thinking will be detrimental to persuasion if the arguments are found to be specious.

As outlined in Fig. 5.2, having the necessary motivation to process a message is not sufficient for the central route to persuasion to occur. People must also have the ability to process a message. For example, a complex or long message might require more than one exposure for maximal processing, even if the recipient was highly motivated to think about it. The increased processing with multiple exposures should lead to more favorable thoughts and attitudes if the arguments are strong, but to more counterarguments and less favorable attitudes if the arguments are weak (Cacioppo & Petty, 1989). Of course, repetition is just one variable that has an impact on a person's ability to think about a message. For example, if a message is accompanied by distraction (Petty, Wells, & Brock, 1976) or if the speaker talks too fast (Smith & Shaffer, 1991), thinking about the message will be disrupted. When strong arguments are presented, disrupting thinking diminish persuasion, but when weak arguments are presented disrupting thinking should enhance persuasion by reducing counterarguing (see Petty & Brock, 1981). Different media sources have an impact on peoples' ability to think about the message. Specifically, people are generally better able to process messages that appear in the print media than those that are controlled externally (e.g., radio and television; Chaiken & Eagly, 1976; Wright, 1981).

A consideration of motivational and ability variables together suggests some interesting effects. For example, research shows clearly that moderate repetition of a message can be beneficial if arguments and cues are positive, but repeating the same message over and over eventually leads to boredom and reduced effectiveness. This "wearout" effect occurs regardless of whether the message is on a topic of high or low interest (Sawyer, 1981). Because of this, a number of investigators have suggested that varying the nature of the repeated ads should forestall the inevitable tedium effect (see Pechman & Stewart, 1989). The ELM suggests that different kinds of message variation should be attempted in a media campaign depending on the recipient's overall motivation to think about the issue of the campaign. In a test of this hypothesis, Schumann, Petty, and Clemons (1990) found that for highly motivated message recipients (those expecting to make an imminent decision about the issue discussed in the communications), repeated presentations on the same topic could be made more effective if the messages varied the substantive arguments that they presented. Variation in peripheral cues made no difference. On the other hand, for recipients low in motivation, variation in simple cues across repeated exposures enhanced the effectiveness of the campaign, but variation in arguments did not.

Objective Versus Biased Thinking. In addition to influencing a person's general motivation or ability to think about a message, Fig. 5.2 indicates that variables can also have an impact on persuasion by influencing the *nature* of the thoughts that come to mind. That is, some features of the persuasion situation increase the likelihood of favorable thoughts being elicited, but others increase the likelihood of unfavorable thoughts coming to mind. Although the subjective cogency of the arguments employed in a message is a prime determinant of whether favorable or unfavorable thoughts are elicited when message thinking is high, other variables can also be influential in determining whether favorable or unfavorable thoughts predominate (Petty & Cacioppo, 1990). For example, instilling "reactance" in message recipients by telling them that they have no choice but to be persuaded on an important issue *motivates* counterarguing even when the arguments used are strong (Brehm, 1966; Petty & Cacioppo, 1979a). Similarly, people who possess accessible attitudes bolstered by considerable attitude-congruent knowledge are better *able* to defend their attitudes than those who have inaccessible attitudes or attitudes with a minimal underlying foundation (Fazio & Williams, 1986; Wood 1982).

Arguments Versus Peripheral Cues. As we noted above, when people have the motivation and ability to think about an issue, they scrutinize the issue-relevant information presented, such as the arguments provided in the communication. An argument is a piece of information that says something about the true merits of the position taken. Although we ordinarily think of arguments as features of the message content itself, source, recipient, and other factors can also serve as arguments. For example, if a spokesperson for a beauty product says that "if you use this product, you will look like me," the source's physical attractiveness serves as relevant information for evaluating the effectiveness of the product. Just as source factors can serve as persuasive arguments in the appropriate context, features of the persuasive message can serve as peripheral cues. A peripheral cue is a feature of the persuasion context that allows favorable or unfavorable attitude formation even in the absence of an effortful consideration of the true merits of the object or issue. Among the variables that have been shown to be capable of serving as simple cues when motivation or ability to process the arguments is low are the credibility of the message source (Petty, Cacioppo, & Goldman, 1981), how likable or attractive the source is (Chaiken, 1980; Petty, Cacioppo, & Schumann, 1983), the mere number of arguments in the message (Alba & Marmorstein, 1987; Petty & Cacioppo, 1984a), the length of the arguments used (Wood, Kallgren, & Priesler, 1985), the number of other people thought to endorse the position (Axsom et al., 1987), and others.[5]

Summary. The ELM holds that as the likelihood of elaboration is increased (as determined by factors such as the personal relevance of the message and the number of times it is repeated), the perceived quality of the issue-relevant arguments presented becomes a more important determinant of persuasion. Effortful evaluation of the message arguments can proceed in a relatively objective or a relatively biased fashion, however. As the elaboration likelihood is decreased, peripheral cues become more important. That is, when the elaboration likelihood is high, the central route to persuasion dominates, but when the elaboration likelihood is low, the peripheral route takes precedence (see Petty, in press, for additional discussion of the operation of central and peripheral processess along the elaboration likelihood continuum).

As we have noted above, the accumulated research on persuasion has pointed to many variables that can be used to either increase or decrease the amount of thinking about a persuasive message and render that thinking relatively favorable or unfavorable. Although we have focused on motivational and ability variables that can be modified by external means (e.g., including rhetorical questions in a message enhances motivation to think about the arguments), other determinants of motivation and ability to process a message are dispositional (e.g., people

---

[5]As depicted in Fig. 5.2 features of the persuasion situation can also influence the extent to which the thoughts elicited by a message are consolidated and stored in long-term memory. For example, arguments that match a person's attitude schema are more easily incorporated into the existing cognitive structure than arguments that do not match (Cacioppo, Petty, & Sidera 1982). Little research has examined this feature of the ELM, however.

high in "need for cognition" tend to chronically engage in and enjoy thinking, Cacioppo & Petty, 1982).

Multiple Roles for Variables
in the Elaboration Likelihood Model

One of the most important features of the ELM is that it holds that any one variable can have an impact on persuasion by serving in different roles in different situations. That is, the same feature of a persuasive message can serve as an issue-relevant argument in some contexts, a peripheral cue in others, affect the motivation or ability to think about the message in other situations, and influence the nature of the thoughts that come to mind in still other domains. For example, in separate studies, the attractiveness of a message source has (a) served as a simple peripheral cue when it was irrelevant to evaluating the merits of an attitude object and participants were not motivated to process the issue-relevant arguments, (b) served as a message argument when it was relevant to evaluating the merits of the attitude object and the elaboration likelihood was high, and (c) affected the extent of thinking about the message arguments presented when the elaboration likelihood was moderate (see Petty, Kasmer, Haugtvedt, & Cacioppo, 1987, for discussion).

If any one variable can influence persuasion by several means, it becomes critical to identify the general conditions under which the variable acts in each of the different roles or the ELM becomes descriptive rather than predictive (cf. Stiff, 1986). The ELM holds that when the elaboration likelihood is high (such as when perceived personal relevance and knowledge are high, the message is easy to understand, no distractions are present, and so on), people typically know that they want to and are able to evaluate the merits of the arguments presented, and they do so. Variables in the persuasion setting are likely to have little direct impact on evaluations by serving as simple peripheral cues in these situations. Instead, when the elaboration likelihood is high, a variable can serve as an argument if it is relevant to the merits of the issue, or the variable can determine the nature of the ongoing information processing activity (e.g., it might bias the ongoing thinking). On the other hand, when the elaboration likelihood is low (e.g., low personal relevance or knowledge, complex message, many distractions, and so on), people know that they do not want to or are not able to evaluate the merits of the arguments presented, or they do not even consider exerting effort to process the message. If any evaluation is formed under these conditions, it is likely to be the result of relatively simple associations or inferences based on salient cues. Finally, when the elaboration likelihood is moderate (e.g., uncertain personal relevance, moderate knowledge, moderate complexity, and so on), people may be uncertain as to whether or not the message warrants or needs scrutiny and whether or not they are capable of providing this analysis. In these situations they may examine the persuasion context for indications (e.g., is the source credible?) of whether or not they are interested in or should process the message. A few examples should help to clarify the multiple roles that a variable can have in different situations.

Multiple Roles for Source Factors. First, consider the multiple processes by which source factors (e.g., expertise, attractiveness) can have an impact on persuasion (see Petty & Cacioppo, 1984c). Some research has found that when the elaboration likelihood was low, source factors such as expertise and attractiveness served as simple positive cues, enhancing attitudes regardless of argument quality. However, when the elaboration likelihood was quite high, source factors did not serve as simple cues. Instead, attitudes were determined primarily by the nature of the arguments presented (Chaiken, 1980; Petty, Cacioppo, & Goldman, 1981). Finally, in two separate experiments in which the elaboration likelihood was not manipulated but was held constant at a moderate level, the source factors of expertise and attractiveness determined how much thinking participants did about the arguments presented (Heesacker, Petty, & Cacioppo, 1983; Puckett, Petty, Cacioppo, & Fisher, 1983). That is, attractive and expert sources led to more persuasion when the arguments were strong, but to less persuasion when the arguments were weak. Interestingly, the self-monitoring scale (see Snyder, 1987) has been used recently to distinguish people who tend to think more about what experts have to say (i.e., low self-monitors) from those who are more interested in what attractive sources have to say (i.e., high self-monitors; DeBono & Harnish, 1988). In any case, the accumulated research has shown clearly that source factors are capable of serving in different roles.

Only one study to date has examined the effects of a source factor across three distinct levels of elaboration likelihood, however. This study (Moore, Hausknecht, & Thamodaran, 1986, Experiment 3) provided support for the ELM notion that variables can serve in different roles in different situations. Specifically, Moore et al. manipulated the likelihood of message elaboration by varying the speed of a radio advertisement for a product. In addition to the speed of the announcement, the credibility of the product endorsers and the quality of the arguments for the product were also varied. This research revealed that when the advertisement was presented at a very rapid pace so that it was difficult to process (i.e., low elaboration likelihood), people were greatly influenced by the credibility of the product endorser, but the quality of the arguments for the product had little effect. When the message was presented at a normal pace and was very easy to process (i.e., high elaboration likelihood), the quality of the arguments in the ad made a difference, but the credibility of the endorser was reduced in importance compared to the fast message conditions. Finally, when the message was presented at a moderately fast pace and processing was possible but challenging, the expertise of the endorser determined how much message processing occurred: the expert source induced more thinking than the nonexpert (see Petty Kasmer, Haugtvedt, & Cacioppo, 1987, for further discussion).

In a more recent study relevant to multiple roles, Mackie, Worth, and Asuncion (1990) examined the persuasive impact of message sources who were ingroup versus outgroup members. In this research, an ingroup source served as a simple positive cue when the persuasive message was rather low in relevance to the group. When issue relevance was increased, however, ingroup sources provoked more message-relevant thinking than outgroup sources.

Multiple Roles for Message Factors.   As we noted above, the mere number of items in a message can serve as a peripheral cue when people are either unmotivated or unable to think about the information. When motivation and ability are high, however, the informational items in a message are not simply counted as cues, but instead the information is processed for its cogency. When the number of items in a message serves as a cue (low elaboration conditions), adding weak reasons in support of a position enhances persuasion, but when the items in a message serve as arguments, adding weak reasons reduces persuasion (Alba & Marmorstein, 1987; Petty & Cacioppo, 1984a).

One recent study examined the multiple roles for message factors at three levels of recipient elaboration likelihood. In this research, a regular advertisement for an unknown product was contrasted with an "upward comparison" ad that compared the new product to a well-established one (Pechman & Estaban, 1990). Unlike a regular message that simply provides support for its position (e.g., You should vote for Candidate X because . . .), an upward comparison message suggests that the critical issue, product, or person is similar to one that is already seen as desirable (e.g., You should vote for Candidate X, who like Person Y, favors . . .). In order to examine the multiple roles for this message variable, regular and upward comparison ads containing either strong or weak arguments were presented following instructions and procedures designed to elicit either a relatively low, moderate, or high motivation to think about the critical ad.

Effectiveness of the ads was assessed by asking participants to rate their intentions to purchase the product advertised. When the low-motivation instructions were used, the upward comparison ad produced more favorable intentions than the regular ad, but strong arguments did not produce more favorable intentions than weak ones. That is, under the low elaboration likelihood conditions, the comparison with the well-known product served as a simple peripheral cue, and argument processing was minimal. When the high motivation conditions were examined, the opposite resulted. That is, under the high elaboration instructions, the strong arguments produced more favorable intentions than the weak ones, but the upward comparison was completely ineffective as a cue for producing more favorable intentions. Finally, when the moderate motivation conditions were analyzed, the use of an upward comparison ad was found to enhance processing of the message arguments. Specifically, when the upward comparison ad employed strong arguments, it led to more persuasion than the direct ad, but when the upward comparison ad used weak arguments, it produced less persuasion than the regular ad.

The results of the Pechman and Estaban (1990) study are quite comparable to the effects observed by Moore et al. (1986), who employed very different experimental operations. When motivation or ability to process the message arguments was low, source credibility and upward comparison claims served as simple cues. When motivation and ability to think about the arguments were high, credibility and upward comparison were unimportant as simple cues. Instead, whether the arguments were strong or weak was the primary determinant of persuasion. Finally, when motivation and ability to process were moderate, people evaluated the arguments only when it seemed worthwhile to do so—when the source was credible or when the unknown product was linked to a desirable one.

Multiple Roles for Recipient Factors. Finally, consider how an individual's mood, a recipient factor, might serve in multiple roles in different situations. If the elaboration likelihood is very low, a pleasant mood should be capable of serving as a simple cue, rendering people more positive toward whatever view is presented. What should happen if the elaboration likelihood is very high and people are clearly motivated and able to think about the arguments presented? Because pleasant moods have been shown to increase the accessibility of positive thoughts and ideas (see Bower, 1981; Clark & Isen, 1982), a pleasant mood under high elaboration conditions might introduce a positive bias to the thoughts generated. Finally, if the elaboration likelihood conditions are moderate, such as when a message is of uncertain relevance and people must decide whether or not to devote effort to thinking about the message, their current mood state might determine whether or not they engage in effortful cognitive activity (e.g., "I won't think if it will destroy my good mood"; cf. Mackie & Worth, 1989; Bless, Bohner, Schwarz, & Strack, 1990; see Petty, Gleicher, & Baker, 1991, for further discussion).

In a partial examination of the multiple ways in which a person's mood can influence attitudes, Petty, Schumann, Richman, and Strathman (1993) exposed participants to an advertisement for a product in the context of a relatively pleasant television program (an episode of a popular situation comedy) or a more neutral program (a segment from a documentary). The likelihood of thinking about the critical ad was varied by telling some participants that they would be allowed to select a free gift at the end of the experiment from a variety of brands of the target product (high involvement), or that they would be allowed to select a free gift from another product category (low involvement). Following exposure to the television program containing the ads, participants reported on their moods, rated their attitudes toward the target product, and listed the thoughts they had during the message. The results of this study revealed that the pleasant program led to a more positive mood and more positive evaluations of the product under both high- and low-elaboration conditions. Importantly, and consistent with the notion that a pleasant mood produces positive attitudes by different processes under high- and low-elaboration conditions, was the finding that a pleasant mood was associated with more positive thoughts about the product when the elaboration likelihood was high, but not when it was low.

Figure 5.4 presents the results from causal path analyses that simultaneously estimated the three paths between (a) manipulated mood and attitude toward the product, (b) manipulated mood and proportion of positive thoughts generated, and (c) proportion of positive thoughts and attitude toward the product. Under low-involvement (low-elaboration) conditions, mood had a direct effect on attitudes, but did not influence thoughts (see left panel). In contrast, under high-involvement (high-elaboration) conditions, mood had no direct effect on attitudes. Instead, mood influenced the production of positive thoughts, which in turn had an impact on attitudes (see right panel).

Consequences of Multiple Roles. Because any one variable can produce persuasion in multiple ways, it is important to understand the process by which the variable has influenced a person's attitude. For example, our discussion of the two routes to persuasion suggests that if a good mood has produced persuasion by serving as a simple cue under

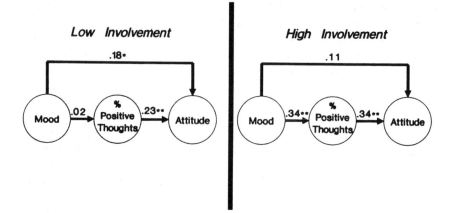

FIG. 5.4. Direct and indirect effects of positive mood on attitudes under high- and low-involvement conditions. Data in the left panel show that when involvement is low and people are not motivated to process the message, mood has a direct effect on attitudes. Data in the right panel show that when involvement is high and people are motivated to process the message, the effect of mood on attitudes is mediated by the generation of positive thoughts (figure adapted from Petty, Schumann, Richman, & Strathman, 1993).

low elaboration conditions, the attitude induced will be less accessible, less persistent, less resistant, and less predictive of behavior than if a good mood produced the same amount of persuasion, but worked by increasing positive thoughts to the message arguments under high-elaboration conditions. In empirical research on media campaigns in a variety of domains (see Rice & Atkin, 1989), many source, message, recipient and contextual variables have been examined. Relatively little attention has been paid, however, to the processes by which these variables work. The ELM holds that source, message, recipient, and contextual factors can work by different processes in different situations, and that the process, central or peripheral, by which the variable induces change is critical for understanding the consequences of any attitude change that occurs (see Fig. 5.2).

Directions for Future ELM Research

Thus far we have reviewed evidence that has supported the primary ELM postulates about the processes responsible for attitude change. Before addressing the links between attitude change and behavior change, it is useful to consider where some future basic research on persuasion processes might be directed. We explained that an important factor in the ELM is how much thinking a person is motivated or able to engage in regarding an attitude issue. Because of this, most of the research on the ELM to date has focused on variables that initiate message processing. Little attention has been paid to variables that determine when that processing will stop. Because most of the messages employed in laboratory research are relatively short (e.g., 1–3 minutes; 1–2 pages of text), it is likely that once individuals embark on the central route, they will continue to think about the message until it stops. On the other hand, the longer the message becomes, the less likely it seems that people will continue to diligently process every argument that is presented. At some point, the individual becomes tired, loses interest, or has considered enough information to come to a reasonable conclusion. Once this point is reached, the person becomes less attentive to the remaining message. As attention begins to wander, the person may become more aware of peripheral features of the persuasion context, or may turn attention completely to noncommunication factors.

On the other hand, consider a person who embarks down the peripheral route because the message initially seems irrelevant and the source is an expert who presumably can be trusted. Thus, minimal attention is paid to the message. What if, however, the first argument when processed in even a cursory manner appears to be silly? This incongruent occurrence might shift the individual from the peripheral to the central route (Maheswaran & Chaiken, 1991). Similarly, an inexpert source on a low relevance topic ordinarily would be resisted via the peripheral route (Petty, Cacioppo, & Goldman, 1981). What if, however, the speaker began to use rhetorical questions rather than statements to frame the arguments? Research suggests that this message factor shifts the individual from the peripheral to the central route (Petty, Cacioppo, & Heesacker, 1981). If a source or other peripheral cue is very salient, greater message processing will be necessary to overcome the cue than if it is not salient. In sum, future research might be directed profitably not only at additional variables and psychological conditions that initiate message processing ("start rules"), but also on those that determine when message processing will cease ("stop rules"), or shift processing from one mode to another ("shift rules").

ATTITUDE–BEHAVIOR LINKS

As we noted above, the ELM provides a framework for understanding persuasion or yielding processes. Once a person's attitude has changed, however, behavior change requires that the person's new attitude rather than the old attitude or previous habits guide action. Considerable research has addressed the links between attitudes and behavior, and a number of situational and dispositional factors have been shown to enhance attitude–behavior consistency (see Ajzen 1988, for a comprehensive review).

Two general models of the process by which attitudes guide behavior have achieved widespread acceptance. One type is exemplified by Fishbein and Ajzen's (1975) "theory of reasoned action," which assumes that "people consider the implications of their actions before they decide to engage or not engage in a given behavior" (p. 5). In this model, people are hypothesized to form intentions to perform or not perform behaviors, and these intentions are based on the person's attitude toward the behavior as well as perceptions of the opinions of significant others (norms). The model focuses on the relatively thoughtful processing involved in considering the personal costs and benefits of engaging in a behavior. In particular, the model focuses on the perceived likelihood that certain benefits will be obtained or costs avoided, and on the desirability or aversiveness of those benefits or costs. The model has accumulated considerable empirical support (Sheppard, Hartwick, & Warshaw, 1988). Recently, Ajzen (1991) expanded the model into a "theory of planned behavior," and has shown that in addition to attitudes and norms, it is important to consider a person's perceptions of control over the behavior.

In contrast to the thoughtful processing highlighted by the theories of reasoned action and planned behavior, Fazio (1990) proposed that much behavior is rather spontaneous and that attitudes guide behavior by a relatively automatic process. That is, if the relevant attitude comes to mind, consistent behavior is likely to follow. Fazio argued that attitudes can guide behavior without any deliberate reflection or reasoning if (a) the attitude is accessed spontaneously by the mere presence of the attitude object, and (b) the attitude colors perception of the object so that if the attitude is favorable (or unfavorable), the qualities of the object appear favorable (or unfavorable). Fazio further noted that motivational and ability factors are important in determining whether the reasoned action or the automatic activation process occurs. That is, for behavioral decisions that are high in perceived personal consequences, attitudes are likely to guide behavior by a deliberate reflection process, but when perceived consequences are low, spontaneous attitude activation should be more important as a determinant of behavior. Similarly, as the time allowed for a decision is reduced, the importance of spontaneous attitude activation processes should increase over more deliberative processes. When there is sufficient motivation and ability to think about one's behavior, a person may reflect upon the costs and benefits of the anticipated action. Interestingly, depending on what costs and benefits are salient at the moment, this process could lead to a behavior that is consistent or inconsistent with the underlying attitude (see Wilson, Dunn, Kraft, & Lisle, 1989). When motivation and ability to reflect are low, however, people's actions are determined by which attitudes are the most accessible.[6]

In some domains an accessible attitude is easily translated into behavior (e.g., I like candidate X, I will vote for this candidate). In other domains, however, translating new attitudes into new behaviors is rather complex even if the person has the desire to act on the attitude (e.g., I want to consume a low fat diet, but how do I do this?). Thus, for some media campaigns, attitude change, though an important first step, may still be insufficient to produce the desired behavioral responses even if appropriate attitudes were formed by the central route. People may also need to acquire new skills and self-perceptions of confidence that allow newly acquired attitudes and intentions to be translated into action. Bandura's (1977, 1986) social-cognitive theory provides a framework to understand these processes (see Bandura, chapter 4, this volume).

SUMMARY AND CONCLUSIONS

Although considerable research on mass media effects has shown that it is possible for media messages to change the knowledge or facts that people have about some object, issue, or person, we have argued that knowledge reception does not invariably result in attitude and behavior change. Our brief review of the ELM and the research supporting it has emphasized that information will only be successful in producing enduring changes in attitudes and behavior if people are motivated and able to process the information, and if this processing results in favorable thoughts and ideas. Furthermore, once attitudes have changed, implementing changes in some behaviors may require learning new skills and perceptions of self-efficacy. Thus, current work on attitude and behavior change may help to account for some unsuccessful media campaigns in which knowledge acquisition failed to have attitudinal and/or behavioral consequences. First, the knowledge acquired may have been seen as irrelevant by the recipients, or may have led to unfavorable rather than favorable reactions. Second, even if appropriate attitude changes were induced, the changes may have been

---

[6]Because attitudes formed by the central route tend to be more accessible than attitudes formed by the peripheral route, peripheral cues in the behavioral environment are likely to have an impact on immediate actions only when the likelihood of reflection in the current situation is low and there are no accessible attitudes to guide behavior.

based on simple peripheral cues rather than on elaborative processing of the message. Third, even if attitude changes were produced by the central route, the people influenced may have lacked the necessary skills or self-confidence to translate their new attitudes into action, or the impact of attitudes on behavior may have been undermined by competing norms.

Perhaps the three most important issues raised in our review are: (a) although some attitudes are based on an effortful reasoning process in which externally provided information is related to oneself and integrated into a coherent belief structure (central route), other attitudes are formed as a result of relatively simple cues in the persuasion environment (peripheral route), (b) any one variable (e.g., source credibility) can be capable of inducing persuasion by either the central or the peripheral route in different situations, and (c) although both central and peripheral route processes can lead to attitudes similar in their valence (how favorable or unfavorable they are), there are important consequences of the manner of attitude change.

If the goal of a mass media influence attempt is to produce long lasting changes in attitudes with behavioral consequences, the central route to persuasion appears to be the preferred persuasion strategy. If the goal is immediate formation of a new attitude, even if it is relatively ephemeral (e.g., attitudes toward the charity sponsoring a telethon), the peripheral route may prove acceptable. Influence via the central route requires that the recipient of the new information have the motivation and ability to process it. As noted previously, one of the most important determinants of motivation to think about a message is the perceived personal relevance of that message. Most of the media messages people receive are probably not perceived as directly relevant and they have few personal consequences. Thus, many of these messages will be ignored or processed primarily for peripheral cues. An important goal of any persuasion strategy aimed at enduring change will be to increase people's motivation to think about the messages by increasing the perceived personal relevance of the communications or employing other techniques to enhance processing (e.g., ending arguments with questions rather than statements; using multiple sources).

In conclusion, we note that research on mass media persuasion has come a long way from the early notions that the mere presentation of information was sufficient to produce persuasion, and the subsequent pessimistic view that media influence attempts were generally ineffective. We now know that media influence is a complex, though explicable process. We know that the extent and nature of a person's cognitive responses to external information may be more important than the information itself. We know that attitudes can be changed in different ways, such as central versus peripheral routes, and that some attitude changes are more accessible, stable, resistant, and predictive of behavior than others. We also know that even apparently simple variables such as how likable a source is or what mood a person is in can produce persuasion by very different processes in different situations.

REFERENCES

Ajzen, I. (1988). *Attitudes, personality, and behavior.* Chicago: Dorsey Press.

Ajzen, I. (1991). The theory of planned behavior. *Organizational Behavior and Human Decision Processes, 50,* 179–210.

Alba, J. W., & Marmorstein, H. (1987). The effects of frequency knowledge on consumer decision making. *Journal of Consumer Research, 13,* 411–454.

Axsom, D., Yates, S., & Chaiken, S. (1987). Audience response as a heuristic cue in persuasion. *Journal of Personality and Social Psychology, 53,* 30–40.

Baker, S. M., & Petty, R. E. (in press). Majority and minority influence: Source advocacy as a determinant of message scrutiny. *Journal of Personality and Social Psychology.*

Bandura, A. (1977). *Social learning theory.* Englewood Cliffs, NJ: Prentice-Hall.

Bandura, A. (1986). *Social foundations of thought and action.* Englewood Cliffs, NJ: Prentice-Hall.

Bem, D. J. (1972). Self-perception theory. In L. Berkowitz (Ed.), *Advances in experimental social psychology* (Vol. 6, pp. 1–62). New York: Academic Press.

Bless, H., Bohner, G., Schwarz, N., & Strack, F. (1990). Mood and persuasion: A cognitive response analysis. *Personality and Social Psychology Bulletin, 17,* 332–346.

Bower, G. H. (1981). Mood and memory. *American Psychologist, 11,* 11–13.

Brehm, J. W. (1966). *A theory of psychological reactance.* New York: Academic Press.

Brickner, M. A., Harkins, S. G., & Ostrom, T. M. (1986). Effects of personal involvement: Thought provoking implications for social loafing. *Journal of Personality and Social Psychology, 51,* 763–769.

Burnkrant, R., & Unnava, R. (1989). Self-referencing: A strategy for increasing processing of message content. *Personality and Social Psychology Bulletin, 15,* 628–638.

Cacioppo, J. T., & Petty, R. E. (1982). The need for cognition. *Journal of Personality and Social Psychology, 42,* 116–131.

Cacioppo, J. T., & Petty, R. E. (1989). Effects of message repetition on argument processing, recall, and persuasion. *Basic and Applied Social Psychology, 10,* 3–12.

Cacioppo, J. T., Petty, R. E., & Sidera, J. (1982). The effects of a salient self-schema on the evaluation of proattitudinal editorials: Top down versus bottom-up message processing. *Journal of Experimental Social Psychology, 18,* 324–338.

Cartwright, D. (1949). Some principles of mass persuasion. *Human Relations, 2,* 253–267.

Chaiken, S. (1980). Heuristic versus systematic information processing and the use of source versus message cues in persuasion. *Journal of Personality and Social Psychology, 39,* 752–756.

Chaiken, S. (1987). The heuristic model of persuasion. In M. P. Zanna, J. Olson, & C. P. Herman (Eds.), *Social influence: The Ontario symposium* (Vol. 5, pp. 3–39). Hillsdale, NJ: Lawrence Erlbaum Associates.

Chaiken, S., & Eagly, A. H. (1976). Communication modality as a determinant of message persuasiveness and message comprehensibility. *Journal of Personality and Social Psychology, 34,* 605–614.

Chaiken, S., Liberman, A., & Eagly, A. H. (1989). Heuristic and systematic processing within and beyond the persuasion context. In J. Uleman & J. Bargh (Eds.), *Unintended thought* (pp. 212–252). New York: Guilford Press.

Clark, M. S., & Isen, A. M. (1982). Toward understanding the relationship between feeling states and social behavior. In A. Hastorf & A. Isen (Eds.), *Cognitive social psychology* (pp. 73–108). New York: Elsevier North Holland.

DeBono, K., & Harnish, R. (1988). Source expertise, source attractiveness, and the processing of persuasive information: A functional approach. *Journal of Personality and Social Psychology, 55,* 541–546.

DeBono, K., & Packer, M. (1991). The effects of advertising appeal on perceptions of product quality. *Personality and Social Psychology Bulletin, 17,* 194–200.

Doob, L. (1935). *Propaganda, its psychology and technique.* New York: Holt.

Eagly, A. H., & Chaiken, S. (1993). *The psychology of attitudes.* Fort Worth, TX: Harcourt, Brace, Jovanovich.

Fazio, R. H. (1990). Multiple processes by which attitudes guide behavior: The MODE model as an integrative framework. In M. Zanna (Ed.), *Advances in experimental social psychology* (Vol. 23, pp. 75–109). New York: Academic Press.

Fazio, R. H., & Williams, C. J. (1986). Attitude accessibility as a moderator of the attitude-perception and attitude-behavior relations: An investigation of the 1984 presidential election. *Journal of Personality and Social Psychology, 51,* 505–514.

Fishbein, M., & Ajzen, I. (1975). *Belief, attitude, intention, and behavior: An introduction to theory and research.* Reading, MA: Addison-Wesley.

Fiske, S. T., & Pavelchak, M. A. (1986). Category-based versus piecemeal-based affective responses: Developments in schema-triggered affect. In R. M. Sorrentino & E. T. Higgins (Eds.), *Handbook of motivation and cognition: Foundations of social behavior* (pp. 167–203). New York: Guilford Press.

Greenwald, A. G. (1968). Cognitive learning, cognitive response to persuasion, and attitude change. In A. Greenwald, T. Brock, & T. Ostrom (Eds.), *Psychological foundations of attitudes* (pp. 147–170). New York: Academic Press.

Harkins, S. G., & Petty, R. E. (1981). The effects of source magnification cognitive effort on attitudes: An information processing view. *Journal of Personality and Social Psychology, 40,* 401–413.

Harkins, S. G., & Petty, R. E. (1987). Information utility and the multiple source effect in persuasion. *Journal of Personality and Social Psychology, 52,* 260–268.

Haugtvedt, C., & Petty, R. E. (1992). Personality and persuasion: Need for cognition moderates the persistance and resistance of attitude changes. *Journal of Personality and Social Psychology, 63,* 308–319.

Heesacker, M., Petty, R. E., & Cacioppo, J. T. (1983). Field dependence and attitude change: Source credibility can alter persuasion by affecting message-relevant thinking. *Journal of Personality, 51,* 653–666.

Hovland, C. I. (1954). Effects of the mass media of communication. In G. Lindzey (Ed.), *Handbook of social psychology* (Vol. 2, pp. 1062–1103). Cambridge, MA: Addison-Wesley.

Hovland, C. I. (1959). Reconciling conflicting results derived from experimental and survey studies of attitude change. *American Psychologist, 14,* 8–17.

Hovland, C. I., Janis, I., & Kelley, H. H. (1953). *Communication and persuasion.* New Haven, CT: Yale University Press.

Hovland, C. I., Lumsdaine, A., & Sheffield, F. (1949). *Experiments on mass communication.* Princeton, NJ: Princeton University Press.

Howard, D. J. (1990). Rhetorical question effects on message processing and persuasion: The role of information availability and the elicitation of judgment. *Journal of Experimental Social Psychology, 26,* 217–239.

Hyman, H., & Sheatsley, P. (1947). Some reasons why information campaigns fail. *Public Opinion Quarterly, 11,* 412–423.

Iyengar, S. & Kinder, D. R. (1987). *News that matters: Television and American opinion.* Chicago: University of Chicago Press.

Katz, D., & Lazarsfeld, P. R. (1955). *Personal influence.* New York: Free Press.

Kitson, H. D. (1922). *The mind of the buyer: A psychology of selling.* New York: Macmillan.

Klapper, J. T. (1960). *The effects of mass communication.* New York: The Free Press.

Lasswell, H. W. (1927). *Propaganda techniques in the world war.* New York: Peter Smith.

Lasswell, H. W. (1964). The structure and function of communication in society. In L. Bryson (Ed)., *Communication of ideas* (pp. 37–51). New York: Cooper Square Publishers.

Lazarsfeld, P., Berelson, B., & Gaudet, H. (1948). *The people's choice.* New York: Columbia University Press.

Lee, A., & Lee, E. B. (1939). *The fine art of propaganda: A study of Father Coughlin's speeches.* New York: Harcourt, Brace.

Leippe, M. R., & Elkin, R. A. (1987). When motives clash: Issue involvement and response involvement as determinants of persuasion. *Journal of Personality and Social Psychology, 52,* 269–278.

Lippmann, W. (1922). *Public opinion.* New York: MacMillan.

Mackie, D., & Worth, L. (1989). Processing deficits and the mediation of positive affect in persuasion. *Journal of Personality and Social Psychology, 57,* 27–40.

Mackie, D. M., Worth, L. T., & Asuncion, A. G. (1990). Processing of persuasive in-group messages. *Journal of Personality and Social Psychology, 58,* 812–822.

MacKuen, M. B. (1981). Social communication and the mass policy agenda. In M. B. MacKuen & S. L. Coombs (Eds.), *More than news: Media power in public affairs* (pp. 19–144). Beverly Hills, CA: Sage Publications.

Maheswaran, D., & Chaiken, S. (1991). Promoting systematic processing in low motivation settings: Effect of incongruent information on processing and judgment. *Journal of Personality and Social Psychology, 61,* 13–25.

McGuire, W. J. (1968). Personality and susceptibility to social influence. In E. F. Borgatta & W. W. Lambert (Eds.), *Handbook of personality theory and research* (pp. 1130–1187). Chicago: Rand McNally.

McGuire, W. J. (1969). The nature of attitudes and attitude change. In G. Lindzey & E. Aronson (Eds.), *Handbook of social psychology* (2nd ed., Vol. 3, pp. 136–314). Reading, MA: Addison-Wesley.

McGuire, W. J. (1985). Attitudes and attitude change. In G. Lindzey & E. Aronson (Eds.), *Handbook of social psychology* (3rd ed., Vol. 2, pp. 233–346). New York: Random House.

McGuire, W. J. (1989). Theoretical foundations of campaigns. In R. E. Rice & C. K. Atkin (Eds.), *Public communication campaigns* (2nd ed., pp. 43–65). Newbury Park, CA: Sage Publications.

Mendelsohn, H. (1973). Some reasons why information campaigns can succeed. *Public Opinion Quarterly, 11,* 412–423.

Moore, D. L., Hausknecht, D., & Thamodaran, K. (1986). Time pressure, response opportunity, and persuasion. *Journal of Consumer Research, 13,* 85–99,

Moore, D. L., & Reardon, R. (1987). Source magnification: The role of multiple sources in processing of advertising appeals. *Journal of Marketing Research, 24,* 412–417.

Paisley, W. (1989). Public communication campaigns: The American experience. In R. E. Rice & C. K. Atkin (Eds.), *Public communication campaigns* (2nd ed., pp. 15–41). Newbury Park, CA: Sage Publications.

Palmerino, M., Langer, E., & McGillis, D. (1984). Attitudes and attitude change:

Mindlessness-mindfulness perspective. In J. R. Eiser (Ed.), *Attitudinal judgment* (pp. 179–195). New York: Springer-Verlag.

Pechman, C., & Estaban, G., (1990). *How comparative claims affect the route to persuasion.* Working paper, Graduate School of Management, University of California, Irvine, CA.

Pechman, C., & Stewart, D. W. (1989). Advertising repetition: A critical review of wearin and wearout. *Current Issues and Research in Advertising, 11,* 285–330.

Peterson, R. E., & Thurstone, L. (1933). *Motion pictures and the social attitudes of children.* New York: MacMillan.

Petty, R. E. (in press). Two routes to persuasion: State of the art. In G. d'Ydewalle, P. Eelen, & P. Bertelson (Eds.) *Current advances in psychological science: An international perspective.* Hillsdale, NJ: Lawrence Erlbaum Associates.

Petty, R. E., Baker, S. M., & Gleicher, F. (1991). Attitudes and drug abuse prevention: Implications of the Elaboration Likelihood Model of persuasion. In L. Donohew, H. E. Sypher, & W. J. Bukoski (Eds.), *Persuasive communication and drug abuse prevention* (pp. 71–90). Hillsdale, NJ: Lawrence Erlbaum Associates.

Petty, R. E., & Brock, T. C. (1981). Thought disruption and persuasion: Assessing the validity of attitude change experiments. In R. Petty, T. Ostrom, & T. Brock (Eds.), *Cognitive responses in persuasion* (pp. 55–79). Hillsdale, NJ: Lawrence Erlbaum Associates.

Petty, R. E., & Cacioppo, J. T. (1979a). Effects of forewarning of persuasive intent on cognitive responses and persuasion. *Personality and Social Psychology Bulletin, 5,* 173–176.

Petty, R. E., & Cacioppo, J. T. (1979b). Issue-involvement can increase or decrease persuasion by enhancing message-relevant cognitive responses. *Journal of Personality and Social Psychology, 37,* 1915–1926.

Petty, R. E., & Cacioppo, J. T. (1981). *Attitudes and persuasion: Classic and contemporary approaches.* Dubuque: Wm. C. Brown.

Petty, R. E., & Cacioppo, J. T. (1984a). The effects of involvement on responses to argument quantity and quality: Central and peripheral routes to persuasion. *Journal of Personality and Social Psychology, 46,* 69–81.

Petty, R. E., & Cacioppo, J. T. (1984b). Motivational factors in consumer response to advertisements. In W. Beatty, R. Geen, & R. Arkin (Eds.), *Human motivation* (pp. 418–454). New York: Allyn & Bacon.

Petty, R. E., & Cacioppo, J. T. (1984c). Source factors and the elaboration likelihood model of persuasion. *Advances in Consumer Research, 11,* 668–672.

Petty, R. E., & Cacioppo, J. T. (1986a). *Communication and persuasion: Central and peripheral routes to attitude change.* New York: Springer/Verlag.

Petty, R. E., & Cacioppo, J. T. (1986b). The Elaboration Likelihood Model of persuasion. In L. Berkowitz (Ed.), *Advances in experimental social psychology* (Vol. 19, pp. 123–205) New York: Academic Press.

Petty, R. E., & Cacioppo, J. T. (1990). Involvement and persuasions: Tradition versus integration. *Psychological Bulletin, 107,* 367–374.

Petty, R. E., Cacioppo, J. T., & Goldman, R. (1981). Personal involvement as a determinant of argument-based persuasion. *Journal of Personality and Social Psychology, 41,* 847–855.

Petty, R. E., Cacioppo, J. T., & Haugtvedt, C. (1992). Involvement and persuasion: An appreciative look at the Sherifs' contribution to the study of self-relevance and attitude change. In D. Granberg & G. Sarup (Eds.), *Social judgment and intergroup relations: Essays in honor of Muzafer Sherif* (pp. 147–174). New York: Springer/Verlag.

Petty, R. E., Cacioppo, J. T., & Heesacker, M. (1981). The use of rhetorical questions in persuasion: A cognitive response analysis. *Journal of Personality and Social Psychology, 40,* 432–440.

Petty, R. E., Cacioppo, J. T., & Schumann, D. (1983). Central and peripheral routes to advertising effectiveness: The moderating role of involvement. *Journal of Consumer Research, 10,* 134–148.

Petty, R. E., Gleicher, F., & Baker, S. M. (1991). Multiple roles for affect in persuasion. In J. Forgas (Ed.), *Affect and judgment* (pp. 181–200). London: Pergamon.

Petty, R. E., Kasmer, J., Haugtvedt, C., & Cacioppo, (1987). Source and message factors in persuasion: A reply to Stiff's critique of the Elaboration Likelihood Model. *Communication Monographs, 54,* 233–249.

Petty, R. E., & Krosnick, J. A. (Eds.). (in press). *Attitude strength: Antecedents and consequences.* Hillsdale, NJ: Lawrence Erlbaum Associates.

Petty, R. E., Ostrom, T. M., & Brock, T. C. (Eds.). (1981). *Cognitive responses in persuasion.* Hillsdale, NJ: Lawrence Erlbaum Associates.

Petty, R. E., Priester, J. R., & Wegener, D. T. (in press). Cognitive processes in attitude change. In R. S. Wyer, & T. K. Srull (Eds.), *Handbook of social cognition* (2nd ed.). Hillsdale, NJ: Lawrence Erlbaum Associates.

Petty, R. E., Schumann, D., Richman, S., & Strathman, A. (1993). Positive mood and persuasion: Different roles for affect under high and low elaboration conditions. *Journal of Personality and Social Psychology, 64,* 5–20.

Petty, R. E., Unnava, R., & Strathman, A. (1991). Theories of attitude change. In H. Kassarjian & T. Robertson (Eds.), *Handbook of consumer theory and research* (pp. 241–280). Englewood Cliffs, NJ: Prentice-Hall.

Petty, R. E., Wegener, D. T., Fabrigar, L. R., Priester, J. R., & Cacioppo, J. T. (in press). Conceptual and methodological issues in the Elaboration Likelihood Model of persuasion: A reply to the Michigan State critics. *Communication Theory.*

Petty, R. E., Wells, G. L., & Brock, T. C. (1976). Distraction can enhance or reduce yielding to propaganda. *Journal of Personality and Social Psychology, 34,* 874–884.

Puckett, J., Petty, R. E., Cacioppo, J. T., & Fisher, D. (1983). The relative impact of age and attractiveness stereotypes on persuasion. *Journal of Gerontology, 38,* 340–343.

Rholes, N., & Wood, W. (1992). Self-esteem and intelligence affect influenceability: The mediating role of message reception. *Psychological Bulletin, 111,* 156–171.

Rice, R. E., & Atkin, C. K. (Eds.). (1989). *Public communication campaigns.* Newbury park, CA: Sage Publications.

Sawyer, A. G. (1981). Repetition, cognitive responses and persuasion. In R. E. Petty, T. M. Ostrom, & T. C. Brock (Eds.), *Cognitive responses in persuasion* (pp. 237–261). Hillsdale, NJ: Lawrence Erlbaum Associates.

Schumann, D., Petty, R. E., & Clemons, S. (1990). Predicting the effectiveness of different strategies of advertising variation: A test of the repetition-variation hypothesis. *Journal of Consumer Research, 17,* 192–202.

Sears, D. O., & Kosterman, R. (in press). Mass media and political persuasion. In T. C. Brock & S. Shavitt (Eds.), *Psychology of persuasion.* Needham Heights, MA: Allyn & Bacon.

Sears, D. O. & Whitney, R. E. (1973). *Political persuasion.* Morristown, NJ: General Learning Press.

Sheppard, B. H., Hartwick, J., & Warshaw, P. (1988). The theory of reasoned action: A meta-analysis of past research with recommendations for modifications and future research. *Journal of Consumer Research, 15,* 325–343.

Shils, E. A., & Janowitz, M. (1948). Cohesion and disintegration in the Wehrmacht. *Public Opinion Quarterly, 12,* 300–06; 308–315.

Smith, S. M., & Shaffer, D. R. (1991). Celebrity and cajolery: Rapid speech may promote or inhibit persuasion via its impact on message elaboration. *Personality and Social Psychology Bulletin, 17,* 663–669.

Snyder, M. (1987). *Public appearances, private realities: The psychology of self-monitoring.* New York: Freeman.

Snyder, M., & DeBono, K. G. (1989). Understanding the functions of attitudes: Lessons from personality and social behavior. In A. Pratkanis, S. Breckler, & A. Greenwald (Eds.), *Attitude structure and function* (pp. 339–359). Hillsdale, NJ: Lawrence Erlbaum Associates.

Staats, A. W., & Staats, C. (1958). Attitudes established by classical conditioning. *Journal of Abnormal and Social Psychology, 67,* 159–167.

Stiff, J. B. (1986). Cognitive processing of persuasive message cues: A meta-analytic review of the effects of supporting information on attitudes. *Communication Monographs, 53,* 75–89.

Swasy, J. L., & Munch, J. M. (1985). Examining the target of receiver elaborations: Rhetorical question effects on source processing and persuasion. *Journal of Consumer Research, 11,* 877–886.

Taylor, S. E. (1981). The interface of cognitive and social psychology. In J. H. Harvey (Ed.), *Cognition, social behavior, and the environment* (pp. 189–211). Hillsdale, NJ: Lawrence Erlbaum Associates.

Wartella, E., & Middlestadt, S. (1991). Mass communication and persuasion: The evolution of direct effects, limited effects, information processing, and affect and arousal models. In L. Donohew, H. E. Sypher, & W. J. Bukoski (Eds.), *Persuasive communication and drug abuse prevention* (pp. 53–69). Hillsdale, NJ: Lawrence Erlbaum Associates.

Wartella, E., & Reeves, B. (1985). Historical trends in research on children and the media: 1900–1960. *Journal of Communications, 35,* 118–133.

Wilder, D. A. (1990). Some determinants of the persuasive power of ingroups and outgroups: Organization of information and attribution of independence. *Journal of Personality and Social Psychology, 59,* 1202–1213.

Wilson, T. D., Dunn, D. S., Kraft, D., & Lisle, D. (1989). Introspection, attitude change, and attitude-behavior consistency: The disruptive effects of explaining why we feel the way we do. In L. Berkowitz (Ed.), *Advances in experimental social psychology* (Vol. 22, pp. 287–343). San Diego, CA: Academic Press.

Wood, W. (1982). Retrieval of attitude relevant information from memory: Effects on susceptibility to persuasion and on intrinsic motivation. *Journal of Personality and Social Psychology, 42,* 798–810.

Wood, W., Kallgren, C., & Priesler, R. (1985). Access to attitude relevant information in memory as a determinant of persuasion. *Journal of Experimental Social Psychology, 21,* 73–85.

Wright, P. L. (1981). Cognitive responses to mass media advocacy. In R. E. Petty, T. M. Ostrom, & T. C. Brock (Eds.), *Cognitive responses in persuasion* (pp. 263–282). Hillsdale, NJ: Lawrence Erlbaum Associates.

6

The Expanding
Boundaries of Political
Communication Effects

JACK M. McLEOD
University of Wisconsin-Madison

GERALD M. KOSICKI
Ohio State University

DOUGLAS M. McLEOD
University of Delaware

Political research, perhaps more than other areas of communication inquiry, cannot evade normative assumptions of how societal institutions "ought to" work. The value of participatory democracy, active and widespread popular participation informed by a free and responsible press, was an important impetus to political communication research from Walter Lippman (1922) onward. Concern for a participatory democracy led naturally to a set of expectations regarding the functioning of news media that might have served as criteria for a broad examination of press performance. The reality, for a variety of reasons, proved to be otherwise. For several decades following World War II, political communication research was confined within a fairly narrow set of topics, focusing on media content and individual voting behavior within relatively stable political systems. Little interest was exhibited during the 1940s through the 1960s in the less tractable issues of institutional evaluation. This situation has changed greatly in recent years. Global and national political systems have shown conflict and instability, thus challenging generalizations based on stable political systems. The rapid evolution of media systems and technologies has made media effects potentially stronger and more complicated. In turn, research on political communication has broadened its scope beyond the individual level to macro-concerns about the role of mass media in democratic systems. In the process, it has also expanded what we mean by effects, and how we look at media content and its effects.

OBJECTIVES, ASSUMPTIONS, AND ORGANIZATION

The purpose of this chapter is to convey a sense of the broadened scope of recent political communication research. The particular argument made here is that understanding political communication effects, because of their dependence on specific sociopolitical environments, requires examination in broader spatial and temporal contexts than required by other types of media effects. This argument is based on five meta-theoretical assumptions:

1. The connection between normative democratic standards for the media and empirical political communication research, which was severed for several decades, should be restored. In democratic societies, normative expectations can serve as useful criteria for evaluating the performance of media institutions and the workings of political communication more generally.

2. Evaluation of media performance requires specification of observable indicators of the adequacy of institutional performance, their formats and processes, and the products and output they produce.

3. Understanding of the performance by media institutions requires examination of their constraints and conventions, both induced and self-imposed. Attribution of effects to the media is dependent on evidence that the media production process was involved in shaping the message and not simply acting as a conduit for other sources.

4. Examination of performance requires going beyond critiques of media content and other institutional outputs to study individual cognitive, affective, and behavioral effects of these products. It is important to examine effects not only on individual citizens but also on key political actors, such as political leaders, information strategists, and journalists.

5. Understanding of political communication necessitates examination of outcomes for the political system resulting from collective reactions of individuals and cumulative consequences of institutional performance.

These assumptions are potentially useful for evaluating institutional sources of political communication influence other than mass media (e.g., families, schools, political parties, governmental agencies, interest groups). Our analysis is necessarily limited to mass media influences, primarily those of news content. We begin by conceptualizing the boundaries of political communication. This is followed by a brief discussion of recent trends in political communication research.

A third section is devoted to the context of changes in the social and political systems and the mass media. Political communication effects are likely to be more vulnerable to such influences than are other types of media influences. Media content and influences on it are the focus of the fourth section. Antecedents of media content are not usually a part of media effects research; our argument is that particularly for political communication a more comprehensive view inclusive of the production process is required for the understanding of such effects.

The fifth section illustrates recent research on political communication effects that is distinctively different from research of the post-World War II decades. The sixth section examines recent work with a more complex O-S-O-R model for the analysis of media effects. A seventh section discusses possible media effects on politicians and policy-makers beyond their impact on ordinary citizens. Finally, we extend the normative standards of Gurevitch and Blumler (1990) by integrating media effects research into a larger media performance model.

UNDERSTANDING POLITICAL COMMUNICATION

Surveying the Boundaries

Defining the boundaries of political communication has become an increasingly difficult task as the contributions from a variety of disciplines and research traditions—including political science, psychology, sociology, linguistics, rhetoric, and mass communication—have broadened the focus of research. Whereas the study of political communication once was confined to the relationship between print media use and voting choices, it has been expanded to other political aspects of communication as researchers incorporated additional facets of the communication process. The theoretical fermentation has been accentuated by the development of new approaches to political communication research and the use of multiple methods. Indeed, it has led to the recognition that all facets of social behavior, including interpersonal relationships shown on entertainment television programming, could be conceived of as political.

For practical purposes, however, the boundaries of political communication must be narrowed. Generally speaking, political communication involves the exchange of symbols and messages between political actors and institutions, the general public, and news media that are the products of or have consequences for the political system (Meadow, 1980). The outcomes of these processes involve the stabilization or alteration of power. In this chapter dealing with media-related research, this definition can be further narrowed by focusing on symbols and messages exchanged via the mass media, particularly in their news content.

Mapping the Territory

To map out the territory within the narrowed boundaries of mass-mediated political communication, one might start with ideas about how representative political systems are designed to balance the ideals of participatory democracy and the practicality of efficient decision making. In theory, the media play an important role as an intermediary between the people and their representatives (McQuail, 1992). Gurevitch and Blumler (1990, p. 270) identified eight normative standards for mass media systems in democratic societies, which can be paraphrased as:

1. Surveillance of contemporary events that are likely to impinge, positively or negatively, upon the welfare of citizens.
2. Identification of key sociopolitical issues including their origins and possibilities for resolution.
3. Provision of platforms for advocacy by spokespersons for causes and interests.
4. Transmission of diverse content across the various dimensions and factions of political discourse, as well as bidirectionally between potential power holders and mass publics.
5. Scrutiny of government officials, their institutions and other agencies of power by holding them accountable for their actions and policies.
6. Incentives and information to allow citizens to become active informed participants rather than spectators in the political process.
7. Principled resistance to external forces attempting to subvert media autonomy.
8. Respectful consideration of the audience as potentially concerned, sense-making, and efficacious citizens.

As Gurevitch and Blumler recognized, the media often fall far short of these democratic standards. They suggested that four major obstacles hinder the attainment of these democratic goals. First, these expectations may themselves conflict, necessitating trade-offs and compromises. For example, the principle of editorial autonomy (Principle 7) may conflict with providing platforms for advocacy (Principle 3). Second, the dialogue of elite political communicators is often distanced from the perspectives of ordinary people, thus limiting the latter's participation. Third, because political participation is voluntary in a democratic society, many citizens may choose to be politically apathetic. Finally, social, political, and economic environments may constrain the media's pursuit of these democratic ideals. These are problems that require closer examination.

It may be useful to extend Gurevitch and Blumler's (1990) eight democratic standards by connecting them to problems of media performance and their possible antecedents and consequences. Some illustrative examples of media performance problems associated with democratic standards are noted in the third column of Table 6.1a. This table also lists some of the prominent constraints and organizational conventions that various authors advance to account for media shortcomings. Table 6.1b identifies some potential outcomes of media performance deficiencies for individual audience members and for the system as a whole.

The descriptions contained in the rows for each standard represent allegations with a range of backing from speculation to substantial empirical evidence. Two problems immediately arise when trying to use Table 6.1 as a base for theoretical development. First, discussions of news media faults too often fail to distinguish criticisms based on unsystematic observation from those based on more solid evidence. Second, specific research programs unfortunately tend to focus on questions found in a single column of Table 6.1—on constraints, performance, effects, or consequences—somewhat separately without linking questions or using research designs that go across columns within a row. Characterizations across any given row, however, may be causally related and could serve as the basis of hypotheses to be tested empirically. The particular aspect of media performance could be connected with its antecedent structural conditions and its individual effects and systemic consequences. The linkages should be regarded, however, not as inclusive statements of what has or should be done but rather as examples of what might be possible. Obviously, one could add much to the various cells and construct linkages in very different ways as well as add other standards to the rows.

Admittedly, there are vertical linkages between factors down each column. For instance, the organizational constraint of limited news budgets may be related to the convention of organizing "news nets" around official sources that provides a constant flow of accessible

TABLE 6.1a
Democratic Standards for Mass Media News, Constraints and Conventions,
and Allegations of Performance Deficiencies

Democratic Standards[a]	Constraints and Conventions	Media Performance
1. Surveillance of relevant events	Budgetary constraints; personnel limitations; audience maximization	Routinized coverage of politically irrelevant events for their high entertainment value; pseudo-event coverage
2. Identification of key issues	Institutional organization of news nets; need for interesting video and photos; lack of news staff specialization	Issue coverage follows institutional agenda; emphasis on events not issues; decontextualized and ahistorical coverage
3. Provision of platforms for advocacy	Ideologies of objectivity and press autonomy; belief that the media must control "air time"	Media access is difficult for marginalized groups; mainstream groups must conform to media practices by "running the news value gauntlet"
4. Transmission of diverse political discourse	Reliance on official sources; ideology of source legitimacy; concern for audience composition	Mainstream content ignores "deviant" groups and less attractive audiences (e.g., the poor and elderly)
5. Scrutiny of institutions and officials	Interdependence of media and other powerful institutions; High cost of investigative reporting	Limited coverage of systematic problems; blame is focused on individuals not the system
6. Activation of informed participation	Ideologies of objectivity and press autonomy	Lack of mobilizing information to avoid accusations of bias
7. Maintenance of media autonomy	Corporate media ownership, particularly by non-media industries; "bureaucratic subsidization of news"; advertising revenue	Content reflects on elite agenda and elite perspectives; as politicians adapt to news imperatives, media transmit official propaganda as news
8. Consideration of audience potential	Audience maximization; consumer-driven news production	Existing preferences and abilities are seen as natural, not learned; news as entertainment

[a]Standards adapted from Gurevitch and Blumler (1990).

information. Despite some overlap between rows, even tentative attempts at separation at least improves the present situation, which tosses all faults into a large confounded pile, undifferentiated as to which performance problems have what causes and what consequences. The table simply attempts to be an organizing device to make explicit what has previously been implicit.

TABLE 6.1b
Individual and System Effects of Media Performance Limitations

Individual Effects (Audience)	System Effects (Society)
Lack of awareness and knowledge of important events and their consequences; political news is viewed as irrelevant	Campaigns focus on events not issues; political events staged for media consumption
Adoption of media agenda; superficial understanding of issue origins and consequences	Sound bites replace political discourse; political decisions are based on immediate appearances as opposed to long-term consequences
Mainstreaming and support for the status quo; lack of participation in the media forum; leaders hesitate to take "advocacy" roles	Power of major institutions and mainstream groups is perpetuated; political participation is an elite activity; leaders hesitate to take "advocacy" roles
Inability to distinguish and consider political alternatives	Narrowed boundaries of the "marketplace of ideas"
Blaming individuals and inability to recognize structural roots of societal problems	Inefficient and dysfunctional structures are perpetuated; structural roots of societal problems are ignored; lack of system accountability
Political apathy, low levels of political involvement, and perceived efficacy	Feedback from the public to policy-makers is limited, indirect, and distorted; concentration of decision-making power
Support for the status quo	Predominance of elite agenda; dominance of values consistent with corporate capitalism
Lack of interest in politics; superficial understanding of events and issues; cultivation of homogeneous tastes	Political discourse is limited, simplistic, and emotional; high ratio of spectators to players in the political arena

Locating Political Effects

Political communication effects are phenomena that have consequences for the political system. Explanation of them involves attributing the effect to some personal or institutional source of influence (e.g., a political leader, advertising message, news media, news story). Thus, news media political effects is a subset of a larger set of political communication effects. The term *media effect* is often used loosely and can be ambiguous or misleading. The role played by media may vary greatly from, say, C-Span carrying U.S. Congressional proceedings live and without commentary to a "60 Minutes" investigation story initiated by journalists with strongly formed conclusions. It may be less important whether we choose to call the C-Span example a "media effect" at all than it is to make clear in a given analysis what the unique contribution of media really is. An effect may arise from the form of different media (e.g., visual & sound vs. sound only vs. text only), formats within a medium (e.g., average length of story, sound bite), amount of time/space devoted to coverage, framing of a story (e.g., labeling, use of metaphors), or extent and type of commentary or intervention in the story (e.g., use of external experts, journalists challenging a story).

Effects can be manifested at the micro level of individual behavior, the intermediary level of political groups, or at the macro level of the system itself. There are also effects that involve cross-level relationships such as the impact of political institutions on individual behavior or the process by which individual political sentiments become translated into social policy. In addition, the term *effect* commonly implies some type of change but can also include processes that maintain stability (McLeod & Reeves, 1980). This review focuses on mass mediated political communication, considering factors that shape the content of mediated messages and the impact that these messages have on the audience, politicians and policy-makers, and the journalists themselves.

THE HISTORICAL DEVELOPMENT OF POLITICAL COMMUNICATION RESEARCH

Political communication research has traditionally played a central role in research on the effects of mass media. Klapper's (1960) conclusion that the effects of mass media are "limited" was based largely on studies of political election campaigns by researchers at Columbia University (Berelson, Lazarsfeld, & McPhee, 1954; Lazarsfeld, Berelson, & Gaudet, 1948). The "limited effects" perspective rests uneasily on several underlying assumptions, including the power of selectivity processes (exposure, attention, perception, and recall), reinforcement and crystallization, social predispositions, interpersonal mediation, and the stability of social systems. Despite its landmark status in the history of the field, sharp criticism has been leveled against the limited effects model (Blumler & McLeod, 1974; Chaffee & Hochheimer, 1985; Gitlin, 1978).

At a minimum, the limited effects model presented an overly stable picture of the "functional" role of politics and the media.

The Rebirth of Political Communication Inquiry

For 20 years following the last Columbia study of the 1948 election, voting studies paid little attention to media influences in political campaigns and highlighted the effects of party affiliation. Lacking alternatives, the limited effects model held sway until the 1970s. The growth and changing nature of political communication inquiry starting in the 1970s was accompanied by marked shifts in the political andmedia environments. Four important historical influences fostered substantial recent growth in political communication research (McLeod, Kosicki, & Rucinski, 1988). First, important sociopolitical changes have made voting a far less predictable behavior. Second, the development of new media, particularly television, has produced concern over their potentially detrimental effects on the political system. Third, the field has benefitted from the influx of European scholarship from a variety of theoretical perspectives. Finally, the "cognitive revolution" in social science has also widened the focus of political communication research.

Trends in Political Communication Research

Several promising trends in political communication research can be noted. First, there has been some progress in connecting audience effects with other parts of the communication process: news sources, media organizations, and content. Second, investigation at the macro-social level of analysis has been revitalized to complement the already extensive research at the individual level. Coinciding with the resurgence of macrolevel concern, research making comparisons between communities, nations, and historical periods has also emerged (Blumler, 1983; Blumler, McLeod, & Rosengren, 1992; Tichenor, Donohue, & Olien, 1980). A fourth trend is a renewed interest in language, not only the language of media content, but language as it relates to the production and interpretation of mediated information. Fifth, there has been an increase in the number of studies that combine methodologies and/or use multiple sources of data to provide more complete answers to research questions. The final trend, likely the result of the previous five trends, is the development of more complex models of political communication processes. Each of the trends has been stimulated by the increasing complexity of the political environment and has facilitated the growth of knowledge in the field.

THE CHANGING CONTEXT
OF POLITICAL COMMUNICATION

The social, political, and media environments in a given society can be expected to influence the character, form, and content of political information available and its impact on the public.

The Changing Social and Political Environments

U.S. society in the post-World War II era has been rapidly evolving in ways driven by increased education, suburbanization, and immigration, as well as increasing disparity between rich and poor. One result of these changing circumstances is increased tension in the political dialogue and a complication of political discourse. As society diversifies, the political system has become less predictable. Party identification, along with voter turnout, is down, and split-ticket voting in a given election and party instability across elections are more common, leading to divided government at almost every level. Accompanying these destabilizing trends is a loss of confidence in institutions and leaders, including government, business, and journalism.

One response to this is the growth of special interest groups. Adept at raising funds and at using public relations strategies, often in consort with other like-minded groups, interest groups seek to dominate discourse by getting their "experts" on news and talk shows, providing "background" information to reporters, and inducing the news media to adopt their "frames" on controversial issues (Gandy, 1982; Pertschuk & Schaetzel, 1989). Playing directly to these organized interest groups are candidates who raise special interest money and build their own organizations largely independent of party influences. Once elected, these individuals are relatively free of party discipline and seem mainly concerned with preserving their own power bases. This new freedom can be translated into national political power on selected issues for those able to use their posts to become recurrent news sources.

The center of the new political system appears to be the media. Presidential candidates, for example, travel incessantly to generate opportunities to appear on the news and to raise campaign funds for advertising. Candidates learn to speak in brief sound bites, and advertisements are increasingly limited in length. Neither affords the opportunity for any sustained political reasoning even if the candidates were inclined to reason. Political ads make sophisticated use of music, symbols, and imagery, particularly to impute negative qualities to opponents. Fear of attacks increasingly dictates that political decisions of all kinds be directed by considerations of how easy a course of action is to explain.

From the demands of the new styles of campaigning, a new set of professional roles have emerged: image managers, spin doctors, photo opportunists, opinion poll readers, media pundits, and so on (Blumler, 1990). A large part of the communicator's job is to design visually compelling scenes that journalists will find irresistible (Altheide & Snow, 1991).

The Changing Media Environment

Although concentration of media ownership has been seen as a problem for more than half a century, recent corporate takeovers have added to the problem. News has increasingly come under the control of executives whose values are shaped by their experiences in financial or entertainment circles. This leads to attempts to make the news more appealing to broader audiences, prompting stronger demands for entertainment values in story selection and structure. Serious political journalism has been reduced, and what is left faces increased competition from cable television.

These social and political trends place considerable strain on the media. Performance expectations have increased as media replace political parties in the center of the political communication process. At the same time, social trends toward change and diversity, political instability, and the dispersion of power forces media to do more with less, and do it in a more difficult environment.

MEDIA CONTENT AND ITS ANTECEDENTS

There are advantages to the usual scheme of studying content in terms of its most manifest features: reliability of measurement, face validity, comparability, and so on (e.g., Berelson, 1952; Stempel, 1989). But there are several reasons to consider alternatives. First, recent research examining more latent forms of political content has suggested ways in which more subtle use of language may shape audience understanding of public issues (Gamson & Mogdigliani, 1989; Glasgow Media Group, 1982; Hallin, 1992; McLeod & Hertog, 1992). Second, the results of skilled strategies that modern political practitioners use to influence news are not likely to be captured by gross manifest content categories. Finally, the usual categories of manifest content analysis are not readily connected with theoretical conceptions of media effects.

Alternatives to Manifest Content

We can study latent aspects of media content by analyzing the frames used to shape the story (Gamson, 1992; Gamson & Lasch, 1983;

McLeod, Kosicki, Pan, & Allen, 1987; Pan & Kosicki, in press; Tuchman, 1978). According to Gamson and Lasch, a frame suggests a "central organizing idea for understanding events related to the issue in question" (p. 398). As part of the "package" containing the core frame there are various framing devices (metaphors, exemplars, catchphrases, depictions, and visual images) and reasoning devices (causal attributions, consequences, and appeals to principles). Linsky (1986) distinguished five stages of the policy process: problem identification, solution formulation, policy adoption, implementation, and evaluation. At least early in the history of an issue, a reporter or editor may have considerable latitude to choose among several frame packages; later the options narrow as elites take positions and media content begins to show consensus in choosing particular frames. Frames are clearly important to the study of effects, as they influence how audiences understand issues and policy options.

Whereas *framing* refers to the organization of content contained in a given story, the term *bracketing* refers to the placement of evaluative information surrounding a story. This can be seen most clearly in instances of reporters "disdaining the news" by commentary that casts scorn or cynical comments on news they have just delivered (Levy, 1981). Disdaining is used when the news must be presented for competitive reasons, but the journalist feels used because the source controls the framing of the story.

Apart from the manifest or latent features of news content, we might consider variations in news format. This can refer to the parameters of story length or size, length of sound bites or quotes within stories, labels or other means of identifying the genre of the story, or congruency of audio and visual tracks. Features of form in entertainment television programs have been shown to have effects independent of content (Watt & Krull, 1977).

Media Content and Its Critics

Media institutions and media workers have developed distinctive organizational procedures, values, and workways to facilitate their tasks of producing the news on a regular basis. Given their proximity to east-coast government and financial centers, and elite universities and think tanks, there is a tendency to draw from sources with geographic and social proximity, thus restricting the range of sources and views (e.g., Gans, 1979; Herman & Chomsky, 1988; Lee & Solomon, 1990). Effects of this range from assessments of the relative importance of presidential primaries (Adams, 1987, p. 46) to a general sense of conformity to establishment priorities and world views (Gitlin, 1980).

Sourcing the news has long been recognized as a central problem in journalism because of the role sources play as "primary definers" (Ericson, Baranek, & Chan, 1989; Hall, Critcher, Jefferson, Clarke, & Roberts, 1978, pp. 58–59). Although choices of sources are generally crucial, the influence of these decisions on what is actually printed or broadcast may be mediated by the overall context in which the story is embedded. For example, although political candidates often set the tone for campaigns by waging low-key or intense, negative campaigns (Jamieson, 1992), these actions by sources will influence decisions about the resources news organizations are willing to commit to coverage of any given race (Clarke & Evans, 1983; Westlye, 1991). Many other factors are cited in the newswork literature, including the values of individual journalists, their organizational deadlines and routines, occupational ideologies, and legal and social constraints (cf. Bennett, 1988; Shoemaker & Reese, 1991).

Much of this literature, however, grows out of sociological concerns, and remains, with certain exceptions, rather uniformed by advances in cognitive and social psychology (Kennamer, 1988; Stocking & Gross, 1989). This arguably has led to an overemphasis on news production as a selection process, and drawn attention away from the constructionist aspects that might link more readily with certain media effects traditions (Ryan, 1991). Nonetheless, Bennett and others such as Iyengar (1991) identified characteristics of news that are helpful in conceptualizing media effects. Iyengar based his experimental studies of framing on differences between episodic and thematic coverage. Episodic coverage, characterizing much of day-to-day journalism, grows out of standard news events and news values. Bennett (1988) also examined episodic news routines and suggested several common flaws in news: *Personalization* is the focus on individuals and incorrectly seeing large social issues in terms of individual actors. *Fragmentation* is the presentation of information in ahistorical capsule summaries, disconnected from each other. *Dramatization* is using news values rather than importance as selection criteria, suggesting that many important but undramatic issues do not make the news unless they reach crisis proportions. Finally, *normalization* is the overlaying of problems with solutions emanating from the political system, thus reinforcing existing power structures.

POLITICAL COMMUNICATION EFFECTS

Political communication effects research has developed in numerous directions as a result of (a) the increased complexity of effects models, (b) augmented conceptions of media messages, and (c) expanded emphasis on diverse types of effects.

Complex models have been developed that go beyond the predispositional demographic forces in the Columbia model and the influences of partisanship in the Michigan model. These complicated models reflect the realities of voters using informational shortcuts and uncertainties of cognitive judgmental processes (Herstein, 1985; Lau & Erber, 1985). Although these cognitive models do not explicitly include media variables, they do assume that the media are major sources of information for judgments included in the models. Although recognizing the complexity of voting decisions, scholars have begun to realize that these additional types of effects (e.g., learning, framing, perceptions of issue salience, etc.) are themselves worthy criteria of effects, not merely pathways to some ultimate political choice.

We distinguish four major classes of individual effects: opinion formation and change, cognitive changes, perceptions of the political system, and political participation. We then turn from individual effects to collective outcomes for the political system.

Opinion Formation and Change

A substantial body of literature concerns media's impact on the formation, change, and stabilization of opinions on political issues and candidates. Opinion change is likely to be what comes to mind when thinking of media effects. The early work of Lazarsfeld et al. (1948) failed to find persuasive media effects. The study of political opinion change has been revitalized, however, by the application of the Elaboration Likelihood Model (ELM) of persuasion (Petty & Cacioppo, 1986) and the Reasoned Action Model (Fishbein & Ajzen, 1975) linking attitudes, perceived social norms, and behavior. At least some success has been noted in their application to campaign effects studies (Fazio & Williams, 1986; Granberg & Brown, 1989; Krosnick, 1988; O'Keefe, 1985; Rice & Atkin, 1989). These models are more applicable to political advertising than to the less intentionally persuasive content of news. More recently, Zaller (1992) proposed, based on cognitive principles, a general political attitude model called Receive–Accept–Sample that appears to have applicability across many topic domains. Examples of opinion change associated with media use are more frequently documented than are instances of its opposite, stabilization. However, debates and other forms of campaign information have been shown to increase the consistency of partisan attitudes (Katz & Feldman, 1962; Sears & Chaffee, 1979).

Cognitive Changes

Here we summarize four types of cognitive effects that have received considerable attention in recent years: agenda setting, priming, knowledge gain and cognitive complexity, and framing.

Agenda Setting. Agenda-setting research is based on two related propositions: (a) the media control the agenda by selecting certain issues for prominent coverage, and (b) prominence subsequently determines which issues are judged as important (McCombs & Shaw, 1972; Weaver, Graber, McCombs, & Eyal, 1981). There is substantial evidence supporting the second proposition that public judgments of the salience (importance) of issues follow the prominence of the media agenda. The early evidence took three distinct forms: time-series comparisons of the national news agenda with aggregated issue ratings from opinion polls (Funkhouser, 1973; MacKuen, 1981; McCombs & Shaw, 1972); panel studies examining the sequencing of changes in the media agenda with corresponding changes in the issue saliences of individual respondents (McCombs, 1977; Tipton, Haney, & Basehart, 1975); and cross-sectional surveys comparing contrasting media agendas with the issue saliences of their respective audiences (McLeod, Becker, & Brynes, 1974). More recently, the evidence has been strengthened by an ingenious series of experiments manipulating the agenda of televised newscasts (Iyengar & Kinder, 1987).

Some words of caution are in order, however. Audience agenda-setting research has become so well recognized that it has become almost synonymous with powerful political effects of media. We should be careful to note that agenda-setting effects are not necessarily powerful, consequential, and universal. Real-world events such as wars and shifts in the economy are more likely to command the agenda than are fluctuations in media coverage. In terms of impact on audiences, news sources may be far more influential than are stories under media control (Iyengar & Kinder). Changes in issue salience, as cognitive effects, may not alter affect and behavior. In political campaigns, for example, advancement of an issue may not change voting preferences unless the issue is more favorable to one candidate than another. The power of the media to control issue salience was undoubtedly overstated as "stunningly successful" in its early formulation (Cohen, 1963) and, as discussed later, the agenda is likely to influence primarily certain sectors of the public.

More ambiguity surrounds the first agenda-setting proposition that the media determine the agenda. The news media certainly serve at least as carriers of the agenda to the public, and clearly selection is involved. Less certain is how the power to control the agenda is distributed between the media and sources and how the news agenda is struggled over. Media-source transactions have been examined (Epstein, 1973; Sigal, 1973) and there is promise in recent research on how news agendas are set (Ericson et al., 1989; Semetko et al., 1991).

Priming. One of the key concepts of the "cognitive revolution" that has transformed the social sciences is that of priming. As applied to media use, exposure to a given type of content or message activates a concept, which for a period of time increases the probability that the concept, and thoughts and memories connected with it, will come to mind again (Berkowitz & Rogers, 1986). As adapted to political communication in a series of experiments, priming effects of television news were shown in shaping the standards by which presidential performance is judged (Iyengar & Kinder, 1987). When primed by stories focusing on national defense, for example, respondents gave disproportionate weight to judgments of how well they thought the president had done on that issue in judging his overall performance. This held across six issues, for presidents from each party and for good news as well as for bad. Additional experiments by the same authors showed priming influences may extend to vote choices. Media coverage of the Iranian hostage crisis late in the 1980 presidential campaign may have primed voters to weigh foreign affairs heavily in judging President Carter's performance. The result may have contributed to the margin of the Reagan victory.

Knowledge Gain. The early voting research focused on persuasion while almost ignoring the media's role in informing the public. Yet, evidence of knowledge gain from news media use can be found in research from the Columbia studies to the present. Special forms of political communication, debates, and conventions, along with standard news coverage, convey discernible if modest amounts of information to their audiences (Conover & Feldman, 1989; Gunter, 1987; McLeod, Bybee, & Durall, 1979). Yet, citizens remain remarkably uninformed about public affairs. Despite a threefold increase in the proportion of Americans who have attended college, factual knowledge of politics has increased only marginally since the 1960s and has actually declined when education is controlled (Delli Carpini & Keeter, 1991). Retention of specific information from news stories is minimal. When interviewed immediately after a television news broadcast that they had watched, viewers freely recalled only 1.2 among the 20 stories on average; less than half were recalled even when the story heads were read to them (Neuman, 1976). Although increments of learning from news are small, Popkin (1991) argued that they may be sufficient for the voter's purposes, for example, to connect issues to offices and to separate the candidates on the issues.

Many reasons have been offered for the relatively weak increments of knowledge conveyed by the news media. Most prominent is the charge that the "horse-race" coverage of political campaigns, focusing on who is winning rather than on issues, deters learning (Arterton, 1984; Patterson, 1980). News content considered more generally may also limit learning. Picking news for its entertainment value rather than for its political importance may prevent more complex issues from reaching the public. Increasingly shorter sound bites on television news and presentation of "nuggetized factoids" devoid of historical or political context in all media may lead to processing information episodically rather than reflectively. For the most part, these charges emanate from critical observation of content alone without systematic tests as to their actual impact on the audience. Recently, however, there have been more systematic efforts to connect psychological theorizing on memory and comprehension with research on news forms and content and their effects on the audience (Ferejohn & Kuklinski, 1990; Gunter, 1987; Robinson & Levy, 1986).

To evaluate learning from the media, researchers have gone beyond the recognition or recall of specific factual knowledge to examine audience understandings of news stories and events more broadly. Techniques of open-ended questions and recording of group discussion are used to measure the complexity and structure of audience thinking on a given issue or news story. The *cognitive complexity* of audience understanding can be measured reliably by counting such features of open-ended responses as the number of arguments, time frames, and causes and implications the person brings into the discussion (McLeod et al., 1987; McLeod, Pan, & Rucinski, 1989). Cognitive complexity so measured is moderately correlated with factual knowledge from closed-ended questions, but the two criteria have distinct sets of social structural and media use antecedents. Complexity of thinking about public issues appears to be a function both of personal characteristics and patterns of news media use.

Framing. Corresponding to the journalist's role in framing news stories discussed earlier (Tuchman, 1978), audiences also can be seen as framing (or perhaps reframing) the news that comes to their attention. Audience framing involves, according to Erving Goffman (1974), invoking "schemata of interpretation" that allow individuals to "locate, perceive, identify, and label" information coming from the environment. Despite the fact that news stories use standard forms such as the summary lead and the inverted pyramid style, audience members assemble the data about a candidate or issue into a causal narrative or story that reflects their point of view or frame (Kinder & Mebane, 1983). This narrative then serves as a framework for understanding other news stories.

Framing of media messages, in most instances, involves low levels of attention and the use of various cognitive shortcuts to make enough sense of a story or issue. Processing is likely to be of "low information rationality," sufficient only to satisfy whatever level of understanding the person considers "good enough" (Popkin, 1991). Information processing typical of most citizens can be categorized into three types of heuristic biases: categorization, selection, and integration of information about an issue or candidate. To analyze such biases, political communication research has borrowed heavily from cognitive psychology, using concepts such as availability (Krosnick, 1989), default values (Lau & Sears, 1986), schema (Graber, 1988), and causal attribution (Iyengar, 1991). Causal attribution, discussed in greater detail later, is particularly relevant in that it connects meaning at the individual level with potential for political action. Audience framing research also has been influenced by recent developments from three quite different directions, from critical (Morley, 1980; Philo, 1990), cultural (Liebes & Katz, 1990), and constructivist perspectives (Gamson, 1992; Gamson & Modigliani, 1989). In cultural studies, for example, the traditional exclusive focus on texts has now been extended to include audience reception analysis. Collectively, these alternatives serve political effects research in at least two ways: They illustrate the subtleties and complexities of the media text as a unit not easily reducible to stimuli and, secondly, they provide examples of the diversity in audience interpretations of media content (Livingstone, 1990; van Dijk, 1988).

Audience framing is a complex construct in that it refers both to the process of individual and interpersonal sense-making and to the content or output of that process. Audience frames are both cognitive representations in an individual's memory and devices embedded in public discourse (Kinder & Sanders, 1990; Pan & Kosicki, in press). They may be elicited in a number of ways: through experimental manipulation of news broadcasts (Iyengar, 1991), reactions to specific news broadcasts, or to types of news stories, to a set of public issues (Neuman, Just, & Crigler, 1992), or to a major issue in the news (McLeod et al., 1987; McLeod et al., 1989). The unit of analysis may be the individual or a natural social grouping such as the family or work group.

One striking feature of the meanings given to news stories and to political issues by individuals is their polysemy—there seem to be almost as many interpretations as there are perceivers. But this overstates their variety. Audience frames can be coded in meaningful ways (e.g., cognitive complexity, personal vs. systemic causation), and the structure of news stories does affect how people think and talk about issues (Iyengar, 1991; Kinder & Sanders, 1990; McLeod et al., 1987). There do seem to be some common frame dimensions that cut across public issues and that members of the audience use to differing degrees: political-ideological (e.g., partisan party, cold-war) frame and a time frame (e.g., bringing in the past history and future consequences) for the event or issue (McLeod et al., 1989). Various influences (e.g., social structural location, values, patterns of media use) are systematically related to the way a given issue is framed.

The origins of audience frames are thus likely to be some combination of the news media "packages" (Gamson & Modigliani, 1989), the person's structural location and values, political beliefs and knowledge, and the political norms and discourse of social groups. The framing of any audience member may be consonant with the news package, it may be in active opposition to the media frame, or it might appear to be independent of the news form and content. Better identification of the influences on framing patterns and the effects of such patterns on subsequent behavior are high priorities for political communication research.

Perceptions of the Political System

Self-Interest and Systemic Perceptions. Making connections between the individual-cognitive and social systems levels is a problem common to all areas of social science (Price, Ritchie, & Eulau, 1991). The problem is particularly acute for political communication, however. Most political action and power relationships operate at the societal or other systemic levels, whereas the bulk of empirical theory and research concentrate on the behavior of the individual citizen. Although we think of voting as a private act (save for the probing of pollsters) based on narrow self-interest, this highly individualized account may be illusory. Citizens may have difficulty recognizing their own self-interest, and their perception of it may not be entirely selfish in that such judgments include concern for the welfare of others (Popkin, 1991). Further, although strength of the evidence is disputed (Kramer, 1983), voting decisions seem to be made less on the basis of perceived "pocketbook" self-interest than on "sociotropic" estimates of how well the country is doing economically (Fiorina, 1981; Kinder & Kiewiet, 1983). People clearly distinguish between their own economic situation and that of the nation. At levels between the nation and the individual lie a host of other entities and groups potentially consequential to individual voting and participation.

The implications of sociotropic conceptions for media effects are quite clear. Given that systemic perceptions are based largely on media inputs, the news media have responsibilities for presenting an accurate and comprehensive picture of governmental operations. Many have expressed doubt as to how well the press plays this role. Although the public is exposed to the moves of the president and prominent members of Congress, little emphasis is given on how government actually works in terms of processes, compromises, and so on (Popkin, 1991).

Causal Attribution. Jones and Nisbett (1972) suggested that actors attribute causality or responsibility for their own behavior to situational factors, whereas observers attribute the actor's behavior to stable dispositions of the actor. Applied to political judgments, this can be seen in the tendency to ascribe weaknesses of public officials to their personal faults and in blaming the poor and the homeless for their condition. Iyengar (1989) showed that failure to link social problems with societal responsibility extends to poverty, racism, and crime. Media coverage may accentuate the attribution of personal causation. Television often portrays politics as conflict between individuals rather than as struggles between institutions and principles (Rubin, 1976; Weaver, 1972). A study of newspapers in congressional campaigns found that they generally focused on personal weaknesses of incumbents, not on the system (Miller, Goldenberg, & Erbring, 1979).

Iyengar (1991) provided important experimental evidence that television influences attribution of responsibility for both the creation of problems (causal) and their resolution (treatment). Adapting the psychological conception of framing from Kahneman and Tversky (1984), Iyengar distinguished between episodic and thematic framing of news stories. Episodic framing uses case-study or event-oriented reports and concrete instances; thematic forms place the issue in a more general or abstract context. Although content analyses showed that few television news stories were exclusively one or the other, nearly 80% of a sample of CBS news stories were predominantly episodic.

Experimental variation of the two types of story frames showed that whereas thematic stories increased the attributions of responsibility to government and society, episodic treatments decreased system-level responsibility overall (Iyengar, 1991). The strength of framing effects varied across the five issues used. The consequences of episodic versus thematic framing have substantial implications for subsequent political behavior. Iyengar found that people who attribute the cause of a problem to systemic forces are more likely to bring that problem into their political judgments than are people citing dispositional causes.

The 30-year trend of increasing dominance of television as the primary news medium may have stimulated a concomitant trend toward nonsystemic attribution. Political stories in the print media are more likely to be thematic than those of television news, and print media use may enhance systemic attribution. McLeod, Sun, Chi and Pan (1990), in a survey of public reactions to the "war on drugs," found responses to open-ended questions about causes of the problem formed three distinct attributional dimensions, each having a dispositional (individual, family-interpersonal, drug supplier) and a systemic (foreign nations, economic conditions, social-legal) end. Frequent and attentive newspaper readers were more likely to invoke systemic causes and responsibilities on two of the three dimensions. Television news use was unrelated to any dimension.

A somewhat different pattern of attributional effects was shown in a 1972-1974 panel study during the Watergate era (McLeod, Brown, Becker, & Ziemke, 1977). During an interval when trust in government declined markedly, the most avid users of both newspaper and television news held relatively stable levels of trust. When rating different sources as to blame for Watergate, they tended to blame Nixon more and the political system less than did other respondents even after partisanship was controlled. This may have been the result of the statements appearing frequently in the news of that period that "the system works." Singling out the "bad apple in the barrel" may be easier than considering the more fundamental problems of system storage.

Climate of Opinion. A crucial assumption in Noelle-Neumann's (1984) *Spiral of Silence* is that people make "quasi-statistical" judgments about which side is ahead and gaining support on controversial issues. According to her theory, this diminishes expression of opinion by the losing side, starting a spiral of silence, and ultimately affects change of opinion and political behavior. Noelle-Neumann claimed that German television news affected electoral outcomes because of newscasters having portrayed the climate of opinion as being unfavorable to the Christian Democratic party.

Other System Perceptions. Other systemic perceptions could be explored as criteria of media effects. There is a connection, for example, between use of public affairs media content and support for the various aspects of the political system: for authority and trust in government but also for the need for the press to criticize government. Attentive news users tend to be more tolerant of political diversity, to have more empathy with various parts of the society, and to hold distinctive perceptions of the legitimacy or marginality of various groups and of how the world works (Amor, McLeod, & Kosicki, 1987).

Political Participation

Media effects on voting preferences have long dominated the political communication agenda. Voting decisions remain the ultimate criterion in much of the research reviewed here; however, recent work no longer looks for direct media effects and instead sees voting as a complex behavior influenced indirectly through the various cognitive influences. Another change is that interpersonal communication has become part of the participation process rather than simply an antecedent of voting.

Voter Turnout. Turnout was once thought to be a rather uninteresting phenomenon simply explained and highly stable, but it seems less predictable and more interesting in recent years. Turnout continues to be predicted by education, partisanship, age, church attendance, community involvement, and marital status (Strate, Parrish, Elder, & Ford, 1989; Wolfinger & Rosenstone, 1980), but abstention from voting continues to rise and television is thought to contribute to the decline of participation (Ranney, 1983). In a panel study of the unusually high abstention rate in the 1970 British general election, media influences were found to be complex (Blumler & McLeod, 1974). Those mostly likely to abstain as a result of disenchantment with the televised image of the person's party leader, surprisingly, tended to be the more educated and better informed voters. Turnout studies in the United States suggest that exposure and attention to hard news in the print media are associated with turnout and with other forms of participation as well (McLeod, Bybee, Leutscher, & Garramone, 1981, McLeod & McDonald, 1985).

Interpersonal Communication. The Columbia studies posed interpersonal communication as an alternative to mass media influence, noting that on an average day 10% more discussed the election than read or heard about it through the media (Lazarsfeld et al., 1948). More recently observers have come to see this as a "synthetic competition" (Chaffee, 1982), arguing that media and interpersonal channels may have convergent, complementary, or other relationships as well. There is substantial evidence that both customary patterns of exposure and attention to newspaper public affairs content, and exposure to the media during the campaign, stimulate interpersonal discussion (McLeod, Bybee, & Durall, 1979). Although not very efficient in conveying information about issues, the media do seem to stimulate interpersonal discussion and interest in the campaign (McLeod et al., 1979). Interpersonal discussion helps people decide how to vote and may stimulate turnout except where the others in the conversational network are of the opposite party. Even discussion with strangers may affect voting. Noelle-Neummann (1984) reported that willingness to express a particular side of an issue in conversations with strangers ultimately led to change in opinion toward that side. Popkin (1990) found that in the early primary states where door-to-door canvassing is still possible, people contacted by one candidate's supporters subsequently paid more attention to all candidates in the news. This had the effect of increasing turnout on primary election day.

Systemic Effects

Several problems are encountered in mapping media effects on individuals onto consequences for the society. First, the size and practicalsignificance of individual effects remain controversial. We can contrast the weak effects position of McGuire (1986) with Iyengar's (1991) view of much stronger effects. Second, there are also individual-level media effects on politicians and journalists that affect systems. Third, systemic consequences are manifested through institutional policies, practices, and outcomes (e.g., laws) that transcend individual judgments. Fourth, systemic consequences are not reducible to the simple aggregation of individual-level effects. The distribution of such effects can be of theoretical significance, as in knowledge gap issues (Tichenor, Donohue, & Olien, 1970). Fifth, democratic practices involve collective forms of action such as social movements whose fate involves the connection of groups to information and power.

These problems point out that political communication must be understood as micro-individual and macro-level system processes. Quite different concepts and theories are appropriate to the analyses at various micro and macro levels (McLeod & Blumler, 1987). To study macro-to-macro and micro-to-macro influences, auxiliary theories are required (Pan & McLeod, 1991). In lieu of more formal attempts at cross-level theorizing, we can take current problems with the political system and work backward to possible ways in which the media might be responsible. In this, we are likely to be frustrated by the confounding of media influences with those of other institutions: political parties, schools, families, and political culture more generally. Alternatively, we can take what is known about individual political effects and extrapolate them to system consequences.

The problems of the American political system are well documented. Knowledge levels, participation, and turnout rates are low and more stratified across education levels than seems desirable (Burnham, 1982; Powell, 1986). Few citizens seem capable of imposing an overarching ideological framework in their understanding of politics (Converse, 1964), and levels of knowledge and discussion of news seem similarly stratified (Popkin, 1991). Evidence of political stratification depicts a political world sharply divided into a small group of sophisticated, involved citizens and a much larger segment of uninterested and largely uninformed persons (Neuman, 1986).

This stratified model of the political system may need qualification. Popkin argued that increases in education have not deepened but nonetheless have broadened the number of issues seen as relevant to citizens' lives. It is likely that television news can be given some credit for this (Blumler & McLeod, 1974). Broadening may have led to an increase in the number of issue publics, that is, relatively small groups of people with intense interest in a particular issue but with much less interest in other issues. This poses problems for political parties desiring to unite these diverse publics. Issue specialization also makes adequate media coverage much more difficult and the identification of media effects more complex.

Critiques of political campaigns identify many systemic problems. The increased importance of money, lack of issue content, shallow media-genic candidates, weakness in party control, and low participation are some of the outcomes attributed to the growing dominance of television in campaigns (Ranney, 1983). The public seems to enter only as a factor to be managed. Yet the effect of television is difficult to disentangle from changes induced by the political parties themselves. Media and political forces are also intertwined in the arena of Congressional elections. Incumbents have their franking privileges and greater opportunities to raise money, and they benefit from more media coverage (Clarke & Evans, 1983).

Another common critical theme is the lack of accountability. Elected and nonelected officials do not seem to be accountable to anyone. This reflects a serious problem of media coverage. Government agencies and the large corporate contractors that supply them are simply too large to be adequately covered by media resources. News judgments may be involved as well. The very costly S & L bank scandals were consigned to the financial pages of elite newspapers until Congress finally began to act on the matter. Problems with accountability seem to be the joint product of political and media faults and inadequacies.

MORE COMPLEX MODELS OF POLITICAL EFFECTS

Recent political communication effects research provides ample evidence that media impact is likely to be conditional rather than universal across audience members. They take the form of O-S-O-R models (Markus & Zajonc, 1985). The first O represents the set of structural, cultural, cognitive, and motivational characteristics the audience brings to the reception situation that affect the impact of the message. They are often referred to as individual differences, although they are likely to be socially determined. The second O denotes what is likely to happen between the reception of the message and the response of the audience member. Activity is the label given to various intervening responses (Hawkins & Pingree, 1986). As is true for the first O, activities may be conceptualized at various levels ranging from a short-term physiological response to the social context of the viewing situation to a complex set of interpersonal interactions after the reception. A few examples of each may convey the importance of these orientations to theory building in political communication.

Prereception Orientations

Political Sophistication and Involvement. Educational and other status factors have produced large differences in how much citizens know and care about politics. These differences can be conceptualized as political sophistication (Neuman, 1986). Evidence that those already informed are more likely to learn new information goes back as far as the UN campaign study in Cincinnati (Star & Hughes, 1950) and recurs in knowledge-gap research (Tichenor et al., 1970). Sophistication also provides more complex schema for the interpretation of ambiguous political campaign events (Graber, 1988). Although enhancing learning effects, education and sophistication may restrain other media effects such as reducing the impact of agenda setting for both newspapers (McLeod et al., 1974; Weaver et al., 1981) and television (Iyengar & Kinder, 1987). More involved citizens may have their own agendas.

Partisanship. Political partisanship generally serves as a conditioner of media effects. Where there is freedom to choose supportive sources of information, for example subscribing to a newspaper that favors one's own party, de-facto selectivity is likely (Katz, 1987). Partisanship may act as a frame to minimize the effects of the media agenda (Iyengar & Kinder, 1987; McLeod et al., 1974). Priming, in contrast, is reduced among partisans when the primed news story is inconsistent with their predispositions (Iyengar & Kinder, 1987).

News Media Images. The images or "common-sense theories" that people hold of news also affect how much they learn from news. Three dimensions of images are particularly pertinent as conditional variables (Kosicki & McLeod, 1990): *news information quality,* a positive evaluation of media as being accurate and complete; *patterning of news,* faith in one's ability to extract patterns from fragmentary news; and *negative aspects of content,* criticism of news as dull, sensational, and dominated by bad news. Contrary to what media managers might predict, higher ratings of news quality are associated with *lower* levels of learning from media (McLeod, Kosicki, Amor, Allen, & Philps, 1986). Those who are somewhat skeptical about news quality appear to process it more critically and thoughtfully and thereby learn more. Those seeing news as having underlying patterns tend to learn more from news, whereas those most critical of its content learn less.

Gratifications Sought from News. Traditionally, uses-and-gratifications research was seen as an alternative rather than a complement to media effects research. However, self-reports of gratifications sought can be viewed as conditions affecting the extent of media impact. The strength of motivation to watch party broadcasts interacted with viewing such broadcasts to enhance information gain in Britain (Blumler & McQuail, 1969) and validated for political effects in the United States (McLeod & Becker, 1974). Gratification seeking has also been shown to deter agenda-setting effects. Readers with the strongest motivation to seek campaign information failed to shift their salience ratings of issues in accordance with the agenda of the newspaper they read (McLeod, Becker, & Byrnes, 1974).

Reception Activity Orientations

Effects are also conditioned by orientations during exposure to news. These can be measured physiologically below the level of the person's awareness (Reeves, Thorson, & Schleuder, 1986), or using self-report measures that suffer the weaknesses of other self-report measures but do reveal substantial variance between persons.

Attention. Attention is the conscious focusing of increased mental effort. As applied to news, it can be measured from closed-ended questions regarding various types of hard news content, and separately for television and for newspapers. Attention is particularly important for television, where exposure takes place under very different levels of attention. In contrast, the reading of a newspaper virtually demands attention. Learning from news is enhanced at higher levels of attention (Chaffee & Choe, 1980; Chaffee & Schleuder, 1986). Exposure to presidential debates conveys minimal knowledge, but it does stimulate campaign interest and discussion in formulating vote-choice decisions (McLeod et al., 1979). In a noncampaign context, exposure to hard news interacted with attention to increase both knowledge about the economy and community participation (McLeod & McDonald, 1985).

Information-Processing Strategies. Audience activity includes strategies people employ to cope with the "flood of information" that threatens to overwhelm them (Graber, 1988). Surveys using a set of nine self-report items have repeatedly found three dimensions of audience news information-processing strategies (Kosicki & McLeod, 1990; Kosicki, McLeod, & Amor, 1987): selective scanning, skimming, and turning out items; active processing, going beyond or "reading through" a story to reinterpret it according to the person's needs; and reflective integration, replaying the story in the person's mind and using it as a topic of discussion. The extent of political learning, political interest, and participation are restricted by selective scanning and enhanced byreflective integration. Active processing has little effect on learning but does stimulate interest and participation. All three processing strategies are related to different conceptual frames that people use to interpret and understand public issues (McLeod et al., 1987).

EFFECTS ON POLITICIANS AND POLICY-MAKERS

Media also influence policy-makers and the public policy process. But, as seen earlier, these effects too are unlikely to be simple and direct. We consider several types of effects on public institutions, on politicians, and on public policy processes.

Protess et al. (1991) considered the effects of investigative reporting on achieving various civic reforms in areas such as health care, crime, and housing. Their coalition model of agenda-building focuses attention on the interactions of investigative journalism with government policy-makers, citizens, and interest groups. The effects of investigative reporting are thus not seen as acting through a mobilization model in which journalists stir up the citizenry to press their elected officials to work for reforms. Instead, the coalition model focuses on the interactions of journalists with a variety of interest groups and public officials to garner public support for necessary reforms.

Kaniss (1991) examined a variety of press procedures and workways on reporting of major civic projects such as the $523 million Philadelphia Convention Center, the most expensive undertaking in the history of the city. Kaniss argued that fundamental media values—metropolitan pride, economic self-interest, and a variety of workways—drive the local media to support such mammoth civic spending projects. Similar points were made by Logan and Molotch (1987).

In the legislative arena, the nomination of Judge Robert Bork to the U.S. Supreme Court provided an unusual focal point for the intersection of media, interest groups, and legislators. Bork's nomination was ultimately rejected by the Senate, but only after one of the most intense information campaigns in history, notable for its use of formative research (Pertschuk & Schaetzel, 1989). Regarding more typical legislative activity, Cook (1989) presented a variety of ways that media influence the legislative process. These range from structural changes in office procedures to accommodate the press to influence the legislative strategies of individual members. Media publicity coupled with the chairmanship of an important committee or subcommittee can be a powerful tool for achieving policy goals (Smith, 1988) and raising large amounts of money to help ward off electoral challengers and wage reelection campaigns (Etzioni, 1988; Goldenberg & Traugott, 1984). The vast amount of money raised by politicians for their campaigns is now thought by some to represent a major antidemocratic force (e.g., Bennett, 1992; Drew, 1983; Etzioni, 1988). This conclusion is controversial, however (e.g., Sabato, 1987).

EVALUATING DEMOCRATIC STANDARDS
FOR NEWS MEDIA PERFORMANCE

We now can assess ways in which political effects research can inform evaluation of the democratic standards proposed by Gurevitch and Blumler (1990, shown in Table 9.1a). We consider each standard in turn, presenting some alleged news performance deficiencies and possible constraints accounting for these deficiencies. We then suggest possible individual effects of the alleged deficiencies and what might be their consequences for the political system. Finally, we re-examine conclusions from evidence of political effects and propose new directions for future research.

Surveillance of Relevant Events

Although surveillance of the environment has long been recognized as a primary function of the press (Lasswell, 1948), the press is not only a simple conduit of events. News coverage involves selecting a few developments that are most likely to impinge on the welfare of citizens (Gurevitch & Blumler, 1990). The many publics in a modern society attach themselves to issues in quite different ways and few stories are similarly relevant to all citizens. Budgetary constraints, grown tighter in recent years, limit the resources available for news coverage. This increases dependence on official sources and presentation as elite versions of events rather than as problems confronting average citizens. The market structure of media not only has limited, less "cost efficient" coverage, but also has shifted news style to short and entertaining "infotainment." Network television news is constrained by shortened sound bites and its rigid "22-minute ration" of time, with fixed placement of commercials (Gurevitch & Blumler).

Political learning research seems to confirm the fear that the problems of media coverage adversely affect audiences. The amount of learning from television is slight. Large numbers of citizens see news as boring and politics as disconnected from their lives. System consequences may include not only a less informed electorate and low voter turnout but also campaigns that focus on pseudo-events and personalities rather than issues (Jamieson, 1992).

A case can be made in defense of media performance, however. The media present a more extensive diet of events than most citizens appear willing to consume. Popkin (1991) argued that people learn from media as much as they think they need to know, or perhaps as much as think they can comprehend. Research techniques may confuse the issue, to the extent that research showing weak learning effects has used specific "factual" information as a criterion. This may paint too bleak a picture of citizen awareness and, by implicitly blaming the audience for its lack of interest, may justify even further shortening and softening of news. Research has recently broadened the criteria to examine how audiences construct the news to fit their own experiences (McLeod et al., 1987; Morley, 1980; Philo, 1990). The resulting protocols are often impressive in their sense-making structure, if not their factual basis. Future research might test whether variations in characteristics of news (e.g., Bennett, 1988) restrict complexity of understanding.

Identification of Key Issues

The media have a responsibility not only to identify key issues but also to analyze the forces that have formed them and the possibilities for their resolution. Critics charge that the agenda set by the media is not broad, balanced, or meaningful. Rather it is set from the agenda of dominant institutions. Decontextualized and ahistorical presentation of issues are said to lead to issues being understood as little more than labels without consequences. Abstract issues that are difficult to portray visually, and those requiring specialized knowledge seldom found among news staffs, may have difficulty getting onto the media agenda. Lack of meaningful agenda setting may have systemic consequences in restricting governmental decisions to immediate appearances and short-term payoffs. Adoption of the media agenda, being most common among those least attached to the political system, has implications for greater system instability.

The media agenda undoubtedly does affect audience judgments of importance of issues. More research is needed, however, on the processes by which the agenda is set, including the struggles of contending powers to control language as well as priorities of the agenda. It matters a great deal, for example, whether an insurgent army is framed in the press as "brave freedom fighters" or as "hired guns," and perhaps even more whether the audience adopts that frame (McLeod et al., 1990).

Provision of Platforms for Advocacy

Democratic change depends on consideration of a wide range of views and proposals. The media thus could be judged on how well they provide for "intelligible and illuminating platforms" from which politicians and spokespersons of various causes can make appeals (Gurevitch & Blumler, 1990). Public access cable channels have very low viewership, and mainstream media are apt to grant access only if the group takes direct action whose illegality or unusual character makes it newsworthy. Even mainstream groups are forced to conform to media practices by "running the news value gauntlet" (Blumler, 1990). The ideologies of objectivity and press autonomy contribute to resist access; journalists tend to see advocacy as a threat to a free press and to control over their own jobs.

Media effects research barely touches on the issues of access, partly because access is so limited. If sufficient variation in access could be found, criteria might include how aware citizens are of nonmainstream groups and positions and their approval of political participation even in less traditional forms. Systemic outcomes might include the popularity of public access programming and participation of lower status groups in the political process.

Transmission of Diverse Political Discourse

Media can be judged by how well they facilitate dialogue between diverse views and two-way communication between power holders and mass publics. Critics charge that the media focus instead on "mainstream currents bounded politically by the two-party system, economically by imperative of private enterprize capitalism, and culturally by the values of a consumer society" (Gurevitch & Blumler, 1990, p. 269). Nonmainstream political groups are marginalized as "deviant" (Gitlin, 1980) and little coverage is given to less attractive audiences like the poor and the elderly. The result may be that citizens are lacking in awareness of political alternatives and unable even to articulate their own views. The implication for the political system is a narrowing of the boundaries of the "marketplace of ideas."

A combination of content analysis and audience research might be useful for evaluating media on this standard. Dialogue may be effective only if the media systematically compare diverse points of view and alternate frames. Media presentations might be expected to help citizens recognize and articulate their own feelings and connect them to larger political contexts. Attentive reading of hard news in the print does seem to facilitate such connections and allows them to be discussed with others (McLeod et al., 1989).

Scrutiny of Institutions and Officials

The media standing as a watchdog over government is one of the cherished images of U.S. journalism. Investigative reporting is a key-mechanism for holding officials accountable for their performance. Critics charge, however, that the growth of government and of economic organizations has far outstripped the ability of the press to engage in costly investigations of these institutions. The result is a general lack of government and corporate accountability. Investigative reporting that is done may aim too low in the chain of corruption, as in focusing on street pushers and users in drug coverage, and in many cases the blame is placed on individuals rather than on fundamental systemic causes.

Research on causal attribution is highly relevant to this standard. Coverage of government wrongdoing, unless placed in a larger structural and historical context, may nullify any beneficial effects the stories might have had on citizens. Future research might investigate whether sustained episodic coverage of government problems lessens interest in knowing how government works and/or increases cynicism about politics.

Activation of Informed Participation

News media might be evaluated by how well they provide incentives for citizens to learn about and become involved in politics. The news media do not appear to pay much attention to this standard, at least to the extent there is a lack of "mobilizing information" (Lemert, Mitzman, Seither, Cook, & Hackett, 1977). Citizen activation may require articulation of the feelings of less involved citizens and transforming them into more organized views. Although techniques of reaching mass voting publics have become more sophisticated, feedback from the public remains limited, indirect, and distorted. The political system pays a price in loss of potential "participatory energy the system might generate" (Gurevitch & Blumler, 1990).

The vast literature on political participation pays little attention to media influences (Verba & Nie, 1972). Media effects findings do have implications for participation, however. The failure to see systemic consequences, limited in part by the episodic and personalized media content of television news, may limit active participation. Political activation is also a matter of media treatment of protest groups. The social movement literature is highly relevant for evaluation of press performance on activation.

Maintenance of Media Autonomy

Protection of the press from governmental interference is a key element of the First Amendment. Without such protection all other democratic standards are in jeopardy. Maintenance of media autonomy, however, is much more than the absence of governmental restraints envisioned by the founding fathers. Government growth and corporate power deserve close scrutiny by the press, but this is made difficult because major media have themselves become such corporate conglomerates. Given the problems of media in the modern marketplace, the autonomy standard demands a "principled resistance to the efforts of forces outside the media to subvert their independence, integrity and ability to serve the audience" (Gurevitch & Blumler, 1990, p. 279). In cases where such resistance has been attempted, as in press attempts to forestall strict governmental controls in the Gulf War, efforts to assert autonomy have failed. At worst, the result is elite perspectives presenting a high proportion of news generated from official bureaucratic sources. Journalists may react to covering stories dominated by manipulative sources by inserting disdaining comments in the stories they cover. This may bolster the self respect of the journalist, but its impact on learning and interest in politics among the viewers is a matter to be investigated.

Consideration of Audience Potential

Each of the first seven Democratic Standards shown in Table 6.1a concerns media performance highly constrained by relationships where individual journalists have limited room to maneuver. Consideration of audience potential is less constrained by production forces and more a matter of how journalists define their audiences. As Gurevitch and Blumler put it, consideration involves "a sense of respect for the audience member, as potentially concerned and able to make sense out of his or her environment" (p. 270). The complaint here is that journalists and media executives, faced with pressures to maximize their audiences and to produce news according to consumer-driven standards, have bought into the hierarchical view that there is only a small elite core of interested citizens and a very large uninterested mass. Existing preferences for light fare and the seemingly limited abilities of most citizens to comprehend news may be seen as being natural and immutable, rather than as functions of life experiences or as stemming from inadequacies in the construction of news. Journalists may use their own working theories that see the information-seeking citizen as a fiction to justify short sound bites, episodic stories, and the blurring of lines between news and entertainment.

Research indicates that most citizens are at least somewhat aware of important public issues and many have greater interest and knowledge in a particular issue that is consequential to them (Krosnick, 1990). Despite low levels of specific knowledge, citizens often develop elaborate frameworks to make sense of the world. Unless news producersmake efforts to develop alternatives to the increasingly homogeneous patterns of news construction, the trend toward lower interest in politics is likely to continue. The long-term consequences for the political system are to erode political discourse toward the simplistic and to increase the social status disparities in political participation.

Some Concluding Remarks

We have presented various ways in which the boundaries of political communication effects research have expanded in recent years. Movement has been "horizontal," connecting individual effects with other parts of the mass communication process: potential problems of media content; institutional and professional forms and practices constraining media content; and consequences of individual effects for political system operation. Broadening of effects also necessitates "vertical" linkages of individual behavior with political system institutions and interpersonal processes. Expansion is also seen in the diversity of media effects considered and in alternative conceptualizations of media messages. Political effects are now more likely to be seen as having varying impact contingent on characteristics of particular segments of the audience and as operating in an indirect and delayed fashion. Finally, we have shown how very different methodological strategies have informed the body of political communication knowledge.

We have noted the particularly close connection of political research to normative assumptions of how societies ought to work. Rather than trying to separate normative assumptions from empirical research, we suggest such assumptions might operate as standards against which we can evaluate media performance. McQuail (1992) used a similar starting point to develop an elaborate system for media evaluation including appropriate empirical research strategies: To illustrate how such standards might help to separate often conflated charges about media performance, we have used eight democratic standards developed by Gurevitch and Blumler. Charges about deficiencies in media performance are often vague and lacking in evidence. It appears, however, that a considerable amount of empirical research on political effects is highly pertinent to particular standards. Many critical assertions about media performance have not been examined empirically and these are appropriate subjects for research. More systematic connections, particularly those between production constraints and media content and those between individual effects and system consequences, will be needed before more comprehensive theories are possible. This will require searching for variance between systems where little is found within systems and using a variety of methods to search out connections.

In conclusion, we should like to point out that the news media are by no means the sole cause nor even a major cause of current problems in the political system. Responsibility must be shared with other social institutions: the family, schools, political parties, and political leaders who have "joint custody" of democracy. That makes systematic study of the media's political effects no less necessary.

REFERENCES

Adams, W. C. (1987). As New Hampshire goes. . . . In G. Orren & N. Polsby (Eds.), *Media and momentum: The New Hampshire primary and nomination politics* (pp. 42–59). Chatham, NJ: Chatham House.

Altheide, D. L., & Snow, R. P. (1991). *Media worlds in the postjournalism era.* Hawthorn, NY: Aldine de Gruyter.

Amor, D. L., McLeod, J. M., & Kosicki, G. M. (1987, May). *Images of the mass media, orientations to the world: Where do public images of the mass media come from?* Paper presented at the meeting of the International Communication Association, Montreal, Quebec.

Arterton, F. C. (1984). *Media politics: The news strategies of presidential campaigns.* Lexington, MA: D. C. Heath.

Bennett, W. L. (1988). *News: The politics of illusion* (2nd ed.). New York: Longman.

Bennett, W. L. (1992). *The governing crisis: Media, money and marketing in American elections.* New York: St. Martin's Press.

Berelson, B. R. (1952). *Content analysis as a tool of communication research.* New York: Free Press.

Berelson, B. R., Lazarsfeld, P. F., & McPhee, W. N. (1954). *Voting: A study of opinion formation in a presidential campaign.* Chicago: University of Chicago Press.

Berkowitz, L., & Rogers, K. H. (1986). A priming effect analysis of media influences. In J. Bryant & D. Zillmann (Eds.), *Perspectives on media effects* (pp. 57–81). Hillsdale, NJ: Lawrence Erlbaum Associates.

Blumler, J. G. (Ed.). (1983). *Communicating to voters: Television in the first European parliamentary election.* London: Sage.

Blumler, J. G. (1990). Elections, media and the modern publicity process. In M. Ferguson (Ed.), *Public communication: The new imperatives: Future directions for media research* (pp. 101–113). London: Sage.

Blumler, J. G., & McLeod, J. M. (1974). Communication and voter turnout in Britain. In T. Legatt (Ed.), *Sociological theory and social research* (pp. 265–312). London, Beverly Hills, CA: Sage.

Blumler, J. G., McLeod, J. M., & Rosengren, K. E. (1992). An introduction to comparative communication research. In J. Blumler, J. McLeod, & K. Rosengren (Eds.), *Compar-*

atively speaking: Communication and culture across space and time (pp. 3–18). Newbury Park, CA: Sage.

Blumler, J. G., & McQuail, D. (1969). *Television in politics: Its uses and influence*. Chicago: University of Chicago Press.

Burnham, W. D. (1982). *The current crisis in American politics*. New York: Oxford University Press.

Chaffee, S. H. (1982). Mass media and interpersonal channels: Competitive, convergent or complementary? In G. Gumpert & R. Cathcart (Eds.), *Inter/media: Interpersonal communication in a media world* (pp. 57–77). New York: Oxford University Press.

Chaffee, S. H., & Choe, S. Y. (1980). Time of decision and media use during the Ford-Carter campaign. *Public Opinion Quarterly, 44*, 53–59.

Chaffee, S. H., & Hochheimer, J. (1985). The beginnings of political communication research in the United States: Origins of the limited effects model. In M. Gurevitch & M. Levy (Eds.), *Mass communication review yearbook* (Vol. 5, pp. 75–104). Beverly Hills, CA: Sage.

Chaffee, S. H., & Schleuder, J. (1986). Measurement and effects of attention to media news. *Human Communication Research, 13*, 76–107.

Clarke, P., & Evans, S. (1983). *Covering campaigns*. Stanford, CA: Stanford University Press.

Cohen, B. C. (1963). *The press and foreign policy*. Princeton, NJ: Princeton University Press.

Conover, P. J., & Feldman, S. (1989). Candidate perception in an ambiguous world: Campaigns, cues and inference processes. *American Journal of Political Science, 33*, 912–939.

Converse, P. E. (1964). The nature of belief systems in mass publics. In D. E. Apter (Ed.), *Ideology and discontent* (pp. 206–261). New York: Free Press.

Cook, T. E. (1989). *Making laws and making news: Media strategies in the U.S. House of Representatives*. Washington, DC: Brookings Institution.

Delli Carpini, M. X., & Keeter, S. (1991). U.S. public's knowledge of politics. *Public Opinion Quarterly, 55*, 583–612.

Drew, E. (1983). *Politics and money: The new road to corruption*. New York: Macmillan.

Epstein, E. J. (1973). *News from nowhere*. New York: Random House.

Ericson, R. V., Baranek, P. M., & Chan, B. L. (1989). *Negotiating control: A study of news sources*. Toronto: University of Toronto Press.

Etzioni, A. (1988). *Capital corruption: The new attack on American democracy*. New Brunswick: NJ: Transaction Books.

Fazio, R. H., & Williams, C. J. (1986). Attitude accessibility as a moderator of the attitude-perception and attitude-behavior relations: An investigation of the 1984 presidential election. *Journal of Personality and Social Psychology, 51*, 505–514.

Ferejohn, J. A., & Kuklinski, J. H. (1990). *Information and democratic processes*. Urbana, IL: University of Illinois Press.

Fiorina, M. P. (1981). *Retrospective voting in American national elections*. New Haven, CT: Yale University Press.

Fishbein, M., & Ajzen, I. (1975). *Belief, attitude, intention and behavior: An introduction to theory and research*. Reading, MA: Addison-Wesley.

Funkhouser, G. R. (1973). The issues of the sixties: An exploratory study in the dynamics of public opinion. *Public Opinion Quarterly, 37*, 62–75.

Gamson, W. A. (1992). *Talking politics*. Cambridge: Cambridge University Press.

Gamson, W. A., & Lasch, K. E. (1983). The political culture of social welfare policy. In S. Spiro & E. Yuchtman-Yaar (Eds.), *Evaluating the welfare state: Social and political perspectives* (pp. 397–415). New York: Academic Press.

Gamson, W. A., & Mogdigliani, A. (1989). Media discourse and public opinion: A constructivist approach. *American Journal of Sociology, 95*, 1–37.

Gandy, O. H. (1982). *Beyond agenda setting: Information subsidies and public policy*. Norwood, NJ: Ablex.

Gans, H. J. (1979). *Deciding what's news: A study of the CBS Evening News, NBC Nightly News, Newsweek and Time*. New York: Vintage Books.

Gitlin, T. (1978). Media sociology: The dominant paradigm. *Theory and Society, 6*, 205–253. Reprinted in G. Wilhoit & H. de Bock (Eds.), *Mass communication review yearbook* (Vol. 2, pp. 73–121). Beverly Hills, CA: Sage.

Gitlin, T. (1980). *The whole world is watching: Mass media and the making and unmaking of the New Left*. Berkeley, CA: University of California Press.

Glasgow Media Group. (1982). *Really bad news*. London: Writers & Readers.

Goffman, E. (1974). *Frame analysis*. New York: Harper & Row.

Goldenberg, E., & Traugott, M. (1984). *Campaigning for congress*. Washington, DC: CQ Press.

Graber, D. (1988). *Processing the news: How people tame the information tide* (2nd ed.). New York: Longman.

Granberg, D., & Brown, T. A. (1989). On affect and cognition in politics. *Social Psychology Quarterly, 52*, 171–182.

Gunter, B. (1987). *Poor reception: Misunderstanding and forgetting broadcast news*. Hillsdale, NJ: Lawrence Erlbaum Associates.

Gurevitch, M., & Blumler, J. G. (1990). Political communication systems and democratic values. In J. Lichtenberg (Ed.), *Democracy and the mass media* (pp. 269–289). Cambridge: Cambridge University Press.

Hall, S., Critcher, C., Jefferson, T., Clarke, J., & Roberts, B. (1978). *Policing the crisis*. New York: Holmes & Meier.

Hallin, D. C. (1992). Sound bite news: Television coverage of elections, 1968-1988. *Journal of Communication, 42*(2). 5–24.

Hawkins, R. P., & Pingree, S. (1986). Activity in the effects of television on children. In J. Bryant & D. Zillmann (Eds.), *Perspectives on media effects* (pp. 233–250). Hillsdale, NJ: Lawrence Erlbaum Associates.

Herman, E. S., & Chomsky, N. (1988). *Manufacturing consent: The political economy of the mass media*. New York: Pantheon Books.

Herstein, J. A. (1985). Voter thought processes and voting theory. In S. Kraus & R. Perloff (Eds.), *Mass media and political thought* (pp. 15–36). Beverly Hills, CA: Sage.

Iyengar, S. (1989). How citizens think about national issues. *American Journal of Political Science, 33*, 878–897.

Iyengar, S. (1991). *Is anyone responsible? How television frames political issues*. Chicago: University of Chicago Press.

Iyengar, S., & Kinder, D. R. (1987). *News that matters*. Chicago: University of Chicago Press.

Jamieson, K. H. (1992). *Dirty politics: Deception, distraction and democracy*. New York: Oxford University Press.

Jones, E. E., & Nisbett, R. E. (1972). The actor and the observer: Divergent perceptions of the causes of behavior. In E. Jones, D. Kanouse, H. Kelley, R. Nisbett, S. Valins, & R. Kidd (Eds.), *New directions in attribution research* (pp. 79–94). Morristown, NJ: General Learning Press.

Kahneman, D., & Tversky, A. (1984). Choice, values and frames. *American Psychologist, 39*, 341–350.

Kaniss, P. (1991). *Making local news*. Chicago: University of Chicago Press.

Katz, E. (1987). On conceptualizing media effects: Another look. In S. Oskamp (Ed.), *Applied Social Psychology Annual* (Vol. 8, pp. 32–42). Beverly Hills, CA: Sage.

Katz, E., & Feldman, J. J. (1962). The debates in the light of research: A survey of surveys.

In S. Kraus (Ed.), *The great debates* (pp. 173–223). Bloomington, IN: Indiana University Press.

Kennamer, J. D. (1988). News values and the vividness of information. *Written Communication. 5*, 108–123.

Kinder, D. R., & Kiewiet, D. R. (1983). Sociotropic politics: The American case. *British Journal of Political Science, 11*, 129–161.

Kinder, D. R., & Mebane, W. R., Jr. (1983). Politics and economics in everyday life. In K. Monroe (Ed.), *The political process and economic change* (pp. 141–180). New York: Agathon.

Kinder, D. R., & Sanders, L. M. (1990). Mimicking political debate with survey questions: The case of white opinion on affirmative action for blacks. *Social Cognition, 8*, 73–103.

Klapper, J. T. (1960). *The effects of mass communications.* Glencoe, IL: Free Press.

Kosicki, G. M., & McLeod, J. M. (1990). Learning from political news: Effects of media images and information-processing strategies. In S. Kraus (Ed.), *Mass communication and political information processing* (pp. 69–83). Hillsdale, NJ: Lawrence Erlbaum Associates.

Kosicki, G. M., McLeod, J. M., & Amor, David L. (1987, May). *Processing the news: Some individual strategies for selecting, sense-making and integrating.* Paper presented at the meeting of the International Communication Association, Montreal, Quebec.

Kramer, G. H. (1983). The ecological fallacy revisited: Aggregate versus individual level findings on economics and elections and sociotropic voting. *American Political Science Review, 77*, 77–111.

Krosnick, J. A. (1988). The role of attitude importance in social evaluation: A study of policy preference, presidential candidate evaluations, and voting behavior. *Journal of Personality and Social Psychology, 55*, 196–210.

Krosnick, J. A. (1989). Attitude importance and attitude accessibility. *Personality and Psychology Bulletin, 15*, 297–308.

Krosnick, J. A. (1990). Government policy and citizen passion: A study of issue publics in contemporary America. *Political Behavior, 12*, 59–93.

Lasswell, H. (1948). The structure and function of communication in society. In L. Bryson (Ed.), *The communication of ideas* (pp. 37–51). New York: Institute of Religious and Social Studies.

Lau, R. R., & Erber, R. (1985). Political sophistication: An information-processing approach. In S. Kraus & R. Perloff (Eds.), *Mass media and political thought: An information-processing approach* (pp. 37–64). Newbury Park, CA: Sage.

Lau, R. R., & Sears, D. O. (1986). Social cognition and political cognition: The past, the present and the future. In R. Lau & D. Sears (Eds.), *Political cognition* (pp. 347–366). Hillsdale, NJ: Lawrence Erlbaum Associates.

Lazarsfeld, P. F., Berelson, B. R., & Gaudet, H. (1948). *The people's choice* (2nd ed.). New York: Columbia University Press.

Lee, M. A., & Solomon, N. (1990). *Unreliable sources: A guide to bias in news media.* New York: Lyle Stuart.

Lemert, J. B., Mitzman, B. N., Seither, M. A., Cook, R. H., & Hackett, R. (1977). Journalists and mobilizing information. *Journalism Quarterly, 54*, 721–726.

Levy, M. R. (1981). Disdaining the news. *Journal of Communication, 31*(3), 24–31.

Liebes, T., & Katz, E. (1990). *The export of meaning: Cross-cultural readings of Dallas.* New York: Oxford University Press.

Linsky, M. (1986). *Impact: How the press affects federal policymaking.* New York: W. W. Norton.

Lippman, W. (1922). *Public opinion.* New York: MacMillan.

Livingstone, S. M. (1990). *Making sense of television: The psychology of audience interpretation.* Oxford: Pergamon Press.

Logan, J. R., & Molotch, H. L. (1987). *Urban fortunes: The political economy of place.* Berkeley, CA: University of California Press.

MacKuen, M. (1981). Social communication and the mass policy agenda. In M. MacKuen & S. Coombs (Eds.), *More than news: Media power in public affairs* (pp. 19–144). Beverly Hills, CA: Sage.

Markus, H., & Zajonc, R. B. (1985). The cognitive perspective in social psychology. In G. Lindzey & E. Aronson (Eds.), *The handbook of social psychology* (3rd ed., pp. 137–230). New York: Random House.

McCombs, M. E. (1977). Newspapers versus television: Mass communication effects across time. In D. Shaw & M. McCombs (Eds.), *The emergence of American political issues: The agenda-setting function of the press* (pp. 89–105). St. Paul, MN: West Publishing.

McCombs, M. E., & Shaw, D. L. (1972) The agenda-setting function of the mass media. *Public Opinion Quarterly, 36,* 176–187.

McGuire, W. J. (1986). The myth of massive media impact: Savagings and salvagings. In W. Comstock (Ed.), *Public communication and behavior* (Vol. 1, pp. 173–257). New York: Academic Press.

McLeod, D. M., & Hertog, J. K. (1992). The manufacture of "public opinion" by reporters: Informal cues for public perceptions of protest groups. *Discourse & Society, 3*(3), 259–275.

McLeod, J. M., & Becker, L. B. (1974). Testing the validity of gratification measures through political effects analysis. In J. G. Blumler & E. Katz (Eds.), *The uses of mass communication: Current perspectives on gratifications research* (pp. 137–164). Beverly Hills, CA: Sage.

McLeod, J. M., Becker, L. B., & Byrnes, J. E. (1974). Another look at the agenda-setting function of the press. *Communication Research, 1,* 131–165.

McLeod, J. M., & Blumler, J. G. (1987). The macrosocial level of communication science. In S. Chaffee & C. Berger (Eds.), *Handbook of communication science* (pp. 271–322). Beverly Hills, CA: Sage.

McLeod, J. M., Brown, J. D., Becker, L. B., & Ziemke, D. A. (1977). Decline and fall at the White House: A longitudinal analysis of communication effects. *Communication Research, 4,* 3–22.

McLeod, J. M., Bybee, C. R., & Durall, J. A. (1979). The 1976 presidential debates and the equivalence of informed political participation. *Communication Research, 6,* 463–487.

McLeod, J. M., Bybee, C. R., Leutscher, W., & Garramone, G. (1981). *Public Opinion Quarterly, 45,* 69–90.

McLeod, J. M., Kosicki, G. M., Amor, D. L., Allen, S. G., & Philps, D. M., (1986, August). *Public images of mass media news: What are they and does it matter?* Paper presented at the meeting of the Association for Education in Journalism and Mass Communication, Norman, OK.

McLeod, J. M., Kosicki, G. M., Pan, Z., & Allen, S. G., (1987, August). *Audience perspectives on the news: Assessing their complexity and conceptual frames.* Paper presented at the meeting of the Association for Education in Journalism and Mass Communication, San Antonio, TX.

McLeod, J. M., Kosicki, G. M., & Rucinski, D. M. (1988). Political communication research: An assessment of the field. *Mass Communication Review, 15*(1), 8–15, 30.

McLeod, J. M., & McDonald, D. G. (1985). Beyond simple exposure: Media orientations and their impact on political processes. *Communication Research, 12,* 3–33.

McLeod, J. M., Pan, Z., & Rucinski, D. (1989, May). *Framing a complex issue: A case of social construction of meaning.* Paper presented at the meeting of the International Communication Association, San Francisco, CA.

McLeod, J. M., & Reeves, B. (1980). On the nature of mass media effects. In S. Withey &

R. Abeles (Eds.), *Television and social behavior: Beyond violence and children* (pp. 17–54). Hillsdale, NJ: Lawrence Erlbaum Associates.

McLeod, J. M., Sun, S., Chi, A., & Pan, Z. (1990, August). *Metaphor and the media: What shapes public understanding of the "war" on drugs?* Paper presented at the meeting of the Association for Education in Journalism and Mass Communication, Minneapolis, MN.

McQuail, D. (1992). *Media performance: Mass communication and the public interest.* London: Sage.

Meadow, R. B. (1980). *Politics as communication.* Norwood, NJ: Ablex.

Miller, A. H., Goldenberg, E. N., & Erbring, L. (1979). Type-set politics: Impact of newspapers on public confidence. *American Political Science Review, 73*, 67–84.

Morley, D. (1980). *The "nationwide" audience* (Television Monograph No. 11). London: British Film Institute.

Neuman, W. R. (1976). Patterns of recall among television news viewers. *Public Opinion Quarterly, 40*, 115–123.

Neuman, W. R. (1986). *The paradox of mass politics: Knowledge and opinion in the American electorate.* Cambridge, MA: Harvard University Press.

Neuman, W. R., Just, M. R., & Crigler, A. N. (1992). *Common knowledge: News and the construction of political meaning.* Chicago: University of Chicago Press.

Noelle-Neumann, E. (1984). *The spiral of silence: Public opinion–our social skin.* Chicago: University of Chicago Press.

O'Keefe, G. J. (1985). "Taking a bite out of crime": The impact of a public information campaign. *Communication Research, 12*, 147–178.

Pan, Z., & Kosicki, G. M. (in press). Framing analysis: An approach to news discourse. *Political Communication.*

Pan, Z., & McLeod, J. M. (1991). Multi-level analysis in mass communication research. *Communication Research, 18*, 140–173.

Patterson, T. E. (1980). *The mass media election: How Americans choose their president.* New York: Praeger.

Pertschuk, M., & Schaetzel, W. (1989). *The people rising: The campaign against the Bork nomination.* New York: Thunder's Mouth Press.

Petty, R. E., & Cacioppo, J. T. (1986). *Communication and persuasion: Central and peripheral routes to attitude change.* New York: Springer-Verlag.

Philo, G. (1990). *Seeing and believing: The influence of television.* London: Routledge.

Popkin, S. L. (1990, September). *The Iowa and New Hampshire primaries: The interaction of wholesale and retail campaigning.* Paper presented at the meeting of the American Political Science Association, Washington, DC.

Popkin, S. L. (1991). *The reasoning voter: Communication and persuasion in presidential campaigns.* Chicago: University of Chicago Press.

Powell, G. B., Jr. (1986). American voter turnout in comparative perspective. *American Political Science Review, 80*(1), 17–44.

Price, V., Ritchie, L. D., & Eulau, H. (1991). Micro-macro issues in communication research (Special Issue). *Communication Research, 18*, 133–273.

Protess, D. L., Cook, F. L., Doppelt, J. C., Ettema, J. S., Gordon, M. T., Leff, D. R., & Miller, P. (1991). *The journalism of outrage: Investigative reporting and agenda building in America.* New York: Guilford Press.

Ranney, A. (1983). *Channels of power.* New York: Basic Books.

Reeves, B., Thorson, E., & Schleuder, J. (1986). Attention to television: Psychological theories and chronometric measures. In Bryant, J. & Zillmann (Eds.), *Perspectives on media effects* (pp. 251–279). Hillsdale, NJ: Lawrence Erlbaum Associates.

Rice, R. E., & Atkin, C. K. (Eds.). (1989). *Public communication campaigns* (2nd ed.). Beverly Hills, CA: Sage.

Robinson, J. P., & Levy, M. R. (1986). *The main source: Learning from television news.* Beverly Hills, CA: Sage.

Rubin, R. (1976). *Party dynamics: The Democratic coalition and the politics of change.* New York: Oxford University Press.

Ryan, C. (1991). *Prime time activism: Media strategies for grassroots organizing.* Boston: South End Press.

Sabato, L. (1987). Real and imagined corruption in campaign financing. In J. Reichley (Ed.), *Election American style* (pp. 155–179). Washington, DC: Brookings Institute.

Sears, D. O., & Chaffee, S. H. (1979). Uses and effects of the 1976 debates: An overview of empirical studies. In S. Kraus (Ed.), *The great debates, 1976: Ford vs. Carter* (pp. 223–261). Bloomington, IN: Indiana University Press.

Semetko, H. A., Blumler, J. G., Gurevitch, M., & Weaver, D. H., with Barkin, S. & Wilhoit, G. C. (1991). *The formation of campaign agendas: A comparative analysis of party and media roles in recent American and British elections.* Hillsdale, NJ: Lawrence Erlbaum Associates.

Shoemaker, P. J., & Reese, S. D. (1991). *Mediating the message: Theories of influence on mass media content.* New York: Longman.

Sigal, L. V. (1973). *Reporters and officials: The organization and politics of newsmaking,* Lexington, MA: D.C. Heath.

Smith, H. (1988). *The power game.* New York: Random House.

Star, S. A., & Hughes, H. M. (1950). Report on an education campaign: The Cincinnati plan for the UN. *American Journal of Sociology, 55,* 389–400.

Stempel, G. H., III. (1989). Content analysis. In G. Stempel & B. Westley (Eds.), *Research methods in mass communication* (pp. 119–131). Englewood Cliffs, NJ: Prentice-Hall.

Stocking, S. H., & Gross, P. H. (1989). *How do journalists think? A Proposal for the study of cognitive bias in newsmaking.* Bloomington, IN: ERIC Clearinghouse on Reading and Communication Skills.

Strate, J. M., Parrish, C. J., Elder, C. D., & Ford, C., III. (1989). Life span and civic development and voting participation. *American Political Science Review, 83*(2), 443–464.

Tichenor, P. J., Donohue, G. A., & Olien, C. N., (1970). Mass media flow and differential growth of knowledge. *Public Opinion Quarterly, 34,* 159–170.

Tichenor, P. J., Donohue, G. A., & Olien, C. N. (1980). *Community conflict and the press.* Beverly Hills, CA: Sage Publications.

Tipton, L. P., Haney, R. D., & Basehart, J. R. (1975). Media agenda-setting in city and state election campaigns. *Journalism Quarterly, 52,* 15–22.

Tuchman, G. (1978). *Making news.* New York: Free Press.

van Dijk, T. A. (1988). *News as discourse.* Hillsdale, NJ: Lawrence Erlbaum Associates.

Verba, S., & Nie, N. H. (1972). *Participation in America.* New York: Harper & Row.

Watt, J. H., & Krull, R. (1977). An examination of three models of television viewing and aggression. *Human Communication Review, 3,* 99–112.

Weaver, D. H., Graber, D. A., McCombs, M. E., & Eyal, C. H. (1981). *Media agenda-setting in a presidential election: Issues, images and interests.* New York: Praeger.

Weaver, P. (1972). Is television news biased? *Public Interest,* Winter, 57–74.

Westlye, M. C. (1991). *Senate elections and campaign intensity.* Baltimore: Johns Hopkins University Press.

Wolfinger, R. E., & Rosenstone, S. J. (1980). *Who votes?* New Haven, CT: Yale University Press.

Zaller, J. R. (1992). *The nature and origins of mass opinion.* Cambridge: Cambridge University Press.

7

The Question
of Media Violence

BARRIE GUNTER
Independent Broadcasting Authority
London, UK

ORIGINS OF CONCERN

Concern about media violence has its roots in the unease that has historically been expressed whenever a new entertainment or communications medium appears on the scene that appeals to the masses. Strong reactions were recorded on the appearance of popular romantic and adventure novels in the 19th century and were observed again in response to the growing popularity of motion pictures in the early part of the present century.

The earliest coordinated social scientific research investigation into the impact of media violence began in the 1920s in the United States, during a period when the motion picture industry became the major source of mass entertainment. During the same period, important developments were taking place in the social sciences. Research techniques were being developed that now enabled researchers to investigate issues they had previously not been equipped to.

Utilizing these new found research methodologies, the Payne Fund Studies tackled such questions as whether the movies eroded moral standards or had an influence on conduct. Findings indicated that many scenes of crime and sex could be found in the movies that were contrary to moral standards of the day, but no conclusive evidence emerged that the movies actually had degenerating effects on their audiences. Studies of movies' influences on delinquency suggested, however, that there might be a link. One study of delinquency-prone youngsters reported that motion pictures played a direct role in shaping delinquent and criminal careers. The methods and strategies of some of this work were highly criticized at the time by criminologists and specialists in the study of deviant behavior; nevertheless the findings caused quite a stir (see Blumer & Hauser, 1933; Dysinger & Ruckmick, 1933).

In the 1950s attention switched to another popular entertainment medium—comics. In his book, *The Seduction of the Innocent*, Wertham (1954) argued that comic books were, contrary to what their name suggested, not the least bit funny. Instead, at their worst, they were turning children into dangerous juvenile delinquents; at best, they were giving children who read them a distorted view of the world. They were also blamed by Wertham for contributing to reading problems.

Throughout his book, Wertham catalogued instances where children supposedly imitated violent acts they found in crime comics. He claimed that there is a significant correlation between crime comics reading and the more serious forms of juvenile delinquency. Reduced to its simplest terms, Wertham's argument was that: (a) comic books were read by a large number of children; (b) because a large component of the comic diet consisted of crime, violence, horror, and sex; (c) children who read the comics were necessarily stimulated to the performance of delinquent acts, cruelty, violence, and undesirable social behavior. Perhaps the most significant impact of Wertham's work was to seriously undermine the comic industry. Theoretically, however, there were inconsistencies in his analysis, and his evidence for comic book effects of delinquent tendencies in youngsters, based as it was on interviews with children in clinical settings, was often unsystematic and ambiguous in its potential interpretations, so as to give rise to more questions than answers.

VIOLENCE ON TELEVISION

The growth of television as a popular mass entertainment and information medium during the 1950s saw similar concerns about potential harms, especially in connection with young audiences. In the United Kingdom, Himmelweit, Oppenheim, and Vince (1958) examined the impact of the new medium on children in communities for whom television was a relatively new phenomenon. A similar research program followed among children in the United States and Canada a few years later (Schramm, Lyle, & Parker, 1961). The North American work found indications of links between watching violence on television and aggressiveness among young viewers, whereas Himmeltweit et al. concluded that whereas regular viewing was associated with evidence of habituation to violence on screen, it was difficult to prove a causal connection between exposure to certain kinds of television content and aggressive behavior.

Television came under even closer scrutiny later on during the 1960s. In the United States, fear about rising crime, concern about inner-city riots and college campus rebellions against the Vietnam war, together with other forms of civil unrest, gave many the impression that the fabric of American society was being ripped apart. These anxieties were brought sharply into focus by the assassinations of four prominent public figures, John F. Kennedy, Malcolm X, Martin Luther King, Jr., and Robert Kennedy. In response to public concerns surrounding these incidents, in 1968 President Johnson set up a National Commission on the Causes and Prevention of Violence. The report by the Commission's Media Action group did not find television to be a substantial cause of social violence.

Following closely behind this report, however, came another large investigation that focused specifically on television's effects on social behavior. The Surgeon General's Scientific Advisory Committee on Television and Social Behavior was set up in 1969 to investigate the effects of television violence on children's and teenagers' attitudes and behavior.

Political controversy surrounded this research program before it got underway because television network representatives on the committee blackballed seven leading social scientists distinguished for their past research and expertise on the subject of television violence. Further arguments followed the publication of the five-volume report and summary document mainly because, according to some analysts, the summary played down the negative findings of some of the studies. The main conclusions were that:

1. Television content is heavily saturated with violence.
2. Children and adults are spending more and more time watching this content.
3. There is some evidence that on balance viewing violent television entertainment increases the likelihood of aggressive behavior among viewers.

Because the publication of the Surgeon General's report a multitude of further studies on the subject of media violence have been published, to say nothing of the ones that appeared before this research, produced in the 1960s largely by the blackballed researchers. In order to assess the major findings of this work, to judge the weight to lend to these findings, and to determine where research in the field is now moving or perhaps more significantly where it ought to be moving, we must first begin by highlighting the major questions, the basic techniques used for investigating them, and the validity and relevance of perspectives that have principally been addressed.

THE MAJOR ISSUES

What are the major questions about media violence? History reveals several major issues that regularly arise in public debates about media violence. These issues tend to include questions about how much violence there is in different media, the extent to which individuals are exposed to violent media content, and what effects media violence has on its consumers. There is a further question that is addressed relatively less often, though this should not be construed as diminishing its importance, and that is what does the public really think and feel about media violence?

The remainder of this chapter explores research on each of these important questions, assessing theories and methodologies that underpin the research as and where appropriate. It finishes by asking, what next? Although considerable academic research effort has been expended on the topic of media violence, much of the evidence on its effects still would not stand up in court. Even in the context of influencing policy, how much notice should media executives take of what research has to say about media violence? Where should research on media violence go next? Are there any new and different ways of studying this complex subject that could usefully build upon and add to the body of research already accumulated?

EFFECTS OF TELEVISION VIOLENCE

A major bone of contention in the ongoing debate about TV violence has focused on whether it causes aggressive behavior among viewers. In examining the effects of television violence, there are two principal questions that need to be considered. First, what kinds of effects are being referred to? Second, how are the effects measured and to what extent can the evidence deriving from these measures be unquestionably accepted?

Over the years, a number of theories and hypotheses have been proposed and tested concerning the mechanisms through which TV violence can supposedly influence viewers' aggressive dispositions. Furthermore, the great body of research studies can be boiled down to a handful of research methods.

Types of effect: TV violence may have an impact on viewers at a number of psychological levels, which can be broadly divided into cognitive, affective, and behaviorial. Behaviorial effects have received the greatest attention, although sometimes these are operationalized as attitudes towards particular forms of behavior as might be deployed in different situations. We focus on behavioral effects initially and turn to cognitive and affective responses to TV violence later.

Behaviorial Effects

Behavioral effects of TV violence have been hypothesized to act via a number of mechanisms, principal among which are: catharsis, arousal, disinhibition, imitation, and desensitization.

Catharsis. According to the catharsis hypothesis, accumulated aggressive impulses can be discharged by individuals if they become absorbed in violent events. Much of the evidence for a catharsis effect linked to watching media violence has derived from the work of Feshbach. In the 1950s and 1960s, his work provided several demonstrations that individuals can harmlessly discharge their aggressive impulses either through fantasizing about violence or through watching fictional portrayals of violence under controlled laboratory conditions (Feshbach, 1955, 1961). Later, Feshbach and Singer (1971) reported a reduction of aggressive tendencies among teenage boys under more natural conditions. Boys in private residential schools and treatment homes were observed before, during, and after a 6-week period during which they had their TV viewing diet manipulated to control the amount of violence-containing programming to which they were exposed. The boys who watched mainly nonviolent material were found to exhibit higher levels of physical aggression against their peers than did boys who watched mainly violent programs.

This research was criticized for failing to control for or take into account a number of important factors, and one attempt to replicate it failed (Wells, 1973). The catharsis notion has not received much support elsewhere. A weak form of the original hypothesis has been suggested in which the ability to discharge aggressive impulses in response to violent media content is conceived to be a dimension of human cognitive skill, which some individuals possess more of than others (Gunter, 1980). Thus, individuals with well-developed imaginative or fantasizing abilities have been found to be more able to reduce experimentally induced anger while watching a violent film compared with individuals who are weak in such abilities (Biblow, 1973).

Arousal. The arousal hypothesis suggests that watching violent television programs can arouse viewers and make them excited. This kind of effect is not restricted to violent content; sexual or humorous content can have the same effect. The emotional arousal itself is conceived as being a nonspecific physiological response; it is defined by the individual in terms of the type of material he or she happens to be watching. Thus, according to the hypothesis, if viewers are watching violent material, they are likely to interpret their arousal as anger and respond aggressively in a situation where they are made angry by someone (Tannenbaum & Zillmann, 1975). There is some suggestion, however, that arousal quickly disperses and that even a short delay between initial emotional arousal and an opportunity to respond aggressively can significantly reduce aggression (Doob & Climie, 1972).

Disinhibition. According to this hypothesis, watching violence on television may legitimize the use of violence by the viewer in real life by undermining social sanctions against behaving violently that normally work to inhibit such behavior. Research carried out under contrived laboratory conditions has supported this hypothesis and been interpreted to show that viewers may behave in a more aggressive manner after watching film violence. This response is especially likely to occur if viewers were already angry before viewing (Berkowitz, 1962, 1965, 1974).

In an important extension of this work, the research of Donnerstein, Malamuth, and associates has investigated the specific effects of violent pornographic media content on male attitudes towards women and the victims of rape, and their propensities to behave aggressively toward women under different circumstances. A host of controlled laboratory and field studies have demonstrated significant effects of single or repeated exposures to such material, even in carefully screened male subjects (Donnerstein, 1980a, 1980b, 1983, 1984; Donnerstein & Berkowitz, 1981; Donnerstein & Malamuth, 1983; Malamuth, 1984; Malamuth & Donnerstein, 1982).

Imitation. This hypothesis assumes that viewers, most especially very young ones, are inclined to learn from behaviors they see performed by TV characters, and copy the actions themselves. It is hypothesized, for example, that children may learn that violence is a useful and appropriate way of overcoming one's problems. Alteratively, young viewers may copy their heroes' behaviors to become more like them, through a psychological process known as identification.

In a series of laboratory-based experiments, Bandura (1978, 1979, 1982, 1985) explored links between exposure to TV or film violence. His findings indicated that children can be encouraged to behave in more aggressive ways following exposure to media violence, with this effect attributed partly to disinhibition and also to observational learning in which children imitate the behaviors of the models they watched. Bandura's experiments showed that witnessing real-life aggression, or a film of the same models, or aggressive cartoon characters all elicited copycat aggressive behavior in children.

Desensitization. According to this hypothesis, repeated viewing of TV violence leads to a reduction in emotional responsiveness to violence on the screen and to an increased acceptance of violence in real life. The argument runs that young viewers become increasingly accustomed to violence in programs if they watch a lot of it. In consequence, demand grows for more and more extreme forms of fictional violence as that that viewers become habituated to loses its "kick" and hence its appeal.

Just a few attempts have been made to provide practical demonstrations of a desensitization effect of TV violence on children. These have investigated either the effect of TV violence on youngsters' own dispositions to act responsibly by trying to stop what they believe to be a real fight or the degree to which they show an emotional response to violence.

Two studies looked at whether watching TV violence affected the response of 8-year-olds who witnessed a real fight between two other children in a playroom. Results showed that children who watched violent material were less likely to seek the help of an adult to stop the fight they thought was taking place (Drabman & Thomas, 1974; Thomas, Horton, Lippincott, & Drabman, 1977). Elsewhere, research has shown that children who are relatively heavy viewers (25+ hours per week) were much less responsive to TV violence in terms of a physiological measure of arousal, than were relatively light viewers (less than 4 hours per week) (Cline, Croft, & Courrier, 1973).

Research Methods

The great body of empirical research published about the effects of television violence can be further boiled down in a manageable way according to the research methodologies employed. Most of the work done so far can be broken down into just a few categories:

- Laboratory experiments
- Field experiments
- Correlational surveys
- Longitudinal panel studies
- Natural experiments
- Intervention studies

Laboratory Experiments.   These have been designed to demonstrate a causal relationship between watching a violent event on television and increased viewer aggressiveness. The findings to emerge from this form of investigation have been taken to provide clear-cut evidence of a causal connection between watching television violence and increased viewer aggressiveness. Typically, however, these studies have tested only small unrepresentative groups of people under highly contrived unnatural viewing conditions. Their measures of television viewing and aggressive behavior tend to be far removed from normal everyday behavior. Thus, whether or not laboratory findings have any meaning in the outside world has been strongly debated.

A series of experiments by Albert Bandura and his associates in the 1960s and 1970s addressed the imitation issue. Bandura believed that children could learn antisocial behavior through observation. In other words, by watching favorite television characters behave violently on screen, young viewers could identify with these actors and their actions, and might, under appropriate circumstances, be inclined to mimic them.

A demonstration of this effect was provided through an experimental design in which children were shown a character on film behaving in an aggressive manner towards a large plastic "Bobo" doll then being placed in a playroom with lots of toys including the doll. Other children were put in the playroom having either seen the same actor behaving nonviolently, or having seen no film at all. While observing the children playing, Bandura and his colleagues noted higher levels of imitative aggressive behaviors (toward the "Bobo" doll) among children who had seen the violent example than among other children. Variations on this general theme were explored over many experiments (Bandura, 1968, 1978; Bandura, Ross, & Ross, 1963a, 1963b; Bandura, Underwood, & Fromson, 1975).

In another series of studies Berkowitz and others (Berkowitz & Alioto, 1973; Berkowitz, Corwin, & Heironimous, 1963; Berkowitz & Geen, 1966; Berkowitz & Rawlings, 1963) provided evidence to suggest that aggressive tendencies among viewers could be sparked off by watching violent film sequences. Viewers in a laboratory setting were shown a violent clip, usually a scene from a dramatic boxing match, and were subsequently given an opportunity to deliver electric shocks to an individual who was in fact a confederate of the experimenter's. For one group of viewers, this individual had been responsible, prior to their watching the film clip, for annoying them in some way. Now they had the chance to get back at him. The research generally showed that viewers of violence were more "aggressive" toward the target individual afterward compared with viewers of nonviolent material, but that this aggressive response was most likely to occur among those who had already been angered. Other variations on the theme found that different factors related to the film clip itself could also affect subsequent responding, for instance the amount of justification for the film violence (e.g., Hoyt, 1970; Meyer, 1973), or the amount of pain suffered by the victim (Hartmann, 1969).

Berkowitz (1964) argued that the mass media can give audiences ideas that may then be translated into open behavior. Violence in the media, especially when portrayed as justified, can offer viewers, especially angry ones, justification to behave violently themselves under intimidating circumstances. In later writings, Berkowitz (1984) gave greater stress to the inner cognitive processes of memory and recall as mediators of media messages' effects on social conduct. He proposed that viewers' reactions to the things they see on television depend on how they interpret what they see; the frames of reference such as background knowledge, social beliefs, and value systems they bring with them to the viewing situation; and the thoughts that are activated by the television experience.

This advance in conceptual thinking by Berkowitz shows an improvement on the initially oversimplistic modeling of television violence effects of his early research. This early work suffered from dubious ecological validity owing to the measures of aggressive behavior, short-duration film clips taken out of context, and special norms and expectations that governed the experimental situation in which viewers' reactions were measured. Does the electric-shock procedure provide a valid and representative indicator of real-life aggressive responding? To what extent did participants in the experiment "know" what was going on? Did participants assume the same responsibility for their actions in this peculiar situation as they normally would in everyday life? These and other question marks still hang over this body of research.

Field Experiments. To avoid some of the problems associated with laboratory research, while retaining a few of its advantages, some researchers have conducted field experiments. In these studies, children or adolescents are generally the object of investigation and are randomly assigned to view either violent or nonviolent television material for a period of a few days to a few weeks. Measures of aggressive behavior, fantasy, or attitudes are taken before, during, and after the period of controlled viewing. In order to ensure control over actual viewing, young people have usually been studied in group or institutional settings. The two most common settings have been nursery schools and residential schools or institutions for adolescent boys. With one exception, all of these studies have confirmed the results of the laboratory studies; in general, children and teenagers who view a diet of violent television exhibit more aggressive behavior than children who view nonviolent television.

In one study, for example, preschool children were shown either violent, neutral or prosocial television for 10 to 20 minutes each day for 4 weeks. Increased levels of aggressiveness during play were found only among those children who were initially more aggressive anyway and who were then shown a diet of violent cartoons (Friedrich & Stein, 1973).

Field experiments with adolescent boys have taken place either in residential boarding schools or in institutions for teenage delinquents. Using several measures of physical and verbal aggression, researchers have found an increase in some measures of aggression for boys watching mainly violent films over a several-week period and an increase in other measures of aggression restricted to those boys initially high in aggression anyway (e.g., Leyens, Parke, Camino, & Berkowitz, 1975; Parke, Berkowitz, Leyens, West, & Sebastian, 1977).

One dissenting finding emerged from a study by Feshbach and Singer (1971), who reported that boys who watched only nonviolent television programs were generally more aggressive than those who watched violent programming over a controlled viewing period of 6 weeks. This study was criticized, however, for failing to control for a number of important factors involving the boys' viewing diets, frustration caused by some boys not being allowed to watch favorite programs (mainly in the nonviolent diet group), and because the results were not in a consistent direction for the boys observed.

Field experiments with adult samples have been rare and not very informative. Loye, Gorney, and Steele (1977) got a number of married couples to agree to participate in an investigation of the effects of viewing a variety of program diets high in violence, high in prosocial content, a mixture of the two, neutral programs, or their normal viewing diet. Program availability was controlled at source via the cable system to which respondents' homes were linked. Each husband was observed during the course of 1 week by his wife, who kept a record of his mood and behavior. No effect of type of programming on mood change was observed. The only significant effect appeared when an analysis of covariance was performed (with initial mood as covariant). This produced a marginally significant effect, with those men in the violent-programs condition becoming more aggressive, those in the prosocial condition becoming less aggressive, and those in other conditions not changing.

An earlier experiment by Milgram and Shotland (1973) had people come into a theatre setting where they were promised a radio set as a reward after watching a program. One version of the program depicted a person stealing from a charity box, whereas the other version did not. After viewing, participants were told to go to another building to pick up their prizes. When they arrived at the designated place, however, the room was empty and a notice informed them that the radios were no longer available. There was also a charity box in the room with money clearly visible in it. Would they take any of the money? There was no indication across eight studies with around 600 people, that the televised example caused viewers to be any more likely to steal the money.

Correlational Surveys. These improve on experimental studies in terms of the representativeness of samples but often fall down in the accuracy of their measures of exposure to television violence. The basic approach in correlational research is to obtain a measure of viewing violent programs and to relate this to a measure or group of measures of aggressiveness. The ultimate goal is to demonstrate a causal relation, with the first step being to find whether or not some relation exists. Viewers often have to identify or recall from lists of program titles which ones they like best or watch most often. Occasionally, more effective diary measures are used, but even then assumptions are made about the probable violent content of programs viewers say they have seen that are not backed up by any better evidence. If some doubt exists about amounts of violence watched on television, there must also be doubts about the evidence offered on the supposed effects of this conduct. In any case, correlational surveys are unable to demonstrate causal relations. They can simply show where degrees of statistical association exist between certain reported sets of behaviors and attitudes. Even then, the small size of most of the correlations indicates some very weak associations.

Positive associations have been recorded between self-reported television viewing habits and peer- and teacher-rated aggressiveness of adolescent boys and girls (Friedman & Johnson, 1972; McLeod, Atkin, & Chaffee, 1972a, 1972b; Robinson & Bachman, 1972). A small correlation was reported between claimed viewing habits and attitudes towards aggressiveness among adolescent boys by Greenberg (1975), whereas Hartnagel and his colleagues have reported small positive correlations between the rated violence of children's favorite programs and self-rated violent behavior (Hartnagel, Teevan, & McIntyre, 1975; McIntyre, Teevan, & Hartnagel, 1972).

Longitudinal Panel Studies. These represent perhaps the best kind of studies of TV effects. They can test causal hypotheses and they usually employ sound sampling methods. The aim of this type of investigation is to discover relationships that may exist or develop over time between TV viewing and social attitudes and behavior. In this respect, such research addresses the notions of the cumulative influence of television violence. This view posits that the link between watching television and personal levels of aggressiveness should increase with age and repeated exposure to televised violence.

So far, however, the evidence from these studies has been equivocal. Some researchers have claimed to have found a strong link between the watching of TV violence containing programs in early childhood and the subsequent development of aggressive tendencies among children and adolescents in later years. Although there is a consistent finding of a small positive correlation between viewing television, violence, and aggressiveness, evidence that viewing television violence in natural settings causes people to be more aggressive is inconclusive (Freedman, 1984).

A series of long-term cross-cultural studies on televised violence and aggressive behavior in children was conducted by Lefkowitz and associates and by Eron and Huesmann and their associates (Eron, Huesmann, Lefkowitz, & Walder, 1972; Huesmann & Eron, 1986). In their initial U.S.-based research, Eron, Huesmann, Lefkowitz, and Walder obtained information from more than 800 8-year-old children about their amount of TV viewing and aggressiveness and 10 years later followed up and reinterviewed around half the original sample. For boys, significant correlations were found between reported watching of TV violence at age 8 and their measures of aggression 10 years later. There was no relationship, however, between early aggression and later TV violence viewing. Two large-scale longitudinal studies conducted in the United States, Finland, and Austria confirmed the relation between televised violence and aggression. Parents' roles, the child's intellectual ability, and social relationships were important variables. Support was found for the theory that there is a sensitive period—probably up to the age of 10—during which television can be especially influential on children's behavior.

These results were confirmed by Viemero (1986) in Finland and challenged by Wiegman, Kuttschreuter, and Baarda (1986) of the Netherlands who first participated in and then pulled out of the Eron et al. (1972) cross-national survey. When the Netherlands' data were subjected to multivariate analysis controlling for a number of variables such as social class and intelligence, only the girls in the study, generally less aggressive than the boys, became more aggressive as they watched more television.

In addition to the above studies, a number of other longitudinal and panel studies have suggested that violence viewing on television is a precursor of aggression (e.g., Belson, 1978; Singer & Singer, 1980).

In the United Kingdom, Belson used a simulated panel survey to study the impact of television violence on the behavior of adolescent boys. In other words, the respondents were not actually studied across separate points in time but were questioned retrospectively at a single point about their habits over previous years. Detailed and lengthy interviews with these teenage boys revealed a relationship between certain aspects of their claimed viewing behavior and self-reported attitudes and dispositions towards the use of violence in their lives. In particular, the extent to which the boys claimed to watch particular types of dramatic television content—classified by Belson as containing violence—the more likely they were to report having used aggression themselves under different circumstances. Belson's results have not been universally accepted, and critics have questioned the validity of the biographical information obtained from his young respondents about not only their current viewing habits and behavior, but also those they tried to recall from 10 years earlier. The study does indicate usefully that certain types of programming may have a more significant impact than other types on antisocial behavior among young viewers, and that it is not sufficient to examine only the overall amount of viewing that is done.

Singer and Singer (1980) provided data on TV viewing and on aggression at four different points in time, and they reported findings separately for boys and girls. The patterns of correlations over time were highly variable; some offered support for the results of Eron et al. (1972), whereas others did not.

Another major panel survey with children was sponsored by the National Broadcasting Company in the United States (Milavsky, Kessler, Stipp, & Rubens, 1982). Some 3,200 elementary-school children and teenagers participated in this research. The primary-age children were surveyed on six occasions and the teenagers on five occasions over a 3-year period (May 1970 through December 1973).

The aim of the research was to find out if there were links, either at any one point in time or over time, between the character of television viewing and the propensity of aggressive tendencies among the children and teenagers under study. Among the primary-school children, evidence about verbal and physical acts of aggression was obtained from school friends, and the teenagers reported on themselves. Television viewing was measured by giving respondents checklists of programs available on the major networks that had been preclassified for their violent content. Thus, not only did the researchers obtain specific information about levels of exposure among these young viewers to violent programs, but information about their aggressive behavior was collected also.

During the analysis phase, the researchers assessed linkages between aggressive behavior and levels of claimed viewing of different types of programming among different subgroups of children as well as among children as a whole. Only small statistical associations were found in any of these cases. Further analyses showed that compared with the influence of family background, social environment, and school perfor- mance, the significance of television viewing as an indicator of aggres- siveness was very weak. This led the authors to conclude that television viewing was not a factor in the development of aggressive behaviors among the children and teenagers in their sample.

Finally, it is worth mentioning a panel study conducted by Atkin, Greenberg, Korzenny, and McDermott (1979) that produced evidence indicating that aggressive predispositions may lead individuals to favor violent TV content. Atkin et al. used a time-order design to draw causal inferences from correlational data. A two-wave panel study of young people across a 1-year interval explored relationships between attitudes and TV viewing patterns over time.

Measures of attitudinal dispositions at Time 1 were used to predict TV viewing patterns at Time 2 one year later. Results showed that although actual viewing patterns changed little in general over the year, there was some evidence for selective exposure to violent programs at Time 2 amongst those respondents who had aggressive attitudes at Time 1. The relationship survived statistical controls for sex, school grade, and initial viewing patterns. The reverse relationship between viewing TV violence at Time 1 and personal aggressiveness at Time 2 was less powerful. These results indicate that a portion of the basic relationship between TV viewing and aggressiveness that has been reported in numerous single- wave field surveys may be attributable to selective exposure rather than the reverse TV influence on violence interpretation.

Natural Experiments. Some researchers have attempted to assess relationships between the presence of television and shifts in social conduct over time in natural environments. These studies fall largely into two categories. The first involves a longitudinal assessment of occurrences of certain forms of conduct, often as documented by the authorities, before and after television was available. A different version of this type of study has attempted to find out if media depictions of certain kinds can spark off subsequent behaviors in real life. The second type of study has taken place in communities in which television has been introduced for the first time. The effects of television on previously unexposed populations can thus be examined.

Hennigan et al. (1982) took advantage of the fact that there was a freeze on the introduction of television into American cities between 1949 and 1952. This meant that some cities had ready access to television for several years, while others did not. The authors compared crime rates in the two types of cities and argued that any effect on crime would appear in a time series analysis as a "bubble" caused by an increase in crime rate in those cities having television relative to those not having it, with this increase eliminated once the other cities had television several years later.

The study found no effect of television on homicide or aggravated assault (violent crime) or on burglary or auto theft (serious instrumental crime), but there was some evidence that the incidence of larceny (minor theft) increased after the introduction of television. The authors suggested that the effect was due not to feelings of aggression or to imitation, but to relative deprivation caused by poorer viewers observing the relatively affluent people who were typically shown on television. Whether or not this explanation is correct, the study offers no evidence for an effect of television viewing on aggression.

A series of studies by Phillips and his colleagues during the 1970s and 1980s investigated specific links between certain acts of violence on television and similar acts in real life (Phillips, 1974, 1979, 1980a, 1980b, 1981, 1982, 1983, 1985).

Phillips (1983) examined the impact of championship heavyweight prizefights on homicides in the United States. Eighteen such fights took place between 1973 and 1978, and the author analyzed the number of homicides that occurred during the 10 days following each fight compared with a computed expected number. The major results are contained in a regression analysis that appears to show that the number of homicides increased on days 3, 4, 6, and 9 after a fight, with the major effect occurring on day 3.

Another analysis indicated that the increase occurred only if the fight took place outside the United States, if it was covered on network news, and if the expected number of homicides on day 3 was high. In addition, if the loser of the fight was White, the number of young, White men who were victims of homicide increased on the day of the fight, and 2 and 8 days later; if the loser was Black, there was an increase in Black homicides 4 and 5 days after the fight. Finally, the football Super Bowl, the most highly publicized and viewed sports event on television, had no effect on homicides.

It is difficult to assess this study because even if the statistical analyses are accepted entirely, the pattern of results appears to be inexplicable. That the effect of a fight might be delayed so that it did not show up until day 3 is conceivable, but what kind of process would cause the effect to reappear on days 6 and 9? Similarly, how can one begin to understand why there is an effect only when the fight takes place outside the United States or when the expected number of homicides on day 3 is high?

Perhaps the most troubling is that in the analysis of the after-effects of a fight, homicides involving a certain race occur on different days depending on the race of the loser, and homicides involving both Whites and Blacks occur on different days from the overall increase in homicides.

Phillips seemed unconcerned by this lack of agreement, but Freedman (1984) argued that it is critical. If one regression analysis is accepted, then all of them must be accepted. Why should homicide increases occur on certain days after a major prizefight but not others? Why should the days differ for White and Black homicides? There is a broader problem. These prizefights are generally shown only on closed-circuit television in theatres and therefore attract a relatively small audience. The later coverage on the news is necessarily brief. In contrast, regular television exposes huge numbers of people to a steady diet of murders and assaults, war reports, and violent sporting events. Yet these championship heavyweight prizefights, to which a relatively small proportion of viewers are exposed, are supposed to increase homicides above and beyond the effects, if any, of all other programming, including the many prizefights that appear on television and that are watched by tens of millions of viewers.

Elsewhere, the research of Phillips has been both replicated and criticized by other investigators (Kessler & Stipp, 1984; Messner, 1986; Stack, 1987). One failure to replicate the teenage suicide findings (Phillips & Paight, 1987) was attributed to the fact that there was a single rather than multiple exposure.

Centerwall (1989) used a population intervention study design in which a case population is compared with external control groups to determine the effects upon aspects of a population's behavior of different interventions. In this study the dependent variable was homicide rates over a 30-year period (1945–1975) among White populations in the United States, Canada, and South Africa. The "intervention" whose inferred influences on homicide rates was under examination was ownership of TV sets. During the period of observation both the United States and Canada experienced a dramatic growth in television ownership, most markedly during the mid-1950s. In South Africa there was no TV set ownership.

In scrutinizing available statistical sources for each country, Centerwall produced graphs that revealed a marked increase in White homicide rates in the United States and Canada in the late 1960s, lagging some 15 years behind a similar growth in TV set ownership. Meanwhile, in South Africa, homicide rates were actually on a par with those in North America but failed to exhibit the same dramatic rise in the 1945–1970 period and during the early 1970s actually fell. Failing to find differences between the three nations in terms of changes in age distribution, urbanization, economic conditions, alcohol consumption, capital punishment, civil unrest, or availability of firearms, which could account for differences in homicide rates, Centerwall made a case for TV as a causal agent. The 10- to 15-year lag between the introduction of TV and changes in homicide rate implies, argued Centerwall, "that the behaviourial effects of TV are primarily exerted upon children" (p. 15).

Two fairly recent studies have investigated the impact of television on previously unexposed populations. Williams (1986) reported a study with small communities in Canada. Among the many measures taken, unobtrusive observations of children's behavior were used in addition to teacher and peer ratings of aggression. This study covered three towns that at the outset either had no television reception (NOTEL), only one channel available (UNITEL), or several channels available (MULTITEL).

The major finding of the study was that the aggressive behavior on the playground of grade-school children (aged 6–11) increased on NOTEL over the 2-year period, whereas playground aggression in UNITEL and MULTITEL showed no increase. This pattern of increased aggression was true for both girls and boys; longitudinal (children aged 6–7 prior to television reception and 8–9 two years after) and cross-sectional (children of same age at each testing) samples; children initially high or low in aggression; and for children who were either heavy or light viewers. In conclusion, the evidence in support of the hypothesis that viewing violence leads to an increase in aggressive behavior is very strong.

In a similar study, Granzberg and Steinbring (1980) compared a Cree Indian community into which television was being introduced with a control Indian community and a control Euro-Canadian community. No pre-post differences in levels of aggression occurred between the experimental and control communities, taken as a whole. But, when children were classified by amount of daily exposure to television, significant differences in aggressive attitudes emerged. The introduction of television into the community increased the aggressiveness of those children who watched a lot of television.

Intervention Studies. In the sphere of violent portrayals, the worst is usually assumed of television. Exposure to televised violence is generally hypothesized to exert potential harms on unsuspecting viewers, especially upon vulnerable young children. A number of studies have started from the assumption that harmful import is contingent upon watching television violence, but have then asked if this is so, what, if anything, can be done to alleviate this undesirable effect. Intervention projects have explored ways of inoculating viewers against television's influences. Such exercises have normally been conducted among children with the aim of improving young viewers' television literacy, that is, their critical appraisal and understanding of television content. Intervention studies have yielded some evidence that increased awareness of television techniques can reduce harmful reaction to TV violence.

In one intervention Singer and Singer (1983) used eight school lessons to teach children, from kindergarten to the fifth grade, about television. They included such topics as: how programs are created, format and program type, commercials, TV as a source of information about the world, violence on TV—its unrealistic nature—and critical viewing skills. Teachers were shown videotapes, including excerpts from current TV programs, demonstrating the concepts to be taught and supported by discussion ideas and activity sheets for class work and for homework. They were trained in the use of the various materials.

Pre- and posttest questions relating to the topics taught and including a television comprehension test were administered to the children, who were divided into experimental and control groups. An attitude measure was used to assess liking for programs and characters and to elicit reasons for watching. Younger children, in kindergarten to second grade, showed improvements in understanding the material taught, especially for camera techniques, video editing, and realism/ fantasy distinctions.

Children in Grades 3–6 were tested in nine schools on all except that to do with the administrative control of television. Singer and Singer (1983) considered that this school was "less enthusiastic" about participating in the study. Local organizational and motivational factors that are largely outside the control of intervention programs can often play a crucial part in determining the pattern of outcomes. The Singers found that it was easier to demonstrate improvements from a low knowledge base. The best improvements were in awareness of production methods and gender-role stereotyping, comprehension of the purpose of commercials, and reality/fantasy distinctions. Small-scale improvements were demonstrated on measures to do with TV violence and critical viewing skills, both of which may have been less successfully taught and which may have required greater teacher training in future studies (Singer & Singer, 1983).

There were few significant changes on the attitude measures but after the intervention there was a tendency to choose a less violent character as a favorite and to base this choice on attributes other than heroism. Third and fourth graders were more likely to choose a realistic rather than fantasy character as their favorite. Reasons for watching TV shifted from "exciting" to judgments like "fun" or "nothing else to do." Singer and Singer suggested that this may indicate less reliance on TV for heightened stimulation.

This type of intervention study, which requires considerable resources and extensive teacher cooperation, demonstrates that substantial knowledge gains, and some changes in social attitudes about TV programs and characters, are possible. The "Freestyle" project, in contrast, used TV to change beliefs and attitudes about a different social issue (i.e., sex role stereotypes). Both show that large interventions (e.g., one lesson a week for a term, supplemented by teacher mediating skills) can achieve measurable, positive improvements. In either case though it is not clear whether the cognitive and attitude changes in turn produced behavioral changes (e.g., more critical TV viewing, less stereotyped career choices).

Huesmann and his co-workers took a different approach in their intervention (see Huesmann & Eron, 1986). They considered it might be possible to change children's attitudes and beliefs about TV violence and thereby modify and attenuate the effects of viewing TV violence. In other words, assuming that there are TV effects, education about TV violence—how it is portrayed, its typically unrealistic nature and unsuitability for coping with many real life problems—should mitigate any social learning resulting from watching it. Their intervention is on a fairly small scale. Children (6- and 8-year-olds) were given six attitudinal questions to rate of a 5-point scale. These included, for example: "How much of what kids see on TV is fake?"; and "Are TV shows with a lot of hitting and shooting harmless for kids?" These sorts of questions are not particularly satisfactory because their wording could be taken as suggesting a particular response to a child. More generally, given the variety of form and content of television programs, simplistic questions about violence tend to elicit global responses, which seem unlikely to get at the details of a child's attitude. On the other hand it could be argued that children's attitudes are fairly unsophisticated anyway and that such measures are quite adequate for the task. However, since most intervention programs do not work with well-articulated models of children's attitudes, it is not possible to estimate accurately the adequacy of these measurement procedures.

Huesmann and colleagues aimed to teach the children in their intervention that watching television violence was undesirable and that such content should not be copied. In two training sessions the children wrote reports about negative aspects of TV violence and read them before a video camera. A comparison group went through the same procedure but their topic was their hobby, rather than TV violence. The results showed that attitudes about TV violence changed in the experimental group but not the comparison group. In the early school years, aggression increases with age (Eron 1980, 1982), and both the experimental and control group showed increased aggression after the intervention, but the increase for the experimental group was significantly less than that for the control group, which was near the population norm.

Although reducing aggression, the intervention did not reduce the children's frequency of violence viewing or perceptions of the realism of TV violence. The best predictor of aggression in the experimental group was a measure of identification with television characters. Stronger identification received more peer nominations of aggressiveness. A positive, but not significant correlation was also found in the comparison group: Violence viewing alone was the best predictor of peer nominations of aggression.

Why was violence viewing no longer a statistically significant predictor of aggression after the intervention? Huesmann et al. explained this by suggesting that change in attitude, as measured by the attitude questionnaire, is not the only cognitive change that reduces aggression. Children who identified least with TV characters also changed their attitudes more (presumably in a positive direction) and became less aggressive, relative to the control group, after intervention. Violence viewing did not change but became uncorrelated with aggression.

The success of the intervention was taken as further support for the Huesmann et al. hypothesis on the TV violence-viewer aggression relationship. However, it could be asked whether teaching about violence in society generally, as opposed to TV violence in particular, would have produced the same result? Finally, it should be noted that the intervention was conducted within the 3-year longitudinal study described earlier, and the children were seen on several occasions during which many measures were taken. Consequently, the effects may not be caused solely by the intervention component of their research program.

More recently, an intervention was conducted in the United Kingdom with the object of modifying 8- to 9-year-old children's comprehension and awareness of violence on TV (Sheppard, Sheehy, & Young, 1989). The intervention included TV show visits, witnessing two male actors demonstrate a fight sequence that was seen on video as well as live, watching educational films about the making of action movies, and discussions of violent TV excerpts. Results showed that even a short-duration intervention program can bring about substantial changes in children's comprehension and awareness of violence on television and in their daily lives.

Cognitive Effects

Effects of television at a cognitive level are those that are envisaged to influence and shape individuals' beliefs and opinions about the world around them. In this context, television is envisaged to represent one among a number of sources of information about the world that people take into account when developing their opinions and impressions of social reality. Although direct experience and second-hand interpersonal sources remain important, increasing amounts of information about conditions and events, near and far, are conveyed by the mass media.

In the more specific context of discussions about public perceptions of crime, the role of the media has achieved prominence. There has been an assumption that television in particular, with its apparently regular portrayal of crime and violence, can have a major impact on public beliefs and concerns about crime (Gerbner & Gross, 1976).

In the 1970s, a series of published studies, based on secondary analyses of national public opinion survey data in the United States, revealed that the amount of television that respondents reported watching was correlated with certain beliefs they had about the world in which they lived. Many of the beliefs examined in this research were related to the prevalence of crime and violence in society (Gerbner, 1972; Gerbner & Gross, 1976; Gerbner, Gross, Eleey, Jackson-Beeck, Jeffries-Fox, & Signorielli, 1977; Gerbner, Gross, Jackson-Beeck, Jeffries-Fox, & Signorielli, 1978; Gerbner, Gross, Signorielli, Morgan, & Jackson-Beeck, 1979; Gerbner, Gross, Morgan, & Signorielli, 1980b).

Content analysis studies reported that fictional drama programming on U.S. prime-time television was filled with scenes of crime and violence, and populated by characters who operated on both sides of the law, who often used violent means to get what they wanted. In their "cultivation hypothesis," Gerbner and Gross (1976) asserted that regular exposure to this overly violent and criminal-infested dramatic world conditioned in viewers an exaggerated impression of the extent of threat and danger in society and could produce excessive anxiety about personal safety.

The Gerbner group argued that viewers learn from stereotyped content patterns on television and draw inferences from them that they then generalize to the real world. Through their research technique called cultivation analysis, Gerbner and his colleagues found that people who watched a great deal of television tended to endorse different beliefs about the world from light viewers of television. Thus, heavy viewers were found to exhibit a measurable television "bias" in their perceptions of the occurrence of crime and violence in society and in their estimates of the number of people working in law enforcement. Heavy viewers exhibited higher estimates of likelihood of personal involvement in violence and great fear of being victims of crime.

This work has not received universal acceptance and has been challenged on a number of counts both within and outside the United States (Blank, 1977a, 1977b; Coffin & Tuchman, 1973; Wober & Gunter, 1988). Two important papers, one by Hughes (1980) and the other by Hirsch (1980), reanalyzed the databases used by Gerbner et al. in an effort to replicate Gerbner's original findings. Both researchers built in extensive methodological and statistical controls for extraneous variables on which information was available but was not taken into account by Gerbner. Both Hughes and Hirsch failed to replicate much of Gerbner's evidence for television cultivation effects.

The Hirsch rebuttal was itself challenged by Gerbner and his colleagues (Gerbner, Gross, Morgan, & Signorielli, 1981a, 1981b) and by researchers independent of the Gerbner group who questioned the validity of Hirsch's arguments based on "third variable controls and the nature of extreme groups of viewers" (Hawkins & Pingree, 1982).

Indeed Gerbner et al. (1980a), in response to both Hirsch and Hughes, reported that different kinds of relationships between television viewing and social beliefs exist within different demographic subgroups that run counter to one another. They thus cancel each other out when the demographic variable in question is statistically partialled out and this, consequently, severely weakens television cultivation effects in the population as a whole.

In a study with residents in Toronto, Canada, Doob and Macdonald (1979) attempted to replicate earlier American findings indicating that television causes people to overestimate the amount of danger that exists in their own neighborhoods, while controlling for a previously uncontrolled factor—the actual incidence of crime in the respondent's neighborhood.

Respondents in a door-to-door survey indicated their media usage and estimated the likelihood of their being victims of violence. Neighborhoods were chosen so as to include a high- and low-crime area in central Toronto and two similar areas in the suburbs of the city. When actual incidence of crime was controlled, no overall relationship emerged between television viewing and fear of being a victim of crime. Across the four areas of the city, those individuals who watched the most television or violent programming tended to be those who were most afraid. But within each area this relationship did not always hold. Although it was present within the high crime area of the city, it tended to disappear in the other areas.

Doob and Macdonald interpreted their data as evidence of the spuriousness of the relationship between television viewing and fear of crime in the real world. However, Gerbner, Gross, Morgan, and Signorielli (1980b) suggested instead that for those urban dwellers who live in high crime centers, television's violent imagery may be most congruent with their real-life perceptions. People who thus receive a "double dose" of messages that the world is violent, consequently show the strongest associations between viewing and fear.

Gerbner et al. analyzed the responses of a large national sample to five questions that were combined together to form a Perceptions-of-Danger index. They also made a distinction similar to that of Doob and MacDonald between residents living in low- and high-crime neighborhoods. It was found that a significant relationship between amount of television viewed and perceptions of danger emerged in the presence of controls for demographic factors for low-income and high-income residents of suburban areas, and also for low-income urban dwellers. No such relationship occurred for high-income urban dwellers. The strongest cultivation effects emerged for the low-income city residents, and this was interpreted as evidence for "resonance," whereby people who already lived in areas where crime levels were presumably high have their fears of falling victim to such crime enhanced by watching a great deal of (violent) television drama.

A challenge to the Gerbner work from further afield has underlined the overly simplistic way in which the nature of television viewing and of public perceptions on violence both as it is shown on television and as it occurs in real life are represented (Gunter, 1985; Wober & Gunter, 1988). In addition, there are important intervening variables related to the personality makeup of individuals that are not taken into account. As a result, this model of television effects comprises many problematic assumptions about causal relationships between what is shown on television and the formation of particular patterns of social perceptions, beliefs, and opinions among viewers about the world in which they live (Wober & Gunter, 1988).

One such assumption is that "messages" inferred from program content profiles concerning various social groups or behaviors are recognized and encoded by audiences, who assimilate them into their existing knowledge structures. It is also assumed that more frequent viewers will be more strongly influenced by television's messages than will less frequent viewers purely as a function of greater volume of exposure to them.

However, measures of the *amount* of viewing may not be valid and sufficient indicators of television effects, because television content and viewers' preferences for that content vary considerably, and two heavy viewers who watch totally different kinds of programs may hold two quite disparate sets of beliefs as a result.

Even though, according to descriptive content analysis, a program contains a good deal of violence, it may not necessarily be perceived as such by its viewers. Content counts can turn out to be poor indicators of audience perceptions (Ceulemans & Fauconnier, 1979; Perloff, Brown, & Miller, 1982). Thus, problems arise when generalizing from statements about or descriptions of television content and the symbolic messages carried by that content to how the content is perceived and understood by the audience. It is necessary to establish the degree of equivalence between the meanings attributed to programs by trained coders and the meaning attributed to them by ordinary viewers. This can be a difficult match to achieve.

In a study of intervening variable effects not included in any previous cultivation effects research, Wober and Gunter (1982) found that zero-order correlations between patterns of viewing television fiction or faction programming and perceptions of violence and crime in reality reduced to nonsignificance in the presence of statistical controls for respondents' scores on a locus control scale (Rotter, 1965). Later research (Gunter & Wober, 1983) revealed that perceptions of social reality were related more to viewing particular categories of programs than to total amount of viewing. This evidence was, in fact, constant with an alternative, "reverse" hypothesis, that viewers with particular beliefs about the world selectively choose to watch certain types of programs that provide reinforcement for their beliefs.

Levels of Judgment. Regardless of the direction of causality that may be inferred from correlational links between television viewing and perceptions of crime or violence, investigators have increasingly recognized that the strength of any such links can be powerfully mediated by a variety of other factors. One author has listed four main categories of intervening variables (Gunter, 1987).

First, relationships between levels of exposure to television and perceptions of crime may be program specific. In other words, any influence of television on beliefs about crime may depend not so much on the total amount of television viewed per se, but more significantly on how much informationally relevant programs (i.e., those with crime-related content) are watched (Weaver & Wakshlag, 1986).

Second, the influence of television may depend not simply on what is watched but on how viewers perceive and interpret the content of programs (Collins, 1973; Pingree, 1983; Teevan & Hartnagel, 1976). Even programs with crime or law enforcement themes may have little impact on beliefs about crime in real life if viewers are not prepared to recognize such programs as having a true reflection of everyday reality (Potter, 1986).

Third, judgments about crime can have different frames of reference. Tyler made a distinction between two kinds of judgments people make about crime (Tyler, 1980, 1984; Tyler & Cook, 1984). First, there are judgments at the societal level that refer to general beliefs about the frequency of crime in the community at large. Then there are personal judgments that refer to beliefs about personal vulnerability to crime and one's own estimated risk of being victimized. Tyler found that these two levels of judgment were not related to media experiences. Estimates of personal risk were primarily determined by direct, personal experience with crime (Tyler, 1980; Tyler & Cook, 1984).

Fourth, at either one of these two levels, the perceived likelihood of other- or self-involvement in crime or the concern about such involvement are situation-specific and may not be the same from one setting to the next. Tamborini, Zillmann, and Bryant (1984), for example, demonstrated that fear of crime is not an undimensional construct. As well as the personal level–societal level distinction, fear of crime in urban areas was found to differ from fear of crime in rural areas.

Emotional Effects

Television can produce both weak and pronounced emotional responses among viewers. These responses may be immediate reactions to the content of specific programs. In addition, longer term relationships have been observed between exposure to television violence over time and the cultivation of fearfulness of personal victimization.

Various researchers over the past 50 years have observed that mass media presentations can produce intense fright reactions in children (Blumer, 1933; Himmelweit, Oppenheim, & Vince, 1958; Preston, 1941; Schramm, Lyle, & Parker, 1961). Movies in the 1930s were thought by one writer to possess children emotionally causing them to lose control over their feelings (Blumer, 1933). Much later, Singer (1975) argued that frightening movies could cause children to have terrible nightmares for a long time after viewing, especially when they had been exposed to content beyond their comprehension.

Recently, a systematic series of studies has been conducted to explore relationships between different types of media materials and the fright responses of children (Cantor & Hoffner, 1987; Cantor & Reilly, 1982; Cantor & Sparks, 1984; Cantor, Wilson, & Hoffner, 1986; Sparks, 1986; Sparks & Cantor, 1986; Wilson, 1985). This research has examined age and developmental differences among children in their responses to frightening media depictions. This work has shown, for example, that very young children are frightened predominantly by characters and events that have an outwardly threatening appearance. As children mature they become more frightened by stimuli that represent realistic and even abstract threats that are independent of the visual grotesqueness of the depiction.

In spite of these developmental differences, children of all ages, as well as adults, have been shown to respond emotionally to violent depictions contained in media presentations. All of the experimental research that has been conducted on fright reactions to media stimuli appears to have involved depictions of violence, injury, or physical danger in one way or another.

Most of the research by Cantor and her colleagues has involved experiments. In the standard research design, children from various age groups are randomly allocated to receive different versions of a coping strategy (or no strategy in a control condition), and they then view a videotaped segment taken from a frightening television program or film. Some of the strategies are contained in a videotape that is viewed prior to watching the frightening program, whereas others involve verbal explanations or instructions provided by the experimenter.

The ages studied have generally been between 3 and 11 years. Thus, a number of important developmental stages are covered. In addition to age, however, the researchers have used tests of memory and comprehension to estimate the child's developmental level.

Four types of measure of emotional response have been used. The first consists of the child's own self-report of emotion obtained via open-ended and forced-choice questions. These are asked immediately after the program has been viewed. Their responses are coded in terms of hedonic tone and mention of specific fear-related words. Following the open-ended question, the children are generally asked how scared they felt and provided with four response options from "not at all scared" to "very, very scared." Other supplementary measures of emotion are facial response as coded from a video-recording of the child's responses while watching. A second supplementary measure is physiological arousal as obtained via small sensors attached to the child's fingers. Some studies have also used behavioral measures of fear. For example, Wilson and Cantor (1987) asked children whether they wanted to see a live snake after viewing the snake pit scene form *Raiders of the Lost Ark.*

Strategies for coping with fear have included noncognitive and cognitive strategies. These strategies broadly differ in terms of the degree to which they require the child to think about or process information about frightening media events.

One noncognitive technique is desensitization. This involves some form of gradual, repeated exposure to a frightening stimulus in a nonthreatening context. This technique has been found to work in a number of studies (e.g., Wilson, 1987; Wilson & Cantor, 1987). In one study by Cantor, Sparks, and Hoffner (1988), the desensitization technique was used to reduce children's fear reactions to the action-adventure series, "The Incredible Hulk." Previous research (Cantor & Sparks, 1984; Sparks & Cantor, 1986) had established that many children were scared by this program, in which a mild-mannered scientist could become transformed into a monstrous 8-feet tall green-skinned creature driven by rage, with superhuman powers.

Reasoning that the fearfulness of children may have been a response to the appearance of the Hulk, a videotape was prepared that went behind the scenes and looked at the way the actor who played the Hulk character was made up. This sequence explained that a great deal of makeup was applied to transform the actor into the monster and revealed the fantasy nature of the show to the children.

It was later found that children who had seen this clip exhibited far less fear while watching the show than did children who had not seen it. Thus, explanation together with gradual, nonthreatening exposure to a fear-arousing media stimulus can alleviate children's fright reactions.

Cognitive strategies require children to think about the fear stimulus. Generally, some type of information is given to the child in order to evoke a change in the interpretation or mental conception of the stimulus. One common variation of this technique is to explain to the child that the mass media character or event is not real. Cantor and Wilson (1984) examined the effectiveness of this technique. Before showing children aged 3–5 years and 9–11 years a scene from the musical fantasy *The Wizard of Oz*, they gave the youngsters different instructional sets. In an unreality condition, children were told to remember that the program was "just a story," that the story was "make believe," and that the witch who appeared in the scene was "just a regular person dressed in a costume." In a control condition, children were given no explanation.

Results indicated that for the older children, the unreality instructions ιᴄᴜᴜced fear reactions while they were viewing the movie scene. In contrast, this instructional set had no appreciable effect on the emotional responses of the younger children. The observed developmental difference in effectiveness was consistent with earlier results on children's perceptions of fear-reducing strategies (Wilson, Hoffner, & Cantor, 1987).

Cognitive strategies that involve supplying children with information about a program generally seem to work better with older children. The reason for this seems to derive from the cognitive demands associated with these techniques. In order to benefit from an informational strategy, the child must encode and comprehend the information being presented. In addition, if the information is provided prior to exposure, the child must store the information in memory so that it can be retrieved during subsequent encounters with the frightening stimulus. Finally, if the information is provided either prior to or during exposure, the child must apply the information while simultaneously attending to the program. Research indicates that younger children have difficulty with any or all of these tasks.

MEASURING VIOLENCE ON TELEVISION

How much violence is usually portrayed on television? Critics often accuse the medium of being too violent. But is there evidence to support this accusation? How to define and measure television violence is a problem that has troubled social scientists for many years.

Most people would probably agree that there is some violence on television, but determining how much violence there is in an objective, systematic fashion presents a real problem. Most researchers choose to use a descriptive content analysis technique in which clearly defined occurrences of violence can be objectively quantified and catalogued. Following this approach, it is the researchers themselves, therefore, who provide the definitional framework that serves as a measuring instrument, which special coders are trained to use in a reliable way. The coders are taught to identify particular phenomena on screen and to record each of the occurrences in an objective fashion without placing any personal value judgments on what is seen.

The study of violence through content analysis may include an examination of many different aspects of its occurrence. For example, coders may not simply count violent incidents, but they might also provide a classification of them in terms of the types of programs in which the violence occurs, the types of characters involved, whether any weapons or special instruments of aggression were used, and the type of observable damage or harm (i.e., to property or people) caused by the violence.

This technique has been used to assess levels of violence on television since the early 1950s. The first quantitative assessments of television violence were carried out in the United States. From the start, crime and violence were found to be prominent features of television prime-time outputs (Schramm, Lyle, & Parker, 1961; Smythe, 1956).

Most early studies of the portrayal of crime and violence on television examined broadcast output at only one point in time. Because the methods used in different investigations often varied, meaningful comparisons between them or trend analyses over time were made very difficult. One attempt to assess violence in television over a long period was made by Clark and Blankenberg (1972). Their analysis ran from 1953 to 1969. However, they used *TV Guide* program synopses rather than samples of actual television output as their source material. This research therefore permitted only very generalized assessments of violence that may have given only a very broad reflection of actual levels of violence on screen. From brief program synopses alone, Clark and Blankenberg found a cyclical pattern to television violence that exhibited several peaks and troughs during the period under analysis.

Perhaps the most extensive analysis of television violence has been carried out by Gerbner and his colleagues at the Annenberg School of Communications, University of Pennsylvania. Using a technique called message system analysis, these investigators have monitored samples of prime-time and weekend daytime television put out for all major U.S. networks every year since 1967. This analysis has come to be regarded by some as the definitive measure of the nature and extent of violence on network television.

The content analysis component of this project involves the monitoring of samples of prime-time and weekend daytime television for all major U.S. networks each year. Analysis is limited to dramatic content, which means that news, documentaries, variety and quiz shows, and sports programs are excluded during coding. A simple, normative definition of violence is employed: "the overt expression of physical force against self or other compelling action against one's will on pain of being hurt or killed or actually hurting or killing" (Gerbner, 1972). This definition is used by trained monitors to record the frequency and nature of violent acts, the perpetrators and victims of violence, and the temporal and spatial settings in which the acts occur. From certain combinations of these measures is derived the "Violence Profile," which purports to represent an objective and meaningful indicator of the amount of violence portrayed in television drama.

The overall picture of the world of television drama revealed by message system analysis is that it is a violent one. For example, Gerbner, Gross, Signorielli, Morgan, and Jackson-Beeck (1979) reported that since monitoring first began in 1967-68, an average of 80% of programs contained violence and 60% of major characters were involved in violence. The average rate of violent episodes was 7.5 per hour, and in weekend, daytime children's programs, violent episodes averaged almost 18 per hour. Indeed, programs directed at children typically score high on most measures of violence except for killing; cartoons, in particular, consistently exceeded all other categories of programs, including adult adventure action and crime-detective shows.

Similar content analysis studies conducted in the United Kingdom have revealed generally smaller volumes of violence on British television (BBC, 1972; Halloran & Croll, 1972). The Halloran and Croll study based its coding scheme for television violence on that used by Gerbner, whereas the BBC study used an extended conceptual framework, with a broader definition of violence and broader spectrum of program types. More recently, a further BBC-funded study has provided an update on the rate at which violence is portrayed on British television (Cumberbatch, Jones, & Lee, 1988).

Interpreting Content Profiles

The portrayal of violence by some individuals and of the propensity of others to fall victim to it was conceived by Gerbner to be a symbolic demonstration of a power relationship between television characters that could be learned by viewers and generalized by them to perceptions of social reality. Thus, through identifying with victims of violence, viewers might develop beliefs about the actual chances of their own involvement in crime.

According to Gerbner et al. (1978), identification of the complex symbolisms and arrays of social and cultural messages conveyed by television programs is essential to any proper measurement of an understanding of the medium's influences on viewers. We need to know what television might be communicating to its audience. In this regard, assessment through descriptive content analysis is an important area of investigation.

The Gerbner group's measures of violence on TV have been challenged on methodological grounds for the representativeness of the program samples as well as for the way different factors are added together to form a single index (Blank, 1977a, 1977b; Coffin & Tuchman, 1973).

There is a more fundamental conceptual problem though. Researchers who use content analysis often go beyond the simple provision of descriptions of what happens on screen to make inferences about the meanings conveyed to the audience by various patterns of television portrayals. The underlying assumption here is that patterns of portrayed events, institutions or social groups may carry the same meanings for audience members as those inferred from this analysis by researchers. Such meanings as are "read" into programs by researchers, however, may not invariably be comprehended by viewers.

Content analysis may be designed to reflect "what large communities absorb over long periods of time" (Signorielli, 1985, p. 241), but whether or not audiences actually perceive and encode such meanings themselves is a quite separate empirical question with which content analysis alone is not equipped to deal (Gunter, 1988; Gunter & Wober, 1988).

Traditionally, descriptive content analysis does not apply different weights to violent incidents, even though violence may be differentially classified in terms of the nature of the incidents, the characters involved, and the type of program or setting in which they occur. All incidents are assumed to have equal intensity despite these varying features. Thus, cartoon violence is treated in the same vein as violence portrayed in contemporary dramatic fiction. This, however, is not how audience members would perceive television violence. Viewers bring a different perspective with them to the television screen and would generally not agree with researchers' a priori assumption about the relative seriousness of different forms of portrayed violence. This fact brings into question the ecological validity of measures of television violence based purely on descriptive techniques.

MEASURING PERCEPTIONS OF TELEVISION VIOLENCE

An alternative approach to classifying television violence is to find out from viewers themselves what they perceive or define as violence. This perspective does not treat violence as a single unitary entity. In other words, it accepts that violence can come in many different forms and with different outcomes. It takes into account what the audience thinks about television violence. It also examines the extent and ways in which viewers agree or disagree about television violence. Some viewers see more violence than others do in programs and react more strongly to particular portrayals of television violence. Audience reactions are connected to the psychological characteristics of viewers and it is important to know if there are particular kinds of viewers who are likely to be especially upset or disturbed by certain forms of violence on television.

Two basic methods have been adopted. One method is to obtain ratings and opinions from viewers about which programs are violent and how seriously so. This can be done by asking individuals to indicate from a list of program titles which ones are violent and which are not (Himmelweit, Swift, & Biberian, 1978; Howitt & Cumberbatch, 1974). One problem with this kind of measure is that it cannot indicate how much violence there is in specific episodes. Are respondents basing their opinions on one particular episode, several episodes, or the whole series?

Adults' Perceptions

Subjective ratings of television violence can also be made for actual program materials. Viewers can be invited to make personal judgments about the violence contained in program excerpts or in entire episodes. This technique allows the researcher to investigate the degree of variation in viewers' opinions about television violence and the specific ingredients of violent portrayals that affect those judgements (Gunter, 1985; Gunter & Furnham, 1982; Van der Voort, 1986).

The ways in which viewers perceive and evaluate characters and events on television do not always match descriptive incident counts or the meanings inferred from them by researchers. Consequently, in order to properly understand the extent to which television content shapes public perceptions of social reality, it may be essential to include some measurement of the meaning of that content for audience members, the extent to which they place their own interpretations on television portrayals, and the significance of such interpretations as mediators of television's impact upon them.

Research has shown that structures such as those monitored in message system analysis are not always perceived by ordinary viewers as salient attributes of programs. For example, a content analysis of British television output, using a fixed definition of violence, showed that the rate of violent incidents per hour was four times as great for cartoon shows as for any other type of program (Halloran & Croll, 1972), whereas a study of the audience's perceptions of television violence indicated that cartoons were not rated as particularly violent (Howitt & Cumberbatch, 1974). Even in films with human characters, violent scenes may not appear as important aspects of content and, unless specifically asked, viewers may often fail to mention violence in follow-up discussions about films containing violent action (BBC, 1972).

More recent research has revealed that adults and children alike are capable of highly refined judgments about television violence. Viewers have their own scales for deciding the seriousness of incidents, and their opinions do not always agree with researchers' categorizations of violence (Gunter, 1985; Van der Voort, 1986). Instead of deciding in advance what violence consists of, these researchers allowed viewers to decide for themselves about the seriousness of violence contained in different television portrayals.

Gunter (1985) reported twelve studies in which groups of people were shown scenes taken from British crime series, American crime series, westerns, science fiction series, and cartoons. Viewers were invited to make a variety of personal judgments about each scene along a set of qualitative rating scales. Scenes were shown singly or in pairs for comparative judgment, in a small lecture theatre. Variations in perceptions of the scenes were related significantly to a number of factors: the types of programs the scenes came from, the types of weapons or instruments of violence used, the physical setting of the action, and the degree of observable harm the violence caused to victims in each scene. The results indicated that viewers may be significantly influenced in their opinions about television violence by many different attributes of portrayals.

A subsequent compilation of public opinion surveys in the United Kingdom concerned with viewers' impressions of television violence extended the above research (Gunter & Wober, 1988). Utilizing a national television viewing panel, these surveys probed viewers' general opinions about violence on television as well as their perceptions of the violence contained in specific programs they had watched. Opinions were found to vary quite a lot, depending on the types of questions being asked and with the types of programs being asked about.

Perhaps the most significant finding was the contrast between general and program-specific opinions. When taking a reflective look over television in general, U.K. viewers were more likely to perceive potential harm than benefit in television violence. Extra special concern was reserved for the impact that televised violence might have on children, and there was widespread public feeling that parents should take greater care and control over what their children watch. Adult viewers felt, for instance, that the reality–fantasy distinction was very important, but that children when very young were not able to make this crucial distinction.

Turning to specific programs, however, and in particular a collection of U.S.-produced and U.K.-produced action–adventure and police-drama series, viewers' opinions mellowed. With respect to programs that they themselves watched and enjoyed, the great majority of viewers could perceive no harm either to themselves or their children. Although involvement in the drama and perceived credibility of characters and storylines varied across different TV series, by and large viewers regarded these programs essentially either as nonviolent in any realistic sense, or if violent at all, not generally in any gratuitous fashion.

Children's Perceptions

Van de Voort (1986) conducted a study of children's perceptions of television violence at three schools in Holland. In all, 314 children were shown full-length episodes of eight television scenes. The episodes varied from realistic crime drama ("Starsky and Hutch" and "Charlie's Angels") to adventure series ("Dick Turpin," and "The Incredible Hulk") and fantasy cartoons ("Scooby Doo," "Tom and Jerry," "Popeye," and "Pink Panther"). Immediately after showing each program, a postexposure questionnaire was filled in measuring ten perception variables: (1) readiness to see violence, (2) approval of violence seen in program, (3) enjoyment of the violence seen, (4) evaluation of the program, (5) emotional responsiveness, (6) absorbtion in the program, (7) detachment while watching, (8) identification with the chief characters, (9) perceived reality of the program, and (10) comprehension and retention of program content.

Van der Voort found that children's perceptions of violence were related to program genre in the same way that Gunter had reported earlier for adults. He made the additional important point, however, that "children's violence ratings do differ from those of content analysts who analyze the amount of violence a program contains by means of the systematic observation of programs recorded on videotape. Programs that are extremely violent according to "objective" content analysis can be seen by children as hardly containing any violence. Thus, although content analyses have identified cartoons as being among the most violent of television programs in terms of numbers of objectively identified incidents per hour or per show (Gerbner, 1972; Gerbner & Gross, 1976), such programs tend to be seen by children as containing hardly any violence at all.

On the basis of the above findings both with adults and children, it is clear that viewers classify program content differently from the descriptive analysis of research frameworks that employ narrow definitions of violence. Although objective cataloguing of incidents in programs has the useful function of providing reliable counts of how often certain categories of items occur, the relevance or meaning of those items for the audience can be properly ascertained only through the perceptions of viewers themselves. There would be some merit in recommending a subjective approach rather than a purely objective one in the analysis at least of televised violence, because those perspectives enable one to identify the programs that viewers themselves take most seriously. A subjective approach can outline ways in which differential weights of seriousness can be applied to programs. This lends usually to the classification of programs that are perceived as most true to life as also being the most serious in the violence they depict.

ATTRACTION TO VIOLENCE ON TELEVISION

Both historically and contemporarily, no broadcast subject has undergone such close public scrutiny and debate or has been the center of as much social scientific research as the portrayal of violence on television. Most often public anxieties have focused on the possible link between watching televised violence and subsequent aggressive or hostile reactions of viewers. A vast literature exists on this topic, and the majority opinion is that screen violence can and does have an impact on levels of real-life violence and interpersonal aggression (Comstock, 1985).

For all the weight of research evidence in support of the harmful effects of television violence, however, violent material is popular with television audiences. This was observed by the Surgeon General's Scientific Advisory Committee on Television and Social Behavior in 1972 and is evidenced by the high viewing figures obtained by many programs portraying violence. Although the latter evidence can be explained in other ways, for instance, violent programs often fill popular schedule slots, where they are virtually guaranteed large audiences, there is nonetheless an almost implicit belief on the part of broadcast schedulers that violence-packed action programming is the kind of fare that mass audiences want to watch. Do such programs attract audiences to them? Is there a link between violent content and entertainment value?

Some observers have noted an advantage of violent content over nonviolent content in the entertainment stakes because violence involves conflict of various kinds, which is an important ingredient of high entertainment value (Berlyne, 1960; Eisenstein, 1949). This observation must color any decisions that are to be taken regarding the amount of violence that is shown on television. If television violence does have harmful effects, it should indeed be strictly controlled. But this may result in taking off the air some of the viewers' favorite programs. One could argue that the supposed harmful effects of television as a whole ought perhaps to be weighed against the important need of the viewer to be entertained when formulating program and schedule policies about the broadcasting of popular adventure-action shows.

Some consideration ought to be given, however, to the empirical question of whether or not violence is indeed entertaining. There has been little research directly testing the link between the violent ingredients of programs and how much they are liked. There is a body of theory and research that bears on this matter indirectly, and recently, a small number of studies have been carried out that have attempted to address the matter in a more direct fashion.

TV Violence and Program Appreciation: Indirect Evidence

Albert Bandura, a leading protagonist of the view that television violence is potentially harmful because it provides models of aggressive behavior that can be copied by viewers, especially children, has suggested that viewing violent program content should not be a pleasurable experience because in our society individuals are usually taught from an early age to suppress their aggressive tendencies. Consequently, any enjoyment derived from watching acts of aggression should give rise to unpleasant, socialized feelings of guilt (Bandura & Walters, 1963). Supporters of the catharsis viewpoint, on the other hand, would suggest that viewing portrayals of violence should be found pleasurable because it provides outlets for the discharge of aggressive energy. Any such discharge typically produces feelings of tension reduction and, thus, satisfaction.

Seymour Feshbach first reported in 1955 that aroused aggressive impulses could be reduced by means of fantasy expression. His participants purged their aggressive feelings towards an annoying experimenter in stories that they wrote about a series of Thematic Appreciation Test pictures; but some 6 years later, the same author showed that they could just as effectively be reduced via the ready-made fantasies provided by filmed representations of violence (Feshbach, 1961).

Following this and further experimental research, however, it became clear that whether or not a viewer is annoyed by the aggressive display concomitantly with the supposed discharge of hostility that it facilitates, can depend very much on mood and experience immediately prior to and during the viewing situation. For instance, Feshbach, Stiles, and Bitter (1967) found that witnessing aggression was pleasurable only if the viewer had just been insulted (and presumably angered); otherwise it was not enjoyed. It is difficult to see how this finding can prove useful when we generalize to the naturalistic viewing situation, because most of us presumably are not angered or intimidated before viewing television.

TV Violence and Program Appreciation: Direct Evidence

The above evidence provides only an indirect indication that television violence is related to program appeal. Is there more direct evidence that such a link exists? A number of studies designed principally to investigate the relationship between television violence and aggressive behavior have indicated that young viewers who are more aggressive in character either watched, said they preferred, or tuned in over a period of time to watch more violence-containing programs (Atkin et al., 1979; Belson, 1978; Friedman & Johnson, 1972; Robinson & Bachman, 1972). Some of these authors have interpreted their results as demonstrating a connection between viewing violence and subsequently behaving more aggressively. Others have argued that it has been aggressive people who have chosen to view violence-containing material (Fenigstein, 1979; Gunter, 1983). Only a handful of studies have dealt with whether the violent aspects of action-adventure series have a significant role in the attraction of their audiences.

One study that has attracted attention among theorists supporting the view that audiences may be drawn to watch programs that contain violence was reported by Boyanowsky, Newtson, and Walster (1974). Following a murder on a university campus, it was observed that students had been more numerous in the audience of a film containing violence than for a less violent film showing at the same time. At this stage it was not possible to interpret this behavior as seeking out violence under conditions of recent anxiety, or seeking out retribution, which the more violent film had shown was the fate of the perpetrator.

Boyanowsky et al. observed that threatened individuals exhibited a distinct preference for viewing potentially fear-inducing events under safe conditions. After a much publicized brutal murder of a first-year, female undergraduate at the University of Wisconsin, attendance at a movie shown locally that featured psychopathic killings (*In Cold Blood*) greatly increased relative to another comparison movie. Girls who had shared a dormitory with the murder victim showed greater preference subsequent to the murder for the murder movie than for a nonviolent romantic film, whereas girls from another dormitory, who were presumably less directly affected by the murder, showed no such preference.

Subsequently, using controlled field experimental conditions, Boyanowsky (1977) reinforced his earlier results and found that threatening conditions, which ostensibly evoke fear or apprehension, enhanced preferences for exciting media content, including some that depicted violence.

According to Zillmann and Wakshlag (1985), one explanation for these results is that females who are anxious about a rapist on the loose locally may enjoy watching a movie featuring violence between men, because it shows some men being victimized. An anxious female may be attracted to sexual themes because a man in the process of making love is rendered "innocuous." However, in the final event, Zillmann and Wakshlag admitted that the findings are difficult to explain.

In the United States, Diener and his colleagues conducted a series of studies that examined, in a more direct fashion, relationships between levels of violent content in programs and how much the programs were liked by viewers. In their first study, Diener and DeFour (1978) looked at 71 episodes from 12 adventure shows and coded them for frequency of occurrence of such events as suspense, emotion, sex, humor, action, and violence over a period of some 3½ months. Most of the shows were "prime-time" broadcasts. The coded items were grouped into four major categories: (a) verbal and physical aggression; (b) drama (suspense, emotion, and romance subcategories combined); (c) action; and (d) humor. After each show the coders rated the episodes on 14 subjective bipolar scales, such as exciting–unexciting and violent–nonviolent. The A. C. Nielsen popularity index was obtained for each week's programs – giving a measure of the percentage of total television-owning households in the United States that was tuned in to the programs. The mean aggression score for the 71 episodes was 30.2 (out of 100), with the most aggressive program rated 92.6 and the least aggressive program rated 4.2. The episodes' scores on the four major categories of content were related to program popularity and were used to predict the Nielsen rating for the show on the following week.

It was found that *none* of these variables served as reliable predictors of a program's popularity. Furthermore, when subjective ratings for each episode on the psychological rating scales were analyzed, it was found that they loaded highly on three principal components, each of which was quite independent of the other: (a) emotional involvement (including ratings of believability, suspense, excitement, drama, entertainment value, and overall liking); (b) violence/action; and (c) nonhumorous. The independence of these measures suggested that subjective liking and ratings of entertainment value were unrelated to the amount of violence in a program.

In a second study, Diener and DeFour (1978) presented 100 male and female college students with two versions of an episode of "Police Woman." One version was uncut, whereas the other consisted of the same episode minus almost all violent scenes. The uncut version was 47 minutes long and scored 40 when coded for violence; the cut version was 44 minutes long and scored only 9 for violent content.

It was found that, generally speaking, the violent version was perceived as being more violent than the nonviolent version, and that it was liked more too, although the difference in liking was nonsignificant. Among the students who saw the violent version, however, those who perceived it as more violent liked it less. Diener and DeFour took this evidence as an indication that violent content may have little impact on the liking of a program. This is a questionable inference though, because their findings are really too weak and lack the internal consistency to show whether violence is related to the degree of like or dislike for a program.

In a later experiment with 62 families in their own homes, in which complete programs from situation comedy and crime-detective series were rated on dimensions such as action, realism, violence, and liking, Diener and Woody (1981) found that higher violence content did not make for greater liking—to a small, nonsignificant extent the reverse was true. Viewers in general, however, did rate high-violence shows as significantly more violent than low-violence shows, whereas other ratings such as action, realism, humor, and romance proved to be poor discriminators.

Although Diener and Woody employed more adequate controls over extraneous variables than the earlier work of Diener and DeFour, even here there was a tendency to treat violence in gross terms only. No attempt was made in any of these studies to examine the possible effects of different kinds of violence portrayals on viewers' evaluations of programs.

WHAT NEXT?

Concerns with the presentation of violent material in the media have characterized the history of the major mass media and their development. As the most salient mass medium, television has attracted by far the most attention and has, in consequence, been the focus of most empirical research. Although accusations have been leveled against television in respect to the amount of violence it contains, ultimately public concern has rested on the effects, mostly of an adverse kind, that television violence may have on the attitudes or social behavior of its regular viewers.

Over the years, a vast body of published research has accumulated documenting empirical studies of the influence of televised violence. As we have seen, however, this substantial number of investigations can be reduced in terms of either methodology or hypothesized effects (or mechanism of effect) to a manageable number of types. Turning to the methodologies in particular, it is clear that question marks can be raised about the accuracy and reliability of the data produced by any of the most commonly applied research procedures. These shortcomings need always to be borne in mind when interpreting the vast body of research data on the subject of the effects of television violence.

This chapter has also differentiated the research according to the psychological nature of the effects being examined. Television has been hypothesized to influence its audiences at a number of levels, principally, cognitive, affective (or emotional), and behavioral. These effects have tended to be investigated quite separately. This pattern has probably been shaped to a great extent by the particular specialties and interests of the researchers concerned. Either the focus of study has been the cognitive effects of media messages, or their effects on usually short-term emotional responses or their short- and long-term behavioral effects. Yet, it is entirely reasonable to assume, and indeed highly probable, that the same media message may have an influence at more than one level. Furthermore, audience responses at these different psychological levels could even be interdependent.

It has been fairly clearly established that audience reactions to television and film content are often mediated by intervening factors. The latter factors may be behavioral, relating to the amount of exposure to a media item, or cognitive, comprising some sort of judgmental response in which the media content is classified in some way by its audience or compared with information from another source. The way in which audiences weigh up media content has a crucial part to play in their subsequent response to it. Thus, television violence that occurs in a fantasy setting will be perceived differently from that that occurs in a contemporary drama setting much closer to real life. This kind of perception will influence the nature of any further cognitive response (shift in belief or knowledge), affective response (fright reaction), or behavioral response (increased aggressiveness).

It could also be the case, however, that the emotional or behavioral responses will also be contingent, at least in part, on the cognitive response. For instance, viewers who watch a great deal of television violence, it could be argued, may become more aware of violence in real life or believe that real-life violence is more commonplace than it really is. In consequence, they also develop a greater fear of falling victim to violence. As a final step in the chain, they also become more security conscious, installing more locks on windows and doors at home, carrying less money around with them, never going out alone, and enrolling in self-defense classes to learn to defend themselves more effectively in the event of an attack. Although some researchers (such as the Gerbner group) have hypothesized and empirically investigated the strength of relationships between reported television viewing and each of these types of response, we need to know more about how these qualitatively different reactions may cluster or occur together and form constellations of psychological responses to media violence.

Although most of this chapter has been devoted to research about television violence, violence can occur in other media—movies, the press, and even on radio. Most individuals in civilized societies today are exposed to information content through a variety of media. Different media are used for particular reasons and in certain characteristic ways, and their contents are perceived differently too. A more comprehensive conceptual model of media effects should be able to take into account the relative influences of different media sources.

The use of media does not occur in a vacuum. Media-related behaviors occur alongside other activities that occupy our time each day. We also have access to other sources of information about the world comprising direct experience and interpersonal experience through conversations and interactions with other people. The role of these social forces in the cultivation of norms and values that govern how we think, feel, and behave cannot and should not be ignored. Understanding the influence of the media on social attitudes and behavior cannot therefore be divorced from the broader social context in which individuals are brought up.

An interesting new approach to the assessment of television violence was employed by Lynn, Hampson, and Agahi (1989). A study of sibling pairs was run to obtain data on the relationship between personal aggression, the viewing and enjoyment of television violence, and the personality traits of extraversion, neuroticism, and psychoticism. This research was designed to test a possible genotype-environment theory explanation of the development of aggression in children. This theory examines the extent to which parents transmit their characteristics to their children by both genetic and environmental mechanisms.

The results of this study failed to support the theory of a causal effect of the amount of viewing of TV violence on aggression. The correlations between siblings for aggression were very low, indicating an absence of shared family environmental effects including the amount of viewing of TV violence; and there were no within-family correlations between the amount of viewing of television violence and aggression, suggesting the absence of a causal relationship. The personality measure of psychoticism was, however, significantly correlated for individuals with their reported amount of TV violence viewing and also to their claimed enjoyment of television violence. Lynn et al. proposed a genotype-environment correlation and interaction theory to explain the results whereby genotypic differences in psychoticism could be posited to generate differences in aggression and the enjoyment of television violence, which could augment aggression.

REFERENCES

Atkin, C., Greenberg, B., Korzenny, F., & McDermott, S. (1979). Selective exposure to television violence. *Journal of Broadcasting, 23,* 5–13.

Bandura, A. (1968). What TV Violence Can Do to Your Child. In Otto N. Larsen (Ed.), *Violence and the mass media* (pp. 123–139). New York: Harper & Row.

Bandura, A. (1978). A social learning theory of aggression. *Journal of Communication, 28*(3), 12–29.

Bandura, A. (1979). Psychological mechanisms of aggression. In M. von Cranach, K. Foppa, W. Lepenies, & D. Ploog (Eds.), *Human ethology: Claims and limits of a new discipline* (pp. 316–356) Cambridge, MA: Cambridge University Press.

Bandura, A., (1982). Self-efficacy mechanism in human agency. *American Psychologist, 37*(2), 122–147.

Bandura, A., (1985). *Social foundations of thought and action,* Englewood Cliffs, NJ: Prentice-Hall.

Bandura, A., Ross, D., & Ross, S. A. (1963a). Imitation of film-mediated aggressive models. *Journal of Abnormal and Social Psychology, 66*(1), 3–11.

Bandura, A., Ross, D., and Ross, S. A. (1963b). Vicarious reinforcement and imitative learning. *Journal of Abnormal and Social Psychology, 67*(6), 601–607.

Bandura, A., Underwood, W., Fromson, M. E. (1975). Disinhibition of aggression through diffusion of responsibility and dehumanization of victims. *Journal of Research in Personality, 9,* 253–269.

Bandura, A., & Walters, R. H. (1963). *Social learning and personality development.* New York: Holt, Rinehart & Winston.

Belson, W. (1978). *Television violence and the adolescent boy.* Hampshire, England: Saxon House.

Berkowitz, L. (1962). Violence in the mass media. In L. Berkowitz (Ed.), *Aggression: A social psychological analysis* (pp. 229–255). New York: McGraw Hill.

Berkowitz, L. (1964). The effects of observing violence. *Scientific American, 210*(2), 35–41.

Berkowitz, L. (1965). Some aspects of observed aggression. *Journal of Personality and Social Psychology, 2*(3), 359–369.

Berkowitz, L. (1974). Some determinants of impulsive aggression: The role of mediated associations with reinforcements for aggression. *Psychological Review, 81*(2), 165–176.

Berkowitz, L. (1984). Some effects of thoughts on anti- and prosocial influences of media events: A cognitive neoassociation analysis. *Psychological Bulletin, 95*(3), 410–417.

Berkowitz, L., & Alioto, J. T. (1973). The meaning of an observed event as a determinant of its aggressive consequences. *Journal of Personality and Social Psychology, 28*(2), 206–217.

Berkowitz, L., Corwin, R., & Heironimous, M. (1963). Film violence and subsequent aggressive tendencies. *Public Opinion Quarterly, 27*(2), 217–229.

Berkowitz, L., & Geen, R. G. (1966). Film Violence and the cue properties of available targets. *Journal of Personality and Social Psychology, 3*(5), 525–530.

Berkowitz, L., & Rawlings, E. (1963). Effects of film violence on inhibitions against subsequent aggression. *Journal of Abnormal and Social Psychology, 66*(3), 405–412.

Berkowitz, L., Parke, R. D., Leyens, J.-P., & West, S. G. (1964). Reactions of juvenile delinquents to "justified" and "less justified" movie violence. *Journal of Research in Crime and Delinquency, 11*(1), 16–24.

Berlyne, D. E. (1960). *Conflict, arousal and curiosity.* New York: McGraw-Hill.

Biblow, F. (1973). Imaginative play and the world of aggressive behaviour. In J. L. Ian (Ed.), *The child's world of make-believe. Experimental studies of imagination play* (pp. 104–128). New York: Academic Press.

Blank, D. A. (1977a). Final comments on the violence profile. *Journal of Broadcasting, 21,* 287–296.

Blank, D. M. (1977b). The Gerbner violence profile. *Journal of Broadcasting, 21,* 273–279.

Blumer, H., & Hauser, P. M. (1933). *Movies, delinquency and crime.* New York: Macmillan.

Boyanowsky, E. O. (1977). Film preferences under conditions of threat, whetting the appetite for violence, information or excitement? *Communication Research, 4,* 33–45.

Boyanowsky, E. O., Newtson, D., & Walster, E. (1976). Film preferences following a murder. *Communication Research, 1,* 32–33.

British Broadcasting Corporation. (1972). *Violence on television: Programme content and viewer perceptions.* London: Author.

Cantor, J., & Hoffner, C. (1987 April). *Children's fear reactions to a televised film as a function of perceived immediacy of depicted threat.* Paper presented at the Convention of the Society for Research in Child Development, Baltimore.

Cantor, J., & Reilly, S. (1982). Adolescents' fright reactions to television and films. *Journal of Communication, 32*(1), 87–99.

Cantor, J., & Sparks, G. G. (1984). Children's fear responses to mass media: Testing some Piagetian predictions. *Journal of Communication, 34*(2), 90–103.

Cantor, J., Sparks, G. G., & Hoffner, C. (1988). Calming children's television fears: Mr. Rogers vs. The Incredible Hulk. *Journal of Broadcasting & Electronic Media, 32,* 271–288.

Cantor, J., & Wilson, B. J. (1984). Modifying fear responses to mass media in preschool and elementary school children. *Journal of Broadcasting, 28,* 431–443.

Cantor, J., Wilson, B. J., & Hoffner, C. (1986). Emotional responses to a televised nuclear holocaust film. *Communication Research, 13,* 257–277.

Centerwall, B. S. (1989). Exposure to television as a cause of violence. *Public Communication and Behaviour, 2,* 1–58.

Ceulemans, M., & Fauconnier, G. (1979). *Mass media: The image, role and social conditions of women* (Report No. 84). Paris, France: UNESCO.

Clark, D. G., & Blankenberg, W. B. (1972). Trends in violent content in selected mass media. In G. Comstock & E. Rubinstein (Eds.), *Television and social behaviour: Vol. 1. Media content and control* (pp. 188–243). Washington, DC: U.S. Government Printing Office.

Cline, V. B., Croft, R. G., & Courrier, S. (1973). Desensitization of children to television violence. *Journal of Personality and Social Psychology, 27*(3), 260–365.

Coffin, T. E., & Tuchman, S. (1973). Rating television programmes for violence: A comparison of five surveys. *Journal of Broadcasting, 17,* 3–22.

Collins, W. A. (1973). Effect of temporal separation between motivation, aggression and consequences: A developmental study. *Developmental Psychology, 8,* 215–221.

Comstock, G. (1985). Television and film violence. In S. J. Apter & A. P. Goldstein (Eds.), *Youth violence: Programs and prospects.* New York: Pergamon Press.

Cumberbatch, G., Jones, I., & Lee, M. (1988). Measuring violence on television. *Current Psychology: Research and Reviews, 7,* 10–25.

Diener, E., & DeFour, D. (1978). Does television violence enhance programme publicity? *Journal of Research and Social Psychology, 36*(3), 333–341.

Diener, E., & Woody, L. W. (1981). TV violence and viewer liking. *Communication Research, 8,* 281–306.

Donnerstein, E. (1980a). Aggressive erotica and violence against women. *Journal of Personality and Social Psychology, 39*(2), 269–277.

Donnerstein, E. (1980b). Pornography and violence against women: Experimental studies. *Annals of the New York Academy of Sciences, 347,* 277–288.

Donnerstein, E. (1983). Erotica and human aggression. In R. G. Geen & E. Donnerstein (Eds.), *Aggression: Theoretical and empirical reviews* (Vol. 2, pp. 127–154). New York: Academic Press.

Donnerstein, E. (1984). Pornography: Its effect on violence against women. In N. M. Malamuth & E. Donnerstein (Eds.), *Pornography and sexual aggression* (pp. 53–81). Orlando, FL: Academic Press.

Donnerstein, E., & Berkowitz, L. (1981). Victim reactions in aggressive erotic films as a factor in violence against women. *Journal of Personality and Social Psychology, 41*(4), 710–724.

Donnerstein, E., & Malamuth, N. (1983). Pornography: Its consequences on the observer. In L. Schlesinger & E. Revitch (Eds.), *Sexual dynamics of anti-social behaviour*. Springfield, IL: C. C. Thomas.

Doob, A. N., & Climie, R. J. (1972). Delay of . . . and effects of film violence. *Journal of Experimental Social Psychology, 8*(2), 136–142.

Doob, A. N., & Macdonald, G. E. (1979). Television viewing and fear of victimisation: Is the relationship causal? *Journal of Personality and Social Psychology, 37*, 170–179.

Drabman, R. S., & Thomas, M. H. (1974). Does media violence increase children's toleration of real-life aggression? *Developmental Psychology, 10*(3), 418–421.

Dysinger, W. S., & Ruckmick, C. A. (1933). *The emotional responses of children to the motion picture situation*. New York: Macmillan.

Eisenstein, S. (1949). *Film Form* (J. Lendon, Trans.). New York: Harcourt, Brace & World.

Eron, L. D. (1980). Prescription for reduction of aggression. *American Psychologist, 35*, 244–252.

Eron, L. D. (1982). Parent-child interaction, television violence, and aggression in children. *American Psychologist, 37*, 197–211.

Eron, L. D., Huesmann, L. R., Lefkowitz, M. M., & Walder, L. O. (1972). Does television violence cause aggression? *American Psychologist, 27*, 253–263.

Fenigstein, A. (1979). Does aggression cause a preference for viewing media violence? *Journal of Personality and Social Psychology, 37*, 2307–2317.

Feshbach, S. (1955). The drive-reducing function of fantasy behaviour. *Journal of Abnormal and Social Psychology, 50*, 3–11.

Feshbach, S. (1961). The stimulating versus cathartic effects of vicarious aggressive activity. *Journal of Abnormal and Social Psychology, 63*, 381–385.

Feshbach, S., & Singer, R. D. (1971). *Television and aggression: An experimental field study*. San Francisco: Jossey-Bass.

Feshbach, S., Stiles, W. B., & Bitter, E. (1967). Reinforcing effect of witnessing agression. *Journal of Research in Personality, 2*, 133–139.

Freedman, J. L. (1984). Effect of television violence on aggressiveness. *Psychological Bulletin, 96*(2), 227–246.

Friedman, H. L., & Johnson, R. L. (1972). Mass media use and aggression: A pilot study. In G. A. Comstock & E. A. Rubinstein (Eds.), *Television and social behaviour: Vol. 3. Television and adolescent aggressiveness* (pp. 336–360). Washington, DC: U.S. Government Printing Office.

Friedrich, L. K., & Stein, A. H. (1973). Aggressive and prosocial television programmes and the natural behaviour of preschool children. *Child Development Monograph 38* (No. 4).

Gerbner, G. (1972). Violence in television drama: Trends and symbolic functions. In G. A. Comstock & E. Rubinstein (Eds.), *Television and social behaviour: Vol. 1. Media content and control* (pp. 28–187). Washington, DC: U.S. Government Printing Office.

Gerbner, G., & Gross, L. (1976). Living with television: The violence profile. *Journal of Communication, 26*, 173–199.

Gerbner, G., Gross, L., Eleey, M. F., Jackson-Beeck, M., Jeffries-Fox, S., & Signorielli, N. (1977). Television violence profile No. 8: The highlights. *Journal of Communication, 27*, 171–180.

Gerbner, G., Gross, L., Jackson-Beeck, M., Jeffries-Fox, S., & Signorielli, N. (1978). Cultural indicators: Violence profile No. 9. *Journal of Communication, 28*, 176–207.

Gerbner, G., Gross, L., Morgan, M., Signorielli, N., & Jackson-Beeck, M. (1979). The demonstration of power: Violence profile No. 10. *Journal of Communication, 29*, 177-196.

Gerbner, G., Gross, L., Morgan, M., & Signorielli, N. (1980a). Some additional comments on cultivation and analysis. *Public Opinion Quarterly, 44*, 408-410.

Gerbner, G., Gross, L., Morgan, M., & Signorielli, N. (1980b). The "mainstreaming" of America: Violence profile No. 11. *Journal of Communication, 30*, 10-29.

Gerbner, G., Gross, L., Morgan, M., & Signorielli, N. (1981a). A curious journey into the scary world of Paul Hirsch. *Communication Research, 8*, 39-72.

Gerbner, G., Gross, L., Morgan, M., & Signorielli, N. (1981b). Final reply to Hirsch. *Communication Research, 8*, 259-280.

Gorney, R., Loye, D., & Steele, G. (1977). Impact of dramatized television entertainment on adult males. *American Journal of Psychiatry, 134*(2), 170-174.

Granzberg, G., & Steinbring, J. (Eds.). (1980). *Television and the Canadian Indians. Impact and meaning among Algon Indians of Central Canada*. Winnipeg, Manitoba: University of Winnipeg.

Greenberg, B. S. (1975). British children and televised violence. *Public Opinion Quarterly, 38*, 531-547.

Gunter, B., (1980). The cathartic potential of television drama. *Bulletin of the British Psychological Society, 33*, 448-450.

Gunter, B. (1983). Do aggressive people prefer violent television? *Bulletin of the British Psychological Society, 36*, 166-168.

Gunter, B. (1985). *Dimensions of television violence*. Aldershots, England: Gower.

Gunter, B. (1987). *Television and the fear of crime*. London: John Libbey.

Gunter, B. (1988). The perceptive audience. In J. A. Anderson (Ed.), *Communication yearbook II* (pp. 22-50). Newbury Park, CA: Sage.

Gunter, B., & Furnham, A. (1982). Perceptions of television violence: Effects of programme genre and physical forms of violence. *British Journal of Social Psychology, 23*, 155-184.

Gunter, B., & Wober, M. (1983). Television viewing and public trust. *British Journal of Social Psychology, 22*, 174-176.

Gunter, G., & Wober, M. (1988). *Violence on television: What the viewers think*. London: John Libbey.

Halloran, J. D., & Croll, P. (1972). Television programmes in Great Britain. In G. A. Comstock & E. A. Rubinstein (Eds.), *Television and social behaviour: Vol. 1. Content and control*. Washington DC: U.S. Government Printing Office, 415-492.

Hartmann, D. P. (1969). Influence of symbolically modelled instrumental aggression and prime clues on aggressive behaviour. *Journal of Personality and Social Psychology, 11*, 280-288.

Hartnagel, T. F., Teevan, J. J., Jr., & McIntyre, J. J. (1975). Television violence and violent behaviour. *Social Forces, 54*, 341-351.

Hawkins, R., & Pingree, S. (1980). Some progress in the cultivation effect. *Communication Research, 7*, 193-226.

Hawkins, R., & Pingree, S. (1982). Television's influence on social reality. In D. Pearl, L. Bouthilet, & J. Lazar (Eds.), *Television and behaviour: Ten years of scientific progress and implications for the eighties* (DHSS Publication No. ADM 82-1190, Vol. 2, pp. 224-247). Washington, DC: U.S. Government Printing Office.

Hennigan, K. M., Del Rosario, M. L., Heath, L., Cook, T. D., Wharton, J. D., & Calder, B. J. (1982). Impact of the introduction of television on crime in the United States: Empirical findings and theoretical implications. *Journal of Personality and Social Psychology, 42*, 461-477.

Himmelweit, H., Oppenheim, A., & Vince, P. (1958). *Television and the child*. London: Oxford University Press.

Himmelweit, H. T., Swift, B., & Biberian, M. J. (1978). The audience as critic: A conceptual analysis of television entertainment. In P. Tannenbraum (Ed.), *The entertainment functions of television* (pp. 67–106). Hillsdale, NJ: Lawrence Erlbaum Associates.

Hirsch, P. (1980). The "scary" world of the non-viewer and other anomalies: A reanalysis of Gerbner et al.'s findings on cultivation analysis: Part 1. *Communication Research, 7,* 403–456.

*Howitt, D., & Cumberbatch, G. (1974). Audience perception of violent television content. *Communication Research, 1*(2), 204–223.

Hoyt, S. (1970). Effect of media violence "justification" on aggression. *Journal of Broadcasting, 16,* 455–465.

Huesmann, L. R. (1982). Television violence and aggressive behaviour. In D. Pearl, L. Bouthilet, & J. Lazar (Eds.). *Television and behaviour: Ten years of scientific progress and implications for the eighties. Vol. 2. Technical reviews* (pp. 220–256). Washington, DC: National Institute of Mental Health.

Huesmann, L. R., & Eron, L. D. (Eds.). (1986). *Television and the aggressive child: A cross-national comparison.* Hillsdale, NJ: Lawrence Erlbaum Associates.

Hughes, M. (1980). The fruits of cultivation analysis: A re-examination of television in fear of victimization, alienation and approval of violence. *Public Opinion Quarterly, 44,* 287–302.

ƒKessler, R., & Stipp, H. (1984). The impact of fictional television suicide stories on U.S. fatalities: A replication. *American Journal of Sociology, 90,* 151–167.

Lefkowitz, M. M., Eron, L. D., Walder, L. Q., & Huesmann, L. R. (1977). *Growing up to be violent: A longitudinal study of the development of aggression.* New York: Pergamon Press.

Leyens, J.-P., Parke, R. D., Camino, L., & Berkowitz, L. (1975). Effects of movie violence on aggression in a field setting as a function of group dominance and cohesion. *Journal of Personality and Social Psychology, 32,* 346–360.

Loye, D., Gorney, R., & Steele, G. (1977). An experimental field study. *Journal of Communication, 27,* 206–216.

Lynn, R., Hampson, S., & Agahi, E. (1989). Television violence and aggression: A genotype-environment, correlation and interaction theory. *Social Behaviour and Personality, 17*(2), 143–164.

Malamuth, N. M. (1984). Aggression against women: Cultural and individual causes. In N. M. Malamuth & E. Donnerstein (Eds.), *Pornography and sexual aggression.* Orlando, FL: Academic Press.

Malamuth, N. M., & Donnerstein, E. (1982). The effects of aggressive pornographic mass media stimuli. In L. Berkowitz (Ed.), *Advances on experimental social psychology* (Vol. 15, pp. 103–136). New York: Academic Press.

McIntyre, J. J., Teevan, J. J., Jr., & Hartnagel, T. (1972). Television violence and deviant behaviour. In G. A. Comstock & E. A. Rubinstein (Eds.), *Television and social behaviour: Vol. 3. Television and adolescent aggressiveness* (pp. 383–435). Washington, DC: U.S. Government Printing Office.

McLeod, J. M., Atkin, C. K., & Chaffee, S. H. (1972a). Adolescents, parents and television use: Adolescent self-report measures from Maryland and Wisconsin samples. In G. A. Comstock & E.A. Rubinstein (Eds.), *Television and social behaviour: Vol. 3. Television and adolescent aggressiveness* (pp. 173–238). Washington, DC: U.S. Government Printing Office.

McLeod, J. M., Atkin, C. K., & Chaffee, S. H. (1972b). Adolescents, parents and television use: Self-report and other measures from the Wisconsin sample. In G. A. Comstock & E. A. Rubinstein (Eds.), *Television and social behaviour: Vol. 3. Television and adolescent aggressiveness* (pp. 239–335). Washington, DC: U.S. Government Printing Office.

Messner, S. (1986). Television violence and violent crime: An aggregate analysis. *Social Problems, 33,* 218–235.

Meyer, T. (1973). Effects of viewing justified and unjustified film violence on aggressive behaviour. *Journal of Personality and Social Psychology, 23,* 21–29.

Milavsky, J. R., Kessler, R. C., Stipp, H. H., & Rubens, W. S. (1982). *Television and aggression: A panel study.* New York: Academic Press.

Milgram, S., & Shotland, R. L. (1973). *Television and antisocial behaviour: Field experiments.* New York: Academic Press.

Parke, R. D., Berkowitz, L., Leyens, J.-P., West, S., & Sebastian, R. J. (1977). The effects of repeated exposure to movie violence on aggressive behaviour in juvenile delinquent boys: Field experimental studies. In L. Berkowitz (Ed.), *Advances in Experimental Social Psychology* (Vol. 8). New York: Academic Press.

Perloff, R., Brown, J., & Muler, M. (1982). Mass media and sex typing: Research perspectives and policy implications. *International Journal of Women's Studies, 5,* 266–273.

Phillips, D. P. (1974). The influence of suggestion on suicide: Substantive and theoretical implications of the Warner Effect. *American Sociological Review, 39,* 340–354.

Phillips, D. P. (1979). Suicide, motor vehicle fatalities, and the mass media: Evidence toward a theory of suggestion. *American Journal of Sociology, 84*(5), 1150–1173.

Phillips, D. P. (1980a). Airplane accidents, murder and the mass media: Towards a theory of imitation and suggestion. *Social Forces, (58)*4, 1001–1023.

Phillips, D. P. (1980b). The deterrent effect of capital punishment: New evidence on an old controversy. *American Journal of Sociology, (86)*1, 139–147.

Phillips, D. P. (1981). Strong and weak research designs for detecting the impact of capital punishment on homicide. *Rutgers Law Review, 33*(3), 790–798.

Phillips, D. P. (1982). The impact of fictional television stories on U.S. adult fatalities: New evidence on the effect of the mass media on violence. *American Journal of Sociology, 87*(6), 1340–1359.

Phillips, D. P. (1983). The impact of mass media violence on US homicides. *American Sociological Review, (48)*4, 560–568.

Phillips, D. P. (1985). The found experiment: A new technique for assessing the impact of mass media violence in real world aggressive behaviour. *Public Communication and Behaviour, 1.*

Phillips, D. P., & Paight, D. (1987). The impact of televised movies about suicide: A replicative study. *New England Journal of Medicine, 317,* 808–811.

Pingree, S. (1983). Children's cognitive processing in constructing social reality. *Journalism Quarterly, 60,* 415–422.

Potter, W. J. (1986). Perceived reality and the cultivation hypothesis. *Journal of Broadcasting and Electronic Media, 30,* 159–174.

Preston, M. I. (1941). Children's reactions to movie horrors and radio crime. *Journal of Pediatrics, 19,* 147–168.

Robinson, J., & Bachman, J. (1972). Television viewing habits and aggression. In G. A. Comstock & E. A. Rubinstein (Eds.), *Television and social behaviour, Vol. 3. Television and adolescent aggressiveness.* Washington, DC: U.S. Government Printing Office.

Rotter, J. B. (1965). General expectancies for internal versus external control of reinforcement. *Psychological Monographs, 80*(1, Whole No. 609).

Schramm, W., Lyle, J., & Parker, E. P. (1961). *Television in the lives of our children.* Stanford, CA: Stanford University Press.

Sheppard, A., Sheehy, N. P., & Young, B. (1989). *Violence on television: An intervention: A report to the Independent Broadcasting authority.* Leeds: University of Leeds.

Signorielli, N. (1985). The measurement of violence in television programming: Violence indices. In J. R. Dominick & J. E. Fletcher (Eds.), *Broadcasting research methods* (pp. 235–250). Boston: Allyn & Bacon.

Singer, J. L., & Singer, D. G. (1983). Implications of childhood television viewing for cognition, imagination and emotion. In J. Bryant & D. R. Anderson (Eds.). *Children's understanding of television research: in attention and comprehension* (pp. 331–353). New York: Academic Press.

Singer, S. L. (1975). *Daydreaming and fantasy.* London: Allen & Unwin.

Singer, S. L., & Singer, D. G. (1980). *Television, imagination and aggression: A study of preschoolers' play.* Hillsdale, NJ: Lawrence Erlbaum Associates.

Smythe, D. W. (1956). *Three years of New York television: 1951–1953.* Urbana IL: National Association of Education Broadcasters.

Sparks, G. G. (1986). Developmental differences in children's reports of fear induced by mass media. *Child Study Journal, 16,* 55–66.

Sparks, G. G., & Cantor, J. (1986). Developmental differences in fright responses to a television programme depicting a character transformation. *Journal of Broadcasting & Electronic Media, 30,* 309–323.

Stack, S. (1987). Celebrities and suicide: A taxonomy and analysis, 1948–1983. *American Sociological Review, 52,* 401–412.

Tamborini, R., Zillmann, D., & Bryant, J. (1984). Fear and victimization: Exposure to television and perceptions of crime and fear. In R. N. Bostrum (Ed.), *Communication Yearbook 8* (pp. 492–513). Beverly Hills, CA: Sage.

Tannenbaum, P. H., & Zillmann, D. (1975). Emotional arousal in the facilitation of aggression through communication. In L. Berkowitz (Ed.), *Advances in experimental social psychology (Vol. 8,* pp. 149–192). New York: Academic Press.

Teevan, J. J., & Hartnagel, T. F. (1976). The effect of television violence on the perception of crime by adolescents. *Sociology and Social Research, 60,* 337–348.

Thomas, M. H., Horton, R. W., Lippincott, E. C., & Drabman, R. S. (1977). Desensitization to portrayals of real-life aggression as a function of exposure to television violence. *Journal of Personality and Social Psychology, (35)6,* 450–458.

Tyler, T. R. (1980). The impact of directly and indirectly experienced events: The origin of crime-related judgments and behaviours. *Journal of Personality and Social Psychology, 39,* 13–28.

Tyler, T. R. (1984). Assessing the risk of crime victimization and socially-transmitted information. *Journal of Social Issues, 40,* 27–38.

Tyler, T. R., & Cook, F. L. (1984). The mass media and judgements of risk: Distinguishing impact on personal and societal level judgements. *Journal of Personality and Social Psychology, 47,* 693–708.

Van der Voort, T. H. A. (1986). *Television violence: A child's eye view.* Amsterdam: Elsevier Science.

Viemero, V. (1986). *Relationships between filmed violence and aggression,* Unpublished doctoral dissertation, Department of Psychology, Abo Akademi, Finland.

Weaver, J., & Wakshlag, J. (1986). Perceived vulnerability to crime, criminal victimization experience, and television viewing. *Journal of Broadcasting and Electronic Media, 30,* 141–158.

Wells, W. D. (1973) *Television and aggression: Replication of an experimental field study.* Unpublished manuscript, Graduate School of Business, University of Chicago.

Wertham, F. (1954). *Seduction of the innocent.* New York: Rinehart.

Wiegman, O. M., Kuttschreuter, B., & Baarda, B. (1986). *Television viewing related to aggressive and pro-social behaviour.* The Hague, The Netherlands: SVO/THT.

Williams, T. M. (1986). *The Impact of Television.* New York: Academic Press.

Wilson, B. J. (1985). Developmental differences in empathy with a television protagonist's fear. *Journal of Experimental Child Psychology, 39,* 284–299.

Wilson, B. J. (1987). Reducing children's emotional reactions to mass media through rehearsed explanation and exposure to a replica of a fear object. *Human Communication Research, 14*, 3–26.

Wilson, B. J., & Cantor, J. (1987). Reducing fear reactions to mass media: Effects of visual exposure and verbal explanation. In M. McLaughlin (Ed.), *Communication Yearbook 10* (pp. 553–573). Beverly Hills, CA: Sage.

Wilson, B. J., Hoffner, C., & Cantor, J. (1987). Children's perceptions of the effectiveness of techniques to reduce fear from mass media. *Journal of Applied Developmental Psychology, 8*, 39–52.

Wober, M., & Gunter, B. (1982). Television and personal threat: Fact or artifact? A British survey. *British Journal of Social Psychology, 21*, 43–51.

Wober, M., & Gunter, B. (1988). *Television and social control.* Aldershot, England: Avebury.

Zillmann, D., and Wakshlag, J. (1985). Fear of victimization and the appeal of crime drama. In D. Zillmann & J. Bryant (Eds.), *Selective exposure to communication.* Hillsdale, NJ: Lawrence Erlbaum Associates.

Fright Reactions to Mass Media

JOANNE CANTOR
University of Wisconsin—Madison

The purpose of this chapter is to investigate fright reactions produced by mass media presentations. First, research findings related to the prevalence and intensity with which feelings of anxiety are experienced as a result of exposure to media drama are reviewed. Then the paradox that fright reactions to media fiction occur at all is discussed, and an explanation is proposed based on principles of stimulus generalization. The theory is then refined to include other factors that are needed to account for observed effects in response to both dramatic and documentary presentations. Finally, developmental differences in the media stimuli that frighten children and in the effectiveness of coping strategies are discussed.

FEELINGS OF FRIGHT IN REACTION
TO THE SCREEN

Anyone who has ever been to a horror film or thriller appreciates the fact that exposure to television shows, films, and other mass media presentations depicting danger, injury, bizarre images, and terror-stricken protagonists can induce intense fright responses in an audience. Most of us seem to be able to remember at least one specific program or movie that terrified us when we were a child and that made us nervous, remained in our thoughts, and affected other aspects of our behavior for some time afterward. And this happened to us even after we were old enough to know that what we were witnessing was not actually happening at the time and that the depicted dangers could not leave the screen and attack us directly. These reactions can also occur when we know that what is being portrayed did not actually happen; at times we may have such reactions even when we understand that there is no chance that the depicted events could ever occur.

The predominant interest in this chapter is fright as an *immediate emotional response* that is typically of relatively short duration, but that may endure, on occasion, for several hours or days, or even longer. The focus here is on emotional reactions involving components of anxiety, distress, and increased physiological arousal that are frequently engendered in viewers as a result of exposure to specific types of media productions. Although the major interest is in reactions of this type that are evoked by exposure to dramatic entertainment fare, there is a good deal of research on adults' reactions to "stressful" documentary films (e.g., by Lazarus and his associates) that is relevant to this issue. A review of the literature reveals that most studies of children's fright reactions deal with responses to fictional or fantasy entertainment programming, whereas most studies of adults deal with responses to extremely upsetting documentary material. This dichotomy is undoubtedly related to ethical issues in the conduct of research. It seems, however, that these two bodies of research should be considered together because, as is discussed later, there is a great deal of overlap in important aspects of the stimuli presented, in the nature of the audience's reactions, and in the processes apparently underlying such reactions.

In this chapter, a distinction is not made between *fear* and *anxiety*. Although different theorists make a variety of distinctions between these two terms, many use the two terms largely interchangeably or consider anxiety to be a vague form of fear (see Hilgard, Atkinson, & Atkinson, 1971). Most experimental studies of adults' responses to stressful films use some form of "anxiety," or "state anxiety" as their major self-report variable (see Lazarus, Speisman, Mordkoff, & Davidson, 1962, for a comparison of effects on major self-report dimensions). Reports of emotional disturbance, tension, degree of upset, and emotional arousal are frequently used as supplementary measures. Physiological responses are also usually employed in studies of adults, the most typical of which include heart rate and a measure of palmar skin conductance (e.g., Falkowski & Steptoe, 1983; Koriat, Melkman, Averill, & Lazarus, 1972). Although there have been studies in which state anxiety was assessed in children (e.g., Kase, Sikes, & Spielberger, 1978), children's self-reports of their fright responses to drama are typically assessed in terms of the degree to which viewers feel scared, worried, or upset (e.g., Sparks & Cantor, 1986), the degree to which they perceive a program as scary (e.g., Osborn & Endsley, 1971), or whether or not their reactions are hedonically "negative" (Wilson & Cantor, 1985). The most prevalent physiological responses used with children have been heart rate and skin temperature (e.g., Wilson & Cantor, 1985; Zillmann, Hay, & Bryant, 1975). In addition, children's facial expressions of fear have been analyzed by some researchers (e.g., Wilson & Cantor, 1987; Zillmann et al., 1975).

Research interest in the phenomenon of fright reactions to mass media has been sporadic at best. Several investigators in the 1930s and 1940s focused primary concerns on fear reactions to mass media (Blumer, 1933; Cantril, 1940; Dysinger & Ruckmick, 1933; Eisenberg, 1936; Preston, 1941). In addition, some major volumes reporting research conducted in the 1950s addressed this issue seriously (Himmelweit, Oppenheim, & Vince, 1958; Schramm, Lyle, & Parker, 1961; Wertham, 1953). But fright responses to mass media were largely ignored in the 1960s and early 1970s. There were only passing references to fright in the Surgeon General's Report (Comstock & Rubinstein, 1972), and in the Surgeon General's Update (Pearl, Bouthilet, & Lazar, 1982), fear was addressed in terms of the long-term effects of media exposure on perceptions of danger, but, for the most part, not in terms of the more transitory emotional effects produced by witnessing a particular program or film.

One reason for the resurgence of interest in fright responses may be that mass media content has become increasingly graphic and horror filled (see Stein, 1982). As anecdotal reports of intense emotional responses to such popular films as *Jaws* and *The Exorcist* proliferated in the press, public attention became more focused on the phenomenon. Although many adults experience such reactions, the major share of public concern has been over children's responses. The furor over children's reactions to especially intense scenes in *Indiana Jones and the Temple of Doom* and *Gremlins* prompted the Motion Picture Association of America to add "PG-13" to its rating system, in an attempt to caution parents that, for whatever reason, a film might be inappropriate for children under the age of 13 (Zoglin, 1984). In addition, the rapid expansion in the number of cable channels has meant that most films produced for theatrical distribution, no matter how brutal or bizarre, eventually end up on television and thus become accessible to large numbers of children, often without their parents' knowledge. Finally, the widespread prior speculation about children's potential emotional responses to the broadcast of the nuclear holocaust film "The Day After" seems to have been unprecedented (see Schofield & Pavelchak, 1985), and similar concerns recently surfaced regarding media coverage of the war in the Middle East (Taylor, 1991).

Although some psychoanalytically oriented observers would seem to argue to the contrary (e.g., Bettelheim, 1975; Smetak, 1986), many researchers have speculated on the potential negative effects on children of exposure to frightening media fare. Blumer (1933) spoke of "emotional possession," during which viewers lose ordinary control over their feelings and perceptions. Preston (1941) contended that exposure to media horrors could become an "addiction" with profound negative effects on children's physical and psychological health. More recently, Singer (1975) argued that children who are exposed to frightening movies may be haunted for years by night terrors and bizarre and weird fantasies. Sarafino (1986) placed a great deal of blame on scary television shows and films for inducing and exacerbating children's fears. His book on children's fears contains countless anecdotes involving the media's negative impact and contends that exposure to "scary portrayals of animals, violence, and monsters on TV and in the movies can impair children's psychological development" (p. 56). Because of such concerns about the potential negative effects of exposure to frightening media on children, research on how to predict and prevent or reduce children's fears can be seen as having immediate practical value.

Research into potential negative effects on children has unique problems, however, in that it is not feasible, for ethical reasons, to demonstrate harmful effects in the experimental laboratory. Thus, what evidence there is for intense emotional disturbances in children comes from anecdotes, case studies, in-depth interviews, and survey research. In these studies, effects observed in the "real world" are reported, but control over variables is impossible, and causal conclusions remain highly tentative. The laboratory research that has been conducted on fright responses to mass media, in contrast, has not been designed to demonstrate negative effects, but rather to determine the variables that contribute to immediate and short-lived fright responses, and those that prevent or mitigate them.

Although the potential practical applications of research on mass media-induced fears seem to have been a major impetus to their study, the value of such research in advancing theory has not been ignored. Because children's fright reactions have been observed to vary as a function of differences in their cognitive processing of mass media stimuli, this research has been helpful in investigating relationships between cognitive development and emotional reactions to mass media, and relationships between cognition and emotion in general.

Prevalence and Intensity
of Media-Induced Fright Reactions

Most researchers who have investigated the issue have found that a
substantial proportion of the respondents questioned admitted having
experienced fright while watching mass media productions, although
the percentages vary greatly as a function of the sample selected and the
specific question asked.[1] Blumer (1933) reported that 93% of the children
in his sample said they had been frightened or horrified by a motion
picture. Approximately 33% of a sample questioned by Himmelweit et
al. (1958) reported having been frightened by something on television.
Lyle and Hoffman (1972) reported that 48% of a sample of first graders
said they were frightened "sometimes or often" by what they saw on
television. In a national survey conducted by Zill (1977), 25% of the
children questioned said they were afraid of TV programs involving
fighting and shooting. Groebel and Krebs (1983) found that 92% of a
representative sample of youths believed that television could evoke
fear. Most recently, about 75% of the respondents in two separate
samples of preschool and elementary school children said that they had
been scared by something they had seen on television or in a movie
(Wilson, Hoffner, & Cantor, 1987).
    Other findings reflect the prevalence of more intense reactions that
last beyond the time of media exposure. Although von Feilitzen (1975),
in summarizing the results of Danish research, concluded that few
children have suffered severe effects in the form of anxiety, nightmares,
or lost sleep, other researchers have reported that enduring and intense
responses are more pervasive. Blumer (1933) stated that the fear induced
by movies "very frequently" lasts beyond the time of viewing. Eisenberg
(1936) found that approximately 43% of a sample of children had
recently dreamed about things they had heard on the radio and that
approximately 50% of these children said that their dreams had involved
witches, murders, crimes, nightmares, and the like. Preston (1941)
reported that among her respondents under the age of 12, sleep
disturbances necessitating intervention by the mother were "common
reactions" to movie horrors and radio crime. When Wall and Simson
(1950) asked adolescents about the films they had seen in the preceding
2 weeks, one film, a thriller, was reported to have produced "lasting
fright" in more than 33% of those who had seen it. Himmelweit et al.
(1958) reported that 18% of the children they questioned thought there

---

[1]Some of the percentages noted here are approximate. For the sake of simplicity, the
percentages reported for separate age groups have been combined without being
weighted by subgroup size.

were things on television that were bad for children, and the most typical reason given was that they cause fright and bad dreams. In a study by Hess and Goldman (1962), 75% of the parents interviewed agreed that children sometimes get nightmares from television programs; 63% agreed *strongly*. Cantor and Reilly (1982) reported that 26% of a group of adolescents said that they experienced enduring fright "sometimes or often" after watching television shows. Moreover, 22% said they sometimes or often *regretted* having seen a scary program because of how much it had upset them. Finally, about 50% of a sample of elementary school children questioned by Palmer, Hockett, and Dean (1983) reported that they experienced enduring fright reactions to television programs "sometimes or frequently," and over 33% said that they sometimes or frequently were sorry they had seen such programs.

In a study designed to assess the severity of typical enduring fright reactions to mass media, Johnson (1980) asked a random sample of adults whether they had ever seen a motion picture that had disturbed them "a great deal." Forty percent replied in the affirmative, and the median length of the reported disturbance was 3 days. Respondents also reported on the type, intensity, and duration of symptoms such as nervousness, depression, fear of specific things, and recurring thoughts and images. Based on these reports, Johnson judged that 48% of these respondents (19% of the total sample) had experienced, for at least 2 days, a "significant stress reaction" of the type identified by Horowitz (1976) and Lazarus (1966) as constituting a "stress response syndrome." When Johnson replicated this survey, using randomly selected moviegoers standing in line outside of theaters, 61% of the sample said they had been greatly disturbed by a movie, and 43% of these respondents (26% of the sample) were judged on the basis of their symptoms, to have had a severe stress reaction. Johnson argued that "it is one thing to walk away from a frightening or disturbing event with mild residue of the images and quite another thing to ruminate about it, feel anxious or depressed for days, and/or to avoid anything that might create the same unpleasant experience" (p. 786). On the basis of his data, he concluded that such reactions were more prevalent and more severe than had previously been assumed.

The most extreme reactions reported in the literature come from psychiatric case studies in which acute and disabling anxiety states enduring several days to several weeks or more are said to have been precipitated by the viewing of horror movies such as *The Exorcist* and *Invasion of the Body Snatchers* (Buzzuto, 1975; Mathai, 1983). Most of the patients in the cases reported had not had previously diagnosed psychiatric problems, but the viewing of the film was seen as occurring in conjunction with other stressors in the patients' lives.

Together, these studies suggest that transitory fright responses to dramatic mass media stimuli are quite typical, that enduring emotional disturbances occur in a substantial proportion of the audience, and that intense and debilitating reactions affect a small but appreciable minority of particularly susceptible viewers.

Parental Knowledge and Children's Exposure

Preston (1941) found that for the most part, the parents of her respondents either were unaware of their children's fright responses to mass media horrors, or minimized their significance. More recent findings are in accord with this generalization. Cantor and Reilly (1982) found that parents' estimates of the frequency of their children's media-induced fright reactions were significantly lower than their children's self-reports. They also found that, generally speaking, the parents' estimates were not even correlated with those of their children.

Cantor and Reilly (1982) further reported that parents' estimates of their children's exposure to frightening media were also significantly lower than children's self-reports. The difference between parents' and children's estimates of exposure is difficult to interpret because it may reflect either the parent's ignorance of what the child has seen or a difference between the parent's and the child's definition of scary programs. Data reported here demonstrate that children often experience fright reactions to programs that most parents would not expect to be scary. Nevertheless, there is evidence that children are widely exposed to televised stimuli that were originally intended for adults and that are considered frightening by a large proportion of adult movie-goers. Sparks (1986b), for example, reported that almost 50% of the 4-to 10-year-olds he interviewed had seen *Poltergeist* and *Jaws*, and substantial proportions of his sample had seen *Halloween* and *Friday the 13th*. Most of this viewing was done in the home, on cable television.

Relationship Between Fright Reactions and Enjoyment

Given the data just cited on the prevalence of immediate fright and other more enduring emotional disturbances produced by exposure to frightening productions, the question obviously arises as to why viewers subject themselves to the risk of such "psychic trauma." Preston (1941) argued that children cannot avoid being exposed to such programs if their parents insist on watching them. She also maintained that children choose such fare themselves so that they can talk about the "hair-raising details" with their friends at school. But in speaking of the

habitual consumption of media horrors as "addiction," Preston implicitly endorsed the notion that such exposure produces intrinsic rewards
as well. In fact, most researchers who have asked the question have
discovered that many children enjoy frightening media presentations, in
spite of the unwanted side-effects that sometimes occur. Blumer (1933)
reported that in a third-grade class he interviewed, 86% of the children
gave instances of being frightened, on occasion severely, by motion
pictures; yet 82% of those who had been frightened said that they liked
to be frightened by movies. Eighty percent of the adolescents interviewed by Cantor and Reilly (1982) and over 50% of the elementary-
school children interviewed by Palmer et al. (1983) said they liked scary
television and films "somewhat or a lot." Sparks (1986b) found that
more than 33% of the elementary-school children he interviewed said
they enjoyed scary programs, and another 25% of the children said they
both enjoyed and disliked them. Finally, in a study by Wilson et al.
(1987), 62% of the children in one sample responded in the affirmative
when asked whether they liked scary programs; about 75% of the
children in another sample stated that they liked them, with about 50%
of the sample saying they liked them "a lot."

Blumer (1933) argued that many children enjoy being frightened
while viewing scary presentations, but suffer unwanted effects afterward. Himmelweit et al. (1958) argued that the child "enjoys being
frightened just a little, but not too much," and that the child "likes the
suspense for the pleasure of the relief that follows it" (p. 210). Zillmann
(1980) provided evidence relevant to the latter mechanism. He argued
that physiological arousal is produced by the anticipation of threatened
negative outcomes and that, through the process of excitation transfer
(e.g., Zillmann, 1978), this arousal intensifies enjoyment of the positive
(or at least nonnegative) outcomes that such presentations usually
provide. Furthermore, Zillmann noted that the enjoyment of suspenseful presentations does not necessarily hinge upon the final outcome, but may occur throughout the presentation as various episodes
within a plot induce and then reduce suspense (Zillmann et al., 1975).

Consistent with Zillmann's reasoning, Cantor and Reilly (1982) presented evidence that undergoing fright reactions to scary presentations
does not necessarily reduce the enjoyment of such presentations, and
that fright may even be positively associated with liking. In a 6th-grade
sample, respondents who reported experiencing enduring fright reactions "sometimes" or "often" did not differ from their less reactive peers
in their liking for scary media. Moreover, in a 10th-grade sample, highly
reactive respondents tended to like scary programs more than less
reactive respondents. Furthermore, respondents who were highly reac-

tive did not differ from those who were less reactive in their reports of frequency of exposure to scary presentations.

An experimental study of adults' appreciation of horror (Zillmann, Weaver, Mundorf, & Aust, 1986) also supports the positive relationship between fright and appreciation. In this study, mean self-report ratings of reactions to *Friday the 13th, Part III* on a "distress" factor were extremely highly correlated with mean ratings on a "delight" factor.

A STIMULUS GENERALIZATION APPROACH TO MEDIA-INDUCED FEAR

As can be seen from the literature summarized here, there is a good deal of evidence regarding viewers' subjective experiences of fear in response to mass media presentations. The next part of this chapter is devoted to speculations about why such fear reactions occur and the factors that promote or inhibit their occurrence. Research data are cited where they are relevant to these speculations. (For a more detailed review of the supporting research, see Cantor, 1991.)

Fear is generally conceived of as an emotional response of negative hedonic tone related to avoidance or escape, due to the perception of real or imagined threat (e.g., Izard, 1977). A classic fear-arousing situation is one in which the individual senses that he. or she is in physical danger, such as upon encountering a poisonous snake on a walk through the woods. Fear can be conceived of as a response involving cognitions, motor behavior, and excitatory reactions that, except under extreme conditions, prepare the individual to flee from the danger.

Using this definition of fear, it is not difficult to explain the public terror that was produced by perhaps the most infamous frightening media drama on record—the 1938 radio broadcast of H. G. Wells' *War of the Worlds*. Many people who tuned in late thought they were listening to a live news bulletin informing them that Martians were taking over the United States (Cantril, 1940). Thus, if they believed what they heard, they justifiably felt that their own lives and indeed the future of their society were in great peril.

But in typical situations in which people are exposed to mass media drama, the audience understands that what is being depicted is not actually happening; in many cases, they know that it never did happen; and in some cases, they know that it never could happen. Objectively speaking, then, the viewer is not in any immediate danger. Why then, does the fright reaction occur? Although fright responses to media presentations are undoubtedly the result of the complex interaction of a variety of processes, a preliminary explanation for this phenomenon is proposed, based on the notion of stimulus generalization (see Pavlov, 1927/1960; Razran, 1949). In conditioning terms, if a stimulus evokes either an unconditioned or conditioned emotional response, other stimuli that are similar to the eliciting stimulus will evoke similar, but less intense emotional responses. This principle implies that, because of similarities between the real and the mediated stimulus, a stimulus that would evoke a fright response if experienced first hand will evoke a similar, but less intense response when encountered via the mass media. In order to evaluate the implications of this explanation, it should be instructive, first, to identify major categories of stimuli and events that tend to induce fear in real-life situations and that are frequently depicted in frightening media productions, and second, to delineate the factors that should promote or reduce the viewer's tendency to respond emotionally to the mediated stimulus.

Stimuli and Events that Generally Produce Fear

Based on a review of the literature on the sources of real-world fears and on the effects of frightening media, three categories of stimuli and events that tend to produce fear in real-life situations and that occur frequently in frightening presentations are proposed. They are (a) dangers and injuries, (b) distortions of natural forms, and (c) the experience of endangerment and fear by others. These categories are obviously not mutually exclusive: On the contrary, a frightening scene usually involves more than one of these categories.[2]

Dangers and Injuries. Stimuli that are perceived as dangerous should, by definition, evoke fear. The depiction of events that either cause or threaten to cause great harm is the stock-in-trade of the frightening film. Natural disasters such as tornadoes, volcanoes,

---

[2]These categories are also not considered exhaustive. Many theorists have proposed additional categories of stimuli that readily evoke fear, such as certain types of animals (especially snakes; see Jersild & Holmes, 1935; Yerkes & Yerkes, 1936) and loud noises, darkness, and stimuli related to loss of support (see Bowlby, 1973). These categories are not discussed separately here because it seems that in mass media productions, such stimuli tend to co-occur with danger or signal its imminence. For example, the snakes, bats, and spiders in horror films are usually depicted as poisonous as well as repulsive. Sudden loud noises and darkness are often used to intensify the perceived dangerousness of situations. Finally, visual stimuli associated with loss of support, such as those experienced when traveling uncontrollably through space in a roller coaster (see Tannenbaum, 1980), are typically presented in horror films to represent threats to a character's safety.

plagues, and earthquakes; violent encounters on an interpersonal, global or even intergalactic level; attacks by vicious animals; and large-scale industrial and nuclear accidents are typical events in frightening media fare. If any of these events were witnessed directly, the onlooker would be in danger, and fear would be the expected response. In addition, because danger is often present when injuries are witnessed, the perception of injuries should come to evoke fear as a conditioned response, even in the absence of the danger that produced the injuries. Through stimulus generalization, one might thus expect mediated depictions of danger or injury to produce fright reactions as well.

Reports of children's fright produced by depictions of dangerous stimuli in media drama abound in the survey literature. Such stimuli include accidents, dangerous animals, and natural disasters (Blumer, 1933), criminal activities (Blumer, 1933; Eisenberg, 1936; Groebel & Krebs, 1983; Himmelweit et al., 1958), and violence (Johnson, 1980; Sparks 1986b). Scenes of danger, injury, and violence have also been shown to produce fear in laboratory situations (Cantor & Hoffner, 1990; Cantor & Omdahl, 1991; Dysinger & Ruckmick, 1933; Hoffner & Cantor, 1990; Kase et al., 1978; Osborn & Endsley, 1971; Wilson & Cantor, 1985; 1987). Moreover, levels of fear have been shown to increase as a function of manipulated levels of depicted danger (Zillmann et al., 1975; Bryant, 1978a, cited in Zillmann, 1980). Finally, the many experiments involving documentary films on such topics as industrial accidents, autopsies, and aboriginal circumcision rituals (e.g., Girodo & Pellegrini, 1976; Lazarus, Speisman, Mordkoff, & Davidson, 1962; Pillard, Atkinson, & Fisher, 1967) have demonstrated that filmed depictions of bodily injuries substantially increase adults' physiological arousal and self-reports of anxiety.

Distortions of Natural Forms.   In addition to dangerous stimuli and the outcomes of dangerous situations, a related set of stimuli that typically evoke fear might be referred to as deformities and distortions, or *familiar organisms in unfamiliar and unnatural forms.* Hebb (1946) observed fear responses to such "deviations from previously experienced patterns" in chimpanzees and argued that such responses are spontaneous, in that they do not require conditioning. Organisms that have been mutilated as a result of injury could be considered to fall into this category as well as the previous category. In addition, distortions that are not the result of injury are often encountered in thrillers in the form of realistic characters like dwarves, hunchbacks, and mutants. Moreover, monsters abound in thrillers. Monsters are unreal creatures that are similar to natural beings in many ways, but deviant from them in other ways, such as through distortions in size, shape, skin color, or facial configuration. In scary movies, monstrous and distorted characters are typically, but not universally, depicted as evil and dangerous.

Monsters, ghosts, vampires, mummies, and other supernatural beings are frequently cited as sources of children's fear in both surveys and anecdotal reports (Blumer, 1933; Cantor & Sparks, 1984; Dorr, Doubleday, & Kovaric, 1983; Leishman, 1981; Lyle & Hoffman, 1976; Sparks, 1986b). Moreover, monstrous characters in "The Incredible Hulk," *The Wizard of Oz*, and *Vampire* have also been shown to increase fear in laboratory studies (Cantor & Wilson, 1984; Cantor, Ziemke, & Sparks, 1984; Sparks & Cantor, 1986).

The Experience of Endangerment and Fear by Others. Although in some cases, viewers seem to respond directly to depictions of fear-evoking stimuli such as dangers, injuries, and distortions, in most dramatic presentations these stimuli are shown to affect the emotional responses and outcomes of depicted characters. In many cases, the viewer can be said to respond *indirectly* to the stimuli through the experiences of the characters. One mechanism underlying such responses is *empathy*. Although there is controversy over the origins of empathic processes (see Berger, 1962; Feshbach, 1982; Hoffman, 1978), it is clear that under some circumstances, people experience fear as a direct response to the fear expressed by others. Many frightening films seem to stress characters' expressions of fear in response to dangers more than the perceptual cues associated with the threat itself.

In a laboratory investigation, Wilson and Cantor (1985) provided evidence of the role of empathic processes in media-induced fright. They found that 9- to 11-year-old children who watched a scene depicting a character's expressions of fear experienced as much fear as did those who watched a scene depicting the frightening stimulus that was responsible for the character's fear. In contrast, preschool children showed significantly less fear in response to the character's emotion than in response to the frightening stimulus, in spite of the fact that almost all of the children who were exposed to the character's emotion were aware of the nature of his feelings. The observed developmental difference is consistent with the notion that true empathy does not occur until the child acquires role-taking skills (see Feshbach, 1982; Selman & Byrne, 1978).

Another indirect mechanism that may be proposed to account for emotional responses to the experiences of others derives from the fact that witnessing other people risk danger can produce the "vicarious" experience of fear, even when the persons at risk do not express fear because they are either unaware of the danger or unafraid. As Zillmann

(1980) argued, much of the tension in suspenseful presentations arises from the fear that something horrible will happen to characters for whom we feel positive affect. The fear evoked may derive, in part, from the anticipation of "separation" from these characters if they should meet their demise (see Bowlby, 1973). Also, Zillmann and Cantor (1977) showed that people respond with dysphoria to the misfortunes of characters for whom they have affection, or at least for whom they do not feel antipathy. Therefore, fear may be seen as deriving from anticipation of the viewer's own distress or from anticipation of empathy with the distress responses of liked characters.

Both survey and experimental findings indicate that the threat of harm to human or animal protagonists increases feelings of anxiety or fear, especially when the viewer feels an affective attachment to the threatened characters (Bryant, 1978b, cited in Zillmann, 1980; Dysinger & Ruckmick, 1933; Himmelweit al., 1958; Leishman, 1981; Schramm et al., 1961; Tannenbaum & Gaer, 1965).

Factors Affecting the Tendency to Respond Emotionally to Mediated Stimuli

Three factors are proposed to have an impact on viewers' tendencies to respond emotionally to mediated fear-evoking stimuli. They are (a) the similarity of the depicted stimuli to real-life fear-evokers, (b) viewers' motivations for media exposure, and (c) factors affecting emotionality, generally.

Similarity of Depicted Stimuli to Real-life Fear-evokers. The notion of stimulus generalization implies that the greater the similarity between a conditioned or unconditioned stimulus and the substitute stimulus, the stronger the generalization response will be. *Perceptually* speaking, realistic depictions of threatening events are more similar to events occurring in the real world than are animated or stylized depictions of the same events. Thus the stimulus generalization notion would predict more intense responses to live-action violence than to cartoon violence, or violence between puppets, for example. Experimental findings involving both adults and children are consistent with this expectation (Gunter & Furnham, 1984; Osborn & Endsley, 1971; Surbeck, 1975).

The *similarity of depicted stimuli to those stimuli that provoke fear in a particular individual* should also enhance stimulus generalization. Himmelweit et al. (1958) argued that "whether an incident will disturb depends less on whether it is fictional or real than on whether it comes within the child's experience and is one with which he can identify himself" (p. 203). Experiments have shown that an individual's fears (e.g., fear of spiders and death) and prior experiences with stressful events (such as childbirth) intensify the emotional effects of related media presentations (Hare & Blevings, 1975; Sapolsky & Zillmann, 1978; Weiss, Katkin, & Rubin, 1968).

Another aspect of similarity that should have an impact on the tendency to generalize from the real to the mediated stimulus has to do with the *perceived similarity between viewing the depicted event and undergoing the corresponding real-world event itself*. At one extreme is the response of the very young child who does not understand the difference between mediated depictions and reality, and who thinks that the frightening stimuli are actually present in the living room or the theater (see Dorr, 1980). At the other extreme is the mature viewer who is well aware that what is being witnessed is only an image being reproduced via media technology. Based on this distinction, one would expect that young children would respond intensely to mediated depictions of things that frighten them because they would react as they would to real-life stimuli. This distinction also leads to the expectation that, due to the process of *stimulus discrimination*, there should be a rapid diminishment of response intensity, with age and with repeated viewing trials, as the viewer increasingly comes to discriminate between the reinforcement contingencies associated with the live and the mediated stimulus.

Consistent with the notion of stimulus discrimination, there is some evidence for short-term habituation through repeated exposure to stressful movie stimuli (Averill, Malmstrom, Koriat, & Lazarus, 1972; Davidson & Hiebert, 1971). There is also some evidence for short-term generalization of habituation to similar but novel stimuli (Pillard et al., 1967; Wilson & Cantor, 1987).

The notion of stimulus discrimination should be considered to be more relevant to the long-term effects of exposure to media than to short-term habituation, however, and in this context, the data are unsupportive of the stimulus generalization model. In contrast to the data on short-term desensitization, studies of long-term effects do not provide evidence of a diminution of emotional responses with repeated exposure to stressful films. Surveys by Himmelweit et al. (1958), von Feilitzen (1975), and Cantor and Reilly (1982) all report that heavy viewing of frightening media is not associated with a lowering of reactivity to such fare. In addition, Sapolsky and Zillmann's (1978) experiment revealed that women who had previously watched a film depicting childbirth reported themselves to be more aroused while witnessing a childbirth film than did those who had never seen such a film.

Because research indicates that fear responses to mass media stimuli are quite common in adults (e.g., Johnson, 1980), and that heavy exposure to frightening media does not necessarily produce a lessening of fright responses, stimulus generalization alone is clearly not a sufficient explanation for fright responses to media stimuli.

Motivations for Media Exposure. One set of factors that the stimulus generalization notion does not take into account are the motivations for media exposure. As Zillmann (1982) argued, mature viewers often seek out media programming for entertainment and arousal. In order to enhance the emotional impact of a drama they may, for example, adopt the "willing suspension of disbelief," by cognitively minimizing the effect of knowledge that the events are mediated. In addition, mature viewers may enhance their emotional responses by generating their own emotion-evoking visual images or by cognitively elaborating on the implications of the portrayed events.

Mature viewers who seek to avoid intense arousal may employ other appraisal processes (see Zillmann, 1978), to diminish fright reactions to media stimuli by using the "adult discount," for example (see Dysinger & Ruckmick, 1933), and concentrating on the fact that the stimuli are only mediated. Although such appraisal processes must be taken into account, they are by no means universally effective. A viewer wanting to enjoy an intense emotional response to a drama may be prevented from downplaying the fact that the events are mediated if, for example, the acting is poor or the special effects are inadequate. On the other hand, a viewer attempting to dampen his or her emotional reactions may nonetheless be "caught off guard" by a particularly arresting or realistic depiction.

Several studies by Lazarus and his co-workers have shown that adults can modify their emotional responses to stressful films by adopting different "cognitive sets" (Koriat et al., 1972; Lazarus & Alfert, 1964; Speisman, Lazarus, Mordkoff, & Davidson, 1964). In a related study, Cantor and Wilson (1984) showed that children in their later elementary school years also can cognitively modify their emotional responses to frightening films.

In addition to seeking entertainment, viewers may expose themselves to media for purposes of acquiring information. If information gain is a goal, it would seem that the viewer would pay particular attention to whether or not the events portrayed are real or fictional. Because part of the emotional response to such stimuli might arise from viewers' *anticipations of future consequences to themselves*, depictions of real threats should evoke more fear than dramatic portrayals. Studies of adults have shown that presentations of violent actions that are perceived to have actually happened are far more arousing than depictions of the same actions that are believed to be fictional (Geen, 1975; Geen & Rakosky, 1973). In addition, most of the researchers studying adults' responses to stressful films, by almost exclusively relying on documentaries as stimulus materials, seem implicitly to assume that responses to real incidents will be more intense than responses to fictional events.

Children have also been reported to respond more intensely to real than to fictional events (Groebel & Krebs, 1983; von Feilitzen, 1975). However, as is discussed in the final section, there is evidence that younger children are less responsive than older children and adults to the distinction between real events and fictional portrayals.

It might also be argued that because of viewers' concerns about their own future safety, depicted threatening agents that are considered to be proximate or imminent should evoke more fear than remote threats. Himmelweit et al. (1958) argued that one reason crime and detective stories were more frightening than Westerns was that the settings were much "nearer to home." Support for this notion comes from anecdotes regarding the especially intense reactions to *Jaws*, a movie about shark attacks, by people who saw the movie while vacationing at the seashore. Similarly, in an experiment (Cantor & Hoffner, 1990), children who thought that the threatening agent depicted in a movie existed in their environment were more frightened by the movie than were children who did not believe that the threat could be found in their local area.

Factors Affecting Emotionality Generally. It is clear from the research reported above that physiological arousal is an important component of viewers' reactions to frightening media. Experiments testing the role of excitation transfer (e.g., Zillmann, 1978) in responses to emotion-evoking films have demonstrated that excitatory residues from prior arousing experiences can combine with responses to unrelated, subsequently presented movie scenes and thereby intensify emotional reactions to the movie (Cantor, Zillmann, & Bryant, 1975; Zillmann, Mody, & Cantor, 1974). Excitation transfer theory also implies that if two unrelated arousal-inducing conditions occur simultaneously, the excitation produced by one source will tend to intensify emotional responses to the other, unless distraction or other factors prevent the misattribution of arousal (see Girodo & Pellegrini, 1976; Schachter & Singer, 1962).

This reasoning leads to the expectation that factors within a frightening presentation that tend to produce arousal may combine with the depiction of fear-evoking stimuli to increase the viewer's arousal and thus the intensity of the fear experienced while viewing. Producers of frightening movies employ a variety of stylistic devices, in addition to plot elements, to intensify the audience's fright. Himmelweit et al. (1958) observed that sound effects, particularly music, were considered by children as frightening elements of scary presentations. Consistent with the effectiveness of such devices, Thayer and Levenson (1983) showed that the addition of different types of music to a stressful film could either intensify or reduce the emotional impact of the film, depending on the nature of the music.

Other studies have investigated the intensification of emotional responses to frightening events through the provision of forewarnings or foreshadowings that the events would occur. Consistent with the reasoning that the physiological arousal produced by the anticipation of the upsetting events intensifies emotional responses to the events when they occur, Cantor et al. (1984) and Nomikos, Opton, Averill, and Lazarus (1968) found that adults' emotional responses to upsetting depictions were more intense when forewarning was provided. A study by Hoffner and Cantor (1990) confirmed that forewarning of upcoming threats in a film sequence increases anticipatory fear in children. It has also been demonstrated (Sparks, 1989), however, that the effects of forewarning may differ as a function of the viewer's preferred style of coping.

DEVELOPMENTAL DIFFERENCES AND MEDIA-INDUCED FEAR

It should be recognized from the above discussion that responses to the mediated depiction of frightening stimuli and events will depend to some extent on characteristics of the viewer. Some researchers have reported that specific personality characteristics, such as sensation seeking or the Machiavellian trait of "deceit" are positively associated with liking for scary media (e.g., Sparks, 1986a; Tamborini, Stiff, & Zillmann, 1987). Others have found that personality factors such as "trait anxiety," or preferred coping style are correlated with emotional responses to frightening media fare (e.g., Girodo & Pellegrini, 1976; Kamen, 1971; Sparks, 1989; Sparks & Spirek, 1988), although several studies have reported inconsistent relationships between personality variables and such responses (e.g., Koriat et al., 1972).

Independent of personality variables, the viewer's chronological age is an extremely important determinant of emotional reactions to frightening media. This is not to say that certain ages are more vulnerable to media-induced fear in general, but rather that there are developmental differences in the types of media stimuli and events that will produce fright.

The expectation of developmental differences is based on several factors. First, research shows that there are consistent developmental trends in the real-world stimuli and issues that evoke fear (e.g., Angelino, Dollins, & Mech, 1956; Maurer, 1965), and such differences should be reflected in responses to mediated depictions. Second, perceptions of danger will depend in some cases on world knowledge or experience. Although an attacking animal might be feared automatically because it provides what Bowlby (1973) referred to as "natural cues" to danger, such as rapid approach, sudden or strange movement, and loud noise, a certain degree of knowledge is necessary to fear such awesome threats as nuclear weapons or AIDS.

A third reason to expect age differences derives from the fact that the perception of stimuli and the comprehension of event sequences are involved, in varying degrees, in the viewer's response. Therefore, developmental differences in information-processing tendencies related to media viewing (see Collins, 1983; Wartella, 1979) should affect the nature and intensity of fright responses to specific depictions. Finally, it has been argued here that certain complex cognitive operations are involved in fright reactions to some types of media stimuli, and the ability to perform such operations is limited in very young viewers and improves throughout childhood.

My collaborators and I have been engaged in a program of research to explore two major developmental issues in fright reactions to media: (a) the types of mass media stimuli and events that frighten children at different ages, and (b) the strategies for preventing or reducing unwanted fear reactions that are most appropriate at different ages. Using observations and theories from developmental psychology as guidelines, particularly theories of cognitive development, we have conducted a series of experiments and surveys. The experiments, of course, have had the advantage of testing rigorously controlled variations in program content and viewing conditions, using a combination of self-reports, physiological responses, the coding of facial expressions of emotion, and behavioral measures. In a complementary fashion, the surveys have investigated the responses of children who had voluntarily exposed themselves to a particular mass media offering in their natural environment, without any researcher intervention (see Cantor, 1989).

Developmental Differences in the Media Stimuli That Produce Fright

It is not true that as children get older they become less and less susceptible to media-produced emotional disturbances. As children mature cognitively, some things become less likely to disturb them, whereas other things become potentially more upsetting. This generalization is consistent with developmental differences in children's fears in general. According to a variety of studies using diverse methodologies, children from approximately 3 to 8 years of age are frightened primarily by animals, the dark, supernatural beings, such as ghosts, monsters, and witches, and by anything that looks strange or moves suddenly. The fears of 9- to 12-year-olds are more often related to personal injury and physical destruction and the injury and death of relatives. Adolescents continue to fear personal injury and physical destruction, but school fears and social fears arise at this age, as do fears regarding political, economic, and global issues (see Cantor, Wilson, & Hoffner, 1986, for review).

A review of these trends suggests that fears in young children derive largely from the direct or mediated experience of perceptually salient stimuli that are either real or fantastic (e.g., animals, monsters). The fears of older elementary school children are characterized by objectively dangerous events that have strong perceptual components when they occur (e.g., kidnapping, accidents, natural disasters), but the fears seem to derive from the anticipation that the events might occur, more often than from the experience of the dangers themselves. The fears of adolescents become even more abstract and diverse (exams, dating, war) and involve the threat of psychological as well as physical harm.

Our findings regarding the media stimuli that frighten children at different ages are consistent with observed changes in children's fears in general. Broad generalizations from our research are summarized here. The first generalization is that *the relative importance of the immediately perceptible components of a fear-inducing media stimulus decreases as a child's age increases.* Research on cognitive development indicates that, in general, very young children react to stimuli predominantly in terms of their perceptible characteristics and that with increasing maturity, they respond more and more to the conceptual aspects of stimuli. Piaget referred to young children's tendency to react to things as they appear in immediate, egocentric perception as *concreteness* of thought (see Flavell, 1963); Bruner (1966) characterized the thought of preschool children as *perceptually dominated.* A variety of studies have shown that young children tend to sort, match, and remember items in terms of their perceptible attributes, and that around the age of 7 this tendency is increasingly replaced by the tendency to use functional or conceptual groupings (e.g., Birch & Bortner, 1966; Melkman, Tversky, & Baratz, 1981).

The notion of a developmental shift from perceptual to conceptual processing has been tested in terms of the impact of visual features of a stimulus. Our research findings support the generalization that preschool children (approximately 3 to 5 years old) are more likely to be frightened by something that *looks* scary but is actually harmless than by something that looks attractive but is actually harmful; for older elementary school children (approximately 9 to 11 years), appearance carries much less weight, relative to the behavior or destructive potential of a character, animal, or object.

One set of data that supports this generalization comes from a survey (Cantor & Sparks, 1984) asking parents to name the programs and films that had frightened their children the most. In this survey, parents of preschool children most often mentioned offerings with grotesque-looking, unreal characters, such as the television series "The Incredible Hulk" and the feature film *The Wizard of Oz*; parents of older elementary school children more often mentioned shows (like *The Amityville Horror*) that involved threats without a strong visual component, and that required a good deal of imagination to comprehend. Sparks (1986b) replicated this study, using children's self-reports rather than parents' observations, and reported similar findings. Both surveys included controls for possible differences in exposure patterns in the different age groups.

A second investigation that supports this generalization was a laboratory study involving an episode of the "Incredible Hulk" series (Sparks & Cantor, 1986). In this study, we concluded that preschool children's unexpectedly intense reactions to this program were partially due to their overresponse to the visual image of the Hulk character.[3] When we tracked participants' levels of fear during different parts of the program, we found that preschool children experienced the most fear after the attractive, mild-mannered hero was transformed into the monstrous-looking Hulk. Older elementary school children, in contrast, reported the least fear at this time, because they understood that the Hulk was really the benevolent hero in another physical form, and that he was using his superhuman powers on the side of "law and order" and against threats to the well-being of liked characters.

In another study (Hoffner & Cantor, 1985), we tested the effect of appearance more directly, by creating a story in four versions, so that a major character was either attractive and grandmotherly-looking or ugly and grotesque. The character's appearance was factorially varied with her behavior—she was depicted as behaving either kindly or cruelly. In judging how nice or mean the character was and in predicting what she would do in the subsequent scene, preschool children were more influenced than older children (6-7 and 9-10 years) by the character's looks and less influenced than older children by her kind or cruel

---

[3]In our survey (Cantor & Sparks, 1984), 40% of the parents of preschool children spontaneously mentioned "The Incredible Hulk" when asked to name a program that had upset their child.

behavior. As the age of the child increased, the character's looks became less important and her behavior carried increasing weight. A follow-up study revealed that all age groups engaged in physical appearance stereotyping in the absence of information about the character's behavior.

A second generalization that emerges from our studies is that *as children mature, they become more responsive to realistic, and less responsive to fantastic dangers depicted in the media.* The data on trends in children's fears suggest that very young children are more likely than older children and adolescents to fear things that are not real, in the sense that their occurrence in the real world is impossible (e.g., monsters). The development of more "mature" fears seems to presuppose the acquisition of knowledge regarding the objective dangers posed by different situations. One important component of this knowledge includes an understanding of the distinction between reality and fantasy. Much research has been conducted on the child's gradual acquisition of the various components of the fantasy–reality distinction (see Flavell, 1963; Kelly, 1981; Morison & Gardner, 1978). Until a child understands the distinction, he or she will be unable to understand that something that is not real cannot pose a threat, and thus, the reality or fantasy status of a media depiction should have little effect on the fear it evokes. As the child comes increasingly to understand this distinction and increasingly appreciates the implications of real-world threats, depictions of real dangers should gain in fear-evoking potential relative to depictions of fantasy dangers.

This generalization is supported by our survey of parents, mentioned earlier (Cantor & Sparks, 1984). In general, the tendency to mention fantasy offerings, depicting events that could not possibly occur in the real world, as sources of fear, decreased as the child's age increased, and the tendency to mention fictional offerings, depicting events that might possibly occur, increased with age. Again, Sparks (1986b) replicated these findings using children's self-reports. Further support for this generalization comes from an experiment (Cantor & Wilson, 1984), in which a reminder that the happenings in *The Wizard of Oz* were not real reduced the fear of older elementary school children but did not affect preschool children's responses.

Our third generalization is that *as children mature, they become frightened by media depictions involving increasingly abstract concepts.* This generalization is clearly consistent with the general sources of children's fears, cited earlier. It is also consistent with theories of cognitive development (e.g., Flavell, 1963), which indicate that the ability to think abstractly emerges relatively late in cognitive development.

Data supporting this generalization come from a survey we conducted on children's responses to the television movie "The Day After" (Cantor, Wilson, & Hoffner, 1986). Many people were concerned about young children's reactions to this movie, which depicted the devastation of a Kansas community by a nuclear attack, but our research led us to predict that the youngest children would be the least affected by it. We conducted a telephone survey (using random sampling) the night after the broadcast of this movie. As we predicted, children under 12 were much less disturbed by the film than were teenagers, and parents were the most disturbed. The very youngest children were not upset or frightened at all. Most of the parents of the younger children who had seen the film could think of other shows that had frightened their child more during the preceding year. Most of the parents of the teenagers could not. We conclude that the findings are due to the fact that the emotional impact of the film comes from the contemplation of the potential annihilation of the earth as we know it—a concept that is beyond the grasp of the young child. The visual depictions of injury in this movie were quite mild compared to what most children have become used to seeing on television. The increase of fear reactions to "The Day After" with increasing age was not expected by organizations such as Educators for Social Responsibility and many school systems that urged that children under the age of 12 not be permitted to watch the movie (Schofield & Pavelchak, 1985).

These developmental generalizations about children's fright reactions to mass media have been confirmed with regard to responses to news reports as well as dramatic presentations. We recently conducted a survey (Cantor, Mares, & Oliver, 1993) to explore the extent of emotional disturbances produced by televised coverage of the 1991 war in the Persian Gulf. In a random sample of parents of children in public school in Madison, Wisconsin, there were no significant differences between first, fourth, seventh, and eleventh graders in the prevalence or intensity of negative emotional reactions to television coverage of the war. However, children in different grades were upset by different aspects of the coverage. Parents of younger children, but not of adolescents, stressed the visual aspect of the coverage and the direct, concrete consequences of combat in their descriptions of the elements that had disturbed their child the most. As the child's age increased, the more abstract, conceptual aspects of the coverage and of the war in general were cited by parents as the most disturbing.

Developmental Differences
in the Effectiveness of Coping Strategies

Developmental differences in children's information-processing abilities produce differences in the effectiveness of strategies to prevent or reduce their media-induced fears (Cantor & Wilson, 1988). The findings of our research on coping strategies can be summed up in the following generalization: *In general, preschool children benefit more from "noncognitive" than from "cognitive strategies"; both cognitive and noncognitive strategies can be effective for older elementary school children, although this age group tends to prefer cognitive strategies.*

Noncognitive Strategies. We have categorized as "noncognitive" those strategies that do not involve the processing of verbal information and that appear to be relatively automatic. The process of visual desensitization is one such strategy that has been shown to be effective for both preschool and older elementary school children in four separate experiments. In one experiment, gradual visual exposure to filmed footage of snakes tended to reduce fear reactions to the "snake pit" scene from the action-adventure film *Raiders of the Lost Ark*. In a second experiment (Wilson, 1987), prior exposure to a realistic rubber replica of a tarantula reduced the emotional impact of a scene involving tarantulas from *Kingdom of the Spiders*. In a third experiment (Wilson, 1989a), prior exposure to a live lizard reduced children's expression of fear while watching a scene involving deadly lizards in *Frogs*. Finally, fear reactions to the Hulk character in "The Incredible Hulk" were reduced by exposure to footage of Lou Ferrigno, the actor who plays the character, having his make-up applied so that he gradually took on the menacing appearance of the character. None of these experiments revealed developmental differences in the technique's effectiveness.

Other noncognitive strategies involve physical activities, such as clinging to an attachment object or having something to eat or drink. Although these techniques are available to viewers of all ages, there is reason to believe they are more effective for younger than for older children. First, it has been argued that the effectiveness of such techniques is likely to diminish as the infant's tendency to grasp and suck objects for comfort and exploration decreases (Bowlby, 1973). Second, it seems likely that the effectiveness of such techniques is partially attributable to distraction, and distraction techniques should be more effective in younger children, who have greater difficulty allocating cognitive processing to two simultaneous activities (e.g., Manis, Keating, & Morison, 1980).

There is no experimental evidence of the effectiveness of physical coping strategies in the mass media situation. However, in a study of children's *perceptions* of the effectiveness of strategies for coping with media-induced fright, preschool children's evaluations of "holding onto a blanket or a toy" and "getting something to eat or drink" were significantly more positive than those of older elementary school children (Wilson, Hoffner, & Cantor, 1987).

Another noncognitive strategy that has been shown to have more appeal and more effectiveness for younger than older children is covering one's eyes during frightening portions of a presentation. In an experiment by Wilson (1989b), when covering the eyes was suggested as an option, younger children used this strategy more often than older children. Moreover, the suggestion of this option reduced the fear of younger children, but actually increased the fear of older children.

Cognitive Strategies.   In contrast to noncognitive strategies, cognitive strategies require the child to think about the fear stimulus in a way that generally casts the threat in a different light. The strategies involve relatively complex cognitive operations, and our research consistently finds such strategies to be more effective for older than for younger children. When dealing with fantasy depictions, the most typical cognitive strategy seems to be to provide an explanation focusing on the unreality of the situation. This strategy should be especially difficult for preschool children, who do not have a full grasp of the implications of the fantasy–reality distinction. In a study mentioned earlier (Cantor & Wilson, 1984), older elementary school children who were told to remember that what they were seeing was not real showed less fear than their classmates who received no instructions. The same instructions had no effect on the fear of preschoolers, however. A more recent study (Wilson & Weiss, 1991) again showed developmental differences in the effectiveness of reality-related strategies.

Children's beliefs about the effectiveness of focusing on the unreality of the stimulus have been shown to be consistent with these experimental findings. In our study of perceptions of techniques, preschool children's ranking of the effectiveness of "tell yourself it's not real" was significantly lower than that of older elementary school children (Wilson et al., 1987). In contrast to children, who apparently view this strategy accurately, parents do not seem to appreciate the inadequacy of this technique for young children. Eighty percent of the parents of both the preschool and elementary school children who participated in another of our studies (Wilson & Cantor, 1987), reported that they employed a "tell them it's not real" coping strategy to reduce their child's media-induced fear.

For media depictions involving realistic threats, the most prevalent cognitive strategy seems to be to provide an explanation that minimizes the perceived severity of the depicted danger. This type of strategy is not only more effective with older than with younger children, in certain situations it has been shown to have a fear-enhancing rather than anxiety-reducing effect with younger children. In the experiment involving the snake-pit scene from *Raiders of the Lost Ark*, mentioned earlier (Wilson & Cantor), a second experimental variation involved the presence or absence of reassuring information about snakes (e.g., the statement that most snakes are not poisonous). Although this information tended to reduce the fear of older elementary school children, kindergarten and first grade children seem to have only partially understood the information, and for them, negative emotional reactions were more likely if they had heard the information than if they had not.

Data also indicate that older children use cognitive coping strategies more frequently than preschool children. In our survey of reactions to "The Day After" (Cantor et al., 1986), we found that the tendency to discuss the movie with parents after viewing increased with the age of the child. In a more recent laboratory experiment (Hoffner & Cantor, 1990), significantly more 9- to 11-year-olds than 5- to 7-year-olds reported spontaneously employing cognitive coping strategies (thinking about the expected happy outcome or thinking about the fact that what was happening was not real). Moreover, in our study of perceptions of techniques (Wilson et al., 1987), the perceived effectiveness of "talk to your mom or dad about the program" increased with age, although nonsignificantly.

We have also conducted studies to determine ways of improving the effectiveness of cognitive strategies for young children, such as by providing visual demonstrations of verbal explanations (Cantor, Sparks, & Hoffner, 1988), and by encouraging repeated rehearsal of simplified, reassuring information (Wilson, 1987). In addition, we have investigated some of the specific reasons for the inability of young children to profit from verbal explanations, such as those involving relative quantifiers (e.g., "some are dangerous, but most are not," Badzinski, Cantor, & Hoffner, 1989) and probabilistic terms ("this probably will not happen to you," Hoffner, Cantor, & Badzinski, 1990). It is clear from these studies that it is an extremely challenging task to "explain away" threats that have induced fear in a child, particularly when there is a strong perceptual component to the threatening stimulus, and when the reassurance can only be partial or probabilistic, rather than absolute (see Cantor & Hoffner, 1990).

The task of reassuring children should be especially difficult when dealing with real threats. Although only a few studies (e.g., Cantor et al., 1993; see also Cantor, 1992) have been conducted on the emotional effects of news and documentary programming on children, the research on children's fright reactions to entertainment programming should be useful in determining when to expect fright reactions to real dangers and in gauging the effectiveness of coping strategies (Cantor, 1994).

Implications for Parental Guidance

One question that arises out of the research on children's fright reactions regards the degree to which fright responses produced by the media are actually detrimental to a child's development. Although many of the researchers cited at the beginning of this chapter have assumed the potential for long-term negative effects, no systematic research has documented the pervasiveness of such effects. The absence of this type of data is no doubt attributable, in part, to ethical considerations. It simply is not possible to carry out an experiment to demonstrate the ability of media horrors to produce long-term emotional scars. Field surveys of children's emotional reactions to real-world disasters and highly publicized media events, such as the Space Shuttle Challenger disaster and "The Day After," have generally reported predominantly mild and short-lived responses on the part of children (see Cantor, 1992).

On the other hand, anecdotal evidence of long-term impact is heard frequently enough to promote concern, and it has been argued that the research process of questioning children about their responses to a traumatic event shortly after it has occurred may have a therapeutic effect and reduce the likelihood of long-term impact (Cantor, 1992). Moreover, long-term retrospective studies are seldom done, and they would necessarily suffer from a heavy reliance on introspection and delayed memory assessments.

A recent study bears on long-term implications, although the data were collected immediately after exposure only (Cantor & Omdahl, 1991). In this experiment, exposure to dramatized depictions of a deadly house fire or a drowning increased children's self-reports of worry about similar events in their own lives. In addition, these fictional depictions affected the children's preferences for normal, everyday activities that were related to the tragedies they had just witnessed: Children who had seen a movie depicting a drowning showed less willingness to go canoeing than other children; those who had seen the program about a house fire were less eager to build a fire in a fireplace. Although the duration of such effects was not measured, the effects were undoubtedly short-lived, especially because debriefings were employed so that no child would experience long-term distress. It is difficult to estimate the long-term effects that occur in children whose viewing is unguided and unobserved, and who do not have the opportunity to discuss unreasonable or disproportionate fears with a concerned adult.

Whatever the long-term implications of children's exposure, the research cited in this chapter indicates that children's reactions will not always be intuitively understandable from a parent's perspective. Developmental issues in perception, comprehension, and interpretation must be taken into account in predicting how children will react to frightening media presentations and how much they will benefit from specific intervention strategies.

SUMMARY AND CONCLUSIONS

This chapter has summarized research indicating that adults and children often experience anxiety and distress while watching mass media productions and that these feelings, in varying intensities, sometimes linger on after exposure. Although these reactions tend to be of negative hedonic tone, the research shows that many people like frightening presentations and that the capacity of such fare to produce fear may be part of their appeal.

An explanation has been proposed to account for the fact that media productions often induce anxiety and fear when the viewer, objectively speaking, is in no immediate danger. It has been argued that through stimulus generalization, stimuli and events that would evoke fear if encountered live, produce fear when depicted in the media. The major stimuli and events producing fear in media presentations have been categorized as dangers, injuries, distortions, and endangerment and fear experienced by others. These categories of stimuli are prevalent in both fictional "horror" shows and in realistic "stressful" documentaries.

The notion of stimulus generalization has further been employed to predict that various types of similarity between real-life fear-evokers and media stimuli will enhance fright reactions to media depictions. But stimulus generalization alone has been found to be an inadequate explanation because it leads to the expectation that media-induced fear responses will extinguish over time. Viewers' various motivations for exposure, such as for entertainment and arousal or for information-gain, have been proposed as important modifying factors. Elements within a media presentation that affect emotionality generally have also been discussed as influential. The findings of surveys and experiments regarding the effects of dramatic media productions as well as realistic documentaries have been discussed in support of these speculations.

Finally, cognitive developmental factors have been discussed as important determinants of the types of media stimuli that evoke fear in children and the effectiveness of strategies for preventing or reducing media-induced fear.

ACKNOWLEDGEMENTS

Much of the research reported in this chapter was supported by Grant RO1 MH 35320 from the National Institute of Mental Health and by grants from the Graduate School of the University of Wisconsin.

REFERENCES

Angelino, H., Dollins, J., & Mech, E. V. (1956). Trends in the "fears and worries" of school children as related to socio-economic status and age. *Journal of Genetic Psychology, 89,* 263–276.

Averill, J. R., Malmstrom, E. J., Koriat, A., & Lazarus, R. S. (1972). Habituation to complex emotional stimuli. *Journal of Abnormal Psychology, 1,* 20–28.

Badzinski, D. M., Cantor, J., & Hoffner, C. (1989). Children's understanding of quantifiers. *Child Study Journal, 19,* 241–258.

Berger, S. M. (1962). Conditioning through vicarious instigation. *Psychological Review, 69,* 450–466.

Bettelheim, B. (1975). *The uses of enchantment: The meaning and importance of fairy tales.* New York: Vintage Books.

Birch, H. B., & Bortner, M. (1966). Stimulus competition and category usage in normal children. *Journal of Genetic Psychology, 109,* 195–204.

Blumer, H. (1933). *Movies and conduct.* New York: Macmillan.

Bowlby, J. (1973). *Separation: Anxiety and anger.* New York: Basic Books.

Bruner, J. S. (1966). On cognitive growth I & II. In J. S. Bruner, R. R. Oliver, & P. M. Greenfield (Eds.), *Studies in cognitive growth* (pp. 1–67). New York: Wiley.

Buzzuto, J. C. (1975). Cinematic neurosis following *The Exorcist. Journal of Nervous and Mental Disease, 161,* 43–48.

Cantor, J. (1989). Studying children's emotional reactions to mass media. In B. Dervin, L. Grossberg, B. O'Keefe, & E. Wartella (Eds.), *Rethinking communication. Vol. 2. Paradigm exemplars* (pp. 47–59). Newbury Park, CA: Sage.

Cantor, J. (1991). Fright responses to mass media productions. In J. Bryant & D. Zillmann (Eds.), *Responding to the screen: Reception and reaction processes* (pp. 169–197). Hillsdale, NJ: Lawrence Erlbaum Associates.

Cantor, J. (1992). Children's emotional responses to technological disasters conveyed by the mass media. In J. M. Wober (Ed.), *Television and nuclear power: Making the public mind* (pp. 31–53). Norwood, NJ: Ablex.

Cantor, J. (1994). Confronting children's fright responses to mass media. In D. Zillmann, J. Bryant, & A. C. Huston (Eds.), *Media, children, and the family: Social scientific, psychodynamic, and clinical perspectives* (pp. 139–150). Hillsdale, NJ: Lawrence Erlbaum Associates.

Cantor, J., & Hoffner, C. (1990). Children's fear reactions to a televised film as a function of perceived immediacy of depicted threat. *Journal of Broadcasting & Electronic Media, 34,* 421–442.

Cantor, J., Mares, M. L., & Oliver, M. B. (1993). Parents' and children's emotional reactions to televised coverage of the Gulf War. In B. Greenberg & W. Gantz (Eds.), *Desert storm and the mass media* (pp. 325–340). Cresskill, NJ: Hampton Press.

Cantor, J., & Omdahl, B. (1991). Effects of fictional media depictions of realistic threats on children's emotional responses, expectations, worries, and liking for related activities. *Communication Monographs, 58,* 384–401.

ʰCantor, J., & Reilly, S. (1982). Adolescents' fright reactions to television and films. *Journal of Communication, 32* (1), 87–99.

ᵗCantor, J., & Sparks, G. G. (1984). Children's fear responses to mass media: Testing some Piagetian predictions. *Journal of Communication, 34* (2), 90–103.

Cantor, J., Sparks, G. G., & Hoffner, C. (1988). Calming children's television fears: Mr. Rogers vs. the Incredible Hulk. *Journal of Broadcasting & Electronic Media, 32,* 271–288.

Cantor, J., & Wilson, B. J. (1984). Modifying fear responses to mass media in preschool and elementary school children. *Journal of Broadcasting, 28,* 431–443.

Cantor, J., & Wilson, B. J. (1988). Helping children cope with frightening media presentations. *Current Psychology: Research & Reviews, 7,* 58–75.

ᵗCantor, J., Wilson, B. J., & Hoffner, C. (1986). Emotional responses to a televised nuclear holocaust film. *Communication Research, 13,* 257–277.

Cantor, J., Ziemke, D., & Sparks, G. G. (1984). Effect of forewarning on emotional responses to a horror film. *Journal of Broadcasting, 28,* 21–31.

Cantor, J., Zillmann, D., & Bryant, J. (1975). Enhancement of experienced sexual arousal in response to erotic stimuli through misattribution of unrelated residual excitation. *Journal of Personality and Social Psychology, 32,* 69–75.

Cantril, H. (1940). *The invasion from Mars: A study in the psychology of panic.* Princeton, NJ: Princeton University Press.

Collins, W. A. (1983). Interpretation and inference in children's television viewing. In J. Bryant & D. R. Anderson (Eds.), *Children's understanding of television* (pp. 125–150). New York: Academic Press.

Comstock, G. A., & Rubinstein, E. A. (Eds.). (1972). *Television and social behavior.* Washington, DC: U. S. Government Printing Office.

Davidson, P. O., & Hiebert, S. F. (1971). Relaxation training, relaxation instruction, and repeated exposure to a stressor film. *Journal of Abnormal Psychology, 78,* 154–159.

Dorr, A. (1980). When I was a child I thought as a child. In S. B. Withey & R. P. Abeles (Eds.), *Television and social behavior: Beyond violence and children* (pp. 191–230). Hillsdale, NJ: Lawrence Erlbaum Associates.

Dorr, A., Doubleday, C., & Kovaric, P. (1983). Emotions depicted on and stimulated by television programs. In M. Meyer (Ed.), *Children and the formal features of television* (pp. 97–143). New York: K. G. Saur.

Dysinger, W. S., & Ruckmick, C. A. (1933). *The emotional responses of children to the motion picture situation.* New York: Macmillan.

Eisenberg, A. L. (1936). *Children and radio programs,* New York: Columbia University Press.

Falkowski, J., & Steptoe, A. (1983). Biofeedback-assisted relaxation in the control of reactions to a challenging task and anxiety-provoking film. *Behavior Research and Therapy, 21,* 161–167.

Feshbach, N. D. (1982). Sex differences in empathy and social behavior in children. In N. Eisenberg (Ed.), *The development of prosocial behavior* (pp. 315–338). New York: Academic Press.

Flavell, J. (1963). *The developmental psychology of Jean Piaget.* New York: Van Nostrand.

Geen, R. G. (1975). The meaning of observed violence: Real vs. fictional violence and consequent effects on aggression and emotional arousal. *Journal of Research in Personality, 9,* 270–281.

Geen, R. G., & Rakosky, J. J. (1973). Interpretations of observed violence and their effects on GSR. *Journal of Experimental Research in Personality, 6,* 289–292.

Girodo, M., & Pellegrini, W. (1976). Exercise-produced arousal, film-induced arousal and attribution of internal state. *Perceptual and Motor Skills, 42,* 931–935.

Groebel, J., & Krebs, D. (1983). A study of the effects of television on anxiety. In C. D. Spielberger & R. Diaz-Guerrero (Eds.), *Cross-cultural anxiety* (Vol. 2, pp. 89–98). New York: Hemisphere.

Gunter, B., & Furnham, A. (1984). Perceptions of television violence: Effects of programme genre and type of violence on viewers' judgements of violent portrayals. *British Journal of Social Psychology, 23,* 155–164.

Hare, R. D., & Blevings, G. (1975). Defensive responses to phobic stimuli. *Biological Psychology, 3,* 1–13.

Hebb, D. O. (1946). On the nature of fear. *Psychological Review, 53,* 259–276.

Hess, R. D., & Goldman, H. (1962). Parents' views of the effects of television on their children. *Child Development, 33,* 411–426.

Hilgard, E. R., Atkinson, R. C., & Atkinson, R. L. (1971). *Introduction to psychology.* New York: Harcourt Brace Jovanovich.

Himmelweit, H. T., Oppenheim, A. N., & Vince, P. (1958). *Television and the child.* London: Oxford University Press.

Hoffman, M. L. (1978). Toward a theory of empathic arousal and development. In M. Lewis & L. A. Rosenblum (Eds.), *The development of affect* (pp. 227–256). New York: Plenum.

Hoffner, C., & Cantor, J. (1985). Developmental differences in responses to a television character's appearance and behavior. *Developmental Psychology, 21,* 1065–1074.

Hoffner, C., & Cantor, J. (1990). Forewarning of a threat and prior knowledge of outcome: Effects on children's emotional responses to a film sequence. *Human Communication Research, 16,* 323–354.

Hoffner, C., Cantor, J., & Badzinski, D. M. (1990). Children's understanding of adverbs denoting degree of likelihood. *Journal of Child Language, 17,* 217–231.

Horowitz, M. J. (1976). *Stress response syndromes.* New York: Appleton-Century-Crofts.

Izard, C. E. (1977). *Human emotions.* New York: Plenum Press.

Jersild, A. T., & Holmes, F. B. (1935). Methods of overcoming children's fears. *Journal of Psychology, 1,* 75–104.

Johnson, B. R. (1980). General occurrence of stressful reactions to commercial motion pictures and elements in films subjectively identified as stressors. *Psychological Reports, 47,* 775–786.

Kamen, G. B. (1971). A second look at the effects of a stress-producing film on adult test performance. *Journal of Clinical Psychology, 27,* 465–467.

Kase, J., Sikes, S., & Spielberger, C. (1978). Emotional reactions to frightening and neutral scenes in story theatre. *Communication Monographs, 45,* 181–186.

Kelly, H. (1981). Reasoning about realities: Children's evaluations of television and books. In H. Kelly & H. Gardner (Eds.), *Viewing children through television* (pp. 59–71). San Francisco: Jossey-Bass.

Koriat, A., Melkman, R., Averill, J. R., & Lazarus, R. S. (1972). The self-control of emotional reactions to a stressful film. *Journal of Personality, 40,* 601–619.

Lazarus, R. S. (1966). *Psychological stress and the coping process.* New York: McGraw-Hill.

Lazarus, R. S., & Alfert, E. (1964). Short-circuiting of threat by experimentally altering cognitive appraisal. *Journal of Abnormal and Social Psychology, 69,* 195–205.

Lazarus, R. S., Speisman, J. C., Mordkoff, A. M., & Davidson, L. A. (1962). A laboratory study of psychological stress produced by a motion picture film. *Psychological Monographs: General and Applied, 76,* (34), Whole No. 553.

Leishman, K. (1981, January 10). When is television too scary for children? *TV Guide,* pp. 5–6, 8.

Lyle, J., & Hoffman, H. R. (1972). Children's use of television and other media. In E. A. Rubinstein, G. A. Comstock, & J. P. Murray (Eds.), *Television and social behavior* (Vol. 4., pp. 129–256). Washington, DC: U. S. Government Printing Office.

Lyle, J., & Hoffman, H. R. (1976). Explorations in patterns of television viewing by preschool-age children. In R. Brown (Ed.), *Children and television* (pp. 45–61). Beverly Hills, CA: Sage.

Manis, F. R., Keating, D. P., & Morison, F. J. (1980). Developmental differences in the allocation of processing capacity. *Journal of Experimental Child Psychology, 29,* 156–169.

Mathai, J. (1983). An acute anxiety state in an adolescent precipitated by viewing a horror movie. *Journal of Adolescence, 6,* 197–200.

Maurer, A. (1965). What children fear. *Journal of Genetic Psychology, 106,* 265–277.

Melkman, R., Tversky, B., & Baratz, D. (1981). Developmental trends in the use of perceptual and conceptual attributes in grouping, clustering and retrieval. *Journal of Experimental Child Psychology, 31,* 470–486.

Morison, P., & Gardner, H. (1978). Dragons and dinosaurs: The child's capacity to differentiate fantasy from reality. *Child Development, 49,* 642–648.

Nomikos, M., Opton, E. Averill, J., & Lazarus, R. (1968). Surprise versus suspense in the production of stress reaction. *Journal of Personality and Social Psychology, 8,* 204–208.

Osborn, D. K., & Endsley, R. C. (1971). Emotional reactions of young children to tv violence. *Child Development, 42,* 321–331.

Palmer, E. L., Hockett, A. B., & Dean, W. W. (1983). The television family and children's fright reactions. *Journal of Family Issues, 4,* 279–292.

Pavlov, I. P. (1960). *Conditioned reflexes* (G. V. Anrep, Trans.). London: Oxford University Press. (Original work published 1927)

Pearl, D., Bouthilet, L., & Lazar, J. (Eds.). (1982). *Television and behavior: Ten years of scientific progress and implications for the eighties* (DHHS Publication No. ADM 82-1196). Washington, DC: U.S. Government Printing Office.

Pillard, R. C., Atkinson, K. W., & Fisher, S. (1967). The effect of different preparations on film-induced anxiety. *Psychological Record, 17,* 35–41.

Preston, M. I. (1941). Children's reactions to movie horrors and radio crime. *Journal of Pediatrics, 19,* 147–168.

Razran, G. (1949). Stimulus generalization of conditioned responses. *Psychological Bulletin, 46,* 337–365.

Sapolsky, B. S., & Zillmann, D. (1978). Experience and empathy: Affective reactions to witnessing childbirth. *Journal of Social Psychology, 105,* 131–144.

Sarafino, E. P. (1986). *The fears of childhood: A guide to recognizing and reducing fearful states in children.* New York: Human Sciences Press.

Schachter, S., & Singer, J. (1962). Cognitive, social, and physiological determinants of emotional state. *Psychological Review, 69,* 379–399.

Schofield, J., & Pavelchak, M. (1985). "The Day After": The impact of a media event. *American Psychologist, 40,* 542–548.

Schramm, W., Lyle, J., & Parker, E. P. (1961). *Television in the lives of our children.* Stanford, CA: Stanford University Press.

Selman, R. L., & Byrne, D. (1978). A structural analysis of levels of role-taking in middle childhood. *Child Development, 45,* 803–807.

Singer, J. L. (1975). *Daydreaming and fantasy.* London: Allen & Unwin.

Smetak, J. R., (1986). Steven Spielberg: Gore, guts, and PG-13. *Journal of Popular Film and Television, 14*(1), 4–13.

Sparks, G. G. (1986a). Developing a scale to assess cognitive responses to frightening films. *Journal of Broadcasting and Electronic Media, 30,* 65–73.

Sparks, G. G. (1986b). Developmental differences in children's reports of fear induced by the mass media. *Child Study Journal, 16,* 55–66.

Sparks, G. G. (1989). Understanding emotional reactions to a suspenseful movie: The interaction between forewarning and preferred coping style. *Communication Monographs, 56,* 325–340.

Sparks, G. G., & Cantor, J. (1986). Developmental differences in fright responses to a television program depicting a character transformation. *Journal of Broadcasting and Electronic Media, 30,* 309–323.

Sparks, G. G., & Spirek, M. M. (1988). Individual differences in coping with stressful mass media: An activation-arousal view. *Human Communication Research 15*, 195–216.

Speisman, J. C., Lazarus, R. S., Mordkoff, A., & Davidson, L. (1964). Experimental reduction of stress based on ego-defense theory. *Journal of Abnormal and Social Psychology 68*, 367–380.

Stein, E. (1982, June 20). Have horror films gone too far? *New York Times* (Arts & Leisure), pp. 1, 21–22.

Surbeck, E. (1975). Young children's emotional reactions to T.V. violence: The effects of children's perceptions of reality. *Dissertation Abstracts International, 35*, 5139–A.

Tamborini, R., Stiff, J., & Zillmann, D. (1987). Preference for graphic horror featuring male versus female victimization: Personality and past film viewing experiences. *Human Communication Research, 13*(4), 529–552.

Tannenbaum, P. H. (1980). Entertainment as vicarious emotional experience. In P. H. Tannenbaum (Ed.), *The entertainment functions of television* (pp. 107–131). Hillsdale, NJ: Lawrence Erlbaum Associates.

Tannenbaum, P. H., & Gaer, E. P. (1965). Mood change as a function of stress of protagonist and degree of identification in a film-viewing situation. *Journal of Personality and Social Psychology, 2*, 612–616.

Taylor, P. (1991, February 6). War may not be news young children can use. *The Washington Post*, p. A3.

Thayer, J. F., & Levenson, R. W. (1983). Effects of music on psychophysiological responses to a stressful film. *Psychomusicology, 3*, 44–52.

von Feilitzen, C. (1975). Findings of Scandinavian research on child and television in the process of socialization. *Fernsehen und Bildung, 9*, 54–84.

Wall, W. D., & Simson, W. A. (1950). The emotional responses of adolescent groups to certain films. *British Journal of Educational Psychology, 20*, 153–163.

Wartella, E. (1979). The developmental perspective. In E. Wartella (Ed.), *Children communicating: Media and development of thought, speech, understanding* (pp. 1–19). Beverly Hills, CA: Sage.

Weiss, B. W., Katkin, E. S., & Rubin, B. M. (1968). Relationship between a factor analytically derived measure of a specific fear and performance after related fear induction. *Journal of Abnormal Psychology, 73*, 461–463.

Wertham, F. (1953). *Seduction of the innocent.* New York: Rinehart.

Wilson, B. J. (1987). Reducing children's emotional reactions to mass media through rehearsed explanation and exposure to a replica of a fear object. *Human Communication Research, 14*, 3–26.

Wilson, B. J. (1989a). Desensitizing children's emotional reactions to the mass media. *Communication Research, 16*, 723–745.

Wilson, B. J. (1989b). The effects of two control strategies on children's emotional reactions to a frightening movie scene. *Journal of Broadcasting & Electronic Media, 33*, 397–418.

Wilson, B. J., & Cantor, J. (1985). Developmental differences in empathy with a television protagonist's fear. *Journal of Experimental Child Psychology, 39*, 284–299.

Wilson, B. J., & Cantor, J. (1987). Reducing children's fear reactions to mass media: Effects of visual exposure and verbal explanation. In M. McLaughlin, (Ed.), *Communication Yearbook 10* (pp. 553–573). Beverly Hills, CA: Sage.

Wilson, B. J., Hoffner, C., & Cantor, J. (1987). Children's perceptions of the effectiveness of techniques to reduce fear from mass media. *Journal of Applied Developmental Psychology, 8*, 39–52.

Wilson, B. J., & Weiss, A. J. (1991). The effects of two reality explanations on children's reactions to a frightening movie scene. *Communication Monographs, 58*, 307–326.

Yerkes, R. M., & Yerkes, A. W. (1936). Nature and conditions of avoidance (fear) response in chimpanzee. *Journal of Comparative Psychology, 21*, 53–66.

Zill, N. (1977). *National survey of children: Summary of preliminary results.* New York: Foundation for Child Development.

Zillmann, D. (1978). Attribution and misattribution of excitatory reactions. In J. H. Harvey, W. Ickes, & R. F. Kidd (Eds.), *New directions in attribution research* (Vol. 2, pp. 335–368). New York: Lawrence Erlbaum Associates.

Zillmann, D. (1980). Anatomy of suspense. In P. H. Tannenbaum, (Ed.), *The entertainment functions of television* (pp. 133–163). Hillsdale, NJ: Lawrence Erlbaum Associates.

Zillmann, D. (1982). Television viewing and arousal. In D. Pearl, L. Bouthilet, & J. Lazar (Eds.), *Television and behavior: Ten years of scientific progress and implications for the eighties* (Vol. 2, pp. 53–67). Washington, DC: U. S. Government Printing Office.

Zillmann, D., & Cantor, J. (1977). Affective responses to the emotions of a protagonist. *Journal of Experimental Social Psychology, 13,* 155–165.

Zillmann, D., Hay, T. A., & Bryant, J. (1975). The effect of suspense and its resolution on the appreciation of dramatic presentations. *Journal of Research in Personality, 9,* 307–323.

Zillmann, D., Mody, B., & Cantor, J. (1974). Empathetic perception of emotional displays in films as a function of hedonic and excitatory state prior to exposure. *Journal of Research in Personality, 8,* 335–349.

Zillmann, D., Weaver, J. B., Mundorf, N., & Aust, C. F. (1986). Effects of an opposite-gender companion's affect to horror on distress, delight, and attraction. *Journal of Personality and Social Psychology, 51,* 586–594.

Zoglin, R. (1984, June 25). Gremlins in the rating system. *Time,* p. 78.

Because not everyone would agree that all of these classes of materials are "pornographic," and because the term *pornographic* is highly value laden but scientifically imprecise, we will instead generally refer to such materials as "sexually explicit" rather than "pornographic."

Clearly, sex also occurs in the media in other than explicitly sexual materials. For example, it is rampant in advertising, particularly for products like perfume, cologne, and after shave, but also for tires, automobiles, and the kitchen sink. Sex in media is not limited to explicit portrayals of intercourse or nudity but rather may include any representation that portrays or implies sexual behavior, interest, or motivation. However, the major focus in this chapter is on the more explicit materials.

History of Sex in Media

Sexual themes in fiction have been around as long as fiction itself. Ancient Greek comedies were often highly sexual in content, such as Aristophanes' *Lysistrata*, an antiwar comedy about women who withhold sex from their husbands in order to coerce them to stop fighting wars. Literary classics like Chaucer's *Canterbury Tales* and Shakespeare's *The Taming of the Shrew* are filled with sexual double entendres and overtly sexual themes, some of which are missed today due to the archaic language and the "classic" aura around such works. Throughout history, the pendulum has swung back and forth in terms of how much explicit sexual expression in literature is tolerated.

Since the advent of electronic media, standards have usually been more conservative for radio and television than for print, because it is easier to keep sexually oriented print media from children than it is to keep radio or TV from them. With the advent of widespread cable and videocassette technology, a sort of double standard has arisen, with greater permissiveness for videocassettes and premium cable channels like Playboy, Tuxxedo, and American Exxxtasy than for network television, on the logic that premium cable and rented movies are "invited" into the home, whereas network programming is there uninvited whenever a TV set is present.

Media Sex Today

Content analyses (Fernandez-Collado, Greenberg, Korzenny, & Atkin, 1978; Greenberg et al., 1993; Greenberg & D'Alessilo, 1985; Lowry & Towles, 1989; Sprafkin & Silverman, 1981) show that, although the sex on network television is not explicit, innuendoes are rampant, often occurring in a humorous context. References to premarital and extramarital sexual encounters far outnumbered references to sex between spouses, as high as 24:1 for unmarried versus married partners in soap operas (Lowry & Towles, 1989) or 32:1 in R-rated movies with teens (Greenberg et al., 1993)! Although more sexual references occurred overall in daytime soaps than on prime-time TV, evening programming contained more references to intercourse and sexual deviance (Greenberg, Abelman, & Neuendorf, 1981). Nudity occurred in one study in all 30 R-rated films popular with teens, with female nudity (especially breasts) exceeding male nudity by a 4:1 margin. R-rated movies and sex magazines had considerably more explicit sex than appeared on television (Greenberg et al., 1993).

Sex in media is one area where we clearly accept some limits on freedom of speech. The sharp differences of opinion surface in deciding just where those limits ought to be. Few are arguing that "Home Improvement" or "Northern Exposure" should be allowed to show frontal nudity or child prostitutes in chains, although of course it is highly unlikely that the producers would ever care to do so. One important issue in discussion of where the limits should be is the age of the viewer or reader. There is far more concern about the effects of sexual media on children than on adults. Even a highly libertarian person might not want their 6-year-old reading *Hustler*, whereas even a morally very conservative person would be less alarmed about adults viewing sexually explicit videos than about children seeing them.

Explicit sexual materials have traditionally been designed by men and for men. As such, they have a distinctly macho and hypermasculinized orientation. Although all varieties of heterosexual intercourse are shown, there is little emphasis on associated foreplay, afterplay, cuddling, or general tenderness. Women are seen eagerly desiring and participating in sex, often with hysterical euphoria. There is little concern with the consequences of sex or the relational matrix within which most adults find it. Quite recently there has been some increase in sexual materials with more emphasis on relationship, pre- and postcoital behaviors, and the woman's point of view generally, developed primarily to be marketed to women. As yet, however, these comprise only a miniscule part of the $5 billion market worldwide (Day & Bloom, 1988; Hebditch & Anning, 1988; Weaver, 1991). Although men are much more active seekers and users of sexual material than are women, this cannot be assumed to be due to greater intrinsic male interest in sex; it may merely reflect the pornography industry's extreme slant to the traditional male perspective.

Media are clearly major sources of information about sex, information that we use to construct our reality of what sexuality and sexual behavior and values are all about. To better understand this reality and its consequences, we now examine some effects of viewing sex in the media. How are we changed after exposure to such material?

EFFECTS OF VIEWING MEDIA SEX

As much as many might wish it otherwise, sex apparently does sell, even very explicit sex. Sexually oriented media of all sorts are highly profitable commercially, and this fact has ramifications for all media. However, this economic effect is not the focus of this book; we turn now to the various psychological effects (see Lyons, Anderson, & Larson, in press, for a careful review of the literature on the effects of viewing sexual media).

Arousal

A fairly straightforward effect of sex in media is sexual arousal, the drive that energizes or intensifies sexual behavior. Sexually oriented media, especially explicit magazines and videos, do tend to arouse people sexually, both in terms of self-rating of arousal level and physiological arousal measures such as penile tumescence (Eccles, Marshall, & Barbaree, 1988; Malamuth & Check, 1980a; Schaefer & Colgan, 1977), vaginal changes (Sintchak & Geer, 1975), and thermography (Abramson, Perry, Seeley, Seeley, & Rothblatt, 1981). Sexual violence is particularly arousing to sex offenders and much less so to normal men, unless the victim is portrayed as being aroused by the assault. These findings are discussed in more detail later.

Sexual arousal to stimuli not naturally evoking such response may be learned through classical conditioning. For example, Rachman (1966) and Rachman and Hodgson (1968) classically conditioned heterosexual men to be sexually aroused by women's boots by pairing the boots with nude photos, thus providing a model of how fetishes could be learned. More generally, this could account for the vast individual differences in which specific stimuli arouse people sexually. Through our different experiences, we have all been conditioned to be "turned on" by different stimuli.

Contrary to what one might expect, the degree of arousal is not necessarily highly correlated with the degree of explicitness of the media. Sometimes one is actually more aroused by a less sexually explicit story than a more explicit one (e.g., Bancroft & Mathews, 1971). Censoring out a sex scene may actually make a film more arousing, because viewers can fill in their own completion. Sexual arousal is highly individual. When people are allowed to use their own imaginations to construct the ending of a romantic scene, they are more likely to construct a reality that is more arousing to them personally than if they view someone else's idea of what is arousing. There is some validity to the old truism that the primary sex organ is the brain.

Attitudes and Values

Some Issues. A large class of effects of media sex have to do with effects on attitudes and values. One frequent concern is a desensitization to certain expressions of sexuality deemed by someone to be "inappropriate." For example, parents may be concerned that sitcoms showing teenagers considering being sexually active may contradict and thus weaken family-taught values against premarital sex. Women may be concerned that car magazines selling auto parts by showing a bikini-clad woman held in mock bondage by a giant shock absorber may desensitize readers about violence toward women.

Sometimes the media may actually change one's value or attitude, rather than merely desensitizing or reinforcing an existing one. It may be that teenage girls watching Roseanne's daughter as she considers having sex with her boyfriend may also come to adopt those values. This is especially likely to happen if the TV characters holding those values are respected characters with whom viewers identify. Sexual promiscuity by a prostitute character is less likely to influence the values of a viewer than promiscuity by a respected suburban wife and mother. This type of concern is reflected, for example, in former U.S. Vice President Dan Quayle's 1992 criticism of the single adult woman sitcom character Murphy Brown as being a poor role model, because she had a baby (and presumably intercourse) outside of marriage.

Another concern about the effects on values and attitudes is that sexually oriented media may encourage people not to take sexual issues as seriously as they should. When a sex magazine has a regular cartoon called "Chester the Molester" featuring a child molester, many argue that this is an inappropriately light treatment of an extremely serious subject. One article in a sex magazine aimed at male teenagers was entitled "Good Sex with Retarded Girls"; this too is open to such criticism. Although few would probably argue that sex should *never* be comedic, there are for most people some sexual subjects, especially those involving children or violence, that do not seem appropriate for light treatment.

Of particular concern are attitudes toward women. One of the major criticisms of sexually explicit media is that they are antiwomen in an ideological sense. It is usually women, not men, who are the playthings or victims of the opposite sex. Although this concern spans the gamut of sexual content in media, it is particularly leveled at sexual violence. What are teenage boys who are first learning about sex going to think that women want when they see a picture of a jackhammer in a woman's vagina as the opening photo to a story called "How to Cure Frigidity?" When *Hustler* magazine runs a photo spread of a gang rape turning into an orgy, showing the women appearing to be aroused by the assault, what is being taught about women and their reactions to forcible sex? Research examining this question will be discussed in detail later.

Finally, in regard to values and attitudes, people sometimes complain that media sex, especially the more explicit varieties, removes some of the mystique, some of the aura, from what is a very mysterious, almost sacred activity. This argument holds that sex is very private and more meaningful and more fun if it is not so public. This is a hard concern even to articulate, even harder to refute or test empirically, but it is one often expressed.

Research Evidence. Several studies have shown effects on attitudes and values about sex as a result of exposure to nonviolent sexually explicit materials. After seeing slides and movies of beautiful female nudes engaged in sexual activity, male subjects rated their own partners as being less physically endowed, though they reported undiminished sexual satisfaction (Weaver, Masland, & Zillmann, 1984). In another study men reported loving their own mates less after seeing sexually explicit videos of highly attractive models (Kenrick, Gutierres, & Goldberg, 1989). Men who had just seen a sexually explicit video responded more sexually in terms of behavior to a female interviewer than those having seen a control video, although this result only held for men holding traditional gender schemata (McKenzie-Mohr & Zanna, 1990). All these studies showed significant attitude changes after a very limited exposure to sexual media.

Using a paradigm of showing participants weekly films and testing them 1-3 weeks later, Zillmann and Bryant (1982, 1984) found that participants seeing the films overestimated the popularity of sexual practices like fellatio, cunnilingus, anal intercourse, sadomasochism, and bestiality, relative to perceptions of a control group seeing non-sexually explicit films. This may reflect the cognitive heuristic of *availability*, whereby we judge the frequency of occurrence of various activities by the ease with which we can generate examples (Taylor, 1982; Tversky & Kahneman, 1973, 1974). Recent vivid media instances thus lead to an overestimation of such occurrences in the real world and a likelihood estimation substantially at odds with reality.

Using the same methodology as Zillmann and Bryant (1982, 1984), Zillmann and Bryant (1988a, 1988b) found effects of such media on attitudes about real people. Respondents seeing the explicit films reported, relative to a control group, less satisfaction with the affection, physical appearance, sexual curiosity, and sexual performance of their real-life partners. They also saw sex without emotional involvement as being relatively more important than the control group did. They showed greater acceptance of premarital and extramarital sex and a lesser evaluation of marriage and monogamy. They also showed less desire to have children and greater acceptance of male dominance and female submission. Results generally did not differ for males versus females or college students versus nonstudents.

The medium may make a difference. Dermer and Pyszczynski's (1978) participants were told to think about their mates before *reading* some explicit passages about a woman's sexual fantasies. They later rated their own partner as more sexually attractive. This inconsistency with the Zillmann and Bryant results may be due to specific procedures of the study, particular materials used, or psychological differences in responses to print versus video material. Nonpictorial descriptions of sex in words in the print medium (e.g., the *Penthouse* Advisor column) or in the relatively newer "phone sex" may actually be more conducive to fantasizing about one's own partner, while photographic sex may encourage unfavorable comparison to that person.

Catharsis

Another alleged effect of media sex is catharsis, that emotional release so important to psychodynamic models of personality (e.g., Freud). Applied to sex, the catharsis argument says that consuming media sex relieves sexual urges, with the magazine or video acting (perhaps in conjunction with masturbation) as a sort of imperfect substitute for the real thing. A catharsis argument is frequently used by libertarians to support appeals for lessening restrictions on sexually explicit material (e.g., Kutchinsky, 1973, 1985). The research support for catharsis as a function of viewing media sex is meager if not totally nonexistent, however (*Final report*, 1986).

Behavioral Effects

Consistent with cultivation theory (Gerbner, Gross, Signiorelli, & Morgan, 1986; Signiorelli & Morgan, 1990), people who watch more sexually oriented media make higher frequency estimates of various sexual behaviors (Greenberg et al., 1993). Beyond this, what are the effects on behaviors themselves?

Teaching New Behaviors. Sometimes sexual media may actually teach new behaviors. As part of sex therapy, a couple may buy a sex manual in order to learn new sexual positions or behaviors that they had not tried before. New behaviors are not always so benign, however. One issue of *Penthouse* contained a series of photographs of Asian women bound with heavy rope, hung from trees, and sectioned into parts. Two months later an 8-year-old Chinese girl in Chapel Hill, North Carolina, was kidnapped, raped, murdered, and left hanging from a tree limb (*New York Times*, 2/4/85, cited in *Final report*, 1986, p. 208). Of course, such examples are not commonplace, and definitively demonstrating a causal relationship in such cases is difficult, but the juxtaposition is nonetheless disturbing.

Some of the rawest material shows extreme sexual violence that might be copied by a viewer. These include very violent and offensive images, including women apparently being killed ("snuff" films) through torturing them with power tools or even such bizarre and twisted images as sexual penetration of eye sockets after death ("skull-fucking"). For obvious ethical reasons, it is difficult to scientifically study the use and effects of such extreme materials.

Disinhibition. Erotic material may also disinhibit previously learned behavior, such as when watching TV's treatment of premarital sex disinhibits a viewer's inhibition against engaging in such behavior. Watching a rape scene where a woman is portrayed as enjoying being assaulted may disinhibit the constraint against some men's secret urge to commit such a crime. This is of particular concern given some evidence suggesting that a surprisingly large number of college men reported they might rape if they were sure they would not get caught (Check, 1985; Malamuth, Haber, & Feshbach, 1980).

Sex Crimes. One of the main concerns about a behavioral effect of viewing sexually explicit materials is a possible relationship with sex crimes. There have been many studies looking at rates of crimes like rape, exhibitionism, and child molestation relative to changes in the availability of sexually explicit materials. In a careful review of such studies, Court (1984; see also Bachy, 1976; Court, 1977, 1982) argued that there is in fact a correlation of availability of sexually explicit materials and certain sex crimes. Court claimed that earlier studies, especially Kutchinsky's (1973) study claiming a drop in reported sex crimes in Denmark after liberalization of pornography restrictions in the 1960s, are not really valid, due to an inappropriate lumping of rape with nonviolent acts like voyeurism, indecent exposure, and homosexual sex. Most Western nations have experienced a large increase both in the availability of sexually explicit media and in the rise in reported rapes in the last 20 years. Court presented some data from the Australian states of Queensland and South Australia that show a sharp increase in rape reports in South Australia but not Queensland after state pornography laws were liberalized in South Australia in the early 1970s. A comparable downturn in reported rapes occurred temporarily in Hawaii between 1974 and 1976 during a temporary imposition of restraints on sexually explicit media. For an interesting apparent counterexample, see Abramson and Hayashi (1984) for discussions of rape and pornography in Japan.

Firmly establishing a causal relationship between the availability of sexually explicit media and the frequency of rape is extremely difficult, due to the many other relevant factors, including the different varieties of sexual material, changes in social consciousness about reporting sexual assaults, and changing norms sanctioning such behavior. Some evidence (see Baron & Straus, 1985; Jaffee & Straus, 1986; Scott & Schwalm, 1985, all cited in *Final report*, 1986) suggests a correlation between rape and circulation of sex magazines, particularly those containing sexual violence. For example, Baron and Straus found a correlation of $+.64$ for rape rates and circulation rates of eight sex magazines in 50 states. Although others argue no demonstrated relationship, very few (Kutchinsky, 1985) currently support a catharsis explanation that sexually explicit material allows open expression of sexual urges and thus decreases the rate of sex crimes.

Prevailing Tone

The effects of media sex are not entirely due to the nature of the material itself. They also depend on the context of the material itself and the context in which the person sees it (Eysenck & Nias, 1978). This diverse collection of variables is called the "prevailing tone." The nature of this prevailing tone can make enormous difference in the experience of consuming sexually explicit media.

One of the relevant variables of the prevailing tone is the degree of playfulness or seriousness of the material. Even a highly explicit and potentially controversial topic may not be particularly controversial when presented seriously. For example, a documentary on rape or a tastefully done TV movie on incest may be considered perfectly acceptable, whereas a far less explicit comedy with the same theme may be highly offensive and considered "too sexual." What is really the concern in such cases is not the sex as such, but rather the comedic, to some flippant, treatment of it. Highly explicit videos, books, and magazines are used routinely and noncontroversially in sex therapy to treat sexual dysfunctions generally and sex offenders specifically. See Quinsey and Marshall (1983) for a review.

A second factor in the prevailing tone is the artistic worth and intent. We react very differently to a sexually explicit drawing from Picasso versus one in *Hustler* magazine. Shakespeare, Chaucer, *The Song of Solomon* in the Bible, and serious sex manuals like *The Joy of Sex* are seen to have serious literary or didactic intentions and thus the sex therein is considered more acceptable and even healthy. One interesting issue in this regard is how to respond to something of clear artistic worth but written at a time when standards differed from what they are today. For example, should Rhett Butler's forcing his attentions on Scarlett O'Hara in *Gone with the Wind* be seen as rape or as the noncontroversial romantic moment that it appeared to be in 1939?

The relation and integration of sex to the overall plot and intent of the piece is also a part of the prevailing tone. A sex scene, even a mild and nonexplicit one, may be offensive if it appears to be "thrown in" merely to spice up the story but having no connection to it. Something far more explicit may be accepted much better if it is necessary and central to the plot. Sex scenes in a story about a prostitute may be much less gratuitous than comparable scenes in a story about a female corporate executive. Sex, of course, is not the only common gratuitous factor in media; for example, contemporary television shows and movies frequently insert car chases and rock video segments completely unrelated to the plot.

Although it is not the overriding factor in predicting reactions to sexual media as many think it to be, the degree of explicitness of the sex is nevertheless a real factor. Sex may be shown explicitly or implied by innuendo. In the latter sense, some of the sexiest television shows are sitcoms like the old "Three's Company" or the more recent "Married . . . with Children," which have constant remarks and double entendres dealing with sex, but never anything explicit. A study of women's reactions to sex in television commercials (Johnson & Satow, 1978) found that older women were more offended by the more explicit material, whereas younger women were more offended by innuendo, especially that which could readily be considered sexist.

The context of the viewing also influences the experience and effect of sex in the media. When watching an erotic film with your parents, your grandparents, your children, by yourself, in a group of close same-sex friends, or with your spouse, the reaction to it may be very different as a function of who one watches it with. It may be seen as more or less erotic or arousing and more or less appropriate or offensive.

The cultural context is also a factor. Some cultures of the world do not consider female breasts to be particularly erotic or inappropriate for public display. We recognize these cultural differences and thus, at least after the age of 14, most readers do not consider topless women from some distant culture in *National Geographic* photos to be the slightest bit erotic, sexual, or inappropriate. Even in Western culture, standards have changed. In much of the 19th century, knees and calves were thought to be erotic, and the sight of a bare-kneed woman would be as scandalous, perhaps even as sexually arousing, as a topless woman is today. As societies go, North America overall is a bit more conservative than many Northwest European or Latin American cultures but far more permissive than many Islamic and East Asian cultures.

Finally, the expectations we have affect our perception of the prevailing tone. Sex is less offensive and shocking if it is expected than if it appears as a surprise. Seeing a photo of a nude women being fed through a meat grinder may be less shocking in *Hustler* magazine than if we were to suddenly encounter it in *Newsweek*. The stimulus may be the same, but the perceived experiential reality of the act of seeing it would differ considerably in the two cases.

We now turn to examine that potent combination of sex and violence in the media—sexual violence.

SEXUAL VIOLENCE

Although neither sex nor violence in the media is at all new, the integral combination of the two has become far more prevalent in recent years. Although sex magazines are not new, some particularly violent publications are relatively new, and even more "established" publications like *Penthouse* and *Playboy* show some evidence of increasing themes of sexual violence (Malamuth & Spinner, 1980). Dietz and Evans (1982) content analyzed the covers of 1,760 sex magazines from 1970 to 1980; they found a huge increase in bondage and domination imagery (up to 17.2% of the covers by 1981).

Another old familiar genre, the horror film, has recently evolved into showing frequent and extensive scenes of violence against women in a sexual context (Palys, 1986; Yang & Linz, 1990). These films are heavily targeted toward teenagers, in spite of the R ratings many of them receive. With all of these, the major concern is not with the sex or violence in and of themselves, but with the way the two appear together. The world constructed in the mind of the viewer of such materials can have some very serious consequences.

Erotica as Stimulator of Aggression

Links between sex and aggression have long been speculated upon, particularly in the sense of sexual arousal facilitating violent behavior.

The research has been inconsistent, however, with some studies showing that erotic materials facilitate aggression (Baron, 1979; Donnerstein & Hallam, 1978) and others showing they inhibit it (Donnerstein, Donnerstein, & Evans, 1975; White, 1979). The resolution of this issue apparently concerns the nature of the material. Sexual violence and unpleasant themes typically facilitate aggression, whereas, nonviolent, more loving and pleasant "soft-core" explicit materials may inhibit it (Zillmann, Bryant, Comisky, & Medoff, 1981). Thus, in considering the effects of sexual media, it is helpful to separate sexual violence from consenting, loving sex.

Effects of Seeing Sexual Violence

Malamuth (1984) reported several studies that showed male participants sexual violence and afterwards measured their attitudes on several topics. Participants seeing the films showed a more callous attitude toward rape and women in general, especially if the women victims in the film were portrayed as being aroused by the assault. In terms of sexual arousal, participants were aroused by the sexual violence only if the victim was shown to be aroused but not if she was not so portrayed.

Individual Differences. Other studies examined convicted rapists and found them to be aroused by both rape and consenting sex, whereas normal participants were aroused only by the consenting sex (Abel, Barlow, Blanchard, & Guild, 1977; Barbaree, Marshall, & Lanthier, 1979). An important exception to this occurred if the victim was portrayed as enjoying the rape and coming to orgasm; in this case normal males (but not females) were equally or more aroused by the rape than by the consenting sex (Malamuth, Heim, & Feshbach, 1980). In further examining this question of individual differences, Malamuth (1981) identified one group of college men who were "force oriented," that is, prone to use force in their own lives. This group, and a group of non-force-oriented men, were shown a film where a man stops his car on a deserted road to pick up a female. Following this, they either have sex in his car with both clearly consenting or he rapes her, although she is depicted as finally enjoying the assault. Students were then asked to create their own sexual fantasies to achieve a high level of arousal. Although non-force-oriented males were more aroused by the consenting scene than the sexual violence, the reverse was true for the force-oriented males!

A similar study (Malamuth & Check, 1983) had men listen to a tape of a sexual encounter with (a) consenting sex or (b) nonconsenting sex where the woman showed arousal, or (c) nonconsenting sex where she showed disgust. Where the woman showed disgust, both force-oriented and non-force-oriented males were more aroused (in both self-report and penile tumescence) by the consenting than the nonconsenting (rape) scene. However, when the woman was portrayed as being aroused, the non-force-oriented males were equally aroused by both consenting and nonconsenting versions, whereas the force-oriented participants actually showed more arousal to the nonconsenting version.

Donnerstein (1980) showed male students either a nonviolent but sexually explicit film or a film where a woman was sexually abused and assaulted. Participants seeing the latter but not the former film were more likely to administer electric shocks to a third party in a subsequent "experiment" on learning and punishment, especially so in participants who had been previously angered. In a similar study (Donnerstein & Berkowitz, 1981), male participants saw a sexually violent film where a woman is attacked, stripped, tied up, and raped. In one version of the film the woman was portrayed as enjoying the rape. Afterwards participants were given a chance to administer electric shocks to a confederate of the experimenter, the same confederate who had earlier angered them. Participants seeing the film where the woman enjoyed being raped administered more shocks to a female confederate, but not to the male. This suggests that the association of sex and violence in the film allowed violent behavior to be transferred to the target confederate.

Most of this research has been conducted on men. However, a few studies testing women have obtained behavioral effects of aggression toward women (Baron, 1979) and desensitization effects of trivialization of rape and rape myths (Malamuth, Check, & Briere, 1986; Zillmann & Bryant, 1982).

Several conclusions emerge from this line of research. One is that a critical aspect of sexual violence is whether the woman is seen as enjoying and being aroused by the assault. Far more undesirable effects generally occur in normal men if the woman is seen to be aroused than if she is seen to be terrorized. This media portrayal of women as being "turned on" by rape is apparently not only a distasteful deviation from reality but also a potentially dangerous one. A second important conclusion is that sexually violent media often affect different men very differently, depending on their own propensity to use force in their own lives. Convicted rapists and other force-oriented men are more likely to become aroused or even incited to violence by sexually violent media, especially if the woman is portrayed as being aroused by the assault.

Slasher Movies. Because the studies discussed above used very sexually explicit materials, the kind that would be considered "hard-core pornography," many might consider them beyond the limits of what they themselves would be exposed to. However, sexual violence is by no means confined to "pornographic" materials restricted from minors. More "mainstream" R-rated films are readily available to teenagers anywhere, in theaters and even more so in video stores. There are the highly successful series like *Halloween, Friday the Thirteenth,* and *Nightmare on Elm Street,* but also many lesser known films. Most are extremely violent, with at least strong sexual overtones. For example, *Alien Prey* shows a blood-stained vampire sucking out a dead woman's entrails through a hole in her stomach. *Flesh Feast* treats us to maggots consuming live human beings, starting with the face and working down. *Make Them Die Slowly* promises "24 scenes of barbaric torture," such as a man slicing a woman in half ("Child's Play," 1987, p. 31). *The Offspring* shows a soldier choking a little-girl captive to death while kissing her. In some countries rape and other acts of violence against women are even more standard entertainment fare; for example, in India, films frequently portray rape in a titillating manner (Pratap, 1990).

Although some of these films have R ratings in the United States, others are released unrated to avoid the "accompanied by parent" restriction of R movies in the United States. Because no restrictions apply in most video stores, anyway, the rating is not a major issue. The viewing of such films is widespread among youth. A survey in the early 1980s of 4,500 English and Welsh children found that almost 20% of the 13- to 14-year-old boys had seen the sexually violent *I Spit on Your Grave,* a film deemed legally obscene and liable to prosecution in the United Kingdom (Hill, Davis, Holman, & Nelson, 1984)! A later American study (Oliver, 1993) found that punitive attitudes toward sexuality and traditional attitudes toward women's sexuality were associated with high school students' greater enjoyment of previews of slasher films. Finally, a study of U.S. college students (mean age = 19) showed that two-thirds of them regularly viewed or rented slasher films (Greenberg et al., 1993).

The major concern with such films is the juxtaposition of erotic sex and violence. For example, one scene from *Toolbox Murders* opens with a beautiful woman disrobing and getting into her bath, with the very romantic music "Pretty Baby" playing in the background. For several minutes she is shown fondling herself and masturbating in a very erotic manner. Suddenly the camera cuts to the scene of an intruder breaking into her apartment, with loud, fast-paced suspenseful music in the background. The camera and sound track cut back and forth several times between these two characters until he finally encounters the woman. He attacks her with electric tools, chasing her around the apartment, finally shooting her several times in the head with a nail gun. The scene closes after seeing her bleed profusely, finally lying on the bed to die with the sound track again playing the erotic "Pretty Baby."

Linz, Donnerstein, and Penrod (1984; Linz, Donnerstein, & Adams, 1989; see also Linz, 1985) examined the effects of such films. Their college-student male participants were initially screened to exclude those who had prior hostile tendencies or psychological problems. The remaining men in the experimental group were shown one standard Hollywood-released R-rated film per day over 1 week. All of the films were very violent and showed multiple instances of women being killed in slow, lingering, painful deaths in situations associated with much erotic content (e.g., the *Toolbox Murders* scene described above). Each day the participants filled out some questionnaires evaluating that day's film and also completed some personality measures.

These ratings showed that these men became less depressed, less annoyed, and less anxious in response to the films during the week. The films themselves were rated over time as more enjoyable, more humorous, more socially meaningful, less violent and offensive, and less degrading to women. Over the week's time, the violent episodes in general and rape episodes in particular were rated as less frequent. A similar study by Krafka (1985) tested women and did not find the same effects. Although these data provide clear evidence of desensitization in men, there is still the question of generalization from the films to other situations.

To answer this question, Linz et al. (1984) arranged to have the same people participate in a later study that the participants did not know had any connection to seeing the slasher movies. For this experiment, they observed a rape trial at the law school and evaluated it in several ways. Compared to a control group, men who had seen the slasher films rated the rape victim as less physically and emotionally injured. These results are consistent with those of Zillmann and Bryant (1984), who found that massive exposure to pornography resulted in shorter recommended prison sentences for a rapist. Such findings show that the world we construct in response to seeing such movies can be at variance with reality and can have dire consequences when actions are taken believing that such a world is reality.

Not surprisingly, this study and others by the authors along the same line (see Donnerstein, Linz, & Penrod, 1987, for a review) have caused considerable concern in the public. They have also caused considerable scientific concern. Some of the major effects have not been replicated in later work (Linz & Donnerstein, 1988), and there have been some methodological criticisms (see Weaver, 1991, in press, for discussions of these criticisms).

The sharp distinction that Donnerstein and Linz made between the effects of violent and nonviolent pornography has been called into question (Weaver, 1991; Zillmann & Bryant, 1988a). Research findings have been somewhat inconsistent in each area; Zillmann and Bryant argued that Linz and Donnerstein were too quick to cite failures to reject the null hypothesis as support for the harmlessness of nonviolent pornography, yet they all but ignored such results in arguing for serious deleterious effects of sexual violence. Check and Guloien (1989) found that men exposed to a steady diet of rape-myth sexual violence reported a higher likelihood of committing rape themselves, compared to a no-exposure control group, but the same result was found for a group exposed to nonviolent pornography. There is considerable controversy about the use and interpretation of data from particular studies. How this will be resolved is still unclear; we clearly need more research, especially on slasher-type movies.

Mitigating the Negative Effects of Sexual Violence

Results from the studies discussed above are disturbing, especially given the widespread viewing of slasher films by children and teens and the recent increase in sexually violent media. Some studies have developed and evaluated extensive preexposure training procedures to attempt to lessen the desensitizing effects of sexual violence (Intons-Peterson & Roskos-Ewoldsen, 1989; Intons-Peterson, Roskos-Ewoldsen, Thomas, Shirley, & Blut, 1989; Linz, Donnerstein, Bross, & Chapin, 1986; Linz, Fuson, & Donnerstein, 1990). These studies have typically shown mitigating effects on some measures and not on others. Linz et al. (1990) found that men were most strongly affected by the information that women are not responsible for sexual assaults perpetrated upon them. There is also some evidence that desensitization can be reduced by introducing pertinent information about rape myths and the inaccuracy of media portrayals after people have seen some of the sexually violent media. At least some participants were more impressed with such arguments after they had felt themselves excited and aroused by the film and they had seen very specific examples to illustrate the point of the debriefing/mitigation information. In the context of having seen such a film, the specific points of the sensitization training have greater impact.

The more potential harm that is identified from viewing sexually explicit, especially sexually violent, materials, the more question is raised about the ethics of doing research by exposing people to such materials. Although we have clearly learned some valuable information, what will the cost of this knowledge be in terms of the lives of the research participants? This issue has been taken seriously by Malamuth, Heim, and Feshbach (1980) and others, who have offered an extensive debriefing, complete with information on the horrible reality of rape and the complete unreality of someone enjoying it. Malamuth, et al. even included a discussion of why the myth of enjoying being raped was so prevalent in sexually violent media. Some studies have included evaluations of such debriefing sessions and shown that, compared to a control group not in the experiment, debriefed people showed less acceptance of rape myths (Donnerstein & Berkowitz, 1981; Malamuth & Check, 1980b).

Using a different approach, measuring the effect of seeing a prosocial TV movie about rape, Wilson, Linz, Donnerstein, and Stipp (1992) found that, compared to a control group, people viewing the film generally showed heightened awareness and concern about rape. However, not all groups were so affected. Unlike women and young and middle-aged men, men over 50 had their preexisting attitudes reinforced and actually blamed women more for rape after seeing the film. This suggests that the attitudes and experiences of the target audience of any intervention must be carefully considered.

We conclude with a brief look at the two U.S. pornography commissions, which provide a fascinating, albeit often unsatisfying, case study of the interaction of politics and social science research.

THE PORNOGRAPHY COMMISSIONS

National Commission on Obscenity and Pornography

This commission was established by U.S. President Lyndon Johnson in 1967 to analyze the (a) pornography control laws, (b) distribution of sexually explicit materials, and (c) effects of consuming such materials, and to recommend appropriate legislative or administrative action. It funded over 80 research studies on the topic, providing important impetus to the scientific study of sexually explicit material. The final report 3 years later (U.S. Commission on Obscenity and Pornography, 1970) recommended stronger controls on distribution to minors but an abolition of all limits on access by adults. The latter recommendation was based on the majority conclusion that there was "no evidence that exposure to or use of explicit sexual materials play a significant role in the causation of social or individual harms such as crime, delinquency, sexual or nonsexual deviancy or severe emotional disturbance" (p. 58). The report also included a series of minority conclusions that argued for some curbs on sexually explicit materials.

Although the composition of the commission has been criticized for being overloaded with anticensorship civil libertarians (Eysenck & Nias, 1978), its majority conclusions were rejected anyway by the new administration of President Richard Nixon, who declared, "so long as I am in the White House there will be no relaxation of the national effort to control and eliminate smut from our national life" (Eysenck & Nias, 1978, p. 94). During the same period, the Longford (1972) and Williams (1979) Commissions in Great Britain issued reports, followed a few years later by the Fraser Commission in Canada (*Report of the Special Committee on Pornography and Prostitution*, 1985). The major conclusion of these commissions was a lack of conclusiveness of the research to date. See Einsiedel (1988) for a discussion of these commissions and their social and political context and interpretations of research.

The "Meese Commission"

The nature of sexual media changed greatly from 1970 to 1985, particularly in the great increase of sado-masochistic themes and the linking of sex and violence, themes relatively rare in 1970, or at least not seriously addressed by the earlier U.S. commission. Additionally, technological advancements like cable and satellite television and VCRs made sexually explicit material available in the home far more easily and privately than formerly had been the case. In 1985 alone, 1,700 new sexually explicit videocassettes were released in the United States, accounting for about one-fifth of videotape rentals and sales (*Final report*, 1986). These changes, plus certain social and political considerations, led to the formation of the new commission.

U.S. Attorney General Edwin Meese charged the newly formed commission in 1985 to "determine the nature, extent, and impact on society of pornography in the United States, and to make specific recommendations . . . concerning more effective ways in which the spread of pornography could be contained, consistent with constitutional guarantees." Although there is a clear political position even in this charge, the part of the *Final Report* (1986) of most interest here concerns the issue of possible harmful effects of exposure to sexually explicit material.

One of the major conclusions of the commission dealt with the effect of sexual violence: "The available evidence strongly supports the hypothesis that substantial exposure to sexually violent materials. . . bears a causal relationship to antisocial acts of sexual violence, and for some subgroups, possibly the unlawful acts of sexual violence" (p. 40).

Groups like the Meese Commission typically have both a scientific and a political agenda (Paletz, 1988; Wilcox, 1987). Sometimes, even if there is relative consensus on the scientific conclusions, there is often strong disagreement about the policy ramifications. For example, Linz, Donnerstein, and Penrod (1987) took exception with some of the conclusions drawn by the Meese Commission using those researchers' own work demonstrating deleterious effects of sexual violence (see earlier discussion). Linz et al. argued that the Commission's call for strengthening obscenity laws was not an appropriate policy change based on the research, because it ignored the strong presence of sexually violent themes in other media not covered by such laws.

Just before his 1989 execution in Florida, convicted serial killer Ted Bundy granted an interview in which he blamed pornography for his brutally violent behavior. Although this deathbed accusation circulated widely in the media, Linz and Donnerstein (1992) argued that a careful reading of Bundy's statement actually blamed violent movies and television. A spokesperson for the FBI told a Surgeon General's panel in 1986 that violent detective magazines, not pornography, were usually found in violent criminals' possession at their arrest.

However, in response to concern over people like Bundy, the U.S. Senate Judiciary Committee approved a bill that would allow rape victims and families of murder victims to sue producers of sexually explicit materials. However, the bill would not cover R-rated "slasher" movies, which research discussed earlier suggests may be just as damaging (Linz & Donnerstein, 1992). Debate on this issue illustrates the double standard in the United States of far greater acceptance of violence than sex in the media. With research increasingly showing deleterious effects of the combination of sex and violence, sorting out policy implications becomes even more complicated.

CONCLUSION

What may we conclude from the research on the perceived reality and effects from viewing sexual media? It is useful to make a distinction between violent and nonviolent sexual media, although this distinction may not be quite as important as Linz and Donnerstein argued. Although there are some negative effects of nonviolent sexual materials, especially on attitudes toward women (Weaver, 1991; Zillmann & Bryant, 1988a, 1988b), the research is especially compelling in the case of sexual violence. Sexual violence is arousing to sex offenders, force-oriented men, and sometimes even to "normal" young men if the woman is portrayed as being aroused by the attack. For a careful review of results from 81 experimental studies on the effects of viewing sexually explicit media, see Lyons, Anderson, and Larson (in press).

Repeated exposure to sexual violence may lead to desensitization toward violence against women and greater acceptance of rape myths. In this sense, the "no effects" conclusion of the 1970 commission must be revised. Not only does this suggest that the combination of sex and violence together is considerably worse than either one separately, but it also matters what the nature of the portrayal is. If the woman being assaulted is portrayed as being terrorized and brutalized, negative effects on normal male viewers are less than if she is portrayed as being aroused and/or achieving orgasm through being attacked. There is nothing arousing or exciting about being raped, and messages to the contrary do not help teenage boys understand the reality of how to relate to girls and women.

The themes of sexual aggression against women are not limited to what is commonly considered pornographic material or even to very violent horror movies. Such images are also found in mainstream television. For example, in a content analysis study, Lowry, Love, and Kirby (1981) found that, except for erotic touching among unmarried persons, aggressive sexual contact was the most frequent type of sexual interaction in daytime soap operas. Some years ago several episodes of *General Hospital* focussed on the rape of one main character by another. Although the woman first appeared humiliated, she later fell in love with the rapist and married him. *Newsweek* ("Soap Operas," 1981, p. 65) reported that producers and actors in soap operas believe the increase in sexual aggression in that genre has attracted more male viewers, who "started watching us because we no longer were wimps. When a woman was wrong, we'd slap her down."

Such images appear in other media as well. A content analysis of detective magazines found that 76% of the covers depicted domination of women, while 38% depicted women in bondage (Dietz, Harry, & Hazelwood, 1986), all of this in a publication never even considered sexual, much less pornographic! Some studies of rock videos (Hansen & Hansen, 1990; Zillmann & Mundorf, 1987) have shown that sexual content is highly appealing but that violent content is not. Although sexual violence may have the negative effects discussed earlier, it may not even be enjoyed! The effect of parental warning labels about sexual content on CDs and tapes is not entirely clear, but in one study (Christenson, 1992) they seemed to decrease appeal to middle school students. However, these sexually violent themes are pervasive in much media and no "quick fix" of stricter pornography laws or warning labels will make them go away entirely.

In this age of rapidly changing technology and ever-expanding possibilities of new forms of sexual media, it is sometimes hard for the research to keep up with all that is available to the user. Nevertheless, the research reviewed in this chapter clearly points to some reliable and often disturbing effects. It is now up to the policymaker, the educator, and the parent to use this research to help guide a new generation learning about sexuality.

REFERENCES

Abel, G. G., Barlow, D. H., Blanchard, E. B., & Guild, D. (1977). The components of rapists' sexual arousal. *Archives of General Psychiatry, 34*, 895–903.

Abramson, P. R., & Hayashi, H. (1984). Pornography in Japan: Cross-cultural and theoretical considerations. In N. M. Malamuth & E. Donnerstein (Eds.), *Pornography and sexual aggression* (pp. 173–183). Orlando: Academic Press.

Abramson, P. R., Perry, L., Seeley, T., Seeley, D., & Rothblatt, A. (1981). Thermographic measurement of sexual arousal: A discriminant validity analysis. *Archives of Sexual Behavior, 10*(2), 175–176.

Bachy, V. (1976). Danish "permissiveness" revisited. *Journal of Communication, 26*, 40–43.

Bancroft, J., & Mathews, A. (1971). Autonomic correlates of penile erection. *Journal of Psychosomatic Research, 15*, 159–167.

Barbaree, H. E., Marshall, W. L., & Lanthier, R. D. (1979). Deviant sexual arousal in rapists. *Behaviour Research and Therapy, 17*, 215–222.

Baron, R. A. (1979). Heightened sexual arousal and physical aggression: An extension to females. *Journal of Research in Personality, 13*, 91–102.

Bigler, M. O. (1989, October/November). Adolescent sexual behavior in the eighties. *SIECUS Report*, pp. 6–9.

Check, J. V. P. (1985). *The effects of violent and nonviolent pornography.* Ottawa: Department of Justice for Canada.

Check, J. V. P., & Guloien, T. H. (1989). Reported proclivity for coercive sex following repeated exposure to sexually violent pornography, nonviolent pornography, and erotica. In D. Zillmann & J. Bryant (Eds.), *Pornography: Research advances and policy considerations* (pp. 159–184). Hillsdale, NJ: Lawrence Erlbaum Associates.

Child's play: Violent videos lure the young. (1987, June 1). *Time*, p. 31.

Christenson, P. (1992). The effects of parental advisory labels on adolescent music preferences. *Journal of Communication, 42*(1), 106–113.

Court, J. H. (1977). Pornography and sex crimes: A re-evaluation in the light of recent trends around the world. *International Journal of Criminology and Penology, 5*, 129–157.

Court, J. H. (1982). Rape trends in New South Wales: A discussion of conflicting evidence. *Australian Journal of Social Issues, 17*, 202–206.

Court, J. H. (1984). Sex and violence: A ripple effect. In N. M. Malamuth & E. Donnerstein (Eds.), *Pornography and sexual aggression* (pp. 143–172). Orlando: Academic Press.

Darling, C. J., & Hicks, M. (1982). Parental influences on adolescent sexuality: Implications for parents as educators. *Journal of Youth and Adolescence, 11*, 231–245.

Day, G., & Bloom, C. (Eds.). (1988). *Perspectives on pornography: Sexuality in film and literature.* London: Macmillan.

Dermer, M., & Pyszczynski, T. A. (1978). Effects of erotica upon men's loving and liking responses. *Journal of Personality and Social Psychology, 36*, 1302–1309.

Dietz, P. E., & Evans, B. (1982). Pornographic imagery and prevalence of paraphilia. *American Journal of Psychiatry, 139*, 1493–1495.

Dietz, P. E., Harry, B., & Hazelwood, R. R. (1986). Detective magazines: Pornography for the sexual sadist? *Journal of Forensic Sciences, 31*(1), 197–211.

Donnerstein, E. (1980). Aggressive erotica and violence against women. *Journal of Personality and Social Psychology, 39*, 269–277.

Donnerstein, E., & Berkowitz, L. (1981). Victim reactions in aggressive erotic films as a factor in violence against women. *Journal of Personality and Social Psychology, 41,* 710–724.

Donnerstein, E., Donnerstein, M., & Evans, R. (1975). Erotic stimuli and aggression: Facilitation or inhibition? *Journal of Personality and Social Psychology, 32,* 237–244.

Donnerstein, E., & Hallam, J. (1978). Facilitating effects of erotica on aggression against women. *Journal of Personality and Social Psychology, 36,* 1270–1277.

Donnerstein, E., Linz, D., & Penrod, S. (1987). *The question of pornography: Research findings and policy implications.* New York: Free Press.

Dorr, A., & Kunkel, D. (1990). Children and the media environment: Change and constancy amid change. *Communication Research, 17,* 5–25.

Eccles, A., Marshall, W. L., & Barbaree, H. E. (1988). The vulnerability of erectile measures to repeated assessments. *Behavior Research and Therapy, 26,* 179–183.

Einsiedel, E. F. (1988). The British, Canadian, and U.S. pornography commissions and their use of social science research. *Journal of Communication, 38*(2), 108–121.

Eysenck, H. J., & Nias, D. K. B. (1978). *Sex violence and the media.* New York: Harper.

Fabes, R. A., & Strouse, J. S. (1984). Youth's perceptions of models of sexuality: Implications for sexuality education. *Journal of Sex Education and Therapy, 10,* 33–37.

Fabes, R. A., & Strouse, J. S. (1987). Perceptions of responsible and irresponsible models of sexuality: A correlational study. *The Journal of Sex Research, 23,* 70–84.

Fernandez-Collado, C., Greenberg, B. S., Korzenny, F., & Atkin, C. (1978). Sexual intimacy and drug use in TV series. *Journal of Communication, 28*(3), 30–37.

Final report of the Attorney General's Commission on Pornography. (1986). Nashville, TN: Rutledge Hill Press.

Gerbner, G., Gross, L., Morgan, M., & Signorielli, N. (1986). Living with television: The dynamics of the cultivation process. In J. Bryant & D. Zillmann (Eds.), *Perspectives on media effects* (pp. 17–40). Hillsdale, NJ: Lawrence Erlbaum Associates.

Greenberg, B. S., Abelman, R., & Neuendorf, U. (1981). Sex on the soap operas: Afternoon intimacy. *Journal of Communication, 31*(3), 83–89.

Greenberg, B. S., Brown, J. D., & Buerkel-Rothfuss, N. L. (1993). *Media, sex, and the adolescent.* Cresskill, NJ: Hampton Press.

Greenberg, B. S., & D'Alessilo, D. (1985). Quantity and quality of sex in the soaps. *Journal of Broadcasting & Electronic Media, 29,* 309–321.

Hansen, C. H., & Hansen, R. D. (1990). The influence of sex and violence on the appeal of rock music videos. *Communication Research, 17,* 212–234.

Harris, R. J. (1993). *A cognitive psychology of mass communication* (2nd ed.). Hillsdale, NJ: Lawrence Erlbaum Associates.

Hebditch, D., & Anning, N. (1988). *Porn gold: Inside the pornography business.* London: Faber & Faber.

Hill, C., Davis, H., Holman, R., & Nelson, G. (1984). *Video violence and children.* London: Report of a Parliamentary Group Video Enquiry.

Intons-Peterson, M. J., & Roskos-Ewoldsen, B. (1989). Mitigating the effects of violent pornography. In S. Gubar & J. Hoff-Wilson (Eds.), *For adult users, only.* Bloomington, IN: Indiana University Press.

Intons-Peterson, M. J., Roskos-Ewoldsen, B., Thomas, L., Shirley, M., & Blut, D. (1989). Will educational materials reduce negative effects of exposure to sexual violence? *Journal of Social and Clinical Psychology, 8,* 256–275.

Johnson, D. K., & Satow, K. (1978). Consumers' reaction to sex in TV commercials. *Advances in Consumer Research, 5,* 411–414.

Jones, S. S., Forrest, J., Goldman, N., Henshaw, S., Lincoln, R., Rosoff, J., Westoff, C., & Wulf, D. (1985). Teenage pregnancy in developed countries: Determinants and policy implications. *Family Planning Perspectives, 17*(2), 53–63.

Kenrick, D. T., Gutierres, S. E., & Goldberg, L. L. (1989). Influence of popular erotica on judgments of strangers and mates. *Journal of Experimental Social Psychology, 25,* 159–167.

Krafka, C. L. (1985). *Sexually explicit, sexually violent, and violent media: Effects of multiple naturalistic exposures and debriefing on female viewers.* Unpublished doctoral dissertation, University of Wisconsin, Madison.

Kutchinsky, B. (1973). The effect of easy availability of pornography on the incidence of sex crimes: The Danish experience. *Journal of Social Issues, 29*(3), 163–181.

Kutchinsky, B. (1985). Pornography and its effects in Denmark and the United States: A rejoinder and beyond. *Comparative Social Research, 8,* 301–330.

Linz, D. (1985). *Sexual violence in the mass media: Effects on male viewers and implications for society.* Unpublished doctoral dissertation, University of Wisconsin, Madison.

Linz, D., & Donnerstein, E. (1988). The methods and merits of pornography research. *Journal of Communication, 38*(2), 180–184.

Linz, D., & Donnerstein, E. (1992, September 30). Research can help us explain violence and pornography. *Chronicle of Higher Education,* pp. B3–B4.

Linz, D., Donnerstein, E., & Adams, S. M. (1989). Physiological desensitization and judgments about female victims of violence. *Human Communication Research, 15,* 509–522.

Linz, D., Donnerstein, E., Bross, M., & Chapin, M. (1986). Mitigating the influence of violence on television and sexual violence in the media. In R. Blanchard (Ed.), *Advances in the study of aggression* (Vol. 2., pp. 165–194). Orlando: Academic Press.

Linz, D., Donnerstein, E., & Penrod, S. (1984). The effects of multiple exposures to filmed violence against women. *Journal of Communication, 34*(3), 130–147

Linz, D., Donnerstein, E., & Penrod, S. (1987). The findings and recommendations of the Attorney General's Commission on Pornography: Do the psychological "facts" fit the political fury? *American Psychologist, 42,* 946–953.

Linz, D., Fuson, I. A., & Donnerstein, E. (1990). Mitigating the negative effects of sexually violent mass communications through preexposure briefings. *Communication Research, 17,* 641–674.

Longford, L. (Ed.). (1972). *Pornography: The Longford Report.* London: Coronet.

Lowry, D. T., Love, G., & Kirby, M. (1981). Sex on the soap operas: Patterns of intimacy. *Journal of Communication, 31,* 90–96.

Lowry, D. T., & Towles, D. E. (1989). Soap opera portrayals of sex, contraception, and sexually transmitted diseases. *Journal of Communication, 39*(2), 76–83.

Lyons, J. S., Anderson, R. L., & Larson, D. B. (in press). A systematic review of the effects of aggressive and nonaggressive pornography. In D. Zillmann, J. Bryant, & A. C. Huston (Eds.), *Media, children, and the family: Social, scientific, psychodynamic, and clinical perspectives.* Hillsdale, NJ: Lawrence Erlbaum Associates.

Malamuth, N. M. (1981). Rape fantasies as a function of exposure to violent sexual stimuli. *Archives of Sexual Behavior, 10,* 33–47.

Malamuth, N. M. (1984). Aggression against women: Cultural and individual causes. In N. M. Malamuth & E. Donnerstein (Eds.), *Pornography and sexual aggression* (pp. 19–52). Orlando: Academic Press.

Malamuth, N. M., & Check, J. V. P. (1980a). Penile tumescence and perceptual responses to rape as a function of victim's perceived reactions. *Journal of Applied Social Psychology, 10,* 528–547.

Malamuth, N. M., & Check, J. V. P. (1980b). Sexual arousal to rape and consenting depictions: The importance of the woman's arousal. *Journal of Abnormal Psychology, 89,* 763–766.

Malamuth, N. M., & Check, J. V. P. (1983). Sexual arousal to rape depictions: Individual differences. *Journal of Abnormal Psychology, 92,* 55–67.

Malamuth, N. M., Check, J. V. P., & Briere, J. (1986). Sexual arousal in response to aggression: Ideological, aggressive, and sexual correlates. *Journal of Personality and Social Psychology, 50,* 330–340.

Malamuth, N. M., Haber, S., & Feshbach, S. (1980). Testing hypotheses regarding rape: Exposure to sexual violence, sex differences, and the "normality" of rapists. *Journal of Research in Personality, 14,* 121–137.

Malamuth, N. M., Heim, M., & Feshbach, S. (1980). Sexual responsiveness of college students to rape depictions: Inhibitory and disinhibitory effects. *Journal of Personality and Social Psychology, 38,* 399–408.

Malamuth, N. M., & Spinner, B. (1980). A longitudinal content analysis of sexual violence in the best selling erotica magazines. *Journal of Sex Research, 16,* 226–237.

McKenzie-Mohr, D., & Zanna, M. P. (1990). Treating women as sexual objects: Look to the (gender schematic) male who has viewed pornography. *Personality and Social Psychology Bulletin, 16,* 296–308.

Oliver, M. B. (1993). Adolescents' enjoyment of graphic horror. *Communication Research, 20,* 30–50.

Paletz, D. L. (1988). Pornography, politics, and the press: The U.S. Attorney General's Commission on Pornography. *Journal of Communication, 38*(2), 122–136.

Palys, T. S. (1986). Testing the common wisdom: The social content of video pornography. *Canadian Psychology, 27,* 22–35.

Pratap, A. (1990, August 13). Romance and a little rape. *Time,* p. 69.

Quinsey, V. L., & Marshall, W. (1983). Procedures for reducing inappropriate sexual arousal: An evaluation review. In J. G. Greer & I. Stuart (Eds.), *The sexual aggressor: Current perspectives on treatment* (pp. 267–289). New York: Van Nostrand Reinhold.

Rachman, S. (1966). Sexual fetishism: An experimental analogue. *Psychological Record, 16,* 293–296.

Rachman, S., & Hodgson, R. J. (1968). Experimentally-induced "sexual fetishism": Replication and development. *Psychological Record, 18,* 25–27.

Report of the Special Committee on Pornography and Prostitution. Vol. 1. (1985). Ottawa: Minister of Supply and Services.

Schaefer, H. H., & Colgan, A. H. (1977). The effect of pornography on penile tumescence as a function of reinforcement and novelty. *Behavior Therapy, 8,* 938–946.

Signorielli, N., & Morgan, M. (Eds.). (1990). *Cultivation analysis: New directions in media effects research.* Newbury Park, CA: Sage.

Sintchak, G., & Geer, J. (1975). A vaginal plethysymograph system. *Psychophysiology, 12,* 113–115.

Soap operas. (1981, September 28). *Newsweek,* p. 65.

Sprafkin, J. N., & Silverman, L. T. (1981). Update: Physically intimate and sexual behavior on prime-time television 1978-79. *Journal of Communication, 31*(1), 34–40.

Strouse, J. S., & Fabes, R. A. (1985). Formal vs. informal sources of sex education: Competing forces in the sexual socialization process. *Adolescence, 78,* 251–263.

Taylor, S. (1982). The availability bias in social perception and interaction. In D. Kahneman, P. Slovic, & A. Tversky (Eds.), *Judgment under uncertainty: Heuristics and biases* (pp. 190–200). Cambridge: Cambridge University Press.

Tversky, A., & Kahneman, D. (1973). Availability: A heuristic for judging frequency and probability. *Cognitive Psychology, 5,* 207–232.

Tversky, A., & Kahneman, D. (1974). Judgment under uncertainty: Heuristics and biases. *Science, 185,* 1124–1131.

U. S. Commission on Obscenity and Pornography (1970). *The report of the Commission on Obscenity and Pornography.* New York: Bantam.

Wartella, E., Heintz, K. E., Aidman, A. J., & Mazzarella, S. R. (1990). Television and beyond: Children's video media in one community. *Communication Research, 17*(1), 45–64.

Weaver, J. B. (1991). Responding to erotica: Perceptual processes and dispositional implications. In J. Bryant & D. Zillmann (Eds.), *Responding to the screen: Reception and reaction processes* (pp. 329–354). Hillsdale, NJ: Lawrence Erlbaum Associates.

Weaver, J. B. (in press). The impact of exposure to horror film violence on perceptions of women: Is it the violence or an artifact? In B. Austin (Ed.), *Current research in film* (Vol. 5). Norwood, NJ: Ablex.

Weaver, J. B., Masland, J. L., & Zillmann, D. (1984). Effects of erotica on young men's aesthetic perception of their female sexual partners. *Perceptual and Motor Skills, 58*, 929–930.

White, L. A. (1979). Erotica and aggression: The influence of sexual arousal, positive affect, and negative affect on aggressive behavior. *Journal of Personality and Social Psychology, 37*, 591–601.

Wilcox, B. L. (1987). Pornography, social science, and politics: When research and ideology collide. *American Psychologist, 42*, 941–943.

Williams, B. (1979). *Report of the Committee on Obscenity and Film Censorship*. London: Her Majesty's Stationery Office.

Wilson, B. J., Linz, D., Donnerstein, E., & Stipp, H. (1992). The impact of social issue television programming on attitudes toward rape. *Human Communication Research, 19*, 179–208.

Yang, N., & Linz, D. (1990). Movie ratings and the content of adult videos: The sex-violence ratio. *Journal of Communication, 40*, 28–42.

Zillmann, D., & Bryant, J. (1982). Pornography, sexual callousness, and the trivialization of rape. *Journal of Communication, 32*(4), 10–21.

Zillmann, D., & Bryant, J. (1984). Effects of massive exposure to pornography. In N. M. Malamuth & E. Donnerstein (Eds.), *Pornorgraphy and sexual aggression* (pp. 115–141). Orlando: Academic Press.

Zillmann, D., & Bryant, J. (1988a). Effects of prolonged consumption of pornography on family values. *Journal of Family Issues, 9*, 518–544.

Zillmann, D., & Bryant, J. (1988b). Pornography's impact on sexual satisfaction. *Journal of Applied Social Psychology, 18*, 438–453.

Zillmann, D., Bryant, J., Comisky, P. W., & Medoff, N. J. (1981). Excitation and hedonic valence in the effect of erotica on motivated intermale aggression. *European Journal of Social Psychology, 11*, 233–252.

Zillmann, D., & Mundorf, N. (1987). Image effects in the appreciation of video rock. *Communication Research, 14*, 316–334.

10

Minorities and the Mass Media: 1970s to 1990s

BRADLEY S. GREENBERG
JEFFREY E. BRAND
Michigan State University

This chapter updates the current state of social research on minorities and the mass media, particularly as it relates to the media and television's particular potential for young people to acquire social information about minorities. Earlier efforts (Greenberg, 1986; Greenberg & Atkin, 1978, 1982) indicated that considerable content in various media had been systematically examined and that a fair body of research in the early 1970s had accompanied some major public television programming efforts directed at youngsters. It concluded that little had been accomplished in terms of isolating the impact of minority characters and minority-dominated programming directed at the larger public or at youngsters. The intervening years have not altered this research pattern substantially; overall, new research efforts appear to be receding at a time when public consciousness about minority issues is rising.

Two reviews, the addition of an excellent annotated bibliography, and recent work largely confirmed these tendencies. One review (Comstock & Cobbey, 1979) yielded these general propositions:

1. Ethnic minority children have a distinctive orientation toward television and other mass media (p. 105).
2. Children of ethnic minorities have different tastes and preferences in television programming (p. 107).

3. The behavioral response of children and adolescents to television portrayals is in part dependent on ethnic minority membership (p. 108).
4. Ethnic minority children have information needs that give particular prominence to television as a source of guidance (p. 110).

The second review did not confine itself to such general statements nor young respondents, although they constitute the prominent set. Poindexter and Stroman (1981) proposed that:

1. Blacks have been underrepresented; there has been a trend toward increased visibility; stereotyping and negative connotations of Blacks continue; and Blacks typically appear in minor roles and in low-status occupational roles on television;
2. Blacks tend to rely heavily on television figures for information, including information about Blacks and the Black community;
3. Blacks have distinct tastes and preferences in TV programs, are among its heaviest consumers, except for news and public affairs, and prefer to watch shows that feature Black characters;
4. Black children tend to believe in the reality of television, to learn behaviors from televised models, and to be influenced by television ads.

Signorielli (1985) compiled an annotated bibliography of studies on a variety of role portrayals on television; it included 307 abstracts of studies on racial and ethnic minorities from the early 1950s to the mid 1980s. That bibliography included reports and studies not previously available, and this chapter adds information from a portion of those studies, as well as more recent ones. Greenberg and Brand (1992a, 1992b, 1993) also add to the consideration of minority portrayals with three recent manuscripts: one combing the literature for research on minorities and their relationship to the news media, one reviewing research about minority adolescents and the mass media, and one qualitative analysis of recent offerings of racial diversity in Saturday morning children's programs. Readers interested in a historical and critical analysis of ethnic and racial images in American film and television would do well to examine a volume by Woll and Miller (1987) that traces the portrayal of 10 different groups in considerable detail.

Here, we can report extensively on the kinds of portrayals of minorities that are found in different media. Mass media content is analyzed to facilitate hypotheses about what may be learned from such programming, what may be believed, and what behavioral orientations may develop. Several recent content studies have been completed and there have been needed improvements in the quality and kinds of content analyses conducted.

We also can look at some studies done at multiple times, across years, and thereby more accurately discern trends, if any. One promising and expanding research approach, given a social learning perspective, examines cross-race portrayals and interactions within the same shows and compares those portrayals with ones that occur in shows that feature single-race interactions. There is also more interest in examining subtle role features, for example, personality characteristics, power dimensions, and family roles.

Another major focus has emerged in examining the content and character preference differences between minority and majority viewers. The large majority of field and experimental studies between 1978 and 1985 focused on young people. The emerging studies on content and character preferences attempt to trace the origins and consequences of those choice patterns for both minority and majority youths. A major segment of those studies uses content and character preferences as a basis for postulating social learning outcomes, and those are assimilated in this review. Thus, this chapter is organized into a rather detailed examination of the content analytic work, followed by a look at research that begins to ask questions about social effects and effectiveness. A final section outlines new research on what appear to be missed and totally new opportunities in a changing mass media environment.

A further addition to this chapter is the integration of one other minority—the physically challenged—based on emerging studies that deal with that subgroup's media portrayals and the effects of those portrayals. Estimates place the proportion of physically challenged at 15%-20% of the U.S. population. This reminds us that minorities are not confined to racial groups, and that in subsequent summaries, one may wish to examine other minorities, for example, by nationality, religious affiliation, and sexual orientation. Here, we look at quantitative research. A critical analysis of what she terms *disability drama* in television and film is available from Klobas (1988).

ENTERTAINMENT PORTRAYALS

The studies reported can be grouped into three major sets. First are those that count the presence or absence of minorities in media content and compare these head counts with those found for other minorities and for the majority. Second are studies that typically attempt to assess whether the presence of a minority is of major or minor significance when compared with majority role holders. Third, a relatively new and incisive approach is the extent to which those minorities are like or unlike majority characters on the same show, and further, the manner and frequency with which the minority characters interact with the majority characters.

Head Counts

One decade-long study conducted by Seggar, Hafen, and Hannonen-Gladden (1981), with content samples from 1971, 1973, 1975, and 1980, included 18,000 character portrayals. The first two periods focused on comedies and dramas, and the latter two added movies. Across this decade, White males increased steadily from 81% to 88% of the television male character population, and Black males fluctuated from 6% in 1971 to 9% in 1980, with no change recorded between 1975 and 1980. Both increases came at the expense of other minorities who decreased from 13% in 1971 to 3% in 1980. The pattern was parallel for females. In 1971, 84% were White, and 91% were White in 1980; Black females fluctuated at a lower level from 5% to 6% across the decade; others dropped from 10% to 2.5%. Thus, Whites expanded their domination in these television content areas, Blacks were below their population percentages, and all others were negligible.

A second decade-long study (1969–1978) is from the University of Pennsylvania cultural indicators project (Gerbner & Signorielli, 1979). In the peak year of minority representation (i.e., 1977), all non-Whites comprised 14% of the television characters in prime-time drama and were males by a 3–1 margin. Across the decade, they averaged 11% per year, with 8% male, but there was a systematic increase from 1969 through 1972, followed by small decreases in the next 2 years, a sharp drop in 1976, and then the peak in 1977.

Gerbner (1993) reported that for the 1991–1992 season, African Americans constituted 11% of the prime-time program characters, 9% on the daytime serials (a substantial increase in the latter), and were less than 3% on Saturday morning; Latino/Hispanic characters were rare and the remaining ethnic U.S. minorities were "most conspicuous by their absence" (p. 4). Ethnic diversity was greatest on network game shows!

From a 1979 program sample, Weigel, Loomis, and Soja (1980) reported that Blacks appeared in half the dramas and half the comedies studied, figures that paralleled estimates made by Roberts (1971). But such gross measures (i.e., mere presence in a show) mask the nature of those appearances, at least in terms of time. Blacks filled 8% of the total human appearance time on those shows. And those appearances were concentrated in very few shows; 75% of the total time Blacks were visible occurred in just 18% of the shows. Further, the Black characters were six times as likely to be presented in comedies as in dramas. Looking at more than 20,000 television characters in primetime and daytime, Signorielli (1983) reported that minorities were underrepresented in every program type, except for Asian Americans (because of "Hawaii Five-O") and male Blacks in situation comedies.

These studies are in relatively strong agreement. By 1980, 8 of every 100 prime-time television characters were likely to be Black, with 3 to 4 characters of other races observed. Black females were infrequent, and other non-White females were essentially absent. These findings reappear in two studies organized by the U.S. Commission on Civil Rights (1977, 1979). It is unlikely that these levels have changed greatly.

These appearances by minority characters in prime-time television do not carry over into the daytime. On soap operas, less than 3% of speaking characters have been identified as non-White (Greenberg, Neuendorf, Buerkel-Rothfuss, & Henderson, 1982), even less than the 5% figure reported earlier by Downing (1974).

An early systematic analysis of handicappers (undefined) was reported by Donaldson (1981); sampling 85 half-hour network prime-time programs, 1% of the characters were handicapped, 3% among major characters. Byrd's (1989) recent analysis of 302 films produced in the United States from 1986 to 1988, as cited in the *Monthly Film Bulletin*, found that 53 included characters with such impairments as alcoholism ($n = 16$), drug addiction (6), emotional disturbances (6), and suicidal attempts (5), in addition to blindness (3), deafness (3), and crippled features (2). Klobas (1988) examined the television and film portrayals of blindness, wheelchair users, deafness, amputees, developmental disabilities, small stature, and multiple disability portrayals. These studies highlight little agreement as to operational definitions of handicaps.

Roles

Seggar et al. (1981) examined role significance among Black and White characters between their 1975 and 1980 studies. White males showed sizable gains in both major and supporting roles and had trivial changes in minor and bit parts. Black males gained only slightly in the latter two categories and dropped more than 50% in major and supporting roles, from 9% to 4.4% and 12% to 4.5%, respectively. White females gained 10% in major roles, whereas Black females decreased in major and supporting roles even more sharply than Black males: In 1980, they comprised 2.4% of the major female roles and 2.7% of the supporting roles.

The particular setting of cross-racial interactions studied by Weigel et al. (1980) indicated that Blacks and Whites were cast together in predominantly egalitarian situations in at least 70% of the episodes they examined. However, only 13% of the interactions could be rated as displaying personal friendliness and/or mutual respect.

The discontinuity in the annual head count of non-Whites reported by Gerbner and Signorielli (1979) is even more striking in terms of major character portrayals, which averaged 10% per year (3.5: 1 male). There were increases in even-numbered years and decreases in odd-numbered years until 1976, when a downward trend continued. In the most recent year presented (1978), non-Whites filled less than 5% of the major roles, although they had 13% of all roles; non-White females had 1% of the major roles, the same as 10 years earlier.

Gerbner and Signorielli elaborated role analyses for specific racial groups. Major roles for Blacks and Hispanics paralleled their presence in prime time, comprising 8.5% and 2.5%, respectively. This study collapses what Seggar et al. (1981) divided into major and supporting roles, and the figures are equivalent. Again, the most recent data for this analysis show a substantial drop (to 6.5%) in major roles for Blacks from immediate past seasons. Whatever increase there was in non-White characters over portions of the decade occurred as minor characters.

The importance of family life to the characters was found to be much higher among non-White males and females. This reflects their relative containment in situation comedies, in contrast to more action-oriented programs. Non-White characters were consistently less serious than Whites in prime-time drama; two thirds of the White characters were portrayed in serious roles, compared to half of all non-White characters and less than half of the non-White females. Gerbner and Signorielli concluded that "minorities . . . generally were in non-serious and/or family-centered roles, limiting their opportunities for action and diminishing their symbolic power" (Signorielli, 1985. p. 110).

Signorielli (1982) also indicated that White women were more likely to be single and less likely to be married than their non-White peers; there was more difficulty in knowing whether White men as compared to non-White men were married or single.

Focus on the villain–hero or aggressiveness dimension of the characters has been a popular feature of role analyses. Non-White characters were more likely depicted as good guys and equivalent to Whites in their presence as bad guys. Success and failure occurred in equal portions as well. Among major characters in the Gerbner and Signorielli (1979) study, these patterns persisted. Earlier samples from Gerbner (1970) showed White males as most powerful, with non-Whites and women as least. Violence was committed by half of all White Americans, 6 in 10 White foreigners and two thirds of the non-Whites; non-Whites were more likely victims and the killer-to-killed ratio for Whites was 4:1

and for non-Whites, it was 1:1. This may have been changing when Gerson (1980) reported that Blacks and Native Americans were more likely to kill than be killed, with Whites, Asians, and Hispanics more likely to be killed than to kill. Dominick (1973) found in 1 week of prime-time programming that non-Whites were 7% of the criminals, 7% of the victims, 14% of the law enforcement agents, and 27% of the murder victims, with the criminal and murder victim proportions far below the levels reported in FBI statistics. A decade later, Lichter and Lichter (1983) found that non-Whites were 12% of all criminals, committing 10% of all violent crimes, and 3% of the murders; they remained 15% of the law enforcement officials. White males were more aggressive and White females less aggressive than their Black counterparts in prime-time series analyzed by Donagher, Poulos, Liebert, and Davidson (1975). Harvey, Sprafkin, and Rubinstein (1979) also reported that Black characters were less aggressive than Whites. In another sample of years, non-White women were least likely to commit violence, but most likely to be the victims (Gerbner, Gross, Jackson-Beeck, Jeffries-Fox, & Signorielli, 1978; U.S. Commission on Civil Rights, 1977).

McNally (1983) added to this potpourri of comparative features in finding that Black nighttime characters were less "playful" and more "content" than their White counterparts, but that Blacks were more likely to be on the receiving end of negative and neutral consequences for their behavior, whereas Whites received more positive consequences for theirs. On a more mundane level, two studies (Kaufman, 1980 Sweeper, 1988) identify that a disproportionate percentage of Blacks were overweight and that 90% of the obese characters were Black, especially Black mothers.

In occupational roles, non-Whites were less often portrayed in white-collar and professional roles (although all were overrepresented in these roles when compared to U.S. census information) and more often portrayed in blue collar and service jobs. Very few Blacks were found in prestigious occupations, and Hispanics were especially missing in occupation roles (Gerbner, Gross, & Signorielli, 1985).

Age results paralleled earlier research as well. One third of the White males were under age 35; three fifths of the non-Whites were in that age group. The same discrepancy existed for females, who overall are consistently younger than males on television. Non-White teenagers were twice as frequent as White ones.

Handicappers in Donaldson's study (1981) were seldom portrayed positively. For most of the characters, their disability was a central feature of their lives. Elliot and Byrd (1982) indicated that 57% of the disabled characters in comic books were found to be villains, whereas 43% were heroes. They also noted that prime-time television portrayals of the disabled depict this group predominantly in lower SES groups, unemployed, single, victims of abuse, and more likely to enjoy a positive outcome than able-bodied characters at the end of the show.

In a study of newspapers and prime-time television over a 3-week period, Gardner and Radel (1978) found that 68% of handicapper portrayals depicted physical handicaps and 22% mental retardation and mental illness. The kinds of physical handicappers included those who were paraplegic, quadriplegic, blind, deaf, with cerebral palsy, epileptic, diabetic, and physically deformed. One third of the characters with physical handicaps were depicted as independent and capable contributors to society or their environment. Handicappers were found more often in entertainment than in news or informational content: In 19 television entertainment programs with portrayals of handicapped persons, 42% were depicted as dependent, 21% were abusers or in some way socially deviant, and 5% were victims of abuse. Major themes in these shows portrayed 48% of the handicappers dealing with problems adjusting to the majority world and 26% projecting strange, bizarre, antisocial, or otherwise deviant attributes of handicapped people or groups.

Byrd (1989) looked at the role portrayals of 67 characters with disabilities in the movies between 1986 and 1988; 73% had abnormal personalities, two thirds were normal in appearance, but more were unattractive (22%) than attractive (12%), 55% were victims in the story, and more (45%) experienced negative consequences in the story than either neutral or positive conclusions. Most handicapper characters have social relationships with other film characters, 90% were not depicted in an institutional setting, about half were shown as members of a family, and about half were given clear middle-class status, with 13% lower class and 4% upper class. More often than not, people with handicapper features were unemployed (55%), with a disproportionate emphasis among those employed as professionals (21%).

Cross-Race Portrayals

A promising approach to content and structural analysis of race on television is examining within-show characterizations of two races. For example, to what extent do direct comparisons between Blacks and Whites paired with (against?) each other on the same show provide findings not discernible from the total television racial composite, as provided by demographic comparisons alone? Young viewers with a need for more concrete referents may be particularly susceptible to observing how two racial groups interact and behave in the same context (i.e., the same show). From a conceptual view, they begin to tackle the issue of whether impact is more likely to emerge from dynamic, interactive images of the races as contrasted with the more static models describable from head count and role attribute investigations.

Reid (1979) compared the behaviors of Black and White characters on 10 half-hour comedies. The comedies selected were groupings of Black-dominated, White-dominated, and racially mixed shows, all with at least one regular Black character. Across a dozen different behaviors examined, the only one to yield racial differences was that Black characters sought recognition for their deeds more often. Further analyses by sex of the characters indicated that Black males did not differ from White males on any of the behaviors studied, whereas Black females were less achieving (e.g., in initiating plans), were less succorant, more boasting, and more dominant—behaviors all indicative of a continuing Black female stereotype. And Black females appeared almost exclusively on the Black-dominated shows.

Reid then analyzed the behaviors of the White characters across the three show types. Whites appearing on Black-dominated situation comedies were more deferent and less autonomous, less nurturing, and less succorant than counterpart Whites on White-dominated comedies. Whites on the former were generally less pleasant characters: They were more aggressive, dependent, and negative in their attitude toward others. Lemon (1977) determined that Whites were more dominant in cross-race interactions in crime shows, whereas Blacks clearly had the more dominant roles in situation comedies.

Banks (1977) looked at series with nearly all Black casts and compared them with racially mixed casts and concluded that the former were more negative, that is, they were more poorly educated and more beset with personal problems, whereas those with mixed casts presented Blacks as of higher social status, more cooperative, and more competent—all attributes alleged to be more often associated with White characters.

Another attempt to look at same-show characterization of the two races compared the 100 Blacks found in a week's sample of programs with a sample of 100 Whites from the same shows (Baptista-Fernandez & Greenberg, 1980). The Blacks were systematically younger (two thirds were 23 or younger), less frequently employed, and funnier. Half the Blacks were in comedies compared to one third of the Whites, and the Blacks were either in programs that were virtually all Black or were isolated Blacks on otherwise White shows. Half the Blacks and none of the Whites appeared on shows with four or more Black characters. In behavioral comparisons across these characters, the Whites had eight conversations with other Whites to every one with a Black character, although there were only five times as many White characters. Blacks interacted with Whites three times as often as the reverse. Both talked equivalently and primarily of domestic matters in these shows, but Whites discussed business issues and crime more often. Blacks discussed no specific topic more often than Whites. There were no significant differences in the extent to which each group gave, sought, or received advice, information, or orders.

Shu (1979) added information about Chinese characters on network television. From 11 shows in 1974-1975 with Chinese characters who were present for at least 15 seconds per half hour, these characters were different from census comparisons on gender, age, marital status, and occupations; by comparison with Whites on the same shows, they were poorer, more likely to be teenagers, criminals, and business owners. They also were more likely to be aggressive with a weapon, submissive in interpersonal interaction, and on the screen less time.

Brown and Campbell (1986) looked at music videos, with one sample from MTV and the second from "Video Soul," on the Black Entertainment Network cable channel in 1984. The MTV collection had 3% Black male leads and 1% Black female, compared with 54% and 19% on the minority-centered channel. They concluded that "White men . . . are the center of attention and power and are more often aggressive and hostile than helpful and cooperative. Women and Blacks are rarely important enough to be a part of the foreground" (p. 104). Thus, the specialized music TV channel for the majority audience continued the pattern found in television series.

A study of race relations on prime-time television focused on examining content variables that reflected social psychological determinants of interracial friendliness and prejudice reduction across racial lines, for example, equal status, cooperative interactions, supportive social norms, and interpersonal intimacy (Weigel et al., 1980). A 1-week 1978 prime-time sample of drama, situation comedies, and movies yielded 91 cross-racial interactions (1.5 per hour), and these were compared with a random sample of 60 White-White interactions. A key finding is that only 2% of the human appearance time involved cross-racial interactions. Although Blacks were in more than half of the situation comedies and dramas, solely White appearances accounted for 99% of the time in the latter and 86% of the former. Thus, although television is not entirely White, it continues to be subdivided into episodes in which Blacks and Whites seldom encounter one another.

In terms of variables that foster positive race relations, the study determined that Black–White interactions were more interdependent than White–White relations with respect to both common goals and interpersonal cooperation. However, relationships between Blacks and Whites were also characterized by less shared decision making, narrower, more formal relationships, less intimate personal relationships, and almost no romantic relationships. Friendships and nonwork relationships were more common in White–White interactions. Blacks and Whites discussed problem alternatives in but 13% of the possible situations, compared to 56% of the White–White decisions. Black–White interactions occurred almost exclusively in job-related contexts, compared to half of the White–White relationships. Thus, cross-racial relationships are infrequent and relatively formal. Blacks and Whites can work together but do not maintain the same degree of voluntary, individualized relationships that Whites do. For the most part, Blacks and Whites appear on different shows; when they do appear together, they largely maintain that separateness.

Although not an analysis of same-show behavior, another promising approach is examining larger units of behavior, such as families or work units. Do Black families and family members behave differently than Whites? Rarely would these families appear together, with some notable exceptions (e.g., "The Jeffersons"). Nevertheless, whether the portrayals of Black and White families are comparable or different provides the basis for potential social learning hypotheses, as would work units consisting of either mixed racial membership (e.g., "LA Law") or the same racial composition.

Across a week of television, one can see a Black family on four or five shows and a White family eight times as often (Greenberg & Neuendorf, 1980). The dominant Black family type consists of a single parent plus children; the primary White family type has two parents and one or more children. One could find the latter composition perhaps in one show a season featuring Blacks. The single Black parent tends to be a mother. Black families seldom have kinfolk, consisting almost entirely of nuclear family members, whereas as many as one-fifth of the White family members would be cousins, uncles, in-laws, and other relatives. As for family interaction, Black sons have had larger roles than daughters and White children. Overall, Black males were more active in family interactions than White males, although the most active role pair in both Black and White families was husband–wife. The major behavioral difference between Black and White families was that of conflict, accounting for one-sixth of the interactions in the former and one-tenth in the latter. In White families, conflict was evenly distributed among role members; in Black families, it was centered in the wives and among siblings. These are substantial differences and provide a potentially important basis for what young viewers may think they know about how Black and White families are composed, interact, and behave.

With a more expansive sample and time frame, Sweeper (1983) studied 93 episodes of six White and six Black family-centered shows from 1970–1980. Black families more often depicted broken homes, households headed by females, lower educated family members employed in lower status occupations; Black adult males were more hostile, ineffectual, self-centered and unreliable than their White counterparts; interactions among Black family members were more abrasive, especially between opposite-sex siblings. Sweeper concluded that earlier Black stereotypes were being replaced by equally demeaning portrayals, in contradistinction to the predominantly positive images of the White family.

Handicappers, according to Donaldson (1981), have not been depicted in professional and social interactions with nonhandicappers, and were never seen in the background as shoppers, spectators, or workers.

NEWS PORTRAYALS

By the early 1970s, Blacks were becoming more visible in the news, and studies suggested more egalitarian coverage and presentation. Blacks were found in 13% of news-magazine pictures by Stempel (1971), in 25% of network television newscasts by Baran (1973), and in 23% of network TV newscasts by Roberts (1975), although primarily in nonspeaking roles on segments dedicated to busing, segregation, and other civil rights issues. In 1977, the U.S. Commission on Civil Rights claimed that there were few Black television news correspondents and that they seldom handled lead stories; by 1979, that same commission in a follow-up study (U.S. Commission on Civil Rights, 1979) reported that less than 2% of the network news stories dealt with minorities, a smaller proportion than 2 years earlier, and that 8% of the correspondents were minorities. In a recent evaluation of news and minorities, Greenberg and Brand (1992b) concluded that recent studies "of minority portrayals in the news media indicate clearly an increased presence of Blacks and Hispanics in news stories and news presentations. They are far more visible than two decades ago, although questions remain as to the qualitative attributes of their presence, that is how they are being presented and in what context" (pp. 14-15). We review research consistent with this conclusion here.

Chaundhary (1980) examined the newspaper coverage of Black and White elected officials during 1974 and 1976 elections in 19 metropolitan cities in which the Black population exceeded 200,000. News coverage on election day and for every other day up to 10 days before each election was analyzed across 2,780 items about elected officials. White elected officials received significantly more coverage on election day and

2 days before the election, and they received more favorable placement on the front page and inside front page above the fold, where most of the election stories were located. However, Black elected officials received longer stories, averaging 300 words compared to 225 for White officials. There were no differences in terms of headline size, photo coverage, or story type. However, there were substantial divergences among the 19 newspapers, indicating that local editorial policy may play a major role in the equity of coverage of Black and White candidates.

Chaudhary had coders rate the degree of positive and negative bias in each story, $r = .84$ between coders, and determined that most items for both sets of candidates were coded as neutral. However, the distribution of stories was such that significantly more negative stories appeared for Black elected officials than for Whites. This study highlights the importance of examining how Blacks are covered, in addition to whether they are covered.

In a progression of analyses of the same data set, Martindale examined the press' portrayal of Black Americans. For her first analysis (Martindale, 1984), she examined the coverage of Black Americans in 66 sampled issues of the *Youngstown (Ohio) Vindicator* between 1950 and 1980. Using three time periods: (1950-1953, before the civil rights movement; 1963-1968, at the height of the movement; and 1972-1980, after confrontations had ceased), her news categories were stereotypic coverage (crimes by Blacks and entertainment figures), everyday life, civil rights (e.g., Black protests, civil rights gains), and minority life (e.g., Black problems, housing programs). For the *Vindicator*, total news hole given to these topics during the 1970s (15%) was half of its 1960s figure (33%) and equivalent to its 1950s level (13%). As to topic emphasis, 6% of its coverage in the 1950s and 1960s was stereotypic, and 15% in the 1970s; in the three time periods, everyday life occupied 73%, 29%, and 62% of the newshole; civil rights stories were in 14%, 61%, and 20% of the newshole; and minority life topics never exceeded 7% in any of the time periods, with coverage of Black problems never greater than 3%. However, of the coverage of local community activities of Blacks, an increasing percentage was stand-alone photos, without stories; 32% in the 1950s, then 66%, and finally 71% of all coverage was photos. Further, Martindale indicated that only 6% of the paper's coverage of Black protest activities in the 1960s gave any information as to the causes underlying the protests. Martindale concluded, "On the one hand, the coverage provided many indications of the . . . management's positive attitudes toward local Blacks, its avoidance of stereotypical coverage, and its efforts to include Blacks in its portrayal of the city's life. But the coverage also suggested the paper made little effort to portray the problems of local Blacks, to explore their contribution to the city" (p. 23).

Martindale then compared the content of the *Vindicator* with that of the *New York Times, Atlanta Constitution, Chicago Tribune, and the Boston Globe* (Martindale, 1985). Using the same time periods, the same content categories, and so on, (we omit the *Vindicator* findings already presented), she found that among these four major newspapers, the coverage of Blacks increased from the 1960s to the 1970s for two of them and remained relatively stable for the other two. As for the major content categories, we will summarize the findings only from the most recent time period: In the 1970s, coverage of Blacks in the everyday life category was the predominant topic in all papers except for the *Globe*, which chose to emphasize civil rights related stories. Stereotyped stories comprised 14% of the *Times* coverage, 18% of the *Constitution*, 9% of the *Globe*, and 15% of the *Tribune's* daily newshole dedicated to coverage of Black Americans in the 1970s sample. The coverage of Black problems ranged from 3% (*Globe*) to 13% (*Tribune*); all these represented substantial increases from prior periods, save for the *Globe*; concurrently, there was little space given to the coverage of causes of Black protest activities. For Martindale, the most noteworthy finding is the continued coverage of Blacks in the 1970s even after the events of the civil rights movement subsided.

Martindale returned to this same data set (Martindale, 1987) and extracted the category of stereotyped news coverage for more intensive analysis. Again, we concentrate here on the 1970s data set for the four major daily newspapers. She compared coverage of Blacks involved in criminal activities, as entertainment figures, and as protesters and then added the category of politicians. Taking as a baseline the total coverage of Blacks in the newspaper, she found that criminal activities' coverage ranged from 3% in the *Globe* to 12% in the *Constitution*; Blacks as entertainers ranged from 5% to 9% across the four papers; Blacks as protesters was exactly 1% in all four papers; and the coverage of Black politicians ranged from 8% in the *Globe* to 20% in the *Constitution*. Overall, there was little change from the 1960s to the 1970s in coverage of Blacks in criminal activities, a sharp increase in coverage as entertainers, a sharper increase in coverage as politicians, and a striking decrease in presenting them as protesters (from 15% of their appearances in the 1960s to 1% in the 1970s).

One systematic examination of the newspaper coverage of a second minority, Mexican Americans, was located. In six southwestern U.S. cities with Hispanic residents comprising 20%-65% of the population, a 2-week sample of local daily newspapers was analyzed in terms of locally written Hispanic news, sports, editorials, photos, and bulletin listings (Greenberg, Heeter, Burgoon, Burgoon, & Korzenny, 1983a). All sites filled their local newshole with local Hispanic news stories in proportion to the percentage of Hispanics in their community, although 75% of these stories qualified solely because they contained a Spanish surname. There were four such stories per issue each day. However, news stories that focused primarily on Hispanics averaged only 10% of the local news. Local Hispanic sports stories filled more of the local sports newshole (42%), averaging two stories a day, with virtually all qualifying because the story contained one or more Spanish surnames. Sports coverage was markedly different by site, with the newshole proportion ranging between 18% and 77%. Bulletins (e.g., births, deaths, community events) indicated an underrepresentation of Mexican Americans as had been demonstrated for Black Americans (Kearl, 1986-1987). Overall, bulletin representation was one-half or less of the proportion of the Hispanic population. Hispanic photos filled 19% of the total local photo newshole, or about 2 in 10 photos, with 1 in 10 on the front page. The primary photo content was that of soft news and sports (82% of all photos), with crime accounting for only 2%. Editorial page content carried one Hispanic referent every other issue, filling 13% of the local editorial page. Half the items identified were Hispanic-authored letters to the editor on non-Hispanic issues; 33% of the items dealt with minority issues, 33% with other hard news issues, and 14% with crime.

Again, the newspapers varied greatly in their coverage of Mexican Americans across the sites and across the different types of news items. Stories primarily on Hispanics were rare in both the news and sports sections. Editorial page coverage was slight. Whether the coverage is adequate seems to depend on the individual newspaper and whether the criterion is that of prominence, representativeness, or content emphasis.

Examining two southwest papers for 1982, 1984, and 1986, Turk, Richard, Bryson, and Johnson (1989) found that Hispanics were present in those newspapers at least in proportion to their presence in the population. The three single-year samples were not different from one another within each paper; the coverage in 1986 was equivalent to the other 2 years. In a community with one-third Hispanics, Albuquerque, half the newspaper space was devoted to Hispanic coverage, Hispanic stories and photos were generally longer, with bigger headlines and more prominent placement. Nevertheless, Hispanic news coverage tended to focus on Hispanics as "problem people." One-fourth of the Hispanic stories and 13% of Anglo stories dealt with judicial or criminal activities. Overall, however, the slant on Anglo stories was more unfavorable than that on Hispanic stories.

Heeter et al. (1983) compared local Hispanic news coverage across newspapers, radio, and television in terms of prominence, content aspects, and representativeness. Local Hispanic community leaders believed that there was an overemphasis on crime and negative news, a shortage of positive news, and that the media just did not cover Hispanic events and individuals as much or as prominently as non-Hispanic activities. They also believed that radio offered the most local coverage and that television coverage was minimal (Korzenny, Griffis, Greenberg, Burgoon, & Burgoon, 1983). On a typical day,news that involved Hispanics averaged a little more than one-half page of text in the daily newspaper, 1 of 5 minutes devoted to local news on the top-rated radio station, and a little more than 3 of the 14 minutes of news on the major local evening television news show. Hispanic reports on both broadcast media were longer than non-Hispanic reports. As for content emphasis, more than one third of the radio stories about Hispanics dealt with crime, in contrast to less than half that figure in the other two media. Newspapers were most varied in the content issues covered. No Hispanic studio newscasters were reported for either radio or television. Radio news stories were far more likely to qualify solely because they contained a Spanish surname. Overall, local radio gave less of its newshole and focused more on crime and name dropping. Newspapers gave newshole, and television gave time equivalent to Hispanic population proportions; newspapers covered many more kinds of issues for more varied reasons; television coverage was present and was at least as strong as radio. These results stand in sharp contrast to the expressed beliefs of Hispanic community leaders about coverage.

More recently, Womack (1986, 1988) determined the extent of Black (and female) participation in network presidential convention broadcasts. He compared 1972 and 1976 with 1984. He found no differences among the networks in their presentation of race and gender, but significantly more Blacks were interviewed in 1984 than earlier. Furthermore, Blacks were interviewed in greater proportion than their relative delegate strength, but those interviewed were most likely to be rank-and-file delegates.

Entman (1992) analyzed local TV news coverage of four Chicago stations for 55 days between December 1989 and May 1990 to determine whether crime and political reporting depicted Blacks as more physically threatening and demanding than Whites. Among other findings about portrayals of Blacks in the news, he found that Blacks, compared with Whites, were less often named, less likely to be shown in motion, more likely to be pictured in custody, less likely to be defended in the story text, and more often talked about by White and Black police officials. Examining political coverage, Entman found that Black leaders were more often shown defending Black community interests, whereas White leaders more often appeared to represent all constituents. He concluded that television news portrayed Blacks in politics as advancing special interests rather than the public interest.

In a relatively strong effort to assess causality, Mathews (1987) counted the number of articles indexed on Black Americans in the *Reader's Guide to Periodical Literature* and then counted the number of films with Black actors in starring or feature roles. He identified a strong positive relationship between the news media agenda (frequency of articles indexed on Black Americans) and the casting of Blacks in featured roles in motion pictures, with a 4-year time lag between the news media agenda and the onset of the films.

In what remains a unique study of broadcast commentary, Rainville and McCormick (1977) examined protocols from 12 National Football League games in which they matched biracial pairs of players and compared the spontaneous commentary of the announcers. Whites received more play-related praise and more favorable comments on aggressive plays, while Blacks were more the subject of unfavorable comparisons to other players, and all 11 negative refe rences to nonprofessional past behaviors were to Black players. With a recent influx of Black commentators into the announcer's booth, this special study should be replicated.

News coverage of and themes related to handicappers were very different for television and for newspapers. Gardner and Radel (1978) noted that newspapers dealt with the theme of special services (44%) for the disabled significantly more than did television (11%). Difficulty in adjusting to the majority world was found in 8% of the newspaper stories and 37% of the television programs. The theme of abuse of the disabled was carried in 14% of the press stories and in no television coverage.

Images of handicappers in newspapers were neither as positive nor as realistic as the thematic coverage. Half the articles portrayed dependency whereas only 22% depicted those with handicapping features as independent. Newspapers represented handicappers as objects of abuse in 19% of the stories and as social outcasts or deviants in 9%.

Sampling national daily newspapers, Keller, Hallahan, McShane, Crowley, and Blandford (1990) analyzed articles covering disabilities to determine whether disabilities were the prominent focus of each article, what types of disability were covered, in what article genres and with what impact to the subject or subjects of the disability. They found 8.3 articles appeared daily in which disabilities were either a major and minor focus of the story. In 63% of those, the disability was the major focus of the story. However, half the stories were soft news features "tending to be more emotionally charged" (p. 275). Physical disabilities were the focus of 27% of the articles, mental impairments 13% of the stories, and generic "handicapped" and "disabled" 12% and 9%, respectively. About half the articles did not discuss the effect of the disability on the life of the story subject, but 48% were negative about the disability's impact, whereas but 1% portrayed positive impact. Most articles (52%) featured no details about potential for improvement in the handicapper, although 44% of articles portraying the negative impact of the disability indicated potential for improvement and 4% portrayed the handicap as unimprovable.

ADVERTISING PORTRAYALS

The portrayal of Blacks in print advertising has been sparse indeed, and it is nonexistent for handicappers. Early studies from the 1940s through the mid-1960s indicated not more than 3% usage of Blacks in major magazine advertising, with their few appearances as entertainers, athletes, and servants (Colfax & Steinberg, 1972; Kassarjian, 1969; Stempel, 1971). An increase to 5% presence in magazine advertisements was identified by Cox (1969-1970) for the last half of the 1960s, yet for 1978, Bush, Resnick, and Stern (1980) again reported 2%. Reviewing ads in 27 issues of *Time, Newsweek, Sports Illustrated, and U.S. News & World Report* between 1975 and 1980, Soley (1983) found but 29; 2 had Black females, 3 had both sexes, and the remainder had Black males only. In an interesting analysis for the 10 years ending in 1977, Reid and Vanden Bergh (1980) specifically examined ads that presented a product or service new to the advertisers in *Time, Cosmopolitan, Reader's Digest,* and *Ladies' Home Journal*. Of the 8,700 ads examined, only 59 (less than 1%) contained any Black characters. There was no apparent trend across the years. Furthermore, in this small subset, only one-sixth characterized the Black in a major role. To the extent there was increased usage of Blacks in print advertising, they did not introduce new products.

In an experimental study of female responses to Black advertising models, controlling for facial features, hair style, and skin pigmentation, Kerin (1979) examined perceived product quality and suitability among Black and White respondents. The Black respondents associated quality most dominantly with Negroid facial features, and the White respondents with Caucasoid facial features. As for suitability, Black and White respondents agreed that maximum suitability derived from models who clustered congruent or stereotypic characteristics, for example, Negroid features with Afro hair styles, and Caucasoid features with wavy hair styles. Several experiments have all reported that White respondents do not respond negatively to the use of Black models in ads (e.g., Block, 1972; Schlinger & Plummer, 1972).

Looking at 962 ads in January and July issues of *Cosmopolitan*, *Glamour*, and *Vogue* fashion magazines from 1986 to 1988, Jackson and Ervin (1991) found that only 23 (2.4%) contained Black women; 12.5% of the female population in the late 1980s was Black as were 15% of subscribers to these magazines. Moreover, 83% of the ads containing Black women portrayed the full body, whereas 9% portrayed only the face conveying, the authors note, that Black women are usually portrayed from a distance if at all.

Pollay, Lee, and Carter-Whitney (1992) completed a census of 540 cigarette ads for 23 brands in *Ebony* magazine between 1950 and 1965 and compared these to a matched sample from *Life* magazine during which 526 ads were published for 33 brands. They found that *Ebony* featured Black models increasingly over the 1950s to the point of exclusivity; most Black models were athletes. *Life*, however, did not carry these ads even though many featured Black athletes and musicians familiar to White readers. *Life* contained more cigarette ads initially, but by the mid-1950s, *Ebony* featured cigarette ads with equal frequency to Life. By 1960, *Ebony* carried more of these ads than *Life*. Yet, Pollay and his colleagues found that cigarette advertising in *Ebony* was two to three years behind *Life* in presenting filtered cigarettes to the Black Audience.

Soley (1983) moved from the laboratory to the field to assess responses to advertising containing Black models. Armed with a sample of ads with Black male models and control sets of ads with White males, he compared Starch readership scores. These measures took into account whether the ad was merely seen, whether the name of the advertiser was read, and whether half or more of the copy was read. In sum, the ethnicity of the model made no difference in ad readership. The absence of Blacks from advertising is bias on the part of the advertiser and/or the client, and not the consumer.

As for broadcast advertising, a sharp increase from 5% to 11% in Black television models was identified from the mid- to late 1960s (Dominick & Greenberg, 1970), with a range from 10% to 13% by the mid-1970s (Bush, Solomon, & Hair, 1977; Culley & Bennett, 1976). In both print and broadcast ads, these studies show that Blacks appeared in "crowd scenes" with Whites or with other Blacks rather than alone; for example, commercials with Blacks averaged 13 people and those without Blacks averaged 4. Further, more than one in three of the Black characters were likely to be children. Atkin and Heald (1977) found that one-fifth of Saturday morning commercials contained Black characters.

Gerbner, Gross, Morgan, and Signorielli (1981) looked at commercials from 1977 to 1979, and found Hispanics in less than 2% during primetime, in less than 1% on weekend daytime television, and in none of the commercials in the evening news. Their sample showed Blacks in one of five commercials, but as the sole participants in less than 2% of all ads.

Using a prime-time sample of 63 hours in 1978, Weigel et al. (1980) used time on air as their key measure of minority presence. Whites were visible in the ads 97% of the time and Blacks were visible 8.5% of the time, with 5% of the time containing cross-racial appearances. Further, cross-racial interactions in the ads occurred slightly less than 2% of the time. Overall, 75% of the commercials were entirely White, and Blacks appeared in less than 20% of the product commercials. In a poignant comparison, they noted that all-Black commercials comprised less than 2% of the items, whereas animated commercials without any human appearances occurred twice as frequently as that figure.

Blacks have yet to make major inroads in print advertising, and the importance of their presence in television advertising may have been overstated by merely counting faces. Certainly, the data verify that there are more Black faces, but they get less time, are less visible, may be buried in a sea of faces, and rarely interact with Whites.

CHILDREN'S TELEVISION PORTRAYALS

In a series of reports for Action for Children's Television, Barcus (1975, 1978) and Barcus and Wolkin (1977) identified the presence of White, Black, and other minority characters in weekday and weekend programs and in advertising directed at children. Then, in 1981, drawing a more extensive sample of programs from television stations in the Boston area, Barcus (1983) compiled an elaborate description of what is available on television about minorities for child viewers. Greenberg and Brand (1993) added to the earlier observations in a qualitative look at Saturday morning portrayals, confirming the persistence of limited minority portrayals aimed at children.

Head Counts

In the mid- to late 1970s, weekday programming for children yielded a 3% Black population of television characters and 1%–4% of other minorities; weekend programming was consistently higher, at 7% for Blacks and 4%–8% for other minorities. This difference can be attributed largely to the extensive use of syndicated programs on weekdays by local stations, many originating in an earlier decade when Blacks were less likely to be part of any television program; weekend programming was largely network offerings. Regardless of day of week, non-White characters on these shows were more likely to be children than adults.

Blacks fared better in commercials during the late 1970s, at about 7% inclusion, whereas other minorities did not exceed 2%. If the stiffer criterion is invoked as to whether a Black was a spokesperson on any ads during children's programming, the answer is no. In contrast, Blacks were featured in no less than 10% of the public service announcements, and during one sample period, reached 23%.

According to Barcus (1983), Blacks evidenced little gain in children's programming. They were 3.6% of 1,145 characters in 1981, whereas all other minorities combined totaled 4% on programs targeted for children. Blacks were clearly cast (perhaps stifled) among much younger characters. On these programs, 25% of all Blacks were children (compared to 11% of all Whites), 20% were teenagers (13% for Whites), 15% were middle-aged (34% for Whites), and none were elderly (4% for Whites), with the remainder as young adults. The other minorities more closely paralleled the White age distribution.

Gerbner and Signorielli (1979) reported one specific analysis of minority character representation in weekend network programming for the period 1970–1976. The underrepresentation of non-Whites found in prime time is exacerbated on the weekends. The proportions of weekend Black characters (6.5%) and of Hispanic characters (1%) are smaller than during prime time; the ratio of Black males to females is larger (8:1), with females constituting less than 1% of the weekend characters. Asians were overrepresented (2.7%) among weekend characters, and Native Americans were negligible (total of five males). Earlier, Mendelson and Young (1972) also had found 7% Blacks among the Saturday morning network characters.

Black characters on weekend programming for children were consistently younger than White characters. More than 40% were teenagers, compared with 25% among White characters. At the opposite end of the age continuum, the situation was reversed. Elderly Blacks could be counted on one hand across 10 television seasons.

Weigel and Howes (1982) used appearance time rather than head count to assess the presence of Blacks on children's programs, examining 15 hours of Saturday morning network programming. They determined that 6.6% of program time contained Black appearances, quite comparable to the 7% character population in weekend shows reported by Barcus during the late 1970s. They elaborated on this by identifying the kind of Saturday morning "ghetto" that exists: 48% of the total Black appearance time was in just one program, and 85% was in but five shows.

Earlier, we indicated that the presence of Blacks and Hispanics in weekend programs is smaller than in prime time. This discrepancy continued in terms of major characters, wherein the proportion of major

characters in each racial grouping is even smaller than their representation in the character population; that is not the case for minority
characters in prime-time programming (Gerbner & Signorielli, 1979).

Network and independent television programs aimed at children on
Saturday mornings and weekday afternoons were analyzed by Barcus
(1978) for images of handicappers. Of the 228 programs in the sample,
only 9 addressed or dealt with handicaps.

Roles

Barcus (1983) then moved from head counts to role depictions of Blacks
and other minorities on children's programs. He found that Blacks were
as often cast as heroes as were Whites, and more so than other minority
characters. They were less likely to be villains and more likely to be
major characters. However, Blacks constituted 2% of all major characters
overall.

Blacks continue to be employed less often than Whites, with one third
of the former and one half of the latter clearly indicated as job holders.
However, more than half of those employed, whether Black or White,
were in professional and managerial jobs, twice the proportion of other
minorities in those jobs. It is the other minorities who have replaced
Blacks in the lower social classes on television. Barcus found the Black
social class distribution on these programs equivalent to that of Whites
and substantially higher than presented for other minorities.

Barcus further examined the goals of all major dramatic characters
and classified them as basically self-goals (self-indulgence, wealth,
power) or altruistic goals (friendship, patriotism, justice). For Whites,
Blacks, and other minorities, altruism comprised two thirds of the
goals sought. Only animal characters, for example, Bugs Bunny, over-
indulged themselves. The primary means used to seek goals were
violence, personal hard work, and intelligence; Whites displayed these
more than minority characters. Ethnic characters attempted to use
personal charm more than did non-ethnic characters.

Taken together, cross-racial interactions totaled just 1% of the children's programming sampled, yielding only 38 consistently brief and
separate interactions. This pool was insufficient to analyze how the
races got along with each other; children's programming was not a basis
for fostering interracial goodwill through vicarious experience unless
you chose to view the single show in which Black–White and White–
White interactions were equally cooperative and interdependent. Barcus
(1983) found that about one in five of the children's program segments
he analyzed contained Whites and Blacks appearing together, but he
failed to tell us what they did.

Barcus' final analysis began to examine personality traits of minority and majority characters. Beset by small samples, the findings can at best be considered suggestive. The most intriguing conclusion is that ethnic heroes and villains tend to be more extreme than non-ethnics; they are either superheroes or archvillains, given more extreme judgments on 10 of 12 personality scales.

Little data are presented dealing with program type. However, a concluding paragraph in Barcus' (1983) analysis of minorities is worth citing: "Cartoon comedy programs contain the most blatant ethnic stereotypes. These programs . . . frequently provide cruel stereotypes of ethnic minorities. And cartoon comedies alone amount to nearly one-half of all program time in children's TV" (p. 115).

On weekend daytime programs, one third of the characters were serious, and the remainder at least partly comical. But Black characters were even more likely to be comical than Whites. This finding applies only to males, inasmuch as the total number of Black female characters identified across 10 years was 15 (Gerbner & Signorielli, 1979). The aggression pattern on Saturday children's programs follows that identified for primetime television; 21% of the Whites were found to be aggressive, compared with 14% of the non-Black minorities and but 2% of the Blacks (Poulos, Harvey, & Liebert, 1976).

In the nine shows with depictions of handicappers identified by Barcus (1978), four dealt with vision disability of the cartoon character, Mr. Magoo. Two were characters with speech impediments (e.g., Porky Pig) and one episode portrayed a character *pretending* to be handicapped in a wheelchair. Only one program included a discussion of problems faced by handicappers. Thus, less than 2% of the segments in Barcus' analysis showed vision impairments and 1% illustrated speech problems.

In a qualitative analysis of 20 Saturday morning television programs on commercial television (Greenberg & Brand, 1993): (a) three programs featured regularly appearing racial minority characters; (b) all racial minority characters who appeared regularly were Black; (c) in 10.5 hours, one Hispanic American was featured, zero Asian Americans and zero Native Americans; and (d) all racial minority characters featured were male—the adult minority woman was invisible, and younger minority females, when present, were background characters. We noted, "Saturday's commercial television program schedule is fairly empty as a carrier of multicultural information" (p. 142).

The preceding discussion, of course, focuses on commercial television; public television has long been an alternative for commercial children's shows and has showed a more profound pattern of minority character integration; with such shows as "Sesame Street," "Mr. Rogers," and "Electric Company," typically one fourth of all characters are minorities (Dohrmann, 1975).

Finally, although a systematic analysis of "Sesame Street" has not been done for content characteristics of handicappers, some portrayals have appeared on the program (Glauberman, 1980). In her experiment looking for changes between viewers (who were exposed to such a segment) and nonviewers in attitudes and behaviors toward handicapped children, Glauberman found that first-grade viewers displayed more positive attitudes toward such children and sat closer to a child in a wheelchair than nonviewers. Glauberman concluded that positive television portrayals of handicappers can improve attitudes and behaviors of children toward their handicapped peers.

EFFECTS: CONTENT AND CHARACTER PERCEPTIONS AND PREFERENCES

In the midst of substantial new research on identification, role-model preferences, and content orientations, there lurk assumptions—some implicit and some tested—about social learning and social effects. These are examined in this section.

Because television has been the most studied medium in research on content and its effects on young people, a brief summary of minority youth television exposure is presented here. Black households watch 23 hours more television than other households each week (Nielsen Media Research, 1988). Brown and her colleagues (Brown, Campbell, & Fischer, 1986) reported from a sample of 1,200 teens (two-thirds White and one-third Black) that the average number of hours of television viewed each week had the following pattern: 25 hours for White females, 27 hours for White males, 31 hours for Black males, and 32 hours for Black females. The ethnic difference was statistically significant; the overall levels of television viewing consisted of 3.6 hours per day at the low end and 4.6 at the high end. In a second study of 1,800 12- to 14-year-olds, Brown, Bauman, Lentz, and Koch (1987) found even higher overall viewing levels, with Whites averaging more than 5 hours and Blacks more than 7 hours per day, but also that television viewing declined with age, with the largest drop occurring between 13 and 14 years of age. That drop in television viewing was offset by increased use of radio in that older age group. Those reported levels of viewing closely match those of Greenberg and Heeter (1987) who identified 5.43 hours per day across an urban sample of 1,100 Black and White 14 to 16-year-olds. Consistent ethnic differences in viewing (Blacks viewed television 1 to 2 hours more each day than Whites) were reported by Greenberg and Linsangan (1993).

Dates (1980) reverified that Black high school students had a stronger preference for Black television shows (e.g., "Good Times") than did White youngsters. The viewing of White situation comedies did not differ by race. The major focus of her study was the extent to which Black and White youngsters identified with, thought favorably of, and perceived greater realism in Black and/or White television characters. The Black youngsters consistently rated Black characters more positively; they rated White characters equally with White students. The same findings held for the other two variables: Perceived reality and personal identification. Blacks exceeded non-Black students in both estimates for Black television characters, with no stable differences between Black and White responses to White characters. Dates also demonstrated no particular relationship between her measure of racial attitudes and character perceptions. Among Blacks, the correlations were nil; among Whites, there tended to be a positive relationship between racial attitudes and Black character evaluation.

Black and White television newscasters in New York City were evaluated by Black and White high school students (Kaner, 1982) in terms of competency and social distance (as potential neighbors and as potential kin). The Black students rated the newscasters of both races the same, whereas White students rated same-race newscasters higher on all attributes, particularly on the social distance estimates. The investigator's assessment of racial attitudes in terms of open minded-ness was not related to the evaluations, nor was frequency of viewing television news.

Elementary school children exhibit the same tendency to select same-race characters as their favorites (Eastman & Liss, 1980). When limited to identifying one favorite television character (during a season in which 85% of all characters were Anglo), 96% of the Anglo youngsters chose same-race characters, compared to 75% of the Black and 80% of the Hispanic youth. When limited to one favorite television program, the minority youth cited a minority-dominant show.

When not limited to a single character, the pattern of same-race selection becomes even more striking. Blacks and Whites are equally likely to identify with White television characters. Across 26 White TV characters, 17% of the Black youths and 16% of the White youths said they want to be like the character; relatively few White or Black children want to be like most of the White models available to them on television. But, Black youths are more than three times as likely to identify with Black characters. Note the findings in Table 10.1 from Greenberg and Atkin (1982).

TABLE 10.1
Percentage of Youths Wanting to be like Black Television Characters

Percentage Wanting to Be Like:	Blacks	Whites
Freddy Washington	57%	27%
Lamont Sanford	45	13
J. J. Evans	45	19
Bill Cosby	43	15
Thelma Evans	43	7
George Jefferson	41	8
Dee Thomas	37	17
Louise Jefferson	30	6
Roger Thomas	28	11
James Evans	29	4
Mrs. Thomas	22	5
Florida Evans	21	3
Average	(37%)	(11%)

Even the scarce Black females on television listed above draw strong identification scores (31% vs. 7%) among the Black youth.

Experimental work supports the ratings' data that minority viewers watch more minority programming, when available. Liss (1981) made two 10-minute excerpts from situation comedies (one Black dominant and one White dominant) simultaneously available to third and sixth graders. Blacks watched the Black situation comedy for 7.5 minutes; Whites watched the White sitcom for 8 minutes of the available 10. Brown et al. (1987) reported that Black and White females prefer sitcoms, White males prefer action-adventure shows, and Black males prefer both program types equally.

The first program preference of Black elementary school children is situation comedies, which should be no surprise because that program type contains the majority of Black characters. Hispanics, for whom no program types contain substantial same-race role models, prefer some program types together with Anglos and others with Blacks, particularly children's shows and cartoons, where racial differences may be less important or less threatening (Eastman & Liss, 1980). The favorite program type among Anglo children was action–adventure shows; it constituted 67% of the favorite shows for Anglo boys compared to 27% for Blacks and 3% for Hispanics. This program type subsumes prime-time shows that have the most violence. That is important in relationship to a finding by Zuckerman, Singer, and Singer (1980) that elementary school Whites with more negative stereotypes (less competent and less obedient) of Blacks spent more time watching violent television shows. The White children who spent more time watching shows with

Black characters, and who watched less violence, had more positive images of Blacks. Only these two television viewing variables were significant correlates of racial prejudice; no demographic or family variables were significant in gauging racial prejudice.

Hispanic youngsters (Grades 2–4) were asked for their favorite television program and favorite characters in research concerned with reactions to television violence (Loughlin, Donohue, & Gudykunst, 1982). The children identified more violent than nonviolent shows and more violent than nonviolent characters. For boys, there was a significant relationship between what they themselves would do in these situations and what their favorite character would do.

Study of media content preferences, across several media, for Hispanic and Anglo youngsters in Grades 5 and 10 is reported by Greenberg, Heeter, Burgoon, Burgoon, and Korzenny (1983b). Although low in absolute level of content preference, Hispanic youths showed a consistent preference for Spanish-relevant content on television, in movies, on radio, and even for more news stories about Mexico and Latin America in the newspapers. Media use gratifications from this content also differed among the groups of youngsters. Newspapers were read more for diversion and for social learning purposes by the Hispanic youngsters; social learning and seeking advice were similarly different in the television gratifications. Hispanic youngsters believed more strongly that the portrayals of both Mexican Americans and Blacks on television were more realistic than did Anglo youth, and they were far more likely to believe that local media and network television portrayed Mexican Americans more often doing good things than did the Anglos. Again, there seems to be a desire to see any Hispanic faces or hear any Hispanic voices in the media that are largely void of such appearances and an abundant belief in the fairness and equity of media presentations.

A Chicago study of Blacks, Hispanics, and Anglos (Faber, O'Guinn, & Meyer, 1987) added perceptions as to the equity of portrayals of minorities. Blacks were most likely to say there were too few Blacks on TV, both Blacks and Hispanics were more likely to perceive too few Hispanics, and there was an overall perception among all that Hispanics were most underrepresented. More interesting is the contradiction between amount of viewing and perceptions of the fairness of these portrayals: Heavy-viewing Anglos were more likely to perceive that the representations of Hispanics were fair; heavy-viewing Hispanics expressed the opposite perception, and for Blacks there was no correlation between viewing and perceived fairness of a different minority. Heavy-viewing Blacks, however, were more likely to say there were too few Blacks on television. The authors argued that the cultivation hypothesis works for members of the host society, but that among minority group members, heavy viewing reminds them that television does not do an adequate job for their particular groups.

These findings can be juxtaposed with Matabane's (1988) results from a sample of Black viewers; the heavy viewers (4 or more hours per day) were more likely than light viewers (0-2 hours) to agree that Blacks fit in, that Blacks and Whites are similar, that they socialize, and in overestimating the size of the Black middle class.

Studies among Blacks continue to confirm this reality perception (Greenberg & Atkin, 1982). Black youths consistently believe that the television portrayals of Blacks and non-Blacks are more real-to-life than Whites believe. Typically, 40% of the Blacks would agree that television's presentation of Black men, women, teenagers, dress, and language are realistic, compared to 30% for Whites. An even greater discrepancy exists when the content referents were not Black (e.g., doctors, wives and husbands, parents).

Additionally, Black youngsters approach television more vigorously with the stated motivation to learn something they can apply in their daily lives. An early study (Greenberg, 1972) indicated that White youngsters depended on television as a major source of information about Black youth. Within this survey, several hundred Black preteens and teens claimed that television taught them most of what they know about jobs (47%), how men and women solve problems (42%), how parents and children interact (57%), how husbands and wives interact (45%), and how teenagers act (48%). Corresponding percentages for White respondents averaged 33% (Greenberg & Atkin, 1982). Whites learn more about Blacks from television; Blacks claim to learn about both Whites and themselves.

In turn, the impact on Black self-esteem in general and racial self-esteem in particular of Black programs on Black fourth and fifth graders was assessed by McDermott and Greenberg (1985) conjointly with the impact of peer and parental communication about the positive characteristics of Black people. Parental communication and the regularity of watching Black shows were both related to the Black students' self-esteem; parental and peer communication were related to racial esteem, with exposure falling just short of significance. On the other hand, when respondents were subdivided into those with more and less positive attitudes toward Black television characters, the correlations between exposure and both self- and racial esteem were significantly larger for those with more favorable perceptions. Strong correlations were found between program exposure and attitudes toward both Black adult and child television characters. Thus, Black youngsters use the televised portrayals to reflect upon themselves, or alternatively, Black youngsters holding stronger self-esteem estimates orient to such programming. The previously reported mediating variable test suggests the former as a more persuasive argument.

Stroman (1986) explored program preferences and the relationship between television viewing and self-concept of 100 Black youngsters, ages 7–13. These Black youth overwhelmingly chose situation comedies to watch; the major gender difference here was the preference for action-adventure shows among males that did not exist among females (an 8–1 margin). Stroman demonstrated a weak, but statistically significant *positive* relationship ($r = .17$) between amount of TV viewing and self-concept, contrary to her hypothesis. This relationship was then determined to exist only among Black females ($r = .24$), and was uncorrelated among the males.

More recently, Whittler (1991) showed that Black college students who identify more strongly with the Black culture also identify more strongly with Black actors in advertising; Blacks with low culture identification did not differ in their orientation toward Black and White actors. High prejudice Whites reacted more strongly to source cues; they identified more with White actors than with Black actors in ads for the same product, whereas low-prejudice Whites showed no differences in their identification with Black and White actors, therefore depending less on source cues.

What do White youth who choose to watch Black television programs on a regular basis learn? Is it program content or predispositions that form the basis for selectively exposing themselves to television programs heavily featuring Black characters? From a sample of fourth-, sixth-, and eighth-grade White children, Atkin, Greenberg, and McDermott (1983) explored the consequences of Black program exposure on a variety of belief areas. Frequent exposure to programs starring Blacks was significantly associated with the motivation to watch television to find out how different people talk, dress, behave, and look, with higher estimates of the numbers of Blacks to be seen in various roles in the real world, and with self-reports that television teaches them most of what they know about Blacks. Show exposure was not related to real-life evaluations of Black people in terms of attractiveness, strength, activity, or to discrepancies in these attributes between Blacks and Whites. Exposure was related to perceptions of funniness among Black television characters. Those traits were all related to what the youngsters perceived the characteristics of television Blacks to be and with the strength of their identification with Black characters.

The White youngsters' interpretation of Black television character traits is closely related to parallel beliefs about the real world. Although this correlation may result in part from selective distortion of the televised portrayals, it is likely that the incoming perceptions exert a stronger influence. Thus, for some sets of beliefs, content is important; for others, predispositions clearly have a greater role. In this manner, television serves both to reinforce what is learned outside the television situation and offers the possibility of new information, where little or none was available. Finally, direct contact with Blacks in real life did not diminish or enhance any of these findings. The interface of vicarious and direct interactions with minority group members has yet to be clarified in any reported research.

More recent attempts to link media exposure to beliefs about Blacks and Whites suggests that heavier exposure to television entertainment by White university students is associated with beliefs that Blacks enjoy a relatively higher income, social class, and educational achievement than census data reveal (Armstrong, Neuendorf, & Brentar, 1992). Conversely, heavier exposure to TV news is associated with the belief that Blacks are worse off than Whites.

An experiment by Elliot and Byrd (1983) determined how televised portrayals of handicappers affected participants' attitudes toward this minority. Using 101 eighth-grade students divided into three groups, they exposed one group to an episode of "Mork and Mindy" featuring a blind actor, a second group to a professional informative film that discussed meeting blind people, and a control group to an episode of "Mork and Mindy" without handicapped characters. The first group did not have significantly more positive attitudes toward blind people than the control group, but the second group (informational film) emerged with more positive attitudes. In a replication with 46 college males, Elliot and Byrd (1984) found, again, that the informational film produced significant attitude change.

DISCUSSION

The abundance of content analyses of minority portrayals in media continues, although it has been centered on television content to the deficit of most other media. Recent analyses of newspaper content are absent, and there have been few examinations of music videos, movies, magazines, or even school books. We searched for any contemporary quantitative analyses of sexual orientation, given recent efforts by gay and lesbian groups to acquire more sensitive presentations on television, and found none. Quantitative analyses of film offerings of minorities are notably absent. We have Black stars (e.g., Eddie Murphy) and Black directors (e.g., Spike Lee) but what is their message and what is its impact? More rare are field and experimental studies that attempt to see if all this content—with its diverse themes, characterizations, and problem posing—makes a difference. The reader is reminded of our opening thesis, that content is typically examined as a basis for generating hypotheses about potential social effects. It is all well and good to use content analytic results to raise awareness among media professionals and the public as to what they are being shown and what they are not being shown, but that remains an insufficient end in itself.

Berry (1980) suggested that there were three stages in television's portrayals of Blacks. The first embodied the most basic stereotypes of laziness, stupidity, and incompetence, among others, and he argued that it ended in the mid-1960s. The second, from the mid-1960s through the early 1970s identified a new awareness in the industry and resulted in Blacks being given very positive traits. The third, continuing at least until he wrote his ideas, reflected a period of stabilization when Blacks were presented in a more "realistic" manner in Black-cast shows; these shows, he contended, provided new and more subtle stereotypes indicative of racial inferiority, irresponsible and absent Black males, esteem given to bad, flashy characters, and a general lack of positive attributes in the Black community. Contemporary analyses suggest that this third stage may well still be dominant. Clark (1969), some 15 years earlier, argued that the introduction of minorities into entertainment content progressed through a different set of stages: First, they were absent or largely invisible in the background of shows, stories, movies, and so on; second, they were introduced in comic roles, but typically as the buffoon or object of ridicule, rather than as the creator of humor; third, they would be cast largely as cops or crooks, on both sides of the regulation of society; and eventually, it was to be hoped but not yet realized, that they would be cast in a much broader variety of roles, a variety that matched those of the larger society. Perhaps the portrayal of Blacks is moving into that final stage; certainly the portrayal of Hispanics, Asian-Americans, and others is not.

As for handicappers, Byrd (1989) concluded that little progress has been made in portraying disabilities with increased realism and accuracy; Elliot and Byrd (1982) said the mass media reinforce negative attitudes toward handicappers through misinformation and stereotypes; Donaldson (1981) found that half the portrayals are positive and the other half are extremely negative, focusing on pitiful lifestyles and evil behaviors related to persons with handicapper characteristics.

For whatever reasons, the research on minorities and media is still heavily reliant on content analysis and subsequent speculation rather than on the demonstration of the impacts of that content. The most likely reason is that funding is not yet systematically available for the kinds of research necessary to study impacts.

Surely there have been some gains in the range of content analyses conducted. Rather than finding only head counts, there are studies that explore the role behaviors of the characters on television programs, look specifically at the kinds of interactions that occur between the races within programs (and find too few to be very meaningful), and examine different content areas. Nonetheless, there remains the gulf between what content projects and what viewers perceive, observe, and learn. This gulf reflects the paucity of social effects research on these kinds of issues: (a) What available images of Blacks and other minorities on television are perceived by majority and minority viewers? (b) Do these perceptions translate into behavioral orientations toward minorities? (c) What is the intersection of what is learned from the media about minorities with what is learned from direct contact with minorities?

Elsewhere, we have argued (Greenberg, 1988) that it may be more important to identify critical portrayals of minority characters or programs that are more significant to large numbers of viewers, rather than to focus on the sheer frequency of what is found. This idea of a "drench" effect is based on the notion that not all exposures are equal to each other, that some portrayals may be sufficiently strong, intense, or memorable, that they create lasting impressions that are not undermined by the fleeting presence of insignificant characters on numerous other shows. Are there key portrayals that stand out above the average occurrence obtained from counting a sample week or month of programming? Are 10 exposures to "A Different World" or "The Fresh Prince of Bel-Air" paramount for some and two exposures to "LA Law" critical for others to form or alter attitudes as to possible or appropriate behavioral interactions between Blacks or Hispanics and Whites? Don't we better remember some media experiences than others, and do these not form the basis for our perceptions?

All these studies ignore the multichannel environment now accessed by more than 60% of the homes in this country via cable, subscription television, or satellite, and the two-thirds of the homes that now use a VCR on a regular basis. Network television audiences are being fragmented; estimates of viewing nonnetwork cable channels range from 30% to 50% of total viewing time. The largest portion of this comes at the expense of the commercial networks. Cable systems with 24–36 channels now serve more than half of the cabled population. Black cable channels, Spanish-language cable channels, and other minority channels are available in areas serving large minority communities.

These new media access points may alter the image-making of minorities. The study by Brown and Campbell (1986) demonstrated a paucity of Black lead singers on MTV, but this was done in the early days of MTV, when Black performers and Black groups were largely excluded. Activist groups and critics identified this shortcoming to little avail. Then came the Michael Jackson phenomenon, a single video ("Thriller") became a national phenomenon, and this cable network discovered that Black performers would be generally popular. MTV viewers are not yet saturated with Black performers, but this is another major access point for content from which young viewers may derive impressions about Black singers, at least (whether for good or for bad has yet to be assessed).

Music, whether from radio, home playback system, or MTV, is an integral part of the adolescent youth culture as are videogames, neither of which receives more than limited research attention (Greenberg & Brand, 1992a). The potential impact of this media set alone is staggering. Brown and Schulze (1990), for example, were interested in differential interpretations of music videos by Black and White adolescents and used two Madonna tapes as stimuli for open-ended interviews. For "Papa Don't Preach," nearly all the White females and 85% of the White males indicated the theme was pregnancy. In contrast, nearly half the Black respondents cited the theme of a father–daughter relationship. For "Open Your Heart," nearly half the White viewers identified the primary theme as one of pornography, involving sexual perversion; only one-fifth of the Blacks cited that theme and, in fact, more than half the Black males and 30% of the Black females (compared with 14% and 8% of the Whites) said there was no theme. There was a gross disparity in interpretation of these music videos, suggesting very different orientations toward music, sexuality, and the lyrics that link them between Black and White adolescents.

Clearly, subsequent research on media and minorities on television cannot focus so heavily or solely on either network or local station offerings. They still constitute the primary source of media experiences, but they no longer monopolize. The mix of messages and the increasingly rich mix of media sources caution against some overall summary of minority portrayals as cultivating a given or singular set of beliefs and attitudes.

In both child and adult programming, the races are separated more than they are brought together. Half the programs contain no minorities, and a television diet can easily be constructed with selective nonexposure to programs with minorities in key roles. Hispanics remain rarely visible in any programming from the networks and are seldom found on reruns or on soaps. Although Blacks have achieved a noticeable presence, studies cited indicate that the overall numbers are confounded by concentration on few shows, very little cross-race interaction, and so forth. Thus, bias can be more subtle in programming, as Berry (1980) suggested. When there are no minorities on television (or any medium), one could claim blatant discrimination through omission. Given the presence of Blacks for more than a decade on a regular basis in prime-time programming and their slight incursion on daytime and weekend shows, counting heads becomes less useful either for social research or for social equity. What Blacks do and in what context are clearly more important observational points. There appear to be two extreme uses: concentrating Blacks in a few comedy programs and isolating them in the midst of waves of non-Blacks in both programming and advertising. Neither yield much cross-race interaction as potential models for viewers. Evidence suggests that the Black characters are not rejected by White viewers and that shows are not rejected because of their inclusion. The evidence is very consistent that Black models in advertising are not considered inferior to White models. There may be no overwhelming enthusiasm among Whites, but latent or manifest fears that such models will detract from programming or from commercials seem unwarranted.

In contrast, clear evidence shows that Blacks, young and old, are very likely to watch shows with Blacks and that this viewing is accompanied by a strong sense of identification. Give the minority viewer a show laced with a subset of minority characters, perhaps even one, and that character is a favored model, perhaps somewhat independently of how positive the portrayal is. Thus, programmers have nothing to lose and likely something to gain by casting minority characters, perhaps even in pairs, rather than as singletons or in large groupings.

Where are the other minorities? Is Pat Morita's short-lived "O'Hara" the only Asian casting to be attempted? What inhibits network programming from casting Hispanic actors and actresses more often? Our sense is that there is no particular increase in casting Hispanics in significant roles in weekly television series, during the decade in which they may surpass Blacks in terms of total population. Among Hispanics, there is a distinct generation gap. Parents still orient themselves more to their cultural heritage in Mexico, Cuba, and Puerto Rico; their offspring turn more to their new culture. For parents, experiences with Spanish-language media are more important and certainly would be more satisfying if they are seeking Spanish images. They are prime candidates for subscribing to Spanish-language cable networks. But their youngsters orient to the new media, and their inability to find multiple, contemporary Hispanic images, at least on television, is ironic given the institution's slow response to the expressed needs of Black Americans. One-trial learning apparently is not sufficient in the television industry. When the first version of this chapter was written nearly a decade ago, a new Norman Lear show starring Hispanics, "A.K.A. Pablo," premiered and failed. It continued Lear's attempts to satirize ethnic stereotypes in the hope of fracturing them, as he had tried with "All in the Family." More prejudiced viewers watching that show were reinforced in their negative impressions, interpreting the actions of the bigoted character literally; less prejudiced viewers could be expected to recognize their own prejudices more clearly and to reduce the strength of their own enthnocentrism (Tate & Surlin, 1976; Vidmar & Rokeach, 1974; Wilhoit & de Bock, 1976). While preparing this chapter, we scanned the 1990, 1991, and 1992 Fall preview editions of *TV Guide*, and located many new shows with prominent Black characters, but not a single one featuring Hispanics.

Programs specifically designed to attack stereotypes and to catalyze more favorable affect toward minorities can be successful. Field surveys and controlled experiments with "Sesame Street" (Gorn, Goldberg, & Kanungo, 1976) demonstrated that, and research on "Freestyle" (Williams, LaRose, & Frost, 1981) did so for sex roles. However, few such programs are available. In most programs, race messages occur solely on the basis of the character's presence and behavior, and one must infer or ascribe racial overtones, feelings, and attitudes. "I'll Fly Away" is a recent exception to these normative presentations. Thus, it seems prudent for programmers to be sensitized to what kinds of imprints these portrayals have for both Black and White viewers, especially young people. Youngsters turn to TV to learn about life, to learn about people, and to learn more about themselves. There is ample evidence that most characterizations of minorities stand out for them, because they are infrequent. They recall them, favor them, and react to them affectively and cognitively. There remains some obligation to provide more variety in Black presentations and to move to other minorities with similar attempts at heterogeneity. Can we not bypass some of the early stages suggested by Berry and Clark and move more directly to variety and representativeness in the presentation of Hispanics, for example?

A more exact research agenda could begin to identify some strains not present or insufficiently pursued to date. Absent from the literature is the impact of television programming and other media content on minority perceptions of the majority world. Research interests in minority perceptions of self and majority responses to minority groups have omitted the flip side of one of those coins: What expectations emerge among minorities from media portrayals of Whites? Inasmuch as Whites seldom interact with minorities on television, what do minorities believe are appropriate behaviors when with Whites, and what do they expect from them? What inferences do minorities derive about wealth, power, jobs, sex roles, or even the possibility of changes in interracial relations?

Inasmuch as there are increasingly more Black-dominated shows telecast in a given season, more intensive examination of just what goes on during those shows over multiple episodes may provide some clues as to their potential influence. This suggests an approach to content beyond those lauded elsewhere in this chapter. Given the 1992–1993 season as a base, what themes occur on "ROC"? What value statements are made by major characters on "I'll Fly Away"? How are problems resolved on the "Fresh Prince of Bel-Air"? Do these occur consistently across episodes of "A Different World"? If so, they are prime candidates for learning and modeling among regular viewers.

The issue can be reversed. The selection process of both Blacks and Whites who regularly watch one or more of the shows featuring minorities can be probed. How did they choose to watch this show? What attributes of the show make it worth watching on a regular basis? Is it solely race for Black viewers? Is race an unlikely response from regular, majority viewers? Is it some character or two who pique the viewer's fancy? What are the character attributes that lead to return viewing? Are those attributes common across favorite shows or across favorite characters on different shows? If one wants to build a case for more minority characterizations, that argument is better made from success than failure. So, similar probing into least-favorite minority characters and rejected shows is warranted. What did they have or do that turned off minority and/or majority viewers?

Do Hispanics resent Blacks because Blacks are visible on television and Hispanics are not? Or do young Hispanics prefer Anglo models to Black models in their attempt to acculturate? Is there some doubly vicarious identification with another minority on television? Without same-ethnicity role models, with whom does the young Hispanic choose to identify and, more important, with what attributes and for what reasons? Does identification with Anglo role models diminish cultural identity and would more available Hispanic role models solidify cultural identity?

No study has yet assessed whether behaviors toward role holders change, and whether that change is consistent with either the general thrust of television portrayals or with the specific behaviors of a particular character? Do Blacks alter or shape their behavior toward Whites on the basis of anything they see on television, and vice versa? The studies reviewed examined attitudes, beliefs, and self-assessments, but they did not explore the physical or verbal behaviors of intergroup relations. Given the infrequent interracial interactions found on television, there may be little basis for expecting those responses, but again the frequency may be less important than the intensity of those that do occur on such shows as "Heat of the Night" or "LA Law."

Programmatic research is absent. We must patch together findings from separate studies conducted in disparate circumstances. The research program that begins with current available content, systematically examines that content, moves to multiwave field work, and supplements that with key experimental studies has yet to be created. Until more systematic research is accomplished, we must continue to fit together a puzzle without knowing how many pieces exist and without a cover on the puzzle box that depicts the finished product.

REFERENCES

Armstrong, G. B., Neuendorf, K. A., & Brentar, J. E. (1992). TV entertainment, news, and racial perceptions of college students. *Journal of Communication, 42*(3), 153–176.

Atkin, C., Greenberg, B., & McDermott, S. (1983). Television and race role socialization. *Journalism Quarterly, 60*(3), 407–414.

Atkin, C., & Heald, G. (1977). The content of children's toy and food commercials. *Journal of Communication, 27*(1), 107–114.

Banks, C. M. (1977). A content analysis of the treatment of Black Americans on television. *Social Education, 41*(4), 336–339.

Baptista-Fernandez, P., & Greenberg, B. (1980). The context, characteristics and communication behavior of Blacks on television. In B. Greenberg (Ed.), *Life on television* (pp. 13–21). Norwood, NJ: Ablex.

Baran, S. (1973). Dying Black/dying White: Coverage of six newspapers. *Journalism Quarterly, 50*(4), 761–763.

Barcus, E. F. (1975). *Weekend children's television.* Newtonville, MA: Action for Children's Television.

Barcus, E. F. (1978). *Commercial children's television on weekend and weekday afternoons: A content analysis of children's programming and advertising broadcasting in October 1977.* Newtonville, MA: Action for Children's Television.

Barcus, E. F. (1983). *Images of life on children's television.* New York: Praeger.

Barcus, E. F., & Wolkin, R. (1977). *Children's television: An analysis of programming and advertising.* New York: Praeger.

Berry, G. L. (1980). Television and Afro-Americans: Past legacy and present portrayals. In S. B. Withey & R. P. Ables (Eds.), *Television and social behavior: Beyond violence and children* (pp. 231–248). Hillsdale, NJ: Lawrence Erlbaum Associates.

Block C. (1972). White backlash to Negro ads: Fact or fantasy. *Journalism Quarterly, 49*(2), 253–262.

Brown, J. D., Bauman, K., Lentz, G. M., & Koch, G. (1987). *Young adolescents' use of radio and television in the 1980s.* Paper presented at the annual conference, International Communication Association, Montreal, Canada.

Brown, J. D., & Campbell, D. (1986). Race and gender in music videos: The same beat but a different drummer. *Journal of Communication, 36*(1), 94–106.

Brown, J. D., & Schulze, L. (1990). The effects of race, gender, and fandom on audience interpretations of Madonna's music videos. *Journal of Communication, 40*(2), 88–102.

Brown, J. D., Campbell, K., & Fischer, L. (1986). American adolescents and music videos—Why do they watch? *Gazette, 37* (1/2), 19–32.

Bush, R., Resnick, A., & Stern, B. (1980). A content analysis of the portrayal of Black models in magazine advertising. In R. Bagozzi et al. (Eds.), *Marketing in the 80's: Changes and challenges.* (pp. 484–487). Chicago: American Marketing Association.

Bush, R. F., Solomon, P., & Hair, J., Jr. (1977). There are more Blacks in TV commercials. *Journal of Advertising Research, 17,* 21–25.

Byrd, E. K. (1989). A study of depiction of specific characteristics of characters with disability in film. *Journal of Applied Rehabilitation Counseling, 20*(2), 43–45.

Chaudhary, A. (1980). Press portrayal of Black officials. *Journalism Quarterly, 57*(4), 636–641.

Clark, C. (1969). Television and social controls: Some observations on the portrayal of ethnic minorities. *Television Quarterly, 8,* 19.

Colfax, D., & Steinberg, S. (1972). The perpetuation of racial stereotypes: Blacks in mass circulation magazine advertisements. *Public Opinion Quarterly, 35,* 8–18.

Comstock, G., & Cobbey, R. R. (1979). Television and the children of ethnic minorities. *Journal of Communication, 29*(1), 104–115.

Cox, K. (1969–1970). Changes in stereotyping of Negroes and Whites in magazine advertisements. *Public Opinion Quarterly, 33,* 603–606.

Culley, J. D., & Bennett, R. (1976). Selling women, selling Blacks. *Journal of Communication, 26*(4), 160–174.

Dates, J. (1980). Race, racial attitudes and adolescent perceptions of Black television characters. *Journal of Broadcasting, 24*(4), 549–560.

Dohrmann, R. (1975). A gender profile of children's educational TV. *Journal of Communication, 25*(4), 56–65.

Dominick, J. (1973). Crime and law enforcement on prime-time television. *Public Opinion Quarterly, 37*(2), 241–250.

Dominick, J., & Greenberg, B. (1970). Three seasons of Blacks on television. *Journal of Advertising Research, 10*(2), 21–27.

Donagher, P. C., Poulos, R. W., Liebert R. M., & Davidson, E. S. (1975). Race, sex, and social example: An analysis of character portrayals on interracial television entertainment. *Psychological Reports, 37,* 1023–1034.

Donaldson, J. (1981). The visibility and image of handicapped people on television. *Exceptional Children, 47*(6), 413–416.

Downing, M. H. (1974). Heroine of the daytime serial. *Journal of Communication, 24*(2), 130–137.

Eastman, H., & Liss, M. (1980). Ethnicity and children's preferences. *Journalism Quarterly, 57*(2), 277–280.

Elliot, T. R., & Byrd, E. K. (1982). Media and disability. *Rehabilitation Literature, 43* (11–12), 348–355.

Elliot, T. R., & Byrd, E. K. (1983). Attitude change toward disability through television portrayal. *Journal of Applied Rehabilitation Counseling, 14*(2), 35–37.

Elliot, T. R., & Byrd, E. K. (1984). Attitude change toward disability through television: Portrayal with male college students. *International Journal of Rehabilitation Research, 7*(3), 320–322.

Entman, R. M. (1992). Blacks in the news: Television, modern racism and cultural change. *Journalism Quarterly, 69*(2), 341–361.

Faber, R. J., O'Guinn, T. C., & Meyer, T. C. (1987). Televised portrayals of Hispanics. *International Journal of Intercultural Relations, 11,* 155–169.

Gardner, J., & Radel, M. S. (1978). Portrait of the disabled in the media. *Journal of Community Psychology, 6,* 269–274.

Gerbner, G. (1970). Cultural indicators: The case of violence in television drama. *The Annals of the American Academy of Political and Social Science, 388,* 69–81.

Gerbner, G. (1993, June). *Women and minorities on television* (a report to the Screen Actors Guild and the American Federation of Radio and Television Artists). Philadelphia: Annenberg School, University of Pennsylvania.

Gerbner, G., Gross, L., Jackson-Beeck, M., Jeffries-Fox, S., & Signorielli, N. (1978).

Cultural indicators: Violence profile no. 9. *Journal of Communication, 28*(3), 176–207.

Gerbner, G., Gross, L., Morgan, M., & Signorielli, N. (1981). *Aging with television commercials: Images on television commercials and dramatic programming, 1977–1979.* Philadelphia: Annenberg School of Communication, University of Pennsylvania.

Gerbner, G., Gross, L., & Signorielli, N. (1985). *The role of television entertainment in public education about science.* Philadelphia: Annenberg School of Communication, University of Pennsylvania.

Gerbner, G., & Signorielli, N. (1979). *Women and minorities in television drama 1969–1978.* Philadelphia: Annenberg School of Communication, University of Pennsylvania.

Gerson, M. (1980). Minority representation in network television drama, 1970–1976. *Mass Communication Review, 7*(3), 10–12.

Glauberman, N. R. (1980). The influence of positive TV portrayals on children's behavior and attitude toward the physically disabled. *Dissertation Abstracts International, 41*(04), 1386A–1387A.

Gorn, G., Goldberg, M., & Kanungo, R. (1976). The role of educational television in changing the intergroup attitudes of children. *Child Development, 47,* 277–280.

Greenberg, B. S. (1972). Children's reactions to TV Blacks. *Journalism Quarterly, 49*(1), 5–14.

Greenberg, B. S. (1986). Minorities and the mass media. In J. Bryant & D. Zillmann (Eds.), *Perspectives on media effects* (pp. 165–188). Hillsdale, NJ: Lawrence Erlbaum Associates.

Greenberg, B. S. (1988). Some uncommon television images and the drench hypothesis. In S. Oskamp (Ed.), *Applied social psychology annual (Vol. 8): Television as a social issue.* Newbury Park, CA: Sage.

Greenberg, B. S., & Atkin, C. (1978). *Learning about minorities from television.: A research agenda.* Paper presented at a conference on Television and the Minority Child, Center for Afro-American Studies, University of California at Los Angeles.

Greenberg, B. S., & Atkin, C. (1982). Learning about minorities from television: A research agenda. In G. Berry & C. Mitchell-Kernan (Eds.), *Television and the socialization of the minority child* (pp. 215–243). New York: Academic Press.

Greenberg, B. S., & Brand, J. E. (1992a, April). *Minority adolescents and the mass media.* Paper presented at "Are the Kids Alright? Early Adolescence and the Media" Conference organized by the Program for Policy, Research, and Intervention for Development in Early Adolescence (PRIDE), Penn State University.

Greenberg, B. S., & Brand, J. E. (1992b, April). *U.S. minorities and the news.* Paper presented at "Television News Coverage of Minorities: Models and Options for the Commission on Television Policy" Conference organized by the Communications and Society Program of the Aspen Institute and the Carter Center at Emory University at the Wye River House Conference Center, Maryland.

Greenberg, B. S., & Brand J. E. (1993). Cultural diversity on Saturday morning television. In G. Berry & J.K. Asamen (Eds.), *Children and television in a changing socio-cultural world* (pp. 132–142). Newbury Park, CA: Sage.

Greenberg, B. S., & Heeter, C. (1987). VCRs and young people: The picture at 39% penetration. *American Behavioral Scientist, 30*(5), 509–521.

Greenberg, B. S., & Heeter, C., Burgoon, J., Burgoon, M., & Korzenny, F. (1983a). Local newspaper coverage of Mexican Americans. *Journalism Quarterly, 60*(4), 671–676.

Greenberg, B. S., Heeter, C., Burgoon, M., Burgoon, J., & Korzenny, F. (1983b). Mass media use, preferences and attitudes among young people. In B. Greenberg, M. Burgoon, J. Burgoon, & F. Korzenny (Eds.), *Mexican Americans and the mass media* (pp. 147–201). Norwood, NJ: Ablex.

Greenberg, B. S., & Linsangan, R. (1993). Gender differences in adolescents' media use, exposure to sexual content, parental mediation and self-perceptions. In B. S. Greenberg, J. Brown, & N. Boerkel-Rothfoss (Eds.), *Media, sex and the adolescent* (pp. 134–144). Cresskill, NJ: Hamilton Press.

Greenberg, B. S., & Neuendorf, K. (1980). Black family interactions on television. In B. S. Greenberg (Ed.), *Life on television* (pp. 173–182). Norwood, NJ: Ablex.

Greenberg, B. S., Neuendorf, K., Buerkel-Rothfuss, N., & Henderson, L. (1982). The soaps: What's on and who cares? *Journal of Broadcasting, 26*(2), 519–535.

Harvey, S. E., Sprafkin, J. N., & Rubinstein, E. (1979). Prime- time TV: A profile of aggressive and prosocial behaviors. *Journal of Broadcasting, 23*(2), 179–189.

Heeter, C., Greenberg, B., Mendelson, B., Burgoon, J., Burgoon, M., & Korzenny, F. (1983). Cross media coverage of local Hispanic American news. *Journal of Broadcasting, 27*(4), 395–402.

Jackson, L. A., & Ervin, K. S. (1991). The frequency and portrayal of Black families in fashion advertisements. *Journal of Black Psychology, 18*(1), 67–70.

Kaner, G. (1982). *Adolescent reactions to race and sex of professional television newscasters.* Unpublished doctoral dissertation, New York University, New York.

Kassarjian, H. (1969). The Negro and American advertising: 1946–1965. *Journal of Marketing Research, 6,* 29–39.

Kaufman, L. (1980). Prime time nutrition. *Journal of Communication, 30*(3), 37–46.

Kearl, M. C. (1986–87). Death as a measure of life: A research note on the Kastenbaum-Spilka strategy of obituary analyses. *Omega: Journal of Death & Dying, 17*(1), 65–78.

Keller, C. E., Hallahan, D. P., McShane, E. A., Crowley, E. P., & Blandford, B. J. (1990). The coverage of persons with disabilities in American newspapers. *Journal of Special Education, 24*(3), 271–282.

Kerin, R. (1979). Black model appearance and product evaluations. *Journal of Communication, 29*(1), 123–128.

Klobas, L. E. (1988). *Disability drama in television and film.* Jefferson, NC: McFarland.

Korzenny, F., Griffis, B. A., Greenberg, B., Burgoon, J., & Burgoon, M. (1983). How community leaders, newspaper executives and reporters perceive Mexican Americans and the mass media. In B. Greenberg, M. Burgoon, J. Burgoon, & F. Korzenny (Eds.), *Mexican Americans and the mass media* (pp. 55–75). Norwood, NJ: Ablex.

Lemon, J. (1977). Women and Blacks on prime-time television. *Journal of Communication, 27*(4), 70–79.

Lichter, L. S., & Lichter, S. R. (1983). Criminals and law enforcers in TV entertainment. In *Prime time crime.* Washington, DC: The Media Institute.

Liss, M. (1981). Children's television selections: A study of indicators of same-race preference. *Journal of Cross Cultural Psychology, 12*(1), 103–110.

Loughlin, M., Donohue, T., & Gudykunst, W. (1982). Puerto Rican children's perceptions of favorite television characters as behavioral models. *Journal of Broadcasting, 24*(2), 159–171.

Martindale, C. (1984, August). *Being Black in America : The press portrayal.* Paper presented at the 67th annual meeting of the Association for Education in Journalism and Mass Communication, Gainesville, FL.

Martindale, C. (1985). Coverage of Black Americans in five newspapers since 1950. *Journalism Quarterly, 62*(2), 321–328, 436.

Martindale, C. (1987, August). *Changes in newspaper images of Black Americans.* Paper presented at the 70th annual meeting of the Association for Education in Journalism and Mass Communication, San Antonio, TX.

Matabane, P. W. (1988). Television and the Black audience: Cultivating moderate perspectives on racial integration. *Journal of Communication, 38*(4), 21–30.

Mathews, W. T. (1987). *The relationship of news media agenda setting and the production of U.S. produced motion pictures featuring black actors.* Unpublished doctoral dissertation, Michigan State University, East Lansing.

McDermott, S., & Greenberg, B. (1984). Parents, peers and television as determinants of Black children's esteem. In R. Bostrom (Ed.), *Communication yearbook 8* (pp. 164–177). Beverly Hills, CA: Sage.

McNally, D. P. G. (1983). *Blacks and television: A comparison of the portrayal of Black and White characters on television.* Unpublished doctoral dissertation, University of Maryland, College Park.

Mendelson, G., & Young, M. (1972). *A content analysis of Black and minority treatment on children's television.* Boston, MA: Action for Children's Television.

Nielsen Media Research (1988). *Television viewing among Blacks* (4th annual report). Neilsen Research, Inc.

Poindexter, P. M., & Stroman, C. (1981). Blacks and television: A review of the research literature. *Journal of Broadcasting, 25*(2), 103–122.

Pollay, R. W., Lee, J. S., & Carter-Whitney, D. (1992). Separate but not equal: Racial segmentation in cigarette advertising. *Journal of Advertising, 21*(1), 45–57.

Poulos, R. W., Harvey, S. E., & Liebert, R. M. (1976). Saturday morning television: A profile of the 1974–75 children's season. *Psychological Reports, 39*, 1047–1057.

Rainville, R. E., & McCormick, E. (1977). Extent of covert racial prejudice in pro football announcers' speech. *Journalism Quarterly, 54*(1), 20–26.

Reid, L., & Vanden Bergh, B. (1980). Blacks in introductory ads. *Journalism Quarterly, 57*(3), 485–489.

Reid, P. T. (1979). Racial stereotyping on television: A comparison of the behavior of both Black and White television characters. *Journal of Applied Psychology, 64*(5), 465–489.

Roberts, C. (1971). The portrayal of Blacks on network television. *Journal of Broadcasting, 15*(1), 45–53.

Roberts, C. (1975). The presentation of Blacks in television network newscasts. *Journalism Quarterly, 52*(1), 50–55.

Schlinger, M. J., & Plummer, J. (1972). Advertising in Black and White. *Journal of Marketing Research, 9*, 149–153.

Seggar, J. F., Hafen, J., & Hannonen-Gladden, H. (1981). Television's portrayals of minorites and women in drama and comedy drama, 1971–80. *Journal of Broadcasting, 25*(3), 277–288.

Shu, J. I. (1979). *The portrayal of Chinese on network television as observed by Chinese and White raters.* Unpublished doctoral dissertation, State University of New York at Stony Brook, New York.

Signorielli, N. (1982). Marital status in television drama: A case of reduced options. *Journal of Broadcasting, 26*(2), 585–597.

Signorielli, N. (1983). The demography of the television world. In G. Melischek, K. E. Rosengren, & J. Stappers (Eds.), *Cultural indicators: An international symposium* (pp. 53–73). Vienna, Austria: The Austrian Academy of Sciences.

Signorielli, N. (1985). *Role portrayal and stereotyping on television: An annotated bibliography of studies relating to women, minorities, aging, sexual behavior, health, and handicaps.* Westport, CT: Greenwood Press.

Soley, L. (1983). The effect of Black models on magazine and readership. *Journalism Quarterly, 60*(4), 686–690.

Stempel, G. (1971). Visibility of Blacks in news and news-picture magazines. *Journalism Quarterly, 48*(2), 337–339.

Stroman, C. A. (1986). Television viewing and self-concept among black children. *Journal of Broadcasting and Electronic Media, 30*(1), 87–93.

Sweeper, G. W. (1983). *The image of the Black family and the White family in American prime time television programming 1970 to 1980.* Unpublished doctoral dissertation, New York University, New York.

Tate, E., & Surlin, S. (1976). Agreement with opinionated TV characters across culture. *Journalism Quarterly, 53*(2), 199–203.

Turk, J. V., Richard, J., Bryson, R. L., Jr., & Johnson, S. M. (1989). Hispanic American in the news in two southwestern cities. *Journalism Quarterly, 66*(1), 107–113.

United States Commission on Civil Rights. (1977). *Window dressing on the set: Women and minorities in television.* Washington, DC: U.S. Government Printing Office.

United States Commission on Civil Rights. (1979). *Window dressing on the set: An update.* Washington, DC: U.S. Government Printing Office.

Vidmar, N., & Rokeach, M. (1974). Archie Bunker's bigotry: A study in selective perception and exposure. *Journal of Communication, 24*(1), 35–47.

Weigel, R., & Howes, P. (1982). Race relations on children's television. *The Journal of Psychology, 111,* 109–112.

Weigel, R. H., Loomis, J., & Soja, M. (1980). Race relations on prime time television. *Journal of Personality and Social Psychology, 39*(5), 884–893.

Whittler, T. (1991). The effects of actors' race in commercial advertising: Review and extension. *Journal of Advertising, 20*(1), 54–60.

Wilhoit, G. C., & de Bock, H. (1976). "All in the Family" in Holland. *Journal of Communication, 26*(1) 75–84.

Williams, F., LaRose, R., & Frost, F. (1981). *Children, television and sex-role stereotyping.* New York: Praeger.

Woll, A. L., & Miller, R. M. (1987). *Ethnic and racial images in American film and television.* New York: Garland.

Womack, D. L. (1986). ABC, CBS, and NBC live interview coverage during the Democratic National Conventions of 1972, 1976, and 1984: A content analysis. *Dissertation Abstracts International, 47* (6-A), 2786.

Womack, D. L. (1988, July). *Black participation in live network television interviews at the 1984 Democratic Convention.* Paper presented at the 71st annual meeting of the Association for Education in Journalism and Mass Communication, Portland, OR.

Zuckerman, D., Singer, D., & Singer, J. (1980). Children's television viewing, racial and sex role attitudes. *Journal of Applied Social Psychology, 10*(4), 281–294.

11

Media Effects on Advertising

DAVID W. STEWART
University of Southern California

SCOTT WARD
University of Pennsylvania

In this chapter, we examine research and theory pertaining to the issue of how the characteristics of media affect individual responses to advertising, and the processes by which those effects occur. More specifically, we examine the unique and interactive effects of particular media types and vehicles on how advertising affects individuals. We also suggest that the continuing rapid evolution of media presents new opportunities for research, but such research may require a change of focus from analysis of the stimulus, media characteristics, to analysis of the ways in which individuals interact with and act upon media. This latter focus would also lead to an examination of the purposes and functions served by various media for individuals. Even with this relatively focused mission for this chapter, further explanation and delineation is in order.

The effect of media context on advertising response is a topic that has received considerable attention. A number of review papers have been previously published. Given the complexity of the topic, it is not surprising that a variety of disciplines have contributed to theory and research. Schramm (1965) and Klapper (1965) offered reviews of research from the perspective of communications research. Corlett and Richardson (1969); Corlett (1971); Corlett, Lannon, and Richardson (1971); Richardson (1972); Nolan (1972); and Clemens (1972) offered practical perspectives from the advertiser's viewpoint. Gensch (1970) provided a treatment of media factors for purposes of building quantitative media scheduling models. Guggenheim (1984) reviewed media effects from the standpoint of media scheduling but drew heavily on empirical and theoretical work. Schumann and Thorson (1990) provided a model of how television programs affect consumer responses to advertising. Each of these reviews provides a useful and somewhat unique summary of a portion of the large literature on media effects on advertising response.

Our objective is to offer a rather different perspective based on previous research. We draw from various disciplines and viewpoints, including traditional academic disciplines (psychology and communications research), applied academic fields (marketing and consumer research), and useful perspectives and findings offered by advertising and marketing practitioners. Nonetheless, our focus is more on the effects of media on individual processes, rather than on groups or cultures, and more on data from empirical studies or perspectives from theoretical work, rather than on essays or commentaries. Our goal is to summarize what is known about how media influence responses of individual viewers, listeners, or readers, to advertising messages and to suggest important directions for future research.

We begin with a preliminary discussion of managerial perceptions of media influences that affect advertising decisions, and the changing nature of "mass media" caused by technological advances in recent years. We then structure our review of research in terms of individual characteristics that influence uses of media and advertising embedded in media, and in terms of structural factors that shape responses, such as timing, repetition, and frequency of advertising exposure. We conclude with a discussion of the implications of the changing media environment for assessing advertising effects and suggest that future research should focus on individual uses of media, rather than on media characteristics, in order to gain a more complete understanding of how advertising in different media affects individuals.

DIRECTION OF MEDIA EFFECTS

Our concern is with media effects on individuals exposed to advertising, rather than with the effects of specific media characteristics on advertising decisions. That is, it is not unusual for the characteristics of particular media to influence managerial advertising decisions: whether to advertise or not, how much to spend on it, what particular media types and/or vehicles to use. Nonetheless, it is necessary that we address some issues related to the way in which perceptions of media effects influence advertising media decisions, if only to distinguish these issues from our primary mission.

Advertising Clutter and Media Fragmentation

Some advertising media decisions are based on a manager's desire to achieve some relative isolation of advertising exposure. Stated somewhat differently, a goal of advertisers is often exposure to advertising in a context that is free of distractions. Among advertising managers and media buyers, there is increasing concern with "advertising clutter" and with "media fragmentation." These notions are rooted in the belief that advertising messages and advertising campaigns do not have the same impact as in earlier times, due to increases in the volume of advertising, the nature of advertising (viz., the trend toward strings of 10-second commercials on television), and the increased diversity of advertising media (viz., increasing household penetration of cable television). Consequently, some advertisers seek alternatives to traditional mass media advertising vehicles, whereas others have been persuaded that increases in mass media advertising budgets are necessary to achieve advertising objectives in the cluttered media environment.

"New" Media

Media influences on advertising decisions are also influenced by the existence of new media, such as television shopping networks, computer information services such as Prodigy and CompuServe, and event sponsorship. Other media vehicles also influence subjective and objective decisions of advertisers, such as the Super Bowl's vast quantitative reach, plus the subjective effects that advertisers may believe accrue to them by being a Super Bowl sponsor. In spite of the concerns of advertisers with advertising clutter and media fragmentation, most research in the area of advertising media effects has traditionally focused on traditional mass media: television, radio, and print. It is an empirical question as to whether or not results of past research apply to new media forms, and, in any case, the changing and more complex media environment requires that findings from earlier research be assessed in light of this new environment.

Advertising Medium Defined

At the most general level, a *medium* refers to any transmission vehicle or device through which communication may occur. In the context of advertising communication, the term has traditionally been applied to mass communication media, to distinguish advertising from personal selling, which occurs through the medium of interpersonal communication, and from sales promotion activities, which can occur through various media forms. Additionally, advertising media have traditionally been characterized as "measured" media, referring to the availability of quantitative information to assess the number of viewers or readers potentially exposed to advertising messages.

Both the practice of marketing management—the organizational domain in which advertising decisions are generally made—and the technological environment have made traditional conceptions of advertising media open to discussion. Organizations are increasingly aware that there are significantly more opportunities for controlled communications with consumers and other corporate stakeholders than simply advertising communication, and that many communication decisions must be coordinated and rationalized in terms of the organization's objectives. For example, the choice of retail outlets represents a kind of "advertising medium" decision. Whether a good is sold through Tiffany's or through discount merchandisers is an issue that is conceptually similar to whether an advertisement has the same impact in *The New Yorker* as it does in *Tennis* magazine. The sales person is an advertising medium in the same sense as an ad in a weekly newsmagazine, although the nature of the medium is quite different.

In addition to these trends toward expanded views of organizational communications media, trends and developments have extended the traditional definition of advertising media beyond the mass media. For example, cable television, computer information services, technologies such as the FAX machine and automatic dialers for telemarketing enable advertisers to reach much more concentrated and focused audiences than with traditional mass media. Additionally, new ways of communicating with consumers may supplant or complement traditional media advertising. For example, sponsorship of events such as marathons, golf tournaments, and the like, is increasing as advertisers seek to avoid the cluttered media environment and find more effective and efficient means for communicating with customers.

The communication objectives associated with using these newer media are similar to those for traditional mass media, however. For example, sponsorship of an event may influence attitude formation and change because an advertiser is associated with a particular event. At the very least, advertisers hope for very high levels of brand name exposure, as event audiences, as well as audiences that may witness the event on television, are repeatedly exposed to the sponsor's brand name via messages during the event, billboards at the event, or attachment of the brand name to the object of the event (such as a cigarette company's name painted on a race car).

This expanded view of "advertising media" reflects the complexity and diversity of the contemporary media environment and makes the media decisions of advertisers daunting, indeed. One Philadelphia news distributor reported that he distributed about 200 non-newspaper titles each month in the 1950s, but he distributes over, 2,500 titles each month today. To a large extent, the decline of "mass" magazines such as *Life* and *Saturday Evening Post* are the result of two trends: the increasing desires of organizations to segment markets, and technological advances making such specialized publications more financially feasible than was the case 20 or 30 years ago.

Audience Segmentation

The segmentation mentality among organizations has culminated in an apparent oxymoron: highly personalized mass media. Direct mail advertising is a case in point. Direct mail has been joined by a wide array of other such media, however. The advent of selective binding among publishers has provided considerable opportunity to customize a variety of publications ranging from magazines to catalogs. In turn, these highly "targeted" media vehicles are made possible by advances in market research technology, such as the ability to purchase lists of households in five-digit and even nine-digit postal (ZIP) code areas, in order to reach households with highly defined demographic characteristics.

Of necessity, the focus of this chapter is on the effects of relatively traditional mass media advertising types and vehicles, reflecting existing research and theory in the area of media effects. Suffice it to say at this point that the expanded advertising media environment invites researchers to examine the effectiveness of advertising in the "new" media. We will suggest that much of what is known about the influence of more traditional media on advertising response is generalizable to the "new media" under appropriate circumstances, although the new media may alter traditional uses of mass media, and we need to understand how individuals will integrate their uses of mass media in the changing environment. We pursue this point at the conclusion of the chapter. First, we consider the extant body of empirical and theoretical literature on more traditional media.

NATURE OF ADVERTISING MEDIA EFFECTS

It is probably safe to say that the early advertisers were less concerned with media choices and effects than they were with simply initiating communication. Not only were mass media choices limited until the advent of commercial radio in the 1920s, but early advertisers probably also assumed that advertising was very powerful: What is said "gets through" and achieves the intended persuasive objectives. Mass communications historians tell us that the earliest models of communication effects posited that communications were very powerful: the early "bullet" or "hypodermic needle" models of mass communication (Katz & Lazarsfeld, 1955, p. 16) that gave rise to the earliest conception of communication effects: Who says What to Whom through What Medium with What Effects.

Very quickly, advertisers learned that advertising effects are not so powerful. Virtually all advertising textbooks recall John Wanamaker's lament, after witnessing the failure of advertising to stimulate sales in his department store chain: "I know that half of my advertising budget is wasted; the trouble is, I don't know which half." The problem, of course, is that the effects of advertising are due to a myriad of factors, some pertaining to the advertising itself (and, therefore, under the control of the advertiser), and some to relatively uncontrollable factors, such as consumer characteristics, competitive advertising, and so forth. Further complicating the problem is the fact that advertising effects are inherently interactive. That is, it is exceedingly difficult to separate the effects of media from message variables effects, both in the day-to-day practice of advertising management and in empirical research on media effects. Advertising and consumer factors are also inherently interactive: It is difficult to partial out the unique effects of advertising messages from the prior attitudes and experiences of consumers who see or hear the advertisements.

With the advent of commercial television and printing technologies to make segment-specific magazines possible, advertisers came to believe that individual media have unique capabilities and effects. Advertising managers evolved rules of thumb to account for these effects; for example, print media are better to explain complex products, television is better because it can show product demonstrations, and so on. There was an evolving idea that there are "qualitative" media factors, but generally these were—and are today—relegated to the subjective judgment of media influences on advertising effects.

Managerial Approaches to Understanding Media Effects: Media Planning Models

Advertisers' early rules of thumb about media effects evolved into attempts to explicitly model these effects. This evolution may have been stimulated at least as much by the availability of large data bases on media habits of individuals, and by computer technology, as by communication or psychological theory. In any case, there exist today many databases and computer-based models that managers use to plan advertising campaigns. These models are a blend of technological capabilities and algorithms generated by theory, experience, and rules of thumb. These models are often operationalized rather differently, but there are some common characteristics. Most attempt to account for the fact that various media have overlapping audiences. Most such models include an explicit advertising response function designed to capture the relationship between advertising exposure and some measure of audience response. Finally, most models provide a means for incorporating data or subjective judgments of the "quality" of given media as a vehicle for delivering the advertiser's particular message.

Media Overlap. Generally, media models contain information concerning readership, viewership, and listenership among households, and data about household purchasing behavior. It is possible to profile households that subscribe to *Time* and *Good Housekeeping* magazines, watch "60 Minutes" and "The Wonder Years," listen to certain radio programs, and buy particular quantities and brands of specific products. Armed with such information, an advertising planner can quickly identify the characteristics of heavy users of a brand or product category and determine the media habits of such buyers. The media planner can also calculate "internal" and "external" overlap: households that subscribe to a particular magazine, and/or repeatedly watch a television program, and so can be reached multiple times with an advertisement in the same medium (internal overlap). Similarly, because data are available that indicate the variety of media used by households, it is possible to buy advertising space in multiple publications and time on multiple television programs in order to achieve "external overlap."

Advertising Response Function. At the heart of most media planning models is an *advertising response function*. This is the hypothesized relationship between the cumulative number of exposures of an individual (or aggregate of individuals) to an advertisement for a product (within the same medium or across different media), and some dependent variable, such as purchase probability, product knowledge, and so on. The specific form of this response function has been the subject of considerable debate. In general, however, one of two functions is thought to apply (Stewart, 1989). In one of these the advertising response function is a gentle S-curve (see line Z in Fig. 11.1) indicating that advertising generally requires a few exposures to have any impact at all (hence a threshold for any effect at all), a few more exposures to

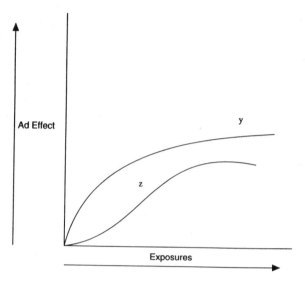

FIG. 11.1. Advertising response functions.

reach its maximum impact, and then a declining marginal impact. The second candidate advertising response function is a simple ogive, which is represented by line Y in Fig. 11.1. This response function also consists of a rapidly rising level of effectiveness with each additional exposure, followed by diminishing marginal impact of each subsequent exposure. This response function differs from the first in that no threshold effect is assumed. Rather, response to advertising is assumed to begin with the very first exposure. The two response functions have much in common, but differ with respect to the presence of a threshold effect.

Both functions have been documented extensively in the literature, which suggests that the specific form of the function may be contingent on other factors. Consistent with this contingency perspective is the suggestion by Burke and Srull (1988) that the threshold portion of the model is observed under conditions of competitive advertising. Their reasoning is consistent with a long tradition of research on interference effects in the learning literature. Simply put, Burke and Srull argued that the threshold effect represents the minimal advertising for a product to overcome the interference created by the advertising for competitive products. Thus, the threshold is likely to be most prominent in heavily advertised product categories and may disappear altogether when competitive advertising is relatively modest. This suggests that at least one dimension of the broader media context, the density of competing messages, may influence the very shape of the advertising response function.

Some have also hypothesized that very long exposure cycles for the same advertisement will result in consumer resentment and irritation, which results in an actual decline in effectiveness (Calder & Sternthal, 1980; Petty & Cacioppo, 1986). This latter effect is generally referred to as *advertising wearout*. Pechmann and Stewart (1988) reviewed the extensive literature on this effect and concluded that it was most likely to occur under conditions of mass repetition, such as those most typically employed in laboratory studies of advertising repetition. Although they do not dismiss the possibility that such a wearout effect might occur in more natural viewing contexts, these authors do suggest that such an effect is less likely in such contexts.

Of course, the advertising response function may also vary as a function of the complexity of the product being advertised, the relative experience or intelligence levels of the target audience, and other factors. In any case, media planners use computer models to specify the intended response function, and the models will "buy" advertising time and space in proper frequencies to approximate the specified response function.

Media Impact. Finally, most media planning models include a capability for the media planner to specify "impact" factors. These are subjective weights that the planner can assign to certain factors, such as media types and vehicles, and types of consumers, that will influence the model to buy particular media types and/or vehicles, and to reach specified audience segments (such as women between 35 and 54, with three or more children at home). The important point is that media vehicle weights represent subjective judgments that some media types (broadcast vs. print) and/or vehicles (*New Yorker* vs. *People*) have more impact or are more effective than others for a given purpose.

There is a general consensus among advertisers and media planners that media do differentially impact the effectiveness of communications embedded within them. Research in a number of different disciplines has provided a rather large catalog of dimensions along which media may differ. For an Advertising Research Foundation (ARF) conference on intermedia comparisons, Chestnut (1983) reviewed some of this literature and concluded that although the literature on intermedia comparisons is small, it is respectable and useful. In fact, he found 111 references to intermedia comparisons in the 1978 ARF bibliography, *Evaluating Advertising*. Among the dimensions of media that have been identified and at least occasionally studied are those in Table 11.1.

General recognition that there exist qualitative differences among media that may influence response to advertising has not brought with it substantial skill in identifying and accommodating these differences,

TABLE 11.1
An Inventory of Media Factors

Active vs. passive	Prestige
Involvement	Arousal propensity
Imbeddedness	Duration of effect
Obtrusiveness/intrusiveness	Hot vs. cold
Informativeness	identification
Mood	Expertise
Reality vs. fantasy orientation	Intimacy
Immediacy	Degree of interaction
Permanence	Entertainment value
Credibility	Utility
Complexity	gratification
Vividness	Social context
Objectivity	participation
Control	Relation to self

Source. Stewart (1992, p. 9).

however. Not only is there some debate as to how to characterize different media across various dimensions, rather little is actually known about how people interact with different media. In the advertising profession media effects, including differences associated with the way in which people interact with specific media, have been collectively referred to as media quality, impact, or mood. Media planners have tried to capture these effects through the use of subjective judgments. Unfortunately, subjective media judgments are not reliable, even in simple cases.

For example, Russ Haley (1985) reported a study on the agreement of 60 experienced media professionals from 10 agencies on the weights to assign the media impact of television vehicles. Even with a thorough briefing on the objectives of the advertising and a single standardized rating form, differences in weighting varied by 250%. In fact, there was not even good agreement within agencies. Among media professionals from the same agency, impact weights differed by 200%. Note that in this particular study the question revolved around the impact of vehicles within one particular medium, television. It is likely that enlarging the problem to include other media would produce even larger variances.

This discussion of computer-based models actually used by media planners provides an overview of how advertisers estimate the nature of media effects, and the knowledge advertisers use in accounting for variance in media effects. As we have seen, there is little empirical guidance to indicate with much precision the unique effects of media types and vehicles. Again, this is due to the inherently interactive nature of media vehicle effects—the difficulty of isolating their unique effects from the total "gestalt" of message characteristics, repetition effects, and the like, on consumer responses.

The models do require subjective judgments about *receivers* of advertising messages in different media. For example, media vehicle weights demand that the media planner weight characteristics of individuals who attend to particular media vehicles. However, these characteristics are normally only understood in terms of demographic characteristics or, in some cases, "psychographic" characteristics that attempt to characterize individuals in terms of attitudes, opinions, beliefs, and lifestyle habits. In contrast, academic research has focused on individual characteristics that may be correlated with demographics, but are oriented more toward processes by which individuals interact with communication media. We turn now to these research streams.

THEORETICAL AND EMPIRICAL APPROACHES TO UNDERSTANDING MEDIA EFFECTS

The guiding hypothesis of this chapter reflects the experience and judgments of advertisers that media do vary and contribute uniquely to advertising effects. Stated more broadly, Marshall McLuhan is well known for his "Medium is the Message" statement, which implies that a medium communicates an image or generates effects independent of any single message it contains (McLuhan & Fiore, 1967). Our framework for assessing media effects is provided in Fig. 11.2. It posits that consumer characteristics influence the effectiveness of advertising in particular media, and it shows four key linkages between consumers and the medium:

1. Attitudes toward the medium;
2. Uses of the medium;
3. Involvement while using the medium; and
4. Mood states affecting media usage.

Further, the framework posits that media scheduling decisions condition media effects through differences in the repetition of the same message in all media and differences in the frequency of exposure to advertisements in any one medium.

The Role of Selective Exposure.   Research is rather clear on the point that characteristics of consumers directly influence media effects. For example, in their review of consumer processing of advertising, Thorson

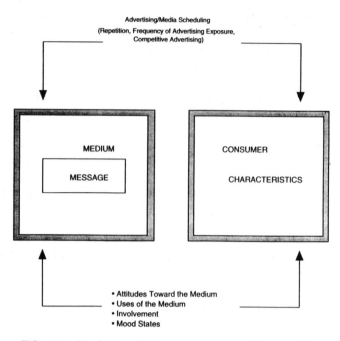

FIG. 11.2. Key linkages between consumers and mass media.

and Reeves (1990) identified such individual difference factors as motivation (involvement), ability, prior learning, and emotion, among others.
The theoretical foundation for these effects is *selective exposure*: the proposition that consumers tend to see and hear communications that are
favorable, congenial, or consistent with their predispositions and interests (Zillmann & Bryant, 1985). The concept of selective exposure is well
established, dating to studies in the 1940s that showed individuals predisposed to a particular political party are more likely to expose themselves to advertisements and other messages of their own party (Berelson, Lazarsfeld, & McPhee, 1954; Lazarsfeld, Berelson, & Gaudet, 1948).
Early research also suggested that people who heavily use one medium
of communication also use other media heavily. Media usage is supplementary, rather than complementary. Finally, early research also established the relationship between demographic characteristics and media
usage, for example, more highly educated individuals are predisposed to
use print media, whereas less educated people disproportionately use
aural and visual media (Berelson & Steiner, 1964).

Such gross characterizations of demographic characteristics and
media usage are anachronistic in today's heavily segmented media
environment. Data are available that profile "psychographic" segments
in the U.S. population that use various media types and vehicles. These

classifications go far beyond demographic characteristics and classify individuals and households by multiple factors related to a broad array of attitudes, activities, and opinions that are associated with variations in purchase behavior.

Attitudes Toward Mass Media.   Beyond these early studies of demographic characteristics related to media usage, studies turned to attitudes and uses of mass media types as partial determinants of media usage and effects. Considering first media types, the characteristics of media and the presumed conditions of exposure shape the conventional wisdom about effects of different media types, for example, the idea that effects of advertising in print media will generally be more enduring than those of broadcast media, because readers may have repeated exposure to magazine ads as they leaf through the publication several times (Coffin, 1975). (See gross media comparisons in Table 11.2.)

More compelling empirical data directly examine influences of attitudes on media vehicle effects, rather than simply assuming different kinds of effects based on surface media characteristics. In a landmark study, the Politz Research Organization compared the vehicle effects of *McCall's* with that of *Look* and *Life* magazines (Politz Research, Inc., 1962). Matched samples of readers were shown the same sets of advertisements, controlling for copy effects, but were told that they appeared in one magazine or the other. There were no differences in brand awareness and knowledge of brand claims, but there were significant differences in brand quality rating and in brand preference. For example, the gain attributed to one advertised brand as the "very highest quality" was 3.8% when the advertisement was said to run in *McCall's* magazine, but only 1.0% when the ad was said to run in the other two magazines.

In a similar vein, Aaker and Brown (1972) examined the interactive effects of media vehicle types ("prestige" vs. "expert" magazines) and copy appeals ("image" advertisements vs. "reason-why" advertisements). The dependent variables were expected price, quality, and reliability. Omitting analysis of participants in their sample who had used the advertised products previously, results show strong interaction effects. Image advertisements performed better in prestige magazines than did reason-why advertisements. However, reason-why advertisements did not perform better in expert magazines than in prestige magazines in terms of the dependent variables. Nonetheless, this study provides some empirical basis for the notion that individual attitudes toward, and uses of, media vehicles condition their responses to advertisements in those vehicles.

It is certainly clear that audiences have different perceptions of and

TABLE 11.2
Gross Media Comparisons

	TV	Radio	Magazines	Newspapers
Total population reach (adults & children)	very strong	good	fair	good
Selective upscale adult reach	fair	good	very strong	good
Upscale adult selectivity (per ad exposure)	poor	fair	very strong	good
Young adult selectivity (per ad exposure)	fair	very strong	very strong	fair
Local market selectivity	good	good	poor	very strong
Ability to control frequency	fair	good	good	very strong
Ability to pile frequency upon reach base	very strong	very strong	good	fair
Seasonal audience stability	poor	very strong	good	good
Predictability of audience levels	fair-poor	good	good	very good
Depth of demographics in audience surveys	poor	poor	very strong	fair-good
Opportunity to exploit editorial "compatibility"	poor	fair	very strong	good
Selective ad positioning	poor	fair	good	very strong
Advertising exposure	good	good	good	good
Advertising intrusiveness	very strong	good	fair	poor
Audience concern over ad "clutter"	very high	high	almost none	almost none
Emotional stimulation	very strong	fair	fair	poor
Sensory stimulation	fair-good	fair	very strong	fair
Brand name registration	very strong	good	fair	fair
Product or efficacy demonstrations	very strong	poor	fair	fair
Ability to exploit attention-getting devices	very strong	poor	very strong	good
Ability to use humor	very strong	good	poor	poor
Ability to use slice-of-life approach	very strong	good	poor	poor
Ability to convey detail and information	fair	fair	very strong	very strong
Ability to stimulate imagination	fair-good	very strong	fair	poor
Package identification	good	poor	very strong	good
Prestige & respectability of medium	fair	fair	very strong	strong
Ability to talk person-to-person with audience	fair-good	very strong	poor	poor

Source. *The Media Book* (1978, pp. 433, 436).

attitudes toward different media. Two examples of such attitudinal differences are given in Table 11.3. Knowing that consumers of various media perceive them differently and have different attitudes toward them still does not tell us how people interact with a given medium or how this interaction influences response to advertising stimuli. Chook (1983) made just this point when he stated that "the attitudinal approach is simple and relatively inexpensive, but at the same time is one that raises a number of critical questions. For one thing, measures of media interest, confidence, and enjoyment have no proven bearing on the performance of advertising. For another, such measures are too generalized for application to specific types of advertising" (p. 250). Spaeth (1983) made a similar point when he suggested that the only stage at which measures between media are comparable is at the point of sales response.

Uses of Mass Media. In a broader sense, media effects may be considered in the context of the stream of research examining uses and

TABLE 11.3
Comparisons of Print Versus Broadcast Media

Consumers Who Describe Advertisements As:[a]	Press	Television
Useful	60	40
Entertaining	20	51
Truthful	40	18
Interesting	54	40
Informative	64	41
Helpful	59	29
Clever in approach	21	56
Trying to interfere with habits	6	26
Annoying	4	41
Stupid	4	38

Consumer Reaction To Advertisements[b]	Annoying	Enjoyable	Informative	Offensive
All media	23%	36%	36%	5%
Magazines	9%	37%	48%	6%
Newspapers	12%	23%	59%	6%
Radio	24%	33%	40%	3%
Television	27%	38%	31%	4%

[a]From Institute of Practitioners in Advertising (1969), "As Others See Us," Occasional Paper No. 17. [b]From *Appraising the Economic and Social Effects of Advertising, A Review of Issues and Evidence*, Marketing Science Institute Staff Report, October, 1971 (Cambridge, MA: Marketing Science Institute), p. 2.63.

gratifications that individuals obtain from using mass media. This paradigm holds that social and psychological needs generate expectations of the mass media that lead to differential patterns of exposure, need gratification, and other outcomes (Atkin, 1985; Katz, Blumler, & Gurevitch, 1974; Rubin, 1986). Although this research approach has been criticized on many grounds (see O'Guinn & Faber, 1991), the notion is appealing that people have uses for, and obtain gratifications from, exposure to advertising in different media. Some research suggests that this may be the case. For example, research has found that "social utility" motives influence watching commercials on television. O'Guinn and Faber suggested that uses and gratification approaches may be most usefully applied to media such as special interest magazine readership.

Evidence for different uses and gratifications from mass media is seen in studies of differential loyalty among consumers of media types and vehicles. In addition, there are selective patterns of exposure or preferential attitudinal dispositions toward certain kinds of media and vehicles within media that are not constant across all viewers (Gunter, 1985). How people think and feel about various vehicles or the extent to which the audience flows toward or across certain programs varies between demographic divisions of the population. More significant, however, are findings that indicate differences in viewing patterns or attitudinal preferences for programs associated with enduring psychological characteristics of viewers (Gunter, 1985).

There is also strong evidence that people selectively attend to information based on its relevance to them at a given point in time (Broadbent, 1977; Greenwald & Leavitt, 1984; Krugman, 1988; Pechmann & Stewart, 1990; Tolley, in press). Individuals who endorse information needs do watch more information programs. Those who endorse social and personal identity needs do watch more of those programs such as popular dramas and movies that can be seen to serve those needs related to vicarious social contact (Murray, 1980). However there are no specific programs that particularly serve those individual viewers with escapist needs. For the escapist, any program may do (p. 28).

Although it is perhaps obvious that people are purposive in their selection and use of media, the full range of purposes and uses, and their effects on responses to advertising, have not been explored. Indeed, there is evidence that the processes of selection may be fundamentally different across media. For example, Rust, Kamakura, and Alpert (1991) reported results of a large-scale study that suggests television viewers seek the least objectionable alternative when deciding what to watch rather than seeking out particularly well-liked programs. Stated somewhat differently, viewers appear to avoid programs they do not like rather than select programs that they do like. In contrast to the selection of a specific magazine or book, the critical decision for the television viewer appears to be whether or not to turn on the television. The choice of program is clearly secondary. What effect such processes have on advertising in the different media remains to be determined.

In summary, research in the area of uses and gratifications of mass media extends our knowledge of media effects in important ways. It is far more explanatory than simply assuming different responses to media based on demographic or psychographic characteristics of consumers in media planning models. The concept of uses and gratifications is also a more compelling, process-oriented explanation for different media effects than the relatively static concept of attitudes toward mass media. However, the progressively more powerful research streams have focussed on media generally, rather than advertising specifically. For our purposes, the key issue is whether these findings are in some way related to advertising effectiveness in different media. It may be that effects of commercial messages will differ substantially depending on the use a particular consumer is making of a given medium. For example, readers of certain publications and viewers of certain programs indicate that advertising content is an important reason for selecting a given vehicle, and in some cases is the sole reason for using a particular medium. On the other hand, it is likely that some commercial messages will not even gain an individual's attention if they are inconsistent with the individual purpose in using a mass medium; that is, they may spoil the mood, distract from the flow, and so on. Evidence on these hypotheses stems from research on the concept of *involvement*, which we address next.

Involvement. Closely related to the preceding notions is the construct of involvement. Originally suggested by Krugman (1965, 1966), this construct is interactive, referring to consumer and media characteristics and to the inherent nature of the advertised products. The concept of involvement has become a key construct in a number of theories of attitude formation and change (Chaiken, 1980; Chaiken, Liberman, & Eagly, 1989; see Greenwald & Leavitt, 1984; Petty & Cacioppo, 1986). It has also been one of the most frequently researched and more controversial constructs within the disciplines of social psychology, advertising, and communication (see Zaichowsky, 1985).

One problem with an examination of the research on the effects of involvement is the lack of a generally accepted definition for the construct. Researchers have used the term to mean a number of distinctly different things. For example, Scherwin (1958) defined *involving programs* as "tense" programs. Kennedy (1971) defined *involve-*

ment as interest in the program storyline, whereas Soldow and Principe (1981) interpreted involvement as suspense. More recently, Thorson, Reeves, Schleuder, Lang, and Rothschild (1985) used liking for a television program and an assessment of cortical arousal as measures of involvement.

Related to these differences in operationalization of the involvement construct is the issue of where to measure involvement. Researchers have defined involvement in terms of the medium (or specific vehicle), in terms of the advertisement, and in terms of the product being advertised. It is likely that the general inconsistency of research findings regarding involvement is due to differences in the way involvement has been defined and operationalized across studies (see Singh & Hitchon, 1989, for a review of this literature). With these caveats in mind, research in this area has yielded important findings on media effects.

Originally, Krugman posited the involvement notion to counter the prevalent model of mass communications effects in the late 1950s and early 1960s, sometimes called the "transactional" model. In contrast to the earlier "hypodermic needle," or "bullet" model that posited strong communications effects, the essential notion in the transactional model is that mass media effects are quite limited. Individual characteristics, attitudes, experiences, predispositions, and so on, all mediate mass media effects. As some have put it, the conceptual shift was to change the focus from "what media do to people," to "what people do to mass media."

Contemporary versions of the transactional model are still popular among attitude researchers today under the general rubric of cognitive response theory. Cognitive response theory posits that the receivers of communications actively process information as it is received by generating thoughts (Greenwald, 1968). Cognitive response theory, of which there are a number of variations, suggests that people are not so much persuaded by communication as they persuade themselves through their own idiosyncratic thoughts in response to communications. The best known cognitive response theory in advertising research is the Elaboration Likelihood Model (ELM) associated with Petty and Cacioppo (1986). ELM posits a number of specific characteristics of receivers of communication that influence the likelihood of cognitive response (hence the name, elaboration likelihood). The two characteristics that have received the most attention from researchers are the ability of the receiver to use the information and the involvement of the receiver.

Krugman suggested that early transaction models may be flawed, however, because mass media "effects" are most often viewed as attitude changes regarding important issues—the focus of most empirical research in the area. Krugman argued that people are much less involved with advertising content, especially in what he called "low involvement" media, such as television.

Cognitive response theory has not, by any means, ignored low-involvement situations. It suggests that there are differences between high-involvement and low-involvement situations. The underlying cognitive response mechanism is the same in both situations, however. What is hypothesized to differ is the content of the thoughts elicited by the communication. More involving situations elicit more thoughts directly related to the message, whereas less involving situations elicit more thoughts related to such nonmessage cues as source expertise, liking for the source, and so forth. In both high- and low-involvement circumstances, the message recipient is viewed as an active information processor. What changes as a function of involvement is the nature of the information attended and processed.

In large measure, cognitive response theory defines involvement in terms of its effect. If message-related thoughts are elicited, the situation is by definition highly involving; if thoughts only peripherally related to the message are elicited, the situation is defined as low involvement. Krugman took a somewhat different perspective. He used the term *involvement* to apply to media characteristics, to consumer characteristics, and to product characteristics. For example, he described broadcast media as "cool" or low-involvement media, and print media as "hot" or high-involvement media. Television, in particular, is a low-involvement medium because the rate of viewing and understanding is not controlled by the viewer. In contrast, exposure to print media is under the control of readers, who may pause and make connections between what is being read and personal experiences and attitudes. Learning occurs in a more traditional way. Information can be selected, evaluated, and integrated into one's existing attitude and knowledge frameworks.

Turning to involvement as a personal characteristic, Krugman defined involvement as the number of conscious "bridging experiences" connections, or personal references per minute that the viewer makes between his or her own life and the stimulus (Krugman, 1966). He argued that television is a low-involvement medium, and that most products advertised on television are of a low-involvement sort. In a harbinger of many recent experiments that have examined media and advertising effects via measurement of brain-wave activity, Krugman reported that:

> Our initial EEG data supports McLuhan in the sense that television does not appear to be communication as we have known it. Our subject was working to learn something from a print ad, but was passive about

television . . . (it is not that) print or television is "better" . . . the response to television is more passive simply because it is an easier form of communication. (p. 25)

Wright (1981) provided support for this proposition in an interesting experimental study employing cognitive response methodology. He offered evidence that thought outputs may approach zero for broadcast ads and suggested that the rather substantial clutter of the broadcast medium environment may actually suppress cognitive response. Thus, if attitudes are formed or changed in response to exposure to television, it is unlikely that the mechanism is cognitive response. Some other mechanism may be at work.

Krugman went on to argue that effects of advertising on television will not be found in traditional, one-shot, after-exposure surveys or experiments, because effects are subtle, emerge over time, and are not likely to be reflected in measures of attitude change. Rather, advertising on television is more likely to affect brand perceptions. Thus, he suggested, measures of effects such as recognition are more appropriate.

Several studies have specifically examined the effect of various kinds of involvement on responses to advertising. Lloyd and Clancy (1989) and Audits and Surveys (1986) reported large-scale studies that demonstrate that more highly involving media (i.e., print) are better vehicles for delivering product messages. This is true regardless of whether the measure of advertising performance is recall, persuasion, or message credibility. Buchholz and Smith (1991) investigated the effect of the interaction of involvement and type of medium on a variety of measures. For these authors, involvement is a situational variable that they induced by instructions that either directed respondents to pay careful attention to an ad or to pay attention to material surrounding the advertisement of interest. Their research demonstrated that in high-involvement situations message recipients were equally likely to process and remember advertising messages embedded in radio and television commercials. Under high-involvement situations, message recipients tended to generate more thoughts, and especially personally relevant thoughts, about the commercial message. In low-involvement situations, television, with its dual channel input (audio and visual), was the superior medium. Cognitive responses and the number of personally relevant connections were substantially reduced in the low-involvement situation. Television was nonetheless superior to radio in low-involvement circumstances.

In sum, the involvement notion is an important one for the present topic because it has formed the basis for research that attempts to directly compare media effects. In general, findings show that media differ in the extent to which they invite different kinds of attentiveness and information-processing of advertising. Additionally, despite the ambiguity of the construct, research has directly examined the complex interactions between effects of the medium itself, viewer characteristics, products advertised, and, perhaps, the situation in which advertising communication occurs.

Mood. The final consumer characteristic influencing media effects that we examine is the concept of mood, or feelings. The term *mood* denotes specific subjective feeling states at the time of advertising exposure. A rather substantial body of research makes it quite clear that mood influences an array of psychological processes—attention, information processing, decision making, memory, attitude formation. Srull (1990), Isen (1989), and Gardner (1985) provided recent reviews of much of this work and its implications for advertising and consumer behavior.

Conceptually related to "uses-and-gratifications" research, discussed earlier, the concept of mood and the related construct of arousal focus on affective rather than cognitive factors that link individuals with mass media. The essential idea is that people use mass media to maintain or change feeling states (moods) or excitatory states (arousal). Self-report data suggest that people use television to both increase and decrease arousal (Condry, 1989), and physiological studies have shown that television viewing can alter blood pressure, heart rate, and other physiological states that presumably reflect arousal states (Klebber, 1985).

Because viewing television programming can lead to changes in arousal, it may also be that such shifts take time to dissipate. This is the notion of "excitation-transfer" (Zillmann, 1971). To the extent excitation-transfer exists, it may be that certain kinds of advertisements have different effects, depending on their placement in a television program. Indeed, as we see in the next section, some studies have shown that reactions to television influence reactions to subsequent commercials and the advertised products.

There is certainly evidence that moods induced by television programs interact with commercials embedded within the programs to produce differential responses among viewers. For example, Kennedy (1971) found that viewers of suspense programs had poorer recall of a brand name in an embedded commercial than viewers of a comedy. However, attitudes toward the advertised brand were more positive among viewers of the suspense program than among viewers of a comedy. Similar results for recall were reported by Soldow and Principe (1981).

Goldberg and Gorn (1987) found that, compared to commercials viewed in the context of a sad program, commercials viewed in the context of a happy television program resulted in happier moods during viewing of both the program and commercials, more positive cognitive responses about the commercials, and higher evaluations of commercial effectiveness. They also found that the mood induced by the program had a greater effect on commercials with a greater emotional appeal than commercials with more informational appeals. These investigators did not examine whether there was an interaction between the emotional tone of the commercials and the programs in which they were embedded.

The potential interaction of the emotional tone of commercials and programs was investigated by Kamins, Marks, and Skinner (1991). They found that a "sad" commercial embedded within a "sad" program was rated by viewers as more likeable and produced higher ratings of purchase intention than a humorous commercial embedded within a "sad" program. Conversely, a humorous commercial embedded within a humorous program performed better than a humorous commercial embedded within a "sad" program. The authors interpreted these results in terms of consistency theory, which suggests that viewers seek to maintain a mood throughout a program. Because commercials represent interruptions, Kamins, Marks, and Skinner suggested that commercials that are more consistent in emotional tone with the program will perform better than those that are inconsistent in tone.

In an earlier study, Krugman (1983) also examined the relationship between responses to advertising and the programming context. Although he did not explicitly address the question of mood, his hypotheses reflect processes that would seem to be conceptually related to the construct of mood: He tested the conventional wisdom that "commercials are particularly objectionable when they interrupt interesting programs." Thus, some reasoned, "the more interesting the program, the less effective the commercial" (Soldow & Principe, 1981). Krugman first distinguished between viewer opinion and impact on viewers as separate phenomena. Then, he examined the impact of advertising in 56 television programs that were determined to vary in interest level. He found a pattern that is just the reverse of the conventional wisdom: Commercials that interrupt interesting programs are more effective. This is consistent with Krugman's earlier hypothesis that involvement with advertising tends to be consistent with interest in the editorial environment. Although this study does not make comparisons with other media, and the notion of interest relates as much to message variables as it may relate to media effects, the finding is indicative of the importance of the media viewing context as a mediator of advertising effects.

Finally, a major field experiment (Yuspeh, 1977) examined the programming context as a determinant of responses to television advertising. This time the programming context was manipulated by having viewers watch either situation comedies or action programs. No explanatory concepts are offered to suggest what it is about the different programming types that might account for different effects, but the implicit idea seems to be that linkage between programming stimuli and advertising responses is attributable to variations in mood or excitatory states experienced while watching. Individuals were asked to watch particular programs that were experimentally manipulated so that half watched three action programs and half watched three situation comedies.

Commercials for six products were embedded in the programs, and effects were measured with multiple indicators such as brand recall, attitudes and buying intention, and commercial element playback. Interestingly, there were only slight differences between the two types of programming contexts on commercial effectiveness. However, there were significant differences among specific episodes with each program type, across products and performance measures. It appears that different episodes of the same program may have different effects on the performance of commercials appearing in those programs. It is likely that such an effect is the outcome of a complex set of interactions between program type, advertising message, and viewer characteristics, especially programming-induced moods.

None of the studies that explore the relationship between programming context and advertising response clarify whether the effects of prior moods differ from programming-induced moods. Nor is it clear whether the types of mood effects that occur in a television context occur in other media, although it is certain that other media are capable of creating or changing moods (Gardner, 1985; Isen, 1989). These topics may be a logical next step for researchers who have examined the processes and effects of feelings generated by advertising exposure, as part of a stream of research that has examined the role of affect in marketing communications (Agres, Edell, & Dubitsky, 1990; Edell & Burke, 1987; Holbrook, 1978; Holbrook & Batra, 1988; Mitchell & Olson, 1981).

MEDIA CONTEXT AS A MEDIATOR OF ADVERTISING EFFECTS

In the broadest sense, the four consumer characteristics discussed to this point form a complex context for media exposure. That is, attitudes toward media types and vehicles, uses and gratifications from media, involvement, and mood states motivating and characterizing media use, all form the context in which we decide whether or not to attend to media and which media to choose, and influence cognitive and affective states while attending to media.

A few studies focus more on media stimuli themselves than on consumer characteristics that determine advertising effects in different media. We refer to these studies as focusing on the "media context." Studies in this area seek to explain relatively immediate outcomes of exposure to advertising, such as cognitive responses, attention behavior, and physiological responses, in terms of exposure to different media types. Other studies examine longer term responses to advertising as a function of frequency and timing of exposure, and these are reviewed in the next section.

Krugman's involvement construct, discussed earlier, suggests that the inherent characteristics of mass media, in addition to consumer characteristics and product characteristics, interact in order to determine one's "involvement" with mass media. Terms such as *hot* (broadcast media) or *cool* (print media), however, do not tell us much about particular media characteristics that may be functionally related to different effects on individuals. A first question is whether the media context affects consumer responses to advertising, and if so, what is the nature of these responses? Research that addresses this question falls into several types: studies of cognitive response, observational studies, studies employing physiological measures, studies of "priming," and research on the mediating effects of various situational or environmental factors.

Cognitive Response

A classic study by Wright (1973) examined the interactive effects of media and receiver involvement on a range of cognitive responses. Drawing heavily on previous research in psychology, Wright argued that individuals may experience an array of responses when exposed to advertising, and the nature and intensity of these responses is directly related to degree of involvement. These cognitive responses include counterarguments, source derogation, support arguments, and, in other research, "connections"—a construct very similar to Krugman's discussion of "bridging" that may occur as individuals relate what they see in advertising to some aspect of their personal lives.

Wright was interested in the mediating role these cognitive response variables might play in determining consumer responses to advertising in different media, under different involvement conditions. Receiver involvement was manipulated by telling some participants that they would have to make a short-term decision after viewing advertising for a new soybean-based product (high involvement). Other participants were not told of the impending decision (low involvement). Messages were transmitted by either audio means, similar to radio advertising, or by print means, similar to newspaper or magazine advertising. Wright found significantly more total cognitive responses, less source derogation, and more support arguments for a print version of an advertisement than for a radio version. Although acceptance of the ad message was not affected by the medium, buying intention was higher for the print condition than for the radio condition.

In addition to the immediately measured cognitive response activity, delayed responses were elicited 2 days later; among the involved women, supportive responses to the radio ad increased, but not for the print ad. Initially, the rapid transmission rate of broadcast media, compared to the more audience-controlled input of print, probably inhibits both the amount and variability of response activity. Over time, relatively more opportunity exists for increases in cognitive responses to broadcast media; the responses may, in turn, be related to different amounts of persistence of attitude change and behavior.

Observational Studies

Other studies also directly examine consumer responses while viewing advertising in a media context. Whereas Wright examined self-reports of cognitive responses while viewing advertising in different media, some researchers have examined actual behaviors while attending to media. For example, Ward, Levinson, and Wackman (1972) and Anderson and his colleagues (Bryant & Anderson, 1983), among others, examined actual behavior while watching television. Tolley (in press) used a unique lamp-like device to unobtrusively track the eye-movements of readers of newspapers. Rothschild and others (Rothschild & Hyun, 1990; Rothschild, Hyun, Reeves, Thorson, & Goldstein, 1988) measured physiological responses among individuals exposed to television commercials. Unfortunately, most of these behavioral studies do not compare responses across media, unlike Wright's study, which compared responses to print and audio advertising.

In the Ward et al. research, mothers observed one of their children watching television, and coded attention behavior. Results show a great deal of activity while watching television generally, ranging from not attending to the television set at all to full attention. During strings of commercials, children's attention initially increases when commercials interrupt programming, but decreases steadily over the "pod" of commercials. Interestingly, there is some tendency for attention to increase later in commercial pods, apparently because children anticipate the return of programming.

Anderson's (Bryant & Anderson, 1983) work sought to identify those attributes of television programs that attract the attention of children. Attention was operationalized as visual selection, that is time the child's eyes were directed toward the television screen. Program characteristics most likely to draw attention to the television screen include movement, high levels of physical activity, and auditory changes in the program. Such findings have not been lost on the creators of children's advertising. Most such advertising routinely includes those elements that draw attention. Simply focusing on a television screen does not, however, assure that information is processed by the viewer. Indeed, research has made it increasingly clear that television viewers do not simply react to the medium, but rather engage in a purposeful search for meaning and personal relevance (Reeves, Thorson, & Schleuder, 1986).

Tolley (in press) found that readers of newspapers scan pages to decide whether and to what they will attend. Most individual newspaper pages receive no attention. Debriefings with readers suggested that they were using the quick scan as a means of identifying those items, editorial matter, ads, and so on, that were personally relevant. Such findings are consistent with research that suggests there exists a preattentional process that acts to filter irrelevant information and helps the individual determine those environmental elements for which information processing is worth the effort (Broadbent, 1977; Greenwald & Leavitt, 1984). Tolley also observed that individuals appear to have consistent, but idiosyncratic styles of reading. Whether such individual differences exist for other media and the extent to which such differences are consistent across media and influence other types of viewer response are empirical questions that have not been addressed by researchers.

Physiological Measures

Rothschild et al. (1988) examined physiological (EEG: electroencephalographic) responses of individuals watching television commercials and examined the relationship between EEG responses and memory for components of television commercials (Rothschild & Hyun, 1990). They found significant EEG activity during commercial exposure, and some differences in hypothesized directions for greater dominance by one brain hemisphere or the other. The latter is the topic of "hemispheric lateralization," referring to specialization of the right and left sides of the brain in information processing (Hellige, 1990). Some advance the idea that the right side of the brain is "better" at processing stimuli such as pictures and music, whereas the left side of the brain is better at processing words and numbers.

Krugman (1977) hypothesized that print advertising is left-hemisphere dominated and television processing is right-hemisphere dominated. Unfortunately, this hypothesis has not been supported by research (Weinstein, Appel, & Weinstein, 1980), but, as Rossiter noted (1982), most media contain both visual and verbal elements, which also interact with individual differences.

One study did compare brain-wave activity during exposure to print and broadcast media advertising, and explored the relationship between patterns of EEG activity and three measures of advertising recall (Rust, Price, & Kumar, 1985). The results of this study show significant participant-by-medium interactions in 14 of 16 analyses, indicating that different participants have different patterns of brain responses to media. There were no clear findings with respect to brain wave activity and advertising recall, however, and results were not clear concerning hemispheric lateralization—more or less active processing by one side of the brain or the other while processing print or broadcast ads. Analysis did show that magazines produced the most beta waves—thought to indicate high levels of processing—and radio and television produced high levels of alpha waves. These types of brain waves are thought to indicate the absence of processing.

Priming

Another stream of research on the effects of media context examines the degree to which media "prime" attention to specific elements of advertising (Herr, 1989; Higgins & King, 1981; Wyer & Srull, 1981; Yi, 1990a, 1990b). Research in contexts other than advertising (Berkowitz & Rogers, 1986) suggests the presence of such an effect. The notion of priming suggests that the media context may predispose an individual to pay more attention to some elements of an ad than others and may influence the interpretation that a viewer gives a complex or ambiguous advertising stimulus.

For example, the presence of an older model in an advertisement could be interpreted in terms of maturity, experience, conservatism, sophistication, steadfastness,or any of a number of other more or less positive attributes. Depending on the product, some of these interpretations would be more desirable than others. For a perfume product, associations of experience and sophistication might be appropriate, whereas conservatism and steadfastness would be less appropriate (although they might be appropriate for a different "product" such as a bank). The media context might serve to prime one or more of these interpretations. For example, if the advertising were embedded in a program about a sensuous older woman, the associations elicited by an older female model in an ad might well include sophistication and experience. On the other hand, if the program in which the advertising was embedded dealt with the struggle of an older woman to adjust to a near fatal illness, rather different associations might be elicited.

Several empirical studies demonstrate that such priming may occur. Further, this priming may occur for both cognitive and affective responses. For example, Yi (1990a) showed that a media context that emphasized one particular interpretation of an automobile attribute (size) resulted in greater salience for the primed interpretation. Ads were embedded in a mock-up of a magazine that carried editorial matter that either emphasized safety (in the context of a story on airline safety) or fuel economy (in the context of a story on entrepreneurial oilmen). The study found support for the cognitive priming hypothesis. This result was attributed to a temporary increase in the accessibility of a given attribute arising from the recent media exposure. This finding is consistent with Wyer and Srull's (1981) model of cognitive accessibility and with recent research on framing effects (Bettman & Sujan, 1987). Similar effects have also been identified in other studies (Herr, 1989; Yi, 1990b).

In the same study, Yi (1990a) also demonstrated affective priming. Affective priming is a type of mood effect in that a mood is induced by the media context, in contrast to a mood that the individual brings to the medium. Yi found that a more positive tone of the editorial matter resulted in a more effective ad (as measured by attitude toward the brand and purchase intention). He further demonstrated that this effect appeared to be mediated by more positive attitudes toward the ad.

Research on priming has generally assumed that priming is unidirectional, that is, that the effect is induced by media context on advertising response. This is probably not an unreasonable assumption under most circumstances, given the embeddedness of commercials within the more dominant media environment. It may be possible for the effect to work in the opposite direction, however, with a commercial (say prior to the beginning of a television program) serving to prime response to the medium. This would be an interesting avenue of future research. Another related question is the degree to which advertisements in the same medium or the same pod of commercials or page in a magazine might prime response to other advertisements.

Again, research on priming has focused more on within-media comparisons and effects of other variables than on cross-media comparisons. We can conclude that priming occurs and identify some of the message and media context variables associated with priming, but research has not explicitly addressed priming effects in different media.

Situational Mediators

A final facet of the effects of media context on responses to advertising is the condition under which people view advertising in different media. The acts of attending to mass media are mediated by situational factors in the exposure environment, beyond consumer characteristics, or stimuli-specific media context factors that we have discussed to this point. These situational effects are the environmental conditions of exposure, such as the presence of others while attending to media, the presence of outside noise, the division of attention between the media and some other task, and other situational factors that may affect responses to advertising in different media.

As with much of the research on other dimensions of media effects, most research of situational determinants of advertising response has focussed on environmental conditions during exposure to advertising in a particular medium, rather than cross-media comparisons. For example, Ward and Ray (1976) found that cognitive processing (counterarguments, connections, and the like) during exposure to anti-drug abuse public service commercials was greatest under conditions of medium levels of distraction. It may be that high levels of distraction while attending to television inhibit one's abilities to attend, whereas conditions of no distraction do not force individuals to pay attention.

To summarize this discussion of media context influences on responses to advertising, the studies we cite have focused on relatively short-term effects of exposure to advertising in different media. Only one study (Wright, 1973) directly compares effects resulting from different media, and we are forced to speculate about media differences from other studies that have examined effects resulting from exposure to advertising in a single medium. Results from Wright's study show differences in cognitive responses depending on media in which advertising appears, and other studies suggest that the viewing context may also affect these cognitive outcomes. Still other studies show effects on physiological processes and attention behavior resulting from exposure to television advertising. Finally, there are studies that show "priming" effects in print advertising.

The key issues for the present chapter revolve around the kinds of effects generated by advertising in different media, and the processes associated with those effects. The variables examined in studies we review, such as cognitive responses, attention, and priming, may occur in response to advertising in any medium. The issue would seem to be whether some of these processes are more likely to occur in response to advertising in some media more than others, and lead to different magnitudes of effects. The influence of media context is especially important due to the increasing diversity of media and, therefore, opportunities for advertising exposure. If individuals see similar advertising for the same product or service in multiple media, are effects different than if the advertising is seen in only one medium? Research reviewed in this section suggests that the answer to the question is more likely to be found by studying audience behavior, rather than by merely describing different outcomes of exposure to advertising in different media. Similarly, different outcomes of advertising and different processes by which advertising affects individuals may result from differences in the frequency and repetition of advertising messages in various media, and we turn now to research and theory on that topic.

EFFECTS OF MEDIA SCHEDULING
ON ADVERTISING EFFECTS

In our pictorial model (Fig. 11.2), individuals and mass media are linked by consumer characteristics and by media scheduling factors. Evidence suggests that there are different effects of advertisements in different media, depending on media scheduling: how often individuals are exposed to advertising in a given time frame (frequency and repetition effects).

An important implication of scheduling revolves around effects of media scheduling on initial learning. As we discussed earlier, growth in new information technologies and media forms has resulted in increased levels of potential advertising exposure for individuals. Some estimate that we are potentially exposed to over 1,000 advertisements and promotions each day. Obviously, advertisers rely on creative techniques to attempt to gain consumer attention, but media selection and scheduling decisions are also important in gaining attention and influencing later learning.

Krugman hypothesized that three exposures to advertising are key. The first exposure elicits what he calls a "what is it?" cognitive response, in which audience members attempt to understand the communication and perhaps decide if it is of interest or not. The second exposure may continue the process of understanding initiated by the first exposure, or it may elicit a "what of it?" response, in which the audience member seeks to determine if the advertisement is relevant and important. The second communication may also prompt the audience member's recognition that the ad has been seen before: what Krugman called the "Aha,

I've seen this before" response. The third exposure is basically a reminder—if the consumer has not acted on the basis of the first two exposures. Obviously, it may not always be so simple. For example, Aaker and Myers (1975) suggested that some audience segments may screen out exposures following the first one until they are ready to process another exposure. This may be particularly true, Aaker and Myers speculated, in the case of television advertising because of the low involvement nature of exposure to that medium.

Pechmann and Stewart (1988), after reviewing the substantial literature on advertising wearout, suggested that three "quality" exposures to a communication are probably sufficient for an advertising message to have its effect, but they noted that it may take many exposure opportunities to produce the effect of three quality exposures. This is because potential message recipients may elect not to attend to an advertising message even when it is present or may see or hear only a portion of the total advertising message. It is also likely that other advertising for competing products, as well as advertising in general, may interfere with the processing of a commercial message at any given point in time.

Two large field studies tend to support the view that there are rapidly diminishing returns to repeated exposures. Blair (1987/1988) reported that in tests of 20 different television commercials, increased spending on advertising (with a concomitant increase in the average number of exposures and gross rating points) in a market increased sales in those cases where the commercial scored well on a measure of persuasion. Spending differences seemed to make no difference when persuasion was low. In other words, if an ad was not persuasive to begin with, even an infinite number of exposures was insufficient to produce a response. More relevant to the current discussion is the finding that the persuasive effect of advertising took place quickly and this effect was in direct proportion to the number of gross rating points purchased for the commercial. Further, once commercials had reached their targeted consumers, there was no further effect of additional exposures. Once consumers were exposed to the advertising and had been persuaded or not, that was the end of the matter. Consumers did not become "more persuaded" with additional exposures.

Whereas Blair's research examined television advertising, a study carried out in the early 1980s by Time, Inc., in collaboration with Joseph E. Seagram & Sons, Inc. (Time, Inc., 1981), examined repetition and frequency effects of print advertising. Although this study was restricted to one product category, liquor, and only two magazines, *Time*, and *Sports Illustrated*, the study was well controlled and extended over a 48-week period. It also examined a range of measures of advertising effects: brand awareness, advertising awareness, attitude toward brand, willingness to buy the brand, and product purchase and use. The study not only examined the effect of advertising exposure versus nonexposure, but it also examined the effects of advertising frequency.

The results of this study found that measures of brand awareness, brand attitude, and willingness to buy increased sharply after the very first "opportunity to see" the advertising. All measures tended to level off, then remain constant, in the latter weeks of the campaign for brands that had a high level of awareness at the beginning of the campaign. However, for brands that began with a low level of initial awareness, all measures tended to show a steady increase over the 48 weeks of the campaign. Further, more frequent "opportunities to see" the ads, that is, a higher frequency of advertising, produced greater results. The influence of greater advertising frequency was greater for low-awareness brands than for high-awareness brands. These results are consistent with a learning view of advertising (Pechmann & Stewart, 1988). Thus, it is useful to compare processes of learning and forgetting media advertising with basic research in memory processes.

Learning and Memory Effects

Most studies of media scheduling on advertising effects examine recall and other variables (especially attitude change) as a function of frequency of exposure and/or repetition of advertising stimuli. This is quite similar to the methods of research on the psychology of learning. One of the pioneers of learning research, Ebbinghaus (1902), identified three basic memory processes:

- A negatively accelerating forgetting curve. After 20 minutes, Ebbinghaus observed, participants forgot one third of what was learned: After 6 days, another one-fourth of the material was forgotten, and a full month later, yet another fifth was forgotten.
- Serial position effects. Items at the beginning or end of a series were most easily learned: Items in the middle were learned most slowly and forgotten most rapidly.
- Overlearning. Overlearning or repetition beyond the point of repetition made very long conscious memory possible (for example: Things go better with _____").

The processes of learning and forgetting advertising stimuli are considerably more complex than learning simple stimuli in the laboratory, of course. Consumer characteristics, such as prior experiences, shape these processes. Advertising factors, including message variables and media effects, also play an important role in determining these proceses.

Nevertheless, much of the laboratory research on verbal learning and forgetting appears to generalize well to an advertising context. For example, studies have shown that after being shown a large number of ads, participants can recognize a specific ad 87% of the time 7 days after initial exposure and 58% of the time after 129 days (Lodish, 1971). Unlike the laboratory setting, the advertising context provides less control over the frequency of repetition. Media in which advertising appear are often defined by their frequency of appearance—nightly news, monthly magazine, daily newspaper. These characteristics of media limit the advertiser's flexibility for scheduling repetitions. Further, as noted earlier in this chapter, an exposure opportunity (the placement of an advertisement in a particular medium) is not the same as an actual exposure. It is likely that there are many more exposure opportunities than actual exposures to advertising. This fact, coupled with the temporal characteristics of various media, create problems for the advertiser that are not present in the laboratory. Thus, a considerable body of research has addressed the issue of scheduling.

Advertising Scheduling

Strong (1974, 1977) examined the scheduling and repetition effects of print advertising and found that greater advertising recognition occurred when consumers were exposed to weekly intervals of magazine advertising than to monthly or daily intervals. Another classic study used direct mail advertising. Zielske (1959) found that repetition was very effective in increasing advertising recall, both when repetitions occurred over a relatively short period of time, and when repetitions occurred in a "pulsed" fashion, over 1 year (see Fig. 11.3). Shortly after the 13th exposure, 63% of the people who had been mailed ads weekly recalled some of the content, as did 48% of those receiving monthly ads. After the monthly ads stopped, that group showed decay of recall, similar to the negatively accelerating forgetting curve observed by Ebbinghaus. In a later study, Zielske and Henry (1980) demonstrated similar effects for television advertising.

Ray and Sawyer (1971) found that the percentages of participants recalling an ad increased from 27% to 74% as the number of repetitions increased from one to six. Although recognition and recall increase as the number of repetitions increases, there are diminishing returns: Additional repetitions result in decreasing magnitudes of gains in recall and recognition. Similar results have been found by a number of other researchers (see Pechmann & Stewart, 1988, for a review of this research).

There may be circumstances in which repetitions have a negative

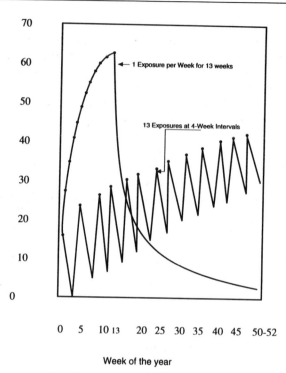

FIG. 11.3. Advertising recall as a function of the timing and number of exposures (from Zielske, 1959).

effect on recall and recognition. When consumers have negative attitudes toward a product, increased repetitions may result in more negative attitudes. Negative effects may also result from very high levels of repetition, regardless of consumer attitudes, a phenomenon termed *wearout* in the advertising industry (Pechmann & Stewart, 1988). As in many other areas of advertising research, most studies of media scheduling effects do not compare effects of various media, and they do not isolate media effects from interactions. As Sawyer and Ward (1976) put it:

> Little systematic evidence exists concerning the effects of advertising medium on persistence of communication effects. The existing evidence suggests that the audience-controlled input of print advertising may generate more immediate learning and cognitive responses than "low involvement" broadcast exposures. Over time, however, increases in reactions to broadcast advertising may occur, which could be related to persistence effects. (p. 125)

Few longitudinal studies have been conducted that would provide a basis for definitive statements about repetition and frequency effects of advertising in different media. Additionally, scheduling and repetition factors cannot be separated from message variables. Particularly compelling or particularly dreary advertisements may accelerate or hamper the kinds of results found in studies reviewed here. Greenberg (1988), for example, suggested that "critical images" in television programming may have profound affects, in contrast to the view that television effects occur slowly and incrementally. He called these strong effects the "drench" hypothesis:

> The drench hypothesis, in its current, primitive form, asserts that critical images may contribute more to impression-formation and image-building than does the sheer frequency of television and behaviors that are viewed. The hypothesis provides an alternative to the no-effects hypothesis and to the view that the slow accretion of impressions cumulate across an indefinite time period. Finally, it also suggests that striking new images can make a difference—that a single character or collection of characters may cause substantial changes in beliefs, perceptions, or expectations about a group or a role, particularly among young viewers. (pp. 100–101)

MEDIA-RELATED OUTCOMES
OF ADVERTISING EXPOSURES

To this point, we have related results from a number of studies, focusing more on independent variables than on dependent variables. Our focus has been on the independent and joint effects of advertising in various mass media types and vehicles on a variety of outcomes. Selection of dependent variables in many of these studies has been driven by the interests of consumer and advertising researchers. Therefore, dependent variables usually pertain to effects having to do with consumption, such as "hierarchy of communication" effects (McGuire, 1969) thought to lead up to purchase behavior, cognitive processes mediating advertising effects, and learning outcomes (effects on long- and short-term memory). These variables include various recognition and recall measures, measures of product knowledge, interest and attitude, and purchase intention and brand choice (see Stewart, Furse, & Kozak, 1983, and Stewart, Pechmann, Ratneshwar, Stroud, & Bryant, 1985, for a review of the use of these measures for assessing the effectiveness of advertising).

Advertising Comprehension and Miscomprehension

One other dependent variable has been studied in relation to different media effects: comprehension and miscomprehension of advertising. A major study of comprehension and miscomprehension of television commercials (Jacoby & Hoyer, 1982; Jacoby, Hoyer, & Sheluga, 1980) was followed by various studies of effects of print advertising (Jacoby & Hoyer, 1989; Jacoby, Hoyer, & Zimmer, 1983; Russo, Metcalf, & Stephens, 1981). In one such study (Russo, Metcalf, & Stephens, 1981), an average miscomprehension rate of 80% was found in advertisements from 10 magazines. Even when the claims were excised and the same ads were shown in "corrected" form, another group of respondents exhibited a 50% miscomprehension rate.

Two studies attempted to compare comprehension and miscomprehension in response to print and televised advertising. Jacoby, Hoyer, and Zimmer found lower miscomprehension for the print versions of advertisements than for televised (or radio) counterparts. All the advertisements were for the same products and were carefully constructed to be equivalent, except for media vehicle exposure conditions. Another cross-media study (Morris, Brinberg Klimberg, Rivera, & Millstein, 1986) found very similar miscomprehension rates to those in the Jacoby et al. study, but somewhat greater miscomprehension rates were found for magazine ads, compared to televised commercials.

In a related study, Jacoby and Hoyer (1989) focussed on print communication. They compared comprehension and miscomprehension rates for editorial and advertising content. On average, 21% of the material was miscomprehended, with an additional 15.5% of "don't know" responses. Editorial content was associated with slightly higher rates of miscomprehension than was advertising content. Comprehension was associated with age, education, and income, but not with other sociodemographic variables.

Jacoby and his colleagues posited a conceptual scheme whereby a communication involves a complex process of sensory and semantic analysis. The former involves features of the communication; the latter involves what they call morphemic representations (i.e., assigning molecular representations into a larger, holistic meaningful structure). They also differentiated between asserted and implied meanings in advertising and other communication content.

Jacoby and Hoyer suggested that expectations and the existence of an information processing schema may be important determinants of the extent to which individuals comprehend or miscomprehend communications, including advertising content. They also asserted that characteristics of media and messages may be important determinants of miscomprehension, noting that there is some evidence for higher levels of miscomprehension associated with verbal communication content than with pictorial or graphic content (Kuss, 1985). Hoyer, Srivastava, and Jacoby (1984) found that the presence of music tended to lower the incidence of communication, a finding that may be consistent with Ward and Ray's finding discussed earlier (Ward & Ray, 1976), that medium levels of distraction during communication heighten attention behavior compared to low or high distraction levels.

Studies concerned with comprehension and miscomprehension of advertising have largely been descriptive and cross-sectional in nature. They describe the presence and frequency of comprehension and miscomprehension but do not identify the effects of these phenomena on other advertising-related responses such as product-related beliefs, attitude formation, purchase intent, or brand choice. Comprehension and miscomprehension no doubt influence these types of outcomes. It would also be of interest to determine whether rates of miscomprehension are rising or declining. Given the increasing number of media and messages confronting the consumer, there may be reason to speculate the rate of miscomprehension is rising.

In addition, studies of comprehension and miscomprehension have not sought to systematically identify the conditions under which comprehension (or miscomprehension) is greatest, and the relationship of comprehension effects on some measure of persuasion. Such conditions are, no doubt, a complex interaction of the individual receiver, media, and media scheduling characteristics that have been identified in this chapter. Comprehension has long been identified as a potential, if not always necessary, mediator of persuasion (Hovland, Janis, & Kelley, 1953; McGuire, 1972). Recent research also suggests that comprehension or miscomprehension may moderate the persuasive impact of other persuasion variables (Ratneshwar & Chaiken, 1991). Thus, future research might fruitfully examine processes that facilitate or retard comprehension of advertising messages in different media, and the relationship of comprehension and miscomprehension to other outcomes, such as persuasion.

SUMMARY AND DIRECTIONS FOR RESEARCH IN THE NEW MEDIA ENVIRONMENT

We have attempted to review a rather large body of research in the area of advertising media effects. We have presented our review loosely around a pictorial model that represents many of the chief streams of research and provides a vehicle for structuring our review (Fig. 11.2). Another way of viewing research in the area is to classify studies in three categories. The first category is comprised of the majority of studies in the area, which focus more on individual responses to advertising messages in various media. The literature suggests that these individual responses are determined primarily by four interrelated factors: attitudes toward specific media, uses and gratifications obtained from using media, involvement, and mood states that affect media usage or are affected by media usage. The second category consists of studies that focus less on individual characteristics and more on media characteristics, or the communication context formed by different mass media.

The third category consists of studies we reviewed in the latter part of this chapter, which deal with structural aspects of exposure to advertising in various media: issues of scheduling, repetition, frequency, and studies that suggest that the structural characteristics of media affect basic comprehension of advertising messages. Clearly, the medium in which advertising is encountered by individuals is a determinant of a variety of responses. What we would like to know are the kinds of responses that occur among different kinds of individuals as a function of exposure to different media, media combinations, and exposure conditions. Our review suggests that we have a patchwork of findings that bear on the dimensions of this overall statement. Although most of the research that we have reviewed has examined only one or a few effects, and usually within a single medium, it is clear that different mass media generate a variety of cognitive, affective, and behavioral responses among individuals, and that individual characteristics, predispositions, and preferences determine the incidence and probably the magnitude of these responses. It is also clear that situational factors associated with the media exposure environment influence responses. The conditions under which people are exposed to advertising influence effects of that advertising.

Two key elements are missing for a more definitive picture of advertising media effects. First, the "patchwork" of findings needs to be replaced by greater integration of research approaches and findings. For example, we would like to know the ranges of responses to advertising in different media, and how individual characteristics and situational factors influence responses. This is a daunting proposition, because it is difficult to isolate the effects of advertising media from the other variables that make up the advertising that individuals see (i.e., message factors). The solution would seem to be to focus more on recipients of advertising than on characteristics of the advertising. Rather than trying to isolate the media context for advertising, it is probably more fruitful to study individual responses to advertising *in* the media context.

The second key element for a more definitive picture of media effects is an understanding of how individuals interact with various forms of media. That is, it may be possible to characterize individuals in terms of the nature of their mass media use, beyond the kinds of attitudinal and uses and gratifications approaches reviewed here. The issue is particularly important, given greater diversity in the contemporary media environment, but greater integration of media, at the same time. That is, there are more forms of media in the environment today compared to the past, but individuals have greater opportunities to use them in an integrated way. For example, "passive" media, such as television, may be on the verge of becoming interactive. The "new" media and media technologies compete with more traditional media for the consumer's attention. The result has been a reduction in the "mass" that can be delivered by mass media.

We began this chapter by noting that the media environment has become highly fragmented. Statistics tell a part of this story. Twenty years ago, 90% of all households watched prime-time television on any given night; today it is only 68% (Russell, 1989). Similarly, 78% of all households regularly read the daily newspaper 20 years ago; today it is only 64% (Russell, 1989). And it appears that only the leading edge of this fragmentation is currently visible. Each new technological advance seems to increase fragmentation. This appears to be particularly true for broadcast media, where until a few short years ago three major networks and a few hundred local television stations dominated the broadcasting landscape.

These new media include such things as 900 telephone services interactive television, computer bulletin boards, and on-line information services. Table 11.4 provides a partial, but representative list. Each of these new technologies and media formats serves to reduce exposure to more traditional broadcast and print media. Almost all would be considered a type of "broadcast" medium, though it is not clear how much longer the classification of media as print or broadcast will be useful. In fact, it has been suggested that print is now little more than a hard copy of electronic broadcast media (Brand, 1988).

Cutler (1990) called the new interactive media the fifth medium (radio, television, newspapers, and magazines are the first four media). In contrast to the other media, the fifth medium provides the opportunity to advertise, transact the sale, and collect payment at the same time and place. It also has one other important advantage: memory. What an individual has acquired, in terms of information, products, or services, can be captured for future use by either the individual or the marketer. Thus, individuals can automate grocery shopping by storing a shopping list that is automatically called from memory every week. At the same time, marketers can identify who inquired about what product or who bought what item, a prospect that some feel raises issues surrounding individual rights to privacy.

More than 20 years ago E. B. Parker (1970) described a new communications environment that has proven prescient:

TABLE 11.4
The New Media

Television	Telephone
High definition television	Information services
Interactive television	Entertainment services
Videocassette	Conversation lines
Pay-per-view	
Televised "magazines"	
Shopping networks and	
video catalogs	Radio
	Magazines
Televised yellow pages	Conversation radio
"Pocket" television	
Computer	
Information services	Audio
Bulletin boards	Customized recordings
Shopping services	
Messaging and electronic mail	
Conversation channels	

Source. Stewart (1992, p. 9).

This new communication medium can be described as looking like a combination of a television set and a typewriter, functioning like a combination of a newspaper and a library, and permitting a communication network that is something of a combination of a telephone and telegraph system. It has one radical new property that previous mass media lack: what is transmitted over the communication channel is controlled more directly by the receiver than the sender of the message. (p. 53)

The key to Parker's insight is not so much the technology he described. Rather, it is the importance of self-selection on the part of the receiver. Technology has simply facilitated the development of a greater number of options for the consumer, and it is likely that more options will develop in the future. As we noted at the beginning of this chapter, in our discussion of media planning models, advertisers have a rich array of market research information to use in selecting and reaching various types of individuals via mass media.

Increasingly, it is the individual who is doing the selecting. Individuals make selections among media, within media, and even within specific vehicles. Technologies such as VCRs make it possible for viewers to "zap" (mute) television commercials when they interrupt viewing. The link between potential for advertising exposure and actual exposure—always a tenuous one—is weakened all the more in the more diverse and complex media environment and, we suggest, by individual desires for more selectivity in attending to media types, vehicles, content within vehicles, and advertisements.

The range of media options from which consumers can choose is not really the problem, however. The consumer also chooses how he or she will interact with a given medium. The same medium can be highly involving and personally relevant, or little more than background noise depending on the purpose of the consumer. Research on media effects makes it clear that advertising effects will vary considerably depending on what the individual brings to the media usage situation and how the individual chooses to interact with the medium. This suggests that there is a need to measure the ways in which individuals interact with media, in addition to existing measures that merely sort and count individuals that may attend to different media. All of the factors we have reviewed— characteristics of the receiver, characteristics of the medium, characteristics of the message, and media scheduling—play an important role in this interaction. Although this has important theoretical implications, it also has a practical dimension for the advertiser: It is the nature of the interaction with media that increasingly determines its efficiency and effectiveness as a communications tool.

Several conferences and surveys of the advertising community have suggested the need for a set of measures that could be used for making decisions among different media (Advertising Research Foundation, 1961, 1983; Schmalensee, 1983; Schultz, 1979). More than a decade ago Raymond (1976) noted that no acceptable measures of response to advertising exist for comparing vehicles in different media. Raymond was referring only to traditional advertising media, but his comment is even more valid when newer media forms are considered and more selective audiences are hypothesized.

Greater selectivity exercised by individuals means, on the one hand, that it will be more difficult to reach target audiences through traditional mass media. On the other hand, the increase in the number of media vehicles available to consumers and consumers' selectivity in using these vehicles may also provide more opportunities to reach precisely defined audiences with the "optimal" message for the medium and the media use occasion. Realizing this possibility requires several things: (a) a better understanding of how and when people use and interact with various media, (b) a better understanding of how the mode of interaction with various media influences the processing of commercial messages, and (c) a better understanding of how to create commercial messages and distribution strategies that are appropriate in the context of specific media uses. Note that what is needed is not a better understanding of *media*, but a better understanding of how people interact with various forms of media and embedded commercial messages.

A single measure of media quality is not enough. What is needed is a broad set of measures of media interaction. Moeller (1988) in *Beyond Media*, argued that a set of "Media Indicators" are needed, much like we now have social indicators and economic indicators. This would require a comprehensive research program designed to transform qualitative channel characteristics into quantitive scales. In effect, what is needed is a matrix that includes media types on one axis and dimensions of interaction, like those in Table 11.1, on the other axis. Table 11.5 provides a stylistic example of such a matrix. It would probably also be necessary to include some type of measure of use occasion for some channels, because such "uses" are likely to establish the mode of interaction with media.

Although many of the dimensions that may need to be considered have been identified, there is not a large amount of empirical research at this point in time to help us fill in much of the matrix suggested in Table 11.5. Even if the cells of the matrix could be filled, however, there still would not be sufficient information to make well-informed advertising decisions. What is required is a second matrix, like the one illustrated in Table 11.6.

The linking pins between channels of communication and marketing outcomes are the factors that influence the individual's self-selection process and the dimensions of interaction with media. The goals and purposes of the users of media are primary determinants of media effects when users have options. Unfortunately, this is an area that has received rather little attention from researchers (Becker & Schoenbach, 1989). We do not believe that this is the result of lack of theory to guide such research. Rather, it appears to be an artifact of the fact that until recently their were relatively few genuinely different media options available. In such situations the behavior of individuals is restricted and largely dwarfed by such differences in media as do exist.

In closing, we suggest that there are numerous candidate theories for

TABLE 11.5
Media by Dimensions of Interaction

	Involvement	Intrusiveness . . .
Medium 1		
Medium 2		
Medium 3		
.		
.		
.		
Medium n		

TABLE 11.6
Measures of Advertising Effectiveness By Dimensions of
Media Interaction

	Involvement	Intrusiveness . .
Recall		
Comprehension		
Attitude Change		
Persuasion		
Reinforcement		
.		
.		
.		

guiding future research on the use of media and subsequent effects on advertising response. Control theory (Powers, 1973, 1978), with its origins in human factors research and its emphasis on purpose as the link between stimulus inputs and behavioral outcomes, may be particularly appropriate given its emphasis on how people get things done. Bandura's (1986) notion of self-efficacy and Azjen and Madden's (1986) work on goal-directed behavior are also potential candidates. In any case, theoretical approaches to future studies of "media effects" should surely focus on individual characteristics that determine media usage patterns, and dependent measures should be selected to reflect the diversity of outcomes seen in research to date.

ACKNOWLEDGMENTS

The authors gratefully acknowledge the comments of Valerie Folks and Michael Kamins who reviewed earlier drafts of this chapter.

REFERENCES

Aaker, D. A., & Brown, P. K. (1972). Evaluating vehicle source effects. *Journal of Advertising Research, 12,* 11–16.
Aaker, D. A., & Myers, J. G. (1975). *Advertising management.* Englewood Cliffs, NJ: Prentice-Hall.
Advertising Research Foundation. (1983). *1983 member representative questionnaire* (Report 1R). New York: Author.
Advertising Research Foundation, Audience Concepts Committee. (1961). *Toward better media comparisons.* New York: Author.
Agres, S. J., Edell, J. A., & Dubitsky, T. M. (1990). *Emotion in advertising.* New York: Quorum Books.
Ajzen, I., & Madden, J. T. (1986). Prediction of goal-directed behavior: Attitudes, intentions and perceived behavioral control. *Journal of Experimental Social Psychology, 22,* 453–474.

Atkin, C. K. (1985). Informational utility and selective exposure to entertainment media. In D. Zillmann & J. Bryant (Eds.), *Selective exposure to communication* (pp. 63–92). Hillsdale, NJ: Lawrence Erlbaum Associates.

Audits & Surveys, Inc. (1986). *A study of media involvement.* New York: Author.

Bandura, A. (1986). *Social foundations of thought and action: A social cognitive theory.* Engelwood Cliffs, NJ: Prentice-Hall.

Becker, L. B., & Schoenbach, K. (1989). When media content diversifies: Anticipating audience behaviors. In L. B. Becker & K. Schoenbach (Eds.), *Audience response to media diversification, coping with plenty* (pp. 1–28). Hillsdale, NJ: Lawrence Erlbaum Associates.

Berelson, B., Lazarsfeld, P. F., & Mcphee, W. N. (1954). *Voting: A study of opinion formation in a presidential campaign.* Chicago: University of Chicago Press.

Berelson, B., & Steiner, G. A. (1964). *Human behavior: An Inventory of findings.* New York: Harcourt, Brace, & World.

Berkowitz, L., & Rogers, K. H. (1986). A priming effect analysis of media influences. In J. Bryant & D. Zillmann (Eds.), *Perspectives on media effects* (pp. 57–81). Hillsdale, NJ: Lawrence Erlbaum Associates.

Bettman, J. R., & Sujan, M. (1987). Effects of framing on evaluation of comparable and noncomparable alternatives by expert and novice consumers. *Journal of Consumer Research, 14,* 141–154.

Blair, M. H. (1987/1988). An empirical investigation of advertising wearin and wearout. *Journal of Advertising Research, 27,* 45–50.

Brand, S. (1988). *The media lab.* New York: Penguin Books.

Broadbent, D. (1977). The hidden pre-attentive processes. *American Psychologist, 32,* 109–118.

Bryant, J., & Anderson, D. (1983). *Children's understanding of television: Research on attention and comprehension.* New York: Academic Press.

Buchholz, L. M., & Smith, R. E. (1991). The role of consumer involvement in determining cognitive response to broadcast advertising. *Journal of Advertising, 20,* 4–17.

Burke, R. R., & Srull, T. K. (1988). Competitive interference and consumer memory for advertising. *Journal of Consumer Research, 15,* 55–68.

Calder, B. J., & Sternthal, B. (1980). Television commercial wearout: An information processing view. *Journal of Marketing Research, 17,* 173–186.

Chaiken, S. (1980). Heuristic versus systematic information processing and the use of source versus message cues in persuasion. *Journal of Personality and Social Psychology, 29,* 751–766.

Chaiken, S., Liberman, A., & Eagly, A. H. (1989). Heuristic and systematic information processing within and beyond the persuasion context. In J. S. Uleman & J. A. Bargh (Eds.), *Unintended thought: Limits of awareness, intention and control* (pp. 212–252). New York: Guilford.

Chestnut, R. W. (1983). Many issues, few answers: A state of the art review of the intermedia literature. *Advertising research foundation transcript proceedings of the intermedia comparisons workshop.* New York: Advertising Research Foundation.

Chook, P. H. (1983). ARF model for evaluating media, making the promise a reality. *Advertising research foundation transcript proceedings of the intermedia comparisons workshop.* New York: Advertising Research Foundation.

Clemens, J. (1972). The effect of media on advertisement reception. In *Ten years of advertising media research, 1962–1971* (pp. 31–52). London: The Thomson Organization Ltd.

Coffin, T. (1975). *Some notes regarding the design of an ARF study of the automated checkstand as a tool for advertising research.* Unpublished memo.

Condry, J. (1989). *The psychology of television.* Hillsdale, NJ: Lawrence Erlbaum Associates.

Corlett, T. (1971, March). Using media research-perspectives from campaign planning (Media research group seminar, January, 1970). *ADMAP.*

Corlett, T., Lannon, J., & Richardson, D. (1971, April). The use of media. *ADMAP World Advertising Workshop 4*.

Corlett, T., & Richardson, D. (1969). The inter-related effects of press and television advertising. *The Thomson Medals and Awards for advertising research 1969*. London: The Thomson Organization Ltd.

Cutler, B. (1990). The fifth medium. *American Demographics, 12*, 24–29.

Ebbinghaus, H. (1902). *Grundzuge der psychologie [Principles of psychology]*. Leipzig: Viet.

Edell, J. A., & Burke, M. C. (1987). The power of feelings in understanding advertising effects. *Journal of Consumer Research, 14*, 421–433.

Gardner, M. P. (1985). Mood states and consumer behavior: A critical review. *Journal of Consumer Research, 12*, 281–300.

Gensch, D. H. (1970). Media factors: A review article. *Journal of Marketing Research, 7*, 216–225.

Goldberg, M. E., & Gorn, G. J. (1987). Happy and sad TV programs: How they affect reactions to commercials. *Journal of Consumer Research, 14*, 387–403.

Greenberg, B. S. (1988). Some uncommon television images and the drench hypothesis. In S. Oskamp (Ed.), *Television as a social issue* (pp. 88–102). Newbury Park, CA: Sage.

Greenwald, A. C. (1968). Cognitive learning, cognitive response to persuasion, and attitude change. In A. G. Greenwald, T. C. Brock, & T. Ostrom (Eds.), *Psychological foundations of attitudes* (pp. 147–170). New York: Academic Press.

Greenwald, A. C., & Leavitt, C. (1984). Audience involvement in advertising: Four levels. *Journal of Consumer Research, 11*, 581–592.

Guggenheim, B. (1984). *Advertising media planning and evaluation: Current research issues. Vol. 7. Current issues and research in advertising*. Ann Arbor, MI: University of Michigan Graduate School of Business Administration.

Gunter, B. (1985). Determinants of television viewing preferences. In D. Zillmann & J. Bryant (Eds.), *Selective exposure to communication* (pp. 93–112). Hillsdale, NJ: Lawrence Erlbaum Associates.

Haley, R. I. (1985). *Developing effective communications strategy*. New York: Wiley.

Hellige, J. B. (1990). Hemispheric asymmetry. *Annual Review of Psychology, 41*, 55–80.

Herr, P. M. (1989). Priming price: Prior knowledge and context effects. *Journal of Consumer Research, 16*, 67–75.

Higgins, E. T., & King, G. (1981). Accessibility of social constructs: Information processing consequences of individual and contextual variability. In N. Cantor & J. Kihlstrom (Eds.), *Personality, cognition, and social interaction* (pp. 69–122). Hillsdale, NJ: Lawrence Erlbaum Associates.

Holbrook, M. B. (1978). Beyond attitude structure: Toward the information determinants of attitude. *Journal of Marketing Research, 15*, 545–556.

Holbrook, M. B., & Batra, R. (1988). Toward a standardized emotional profile (SEP) useful in measuring responses to the nonverbal components of advertising. In S. Hecker & D. W. Stewart (Eds.), *Nonverbal communication in advertising* (pp. 95–109). Lexington, MA: Lexington Books.

Hovland, C. I., Janis, I. L., & Kelley, H. H. (1953). *Communication and persuasion: Psychological studies of opinion change*. New Haven, CT: Yale University Press.

Hoyer, W. D., Srivastava, R. K., & Jacoby, J. (1984). Examining the sources of advertising miscomprehension. *Journal of Advertising, 13*, 17–26.

Isen, A. M. (1989). Some ways in which affect influences cognitive processes: Implications for advertising and consumer behavior. In P. Cafferata & A. Tybout (Eds.), *Cognitive and affective responses to advertising* (pp. 91–118). Lexington, MA: Lexington Books.

Jacoby, J., & Hoyer, W. D. (1982). Viewer miscomprehension of televised communication: Selected findings. *Journal of Marketing, 46*, 12–26.

Jacoby, J., & Hoyer, W. D. (1989). The comprehension/miscomprehension of print communication: Selected findings. *Journal of Consumer Research, 15,* 434–443.

Jacoby, J., Hoyer, W. D., & Sheluga, D. A. (1980). *Miscomprehension of televised communications.* New York: American Association of Advertising Agencies.

Jacoby, J., Hoyer, W. D., & Zimmer, M. A. (1983). To read, view or listen? A cross-media comparison of comprehension. In J. H. Leigh & C. R. Martin (Eds.), *Current issues and research in advertising* (Vol. 6, pp. 201–218). Ann Arbor: University of Michigan.

Kamins, M. A., Marks, L. J., & Skinner, D. (1991). Television commercial evaluation in the context of program induced mood: Congruency versus consistency effects. *Journal of Advertising, 20,* 1–14.

Katz, E., Blumler, J. G., & Gurevitch, M. (1974). Utilization of mass communication by the individual. In J. Blumler & E. Katz (Eds.), *The uses of mass communication* (pp. 19–32). Beverly Hills, CA: Sage.

Katz, E., & Lazarsfeld, P. F. (1955). *Personal influence: The part played by people in the flow of mass communications.* New York: Free Press.

Kennedy, J. R. (1971). How program environment affects TV commercials. *Journal of Advertising Research, 11,* 33–38.

Klapper, J. T. (1965). The comparative effects of the various media. In W. Schramm (Ed.), *The process and effects of mass communication* (pp. 91–105). Urbana, IL: University of Illinois Press.

Klebber, J. M. (1985). Physiological measures of research: A review of brain activity, electrodermal response, pupil dilation, and voice analysis methods and studies. In J. H. Leigh & C. Martin, Jr. (Eds.), *Current issues and research in advertising* (Vol. 8, pp. 53–76). Ann Arbor, MI: University of Michigan.

Krugman, H. E. (1965). The impact of television advertising: Learning without involvement. *Public Opinion Quarterly, 29,* 349–356.

Krugman, H. E. (1966). The measurement of advertising involvement. *Public Opinion Quarterly, 30,* 583–596.

Krugman, H. E. (1977). Memory without recall, exposure without perception. *Journal of Advertising Research, 17,* 7–12.

Krugman, H. E. (1983). Television program interest and commercial interruption: Are commercials on interesting programs less effective? *Journal of Advertising Research, 23,* 21–23.

Krugman, H. E. (1988). Point of view: Limits of attention to advertising. *Journal of Advertising Research, 28,* 47–50.

Kuss, A. (1985). Missverständnis von Fernsehwerbung [Misunderstanding of television advertising]. *Werbeforschung und Praxis, 6.*

Lazarsfeld, P. F., Berelson, B., & Gaudet, H. (1948). *The people's choice.* New York: Columbia University Press.

Lloyd, D. W., & Clancy, K. J. (1989). The effects of television program involvement on advertising response: Implications for media planning. *Proceedings of the first annual Advertising Research Foundation Media Research Workshop.* New York: Advertising Research Foundation.

Lodish, L. M. (1971). Empirical studies on individual responses to exposure patterns. *Journal of Marketing Research, 8,* 214–216.

McGuire, W. J. (1969). The nature of attitudes and attitude change. In G. Lindzey & E. Aronson (Eds.), *The handbook of social psychology* (Vol. 3). New York: Random House.

McGuire, W. J. (1972). Attitude change: The information-processing paradigm. In C. G. McClintock (Ed.), *Experimental social psychology* (pp. 108–141). New York: Holt, Rinehart & Winston.

McLuhan, M., & Fiore, Q. (1967), *The medium is the message.* New York: Bantam Books.

The Media Book, 1978. (1978). New York: Min-Mid Publishing.

Mitchell, A. A., & Olson, J. C. (1981). Are product attribute beliefs the only mediator of advertising effects on brand attitude? *Journal of Marketing Research, 18*, 318–332.

Moeller, L. G. (1988). In R. W. Budd & B. D. Ruben (Eds.), *Beyond media: New approaches to mass communication* (rev. ed). New Brunswik, NJ: Transaction Books.

Morris, L. A., Brinberg, D., Klimberg, R., Rivera, C., & Millstein, L. G. (1986). Miscomprehension rates for prescription drug advertisements. In J. H. Leigh & C. R. Martin (Eds.), *Current issues and research in advertising* (Vol. 9, pp. 93–118). Ann Arbor: University of Michigan.

Murray, J. P. (1980). *Television and youth: 25 years of research and controversy*. Boys Town, NE: Boys Town Center for the Study of Youth Development.

Nolan, J. (1972). Combined media campaigns. In *Ten years of advertising media research, 1962–1971* (pp. 319–349). London: The Thomson Organization Ltd.

O'Guinn, T. C., & Faber, R. J. (1991). Mass communication and consumer behavior. In T. S. Robertson & H. Kassarjian (Eds.), *Handbook of consumer behavior* (pp. 349–400). Englewood Cliffs, NJ: Prentice-Hall.

Parker, E. B. (1970). Information utilities and mass communication. In H. Sackman & N. Nie (Eds.), *Information utility and social choice*. Montvale, NJ: AFIPS Press.

Pechmann, C., & Stewart, D. W. (1988). A critical review of wearin and wearout. *Current Issues and Research in Advertising, 11*, 28–330.

Pechmann, C., & Stewart, D. W. (1990). The role of comparative advertising: Documenting its effects on attention, recall, and purchase intentions. *Journal of Consumer Research, 17*(2) 180–191.

Petty R. E., & Cacioppo, J. T. (1986). *Communication and persuasion: Central and peripheral routes to attitude change*. New York: Springer-Verlag.

Politz Research, Inc. (1962, November). *A measurement of advertising effectiveness: The influence of audience selectivity and editorial environment*. New York: Author.

Powers, W. T. (1973). Feedback: Beyond behaviorism. *Science, 179*, 351–356.

Powers, W. T. (1978). Quantitative analysis of purposive systems: Some spadework at the foundations of scientific psychology. *Psychological Review, 85*, 417–435.

Ratneshwar, S., & Chaiken, S. (1991). Comprehension's role in persuasion: The case of its moderating effect on the persuasive impact of source cues. *Journal of Consumer Research, 18*, 52–62.

Ray, M. L., & Sawyer, A. G. (1971). Repetition in media models: A laboratory technique. *Journal of Marketing Research, 8*, 20–29.

Raymond, C. (1976). *Advertising research: The state of the art*. New York: Association of National Advertisers.

Reeves, B., Thorson, E., & Schleuder, J. (1986). Attention to television: Psychological theories and chronometric measures. In J. Bryant & D. Zillmann (Eds.), *Perspectives on media effects* (pp. 251–280). Hillsdale, NJ: Lawrence Erlbaum Associates.

Richardson, D. (1972). Measuring the role of media in people's lives. In *Ten years of advertising media research, 1962–1971* (pp. 443–464). London: The Thomson Organization Ltd.

Rossiter, J. R. (1982). Point of view: Brain hemisphere activity. *Journal of Advertising Research, 22*, 75–76.

Rothschild, M. L., & Hyun, Y. J. (1990). Predicting memory for components of TV commercials from EEG. *Journal of Consumer Research, 16*, 472–479.

Rothschild, M. L., Hyun, Y. J., Reeves, B., Thorson, E., & Goldstein, R. (1988). Hemispherically lateralized EEG as a response to television commercials. *Journal of Consumer Research, 15*, 185–198.

Rubin, A. M. (1986). Uses, gratification, and media effects research. In J. Bryant & D. Zillmann (Eds.), *Perspectives on media effects* (pp. 281–302). Hillsdale, NJ: Lawrence Erlbaum Associates.

Russell, C. (1989). People who lust after big numbers *American Demographics, 11,* 2.

Russo, J. E., Metcalf, B. L., & Stephens, D. (1981). Identifying misleading advertising. *Journal of Consumer Research, 10,* 119–131.

Rust, R. T., Kamakura, W. A., & Alpert, M. I. (1991). *Preference segmentation and viewing choice models for network television* (working paper). Owen Graduate School of Management, Vanderbilt University, Nashville, TN.

Rust, R. T., Price, L. L., & Kumar, V. (1985). *EEG response to advertisements in print and broadcast media* (Rep. No. 85–111, December). Cambridge, MA: Marketing Science Institute.

Sawyer, A. G., & Ward, S. (1976). *Carry-over effects in advertising communication: Evidence and hypotheses from behavioral science* (working paper, No. 76–122). Cambridge, MA: Marketing Science Institute.

Schmalensee, D. H. (1983). Today's top priority advertising questions. *Journal of Advertising Research, 23,* 49–60.

Schramm, W. (1965). *The process and effects of mass communication.* Urbana, IL: University of Illinois Press.

Schultz, D. E. (1979). Media research users want. *Journal of Advertising Research, 19,* 13–17.

Schumann, D. W., & Thorson, E. (1990). The influence of viewing context on commercial effectiveness: A selection-processing model. In *Current issues and research in advertising* (Vol. 13, pp. 1–24). Ann Arbor, MI: The University of Michigan.

Schwerin, H. (1958). Do today's programs provide the wrong commercial climate? *Television Magazine, 15,* 45–47, 90–91.

Singh, S. N., & Hitchon, J. C. (1989). The intensifying effects of exciting television programs on the reception of subsequent commercials. *Psychology and Marketing, 6,* 1–31.

Soldow, G. F., & Principe, V. (1981). Response to commercials as a function of program context. *Journal of Advertising Research, 21,* 59–65.

Spaeth, J. (1983, December). Intermedia and intramedia comparisons, evaluations, and needs. *Communication Options,* 21–27.

Srull, T. K. (1990). Individual responses to advertising: Mood and its effects from an information processing perspective. In S. J. Agres, J. A. Edell, & T. M. Dubitsky (Eds.), *Emotion in advertising: Theoretical and practical explorations* (pp. 19–34). New York: Quorum Books.

Stewart, D. W. (1989). Measures, methods, and models of advertising response. *Journal of Advertising Research, 29,* 54–60.

Stewart, D. W. (1992). Speculations on the future of advertising research. *Journal of Advertising, 21,* 1–18.

Stewart, D. W., Furse, D. H., & Kozak, R. (1983). A descriptive analysis of commercial copytesting services. In C. Martin & J. Leigh (Eds.), *Current issues and research in advertising* (Vol. 6, pp. 1–44). Ann Arbor, MI: University of Michigan.

Stewart, D. W., Pechmann, C., Ratneshwar, S., Stroud, J., & Bryant, B. (1985). Methodological and theoretical foundations of advertising copy testing: A review. In *Current issues and research in advertising* (Vol. 8, pp. 1–74). Ann Arbor, MI: University of Michigan.

Strong, E. C. (1974). The use of field experimental observations in estimating recall. *Journal of Marketing Research, 11,* 369–378.

Strong, E. C. (1977). The spacing and timing of advertising. *Journal of Advertising Research, 16,* 25–31.

Thorson, E., & Reeves, B. (1990). Consumer processing of advertising. In J. H. Leigh & C. Martin, Jr. (Eds.), *Current issues and research in advertising* (Vol. 12, pp. 197–230). Ann Arbor, MI: University of Michigan.

Thorson, E., Reeves, B., Schleuder, J., Lang, A., & Rothschild, M. L. (1985). Effect of program context on the processing of television commercials. *Proceedings of the American Academy of Advertising*, R58–63.

Time Inc. (1981). *A study of the effectiveness of advertising frequency in magazines, the relationship between magazine advertising frequency and brand awareness, advertising recall, favorable brand rating, willingness to buy, and product use and purchase.* New York: Research Department, Magazine Group, Time Inc.

Tolley, B. S. (in press). The search. In E. Clark, T. Brock, & D. W. Stewart (Eds.), *Advertising and consumer psychology.* Hillsdale, NJ: Lawrence Erlbaum Associates.

Ward, S., Levinson, D., & Wackman, D. (1972). Children's attention to television advertising. In G. A. Comstock & J. P. Murray (Eds.), *Television and social behavior: Vol. IV. Television in day-to-day life.* Washington, DC: Department of Health, Education and Welfare, HSM 70–9059.

Ward, S., & Ray, M. L. (1976). Experimentation for pre-testing public health programs: The case of the anti-drug abuse campaigns. *Advances in Consumer Research, Vol. 3, Proceedings of the 1975 Association for Consumer Research conference*, 121–126.

Weinstein, S., Appel, V., & Weinstein, C. (1980). Brain activity responses to magazine and television advertising. *Journal of Advertising Research, 20*, 57–63.

Wright, P. L. (1973). The cognitive processes mediating acceptance of advertising. *Journal of Marketing Research, 10*, 53–62.

Wright, P. L. (1981). Cognitive responses to mass media advocacy. In R. E. Petty, T. M. Ostrom, & T. C. Brock (Eds.), *Cognitive responses in persuasion* (pp. 263–282). Hillsdale, NJ: Lawrence Erlbaum Associates.

Wyer, R. S., & Srull, T. K. (1981). Category accessibility: Some theoretical and empirical issues concerning the processing of social stimulus information. In E. T. Higgins, C. P. Herman, & M. P. Zanna (Eds.), *Social cognition: The Ontario Symposium* (pp. 161–197). Hillsdale, NJ: Lawrence Erlbaum Associates.

Yi, Y. (1990a). Cognitive and affective priming effects of the context for print advertisements. *Journal of Advertising, 19*, 40–48.

Yi, Y. (1990b). The effects of contextual priming in print advertisements. *Journal of Consumer Research, 17*, 215–222.

Yuspeh, S. (1977, October). *On-air: Are we testing the message or the medium?* Paper delivered to J. Walter Thompson Research Conference, New York.

Zaichowsky, J. (1985). Measuring the involvement construct. *Journal of Consumer Research, 12*, 341–352.

Zielske, H. A. (1959). The remembering and forgetting of advertising. *Journal of Marketing, 23*, 239–243.

Zielske, H. A., & Henry, W. (1980). Remembering and forgetting television ads. *Journal of Advertising Research, 20*, 7–13.

Zillmann, D. (1971). Excitation transfer in communication-mediated aggressive behavior. *Journal of Experimental Social Psychology, 7*, 419–434.

Zillmann, D., & Bryant, J. (1985). *Selective exposure to communication.* Hillsdale, NJ: Lawrence Erlbaum Associates.

12

Principles of Successful Public Communication Campaigns

RONALD E. RICE
Rutgers University

CHARLES ATKIN
Michigan State University

Public communication campaigns can be broadly defined as

> (1) purposive attempts (2) to inform, persuade, or motivate behavior changes (3) in a relatively well-defined and large audience, (4) generally for noncommercial benefits to the individuals and/or society at large, (5) typically within a given time period, (6) by means or organized communication activities involving mass media, and (7) often complemented by interpersonal support. (Rice & Atkin, 1989, p. 7, adapted and expanded from Rogers & Storey, 1987, p. 821)

The following sections suggest ways in which communication campaign developers, implementors, and researchers can improve the likelihood of campaign success. These 10 principles are naturally based on considerable and diverse theoretical developments, research efforts, and practical experience. Yet many current campaigns still fall far below expectations, many theoretical aspects of campaigns are still only partially understood, and many (often unexpected or uncontrollable) factors may influence the direction, implementation, and outcomes of campaigns. Because campaigns are pragmatically goal oriented, this chapter features a prescriptive tone in presenting the basic principles.

UNDERSTAND HISTORICAL
AND CONCEPTUAL DIMENSIONS

Paisley (1989) proposed that campaigns can be understood through a variety of related concepts:

1. *Objectives* or *methods*: Campaigns can be seen as strategies of social control in order to achieve certain objectives, such as one group's intention to influence another groups' beliefs or behavior (e.g., smoking, abortion, AIDS). This is often the case when social benefits are primary. But campaigns can also be viewed as a genre of communication, including the methods and media that the campaign employs, typically in education strategies.

2. *Strategies of change*: Forest fire prevention researchers at the U.S. Forest Service identified three general classes of strategies, called the Three Es: education, engineering, and enforcement. The relative emphasis of these three strategies of social control varies over time, governments, and cultures. If society has common values, education may be the most effective strategy, but the link between knowledge change and behavior change is tenuous. If government is authoritative and cannot be challenged, enforcement may be the most likely strategy, but it emphasizes costs of noncompliance rather than benefits of compliance. If technology is suitable, an engineering strategy may be applied, but social problems generally exceed the constraints of technology. Thus, each strategy has its strengths and weaknesses.

3. *Individual* or *collective* benefits: Campaigns differ in the explicit and implicit relative costs and benefits of the objectives to individuals and to society.

4. *First-party* and *second-party* entitlement: Central to a campaign's influence on the public at large is the question of who has the right to make claims or attempt public persuasion, and is this source accepted as such by the public? What does the social contract imply about these rights to place a topic on the public agenda? Second-party groups can increase their entitlement by public sacrifice (e.g., Greenpeace's risky defense of whales, civil rights demonstrations by Whites).

5. *Stakeholders*: Diverse interests of associations, government agencies, mass media, and social scientists differentially affect the public agenda, funding sources, campaign design, access to media, objectives, and audiences. More effective campaigns involve relevant stakeholders in the design and operation of the campaign.

In the United States, there is an extensive history of public communication campaign efforts, spanning four eras with their own set of stakeholders: associations, government agencies, mass media, and social science (Paisley, 1989).

Associations: In the 1700s and 1800s, initial reform movements and campaign activities were the results of efforts by individual reformers and voluntary associations, filling gaps left by the limited authority of early American governments. Example reform movements led by prominent individuals included Cotton Mather's campaign for smallpox inoculation, Thomas Paine's defense of women's rights, Benjamin Rush's writings for temperance and women's education, and Carrie Nation's push for women's voting rights. Associations developed local chapters to support abolition, women's suffrage, and liquor prohibition. Strategies of suffragists included grass-roots organizing, legislative testimony, mass communication first through pamphlets and then through newspapers, and confrontations that brought publicity. These early efforts established principles and models for successful reform activities.

Media: By the end of the 19th century, the mass media took the initiative for social reform. Muckraking was not only a response to work, health, and political evils, but also a response by newspapers to growing competition in the marketplace, and was thus a means to increase circulation, not too different in purpose from yellow journalism. Muckrakers emphasized the concept of social responsibility by employers, government, and the media itself.

Government: The efforts of these early reformers led to greater government involvement in reform because the nature of the problems required formal, ongoing regulations, policies, and enforcement. By the turn of the century, the Interstate Commerce Act was the justification for many major laws concerning food, child labor, occupational health, and so on. The New Deal and the Great Society sustained this incursion of government as a powerful stakeholder in campaign activities.

Social scientists: The most recent era is the most familiar, that of applying social science to the development and evaluation of campaigns. As a reaction to the extensive propaganda of World War I, policy makers and researchers initially felt that the mass media had the power to influence large segments of society.

Early social science campaign research was generally pessimistic, leading to an academic era of "minimal effects." Unsuccessful campaigns such as the Cincinnati effort to develop support for the United Nations, along with Lazarsfeld et al.'s "two-step flow" model of interpersonal influence, led researchers to conclude that mass media campaigns had no direct effect, that audiences were largely uninterested or applied selective exposure and perception, and that most effects operated indirectly through opinion leaders.

However, with more specified research on the persuasion process and characteristics of message, source, and medium by Hovland and colleagues, along with some successful campaigns in the 1960s and 70s, researchers began to conclude that campaigns could achieve moderate success if well designed and targeted.

Currently, there is a large and growing body of research on campaign principles that supports this conclusion. However, both empirical, and critical analyses have also challenged some of the long-held beliefs and assumptions about causal relations, the efficacy of the mass media, the role of interpersonal channels, and traditional ways of identifying audience needs.

This chapter summarizes some of these principles for successful campaigns, as well as some of the criticisms and challenges to campaign research, design, and implementation.

APPLY AND EXTEND RELEVANT THEORY

While campaigns are typically viewed as merely applied communication research, the most effective campaigns carefully review and apply relevant theories; further, campaign results can be used to extend and improve theories about media effects and social change. (Rice & Atkin, 1989, p. 9)

Campaign designers, especially those with considerable expertise in the creative and production areas, naturally rely on their personal experience and insights, but they often discount academic theory as too abstract or inapplicable. Although there is some truth to this perception, we should remember Lewin's dictum that there is nothing so practical as good theory. For only when we understand underlying general principles of communication, persuasion and social change, and the relationships among the components of a campaign, can we properly design and evaluate campaign efforts. This is especially true precisely for the reasons social science is often criticized by practitioners: Reality is too complex for an individual's perceptions, especially when based solely on experience gained in a few campaigns, to identify what really causes what and what is and is not effective.

There is a wide range of communication and persuasion theories used to guide campaign efforts. One framework for understanding these processes is McGuire's communication/persuasion model (McGuire, 1989). This model is based on the "hierarchy-of-effects" theory, that any particular step in an individual's processing of a message relies on the outputs from a prior step. The 12 output steps range from (1) exposure to the communication through (12) postbehavioral consolidation. Further, communication inputs include source, message, channel, receiver, and destination variables. So the response steps interact with themselves and with the communication variables to mediate the persuasive response (see Fig. 12.1).

Variants to the straightforward communication/persuasion matrix include:

1. *Elaboration likelihood model* (Petty & Cacioppo, 1986): Messages have greater or longer term effect or are more strongly rejected if the individual is motivated to cognitively process (called elaboration) the message. This is the "central" route to persuasion. Messages may also have modest short-term attitudinal or behavioral effects without knowledge change if the individual is not motivated to cognitively process the message. This is the "peripheral" route.

2. *Self-persuasion*: Rather than relying solely on new, external messages, persuasion attempts may also turn to activating information already accepted, but perhaps without great salience. Thus, resistance

INPUT: Independent (Communication) Variables / OUTPUT: Dependent Variables (Response Steps Mediating Persuasion)	SOURCE (number, unanimity, demographics, attractiveness, credibility ••)	MESSAGE (type appeal, type information, inclusion/omission, organization, repetitiveness)	CHANNEL (modality, directness, context)	RECEIVER (demographics, ability*, personality, life style ••)	DESTINATION (immediacy/delay, prevention/cessation, direct/immunization ••)
1. Exposure to the communication					
2. Attending to it					
3. Liking, becoming interested in it					
4. Comprehending it (learning what)					
5. Skill acquisition (learning how)					
6. Yielding to it (attitude change)					
7. Memory storage of content and /or agreement					
8. Information search and retrieval					
9. Deciding on basis of retrieval					
10. Behaving in accord with decision					
11. Reinforcement of desired acts					
12. Post-behavioral consolidating					

FIG. 12.1. Communication/persuasion matrix (from McGuire, 1989).

to persuasion may be increased by providing prior exposure to threatening messages. Or, internal values may be changed by causing the individual to confront those values, to inspect associated issues, or to evoke new arguments (McGuire, 1960).

3. *Alternate causal chains*: Rather than the simple sequence that knowledge changes attitudes that in turn change behavior, it may well be that changed behavior alters one's attitudes, which then causes one to seek out supportive knowledge (Bem, 1970). Both cognitive dissonance and self-perception theories support this altered causal path.

Whereas McGuire's chapter summarizes 16 classes of theories used to explain persuasion, several of the theories most commonly invoked to guide successful campaigns include the following:

Social learning (Bandura, 1977b): Individuals are likely to exhibit behavior similar to that of role models who are credible, who explicitly model intended behaviors, and who receive appropriate negative or positive reinforcements.

Reasoned action (Ajzen & Fishbein, 1980): A combination of one's personal attitudes, perceived norms of influential others, and motivation to comply provides a parsimonious model of predictors of intended behavior. This model is derived from *expectancy-value* theory, which postulates that one's beliefs about how likely a given behavior leads to certain consequences, multiplied by one's evaluation of those consequences, are likely to predict attitudes and behavior.

Instrumental learning (Hovland, Janis, & Kelley, 1953): The classic model of persuasion combines characteristics of the source (such as attractiveness and credibility), incentives of the message appeal (such as fear, social acceptance, correct knowledge), and repetition and placement of the message to predict changes in knowledge, attitude, and behavior.

Self-efficacy (Bandura, 1977a): The extent to which one feels one has control over one's actions, or can in fact accomplish a task, affects the extent to which one engages in changing one's own attitudes and behaviors. Thus an intermediary goal of a campaign would be to improve the self-efficacy of the at-risk group, such as those attempting to stop smoking (McAlister, Ramirez, Galavotti, & Gallion, 1989) or adolescents attempting to learn and practice behaviors that reduce their risk of AIDS. Crucial to increasing self-efficacy is providing explicit strategies through role models (for children, peers are especially influential) and social comparisons to admired others (Reardon, 1989).

Reardon suggested a variety of other perspectives that can be used in campaigns intended to alter unhealthy behaviors by adolescents: *counterattitudinal advocacy* (observing oneself behaving contrary to one's initial beliefs), learning modes of *reasoning* to use against others pressuring them to take health risks as well as identifying those others' reasoning strategies, *mild fear appeals* focused on valued concerns (such as personal appearance and acceptance by peers) instead of extreme or chronologically distant outcomes, and encouragement of deeply held but possibly unrealistic *illusions* that can be anchors for positive behaviors.

UNDERSTAND THEORETICAL IMPLICATIONS
AND INTERACTIONS OF CAMPAIGN COMPONENTS

Characteristics of the message source or medium—such as viability as a social role model, or credibility—influence a campaign's effectiveness; however, this influence may be in the opposite direction than intended or may conflict with other message components (Rice & Atkin, 1989, p. 10)

Using the communication/persuasion matrix (Fig. 12.1), McGuire (1989) identified some fallacies to avoid.

1. *Attenuated-effects*: Given that each of the 12 steps is likely to be only partially effective, the net multiplicative effect is likely to be quite low. So campaign goals should be modest.

2. *Distant-measure*: Few campaigns are explicit as to the final destination: Is it immediate exposure, liking the message, short-term knowledge change, moderate-term attitude change, or long-term behavioral change? Measuring effects at an early stage has no necessary validity for longer term effects. For example, although the majority of smokers has tried to stop smoking for a short period of time, only a small percentage has been able to maintain cessation. Thus, avoiding relapse is a considerably longer term, but more valid measure of the effect of antismoking campaigns (McAlister et al., 1989).

3. *Neglected-mediator*: It may appear that an attractive source increases step 3 (liking, becoming interested), but the attractiveness may simultaneously distract the comprehension process (Step 4). Or, production standards may predominate in making the source credible and familiar (such as Smokey the Bear) but submerge the message content (as Smokey really doesn't tell us how to prevent forest fires).

4. *Compensatory principle*: Different variables may affect behavior outcome in opposite directions because of their mediating effect. For example, if the audience is aware of the persuasive intent of the source,

perceived trustworthiness may decrease, but clarification of the message may increase.

5. *Golden mean*: Because of some of the other principles and interactions among stages, the eventual outcome may be highest at middle levels of several inputs.

PLAN THE CAMPAIGN: MATCH OBJECTIVES
TO INDIVIDUAL COST-BENEFITS

Campaign objectives must, in some way, appeal to the values and cost-benefits of individuals rather than abstract collective benefits. . . . Long-term prevention objectives seem more difficult to achieve than more immediate campaign benefits; so campaigns aimed at prevention need to link future benefits to present benefits or currently held values. (Rice & Atkin, 1989, p. 10)

Part of the process of identifying campaign objectives is to explicitly plan the campaign (Alcalay & Taplin, 1989), stating the following:

Goals: What do you want the audience to do? Identify where along the hierarchy of effects the campaign objectives lie. It is generally more effective to emphasize current rewards and positive behavior changes rather than distant outcomes and negative consequences (Backer, Rogers & Sopory, 1992). Decide whether the objectives are short term or long term.

Media objectives: What percentage of what subaudience in what area do you want to have access to how many messages? Use broadcast ratings for the specific region and audience, and tracking surveys to determine delivery, exposure, and recall.

Media timing: What media channels and what media content are used at what times in the campaign process? In a Honduras health communication campaign, during the rainy season, rehydration treatment messages were provided, whereas before the rainy season, underlying concepts about health, cleanliness, and causes of diarrhea and dehydration were more important.

Media choice: Which specific media will be used, for what specific characteristics? Consider the competition these media and the messages will be facing. For example, in a Gambian campaign, few villagers could read, so a variety of nontext media were used. Colorful posters were distributed that graphically showed how an infant rehydration mix should be used; these posters were valued visual additions to modest living quarters, but also provided continuing reinforcement of the message (Rice & Foote, 1989).

McGuire suggested that three criteria should be applied before campaign efforts are expended on specific objectives: Is the problem serious?; is the solution effective?; and is mass persuasion an appropriate way to achieve the objectives? If these criteria cannot be met, perhaps the objectives should be changed.

Solomon (1989) described another approach to campaigns that builds upon the experience in marketing and advertising fields: *social marketing*. It applies a marketing approach to social concepts. It is based on the fundamental principle of exchange theory: Individuals will engage in transactions to the extent that the exchange is fair and useful. Campaigns that simply transmit a message fail to accommodate this principle. Or, campaigns that attempt to induce individual sacrifice for a collective benefit will, in general, and unfortunately, achieve minimal results. Analyses of the famous Chinese campaigns show clearly that even the Chinese have realized this principle: Campaigns ostensibly identified as successful examples of collective sacrifice have generally been shown later to be failures or misrepresentations. The most successful major Chinese campaign, to reduce childbearing to one or two per family, has come to depend on both incentives and sanctions at the individual level (Rice, 1989).

Campaigns applying a social marketing perspective would attempt to identify and respond to all these primary marketing challenges (Solomon, 1989):

1. *Product*: An associated physical product (such as condoms) may help to make a concept (such as family planning) more concrete. A campaign may develop a "product line" of concepts, so that different audiences can enter into the transaction at their level of expertise, motivation, or effort.

2. *Price*: Every product and campaign objective has a variety of costs to the potential audience member, such as time, money, cultural constraints, peer acceptance, conflict with personal desires, and so on. These must be identified, accommodated, and dealt with in the full campaign context. Price may signal value; for example, family planning campaigns in India were much more successful when condoms were sold for a small price instead of given away.

3. *Place*: What are the campaign's distribution channels? The audience should be able to obtain the information, product, or service easily, and the service provider should be prepared for a successful response.

4. *Promotion*: How should the social concept be promoted, and how can the audience be continually motivated to obtain it? Formative evaluation, audience analysis, and media analysis must be involved.

5. *Positioning*: Any product, whether commercial or social, must compete for mental mindspace with other products and will be associated with others, whether positively or negatively. A campaign should

identify how the concept is already positioned, and how that position can be improved. For example, is family planning perceived as a legal, moral, health, and/or personal issue? Where in the scheme of popular food products are "heart-healthy" foods positioned in the public's mind?

Other important social marketing precepts discussed by Solomon include: Segment the audience, understand all relevant markets, develop information and feedback systems, mix interpersonal and mass communication, utilize commercial resources, and understand the competition.

APPLY FORMATIVE EVALUATION

Formative evaluation of specific campaign objectives and media messages is crucial to developing effective campaigns; it is also necessary to identify and understand the needs and media habits of the relevant audiences. (Rice & Atkin, 1989, p. 10)

As part of campaign management, information and feedback systems should be implemented. After all, campaigns are complex, longitudinal projects. They must be monitored for ongoing administration, scheduling, delivery of materials, effectiveness, diagnosis, and improvement.

An important part of this campaign planning and design is *formative evaluation*, which "provides data and perspectives to improve messages during the course of creation" (Atkin & Freimuth, 1989, p. 131).

A general goal of formative evaluation is to understand the "sociocultural situation," what McGuire called "the situational circumstances [whether economic, cultural, political, psychological, etc.] that instigate and maintain the undesirable target behavior or that sustain the desired target behavior" (p. 63). This understanding is obtained through *preproduction research*. Messages are then revised based on *production testing* (pretesting).

Atkin and Freimuth identified these stages in preproduction research:

1. *Identify the target audiences*: Who is at risk, who is accessible through communication channels, who can influence others at risk, and who is most and least persuasible?

2. *Specify the target behavior*: Insofar as most global behaviors consist of component behaviors (i.e., pregnancy can be prevented in a variety of ways, and responded to in a variety of ways) that are influenced by contextual factors (i.e., religion, socioeconomic status, support groups, information about family planning, etc.), campaign messages should

focus on specific effective component behaviors. For example, formative evaluation of weight-loss messages found that whereas women were aware of their weight problems and motivated to change, men greatly underestimated their weight problem, were not generally motivated to change, and had low self-efficacy about their ability to lose weight (Flora, Maccoby, & Farquhar, 1989). Indeed, McAlister, Ramirez, Galavotti, and Gallion (1989) argued that in addition to *informing* audiences about behaviors and their consequences and *persuading* audiences to change those unhealthy or dangerous behaviors, campaigns must also provide specific *training* of skills necessary to change behavior and maintain that changed behavior, as well as resist opposing influences from the mass media or peers.

3. *Elaborate intermediate responses*: As the hierarchy-of-effects model suggests, there is a long causal chain between exposure and integrated behavior. Formative evaluation can identify how these steps are linked and what intermediate steps are most amenable to campaign efforts. Some of the intermediate responses include knowledge and lexicon, beliefs and images, attitudes and values, salience, priorities, and skills. For example, Cialdini (1989, p. 222) argued that campaigns must distinguish between portraying *prescriptive* norms (perceptions of what behaviors are societally approved) and *popular* norms (perceptions of which behaviors are typically performed). Some campaigns may have been unintentionally providing persuasive models of undesirable but popular norms while explicitly concentrating on desirable but unpopular prescriptive norms.

4. *Ascertain channel use*: Using any kind of media without knowing which media the target audience uses, at what times, for how long or how many times, and in what combination is an ineffective use of campaign resources. Formative evaluation can identify media exposure and attitudes toward the different media. (See the sections on media and audience analysis.)

Then these stages of pretesting research can be applied (Atkin & Freimuth, 1989):

1. *Develop the concept*: Although some campaigns have a very specific understanding of the concept to be communicated, often test audiences can suggest and amplify new or more appropriate concepts. Or, more relevant message sources (e.g., should the source be a doctor or a neighbor?) can be identified. Words, phrases, or descriptions used by target audiences in their discussions about the campaign topic can also be incorporated into message content.

2. *Execute the test message*: Rough, preliminary versions of messages can be tested for the following attributes: attention, comprehensibility, relevance, or controversial aspects.

Several methods are useful, in pretesting messages, including focus group interviews, in-depth interviews, central-location intercept interviews, self-administered questionnaires, theater testing, day-after recall, media gatekeeper review, and physiological response analysis. The Health Message Testing Service, sponsored by the U.S. Department of Health and Human Services, was a standardized system of questionnaire items and theater testing to pretest radio and television messages.

ANALYZE AND UNDERSTAND THE AUDIENCES

The campaign message must reach a sufficiently large proportion of the desired audience, but the message must be a product of individuals' needs and must contribute to their own goals. (Rice & Atkin, 1989, p. 10)

Audience segmentation is necessary to identify internally homogeneous subaudiences, both to be able to provide a relevant message for that audience, and to efficiently use mass media channels. Segmentation may involve analyses of demographics, media ratings, lifestyle, psychographics, ZIP code, uses and gratifications, and channel accessibility.

Dervin (1989) proposed an alternative to the traditional approaches to identifying audience needs and designing appropriate messages. The *sense-making* approach rejects the notion that information is objective content that can be packaged and transmitted, and that audiences simply lack that expert information that can solve their problems.

The sense-making perspective seeks to understand how individuals attempt to make sense out of their world as they move along various situational paths. The core challenge that individuals face, in this approach, is how to "define and bridge gaps in their everyday lives" (p. 40). The objective is to provide informational resources that are context specific and available along those personal routes. Further, campaigns must allow individuals to deal with competing information claims. That is, individuals need to know the motives and reasons for events, rather than just facts about them. Then the individuals can make sense of those new resources and use them in making decisions and taking action. Thus campaigners must conceptualize their efforts as entering into a dialogue with individuals, instead of as transmitting content. "The researcher is mandated to attend to what is called the sense-making triangle: How the respondent sees the situation, what gaps the respondent sees self as facing and/or bridging, and what ways the respondent saw self as helped by the bridge he or she built" (p. 77).

The sense-making approach is less well suited to large-scale mass media campaigns, though results from its intensive, qualitative and quantitative, ethnographic, and systematic procedures in specific contexts may be useful in broader applications.

ANALYZE AND UNDERSTAND MEDIA CHOICES

Campaigns must make their messages available through a variety of communication channels that are accessible and appropriate for the target audience, but the message must also communicate specific information, understandings, and behaviors that are actually accessible, feasible, and culturally acceptable. (Rice & Atkin, 1989, p. 10)

We have seen that the communication/persuasion matrix, along with formative evaluation, can be used to design or identify persuasive and informational attributes of source, message, and channel. A social marketing perspective also emphasizes the need to understand the competition: Design the campaign objective to be attractive, desirable, and accessible relative to other media, other messages, and other behaviors. Any mass media message competes with hundreds of other messages. Any concept competes with dozens of related mental concepts. So, there is a need to identify the "competitive advantage" of the particular campaign objective. For example, exercising as a means of preventing heart disease can also be advertised as a social activity.

Alcalay and Taplin (1989) highlighted the importance and utility of *public relations* ("news about an issue, service, client, or product," p. 116) and *public affairs* ("lobbying and working on regulatory or legislative issues with administrators and legislators," p. 122). Because it is free and has "third party" credibility, public relations can be very useful in not only increasing public awareness of a campaign, but also in deterring opposition to an otherwise controversial issue, such as family planning. Public affairs is important not only in shaping legislation that may affect campaign objectives, but also in gaining support for resources and spokespeople. Editorials, press releases, and hard news coverage may also be powerful media outlets, when managed properly.

It is common practice to request local and sometimes national media to provide *public service announcements* (PSAs). The practice of broadcasting PSAs was in large part an outgrowth of Federal Communication Commission requirements that stations using the broadcasting frequencies served the public interest and necessity. With the increase in media outlets and the movement toward deregulation of the media, opportunities to broadcast PSAs have declined. It can be argued that PSAs are typically of limited value anyway, because they cannot be scheduled for times when the specific target audience is most likely to be watching or listening, or in known amounts of exposure. Nevertheless, PSAs can be placed on local radio stations or in print media that are more likely to reach a target audience, such as teenagers or retired people, if the campaign implementors understand the audience's media usage patterns.

Commercial *broadcast rating* services (such as Nielsen, Arbitron, AGB, Standard Rate and Data Services, Birch, etc.) can help identify the most effective and efficient channels. For example, media books can be used to calculate the effective *CPM*—the cost to reach 1,000 of your target audience through one presentation of your message via a mass medium. Similar data are available for newspapers, magazines, billboards, mailing lists, and even bus posters. By providing figures to calculate the percentage of the target audience exposed to the program or channel at specific time periods, as well as the extent to which audiences change across time periods or are consistent, campaign implementors can determine the *reach* (number of different individuals in the audience) or *frequency* (number of times any individual may be exposed). Different campaign objectives would be achieved through increased reach or increased frequency. For example, increasing awareness about a common issue by the public at large could be achieved more cost effectively through using a specific time/channel combination to maximize reach. However, achieving and maintaining learning or attitude change in a specific at-risk audience would require increased frequency, which may involve a different time/channel mix. A jazz or classical music station, for example, may have high frequency but low reach.

The Advertising Council provides in-kind creative and agency services to support approximately 36 public communication campaigns a year in the United States. Further, in-place commercial distribution channels can be used to support delivery of campaign messages and materials. For example, getting 7-11 or Sears stores involved in a campaign would provide immediate delivery channels across the United States.

Finally, recent campaigns, such as a sexual abstinence campaign in Mexico, and the Be Smart! Don't Start! anti-alcohol campaign in the United States, have begun to engage in cooperative efforts with the entertainment industry to produce attractive and popular music videos or PSAs with celebrities, rock stars, and commercial production teams. These are extensions, or derivations, of prosocial television programs such as *Freestyle* in the United States (LaRose, 1989), and *Hum Log* in India (Singhal & Rogers, 1989). This form of campaign, sometimes called *infotainment* or *edu-entertainment*, consciously mixes theories of social modelling (providing role models for behavior and attitudes), parasocial interaction (getting the audience personally involved in the characters and content), and expectancy value (combining perceived social norms with beliefs about the source's normative expectations concerning those norms) with commercial entertainment values, media personalities, and wide-scale distribution. Celebrities often provide credible and influential sources, especially for certain at-risk populations who distrust, or are not otherwise exposed to, traditional authority figures.

MIX MULTIPLE MEDIA
AND INTERPERSONAL CHANNELS
WHEN COST-EFFECTIVE

Behavioral change is more likely generated and maintained through interpersonal support, especially through preexisting social networks, but for many campaigns this approach may not be cost-effective. (Rice & Atkin, 1989, p. 10)

Examples such as organized listening groups in Tanzania's health campaigns, peer moderators for televised smoking cessation programs, and counseling groups that support disease prevention efforts all show that although mass media can be independently successful, greater and longer lasting effects typically follow from interpersonal communication support. The underlying principle here is that individuals' social contexts provide strong influences—and often strong constraints—on the individuals' attitudes and behavior. For example, a videotape teaching self-management techniques for smoking cessation, accompanied by a live peer moderator who provides social reinforcement and encourages the audience to discuss the content and imitate those techniques, can be a quite effective component of smoking cessation campaigns (McAlister et al., 1989). Further, there is evidence not only that mass media can stimulate interpersonal communication about a campaign topic, but that interpersonal communication can stimulate common use of the mass media as well (Rice & Foote, 1989).

Hornik (1989) challenged this argument, however, by critiquing assumptions underlying measurement, theory, data, and practice of much campaign research on the mass media/interpersonal mix. First, in many contexts, especially development campaigns, it is quite difficult to recruit, pay for, train, manage, and retain interpersonal support, especially over a wide area with complex logistical constraints. Second, it is not necessarily true that media are "more" effective when combined with interpersonal communication; Hornik provided evidence that the two channels have independent effects. Thus mass media not only have the obviously greater reach compared to interpersonal communication, but they are generally more effective (per unit of exposure) and cost effective (per unit of cost) as well. Hornik's arguments also challenge the traditional assumption that mass media are useful only to raise awareness, whereas interpersonal communication is necessary to inform and persuade.

Another means of integrating media and interpersonal communication is to conduct and involve campaign activities at the community level. As Alcalay and Taplin (1989) suggested, "By working with local resources, health care practitioners involved in an intervention can translate general health education project goals into locally meaningful ones and project activities into culturally acceptable and affordable ones" (p. 106).

Flora, Maccoby, and Farquhar (1989) emphasized community-level approaches in the Stanford Five-City Multifactor Risk Reduction (heart disease prevention) Program. Three models of community mobilization were applied as appropriate: (a) *consensus development*, or participation by diverse community members; (b) *social action*, or mobilizing the community to create new social structures and engage in the political process; and (c) *social planning*, or using expert data to propose and plan system-wide change. Campaign messages, resources, and activities were planned through media, training instructors, workplace contests and workshops, schools, restaurants and grocery stores, health professionals, and contests or lotteries.

UNDERSTAND USES AND CONTRADICTIONS OF MASS MEDIA

Mass media can be used to improve awareness and knowledge, to stimulate interpersonal communication, and to recruit others to join in, but commercial media may also help to create or reinforce the initial problems. (Rice & Atkin, 1989, p. 10)

Media can present a wide variety of contradictions for public communication campaigns (Wallack, 1989).

1. *Unhealthy agendas*: Some have claimed that the single most negative health influence in the United States is the portrayal of a wide

variety of unhealthy behaviors, incorrect medical information, and antisocial attitudes on television—in both programs and commercials.

2. *Commercial concerns*: There are many instances of both explicit and implicit advertiser control over program content. Sponsors of alcoholic beverages or drugstore remedies are not likely to encourage either program content that attempts to reduce or question such consumption, or counter advertisements.

3. *Social norms*: Stereotypes of male–female roles, race relations, age-specific behaviors, behavior by medical personnel, and treatments of physical and mental problems are all developed and reinforced through media portrayals that overwhelm attempts by other messages to reduce such stereotypes.

4. *Violent and sexual content*: It has been argued that perceived higher levels of fear, and submissive behavior toward authority, are reported by those who watch more television, especially television with violent content. Greater acceptance of aggressive sexual acts against women have been reported for viewers of films with violent sexual content. It is difficult for family planning or AIDS prevention campaigns to compete with regular program and advertising content that portrays and glamorizes irresponsible or promiscuous sexual behaviors.

5. *Maintaining the consumption ethic*: The media are businesses, and their business is to sell consumers to advertisers. So the underlying message is that consumption is good. Complex matters must be dealt with in simplistic ways that do not alienate large audiences. For instance, televised dramas about AIDS may show the effects on a normal family of the accidental contraction by a child of AIDS through blood transfusion, rather than deal with more likely causes in the United States such as unsafe sexual practices or intravenous drug use.

6. *Individual blame and simplification of complex issues*: Because consumption is an individual choice in a free-market economy, health and social problems are also seen as individually caused and individually solved. The social and economic causes—such as government policies or corporate irresponsibility—of many of our social ills are rarely dealt with at those levels by the mass media in general or even in campaigns in particular.

IDENTIFY REASONABLE CRITERIA FOR CAMPAIGN SUCCESS, AND USE SUMMATIVE EVALUATION TO ASSESS BOTH THEORY AND PROGRAM SUCCESS

Campaign objectives and criteria for success should be reasonable; not only is it difficult to pass through all the individual's information processing stages and to overcome constraints on resources, beliefs, and behavior, but many public communication campaigns have typically set higher standards for success than the most successful commercial campaigns. (Rice & Atkin, 1989, p. 10)

As Flay and Cook (1989) proposed, *summative evaluation* consists of identifying and measuring answers to question about six campaign aspects: (a) the *audience* (e.g., size, characteristics), (b) *implementation* of the planned campaign components (e.g., as exposure of the audience to messages and/or services), (c) *effectiveness* (e.g., influence on attitudes, behaviors, and health conditions), (d) *impacts* or effects on larger aggregations (e.g., families or government agencies), (e) *cost* (e.g., total expenditures, and cost-effectiveness), and (f) *causal* processes (e.g., isolating the reasons why effects occurred or not).

Proper summative evaluation can distinguish between *theory failure*, the extent to which underlying causal chains are rejected by the evaluation results, and *program failure*, the extent to which the implementation of the campaign was inadequate or incorrect, thus allocating blame, credit, and lessons for future campaigns accordingly.

Flay and Cook identified six challenges to summative evaluators:

1. There are inherent *trade-offs* in abilities to answer any given subset of the six questions.
2. Different evaluator *stakeholders* are interested in different subsets of the six questions.
3. It is difficult to identify and reach the small *subaudiences* that are at risk.
4. The *salience* of, and exposure to, campaign messages, is generally low.
5. *Casual chains* in the theoretical foundations of a specific campaign are long, complex, and often questionable.
6. *Sample sizes* tend to be low; indeed, good research design calls for different treatment and control conditions at the community level, generally resulting in analysis sample sizes of a half-dozen or less.

There are three general evaluation models that attempt to respond to these challenges in different ways.

The *advertising* model focuses on the early stages of the communication hierarchy of effects: exposure, recall, liking, self-reported behavioral intentions, and message characteristics. Through the use of cross-sectional surveys, the success of a campaign in these stages can be assessed, especially at the individual level of analysis, but few causal inferences or evidence of behavioral outcomes are possible.

The *impact-monitoring* model focuses on the more distal stages and social impacts in the hierarchy of effects, through tracking of archival data such as population trends, consumption behaviors, epidemiological information, and so on. Such analyses cannot unravel causal factors leading up to these distal outcomes, so it is difficult to unambiguously detect significant effects.

The *experimental* model focuses on testing hypothesized casual chains through controlled manipulation of treatments, often requiring lengthy and complex campaigns. To insure valid analyses, units of analysis should consist of communities or regions, greatly reducing the power of the analysis and highlighting challenges to controlling for confounding explanations.

Flay and Cook suggested that the greatest insights will come from meta-evaluations of different approaches to similar problems, which will overcome the specific but often different weaknesses of the individual studies.

Rice and Foote (1989) suggested a *systems-theoretical* approach to planning campaign evaluation, with particular application to health communication campaigns in developing countries. The approach includes these stages:

1. Specifying the goals and underlying assumptions of the project.
2. Specifying the process model at the project level.
3. Specifying prior states, system phases, and system constraints.
4. Specifying immediate as well as long-term intended poststates.
5. Specifying the process model at the individual level.
6. Choosing among research approaches appropriate to the system.
7. Assessing implications for design.

Similarly comprehensive programs of systems planning and integrated campaigns have been applied to complex problems such as rat control in grain-producing countries (Adhikarya, 1989).

The basic assumption is that campaign inputs intended to alter prior states are mediated by a set of system constraints, enter into a process whereby some inputs are converted into outputs, and evolve into a new poststate, including altered system constraints. Further, this dynamic system occurs at the global project level, the community level, and the individual level of analysis. Campaign evaluation planning must match the timing and nature of inputs (such as media channels, messages, and material resources) and measurements with relevant phases of the system. Rice and Foote distinguished between *planned, real,* and *engaged* inputs. A campaign may plan four radio spots per day on a particular station, whereas only three are actually broadcast, only 40% of the audience had the radio turned on during the day, and only 60% of those could recall any campaign messages. Informed campaign evaluations should measure and analyze these kinds of inputs separately.

Figure 12.2 provides an example summary of inputs, short-term individual-level responses, and longer term individual and system poststates.

CONCLUSION

We would like to end simply by noting that a variety of theoretical and practical challenges and tensions continue to exist in the design, implementation, and evaluation of public communication campaigns.

Many important social problems involve *collective benefits* (such as littering), yet most campaigns have succeeded only when they promote *individual benefits*. How can campaigns increase the salience of collective benefits?

What is the proper mix of *education* and *entertainment?* Will or should new "infotainment" campaigns be embedded in the commercial media mainstream?

How can campaigns, which generally use the mass media, overcome the *simultaneous pervasive negative influence of the mass media* on the campaign issue (such as alcoholism or violence)?

Few theories or campaign designs explicitly distinguish *short-term* from *long-term* effects and objectives. What should be the relative

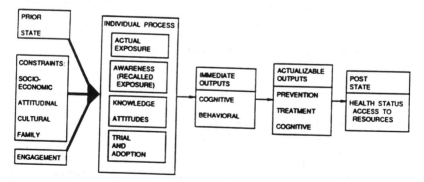

FIG. 12.2. System-theoretic model of prior states, constraints, individual-level process, outputs, and poststate in campaign evaluation (from Rice & Foote, 1989).

emphasis on each, and how can campaigns achieve longer term outcomes?

What is the proper mix of *interpersonal* and *mass media* communication for specific campaign goals?

How can campaigns successfully promote a *prevention* approach in order to avoid the generally more expensive and less effective *treatment* approach typically favored by organizations, government agencies, and the electorate?

What are the relative influences of *individual differences* versus *social structure* on the problems targeted by communication campaigns?

What are the potential roles of *new communication media*, such as electronic mail, voice response systems, interactive video, and computer games, in reaching particular at-risk populations and in influencing learning, attitudes, and behaviors (Rice and Associates, 1984)?

Future campaign research and policy debates should explicitly consider these important challenges. Finally, of course, researchers should seek out, replicate, and document campaign approaches and results. Adhikarya (1989), as did Flay and Cook (1989), Flora, Maccoby, and Farquhar (1989), and Rice and Foote (1989), argued that only with continual documentation of campaign processes and results, and comparisons of results across campaigns, can future campaigns apply the lessons learned from such systematic campaigns. Additional annotated sources for such summaries and reviews are provided in the Appendix by Rice and Atkin (1989), as well as in Backer, Rogers, and Sopory (1992), who also suggested 27 generalizations about successful health communication campaigns (pp. 30–32).

ACKNOWLEDGMENT

The preparation of this chapter was supported by a Visiting Research Fellowship awarded to Dr. Rice, Summer, 1989, c/o Dr. Elizabeth More School of English and Linguistics, MacQuarie University Sydney, New South Wales 2109. The manuscript for this chapter was submitted to the editors in 1990.

REFERENCES

Adhikarya, R. (1989). Rat control in Bangladesh. In R. E. Rice & C. Atkin (Eds.), *Public communication campaigns* (2nd ed., pp. 230–232). Newbury Park, CA: Sage.

Ajzen, I., & Fishbein, M. (1980). *Understanding attitudes and predicting social behavior.* Englewood Cliffs, NJ: Prentice-Hall.

Alcalay, R., & Taplin, S. (1989). Community health campaigns: From theory to action. In R. E. Rice & C. Atkin (Eds.), *Public communication campaigns* (2nd ed., pp. 105–130). Newbury Park, CA: Sage.

Atkin, C., & Freimuth, V. (1989). Formative evaluation research in campaign design. In R. E. Rice & C. Atkin (Eds.), *Public communication campaigns* (2nd ed., pp. 131–150). Newbury Park, CA: Sage.

Backer, T., Rogers, E. M., & Sopory, P. (1992). *Designing health communication campaigns: What works?* Newbury Park, CA: Sage.

Bandura, A. (1977a). Self-efficacy: Toward a unifying theory of behavioral change. *Psychological Review, 84*(2), 191–215.

Bandura, A. (1977b). *Social learning theory.* Englewood Cliffs, NJ: Prentice-Hall.

Bem, D. (1970). *Beliefs, attitudes and human affairs.* Belmont, CA: Brooks/Cole.

Cialdini, R. (1989). Littering: When every litter bit hurts. In R. E. Rice & C. Atkin (Eds.), *Public communication campaigns* (2nd ed., pp. 221–223). Newbury Park, CA: Sage.

Dervin, B. (1989). Audience as listener and learner, teacher and confidante: The sense-making approach. In R. E. Rice & C. Atkin (Eds.), *Public communication campaigns* (2nd ed., pp. 43–66). Newbury Park, CA: Sage.

Flay, B., & Cook, T. (1989). Three models for summative evaluation of prevention campaigns with a mass media component. In R. E. Rice & C. Atkin (Eds.), *Public communication campaigns* (2nd ed., pp. 175–196). Newbury Park, CA: Sage.

Flora, J., Maccoby, N., & Farquhar, J. (1989). Communication campaigns to prevent cardiovascular disease: The Stanford community studies. In R. E. Rice & C. Atkin (Eds.), *Public communication campaigns* (2nd ed., pp. 233–252). Newbury Park, CA: Sage.

Hornik, R. (1989). Channel effectiveness in development communication programs. In R. E. Rice & C. Atkin (Eds.), *Public communication campaigns* (2nd ed., pp. 309–330). Newbury Park, CA: Sage.

Hovland, C., Janis, I., & Kelley, H. (1953). *Communication and persuasion.* New Haven, CT: Yale University Press.

LaRose, R. (1989). Freestyle, revisited. In R. E. Rice & C. Atkin (Eds.), *Public communication campaigns* (2nd ed., pp. 206–209). Newbury Park, CA: Sage.

McAlister, A., Ramirez, A., Galavotti, C., & Gallion, K. (1989). Antismoking campaigns: Progress in the application of social learning theory. In R. E. Rice & C. Atkin (Eds.), *Public communication campaigns* (2nd ed., pp. 291–308). Newbury Park, CA: Sage.

McGuire, W. (1960). A syllogistic analysis of cognitive relationships. In C. Hovland & M. Rosenberg (Eds.), *Attitude organization and change* (pp. 65–111). New Haven, CT: Yale University Press.

McGuire, W. (1989). Theoretical foundations of campaigns. In R. E. Rice & C. Atkin (Eds.), *Public communication campaigns* (2nd ed., pp. 43–66). Newbury Park, CA: Sage.

Paisley, W. (1989). Public communication campaigns: The American experience. In R. E. Rice & C. Atkin (Eds.), *Public communication campaigns* (2nd ed., pp. 15–38). Newbury Park, CA: Sage.

Petty, R., & Cacioppo, J. (1986). *Communication and persuasion: Central and peripheral routes to attitude change.* New York: Springer-Verlag.

Reardon, K. (1989). The potential role of persuasion in adolescent AIDS prevention. In R. E. Rice & C. Atkin (Eds.), *Public communication campaigns* (2nd ed., pp. 273–290). Newbury Park, CA: Sage.

Rice, R. E. (1989). Mass campaigns in the People's Republic of China during the Mao era. In R. E. Rice & C. Atkin (Eds.), *Public communication campaigns* (2nd ed., pp. 212–215). Newbury Park, CA: Sage.

Rice, R. E. and Associates. (1984). *The new media: Communication, research and technology.* Newbury Park, CA: Sage.

Rice, R. E., & Atkin, C. (Eds.). (1989). *Public communication campaigns* (2nd ed.). Newbury Park, CA: Sage.

Rice, R. E., & Foote, D. (1989). A systems-based evaluation planning model for health communication campaigns in developing countries. In R. E. Rice & C. Atkin (Eds.), *Public communication campaigns* (2nd ed., pp. 151–174). Newbury Park, CA: Sage.

Rogers, E. M., & Storey, D. (1987). Communication campaigns. In C. Berger & S. Chaffee (Eds.), *Handbook of communication science* (pp. 817–846). Newbury Park, CA: Sage.

Singhal, A., & Rogers, E. M. (1989). Prosocial television for development in India. In R. E. Rice, and C. Atkin (Eds.), *Public communication campaigns* (2nd ed., pp. 331–350). Newbury Park, CA: Sage.

Solomon, D. (1989). A social marketing perspective on communication campaigns. In R. E. Rice & C. Atkin (Eds.), *Public communication campaigns* (2nd ed., pp. 87–104). Newbury Park, CA: Sage.

Wallack, L. (1989). Mass media and health promotion: A critical perspective. In R. E. Rice & C. Atkin (Eds.), *Public communication campaigns* (2nd ed., pp. 353–368). Newbury Park, CA: Sage.

13

Effects of Media on Personal and Public Health

JANE D. BROWN
University of North Carolina-Chapel Hill

KIM WALSH-CHILDERS
University of Florida

Both health professionals and communication researchers are interested in the mass media's potential to affect health. Studies typically have focused on the negative effects of advertising and the entertainment media, particularly television, on unhealthy behaviors, and the possibilities for health educators to use the mass media to encourage people to live healthier lives. Although these two types of health effects have received the most research attention, they do not represent the only, nor even necessarily the most important, influences on health. As health policy expert Nancy Milio (1986) pointed out, the mass media can influence health at both a personal and public level. At the personal level, the mass media may provide information and models that stimulate changes—either positive or negative—in health-related attitudes and behaviors. At the public level, the mass media also may raise awareness of health issues among policy makers and, thus, may contribute to changing the context in which people make choices about their health.

These effects of the media may be intended by the message producer, as is the case when health educators develop public information campaigns, or may be unintended, as is the case when viewers adopt unhealthy behaviors that are portrayed only for entertainment value on television programs. Clearly, these effects are not always positive, at

TABLE 13.1
Examples of the Potential Effects of the Mass Media on Personal and Public Health

		Personal
Intended	Positive	More people designate a non-drinking driver after seeing TV characters do it.
	Negative	
Unintended	Positive	A TV news report on Pres. Reagan's colon cancer stimulates people to be tested.
	Negative	Adolescent girls begin smoking cigarettes after repeated exposures to cigarette ads.
		Public
Intended	Positive	A referendum for strict air quality controls passes after a media campaign sponsored by a coalition of health and environmental groups.
	Negative	
Unintended	Positive	A state legislator introduces a bill to provide low-cost prenatal care after a series of newspaper articles on infant mortality.
	Negative	Increased funding for antidrug campaign following media coverage results in decreased funding for other health-related education.

least from a public health point of view. The three dimensions—level (personal/public), intention of the message producer (intended/ unintended), and value (positive/negative)—can be plotted together to form a typology of the potential effects of the media on health. The typology and examples of the kinds of effects are presented in Table 13.1.

Two cells of the typology are empty because as far as we know no public or private health agency, advertiser, or media producer would produce messages that were intended to cause harmful health behaviors. At the public level, it also is unlikely that the media would be used intentionally to promote unhealthy policies, although some policies proposed for some issues—such as abortion—are not accepted universally as health promoting.[1]

The distinction between intended and unintended consequences is

---

[1]We are tempted to put cigarette advertising in this category because cigarettes are the only advertised product that is lethal when used as directed. Cigarette companies, however, insist that the link between cigarette smoking and cancer has not been proved and that their advertising of this legal product is intended only to develop brand loyalty among committed smokers. Thus, from the message producer's point of view, we would have to put cigarette advertising in the personal, unintended negative-effects cell.

important because it explains much of the conflict between health and media professionals. Fundamentally, media professionals operate in businesses in which the primary goals/intentions are increasing company profits through increased audience and circulation shares. If health-related content contributes to that goal, fine, and by the same token, in general, if there are negative effects, too bad, because health promotion is not the media's responsibility. It is easy to understand why such a perspective is at the least frustrating for health professionals who would like to see more intentional use of the media for reaching the public and policy makers about health issues.

REVIEW OF RESEARCH

In this chapter, we discuss what research has shown about the intended and unintended, positive and negative consequences the media can have on both personal and public health. The first three sections deal with types of media in which health consequences most often are unintended and occur at the personal health level—commercial product advertising, entertainment programming, and news. A fourth section reviews briefly the intentional use of the mass media in health promotion because public information campaigns are dealt with in greater detail in chapter 12. In the final section, we discuss ways in which the boundaries separating intended and unintended mass media health effects may be blurring as health educators work to persuade the media to take a more active role in health promotion.

COMMERCIAL PRODUCT ADVERTISING

Virtually all of the research conducted so far on the effects of advertising on health have focused on the personal level—effects on individual users of the advertised products. This section reviews some of the most important research on the health effects of advertisements for cigarettes, alcoholic beverages, and foods.[2]

---

[2]The influence of advertising for over-the-counter medicines was investigated in a few studies in the late 1970s. These studies found that such advertising is correlated with belief that the advertised medicines are effective, and intention to take medicine when sick (Robertson, Rossiter, & Gleason, 1979). A longitudinal study found no evidence that among adolescent boys exposure to advertising for legal drugs is related to subsequent use of illegal drugs (Milavsky, Pekowsky, & Stipp, 1975–76).

Cigarettes

Despite a relatively steady decline in cigarette smoking since the early 1970s, by the year 2000 about 22% of American adults still will smoke, and cigarette smoking will continue to be the major preventable cause of death (Pierce, Fiore, Novotny, Hatziandreu, & Davis, 1989; U.S. Dept. of Health and Human Services, 1989). Recognition of the harmful effects of smoking has led many countries, including the United States, to restrict cigarette advertising. In 1982, legislation or voluntary agreements restricted cigarette advertising in 47 countries, including 21 that had either banned or never permitted tobacco advertising (Chapman, 1986). In the United States, cigarette advertising has been banned on television and radio since 1971, so tobacco companies have turned instead to the print media and other forms of promotion such as sponsorship of sporting events. In 1990, despite the broadcast ban and a declining domestic market, more money was spent promoting tobacco than any other consumer product in the country (Babington, 1990).

Advertising Appeals. As consumption among White middle-class men has declined, the tobacco companies increasingly have targeted advertising toward adolescents who have not yet become smokers and to adult population segments that have not had high rates of smoking— most notably women and minorities (Davis, 1987). Black and youth-oriented popular magazines have received an increasing number of cigarette ads since 1965 (Basil & Schooler, 1990).

Cigarette companies argue that they do not advertise to children or adolescents, but research suggests that cigarette advertising does increase smoking among the young. Children and adolescents pay attention to cigarette advertising and readily recognize tobacco symbols and slogans (Aitken, Leathar, & O'Hagan, 1985; Aitken, Leathar, & Squair, 1986), and ad recognition is correlated with frequency of smoking (Goldstein, Fischer, Richards, & Creten, 1987). A series of studies in Australia shows that "life-style" appeals may be especially effective with adolescents because they present images attractive to adolescents who are in the process of developing personal identities. Of more than 130 different brands of cigarettes sold in Australia, just four brands that use such appeals were smoked by more than three-fourths (78.9%) of adolescent smokers (Chapman & Egger, 1980; Chapman & Fitzgerald, 1982). In another study of Australian school children, smoking behavior was best predicted by friends' smoking behavior and second best by approval of cigarette advertising, suggesting that advertising also may serve as a cue for smoking among the young (O'Connell et al., 1981).

Effects on Editorial Content. An alarming indirect effect of tobacco advertising has been the stifling of news coverage of tobacco-related health risks. The typical magazine, dependent on advertising for at least 50% of its revenue, is vulnerable to pressure from advertisers who want their messages in a "supportive editorial atmosphere." Magazines that accept cigarette advertising are less likely to print articles discussing the harmful effects of tobacco than magazines that do not run cigarette advertising (Hesterman, 1987). One content analysis of 12 women's magazines over a 12-year period showed that the magazines that did not accept tobacco advertising were significantly more likely to run articles that addressed the health hazards of smoking (Whelan, Sheridan, Meister, & Mosher, 1981). Another investigation, entitled "The Cigarette Companies: How They Get Away With Murder, Part II," ironically, was commissioned originally by *The New Republic* but was not printed there because of the possibility of "massive losses of advertising revenue" (Owen, 1985, p. 50). Such economically driven silencing of the print media may have contributed to the public's continuing ignorance of the harmful effects of tobacco. Surveys of the American public show that adolescents and adults continue to underestimate the dangers of smoking and the benefits of quitting (Weis & Burke, 1986).

Warning Labels. Since 1966 cigarette manufacturers in the United States have been required to print health warnings on packages and since 1972 also on all cigarette advertising. The warnings have presented increasingly explicit health-risk information in an attempt to affect consumers' attitudes toward smoking. The warnings probably are ineffective, however, primarily because few people notice them. An eye-tracking study found that the average time adolescents viewed warnings in magazine ads amounted to only 8% of the total ad viewing time. In 43.6% of the cases, the warning was not viewed at all (Fischer, Richards, Berman, & Krugman, 1989). People also often are unable to read warning labels in outdoor advertisements. In two field tests of outdoor advertisements, observers were able to read the entire warning on fewer than half of the billboard ads located next to city streets, only 5% of the billboard ads on highways and none in cigarette ads positioned on the top of taxi cabs; they were able to identify the brand name of the cigarette in all 100 taxi ads observed (Davis & Kendrick, 1989).

Paradoxically, the most important effect of the warnings may occur at the public health level by helping to protect cigarette companies from stricter regulation. In three out of the four court cases heard by the end of 1988, in which tobacco companies were charged with damaging cigarette smokers' health, the courts upheld the industry's contention that the warnings provide adequate information about the potential hazards of tobacco use, thus eliminating the industry's responsibility for harmful effects (Fischer et al., 1989).

Counteradvertising. From mid-1967 through 1970, television and radio broadcasters were required by the Federal Communication Commission's Fairness Doctrine to donate air time for anti-smoking messages because smoking was considered a controversial issue. During that time, antismoking groups such as the American Cancer Society were able to broadcast up to one antismoking message for every three cigarette ads. The 3 years of counteradvertising probably contributed to the more than 10% decline in per capita consumption of cigarettes that occurred in the period. When cigarette ads and counterads were removed from the airwaves in 1971, the decline in consumption slowed (Warner, 1979). Recently antismoking forces have begun looking elsewhere for the resources necessary to mount media campaigns of the magnitude assumed necessary to counter the positive image of smoking promoted by the tobacco industry. Several states, including Minnesota and California, now have designated portions of revenues from cigarette taxes for tobacco education programs, and it is likely that such trends will continue (Schultz et al., 1986).

Alcohol

Promotion of alcohol products has been almost as controversial as cigarette advertising.[3] Alcoholism exacts a psychological, physical, and financial toll on millions of individuals and families; more than half of all adolescent deaths are caused by motor vehicle accidents, most of which involve an intoxicated driver (Vital statistics, 1985). Beer and wine are among the most heavily advertised products on television and radio, and although the broadcast media have voluntarily restricted liquor advertising, it is a major source of revenue for magazines and some newspapers (Novelli, 1990).

Research has addressed two questions: Does alcohol advertising encourage nondrinkers (primarily adolescents) to begin drinking, and

---

[3]In 1976 the U.S. Senate Subcommittee on Alcoholism and Narcotics held hearings that raised questions about the effects of alcohol advertising. In 1979 Sweden banned all domestic advertising of alcohol, and in 1981 Canada banned lifestyle alcohol advertising and ads that portray drinking as desirable behavior (Atkin, Hocking, & Block, 1984). The issue has not been resolved in the United States.

does advertising encourage drinkers to drink more and in more dangerous circumstances, such as before or while driving a car?

In a recent review of the research, Atkin (1990) concluded that despite methodological limitations, the cumulative evidence suggests that alcohol advertising on television does stimulate drinking, especially among adolescents. In one key survey, adolescents' exposure to alcohol ads on television was found to be more strongly correlated with both beer and liquor drinking than were parental influence, age, sex, church attendance, social status, or viewing alcohol in entertainment programming (Atkin, Hocking, & Block, 1984).

Despite a number of survey, experimental, and econometric studies, it is still not clear that advertising increases alcohol consumption or dangerous drinking behaviors such as drunk driving. Some survey evidence suggests that exposure to alcohol advertising is correlated with excessive alcohol consumption and drunk driving (Atkin, Neuendorf, & McDermott, 1983), but other studies have produced conflicting results. In one experimental study, for example, Kohn and Smart (1984) found that young men exposed to alcohol ads while watching a televised football game drank more after viewing the first few commercials than men not exposed to the commercials, but they did not continue the increased consumption over the course of the program and exposure to more alcohol commercials. They concluded that ads thus may serve as a cue to drink but do not necessarily lead a viewer to drink more than he would otherwise. Further study of the effect of alcohol ads on dangerous drinking is in order.

Food

It has been estimated that the average child views more than 200,000 television commercials a year, and more than half of them are for foods—primarily sugared snacks and cereals (Barcus, 1975a, 1975b). Does this barrage of nonnutritious images affect children's diets? Research suggests that although parents' diets are significantly more influential than television advertising, exposure to food commercials does affect children's short- and long-term food preferences (Goldberg, Gorn, & Gibson, 1978), and because most of the advertising is for nonnutritious products, the overall effect on children's health is negative. One recent advertising campaign suggests, however, that this need not always be the case.

Collaborations. In 1984 the Kellogg Company introduced a new media campaign for their All-Bran cereal that emphasized the cereal's high fiber content. The ads stated that the National Cancer Institute recommends a high-fiber/low-fat diet because it "may reduce the risk of some types of cancer." Two evaluations of the campaign showed that the public's awareness of the link between nutrition and cancer increased, and more people than before the campaign were eating high-fiber foods, including All-Bran (Freimuth, Hammond, & Stein, 1988; Levy & Stokes, 1987).

This collaboration illustrates how health professionals and food producers might work together to improve consumers' health. However, it also raises a number of questions about the wisdom of allowing food manufacturers to capitalize on the health benefits of their products. As Freimuth et al. (1988) pointed out, most chronic diseases have multiple causes, and rarely will a specific food or nutritional factor be as substantial a health benefit as food producers might claim. Producers also are likely to fail to mention negative attributes of their products (e.g., milk is good for providing calcium but also is high in fat). Nonetheless, we are likely to see more collaborations of this sort because health agencies are impressed by advertising's power to change consumer behavior and because they often lack the resources to mount widespread media campaigns.[4] Food producers also benefit from the credibility that association with a government agency or major nonprofit health organization gives them (Novelli, 1990).

ENTERTAINMENT MEDIA

Many of the same health issues that have attracted research interest in advertising have been investigated in various kinds of entertainment media, with television and music subject to most of the scrutiny.[5]

Television

In the television world in the United States, the relatively few characters who experience physical illnesses outnumber doctors by only about a 2:1 ratio (Signorielli, 1990). The patients typically suffer from acute illnesses that can be cured using the latest in drugs and/or technology

---

[4]The U.S. Food and Drug Administration also has loosened restrictions on health claims in product labeling (Silverglade, 1990).

[5]We discuss here only some of the health-related topics in entertainment media that have received research attention. Some other relevant topics reviewed recently include: TV violence and aggressive behavior (Comstock & Strasburger, 1990); mental illness (Gerbner, Morgan, & Signorielli, 1982; Neuendorf, 1990); and aging (Neuendorf, 1990). For a complete review of the role of music in early adolescence with an emphasis on health implications, see Christenson and Roberts (1990) and Flora (1990).

without concern for cost, which is far from an accurate picture of American health care (Turow & Coe, 1985).

Nutrition. On a typical week's prime-time dramatic programs, eating, drinking, or talking about food occurs about nine times per hour (Gerbner, Gross, Morgan, & Signorielli, 1981). Content analyses show that television characters are engaging in more nutritious eating patterns than they used to. In 1977, almost three-fourths (72.2%) of food references were for less nutritious foods such as potato chips and soft drinks (Kaufman, 1980), but a decade later, almost two-thirds (64.3%) of the 210 servings of food coded in three top-rated shows were nutritious (Larson, 1991).

Research continues to show, however, that the overall nutritional impact of television viewing is not positive. Dietz found consistent moderate correlations between the time spent watching television and obesity among adolescents (Dietz, 1990). In one study of 12- to 17-year-olds, the prevalence of obesity increased by 2% for each additional hour of television viewed (Dietz & Gortmaker, 1985). This effect may be due not only to increased viewing of food advertising and food consumption in the shows but also to the lower energy expenditure by children who watch more television. Children who watch more television also eat more between-meal snacks (Clancy-Hepburn, Hickey, & Nevill, 1974).

The paradox of the nutritional patterns presented on television is that despite frequent snacking and drinking, few people on television are fat. In contrast to the real world, where about 25% of adults are obese, only 12% of televised characters are overweight or obese (Kaufman, 1980). The current standard of body weight in the media is slimmer for women than for men and is the slimmest it has been since the last epidemic of eating disorders occurred in the mid-1920s (Silverstein, Perdue, Peterson, & Kelly, 1986). Dietz (1990) argued that in this context bulimia may be an adaptive response "because only bulimics can eat everything they wish and remain thin" (p. 76). The link between media exposure and eating disorders other than obesity has yet to be established, however.

Substance Use and Abuse. Cigarette smoking has virtually disappeared from current television programming (Breed & DeFoe, 1984; Gerbner, Gross, Morgan, & Signoreilli, 1981), and illegal drugs rarely are used (Greenberg, 1981). Alcohol, however, appears more often than any other beverage (DeFoe, Breed, & Breed, 1983), and in the 1980s, alcohol appeared in more than 70% of prime-time network dramatic programs. More than one third (37%) of all major characters drink alcohol, but only 1% to 2% are characterized as alcoholics. Only about 13% of prime-time programs contain references to the harmful effects of alcohol. Interestingly, the few alcoholics who appear are almost always portrayed negatively, that is, as unsuccessful, physically or mentally ill, or also addicted to drugs (Signorielli, 1987). Unfortunately, we know very little about how portrayals of alcoholics and nonalcoholic drinkers affect viewers, but the content analyses suggest that such frequent and generally positive portrayals of drinking could lead viewers to believe that drinking is a normative and relatively risk-free behavior. Young viewers, especially, are likely to be affected by such portrayals because they have less conflicting real-world experience and typically are seeking information about how they might become part of the adult world.

Safe Sex. Early studies of the sexual portrayals on television were undertaken primarily from a moral standpoint, so these studies paid relatively little attention to health-related issues such as pregnancy or sexually transmitted disease prevention (Neuendorf, 1990). Content analyses consistently have shown, however, that heterosexual interaction occurs primarily in the context of casual relationships and usually is associated with humor, except in action/adventure programs and music videos, in which sexual interaction frequently is accompanied by displays of power or violence (Greenberg & D'Alessio, 1985; Sherman & Etling, 1991). Recent studies show that sexual activity on television is increasingly common and increasingly explicit. Between 1980 and 1985, the number of references to or depictions of sexual activity increased 103%, so that an average adolescent viewer in 1985 was exposed to 1,900 to 2,400 sexual references, depending on his or her viewing patterns (Greenberg, Brown, & Buerkel-Rothfuss, 1991).

Discussion of potentially harmful health outcomes of sex has not kept pace with the increase in sexual activity on television, however. In an analysis of a sample of 1987 afternoon soap operas, Lowry and Towles (1989) found no verbal, implied, or visually depicted mentions of efforts to prevent either pregnancy or sexually transmitted diseases. A study of 1987-1988 prime-time programming found no references to contraception in the entire sample of 232 half-hour segments from 129 shows. References to sexual intercourse appeared, on average, at a rate of two per hour of programming, but viewers had to watch about 10 hours to encounter any reference to sexually transmitted diseases (Louis Harris and Associates, 1987). Anecdotal evidence suggests that, in the wake of the AIDS epidemic, television program producers may have begun to incorporate the use of at least one contraceptive product—condoms—into their scripts. For instance, during a 1987 episode of "L.A. Law," the resident playboy advised another character that he should use condoms during sex because "any time you hit the sheets with someone new, you link yourself up virally to about half the world population" (Mondello, 1987).

Television may have significant potential for influencing adolescents' sexual attitudes and behaviors because they receive relatively little information from other sources. According to a 1986 poll of U.S. teenagers, only one third had talked with their parents about birth control, and only 35% had taken comprehensive school sex education courses that included such information as how contraceptives work and where to get them (Louis Harris and Associates, 1986).

Studies have shown that television can affect older adolescents' beliefs about sexual attractiveness (Kenrick & Gutierres, 1980) and the frequency and acceptability of sexual behaviors. Zillmann and Bryant (1988) found that watching sexually explicit, nonviolent films increased college students' and nonstudent adults' acceptance of promiscuity and sexual infidelity. They also found that after watching sexually explicit films (now available on cable channels), college students expressed greater sexual callousness toward women and trivialized rape as a crime (Zillmann & Bryant, 1982). Other researchers have found such effects only for sexually explicit films that also contained violence (Linz, Donnerstein, & Penrod, 1988), so at this point it is not clear which aspects of the programming are necessary to stimulate undesirable effects.

Two studies have provided evidence that watching sexual content on television may influence adolescent sexual behavior. Brown and Newcomer (1991) found that teenagers whose television viewing included higher proportions of "sexy" shows were more likely to have had sexual intercourse in the previous year. In a longitudinal study, Peterson, Moore, and Furstenberg (1991) found a significant correlation between heavy "sexy" television viewing in 1977 and initiation of intercourse by 1981, but only for boys.

Music and Music Videos

Parents and academics alike argue that the increasingly explicit sexual and violent lyrics and images heard and, since the introduction of music videos in 1980, seen in contemporary rock music (especially heavy metal and rap) are contributing to an increase in adolescent health problems, including teenage pregnancy, sexual assault, drug abuse, depression, and suicide (Brown & Hendee, 1989; Gore, 1987).

Content analyses show that popular songs in the 1950s and early 1960s tended toward the romantic, but now songs emphasize the more physical side of sex (Fedler, Hall, & Tanzi, 1982). Music videos, especially those shown on the MTV cable channel, reflect the shift in emphasis and often portray sexual encounters in a violent context (Sherman & Etling, 1991). But we still know very little about how such depictions affect listeners and viewers. In the one available experimental study, Greeson and Williams (1986) found that adolescents who watched 10 rock music videos were more likely than control group teens to agree that premarital sex is acceptable.

Other research has found correlations between various indicators of "deviant" behavior and music use. For example, in a study of 60 adolescents hospitalized for "dysfunctional psychosocial behaviors" (depression, conduct disorder, and/or substance abuse), Weidinger and Demi (in press) found that those with a longer history of such problems were more likely to listen to heavy metal music and music with negative lyrics or themes. In a large sample of 14- to 16-year-olds, those who engaged in more risky health-related behaviors (such as sexual intercourse, drinking, and smoking cigarettes) listened to the radio and watched music videos more frequently than those who had engaged in fewer risky behaviors, regardless of their race, gender, or parents' education. White males who reported engaging in five or more risky behaviors were most likely to name a heavy metal music group as their favorite (Klein et al., in press).

Causality. We must be cautious about assuming the direction of causality in relationships between health behaviors and consumption of television, music, and other entertainment media. For instance, studies indicate that factors such as the peer group and commitment to school may be intervening factors in the relationship between music media and unhealthy behaviors. Adolescents often employ specific music genres as emblematic of social identities that differ depending on their success with and commitment to mainstream values and peer groups. Correlational studies of both Swedish and Canadian youth suggest that when adolescents are not doing well in school, they turn to non-normative peer groups as an alternative source of self-esteem. These peer groups typically prefer nonmainstream forms of music and may also model and reinforce deviant and unhealthy behaviors (Roe, 1987; Tanner, 1981).

Other studies show that all adolescents do not "see" the same things in music videos or other types of television. Age, gender, race, and the viewer's previous experience with and attitudes toward the topic depicted in the video have been found to affect interpretations of the often ambiguous stimuli (Brown & Schulze, 1990; Walsh-Childers, 1990). Thus, the link between entertainment media and unhealthy behavior may be more complicated than critics suggest.

NEWS

Although research has shown that the news media are important sources of health information for both private individuals (Freimuth, Greenberg, DeWitt, & Romano, 1984; Simpkins & Brenner, 1984; Wallack, 1990a) and policy-makers (Weiss, 1974), few, if any, studies have investigated explicitly the links between news media coverage of health issues and positive or negative health consequences for either individuals or health policies. Studies of the news media's impact on health have tended to rely on content analyses and agenda-setting studies in which media coverage of particular health issues is related to public opinion about the importance of those health issues.

Analyses of health news, both print and broadcast, have shown that "the health message of the mass media is that the answer to modern disease is to be found in the world of medical expertise or . . . in individuals' personal lives through their own habits or life style" (Milio, 1985, p. 126). For example, in a study of three national magazines' coverage of coronary heart disease between 1959 and 1974, Fisher, Gandy, and Janus (1981) found that 21.3% of the articles mentioned behavioral causes or predispositions to heart disease, whereas only 15.1% mentioned social or environmental factors that might contribute to heart disease. The three magazines almost never discussed heart disease as a serious problem for women, although heart disease was then the major killer of women older than 50, but women were given the responsibility for both causing and preventing males' heart disease. Fisher et al. (1981) concluded that *Time, Readers' Digest,* and *Ladies Home Journal* were "consistent in their adoption of victim-blaming models of causality and treatment" (p. 256).

Victim-blaming has been particularly widespread in media coverage of AIDS (Albert, 1986; Baker, 1986). In his analysis of AIDS coverage in national circulation magazines between May 1982 and December 1983, Albert found that many stories linked AIDS to behaviors such as "anonymous sexual contacts" and "recreational use of drugs." He noted that blame was linked not to risky behaviors per se, but rather to nonnormative risky behaviors: "sex is sanctionable, smoking is not" (p. 175).

Baker contended that the media "virtually ignored the problem of AIDS until research showed that populations outside the gay world could contract the disease" (p. 182). Baker's study of *The New York Times* AIDS coverage showed that the peak number of AIDS articles corresponded with public health officials' discussions of cases of AIDS contracted by monogamous female partners of male drug users and by children who seemed to have caught the disease from "routine" contact with AIDS-infected parents. A more comprehensive study, beginning with the earliest media mentions of the disease in 1981, showed that AIDS coverage in the United States was related to the extent to which the disease seemed to threaten mainstream Americans, not to the number of people who had died from the disease or to AIDS-related scientific developments (Kinsella, 1990).

At least one analyst argued that this attention to only those health problems that threaten the mass media's primary consumers—the middle-class mainstream—is the rule rather than the exception. Klaidman (1990) argued that the news media's emphasis on stories that affect the largest numbers of people within the media audience causes reporters and editors to ignore health problems affecting narrow or powerless segments of the population.

Although media coverage of health issues often demonstrates a belief in individual responsibility for health, those same stories often provide little information about how people can reduce their risks of contracting particular diseases, how to detect disease symptoms, or where to go for treatment or other help (Freimuth et al., 1984; Kristiansen & Harding, 1984). In their study of coverage of cancer in the 50 largest daily newspapers in 1977 and 1980, Freimuth et al. found that stories rarely provided information on prevention, risks, detection, or treatment of particular types of cancer. Prevention was mentioned in only 6% of the 1980 stories and only 4% of the 1977 stories. Kristiansen and Harding reported a similar dearth of "mobilizing information"—including details about health facilities and ways of preventing or treating diseases through individual efforts or changes in the environment—in their study of health coverage in the seven British national newspapers.

Another, related flaw in the content of health news reports is that coverage tends to ascribe the power to control individuals' health to medical experts using high-technology equipment. A study of *Time* and *Newsweek* health news stories from 1978, for instance, showed that biomedical research was discussed in one of every four articles, whereas preventive medicine received attention in only 15% of the stories, and environmental or occupational health issues were mentioned in only 3% of the articles (Levin, 1979). Similarly, Fisher et al.'s (1981) study of coverage of coronary heart disease showed that medical hardware used in treating heart disease was mentioned in 39.4% of all articles, and drug treatments appeared in 78.5% of all articles. The authors concluded that when the media supported changes in the system of treating coronary heart disease, the support was for the introduction of expensive technology.

Analyses of the health content of news media, then, suggest that such content would encourage health news consumers to blame themselves for poor health but to rely on medical experts, armed with expensive, elaborate techniques, drugs, and devices to restore their health. Whether consumption of health news actually has such effects remains unclear; to our knowledge, no studies have tested the relationship between health news consumption and health-related attitudes or behaviors.

In fact, the media may be less likely to influence individuals' agendas regarding health than they are for non-health-related issues. In a study linking health news coverage in Ohio newspapers to Ohioans' ratings of the importance of health issues, Culbertson and Stempel (1984) found that survey respondents mentioned medical costs and insurance matters 10 times more often than any other health-related problem. But health-care financing accounted for only 12% of the mentions of the same eight topics in the newspaper stories analyzed for the study. Culbertson and Stempel concluded that the media tend to concentrate on coverage of specific diseases, but readers more often are concerned about problems such as the costs of health care, with which more people are likely to have had personal experience. However, other data from the same survey of Ohioans showed that people may rely more heavily on media coverage in evaluating society-wide health care than they do for assessing their own health care (Culbertson & Stempel, 1985). This greater reliance on health news for evaluations of societal health care does not necessarily mean that news coverage does not affect individuals' health; rather, the impact may be more widespread if people's use of the news media influences their support for or demands for public health policies (e.g., support for limitations on smoking in public places).

Few studies have documented news media influences on public health policy. A few examples, however, suggest that the media can have positive effects on health policy. For instance, the Montgomery (AL) *Journal*'s Pulitzer Prize-winning series on infant mortality led both the Alabama Department of Public Health and some private agencies to increase attention to prenatal care programs for poor women. *Journal* executive editor Bill Brown, who oversaw the development of the series, said he believes the series helped provide the state's public health director with the "firepower" he needed to make changes in the state's programs for infants and pregnant women (W. Brown, 1990).

Media coverage of a health problem may lead directly to policy-maker actions, or the influence on policy makers may result from media coverage of health-related political protests that show that mainstream constituents are concerned about the problem. Baker (1986) reported, for instance, that the number of positive policy actions taken by federal, state, and local politicians in response to the AIDS crisis fluctuated in accordance with *The New York Times* coverage of protests by gay and especially nongay organizations.

The storm of media coverage of drugs during the summer of 1986 probably helped encourage Congress' relatively rapid development and approval of a $1.7 billion antidrug legislation package (Shoemaker, Wanta, & Leggett, 1989). Coverage of the drug problem in three major newspapers (*Chicago Tribune, The New York Times,* and *The Los Angeles Times*), three national news magazines (*Time, Newsweek,* and *U.S. News and World Report*), and on the three television networks accounted for half of the variance in public concern with drugs, as expressed in 46 Gallup polls conducted from 1972 through 1986, with coverage in the New York and Los Angeles newspapers accounting for virtually all of the media-explained variance (Shoemaker, Wanta, & Leggett). Thus, although the impact of media coverage of drugs on governmental drug policies may not be explicitly demonstrable, the implications seem obvious: If public concern about a health issue, which probably increases public support for intervention policies, is itself influenced by media coverage of the health issue, then greater media attention to the issue probably will tend to increase policy makers' interest in developing intervention policies. Reese and Danielian (1989) pointed out, however, that rapid development of new policies is not necessarily positive if the media pressure encourages policy-makers to implement policies that have not been considered carefully (a charge many leveled at the Congressional antidrug initiative in the fall of 1986).

In some cases, then, media coverage of health issues, such as infant mortality or drugs, may influence policy-makers to develop new programs or policies that produce health benefits. Perhaps more often, however, media coverage of health issues tends to support the status quo, framing health problems as residing in individual behaviors, rather than social-environmental-structural factors over which individuals have little control (Atkin & Arkin, 1990; Wallack, 1990a, 1990b). In a study of major news media coverage of health hazards, Singer and Endreny (1987) found that both print and broadcast stories about health controversies (such as abortion, euthanasia, and recombinant DNA research) "tended to accept the frames provided by the dominant institutions currently active in the debate" (p. 22). In a similar study of media coverage of the Bhopal, India, chemical disaster and the meltdown of the Chernobyl nuclear power plant, Wilkins and Patterson (1987) found that the media treated both events as novelties, rather than as symptoms of particular social-industrial systems, failed to analyze the systems that produced the disasters, and did not use sufficiently analytical language to explain the events properly. Wilkins and Patterson argued that "the media need to view risky events as primarily political stories with scientific and technological underpinnings" (p. 90).

The key problem with media coverage of health issues may be that reporters often allow industry representatives to define the terms of the debate, sometimes to the extent that dissident views are excluded entirely. In a study of newspaper, magazine, and scientific journal coverage of recombinant DNA research from 1976 to 1980, for instance, Pfund and Hofstadter (1981) found that early coverage included opinions from dissenting experts and laypersons. By the end of 1977, however, the views of dissenting scientists or environmentalists largely were replaced by those of corporate executives; press representation of these views "lost none of the objective and definitive flavor . . . customarily denied to industrial spokespersons" (p. 42). As the views of dissenting experts disappeared from coverage, so did arguments about the potential risks of recombinant DNA research and technologies.

INFORMATION CAMPAIGNS

Mass media campaigns aimed at improving specific health conditions have been used around the world and have targeted a wide variety of health problems. The success of these campaigns has been mixed.[6] Campaigns aimed at encouraging people to stop smoking (O'Keefe, 1971), to use contraceptives (Udry, 1974), and to wear seatbelts (Robertson et al., 1974) often have been cited as evidence that mass media campaigns cannot produce long-term behavior change. On the other hand, other campaigns aimed at improving cardiovascular health by getting people to stop smoking and modify their diets have proved successful (Farquhar et al., 1977; Flay, 1987; Puska et al., 1979; Truett, Cornfield, & Kannel, 1967).

These successes, coupled with the threat of an AIDS epidemic that may be stopped only through changing individual behavior, have stimulated increased interest in intentional use of the mass media for health education. However, evaluations of AIDS education media campaigns conducted in Australia, Sweden, and the United Kingdom have not shown the campaigns to be effective in changing people's behavior (encouraging them to have fewer sex partners or use condoms more often) (Hornik, 1987; Wober, 1987). In addition, evaluation have shown that these campaigns, intended to produce positive effects at the

---

[6]For further discussions of the use of mass media for health promotion and disease prevention, see DeJong and Winsten (1989), Flay and Burton (1990), and a number of relevant chapters in Rice and Atkin (1989). Also see chapter 12, this volume.

individual level, also may have had negative effects. Officials in Great Britain concluded from extensive evaluation of their $32 million campaign that it had needlessly raised general anxieties about AIDS and had missed those individuals in the highest risk population groups (e.g., drug users) (Department of Health and Social Security and the Welsh Office, 1987). Similar evaluations of the U.S. "Understanding AIDS" campaign, which included a mass mailing of brochures to every household in the United States, suggested that the brochure did not reach or was forgotten more quickly by those at highest risk for contracting the virus (Snyder, Anderson, & Young, 1989).

Thus, even campaigns that successfully accomplish some of their positive goals (such as increasing knowledge about AIDS) may also produce unintended negative effects (such as unnecessarily increasing fear of AIDS). These are not the only problems with mass media health campaigns as they are most commonly practiced, however. Many of the same criticisms leveled at news coverage of health issues also have been applied recently to media campaigns intended to improve public health.

Wallack (1989) complained, for instance, that most media health campaigns are based on an "understanding of (health) problems as inherently individual in nature and thus responsive to information and education approaches" (p. 354). This belief leads health campaigners to attempt to break complex problems down into discreet, smaller parts, so that campaigns can be designed to address each of the smaller parts. Campaign planners believe that consumers, armed with the appropriate health information, will be able to "choose" healthier lifestyles. But this approach does little to address the important external contributory causes of unhealthy behaviors such as alcohol and cigarette advertising aimed at the young, a lack of comprehensive sex education courses in the schools, or the high cost of health care.

One reason that such "victim-blaming" campaign approaches are so popular, according to Wallack, is that they are less risky. Turning the spotlight on individuals' risky behaviors keeps the focus away from the social and political structures that support poorer health among the poorer segments of society and, thus, does not challenge existing power distributions. Both Wallack (1990a, 1990b) and Milio (1988) argued that health campaigns aimed at producing changes only in individual behaviors are likely to have the weakest overall effect on health. Rather than attempting to persuade individuals to abandon unhealthy behaviors while advertisers spend billions encouraging people to continue those same behaviors, health planners should seek public policy changes that can provide the necessary support for individuals who wish to adopt healthier behaviors and make more health options available to those at greatest risk of health problems.

THE FUTURE

Health educators are beginning to use two new strategies to affect changes in personal and public health. Both strategies challenge traditional notions about intentions of the message producers and begin to address some of the problems of traditional campaigns. The first strategy has been called "edutainment" and involves imbedding health-related messages in entertainment content. The second strategy is called "media advocacy" and involves health professionals taking an active part in news coverage of health issues.[7]

Edutainment

A number of health-related agencies and groups have begun to work with producers of entertainment content, primarily in the broadcast media, to develop positive health portrayals. A recent effort by Harvard University's School of Public Health did much to put the idea of a "designated driver" in the public's consciousness (Montgomery, 1989; Rothenberg, 1990). Other groups, such as the American Cancer Society and the Center for Population Options, have been working with Hollywood producers to develop programs that include antismoking scenes and dialogue, and sexually responsible portrayals. In other countries, music videos and soap operas have been used extensively in the promotion of sexual abstinence and family planning (Church & Geller, 1989; Singhal & Rogers, 1989).

We know very little at this point about how successful these efforts have been, but there are at least three reasons to believe that such embedded messages may be more effective than the public service announcements traditionally used in public health campaigns. First, dramatic or musical formats are much more likely to capture and hold the attention of target audiences. Second, dramatic programs and music media are much more likely to reach larger and more appropriate audiences than PSAs, and third, they also allow more time for developing complex informational and persuasive messages. Some media health program developers, for example, have been able to integrate social learning/social modeling strategies into both documentary and dramatic programming, something that is more difficult in shorter formats (Puska et al., 1979; Ramirez & McAlister, 1988).

---

[7]For a summary of recent initiatives and recommendations for future efforts from a public health perspective, see the special section "Health communication for the 1990s" in the May-June (1990) issue of *Public Health Reports* and a Public Health Service publication: *Mass media and health* (1990).

Reliance on the entertainment media for communication of health messages is not without its problems, however. As Montgomery (1990) pointed out, the dependence of entertainment media on advertising (particularly in the United States) makes them unlikely to tackle sensitive health issues. In the United States, despite the frequent sexual content of much entertainment programming and advertising, any health issue related to sex is considered sensitive. Thus, programs about abortion and AIDS, as a sexually transmitted disease, have been scrapped due to lack of advertiser support (Montgomery, 1989).

Interestingly, the U.S. entertainment industry has been very cooperative around the issue of substance abuse, but not totally without ulterior motive. In 1984, when a coalition of public health proposed legislation that would ban alcohol advertising from radio and TV, the broadcast industry used excerpts from programming to document their socially responsible stance (Montgomery, 1989). Thus, short-term gains may work against more permanent solutions.

Finally, as we have discussed above, the entertainment media are unlikely to deal with fundamental policy issues, such as advertising bans or excise taxes, preferring instead to emphasize personal solutions to health problems. Increasingly aware of this problem, health promoters have turned to media advocacy as another strategy for increasing the role of the media in health education.

Media Advocacy

Media advocacy is "the strategic use of mass media for advancing a social or public policy initiative" (National Cancer Institute, 1988). The approach is designed to use media coverage to focus attention on policy-level influences on health problems, rather than on individuals' unhealthy behaviors. As we have discussed, corporations more concerned about profits than public health frequently have been allowed to define the terms of debates about public health issues (Gandy, 1981). The tobacco industry, for instance, has had some success in framing the debate over cigarette advertising as a free speech or free press issue. Tobacco control media advocates, on the other hand, are attempting to reframe the battle as one pitting the tobacco industry's desire for profit against individuals' need for good health. Successful reframing, according to Wallack (1990a), depends on two key strategies: focusing on industry practices rather than on individual behaviors and delegitimizing the industry by showing how it engages in unethical or exploitive practices.

Another key difference between traditional health campaigns and media advocacy is that media advocates do not wait for media outlets to run public service announcements or to cover health issues. Media advocates attempt to create news about research results and to build on breaking news stories by providing local statistics or local reactions relevant to the story, by comparing the risks of using the target product (e.g., cigarettes) to other health risks currently in the news (e.g., chemically treated fruit). Wallack (1990a) pointed out, however, that media advocacy has several limitations: It has not been fully defined or tested, it requires more subtle and complex skills than other health promotion approaches, and it may require more time than public health agents can spend conducting research and cultivating media gatekeepers. In addition, because media advocacy focuses on social and structural influences on health, it may be more difficult to attract and hold media attention, and confrontations with powerful vested interests, both political and corporate, are virtually guaranteed.

CONCLUSIONS

In summary, large bodies of research point to the conclusion that the largely unintended health consequences of advertising for tobacco, alcohol, and food products are negative. Similar conclusions, although somewhat more tentative, can be drawn regarding entertainment media. If we step back and look at the general picture of health provided in these most pervasive of media, we find a world in which people eat, drink, and have sex with abandonment but seldom suffer the consequences. Research shows that the audience does learn from these images and that, in general, what they learn is not good for their health.

Virtually none of the existing research on the news media deals explicitly with the influence of health coverage on either individual health decisions or the development of public health policy. However, content analyses of health reporting have shown that, although media coverage may raise awareness of particular health problems, such as AIDS or drug abuse, among both private individuals and public policy makers, health coverage tends to focus on individual responsibility for healthy or unhealthy behaviors and on medical cures rather than prevention. Health stories often blame victims for their own poor health but fail to provide information that would help individuals improve their health, and reporters and editors often allow those who benefit either financially or ideologically from public health policy decisions to define the terms of debates about those policies.

Many of the same criticisms have been leveled at traditional public health information campaigns. Most are based on an acceptance of individual responsibility for health; they rely on changes in personal behavior, rather than public policy, to improve people's health. These campaigns at best ignore and at worst obscure the important environmental and social-structural contributors to poor health.

What this review has demonstrated most clearly is the need for more research in other areas of the typology discussed in Table 13.1. Researchers need to go beyond simple analyses of the content of advertisements, entertainment programs, and news reports to study the ways in which consumption of these media actually influences both individual health decisions and the development of public health policy.

REFERENCES

Aitken, P. P., Leathar, D. S., & O'Hagan, F. J. (1985). Children's perceptions of advertisements for cigarettes. *Social Science Medicine, 21,* 785–797.

Aitken, P. P., Leathar, D. S., & Squair, S. I. (1986). Children's awareness of cigarette brand sponsorship of sports and games in the UK. *Health Education Research, 1,* 203–211.

Albert, E. (1986). Illness and deviance: The response of the press to AIDS. In D. A. Feldman & T. M. Johnson (Eds.), *The social dimensions of AIDS: Method and theory* (pp. 163–178). New York: Praeger.

Atkin, C. (1990). Effects of televised alcohol messages on teenage drinking patterns. *Journal of Adolescent Health Care, 11,* 10–24.

Atkin, C., & Arkin, E. B. (1990). Issues and initiatives in communicating health information to the public. In C. Atkin & L. Wallack (Eds.), *Mass communication and public health: Complexities and conflicts* (pp. 13–40). Newbury Park, CA: Sage.

Atkin, C., Hocking, J., & Block, M. (1984). Teenage drinking: Does advertising make a difference? *Journal of Communication, 34*(2), 157–167.

Atkin, C., Neuendorf, K., & McDermott, S. (1983). The role of advertising in excessive and hazardous drinking. *Journal of Drug Education, 13*(4), 313–325.

Babington, C. (1990, August 26). Tobacco still healthy but not immortal. *The News and Observer,* pp. 1J, 8J.

Baker, A. J. (1986). The portrayal of AIDS in the media: An analysis of articles in the *New York Times.* In D. G. Feldman & T. M. Johnson (Eds.), *The social dimensions of AIDS: Method and theory* (pp. 179–194). New York: Praeger.

Barcus, R. E. (1975a). *Television in the afternoon hours.* Newton, MA: Action for Children's Television.

Barcus, R. E. (1975b). *Weekend commercial children's television.* Newton, MA: Action for Children's Television.

Basil, M., & Schooler, C. (1990, May). *How cigarettes are sold in magazines: Special messages for special markets.* Paper presented at the meeting of the International Communication Association, Dublin, Ireland.

Breed, W., & DeFoe, J. R. (1984, June). Drinking and smoking on television, 1950–1982. *Journal of Public Health Policy,* 257–270.

Brown, E. F., & Hendee, W. R. (1989). Adolescents and their music: Insights into the health of adolescents. *Journal of the American Medical Association, 62,* 1659–63.

Brown, J. D., & Newcomer, S. (1991). Television viewing and adolescents' sexual behavior. *Journal of Homosexuality, 21* (1/2), 77–91.

Brown, J. D., & Schulze, L. (1990). The effects of race, gender and fandom on interpretations of Madonna's music videos. *Journal of Communication, 40*(2), 88–102.

Chapman, S. (1986). *Great expectorations: Advertising and the tobacco industry.* London: Comedia.

Chapman, S., & Egger, G. (1980). Forging an identity for the non-smoker: The use of myth in promotion. *International Journal of Health Education, 23*(3), 2–16.

Chapman, S., & Fitzgerald, B. (1982). Brand preference and advertising recall in adolescent smokers: Some implications for health promotion. *American Journal of Public Health, 72,* 491–494.

Christenson, P. G., & Roberts, D. F. (1990). *Popular music in early adolescence.* New York: Carnegie Corporation.

Church, C. A., & Geller, J. (1989). Lights! Camera! Action! Promoting family planning with TV, video, and film. *Population reports* (No. 38). Baltimore: Johns Hopkins.

Clancey-Hepburn, K., Hickey, A. A., & Nevill, G. (1974). Children's behavior responses to TV food advertisements. *Journal of Nutrition Education, 6,* 93–96.

Comstock, G., & Strasburger, V. C. (1990). Deceptive appearances: Television violence and aggressive behavior. *Journal of Adolescent Health Care, 11,* 31–44.

Culbertson, H. M., & Stempel, G. H., III. (1984). Possible barriers to agenda setting in medical news. *Newspaper Research Journal, 5*(3), 53–60.

Culbertson, H. M., & Stempel, G. H., III. (1985). "Media malaise": Explaining personal optimism and societal pessimism about health care. *Journal of Communication, 35*(2), 180–190.

Davis, R. M. (1987). Current trends in cigarette advertising and marketing. *New England Journal of Medicine. 316,* 725–732.

Davis, R. M., & Kendrick, J. S. (1989). The Surgeon General's warnings in outdoor cigarette advertising. *Journal of the American Medical Association, 61*(1), 90–94.

DeFoe, J. R., Breed, W., & Breed, L. A. (1983). Drinking on television: A five-year study. *Journal of Drug Education, 13*(1), 25–38.

DeJong, W., & Winsten, J. A. (1989). *Recommendations for future mass media campaigns to prevent preteen and adolescent substance abuse.* (Special Report). Cambridge, MA: Harvard School of Public Health Center Health Communication.

Department of Health and Social Security and the Welsh Office. (1987). *AIDS: Monitoring response to the public education campaign, Feb. 1986-Feb. 1987.* London: Her Majesty's Stationery Office.

Dietz, W. H. (1990). You are what you eat—what you eat is what you are. *Journal of Adolescent Health Care, 11,* 76–81.

Dietz, W. H., & Gortmaker, S. L. (1985). Do we fatten our children at the TV set? Television viewing and obesity in children and adolescents. *Pediatrics, 75*(5), 807–12.

Farquhar, J. W., Maccoby, N., Wood, P., Alexander, J., Breitrose, H., Brown, B., Haskell, W., McAlister, A., Meyer, A., Nash, J., & Stern, P. (1977, June 4). Community education for cardiovascular health. *The Lancet,* pp. 1192–1195.

Fedler, F., Hall, J., & Tanzi, L.A. (1982 Spring/Fall). Popular songs emphasize sex, de-emphasize romance. *Mass Communication Research,* 10–15.

Fischer, P. M., Richards, J. W., Berman, E. J., & Krugman, D. M. (1989). Recall and eye tracking study of adolescents viewing tobacco advertisements. *Journal of the American Medical Association, 261*(1), 84–89.

Fisher, J., Gandy, O. H., Jr., & Janus, N. Z. (1981). The role of popular media in defining sickness and health. In E. G. McAnany, J. Schnitman, & N. Z. Janus (Eds.), *Communication and social structure: Critical studies in mass media research* (pp. 240–257). New York: Praeger.

Flay, B. R. (1987). *Selling the smokeless society: Fifty-six evaluated mass media programs and campaigns worldwide.* Washington, DC: American Public Health Association.

Flay, B. R., & Burton, D. (1990). Effective mass communication strategies for health campaigns. In C. Atkin & L. Wallack (Eds.), *Mass communication and public health* (pp. 129–146). Newbury Park, CA: Sage.

Flora, J. A. (1990). *Strategies for enhancing adolescents' health through music media.* New York: Carnegie Corporation.

Freimuth, V. S., Greenberg, R. H., DeWitt, J., & Romano, R. M. (1984). Covering cancer: Newspaper and the public interest. *Journal of Communication, 34*(1), 62–73.

Freimuth, V. S., Hammond, S. L., & Stein, J. A. (1988). Health advertising: Prevention for profit. *American Journal of Public Health, 78*(5), 557–561.

Gandy, O. H., Jr. (1981). The economics of image building: The information subsidy in health. In E. G. McAnany, J. Schnitman, & N. Janus (Eds.), *Communication and social structure: Critical studies in mass media research* (pp. 204–239). New York: Praeger.

Gerbner, G., Gross, L., Morgan, M., & Signorielli, N. (1981). Health and medicine on television. *The New England Journal of Medicine. 305*(15), 901–904.

Gerbner, G., Morgan, M., & Signorielli, N. (1982). Programming health portrayals: What viewers see, say, and do. In D. Pearl, L. Bouthilet, & J. Lazar (Eds.), *Television and behavior: 10 years of scientific progress and implications for the 80's* (pp. 291–307). Washington, DC: U.S. Government Printing Office.

Goldberg, M. E., Gorn, G. J., & Gibson, W. (1978). TV messages for snack and breakfast foods: Do they influence children's preferences? *Journal of Consumer Research, 5,* 73–81.

Goldstein, A. O., Fischer, P. M., Richards, J. W., & Creten, D. (1987). *The Journal of Pediatrics, 110*(3), 488–491.

Gore, T. (1987). *Raising PG kids in an X-rated society.* Nashville: Abingdon Press.

Greenberg, B. S. (1981). Smoking, drugging and drinking in top rated TV series. *Journal of Drug Education, 11*(3), 227–233.

Greenberg, B. S., Brown, J. D., & Buerkel-Rothfuss, N. (1991). *Media, sex and the adolescent.* Norwood, NJ: Ablex.

Greenberg, B. S., & D'Alessio, D. (1985). Quantity and quality of sex in the soaps. *Journal of Broadcasting and Electronic Media, 29*(3), 309–321.

Greeson, L. E., & Williams, R. A. (1986). Social implications of music videos for youth. *Youth & Society, 18*(2), 177–189.

Hesterman, V. (1987 August). *You've come a long way, baby—or have you?* Paper presented at the meeting of the Association for Education in Journalism and Mass Communication, San Antonio, TX.

Hornik, R. (1987). *Review of recent AIDS evaluation programs: United Kingdom, Australia, Sweden* (unpublished report). Washington, DC: AIDSCOM.

Kaufman, L. (1980). Prime-time nutrition. *Journal of Communication, 30*(3), 37–46.

Kenrick, D. T., & Gutierres, S. E. (1980). Contrast effects and judgements of physical attractiveness: When beauty becomes a social problem. *Journal of Personality and Social Psychology, 38*(1), 131–140.

Kinsella, J. (1990). *Covering the plague: AIDS and the American media.* New Brunswick, NJ: Rutgers University Press.

Klaidman, S. (1990). Roles and responsibilities of journalists. In C. Atkin & L. Wallack (Eds.), *Mass communication and public health: Complexities and conflicts* (pp. 60–70). Newbury Park, CA: Sage.

Klein, J. O, Brown, J. D., Walsh-Childers, K., Oliveri, J., Porter, C., & Dykers, C. (in press). Adolescents' risky behavior and mass media use. *Pediatrics.*

Kohn, P. M., & Smart, R. G. (1984). The impact of television advertising on alcohol consumption: An experiment. *Journal of Studies on Alcohol, 45*(4), 295–301.

Kristiansen, C. M., & Harding, C. M. (1984). Mobilization of health behavior by the press in Britain. *Journalism Quarterly, 61*(2), 364–370, 398.

Larson, M. S. (1991). Health related messages in prime time entertainment. *Health Communication, 3*(3), 175–184.

Levin, A. (Ed.). (1979). *Focus on health: Issues and events of 1978 from the New York Times Information Bank.* New York: Arno Press.

Levy, A., & Stokes, R. (1987). Effects of a health promotion advertising campaign on sales of ready to eat cereals. *Public Health Reports, 102*(4), 398–403.

Linz, D. G., Donnerstein, E., & Penrod, S. (1988). The effects of long-term exposure to violent and sexually degrading depictions of women. *Journal of Personality and Social Psychology, 55*(5), 758–768.

Louis Harris and Associates, Inc. (1986). *American teens speak: Sex, myths, TV, and birth control.* New York: Planned Parenthood Federation of America, Inc.

Louis Harris and Associates, Inc. (1987). *Sexual material on American network television during the 1987–88 season.* New York: Planned Parenthood Federation of America, Inc.

Lowry, D. T., & Towles, D. E. (1989). Soap opera portrayals of sex, contraception, and sexually transmitted diseases. *Journal of Communication, 39*(2), 76–83.

Milavsky, J. R., Pekowsky, B., & Stipp, H. (1975–76). TV drug advertising and proprietary and illicit drug use among teenage boys. *Public Opinion Quarterly, 39*, 457–481.

Milio, N. (1985). Health education = health instruction + health news: Media experiences in the United States, Finland, Australia, and England. In J. D. Brown & E. Rubinstein (Eds.), *The media, social science, and social policy for children* (pp. 118–236). Norwood, NJ: Ablex.

Milio, N. (1986). Health and the media in Australia—An uneasy relationship. *Community Health Studies, 10*(4), 419–422.

Milio, N. (1988). "Political" information is essential. *World Health Forum, 9*, 501–504.

Mondello, B. (1987, December 29). Rewriting the script: From Broadway to Hollywood, the imprint of AIDS on modern drama. *Washington Post Health*, pp. 10–14.

Montgomery, K. (1989). *Target: Prime time. Advocacy groups and the struggle over entertainment television.* New York: Oxford University Press.

Montgomery, K. (1990). Promoting health through entertainment television. In C. Atkin & L. Wallack (Eds), *Mass communication and public health* (pp. 114–128). Newbury Park, CA: Sage.

National Cancer Institute. 1988 *Media Strategies for smoking control* (NIH Publication No. 89-3013). Washington, DC: U.S. Government Printing Office.

Neuendorf, K. A. (1990). Health images in the mass media. In E. B. Ray & L. Donohew (Eds.), *Communication and health: Systems and applications* (pp. 111–135). Hillsdale, NJ: Lawrence Erlbaum Associates.

Novelli, W. (1990). Controversies in advertising of health-related products. In C. Atkin & L. Wallack (Eds.), *Mass communication and public health* (pp. 78–87). Newbury Park, CA: Sage.

O'Connell, D. L., Alexander, H. M., Dobson, A. J., Lloyd, D. M., Hardes, G. R., Springthorpe, J. J., & Leeder, S. R. (1981). Cigarette smoking and drug use in schoolchildren. 11 factors associated with smoking. *International Journal of Epidemiology 10*(3), 223–231.

O'Keefe, M. (1971). The anti-smoking commercials: A study of television's impact on behavior. *Public Opinion Quarterly, 35*, 242–248.

Owen, D. (1985, March). The cigarette companies: How they get away with murder Part II. *Washington Journalism Review*, pp. 48–54.

Peterson, J. L., Moore, K. A., & Furstenberg, F. F. (1991). Television viewing and early initiation of sexual intercourse: Is there a link? *Journal of Homosexuality, 21*(1/2), 92–118.

Pfund, N., & Hofstadter, L. (1981). Biomedical innovation and the press. *Journal of Communication, 31*(2), 138–154.

Pierce, J. P., Fiore, M. C., Novotny, T. E., Hatziandreu, E. J., & Davis, R. M. (1989). Trends in cigarette smoking in the United States. *Journal of the American Medical Association, 26*(1), 61–65.

Puska, P., Tuomilehto, J., Salonen, J., Neittaammaki, L., Maki, J., Virtumo, J., Nissinen, A., Koskela, K., & Takalo, T. (1979). Changes in coronary risk factors during a comprehensive five-year community program to control cardiovascular diseases (North Karelia Project). *British Medical Journal, 2,* 1173–1178.

Ramirez, A. G., & McAlister, A. L. (1988). Mass media campaign – A Su Salud. *Preventive Medicine, 17,* 608–621.

Reese, S. D., & Danielian, L. H. (1989). Intermedia influence and the drug issue: Converging on cocaine. In P. Shoemaker (Ed.), *Communication campaigns about drugs: Government, media and the public* (pp. 29–45). Hillsdale, NJ: Lawrence Erlbaum Associates.

Rice, R. E., & Atkin, C. (1989). *Public communication campaigns* (2nd. Ed.). Newbury Park, CA: Sage.

Robertson, L. S., Kelley, A. B., O'Neill, B., Wixom, C. W., Eiswirth, R. S., & Haddon, W., Jr. (1974). A controlled study of the effect of television messages about safety belt use. *American Journal of Public Health, 64,* 1071–1080.

Robertson, T. S., Rossiter, J. R., & Gleason, T. C. (1979). Children's receptivity to proprietary medicine advertising. *Journal of Consumer Research, 6,* 247–255.

Roe, K. (1987). The school and music in adolescent socialization. In J. Lull (Ed.), *Popular music and communication* (pp. 212–230). Beverly Hills, CA: Sage.

Rothenberg, R. (1990, February 16). Speaking softly of life's dangers. *New York Times,* C1, C7.

Schultz, J. M., Moen, M. E., Pechacek, T. F., Harty, K. C., Skubic, M. A., Just, S. W., & Dean, A. G. (1986). The Minnesota plan for nonsmoking and health: The legislative experience. *Journal of Public Health Policy, 7,* 300–313.

Sherman, B. L. & Etling, L. W. (1991). Perceiving and processing music television. In J. Bryant & D. Zillmann (Eds.), *Responding to the screen: Reception and reaction processes* (pp. 373–388). Hillsdale, NJ: Lawrence Erlbaum Associates.

Shoemaker, P. J., Wanta, W., & Leggett, D. (1989). Drug coverage and public opinion, 1972–1986. In P. Shoemaker (Ed.), *Communication campaigns about drugs: Government, media and the public* (pp. 67–80). Hillsdale, NJ: Lawrence Erlbaum Associates.

Signorielli, N. (1987). Drinking, sex, and violence on television: The cultural indicators perspective. *Journal of Drug Education, 17*(3), 245–260.

Signorielli, N. (1990). Television and health: Images and impact. In C. Atkin & L. Wallack (Eds.), *Mass communication and public health* (pp. 96–113). Newbury Park, CA: Sage.

Silverglade, B. A. (1990). Regulatory policies for communicating health information. In C. Atkin & L. Wallack (Eds.), *Mass communication and public health* (pp. 88–95). Newbury Park, CA: Sage.

Silverstein, B., Perdue, L., Peterson, B., & Kelly, E. (1986). The role of the mass media in promoting a thin standard of bodily attractiveness for women. *Sex Roles, 14,* 519–532.

Simpkins, J. D., & Brenner, D. J. (1984). Mass media communication and health. In B. Dervin & M. J. Voigt (Eds.), *Progress in communication sciences* (pp. 275–297). Norwood, NJ: Ablex.

Singer, E., & Endreny, P. (1987). Reporting hazards: Their benefits and costs. *Journal of Communication, 37*(3), 10–26.

Singhal, A., & Rogers, E. M. (1989). Prosocial television for development in India. In R. E. Rice & C. K. Atkin (Eds.), *Public communication campaigns* (pp. 331–350). Newbury Park, CA: Sage.

Snyder, L. B., Anderson, K., & Young, D. (1989). *AIDS communication, risk, knowledge and behavior change: A preliminary investigation in Connecticut*. Paper presented to the International Communication Association, San Francisco.

Tanner, J. (1981). Pop music and peer groups: A study of Canadian high school students' responses to pop music. *Canadian Review of Sociology and Anthropology, 18*(1), 1–13.

Turow, J., & Coe, L. (1985). Curing television's ills: The portrayal of health care. *Journal of Communication, 35*(4), 36–51.

Truett, J., Cornfield, J., & Kannel, W. (1967). A multivariate analysis of the risk of coronary heart disease in Framingham. *Journal of Chronic Disorders, 20*, 511–524.

Udry, J. (1974). *The mass media and family planning*. New York: Ballinger.

U.S. Department of Health and Human Services. (1989). *Reducing the health consequences of smoking: 25 years of progress. A report of the Surgeon General*. Rockville, MD: U.S. Dept. of Health and Human Services, DHHS Pub. No. 89-8411.

Vital statistics of the United States. (1985). PHS 85-1101, Washington, DC: U.S. Department of Health and Human Services.

Wallack, L. (1989). Mass communication and health promotion: A critical perspective. In R. E. Rice & C. K. Atkin (Eds.), *Public communication campaigns* (2nd ed., pp. 353–367). Newbury Park, CA: Sage.

Wallack, L. (1990a). Improving health promotion: Media advocacy and social marketing approaches. In C. Atkin & L. Wallack (Eds.), *Mass communication and public health: Complexities and conflicts* (pp. 147–163). Newbury Park, CA: Sage.

Wallack, L. (1990b). Mass media and health promotion: Promise, problem, and challenge. In C. Atkin & L. Wallack (Eds.), *Mass communication and public health: Complexities and conflicts* (pp. 41–51). Newbury Park, CA: Sage.

Walsh-Childers, K. (1990). *Adolescents' sexual schemas and interpretations of male-female relationships in a soap opera*. Unpublished doctoral dissertation, University of North Carolina at Chapel Hill.

Warner, K. E. (1979). Clearing the airwaves: The cigarette ad ban revisited. *Policy Analysis, 5*, 435–50.

Weidinger, C. K., & Demi, A. S. (in press). Music listening preferences and preadmission dysfunctional psychosocial behaviors of adolescents hospitalized on an in-patient psychiatric unit. *Journal of Child and Adolescent Psychiatric and Mental Health Nursing*.

Weis, W. L., & Burke, C. (1986). Media content and tobacco advertising: An unhealthy addiction. *Journal of Communication, 36*(4), 59–69.

Weiss, C. H. (1974). What America's leaders read. *Public Opinion Quarterly. 38*, 1–21.

Whelan, E. M., Sheridan, M. J., Meister, K. A., & Mosher, B. A. (1981). *Journal of Public Health Policy, 2*, 28–35.

Wilkins, L., & Patterson, P. (1987). Risk analysis and the construction of news. *Journal of Communication, 37*(3), 80–92.

Wober, J. M. (1987). *Informing the public about AIDS: Measurements of knowledge, attitudes and behavior*. (unpublished research paper). London: Independent Broadcasting Authority.

Zillmann, D., & Bryant, J. (1982). Pornography, sexual callousness and the trivialization of rape. *Journal of Communication, 32*(4), 10–21.

Zillmann, D., & Bryant, J. (1988). Effects of prolonged consumption of pornography on family values. *Journal of Family Issues, 9*(4), 518–544.

Media Uses and Effect
A Uses-and-Gratifications
Perspective

ALAN M. RUBIN
Kent State University

Mass-media effects investigators seek to isolate communicator or message elements that explain the effects of messages on receivers. One view of this process emanates from a mechanistic perspective and assumes direct influence on message recipients. Primary components of mechanistic effects research are: seeing audience members as passive and reactive; focusing on short-term, immediate, and measurable changes in thoughts, attitudes, or behaviors; and assuming direct media influence on audiences.

Some, however, have suggested that other elements intervene between media messages and effects. Over three decades ago, Klapper (1960) questioned the validity of mechanistic approaches. In his phenomenistic approach he proposed that several elements intercede between a message and one's response so that, in most instances, media messages that are intended to persuade actually reinforce existing attitudes. These mediating factors are: individual predispositions and selective perception processes, group norms, message dissemination via interpersonal channels, opinion leadership, and the free-enterprise nature of the mass media in some societies. Accordingly, it can be argued that: (a) by themselves, mass media are usually not necessary or sufficient causes of audience effects; and (b) a medium or message is only one (albeit, at times, an important and crucial) source of influence in the social and psychological environment.

A PSYCHOLOGICAL PERSPECTIVE

Uses and gratifications also sees media as sources of influence amid other sources and sees media audiences as variably active communicators. It underscores the role of social and psychological elements in mitigating mechanistic effects. Mediated communication is psychologically and socially constrained. Rosengren (1974) observed that uses and gratifications rests on a mediated view of communication influence that stresses the role of individual differences in lessening direct media effects. To explain media effects, we must first understand audience motivation and behavior.

Uses and gratifications is a psychological communication perspective that shifts the focus of inquiry from the mechanistic perspective's interest in direct effects of media on receivers to assessing how people use the media: "that is, what purposes or functions the media serve for a body of active receivers" (Fisher, 1978, p. 159). The psychological perspective stresses individual use and choice. As adherents to this perspective, researchers seek to explain media effects "in terms of the purposes, functions or uses (that is, uses and gratifications) as controlled by the choice patterns of receivers" (p. 159).

In contrast to mechanistic views, writers have suggested both functional and psychological views of media influence. Functional orientations are mentioned below, whereas the next section explains uses and gratifications. Following a description of the uses-and-gratifications paradigm, criticisms, research investigations, and media uses and effects links are considered.

MEDIA ACTIVITIES
AND FUNCTIONAL ANALYSIS

The work of Lazarsfeld and Merton (1948) and Lasswell (1948) exemplifies early studies of media functions. Lazarsfeld and Merton proposed status-conferral and ethicizing functions, and a narcotizing dysfunction, of the mass media. Lasswell suggested that by performing certain activities (i.e., surveillance of the environment, correlation of environmental parts, and transmission of social heritage), media content has common effects on people in a society. Later, Wright (1960) added entertainment as a fourth activity and assessed manifest and latent functions and dysfunctions.

Around the same time, researchers proposed that the media serve many functions for people and societies. Horton and Wohl (1956), for example, suggested that television provides viewers with a sense of parasocial interaction with media personalities. Pearlin (1959) argued that viewing television gives people the opportunity to escape from unpleasant life experiences. Mendelsohn (1963) noted that media entertainment reduces anxiety created by media news. Stephenson (1967) argued that television provides people the opportunity for play. And McCombs and Shaw (1972) saw agenda-setting as an important function of the media in election campaigns.

Research focusing on audience motives for using media surrounded these functional studies. The belief that something is best defined by its use guided such study. Klapper (1963) argued that mass communication research "too frequently and too long focused on determining whether some particular effect does or does not occur" (p. 517). He noted that mass communication research had found few clear-cut answers to media-effects questions. Consistent with Katz's (1959) suggestion that a media message ordinarily cannot influence a person who has no use for it, Klapper called for an expansion of uses-and-gratifications inquiry.

THE USES-AND-GRATIFICATIONS PARADIGM

Uses and gratifications' principal elements include people's needs and motives to communicate, the psychological and social environment, the mass media, functional alternatives to media use, communication behavior, and the consequences of such behavior. Katz, Blumler, and Gurevitch (1974) outlined the objectives of uses and gratifications: (a) to explain how people use media to gratify their needs, (b) to understand motives for media behavior, and (c) to identify functions or consequences that follow from needs, motives, and behavior. Uses and gratifications focuses on:

(1) the social and psychological origins of (2) needs, which generate (3) expectations of (4) the mass media or other sources, which lead to (5) differential patterns of media exposure (or engagement in other activities), resulting in (6) need gratifications and (7) other consequences, perhaps mostly unintended ones. (p. 20)

Rosengren (1974) and Katz and his colleagues (1974) sketched the initial tenets of uses and gratifications. These assumptions have been revised since then to reflect learning about media audiences (see Palmgreen, 1984; Palmgreen, Wenner, & Rosengren, 1985; A. Rubin, 1986). A contemporary view of uses and gratifications is grounded in five assumptions:

(a) Communication behavior, including media selection and use, is goal-directed, purposive, and motivated. People are relatively active communication participants who choose media or content. The behavior is functional and has consequences for people and societies.

(b) People take the initiative in selecting and using communication vehicles to satisfy felt needs or desires. Instead of being used by the media, people use and select media to gratify their needs or wants (Katz, Gurevitch, & Haas, 1973). Media use may be a response to basic needs, but also satisfies wants or interests such as seeking information to solve a personal dilemma.

(c) A host of social and psychological factors mediate people's communication behavior. Predispositions, interaction, and environment mold expectations about the media. Behavior responds to media or messages as filtered through one's social and psychological circumstances such as the potential for interpersonal interaction, social categories, and personality.

(d) Media compete with other forms of communication (i.e., functional alternatives) for selection, attention, and use to gratify our needs or wants. There are definite relationships between mass and interpersonal communication in this process. How well media satisfy our motives or desires varies among individuals based on their social and psychological circumstances.

(e) People are typically more influential than the media in the relationship, but not always. One's initiative mediates patterns and consequences of media use. Through this process, media may affect individual characteristics or social, political, cultural, or economic structures of society. (Rosengren, 1974; A. Rubin & Windahl, 1986)

Katz and his colleagues (1974) listed two other early assumptions of the perspective: (a) methodologically, people can articulate their own motives to communicate (i.e., self-reports provide accurate data about media use); and (b) value judgments about the cultural significance of media content or use should be suspended until motives and gratifications are fully understood. Self-reports are still used, but along with other modes of inquiry. And, because we now have a better understanding of motivation, inquiry can turn to questions of cultural significance.

The suppositions of uses and gratifications underscore the role of audience initiative and activity. Communication is goal directed and purposive. People intentionally participate and select media or messages from communication alternatives in response to their expectations. These expectations emanate from personal traits, social context, and interaction. A person has the capacity for subjective choice and interpretation and initiates behavior such as media selection. This initiative affects outcomes. Initiative or activity, though, has come to be seen as more variable than absolute during the past two decades (e.g., Blumler, 1979; Levy & Windahl, 1984, 1985; A. Rubin & Perse, 1987a, 1987b).

EVOLUTION OF USES-AND-GRATIFICATIONS RESEARCH

Uses-and-gratifications research has focused on audience motivation and consumption. It has been guided by revised research questions shifting our focus to what people do with the media, instead of what the media do to people (Klapper, 1963). Research was unsystematic in its early development, but has become more systematic and has begun to ask about the consequences of media use.

Media-Use Typologies

Early gratifications research sought to learn why people use certain media content. Lazarsfeld (1940), for example, considered the appeals of radio programs. These studies preceded any formal conceptualization of uses and gratifications. They described audience motives rather than the effects of the media. Examples of these studies include: the appeals of a radio quiz program for its listeners (Herzog, 1940); the gratifications obtained by women who listen to radio daytime serials (Herzog, 1944); and the reasons why people read the newspaper (Berelson, 1949). Such research was largely abandoned in favor of studies of personal influence and media functions during the 1950s and 1960s.

In the early 1970s uses-and-gratifications research turned to examine audience motivations, developing typologies of the uses people made of the media to gratify social and psychological needs (Katz et al., 1973). Needs were related to social roles and psychological dispositions and often took the form of strengthening or weakening a connection with a referent such as self, family, or society. Katz et al. developed a typology of the helpfulness of the media in satisfying important needs. This typology included such needs as: strengthening understanding of self, friends, others, or society; strengthening the status of self or society; and strengthening contact with family, friends, society, or culture.

Such typologies intend to explain media consumption. They also say something about connections between goals and outcomes, and suggest the complexities of media uses and effects. McQuail, Blumler, and Brown (1972), for example, categorized types of audience gratifications for using television content. They linked social circumstances and viewer background with gratifications sought. They formulated a typology of media–person interactions, observing that people are motivated to use television for: diversion (i.e., escape, emotional release); personal relationships (i.e., companionship, social utility); personal identity (i.e., personal reference, reality exploration, value reinforcement); and surveillance (e.g., acquiring news and information). They concluded that an escapist view of television use is unconvincing, programs are multidimensional in appeal, and "the relationship between content categories and audience needs is far less tidy and more complex than most commentators have appreciated" (p. 162).

Rosengren and Windahl (1972) also observed links between media and their audiences. They noted that associations among individual and environmental possibilities to satisfy a need can result in satisfactory or unsatisfactory solutions to felt problems. They labeled this as the degree of *dependence* on functional alternatives, that can lead to using alternatives to supplement, complement, or substitute for media use. People may seek these alternatives for various reasons such as compensation, change, escape, or vicarious experience. Also, needs for interaction and identification can result in four degrees of *involvement* with media: detachment, parasocial interaction, solitary identification, or capture. Audience members' needs for interaction also can be seen in terms of the degree of *reality proximity* of media content, ranging from noninformative fictional content to informative nonfictional content.

Rosengren and Windahl (1972) posited a link between dependence, involvement, and reality proximity. They reported that one's interaction potential leads to actual interaction, media consumption, and involvement, that actual interaction leads to media consumption, and that consumption leads to involvement. They argued that the two traditions of media effects and media uses must merge, and that it is possible "to ask what effect a given use made of the mass media, or a given gratification obtained from them, may have" (p. 176). This is one of the earlier statements about linking media uses and effects.

Criticisms

Uses and gratifications has received its share of criticism. Much, though, reflects the state of affairs in the early 1970s and is directed at initial assumptions and early research. In many instances opponents criticize without having attended to published work of the past 15 years. Five of the more substantive criticism are summarized below.

To some, by focusing on audience consumption, uses and gratifications is too individualistic. This makes it difficult to explain or predict beyond the persons studied or to consider societal implications of media use (Carey & Kreiling, 1974; Elliott, 1974). To others, though, the strength of the perspective is its focus on how individual differences affect media uses and effects. Comparison and generalization have become possible with replication and consistent findings across samples, media, and cultures.

Similarly, some argue that studies are compartmentalized, producing separate typologies of motives (Anderson & Meyer, 1975; Swanson, 1979). This hinders conceptual development because separate research findings are not synthesized. This is similar to Fisher's (1978) argument about the pragmatic perspective whereby we have "a proliferation of category systems for analyzing communicative functions" reflecting the interests of the researcher, rather than a "paradigmatic inquiry into communicative phenomena performed by a substantial portion of the scientific community" (p. 232). We have witnessed the development of systematic lines of inquiry since the mid-1970s. To the extent this criticism is still evident, though, it partially reflects the time needed for any perspective to mature.

Some have criticized the lack of clarity among central concepts such as social and psychological background, needs, motives, behavior, and consequences (Anderson & Meyer, 1975; Blumler, 1979; Elliott, 1974). We have witnessed more focused study of these concepts in the past decade. For example, researchers have sought to link loneliness and uncertainty reduction with parasocial interaction (Perse & R. Rubin, 1989; A. Rubin, Perse, & Powell, 1985; R. Rubin & McHugh, 1987), unwillingness to communicate with talk-radio calling (Armstrong & A. Rubin, 1989), and other psychological antecedents with television viewing motivation (Conway & A. Rubin, 1991). Again, systematic inquiry over time will provide further opportunity to examine relationships such as the origins of individual needs that produce motives and behavior, and cultural and societal factors that contribute to media uses and dependency. By focusing on certain relationships, empirical inquiry seldom produces immediate, clear-cut, and sweepingly generalizable answers to questions of communication processes and effects.

Critics also argue that investigators attach different meanings to concepts such as motives, uses, gratifications, and functional alternatives (Elliott, 1974; Swanson, 1977, 1979). This contributes to fuzzy thinking and inquiry. In seeking to explain the sequence of uses-and-gratifications models, certain aspects such as media attitudes are treated as antecedent, intervening, or consequent variables in different studies. In most studies, though, concepts such as needs, motives, uses, and gratifications sought are used in an equivalent manner as antecedents to behavior; effects, consequences, gratifications obtained, and outcomes appear as consequents of the behavior.

Two related assumptions, the active audience and the use of self-report data, also have been criticized (Elliott, 1974; Swanson, 1977, 1979). Uses-and-gratifications researchers have come to treat the audience as less than universally active (Blumler, 1979; Levy & Windahl, 1984, 1985; Windahl, 1981). Activity, itself, has been treated as a variable, rather than as a description or prescription of the audience. For example, we have found that such activity elements as intention and attention helped explain differences in motivation and involvement with entertainment and news programming (A. Rubin & Perse, 1987a, 1987b). Research also has largely supported the consistency and accuracy of self-report data by validating scales (e.g., A. Rubin, 1979, 1981a), and by using experimental (e.g., Bryant & Zillmann, 1984) and ethnographic methods (e.g., Lemish, 1985; Lull, 1980). Yet, we should be cautious about how interpretive processes such as perception and reporting bias can affect self-reports (Babrow, 1988; Swanson, 1987).

All perspectives and methods receive their share of criticism. We could be suspect of validity and reliability in most measuring instruments and modes of observation. Because the individual is usually the unit of analysis, we could question the generalizability of much data beyond the person. And, results of other effects approaches are often not conceptually synthesized. These observations, of course, do not remedy valid criticisms. Indeed, the rationale and design of subsequent uses-and-gratification study have addressed many criticisms. A preoccupation with defending any perspective against such criticisms, however, is counterproductive in seeking to learn about the process and effects of mass communication.

Contemporary Studies

Research since the mid-1970s has addressed several of the criticisms, has helped explain media behavior, and has furthered our understanding of media uses and effects. For example, researchers have provided a more systematic analysis of media processes by adapting similar media-motive measures (e.g., Bantz, 1982; Eastman, 1979; Palmgreen & Rayburn, 1979; Perse, 1986; A. Rubin, 1979, 1981a, 1981b, 1983). Greenberg (1974) developed the scales with British children and adolescents. He found age to be the most significant correlate of the viewing motives (i.e., learning, habit, companionship, arousal, relaxation, escape, pass time), and noted other associations among motives, media behavior, television attitudes, and aggressive attitudes.

A partial replication of that work in the United States identified six reasons why children and adolescents watch television: learning, habit/ pass time, companionship, escape, arousal, and relaxation (A. Rubin, 1979). Age was the most significant correlate of the motives. Habitual viewing related negatively to watching news and positively to television affinity and watching comedies. Viewing to learn related positively to perceived television realism. Viewing for excitement and for companionship was linked with watching action/adventure and comedy programs, respectively. These results were similar to Greenberg's (1974) and present a consistent portrait across cultures. The study also supported stability and consistency of responses via test–retest reliability of viewing-motive items and convergent validity of the motive scales with responses to open-ended queries of viewing reasons. Respondents were able to verbalize their reasons for using media. A similar technique in a later study supported convergent validity for a wider sample, ranging from children to older adults, and continued programmatic development and synthesis (A. Rubin, 1981a).

Other studies also answer criticisms and bear witness to systematic progression. Studies within and across these research programs have included replication and secondary analysis, which further conceptual development. Six research directions are identified below, and some links to media effects research are drawn in the following sections.

1. One direction is the links among media-use motives and their associations with media attitudes and behaviors (Eastman, 1979; Perse, 1986; A. Rubin, 1979, 1981a, 1981b, 1983, 1984, 1985; A. Rubin & Bantz, 1989; A. Rubin & R. Rubin, 1982b). This has provided indications of consistent patterns of media use.

2. A second direction is comparing motives across media or content (Bantz, 1982; Cohen, Levy, & Golden, 1988; Elliott & Quattlebaum, 1979; Katz et al., 1973; Lichtenstein & Rosenfeld, 1983, 1984). The research has produced comparative analyses of the effectiveness of different media to meet needs and wants.

3. A third direction is examining social and psychological circumstances of media use (Adoni, 1979; Dimmick, McCain, & Bolton, 1979; Finn & Gorr, 1988; Lull, 1980; Perse & A. Rubin, 1990; A. Rubin et al., 1985; A. Rubin & R. Rubin, 1982a, 1989; R. Rubin & A. Rubin, 1982; Windahl, Hojerback, & Hedinsson, 1986). This work has addressed how elements such as life position, lifestyle, personality, loneliness, isolation, media deprivation, and family-viewing environment influence media behavior.

4. A fourth direction is analyzing links between gratifications sought and obtained when using media or their content (Babrow, 1989; Babrow & Swanson, 1988; Donohew, Palmgreen, & Rayburn, 1987; Galloway & Meek, 1981; Palmgreen & Rayburn, 1979, 1982, 1985; Palmgreen, Wenner, & Rayburn, 1980, 1981; Rayburn & Palmgreen, 1984; Wenner, 1982, 1986). These studies have addressed how motives people have for using media are satisfied, and have proposed transactional, discrepancy, and expectancy-value models of media uses and gratifications.

5. A fifth direction is assessing how variations in background variables, motives, and exposure affect outcomes such as the effects of exposure or motivation on relational perceptions, cultivation, involvement, parasocial interaction, satisfaction, and political knowledge (Alexander, 1985; Carveth & Alexander, 1985; Garramone, 1984; Perse, 1990; Perse & A. Rubin, 1988; A. Rubin, 1985; R. Rubin & McHugh, 1987).

6. A sixth direction is considering the method for measuring and analyzing motivation including reliability and validity (Babrow, 1988; Dobos & Dimmick, 1988; McDonald & Glynn, 1984).

MEDIA USES AND EFFECTS

Some have proposed a synthesis of uses-and-gratifications and media-effects research (Rosengren & Windahl, 1972; A. Rubin & Windahl, 1986; Windahl, 1981). There is a difference between the two traditions: An effects researcher "most often looks at the mass communication process from the communicator's end," whereas a uses researcher begins with the audience member (Windahl, p. 176). For a synthesis of the traditions, Windahl argued that is more beneficial to stress similarities. One major similarity is that both uses and effects seek to explain the outcomes or consequences of mass communication such as individual attitudes or perceptions (e.g., cultivation), behavioral changes (e.g., dependency), and societal effects (e.g., knowledge gaps). Uses and gratifications does so, however, recognizing the potential for audience initiative and activity.

Audience Activity and Media Orientations

Audience activity is the core concept in uses and gratifications. By audience activity we refer to the utility, intentionality, selectivity, and involvement of the audience with the media (Blumler, 1979). No longer, however, do uses-and-gratifications researchers regard audience members to be universally active. They assume a variably active media audience. In short, all audience members are not equally active at all times.

To test this assumption, Levy and Windahl (1984) identified three activity periods for Swedish television viewers: previewing, during viewing, and postviewing. They found that, although preactivity or intention to watch is weakly related to entertainment media use, it is strongly related to surveillance use. They argued that viewers actively seek news to gain information, but do not actively seek diversion.

This finding is consistent with Windahl's (1981) view that depicting the audience "as superational and very selective . . . invites criticism" (p. 176). It also is similar to other research that has treated motives as interrelated structures rather than isolated entities (Abelman, 1987; Perse, 1986, 1990; Perse & A. Rubin, 1988; A. Rubin, 1981b, 1983, 1984; A. Rubin & Perse, 1987a; A. Rubin & R. Rubin, 1982b). Finn (1992) suggested proactive (mood management) and passive (social compensation) media-use dimensions. Others found that media use can be described as primarily ritualized (diversionary) or instrumental (utilitarian) in nature (A. Rubin, 1984).

Ritualized and instrumental media orientations tell us about the amount and type of media use, and about one's media attitudes and expectations. Ritualized media use is using a medium more habitually to consume time and for diversion. It relates to greater exposure to and affinity with the medium. Ritualized use suggests utility but an otherwise less active or less goal-directed state. Instrumental media use is seeking certain media content for informational reasons. It relates to greater exposure to news and informational content and perceiving that content to be realistic. Instrumental use is active and purposive. It suggests utility, intention, selectivity, and involvement.

Activity depends, to a large extent, on the social context and potential for interaction. Elements such as mobility and loneliness are important. Reduced mobility and greater loneliness, for example, result in ritualized media orientations and greater reliance on the media (Perse & A. Rubin, 1990; A. Rubin & R. Rubin, 1982a). Attitudinal dispositions such as affinity and perceived realism are also important. Attitudes filter media and message selection and use. This is consistent with Swanson's (1979) argument about the importance of "the perceptual activity of interpreting or creating meaning for messages" (p. 42). These attitudes, which result from past experiences with a medium and produce expectations for future gratification-seeking behavior, affect meaning.

Blumler (1979) argued that activity means imperviousness to influence. In other words, activity is a deterrent to media effects. The validity of this conclusion, though, is questionable. Activity plays an important intervening role in the effects process. Because activity denotes a more selective, attentive, and involved state of media use, it may be a catalyst to effects. In two studies, for example, instrumental television viewing led to greater cognitive, affective, or behavioral involvement with news and soap operas (A. Rubin & Perse, 1987a, 1987b). In another study, watching action/adventure programs predicted a cultivation effect of feeling less safe, whereas watching television, in general, led to perceptions of greater safety (A. Rubin, Perse, & Taylor, 1988). Stronger cultivation effects are possible when media content is seen as being realistic.

These differences in activity, as evidenced in ritualized and instrumental orientations, then, have implications for media effects. Windahl (1981) argued that using a medium instrumentally or ritualistically produces different outcomes. He saw *effects* as the outcome of using media content and *consequences* as the outcome of using a medium. Instrumental orientations may produce stronger attitudinal effects because they incorporate greater involvement with the message.

Dependency, Alternatives, and Interaction

The idea of media dependency is derived from the role of functional alternatives (Rosengren & Windahl, 1972). Dependency on a medium results from motives or strategies for obtaining gratifications and restricted functional alternatives. Social and psychological attributes (e.g., health, mobility, interaction, life satisfaction, economic security) affect the availability of alternatives, media motives or orientations, and dependency on a medium. In two studies, for example, we observed a negative link between one's degree of self-reliance and television dependency (A. Rubin & R. Rubin, 1982a; R. Rubin & A. Rubin, 1982).

Dependency results from an environmental context that restricts the use of functional alternatives and produces a pattern of media use. Dependency, then, is an intervening factor in media use. In one study, Miller and Reese (1982) found that certain political effects (i.e., activity and efficacy) are more evident from exposure to a relied-upon medium: "Dependency on a medium appears to enhance the opportunity for that medium to have predicted effects" (p. 245).

The links between dependency and functional alternatives help show how uses and gratifications is a perspective capable of interfacing personal and mediated communication. Besides media consumers, resourceful interpersonal communicators have "a wider availability of alternative channels, a broader conception of the potential channels, and the capacity for using more diversified message- and interaction-seeking strategies" (A. Rubin & R. Rubin, 1985, p. 39). They, too, will less likely be dependent on any given person or communication channel.

The personal and media interface also is apparent in how people use the media in relationship to one another. Lull's (1980) typology of the social uses of television illustrates this. One can use television structurally as an environmental resource (e.g., for companionship) or as a behavioral regulator (e.g., punctuating time). Or, one can use television relationally to facilitate communication (e.g., an agenda for conversation), for affiliation or avoidance (e.g., conflict resolution), for social learning (e.g., behavioral modeling), or for competence or dominance (e.g., role reinforcement). Interpersonal needs result in different media uses, which produce different outcomes for the interactants. So, for example, talk radio provides an accessible and nonthreatening alternative to interpersonal communication especially for those with restricted mobility and who are apprehensive about face-to-face interaction (Armstrong & A. Rubin, 1989; Avery, Ellis, & Glover, 1978; Turow, 1974). We have also hypothesized, but without empirical support, that the lonely are more likely than the nonlonely to develop parasocial relationships with media personalities (A. Rubin et al., 1985).

Uses-and-Effects Models

A few models seek to explain media uses and effects. They usually link media motives, behaviors, and content with other features in the mass communication process. McLeod and Becker (1974) argued that a synthesis of the "hypodermic and limited effects models, in which the exposure characteristics of the message *combine with* the orientation of the audience member in producing an effect, may be able to escape the unwarranted simplicities of each of the parent models" (p. 141). Such a transactional model, they reasoned, would "recognize the erroneousness" of both "content equals effect" and "audience intention equals effect" positions.

McLeod and Becker found support for an additive transactional model whereby the gratification supplements exposure when explaining political effects such as issue accuracy and campaign interest. Wenner (1982, 1986) also found support for an additive model as gratifications explained additional variance beyond exposure for dependency on television news and information programs. McLeod, Becker, and Byrnes (1974), though, noted interaction effects of media gratifications and exposure because most gratifications acted "as deterrents to agenda setting" (p. 161).

A. Rubin and Perse (1987b) proposed a model of gratification seeking and audience activity. According to the model, behavior originates with expectations (i.e., anticipated gratifications and media attitudes). We suggested that the uses and effects process flows from "gratifications sought, through attitudes, to behavioral intention, selective exposure to media and messages, attention to the content when consuming the messages, and involvement with that content" (p. 77). Cognitive, affective, or behavioral effects would follow from involvement.

Expectancy-value models have been included in the gratifications sought and obtained research. According to Palmgreen and Rayburn (1982), behavior, behavioral intention, and attitude are a function of: "(1) *expectancy* (or belief), that is, the probability that an attitude possesses a particular attribute or that a behavior will have a particular consequence, and (2) *evaluation*, that is, the degree of affect, positive or negative, toward an attitude or behavioral outcome" (pp. 562–563). The model predicts gratification seeking from communication channels based on the expectancy of an outcome. Linking the model to effects is possible by interpreting the outcome of behavioral intention in terms of the gratifications obtained, such as attitude formation and behavior. The model permits consideration of expectancy and evaluative thresholds for behaviors, and comparisons of congruence of expectation and outcome. Babrow and Swanson (1988) argued that expectancy-value models need to consider associations between gratifications sought and attitude to predict exposure behavior.

The Uses and Dependency Model proposes another uses-and-effects synthesis (A. Rubin & Windahl, 1986). It does so by placing audience consumption at the center of dependency's systems approach. According to the model, societal structure, the media system, individual needs and motives, media use, functional alternatives, and consequences of behavior are shaped by other components of the system. These elements produce different patterns of media use and dependencies on the media or their content. The model depicts links between needs and motives, information-seeking strategies, media and functional alternative use, and media dependency such that, for example, needs and motives that produce narrow information-seeking strategies might lead to dependency on certain channels. Dependency, in turn, leads to other effects such as attitude change, and feeds back to alter system components and relationships. The model posits different outcomes as the result of ritualized use of a medium and instrumental use of media content.

CONCLUSIONS

Two decades ago, Katz and his colleagues (1974) argued that "hardly any substantive or empirical effort has been devoted to connecting gratifications and effects" (p. 28). Five years later, Blumler (1979) echoed those sentiments: "We lack a well-formed perspective about which gratifications sought from which forms of content are likely to facilitate which effects" (p. 16). Although some precision has been lacking, this state of affairs has changed during the past decade as investigators have sought to link psychological and social antecedents, media motivation, behavior, attitudes, and outcomes. Reformulations of media orientations and audience activity have produced renewed interest in linking gratifications sought and effects. Yet, increased specificity is needed.

Blumler summarized three primary media uses: cognitive, diversion, and personal identity. He proposed three hypotheses about media effects based on these gratifications. First, cognitive motivation will facilitate information gain. Second, diversion or escape motivation will facilitate audience perceptions of the accuracy of social portrayals in entertainment media. Third, personal identity motivation will promote reinforcement effects.

Such hypotheses have received some attention to date. For example, cognitive or instrumental motivation leads to seeking informational content and to cognitive involvement (Perse, 1990; A. Rubin, 1983, 1984; A. Rubin & Perse, 1987b; A. Rubin & R. Rubin, 1982b). Researchers have observed links between cognitive or instrumental information-seeking motivation and information gain during a political campaign (McLeod & Becker, 1974), about political candidates (Atkin & Heald, 1976), and about candidates' stands on issues. They have found that public affairs media use and interest lead to increased political knowledge (Pettey, 1988).

The second hypothesis about diversionary motivation and acceptance of role portrayals, though, must recognize the mediating role of attitudes and experiences in media effects. We have learned that attitude and experience affect audience perceptions more than does ritualistic motivation. Limited research supports cultivation effects contingent on the perceived reality of content (Potter, 1986; A. Rubin et al., 1988), audience members' personal experiences with crime (Weaver & Wakshlag, 1986), and media utility and selectivity (Perse, 1986). As to Blumler's (1979) third hypothesis, we have seen that media function as alternatives to personal interaction for the immobile, dissatisfied, and apprehensive (Armstrong & A. Rubin, 1989; Perse & A. Rubin, 1990; A. Rubin & R. Rubin, 1982a), and that social utility motivation might lead to a reduced sense of parasocial interaction with television personalities (A. Rubin & Perse, 1987a).

Windahl (1981) argued that a synthesis would help overcome limitations and criticisms of uses and effects traditions. Such a synthesis would recognize that: media perceptions and expectations guide people's behavior; besides needs, motivation is derived from interests and externally imposed constraints; there are functional alternatives to media consumption; and media content plays an important role in media effects.

During the past decade, we have begun to address theoretical links among media uses and effects. We have learned more about audience members as variably active communicators. We have seen the contributions of interpersonal communication for understanding media uses and effects. The media uses and effects process is a complex one that requires careful attention to antecedent, mediating, and consequent conditions. Single-variable explanations are appealing, yet distracting from the conceptual complexity of media effects.

REFERENCES

Abelman, R. (1987). Religious television uses and gratifications. *Journal of Broadcasting & Electronic Media, 31*, 293–307.

Adoni, H. (1979). The functions of mass media in the political socialization of adolescents. *Communication Research, 6*, 84–106.

Alexander, A. (1985). Adolescents' soap opera viewing and relational perceptions. *Journal of Broadcasting & Electronic Media, 29*, 295–308.

Anderson, J. A., & Meyer, T. P. (1975). Functionalism and the mass media. *Journal of Broadcasting, 19*, 11–22.

Armstrong, C. B., & Rubin, A. M. (1989). Talk radio as interpersonal communication. *Journal of Communication, 39*(2), 84–94.

Atkin, C. K., & Heald, G. (1976). Effects of political advertising. *Public Opinion Quarterly, 40*, 216–228.

Avery, R. K., Ellis, D. G., & Glover, T. W. (1978). Patterns of communication on talk radio. *Journal of Broadcasting, 22*, 5–17.

Babrow, A. S. (1988). Theory and method in research on audience motives. *Journal of Broadcasting & Electronic Media, 32*, 471–487.

Babrow, A. S. (1989). An expectancy-value analysis of the student soap opera audience. *Communication Research, 16*, 155–178.

Babrow, A. S., & Swanson, D. L. (1988). Disentangling antecedents of audience exposure levels: Extending expectancy-value analyses of gratifications sought from television news. *Communication Monographs, 55*, 1–21.

Bantz, C. R. (1982). Exploring uses and gratifications: A comparison of reported uses of television and reported uses of favorite program type. *Communication Research, 9*, 352–379.

Berelson, B. (1949). What 'missing the newspaper' means. In P. F. Lazarsfeld & F. N. Stanton (Eds.), *Communications research 1948–1949* (pp. 111–129). New York: Harper.

Blumler, J. G. (1979). The role of theory in uses and gratifications studies. *Communication Research, 6*, 9–36.

Bryant, J., & Zillmann, D. (1984). Using television to alleviate boredom and stress: Selective exposure as a function of induced excitational states. *Journal of Broadcasting, 28*, 1–20.

Carey, J. W., & Kreiling, A. L. (1974). Popular culture and uses and gratifications: Notes toward an accommodation. In J. G. Blumler & E. Katz (Eds.), *The uses of mass* communications: Current perspectives on gratifications research (pp. 225–248). Beverly Hills, CA: Sage.

Carveth, R., & Alexander, A. (1985). Soap opera viewing motivations and the cultivation process. *Journal of Broadcasting & Electronic Media, 29,* 259–273.

Cohen, A. A., Levy, M. R., & Golden, K. (1988). Children's uses and gratifications of home VCRs: Evolution or revolution. *Communication Research, 15,* 772–780.

Conway, J. C., & Rubin, A. M. (1991). Psychological predictors of television viewing motivation. *Communication Research, 18,* 443–464.

Dimmick, J. W., McCain, T. A., & Bolton, W. T. (1979). Media use and the life span. *American Behavioral Scientist, 23*(1), 7–31.

Dobos, J., & Dimmick, J. (1988). Factor analysis and gratification constructs. *Journal of Broadcasting & Electronic Media, 32,* 335–350.

Donohew, L., Palmgreen, P., & Rayburn, J. D., II. (1987). Social and psychological origins of media use: A lifestyle analysis. *Journal of Broadcasting & Electronic Media, 31,* 255–278.

Eastman, S. T. (1979). Uses of television viewing and consumer life styles: A multivariate analysis. *Journal of Broadcasting, 23,* 491–500.

Elliott, P. (1974). Uses and gratifications research: A critique and a sociological alternative. In J. G. Blumler & E. Katz (Eds.), *The uses of mass communications: Current perspectives on gratifications research* (pp. 249–268). Beverly Hills, CA: Sage.

Elliott, W. R., & Quattlebaum, C. P. (1979). Similarities in patterns of media use: A cluster analysis of media gratifications. *Western Journal of Speech Communication, 43,* 61–72.

Finn, S. (1992). Television addiction? An evaluation of four competing media-use models. *Journalism Quarterly, 69,* 422–435.

Finn, S., & Gorr, M. B. (1988). Social isolation and social support as correlates of television viewing motivations. *Communication Research, 15,* 135–158.

Fisher, B. A. (1978). *Perspectives on human communication.* New York: Macmillan.

Galloway, J. J., & Meek, F. L. (1981). Audience uses and gratifications: An expectancy model. *Communication Research, 8,* 435–449.

Garramone, G. M. (1983). Issue versus image orientation and effects of political advertising. *Communication Research, 10,* 59–76.

Garramone, G. M. (1984). Audience motivation effect: More evidence. *Communication Research, 11,* 79–96.

Greenberg, B. S. (1974). Gratifications of television viewing and their correlates for British children. In J. G. Blumler & E. Katz (Eds.), *The uses of mass communications: Current perspectives on gratifications research* (pp. 71–92). Beverly Hills, CA: Sage.

Herzog, H. (1940). Professor quiz: A gratification study. In P. F. Lazarsfeld (Ed.), *Radio and the printed page* (pp. 64–93). New York: Duell, Sloan & Pearce.

Herzog, H. (1944). What do we really know about daytime serial listeners? In P. F. Lazarsfeld & F. N. Stanton (Eds.), *Radio research 1942–1943* (pp. 3–33). New York: Duell, Sloan & Pearce.

Horton, D., & Wohl, R. R. (1956). Mass communication and para-social interaction. *Psychiatry, 19,* 215–229.

Katz, E. (1959). Mass communication research and the study of popular culture. *Studies in Public Communication, 2,* 1–6.

Katz, E., Blumler, J. G., & Gurevitch, M. (1974). Utilization of mass communication by the individual. In J. G. Blumler & E. Katz (Eds.), *The uses of mass communications: Current perspectives on gratifications research* (pp. 19–32). Beverly Hills, CA: Sage.

Katz, E., Gurevitch, M., & Haas, H. (1973). On the use of the mass media for important things. *American Sociological Review, 38,* 164–181.

Klapper, J. T. (1960). *The effects of mass communication.* New York: Free Press.

Klapper, J. T. (1963). Mass communication research: An old road resurveyed. *Public Opinion Quarterly, 27,* 515–527.

Lasswell, H. D. (1948). The structure and function of communication in society. In L. Bryson (Ed.), *The communication of ideas* (pp. 37–51). New York: Harper.

Lazarsfeld, P. F. (1940). *Radio and the printed page.* New York: Duell, Sloan & Pearce.

Lazarsfeld, P. F., & Merton, R. K. (1948). Mass communication, popular taste and organized social action. In L. Bryson (Ed.), *The communication of ideas* (pp. 95–118). New York: Harper.

Lemish, D. (1985). Soap opera viewing in college: A naturalistic inquiry. *Journal of Broadcasting & Electronic Media, 29,* 275–293.

Levy, M. R., & Windahl, S. (1984). Audience activity and gratifications: A conceptual clarification and exploration. *Communication Research, 11,* 51–78.

Levy, M. R., & Windahl, S. (1985). The concept of audience activity. In K. E. Rosengren, L. A. Wenner, & P. Palmgreen (Eds.), *Media gratifications research: Current perspectives* (pp. 109–122). Beverly Hills, CA: Sage.

Lichtenstein, A., & Rosenfeld, L. B. (1983). Uses and misuses of gratifications research: An explication of media functions. *Communication Research, 10,* 97–109.

Lichtenstein, A., & Rosenfeld, L. (1984). Normative expectations and individual decisions concerning media gratification choices. *Communication Research, 11,* 393–413

Lull, J. (1980). The social uses of television. *Human Communication Research, 6,* 197–209.

McCombs, M. E., & Shaw, D. L. (1972). The agenda-setting function of mass media. *Public Opinion Quarterly, 36,* 176–187.

McDonald, D. G., & Glynn, C. J. (1984). The stability of media gratifications. *Journalism Quarterly, 61,* 542–549, 741.

McLeod, J. M., & Becker, L. B. (1974). Testing the validity of gratification measures through political effects analysis. In J. G. Blumler & E. Katz (Eds.), *The uses of mass communications: Current perspectives on gratifications research* (pp. 137–164). Beverly Hills, CA: Sage.

McLeod, J. M., Becker, L. B., & Byrnes, J. E. (1974). Another look at the agenda-setting function of the press. *Communication Research, 1,* 131–166.

McQuail, D., Blumler, J. G., & Brown, J. R. (1972). The television audience: A revised perspective. In D. McQuail (Ed.), *Sociology of mass communications* (pp. 135–165). Middlesex, England: Penguin.

Mendelsohn, H. (1963). Socio-psychological perspectives on the mass media and public anxiety. *Journalism Quarterly, 40,* 511–516.

Miller, M. M., & Reese, S. D. (1982). Media dependency as interaction: Effects of exposure and reliance on political activity and efficacy. *Communication Research, 9,* 227–248.

Palmgreen, P. (1984). Uses and gratifications: A theoretical perspective. *Communication Yearbook, 8,* 20–55.

Palmgreen, P., & Rayburn, J. D., II. (1979). Uses and gratifications and exposure to public television: A discrepancy approach. *Communication Research, 6,* 155–179.

Palmgreen, P., & Rayburn, J. D., II. (1982). Gratifications sought and media exposure: An expectancy value model. *Communication Research, 9,* 561–580.

Palmgreen, P., & Rayburn, J. D., II. (1985). A comparison of gratification models of media satisfaction. *Communication Monographs, 52,* 334–346.

Palmgreen, P., Wenner, L. A., & Rayburn, J. D., II. (1980). Relations between gratifications sought and obtained: A study of television news. *Communication Research, 7,* 161–192.

Palmgreen, P., Wenner, L. A., & Rayburn, J. D., II. (1981). Gratification discrepancies and news program choice. *Communication Research, 8,* 451–478.

Palmgreen, P., Wenner, L. A., & Rosengren, K. E. (1985). Uses and gratifications research: The past ten years. In K. E. Rosengren, L. A. Wenner, & P. Palmgreen (Eds.), *Media gratifications research: Current perspectives* (pp. 11–37). Beverly Hills, CA: Sage.

Pearlin, L. I. (1959). Social and personal stress and escape television viewing. *Public Opinion Quarterly, 23,* 255–259.

Perse, E. M. (1986). Soap opera viewing patterns of college students and cultivation. *Journal of Broadcasting & Electronic Media, 30,* 175–193.

Perse, E. M. (1990). Involvement with local television news: Cognitive and emotional dimensions. *Human Communication Research, 16,* 556–581.

Perse, E. M., & Rubin, A. M. (1988). Audience activity and satisfaction with favorite television soap opera. *Journalism Quarterly, 65,* 368–375.

Perse, E. M., & Rubin, A. M. (1990). Chronic loneliness and television use. *Journal of Broadcasting & Electronic Media, 34,* 37–53.

Perse, E. M., & Rubin, R. B. (1989). Attribution in social and parasocial relationships. *Communication Research, 16,* 59–77.

Pettey, G. R. (1988). The interaction of the individual's social environment, attention and interest, and public affairs media use on political knowledge holding. *Communication Research, 15,* 265–281.

Potter, W. J. (1986). Perceived reality and the cultivation hypothesis. *Journal of Broadcasting & Electronic Media, 30,* 159–174.

Rayburn, J. D., II, & Palmgreen, P. (1984). Merging uses and gratifications and expectancy-value theory. *Communication Research, 11,* 537–562.

Rosengren, K. E. (1974). Uses and gratifications: A paradigm outlined. In J. G. Blumler & E. Katz (Eds.), *The uses of mass communications: Current perspectives on gratifications research* (pp. 269–286). Beverly Hills, CA: Sage.

Rosengren, K. E., & Windahl, S. (1972). Mass media consumption as a functional alternative. In D. McQuail (Ed.), *Sociology of mass communications* (pp. 166–194). Middlesex, England: Penguin.

Rubin, A. M. (1979). Television use by children and adolescents. *Human Communication Research, 5,* 109–120.

Rubin, A. M. (1981a). An examination of television viewing motivations. *Communication Research, 8,* 141–165.

Rubin, A. M. (1981b). A multivariate analysis of "60 Minutes" viewing motivations. *Journalism Quarterly, 58,* 529–534.

Rubin, A. M. (1983). Television uses and gratifications: The interactions of viewing patterns and motivations. *Journal of Broadcasting, 27,* 37–51.

Rubin, A. M. (1984). Ritualized and instrumental television viewing. *Journal of Communication, 34*(3), 67–77.

Rubin, A. M. (1985). Uses of daytime television soap opera by college students. *Journal of Broadcasting & Electronic Media, 29,* 241–258.

Rubin, A. M. (1986). Uses, gratifications, and media effects research. In J. Bryant & D. Zillmann (Eds.), *Perspectives on media effects* (pp. 281–301). Hillsdale, NJ: Lawrence Erlbaum Associates.

Rubin, A. M., & Bantz, C. R. (1989). Uses and gratifications of videocassette recorders. In J. Salvaggio & J. Bryant (Eds.), *Media use in the information age: Emerging patterns of adoption and consumer use* (pp. 181–195). Hillsdale, NJ: Lawrence Erlbaum Associates.

Rubin, A. M., & Perse, E. M. (1987a). Audience activity and soap opera involvement: A uses and effects investigation. *Human Communication Research, 14,* 246–268.

Rubin, A. M., & Perse, E. M. (1987b). Audience activity and television news gratifications. *Communication Research, 14,* 58–84.

Rubin, A. M., Perse, E. M., & Powell, R. A. (1985). Loneliness, parasocial interaction, and local television news viewing. *Human Communication Research, 12,* 155–180.

Rubin, A. M., Perse, E. M., & Taylor, D. S. (1988). A methodological examination of cultivation. *Communication Research, 15,* 107–134.

Rubin, A. M., & Rubin, R. B. (1982a). Contextual age and television use. *Human Communication Research, 8,* 228–244.

Rubin, A. M., & Rubin, R. B. (1982b). Older persons' TV viewing patterns and motivations. *Communication Research, 9,* 287–313.

Rubin, A. M., & Rubin, R. B. (1985). Interface of personal and mediated communication: A research agenda. *Critical Studies in Mass Communication, 2,* 36–53.

Rubin, A. M., & Rubin, R. B. (1989). Social and psychological antecedents of VCR use. In M. R. Levy (Ed.), *The VCR age: Home video and mass communication* (pp. 92–111). Newbury Park, CA: Sage.

Rubin, A. M., & Windahl, S. (1986). The uses and dependency model of mass communication. *Critical Studies in Mass Communication, 3,* 184–199.

Rubin, R. B., & McHugh, M. P. (1987). Development of parasocial interaction relationships. *Journal of Broadcasting & Electronic Media, 31,* 279–292.

Rubin, R. B., & Rubin, A. M. (1982). Contextual age and television use: Reexamining a life-position indicator. *Communication Yearbook, 6,* 583–604.

Stephenson, W. (1967). *The play theory of mass communication.* Chicago: University of Chicago Press.

Swanson, D. L. (1977). The uses and misuses of uses and gratifications. *Human Communication Research, 3,* 214–221.

Swanson, D. L. (1979). Political communication research and the uses and gratifications model: A critique. *Communication Research, 6,* 37–53.

Swanson, D. L. (1987). Gratification seeking, media exposure, and audience interpretations: Some directions for research. *Journal of Broadcasting & Electronic Media, 31,* 237–254.

Turow, J. (1974). Talk-show radio as interpersonal communication. *Journal of Broadcasting, 18,* 171–179.

Weaver, J., & Wakshlag, J. (1986). Perceived vulnerability to crime, criminal victimization experience, and television viewing. *Journal of Broadcasting & Electronic Media, 30,* 141–158.

Wenner, L. A. (1982). Gratifications sought and obtained in program dependency: A study of network evening news programs and "60 Minutes." *Communication Research, 9,* 539–560.

Wenner, L. A. (1986). Model specification and theoretical development in gratifications sought and obtained research: A comparison of discrepancy and transactional approaches. *Communication Monographs, 53,* 160–179.

Windahl, S. (1981). Uses and gratifications at the crossroads. *Mass Communication Review Yearbook, 2,* 174–185.

Windahl, S., Hojerback, I., & Hedinsson, E. (1986). Adolescents without television: A study in media deprivation. *Journal of Broadcasting & Electronic Media, 30,* 47–63.

Wright, C. R. (1960). Functional analysis and mass communication. *Public Opinion Quarterly, 24,* 605–620.

15

Entertainment as Media Effect

DOLF ZILLMANN
JENNINGS BRYANT
University of Alabama

Many of the chapters in this volume examine effects of media messages that are not intended by producers of these messages (e.g., distorted perceptions of reality, aggression, obesity, sexual dispositions) and that are the byproduct of trying to attract and maintain large audiences for entertaining, informational, and commercial messages. Other chapters consider the intended effects of messages with primarily persuasive intent (e.g., public communication campaigns, political advertising). Although these types of media effects clearly are important and worthy of the rich research traditions they represent, when considered in terms of normative patterns of media influence, these frequently studied effects are not the primary intended effects of most of today's media messages. From the perspective of producers, the primary purpose of the preponderance of today's electronic media messages is *entertainment*.

CONCEPTUALIZATION OF ENTERTAINMENT

Entertainment is a ubiquitous phenomenon. No culture of which we have an adequate accounting has been entirely without it. As soon as the struggle for survival left human groups with sufficient time for relaxation, some form of communicative activity in which dangers and threats and their mastery and elimination were represented seems to have come into being (e.g., Hauser, 1953; Kuhn, 1962–1963; Malinowski, 1948). By the time permanent records were left for posterity, cultures had developed well-defined rites. These rites, to be sure, served the maintenance of social structure and postmortem welfare. In large measure, however, they also served the cause of amusement, merriment, gaiety, fun, and joyous enlightenment. In other words, they served the cause of entertainment.

If entertainment is crudely defined as any activity designed to delight and, to a smaller degree, enlighten through the exhibition of the fortunes or misfortunes of others, but also through the display of special skills by others and/or self, it becomes clear that the concept encompasses more than comedy, drama, and tragedy. It engulfs any kind of game or play, athletic or not, competitive or not, whether witnessed only, taken part in, or performed alone. It subsumes, for instance, musical performances by self for self or others, of others for self, or with others; similarly, it subsumes dancing by self, of others, or with others.

Given such a broad conceptualization, entertainment happenings must have been obtrusive enough to catch the attention of those inclined to understand social phenomena. And they did. Plato, through the dialogue between Socrates and Protarchus in *Philebus*, reflected on the delight derived from learning about the fortunes and misfortunes of others. He approved of some conditions for delight, but he morally condemned many others. In so doing, he set a trend: Entertainment was to be judged in moral terms, a judgment that tended to give it little social merit and that detracted from studying its function in a neutral fashion. Surely, there were less value-laden analyses. Aristotle, in his *Poetics*, furnished an account of the workings of drama that could stand as a model of morally detached description. Western thinking about entertainment and its usefulness continued in a moral vein, however. Barring sacral contexts, Christian philosophers failed to see any redeeming value in singing and dancing, in merriment and gaiety. Those who reflected about the nature of joy, in particular amusement and laughter, detected nothing but evil. Hobbes (1968), for example, thought that laughter "is incident most to them that are conscious of the fewest abilities in themselves; who are forced to keep themselves in their favour, by observing the imperfections of other men" (p. 125). Pascal is usually singled out (e.g., Lowenthal, 1961) as the Christian philosopher who condemned entertainment in the strongest possible terms. Pascal (1941) thought that humans have an "instinct which impels them to seek amusement" and that this impulsion "arises from the sense of their constant unhappiness" (p. 50), and he obviously deemed entertainment an unacceptable means of relief from such unhappiness. But the avenues toward salvation that he favored were not accepted by many others. Montaigne (1927) tends to be credited (e.g., Mendelsohn, 1966) with the opposing, "modern" conception of entertainment as an effective and acceptable means of relief from discontent and the unavoidable stress of daily life. Though he endorsed the unhappiness premise as well, he thought merriment and enlightenment through entertainment, transitory as they may be, were bona fide blessings.

In emphasizing the recreational value of entertainment, Montaigne is said to have anticipated Freud's (e.g., 1930/1960a, 1915/1960b, 1919/1963a, 1908/1963b) views in these matters. Freud's thinking essentially parallels that of Montaigne, indeed. Persons are viewed as suffering the blockage of uncounted pleasure impulses (not to mention their suffering from numerous profound apprehensions and fears), and the need to repress them is seen to open the door for indirect gratification. Many of these indirect gratifications are projected as attainable through entertainment, and the numerous mechanisms said to accomplish this (e.g., identification with another person who is being gratified) have remained the mainstay in a deluge of popular speculations about how entertainment works.

Much of what Freud proposed seems to have been uncritically and carelessly adopted and adapted to entertainment. It was accepted as gospel that provided unfailing post facto "explanations." Freud had lavishly illustrated his theorizing with examples from drama (e.g., the Oedipus complex). His mechanisms were thus linked to drama. However, Freud did not propose any formal theory of drama or drama appreciation, nor did he articulate specific, testable hypotheses that could have spawned psychological research in this area. The situation is very different for humor. Freud's (1905/1960c) treatise on that subject entailed highly specific mechanisms and, presumably because of it, produced a flurry of research on humor appreciation. Freud's publication, it seems, made the study of humor acceptable, though not entirely respectable, among psychologists. Research on drama and related entertainment forms, on the other hand, has simply remained somewhat suspect for serious and profession-conscious psychologists, despite valiant efforts toward its recognition by investigators such as Berlyne (1971, 1973).

RESEARCH APPROACHES TO ENTERTAINMENT

Whereas psychological research into the entertainment experience stagnated and really failed to get underway, communication researchers started to probe the uses and gratifications of what the mass media offered (e.g., Blumler & Katz, 1974; Katz, Gurevitch, & Haas, 1973; Palmgreen & Rayburn, 1982). Although the realization that radio and television are primarily media of entertainment was slow in coming (cf. Tannenbaum, 1980) and the acknowledgement of this fact continues to disillusion numerous irrepressible media idealists, the specifics of what is being consumed for what reason started to be investigated. The assessments were exploratory and largely nontheoretical. The technique was the interview, and the instrument was mainly the questionnaire. Media users reported their perceptions of why they consumed what they consumed, and they did so in unstructured or moderately to highly structured interviews (e.g., Blumler & Katz).

Assessments of this sort provided valuable insight into the entertainment consumers' beliefs about their motives for choosing this and that, as well as about their distaste for some material. The consumers' perceptions are not necessarily veridical, however, in the sense of reflecting correctly the actual motives that govern their entertainment choices. Consumers may be unaware of the actual determinants of their choices, and should they have reliable introspections of these determinants, they may be unable to articulate them. In addition, they may have cause to distort—in efforts at projecting a favorable image of themselves—whatever they know and can articulate. For these reasons, it would seem prudent to consider many of the survey findings concerning people's motives for consuming entertaining fare suggestive rather than conclusive. The motives projected on the basis of consumers' introspections could be treated as hypotheses that are yet to be subjected to testing that is capable of circumventing the problems and limitations associated with introspective assessments. Such testing is known, of course, as behavioral research.

In the study of communication phenomena, the behavioral approach has been successfully employed for decades by psychologists and communication researchers alike. Research has concentrated on persuasion (e.g., Rosnow & Robinson, 1967), interpersonal communication (e.g., Berscheid & Walster, 1969; Miller, 1966), nonverbal communication (e.g., Harper, Wiens, & Matarazzo, 1978; Knapp, 1978), and on the impact of asocial (e.g., Donnerstein, 1980; Geen, 1976) and prosocial messages (e.g., Rushton, 1979). Oddly enough, until recently nobody saw fit to apply the behavioral approach to the study of why people enjoy whatever they enjoy by way of entertainment. Only recently has research been published that probes the determinants of enjoyment and enlightenment in a behavioral fashion and is designed to test proposals deriving from survey research on motives as well as from motivation and emotion theory generally.

In this chapter, we attempt to provide an overview of what has been accomplished in this behavioral exploration of entertainment consumption and its immediate affective effects. The reader who is interested specifically in the perceptions of what makes consumers choose whatever they choose is referred to up-to-date reviews of the pertinent research by Atkin (1985) and Rubin (chapter 14, this volume). We briefly inspect the exploration of entertainment choices and then turn to theory and research concerning the enjoyment entertaining messages.

SELECTIVE EXPOSURE TO ENTERTAINMENT

In making entertainment choices, people can be very deliberate. A particular program might have attracted their attention, they may have decided to watch it, and they may be determined to turn to it once it becomes available. Such deliberate choices appear to be the exception, however. The choice of entertainment is usually made "on impulse." The program that holds the greatest appeal at a given time and under given circumstances, for whatever particular reasons, is likely to be picked. The factors that determine this appeal tend to be unclear to many if not most respondents. When using traditional, noninteractive media, it would be the rare exception for respondents to engage in formal and explicit evaluative comparisons of the choices before them. It is more likely that they make these choices rather "mindlessly," without using reliable and never-changing criteria in their appeal assessments and ultimately in their choices. Once the proposal is accepted that most entertainment choices are made spontaneously, rather than calculated like business deals, it can be projected that these choices are situationally variable and serve ends of which respondents need not be and probably are not aware.

Excitement Versus Relaxation as Ends

Entertaining fare can produce considerable excitement in respondents (cf. Zillmann, 1982). Such excitement manifests itself in obtrusive sympathetic dominance in the autonomic nervous system, among other things, and it produces intense affective reactions. Hedonically speaking, these reactions can be positive or negative, depending on the respondents' idiosyncratic appraisals of what transpired.

Television's capacity to produce excitement is obviously greater for persons experiencing low levels of excitation than for persons already experiencing high levels. To the extent that this capacity might influence entertainment choices, it should do so more strongly for people who suffered through a hapless day characterized by monotonous and boring chores than for people who were confronted with uncertainty, competition, and other pressures—in short, people who suffer from overstimulation and stress.

Under the assumption that levels of excitation that vary within a normal range constitute a necessary, though not sufficient, condition for an individual's feelings of well-being, it has been proposed (Zillmann & Bryant, 1985b) that entertainment from television or elsewhere might be employed to regulate excitation. Understimulated, bored persons should be eager to expose themselves to exciting television fare. Even if the material is not intrinsically pleasant, such exposure should be pleasantly experienced because it brings these persons back to levels of excitation that are more closely linked to feeling good. If the materials are intrinsically enjoyable, all the better. Thus, for understimulated, bored persons, exposure to exciting television programs can be seen as having the benefit of returning them conveniently (i.e., with minimal effort and safely) to a hedonically superior and, hence, desirable state. Put bluntly, entertainment consumers of this kind should be appreciative of each and every arousal kick that television or any other medium provides (Tannenbaum, 1980).

But entertainment not only has the capacity to excite. It can soothe and calm as well (cf. Zillmann, 1982). This capacity may benefit those who are uptight, upset, annoyed, angry, mad, or otherwise disturbed. All these experiences are associated with sympathetic hyperactivity, and those who experience such hyperactivity obviously would profit from exposure to nonexciting, relaxing entertainment fare because this exposure would lower these persons' excitation and return it to more desirable levels. Stressed persons, then, would do well to avoid exciting fare and to seek out materials capable of calming them down.

Intuitive Grounds

Television's excitation- and mood-altering effects are not in doubt. But can it be assumed that, in selecting programs for viewing, people make choices that serve excitatory homeostasis? Do people do what is good for them spontaneously and without reflection? Can it be assumed that bored persons prefer exciting materials over relaxing ones and that stressed persons display the opposite preference? It can, indeed, based on the premise that bored persons experience relief when watching exciting programs, that stressed people experience relief when watching relaxing programs, and that the experience of relief constitutes negative reinforcement that shapes initially random choice patterns into mood-specific entertainment preferences (cf. Zillmann & Bryant, 1985a).

The proposal that people form mood-specific preferences (i.e., be-have as if they had a tacit understanding of what is good for them under particular affective circumstances) has been supported by experimental research (Bryant & Zillmann, 1984). Research participants were placed into states of boredom versus stress and then, ostensibly in a waiting period, allowed to watch television as they pleased. Their choice was among three exciting and three relaxing programs. Time of program consumption was unobtrusively recorded. The data revealed that ex-citing programs attracted bored participants significantly more than stressed participants and that relaxing programs attracted stressed participants significantly more than bored participants. Effects of self-determined exposure on excitation were assessed as well, and it was found that almost all participants had chosen materials that helped them to escape effectively from undesirable excitatory states. In fact, almost all participants overcorrected, that is, bored participants ended up above base levels and stressed ones below base levels of excitation. The few bored participants that failed to behave in line with expectations elected to watch relaxing fare and, as a result, remained in a state of subnormal excitation.

Affective Relief as an End

The tacit understanding of the benefits that accrue to consuming entertainment fare is not limited to exciting and calming materials, but extends to other message characteristics. Experimental research has provided evidence that people select programs that are involving to different degrees as a function of their affective states. Choices are such that persons who would affectively benefit from distraction (i.e., rid themselves of a bad mood) tend to select highly absorbing fare. Those with less need for distraction show less appetite for this kind of material (cf. Zillmann & Bryant, 1985b). And those confronted with acute problems from which distraction through entertainment cannot offer any escape or prompt relief (e.g., anger from provocation that demands corrective action) tend to stay away from entertainment altogether, at least temporarily (Christ & Medoff, 1984).

In seeking mood changes for the better (i.e., in terminating bad moods, in switching over into good moods, or in facilitating and extending good moods), humor and comedy appear to play a special role. To those in acute need of some cheering up, merriment and laughter must be assumed to hold considerable appeal. Generally speaking, entertainment that seems capable of stimulating positive affect immediately and frequently should be the pick of those suffering from the blahs. These people should be strongly inclined to choose comedy and its kin over alternative, competing offerings.

An investigation that makes this point most compellingly has been conducted with women at different stages in the menstrual cycle (Meadowcroft & Zillmann, 1984). On the premise that the premenstrual syndrome is created mainly by the rapid withdrawal of progesterone and estrogen that afforded anesthetizing protection earlier, it was argued that premenstrual and menstrual women should suffer from bad moods, if not from feelings of depression. As a result, these women should experience the greatest need for relief through merriment and laughter. Midway through the cycle, when estrogen levels are elevated and progesterone levels rise, this need should be less pronounced, if existent at all. As there is little that premenstrual and menstrual women can do about their misery, comedy of any kind offers a most convenient way out and, consequently, should become highly attractive.

To test this proposition, women were asked to select programs they would enjoy watching. They chose from among known situation comedies, action dramas, and game shows. Their position in the cycle was ascertained afterward. On the basis of the latter information, the women were placed into 4-day phase groups throughout the cycle, thus allowing the tracing of programs chosen for consumption as a function of hormonal conditions. In confirmation of the hypothesis, it was found that premenstrual and menstrual women are indeed significantly more eager to expose themselves to comedy than are women in other phases of the cycle. At midcycle, the women exhibited comparatively little interest in comedy and showed appetite for drama instead. On gloomy days, then, comedy becomes hyperattractive. If the behavior of the premenstrual and menstrual women is any indication, all people who are down on their luck may be expected to seek, and obtain, mood lifts from comedy.

The findings concerning cycle position and comedy choice were recently extended by Helregel and Weaver (1989). These investigators addressed the variation in progesterone and estrogen during and after pregnancy and observed that low concentrations of these hormones were associated with depressive moods. More importantly, however, they observed that during these depressed mood states the women exhibited a strong preference for comedy.

But comedy is not by necessity a mood improver. Television comedy, in particular, is laden with teasing and demeaning happenings, even with considerable hostility (Zillmann, 1977). Material of this sort is unlikely to amuse persons who have recently been targets of similarly debasing actions because exposure to the material will tend to reinstate the unpleasantness and the annoyance from the treatments in question.

Acutely angry persons, for example, cannot expect favorable mood changes from comedy that dwells on hostile actions. Angry persons thus would be well advised to refrain from exposure to such comedy, though not from other forms of comedy. Experimental research again shows that people behave as if they had tacit knowledge of these effects. Provoked, angry persons were found to refrain from watching hostile comedy and turn to alternative offerings (Zillmann, Hezel, & Medoff, 1980).

Research by O'Neal and Taylor (1989) revealed an interesting exception to the indicated relief-seeking. It was found that angry men who believe they will get a chance to retaliate against their tormentor selected violent material over alternative, potentially calming choices. This was in contrast to equally angry men who believed they would not encounter their annoyer again. These men preferred calming material. It appears, then, that when the maintenance of a noxious emotion, such as anger, has utility, persons refrain from seeking relief and rather choose material likely to keep their emotion going.

Interestingly, children as young as 4 and 5 years of age are already capable of using television fare to improve their mood states. In an experiment by Masters, Ford, and Arend (1983), boys and girls of this age were placed into a nurturant, neutral, or hostile social environment and then provided with an opportunity to watch children's television programs. In the neutral condition, the participants received the same treatment from an adult supervisor as did a same-gender peer. In the nurturant or good-mood condition, the supervisor repeatedly criticized and belittled the peer; by implication the participant was doing fine. In the hostile or bad-mood condition, the supervisor continually and obtrusively admired and praised the participant's companion. Participants in this condition were thus made to feel unimportant, disliked, and rejected. Once the different affective states had been induced, the participants were allowed to watch television for as long as they pleased. They were free to shut off the monitor on which only one program could be received. This program was either nurturant or neutral. The nurturant one was composed of segments from "Mister Rogers' Neighborhood." Mr. Rogers was highly supportive at all times, making nurturant comments like "I really like you," and "You know, you are a nice person." The neutral program consisted of new shows for children that presented world events devoid of emotional content. The time the children elected to watch one or the other program served as a measure of exposure.

The effects were clear cut and as expected for boys. Boys treated in a hostile manner stayed with the nurturant program more than twice as long as boys treated in a nurturant manner. Boys in a good mood exhibited the least need for exposure to nurturant fare. In contrast, the mood treatment had no appreciable effect on exposure to the neutral program. For girls, the mood treatment had apparently failed. Girls confronted with the supervisor who treated them nonnurturantly coped with this situation by paying minimal attention to the discriminating treatment, and reliable exposure effects could not be observed.

Avoiding Discomfort

The boys in the study by Masters et al. (1983) may have found relief in the exposure experience and tried to extend that experience because it felt so good. The information that was offered in the television program was apparently comforting to those in acute need of being comforted. However, the program that proved comforting might be classified as education rather than entertainment. The question thus arises: Can pure entertainment provide comfort? Is it used to obtain comfort or, at least, to minimize and avert discomfort? The research-based answer is: Surely!

How exposure to entertaining fare can provide comfort and help avoid discomfort in adult respondents has been discussed elsewhere (e.g., Zillmann, 1982; Zillmann & Bryant, 1985a). Here we concentrate on the spontaneous selection of entertaining programs and on the tendency in this selection to choose programs that are likely to minimize discomfort through avoidance of disturbing events and, at the same time, maximize comfort through the provision of pacifying information.

An experiment conducted by Wakshlag, Vial, and Tamborini (1983) shows these selection tendencies most clearly. Male and female adults were placed in a state of apprehension about becoming victims of crime, especially violent crime, and later given an opportunity to select entertaining drama for consumption. The differently apprehensive participants chose from a list of film synopses, which had been pretested and received scores for the degree to which a film was perceived as featuring violent victimization and/or the punitive restoration of justice. Measures of the appeal of violence and justice were obtained by summing the scores across the films that were selected.

The findings revealed strong gender differences in the appeal of both violent victimization and justice restoration. Females responded less favorably to violence than did males. At the same time, they were attracted more strongly than males to justice restoration as a salient theme of drama. Irrespective of these overall gender differences, both crime-apprehensive males and crime-apprehensive females proved equally sensitive to the drama dimensions under consideration. Acutely apprehensive persons selected drama that was lower in violent victimization and higher in justice restoration than did their nonapprehensive counterparts. Apprehensive persons thus exhibited the proposed tendency to minimize exposure to disturbing events. Moreover, they exhibited the proposed tendency to expose themselves to information capable of diminishing their apprehensions. The main message of television crime drama—namely, that criminals are being caught and put away, which should make the streets safer—apparently holds great appeal for those who worry about crime (cf. Zillmann, 1980).

The reader who is interested in a more complete accounting of the research on selective exposure is referred to a recent collection of exposés on that topic (Zillmann & Bryant, 1985a). The purpose of the discussion here is only to highlight recent behavioral research into selective exposure to entertainment and to indicate the emerging choice-controlling variables.

ENJOYMENT OF ENTERTAINMENT

Quite obviously, mass media entertainment does not merely serve the regulation of arousal and associated affect or produce a contagion with merriment for persons in need of overcoming the blahs. Entertaining messages are capable of gratifying respondents because of unique intrinsic properties, along with the respondents' idiosyncratic appraisals of these properties. But what are these properties? What are the ingredients of good entertainment? And what properties spoil enjoyment?

The enjoyment of drama, comedy, and sports is influenced by a multitude of variables, many of which have received considerable attention (e.g., Goldstein, 1979; Jauss, 1982). But none seem to control enjoyment as strongly and as universally as do affective dispositions toward interacting parties, especially parties confronted with problems, conflict, and aversive conditions. The exhibition of human conflict in the raw has often been singled out as the stuff of which all good drama is made (e.g., Smiley, 1971). The focus on conflict constitutes only a starting point, however. The dramatic portrayal of intense conflict, in and of itself, does not with any degree of regularity, certainly not by necessity, lead to enjoyment reactions in the audience. Enjoyment depends not so much on conflict as on its resolution and on what the resolution means to the parties involved. It depends on how much those who come out on top are liked and loved and on how much those who come out on the short end are disliked and hated. Good drama, then, relies on positive and negative sentiments toward the parties in conflict and on the extent to which a resolution can be accepted by the audience. Indifference toward protagonists and antagonists is the antidote to good drama. Positive and negative affective dispositions toward the agents in drama are vital and must be created if drama is to evoke strong emotions, enjoyment included. There need be beloved heroes (regardless of how their definition might change over the years), and there need be villains whom the audience can love to hate.

Dispositions and Affective Reactions

The response side of what is commonly referred to as "character development" is affect. The portrayal of goodness in protagonists is to make them likable and lovable. Analogously, the portrayal of evil in antagonists is to make them dislikable and hateable. To the extent that any intended character development works, it produces positive and negative dispositions toward the agents of a play.

Character development is effective, generally speaking, because respondents bring empathy and, more important, moral considerations to the screen. What the agents in a play do matters the most. It is the basis for the audience's approval or disapproval of conduct. Such approval or disapproval is a moral verdict, of course. The fact that this is not generally recognized by respondents (and those who study their behavior) does not alter that circumstance. Approval of conduct is assumed to promote liking; disapproval is assumed to promote disliking. Affective dispositions toward protagonists and antagonists derive in large measure from moral considerations (cf. Zillmann, 1991c).

Once an audience has thus placed its sentiments pro and con particular characters, enjoyment of conflict and its resolution in drama depends on the ultimate outcome for the loved and hated parties. Positive affective dispositions inspire hopes of positive outcomes and fears of negative ones. Protagonists are deemed deserving of good fortunes and utterly undeserving of bad ones. Negative affective dispositions, on the other hand, activate the opposite inclinations: fear of positive outcomes and hopes for negative ones. Antagonists are deemed utterly undeserving of good fortunes and deserving of bad ones. Such hopes and fears are obviously mediated by moral considerations.

These hopes and fears lead respondents to empathize with the emotions displayed by protagonists. The joys as well as the suffering of liked characters tend to evoke concordant affect in the audience. Positive and negative affect is said to be "shared." In contrast, these hopes and fears prompt counterempathetic reactions to the emotions experienced by antagonists. The villains' joy is the audience's distress, and their suffering, their being brought to justice, and their getting their comeuppance is the audience's delight (cf. Zillmann, 1983, 1991a). These basic dynamics of affect in spectators are summarized in Fig. 15.1.

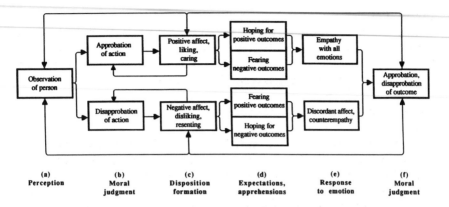

| (a) | (b) | (c) | (d) | (e) | (f) |
| Perception | Moral
judgment | Disposition
formation | Expectations,
apprehensions | Response
to emotion | Moral
judgment |

FIG. 15.1. A model of disposition formation, affective expectations, and emotional responding to benefitted and punished characters in drama (from Zillmann, 1991a; reprinted with permission).

Although these dynamics of affect have been outlined in dichotomous terms, they should not be construed as merely dichotomous. They should be thought of as a dichotomous system underneath which continuous variables exist. Liking and disliking of characters are clearly matters of degree, and the projection of consequences for the enjoyment of events and final outcomes must take this into account. In more formal terms, the following predictions can be stated (cf. Zillmann, 1980):

1. Enjoyment deriving from witnessing the debasement, failure, or defeat of a party, agent, or object increases with the intensity of negative sentiment and decreases with the intensity of positive sentiment toward these entities.
2. Enjoyment deriving from witnessing the enhancement, success, or victory of a party, agent, or object decreases with the intensity of negative sentiment and increases with the intensity of positive sentiment toward these entities.
3. Annoyance deriving from witnessing the debasement, failure, or defeat of a party, agent, or object decreases with the intensity of negative sentiment and increases with the intensity of positive sentiment toward these entities.
4. Annoyance deriving from witnessing the enhancement, success, or victory of a party, agent, or object increases with the intensity of negative sentiment and decreases with the intensity of positive sentiment toward these entities.
5. Propositions 1 through 4 apply jointly. Consequently, all contributions to enjoyment and/or annoyance combine in total enjoyment or annoyance. In this integration of contributions,

annoyance is conceived of as negative enjoyment, and contributions to enjoyment and to annoyance are assumed to combine in an additive fashion.

Predictions from this disposition model have been confirmed not only for the enjoyment of drama, but also for humor appreciation and the enjoyment of sports (Zillmann & Bryant, 1991; Zillmann, Bryant, & Sapolsky, 1979; Zillmann & Cantor, 1976). Comedy can of course be construed as a form of drama that differs from drama proper only in that cues abound that signal that things are not to be taken too seriously (McGhee, 1979). Most tendentious jokes (i.e., hostile and/or sexual ones in which somebody is victimized) can also be construed as dramatic episodes—miniaturized ones, to be sure—in which there is conflict that is resolved in favor of a deserving party and to the detriment of a victim who had it coming. Setting someone up for the punch line is nothing other than making him or her deserving of the humorous knockdown.

The dispositional mechanics of enjoyment are most obvious in sports spectatorship. Sports fans have favorite players and teams. They also have players and teams that they detest with considerable intensity. Seeing a beloved competing party humble and humiliate a resented one obviously constitutes the ultimate in sports enjoyment. And the reverse outcome is the kind of event that can make grown men cry. It is clear, in addition, that indifference toward persons or teams in a contest is the kind of condition under which excitement and intense enjoyment cannot materialize. Hirt, Zillmann, Erickson, and Kennedy (1992) provided compelling evidence for these mechanics and showed that the projected emotions transcend enjoyment or dispair proper. Enjoyment from seeing a beloved team win was found to elevate the fans' self-esteem and enhance confidence in their physical, mental, and social abilities and skills. Despair from seeing their beloved team, defeated, in contrast, deflated self-esteem and diminished confidence in their own talents. Surely, in the enjoyment of athletic events, there are many other factors that must be considered (Zillmann et al., 1979). But the dispositional mechanics seem of overriding significance in the enjoyment of dramatic confrontations of any kind.

On Thrills and Suspense

Upon cursory inspection, the enjoyment of suspenseful drama may strike one as being contradictory, even paradoxical. Such drama tends to be enjoyed despite the fact that for most of its duration the protagonist or protagonists (i.e., those dear to the audience) are seen in duress and in peril; they appear to be doomed (Zillmann, 1980, 1991c). Over considerable periods of time, the heroes are tormented and about to be overpowered and destroyed by evil forces or extraordinary dangers. Dreaded, disastrous happenings are imminent—repeatedly, frequently, and in the latest action-packed raids on the audience, almost continually. How can anybody, under these circumstances, enjoy drama? The dominant affective experience should be one of empathetic distress. Surely, such distress is relieved at times when the feared and seemingly imminent events fail to materialize and, especially in the resolution, when in the grandest of fashions and usually against all odds, the protagonists overcome the dangers that threatened them and destroy the evil forces manifesting these dangers, too. At times, of course, the resolution is less full-fledged, and the protagonists merely get away with dear life (e.g., the survivors of typical disaster movies). Contemporary horror movies tend to take that format also, as tormented ladies barely escape the chain saws, and the villains are spared for the sequel. But even in these resolutions that do not feature the annihilation of evil forces, there is cause for jubilation, and the resolution can be deemed satisfying.

Generally speaking, then, suspenseful drama exhibits much of the condition describable as "hero in peril," but it also offers a resolution that is satisfying, if only minimally so. The indicated paradox consists of the fact that such drama should evoke more empathetic distress than euphoria, at least in terms of time. It should be suffered more—or more accurately, longer—than it should be enjoyed. How can this formula work for nonmasochistic audiences?

One explanation is that the persons attracted to such drama are sufficiently understimulated and bored to appreciate any shake-up of their excitatory state (Tannenbaum, 1980; Zillmann, 1991b; Zuckerman, 1979). If arousal levels are subnormal, excitatory reactions—even those derived from distress—can help return arousal to more pleasantly experienced levels. The safety and convenience of the exposure situation make it unlikely that levels rise to uncomfortable heights. Still, the immediate affective experience associated with any arousal kicks tends to be construed as negative in valence, and this seems to favor a more elaborate explanation.

According to the alternative account, residues of excitation from empathetic distress and/or from the response to the threatening stimuli persist through resolutions and intensify the euphoric experience that is evoked by these resolutions. Because the magnitude of residual excitation is greater the more intense the distressful experience, it follows that the enjoyment of satisfying resolutions will be the more intensified the greater (and more immediate) the preceding distress reaction. The simple consequence of this is that suspenseful drama will be the more enjoyable, the more the audience is initially made to suffer, through empathy with the endangered protagonists and/or any duress induced by those dangers with which the protagonists struggled. Great enjoyment rides the back of great distress. Evidence for this relationship has been provided by numerous experimental investigations of suspenseful drama (Zillmann, 1980, 1991c).

The intensification of the enjoyment of favorable final outcomes by residual excitation from preceding uncertainty and distress should apply to the appreciation of athletic performances, too. A liked team's victory after a close, tense game should be more enjoyable than a similar victory that was decided early in the contest (Sapolsky, 1980). A recent investigation by Bryant, Rockwell, and Owens (1992) supported this contention experimentally. A high school football game was videotaped with multiple cameras, edited, and embellished with different versions of play-by-play and color commentary. Conditions were created under which viewers of the various versions of the game saw play in which the outcome was decided either early in the game or on the very last play of the game—a field goal. Enjoyment of the game was more pronounced when the outcome was decided as the clock expired.

Tragic Events and Bad News

The phenomenon that is most puzzling in the projection of enjoyment from the discussed disposition model is the apparent appeal of tragedy and news reports about disasters and the like. The persons who are witnessed suffering misfortunes and grievous occurrences are, as a rule, not resented and not considered deserving of tragic happenings. However, despite the fact that fiction often entails circumstances that make a tragic outcome more acceptable (e.g., the hero's so-called tragic flaw), it need not be assumed that the immediate affective reactions to the portrayal of tragic events are in any way positive. In all probability, these immediate reactions are negative, even intensely so. Tearjerkers are, after all, known to jerk tears, and negative affect in response to newscasts on tragic events is not in doubt (Veitch & Griffitt, 1976). This makes the fascination with seeing the victimization of parties that are neither disliked nor deemed deserving of what happens to them all the more bewildering. Granted that tragic drama is not exactly the main course of popular drama, it does enjoy a considerable following that needs to be explained. The same applies, outside fiction, to the appeal of bad news in print and broadcast journalism, which is said to be ubiquitous and growing in popularity (Haskins, 1981). Even acutely annoyed men, who would emotionally benefit from exposure to good or affectively neutral news, cannot resist the lure of bad news about misfortunes, mayhem, and disasters (Biswas, Riffe, & Zillmann, in press). What needs might be satisfied by exposure to tragic happenings? And how can such exposure be gratifying, if it is gratifying in some way?

Some have postulated that the fascination with tragic events reflects morbid curiosity (Haskins, 1981). Others have suggested that responding sadly to the sadness of suffering people affords respondents an opportunity to celebrate their own emotional sensitivity (Smith, 1759/1971). Sobbing through a tearjerker is proof to oneself that a valued social skill is abundantly present. Yet others have emphasized that exposure to tragic events invites social comparison, that respondents contrast their own situation with that of the suffering parties they witness, and that this contrasting eventually produces a form of satisfaction (Aust, 1984). Seeing misfortunes befall others and seeing them suffering from it thus may make viewers cognizant and appreciative of how good they have it. And as such positive feelings accrue to seeing tragedy strike, in reality or in fiction, tragedy becomes appealing despite the negative affect that is initially associated with it.

All these explanatory efforts remain conjecture at present. Research has failed to elucidate the response to the exhibition of tragedy in people's lives. Not only does it remain unclear why respondents are initially drawn to watching truly tragic events, but it remains particularly puzzling why exposure is sought repeatedly, as it seems likely that immediate responses were noxious and noxious experiences are generally avoided. Understanding tragedy and, in particular, the popularity of bad news thus poses a formidable challenge to entertainment research.

Audience Influences

Much of the consumption of entertaining messages occurs in particular social situations. Going to the movies is an event that usually involves friends or that happens in the context of dating (Mendelsohn, 1966). Going to see an athletic contest similarly tends to involve well-known others. Television fare is also consumed in the company of such others, but with one big difference: The television audience is limited to comparatively small numbers, in contrast to the backdrop of large audiences composed of unknown others at the movies or, especially, at athletic events.

Given these social circumstances, it should not be surprising to find that a considerable amount of speculation exists that deals with the consequences of specific social conditions for the enjoyment of the entertaining event, even with the consequences of the entertaining event for cohesion in the audience and for affective inclinations among members of that audience. Regarding the latter effect, Ovid (*Artis amatoriae*) was one of the first to propose that audience members' romantic passions might be enhanced by arousing, potentially violent, and bloody entertaining events. His intuition has actually received experimental support in recent years (e.g., White, Fishbein, & Rutstein, 1981). But many other socially relevant effects on the audience have remained unexplored, in spite of the fact that they are highly obtrusive on occasion. For instance, winning an Olympic hockey match against a powerful nation, especially when the victory comes unexpectedly, seems to have the capacity for uniting—for a limited period—a nation in some not so tangible way. In a similar vein, entire communities become high-spirited cities of champions when they have a winning team or fall into gloom if their athletic entertainers fail to defeat the out-of-towners. Effects of this kind have received little attention by researchers. Rigorous exploration is difficult and, presumably for this reason, virtually nonexistent (Schwarz, Strack, Kommer, & Wagner, 1987; Schweitzer, Zillmann, Weaver, & Luttrell, 1992).

The exploration of the effects of social conditions of consumption on the enjoyment of entertaining events has met with greater success, but is quite incomplete nonetheless. The best documented phenomenon of this kind is the facilitative influence of others' laughter on the laughter of respondents (e.g., Chapman, 1973b; Chapman & Wright, 1976; Fuller & Sheehy-Skeffington, 1974; Smyth & Fuller, 1972). Even the canned laughter that accompanies comedy and humorous situations has been found to enhance laughter in child and adult audiences; moreover, it has been found to increase enjoyment in many, though not in all, instances (e.g., Chapman, 1973a; Cupchik & Leventhal, 1974; Leventhal & Cupchik, 1975; Leventhal & Mace, 1970). Persons responding to humor appear to take the reactions of others as a cue that signals the extent to which the events before them are laughable and, ultimately, enjoyable. The facilitative effect of others' laughter on laughter and enjoyment, then, seems to derive from the informational utility of the reactions of others rather than from a mechanical contagion that produces laughter, which, through self-monitoring, eventually leads to a distorted appraisal of enjoyment. Such an interpretation is suggested by the finding that a model's laughter in response to particular stimuli tends to enhance an observer's laughter to these stimuli at a later time; that is, laughter is enhanced in the absence of the laughter of others that could function as an immediate stimulus for laughter in observers and thus serve contagion (Brown, Brown, & Ramos, 1981; Brown, Wheeler, & Cash, 1980).

Applause in response to musical performances functions analogously. As others' laughter makes humor appear funnier, others' applause makes music seem better. Hocking, Margreiter, and Hylton (1977), for instance, succeeded in planting numerous confederates into a nightclub, and members of the audience later evaluated the quality of the band and its music. This quality was deemed higher on nights when the confederates showed delight by applauding enthusiastically than on nights when they failed to do so.

Oddly enough, where the social facilitation of enjoyment is thought to be least in doubt—namely, in the cheering, quasi-hysterical crowds at athletic events—research has failed us, and we must continue to trust journalistic assertions (Hocking, 1982). Research on the effects of the social conditions under which athletic contests are watched on television has proven similarly uninformative. Audience size, for instance, could not be shown to exert an appreciable degree of influence on the enjoyment of a game (Sapolsky & Zillmann, 1978).

Audience size, in and of itself, may not have the impact that many feel it has. What people in the audience do, in contrast, seems to matter greatly. In many instances, the expression of particular emotions may well affect similar emotions in those amidst an expressive audience. The effects can be far more complicated, however, than any model of empathetic contagion and escalation would suggest.

A specific kind of influence of a companion's behavior on the enjoyment of drama has been demonstrated for horror movies. In an investigation by Zillmann, Weaver, Mundorf, and Aust (1984), participants saw terrifying events from the latest horror flicks in the presence of an opposite-gender confederate who gave ample indication of being terrified in a distress condition, gave no indication of affective responsiveness in a neutral condition, or gave clear signs of taking things with the greatest of ease in a mastery condition. Following exposure to the materials, participants reported their enjoyment.

Could their enjoyment be affected by these audience conditions and, if so, in what way? Those who believe in affective contagion might expect the terrified companion to enhance similar reactions in the participants and, because the object of horror movies is to terrify the audience, the film is deemed scarier and, hence, better and, hence, more enjoyable, at least in retrospect. It could also be conjectured that seeing horror with a terrified companion enhances enjoyment in those who enjoy being scared and/or seeing others scared and that it diminishes enjoyment in those who detest being scared and/or seeing others scared. But the findings are consistent with another model that is somewhat more elaborate, yet also more obvious.

On the premise that in our own and in most other societies young men are expected to master fear-arousing situations and, if scared, to deny such a response, whereas young women are allowed, if not encouraged, to express their distress freely, it can be argued that horror films, for better or worse, are a significant socializing institution. The horror genre provides a forum in which persons can confront terrifying happenings such as gruesome maimings and killings, and they can do so safely (i.e., without suffering bodily harm). Respondents can gauge their emotional reactions and in case these reactions should become overly intense, they can curb them by discounting the disturbing events as mere fiction. The reactions are thus always bearable, and thanks to excitatory habituation (cf. Zillmann, 1982), they should grow smaller with repeated exposure to similar stimuli.

Boys and young men apparently benefit most from such habituation. As their distress reactions diminish, they can more readily pretend not to be distressed at all. In fact, they should become proficient in denying any distress by expressing amusement or by similarly belittling the terrifying events before them. How better to exhibit mastery of terror than by waving it off with a smile? And what better companion for showing off this mastery than an apparently terrified female? The presence of such a female, compared to a less expressive one or, worst of all, one that exhibits mastery herself, should make the male feel great because (a) the movie is obviously scary, and (b) he is so cool about it that he could virtually comfort his disturbed companion. Young women, on the other hand, are not burdened with acculturation pressures toward callousness. They can live through and express their dismay. But as they do, an equally frightened male companion renders little comfort. He who effectively pretends not to be disturbed about the terrifying happenings is the one who radiates security, and a terrified female should feel inclined to seek comfort with him rather than with his more sensitive (or less callous) counterparts. The frightened maiden's desire to snuggle up on the macho companion is a cliché for horror movies. If there is any truth to it, we can see why boys want to master, why girls want to scream, and why both parties want to go to such movies in the first place. We can see the implications of entertainment consumption for falling in love. But what about enjoyment of the movies themselves? Here it may be assumed that persons do not fully comprehend what it is that gives them pleasure. They do not neatly identify the sources of their enjoyment and trace different contributions. Rather, they are likely to come to a global assessment of how much they enjoyed a particular movie. Enjoyment that derives from the social circumstances of consumption tends to go unrecognized and is usually misattributed to the entertaining message.

According to this, young men should enjoy horror more in the company of an apparently frightened female companion than in the company of an unexpressive or mastering female. Young women, on the other hand, should enjoy horror more in the company of a mastering male companion than in the company of an unexpressive or distressed male. The experimental investigation (Zillmann et al., 1984) confirmed just that very strongly.

CONCLUDING REMARK

This brief introduction to research into the entertainment experience is necessarily incomplete. The interested reader is referred to the various cited summaries of research in particular domains (i.e., the exploration of enjoyment from suspense, comedy, horror, sports, etc.). But granted incompleteness, this exposition should make the point that it is most meaningful to treat the entertainment experience as an effect. It is, in fact, *the* effect of entertainment consumption. It is the primary effect that is sought out and pursued for the benefits that it entails—benefits such as being distracted from acute grievances, having boredom removed, being cheered up, being given great excitement, being helped to calm down, or being fed pacifying messages. Surely, many media analysts might be inclined to label the attainment of these benefits *escapism*. Heavy consumption of entertainment is indeed likely to be maladaptive in the sense that problems that could be resolved by appropriate action remain unresolved and may grow to calamity levels. The consumption of much entertainment does not fit such an account, however. Consumption is often not just not maladaptive; it can be highly adaptive. This is the case when consumption serves to improve on prevailing moods, affects, and emotions, shifting them from bad to good or from good to better, under conditions in which undesirable states cannot be eliminated and altered through well-targeted action. What should an individual who comes home exhausted from a long day's work in a steel mill or, for that matter, in an executive office do about this undesirable situation? And what can a woman with premenstrual pains do about the pain-inducing conditions? If entertainment consumption manages to calm them down, cheer them up, and get them ready for the next similarly trying day, is it fair to condemn such benefit as escapism? Would it not be more reasonable to accept such effects on mood and emotional well-being as recreational success?

But regardless of how media analysts might elect to characterize the effects in question, the fact remains that much entertainment is consumed to alter moods, affects, and emotions in the specified fashion; moreover, the fact remains that the desired effects come about with considerable regularity. De facto, then, the consumption of much entertainment has beneficial consequences. It is adaptive, recreational, restorative, and in this sense, therapeutic. This is not to say that all of entertainment necessarily has these effects or that massive consumption has benefits. Quite obviously, numerous highly undesirable side-effects exist. This volume gives ample testimony to that. It is to say, however, that entertainment provided by the so-called mass media can provide highly beneficial emotional experiences that are truly recreational and that may be uplifting. These effects of entertainment, presumably because of the ready condemnation of entertainment as cheap escapism, have received very little attention from researchers. We feel that some reevaluation is in order, and we hope that the exploration of the entertainment experience with its consequences for the emotional welfare of the consumers of entertaining fare will receive the attention that it deserves.

REFERENCES

Atkin, C. (1985). Informational utility and selective exposure to entertainment media. In D. Zillmann & J. Bryant (Eds.), *Selective exposure to communication* (pp. 63–82). Hillsdale, NJ: Lawrence Erlbaum Associates.

Aust, C. F. (1984). *The effect of bad news on respondents' satisfaction with their own situation.* Unpublished master's thesis, Indiana University, Bloomington.

Berlyne, D. E. (1971). *Aesthetics and psychobiology.* New York: Appleton-Century-Crofts.

Berlyne, D. E. (1973). The vicissitudes of aplopathematic and thelematoscopic pneumatology (or The hydrography of hedonism). In D. E. Berlyne & K. B. Madsen (Eds.), *Pleasure reward preference: Their nature determinants and role in behavior* (pp. 1–33). New York: Academic.

Berscheid, E., & Walster, E. (1969). *Interpersonal attraction.* Reading, MA: Addison-Wesley.

Biswas, R., Riffe, D., & Zillmann, D. (in press). Mood influence on the appeal of bad news. *Journalism Quarterly.*

Blumler, J. G., & Katz, E. (Eds.). (1974). *The uses of mass communication: Current perspectives on gratifications research.* Beverly Hills, CA: Sage.

Brown, G. E., Brown, D., & Ramos, J. (1981). Effects of a laughing versus a nonlaughing model on humor responses in college students. *Psychological Reports 48,* 35–40.

Brown, G. E., Wheeler, K. J., & Cash, M. (1980). The effects of a laughing versus a nonlaughing model on humor responses in preschool children. *Journal of Experimental Child Psychology, 29,* 334–339.

Bryant, J., Rockwell, S. C., & Owens, J. W. (1992). *Degree of suspense and outcome resolution as factors in the enjoyment of a televised football game.* Unpublished manuscript, University of Alabama, Tuscaloosa.

Bryant, J., & Zillmann, D. (1984). Using television to alleviate boredom and stress: Selective exposure as a function of induced excitational states. *Journal of Broadcasting, 28*(1), 1–20.

Chapman, A. J. (1973a). Funniness of jokes, canned laughter and recall performance. *Sociometry, 36,* 569–578.

Chapman, A. J. (1973b). Social facilitation of laughter in children. *Journal of Experimental Social Psychology, 9,* 528–541.

Chapman, A. J., & Wright, D. S. (1976). Social enhancement of laughter: An experimental analysis of some companion variables. *Journal of Experimental Child Psychology, 21,* 201–218.

Christ, W. G., & Medoff, N. J. (1984). Affective state and selective exposure to and use of television. *Journal of Broadcasting, 28*(1), 51–63.

Cupchik, G. C., & Leventhal, H. (1974). Consistency between expressive behavior and the evaluation of humorous stimuli: The role of sex and self-observation. *Journal of Personality and Social Psychology, 30,* 429–442.

Donnerstein, E. (1980). Pornography and violence against women: Experimental studies. *Annals of the New York Academy of Sciences, 347,* 277–288.

Freud, S. (1960a). Das Unbehagen in der Kultur. In *Das Unbewusste: Schriften zur Psychoanalyse* (pp. 339–415). Frankfurt: Fischer Verlag. (Original work published 1930)

Freud, S. (1960b). Das Unbewusste. In *Das Unbewusste: Schriften zur Psychoanalyse* (pp. 1–40). Frankfurt: Fischer Verlag. (Original work published 1915)

Freud, S. (1960c). *Jokes and their relation to the unconscious.* New York: Norton. (Original work published 1905)

Freud, S. (1963a). Das Unheimliche. In *Das Unheimliche: Aufsatze zur Literatur* (pp. 45–84). Frankfurt: Fischer Doppelpunkt. (Original work published 1919)

Freud, S. (1963b). Der Dichter und das Phantasieren. In *Das Unheimliche: Aufsatze zur Literatur* (pp. 7–18). Frankfurt: Fischer Doppelpunkt. (Original work published 1908)

Fuller, R. G. C., & Sheehy-Skeffington, A. (1974). Effects of group laughter on response to humorous material: A replication and extension. *Psychological Reports, 35,* 531–534.

Geen, R. G. (1976). Observing violence in the mass media: Implications of basic research. In R. G. Geen & E. C. O'Neal (Eds.), *Perspectives on aggression* (pp. 193–234). New York: Academic.

Goldstein, J. H. (Ed.). (1979). *Sports, games, and play. Social and psychological viewpoints.* Hillsdale, NJ: Lawrence Erlbaum Associates.

Harper, R. G., Wiens, A. N., & Matarazzo, J. D. (1978). *Nonverbal communication: The state of the art.* New York: Wiley.

Haskins, J. B. (1981). The trouble with bad news. *Newspaper Research Journal, 2*(2), 3–16.

Hauser, A. (1953). *Sozialgeschichte der Kunst und Literatur* (Vols. 1 & 2). Munchen: C. H. Beck'sche Verlagsbuchhandlung.

Helregel, B. K., & Weaver, J. B. (1989). Mood-management during pregnancy through selective exposure to television. *Journal of Broadcasting & Electronic Media, 33,* 15–33.

Hirt, E. R., Zillmann, D., Erickson, G. A., & Kennedy, C. (1992). Costs and benefits of allegiance: Changes in fans' self-ascribed competencies after team victory versus defeat. *Journal of Personality and Social Psychology, 63*(5), 724–738.

Hobbes, T. (1968). *Leviathan.* Harmondsworth: Penguin. (Original work published 1651)

Hocking, J. E. (1982). Sports and spectators: Intra-audience effects. *Journal of Communication, 32*(1), 100–108.

Hocking, J. E., Margreiter, D. G., & Hylton, C. (1977). Intra-audience effects: A field text. *Human Communication Research, 3*(3), 243–249.

Jauss, H. R. (1982). *Aesthetic experience and literary hermeneutics: Vol. 3. Theory and history of literature* (M. Shaw, Trans.). Minneapolis: University of Minnesota Press.

Katz, E., Gurevitch, M., & Haas, H. (1973). On the use of the mass media for important things. *American Sociological Review, 38,* 164–181.

Knapp, M. (1978). *Nonverbal communication in human interaction.* New York: Holt, Rinehart & Winston.

Kuhn, H. (1962–1963). *Vorgeschichte der Menschheit* (Vols. 1 & 2). Koln: Verlag M. DuMont Schauberg.

Leventhal, H., & Cupchik, G. C. (1975). The informational and facilitative effects of an audience upon expression and evaluation of humorous stimuli. *Journal of Experimental Social Psychology, 11,* 363–380.

Leventhal, H., & Mace, W. (1970). The effect of laughter on evaluation of a slapstick movie. *Journal of Personality, 38,* 16–30.

Lowenthal, L. (1961). *Literature, popular culture, and society*. Englewood Cliffs, NJ: Prentice-Hall.

Malinowski, B. (1948). *Magic, science and religion*. Garden City, NY: Doubleday Anchor Books.

Masters, J. C., Ford, M. E., & Arend, R. A. (1983). Children's strategies for controlling affective responses to aversive social experience. *Motivation and Emotion, 7*, 103–116.

McGhee, P. E. (1979). *Humor: It's origin and development*. San Francisco: Freeman.

Meadowcroft, J., & Zillmann, D. (1984, August). *The influence of hormonal fluctuations on women's selection and enjoyment of television programs*. Paper presented at the meeting of the Association for Education in Journalism and Mass Communication, Gainesville, FL.

Mendelsohn, H. (1966). *Mass entertainment*. New Haven, CT: College & University Press.

Miller, G. R. (1966). *Speech communication: A behavioral approach*. Indianapolis, IN: Bobbs-Merrill.

Montaigne, M. E. de. (1927). *The essays of Montaigne* (Vols. 1 & 2) (E. J. Trechmann, Trans.). London: Oxford University Press.

O'Neal, E. C., & Taylor, S. L. (1989). Status of the provoker, opportunity to retaliate, and interest in video violence. *Aggressive Behavior, 15*, 171–180.

Ovid. (1947). *The art of love, and other poems* (J. H. Mozley, Trans.). Cambridge, MA: Harvard University Press.

Palmgreen, P., & Rayburn, J. D. (1982). Gratifications sought and media exposure: An expectancy model. *Communication Research, 9*, 561–580.

Pascal, B. (1941). *Pensées* (W. F. Trotter, Trans.). New York: The Modern Library.

Plato. (1892). Philebus. In B. Jowett (Ed. and Trans.), *The dialogues of Plato* (3rd ed., Vol. 4, pp. 519–645). New York: Macmillan.

Rosnow, R. L., & Robinson, E. J. (Eds.). (1967). *Experiments in persuasion*. New York: Academic.

Rushton, J. P. (1979). Effects of prosocial television and film material on the behavior of viewers. In L. Berkowitz (Ed.), *Advances in experimental social psychology* (Vol. 12, pp. 321–351). New York: Academic.

Sapolsky, B. S. (1980). The effect of spectator disposition and suspense on the enjoyment of sport contests. *International Journal of Sport Psychology, 11*(1), 1–10.

Sapolsky, B. S., & Zillmann, D. (1978). Enjoyment of a televised sport contest under different social conditions of viewing. *Perceptual and Motor Skills, 46*, 29–30.

Schwarz, N., Strack, F., Kommer, D., & Wagner, D. (1987). Soccer, rooms, and the quality of your life: Mood effects on judgments of satisfaction with life in general and with specific domains. *European Journal of Social Psychology, 17*, 69–79.

Schweitzer, K., Zillmann, D., Weaver, J. B., & Luttrell, E. S. (1992). Perception of threatening events in the emotional aftermath of a televised college football game. *Journal of Broadcasting and Electronic Media, 36*, 75–82.

Smiley, S. (1971). *Playwriting. The structure of action*. Englewood Cliffs, NJ: Prentice-Hall.

Smith, A. (1971). *The theory of moral sentiments*. New York: Garland. (Original work published 1759)

Smyth, M. M., & Fuller, R. G. C. (1972). Effects of group laughter on responses to humorous material. *Psychological Reports, 30*, 132–134.

Tannenbaum, P. H. (1980). An unstructured introduction to an amorphous area. In P. H. Tannenbaum (Ed.), *The entertainment functions of television* (pp. 1–12). Hillsdale, NJ: Lawrence Erlbaum Associates.

Veitch, R., & Griffitt, W. (1976). Good news-bad news: Affective and interpersonal effects. *Journal of Applied Social Psychology, 6*, 69–75.

Wakshlag, J., Vial, V., & Tamborini, R. (1983). Selecting crime drama and apprehension about crime. *Human Communication Research, 10*, 227–242.

White, G. L., Fishbein, S., & Rutstein, J. (1981). Passionate love and the misattribution of arousal. *Journal of Personality and Social Psychology, 41,* 56–62.

Zillmann, D. (1977). Humor and communication. In A. J. Chapman & H. C. Foot (Eds.), *It's a funny thing, humor* (pp. 291–301). Oxford: Pergammon.

Zillmann, D. (1980). Anatomy of suspense. In P. H. Tannenbaum (Ed.), *The entertainment functions of television* (pp. 133–163). Hillsdale, NJ: Lawrence Erlbaum Associates.

Zillmann, D. (1982). Television viewing and arousal. In D. Pearl, L. Bouthilet, & J. Lazar (Eds.), *Television and behavior: Ten years of scientific progress and implications for the eighties: Vol 2. Technical reviews* (pp. 53–67). Washington, DC: U.S. Government Printing Office.

Zillmann, D. (1991a). Empathy: Affect from bearing witness to the emotions of others. In J. Bryant & D. Zillmann (Eds.), *Responding to the screen: Reception and reaction processes* (pp. 135–167). Hillsdale, NJ: Lawrence Erlbaum Associates.

Zillmann, D. (1991b). Television viewing and physiological arousal. In J. Bryant & D. Zillmann (Eds.), *Responding to the screen: Reception and reaction processes* (pp. 103–133). Hillsdale, NJ: Lawrence Erlbaum Associates.

Zillmann, D. (1991c). The logic of suspense and mystery. In J. Bryant & D. Zillmann (Eds.), *Responding to the screen: Reception and reaction processes* (pp. 281–303). Hillsdale, NJ: Lawrence Erlbaum Associates.

Zillmann, D., & Bryant, J. (1985a). Affect, mood, and emotion as determinants of selective exposure. In D. Zillmann & J. Bryant (Eds.), *Selective exposure to communication* (pp. 157–190). Hillsdale, NJ: Lawrence Erlbaum Associates.

Zillmann, D., & Bryant, J. (Eds.). (1985b). *Selective exposure to communication.* Hillsdale, NJ: Lawrence Erlbaum Associates.

Zillmann, D., & Bryant, J. (1991). Responding to comedy: The sense and nonsense of humor. In J. Bryant & D. Zillmann (Eds.), *Responding to the screen: Reception and reaction processes* (pp. 261–279). Hillsdale, NJ: Lawrence Erlbaum Associates.

Zillmann, D., Bryant, J., & Sapolsky, B. S. (1979). The enjoyment of watching sport contests. In J. H. Goldstein (Ed.), *Sports, games, and play: Social and psychological viewpoints* (pp. 297–335). Hillsdale, NJ: Lawrence Erlbaum Associates.

Zillmann, D., & Cantor, J. R. (1976). A disposition theory of humour and mirth. In A. J. Chapman & H. C. Foot (Eds.), *Humour and laughter: Theory, research, and applications* (pp. 93–115). London: Wiley.

Zillmann, D., Hezel, R. T., & Medoff, N. J. (1980). The effect of affective states on selective exposure to televised entertainment fare. *Journal of Applied Social Psychology, 10,* 323–339.

Zillmann, D., Weaver, J., Mundorf, N., & Aust, C. F. (1984). *Companion effects on the enjoyment of horror.* Unpublished manuscript, Indiana University, Bloomington.

Zuckerman, M. (1979). *Sensation seeking: Beyond the optimal level of arousal.* Hillsdale, NJ: Lawrence Erlbaum Associates.

16

Social Aspects of New Media Technologies

FREDERICK WILLIAMS
·SHARON STROVER
AUGUST E. GRANT
The University of Texas at Austin

When we refer to *new media*, we often mean applications of microelectronics, computers, and telecommunications that either offer new services (e.g., mobile cellular telephone) or enhancements of older ones (high definition television). Indeed, many of the new media are not so new as much as they are extensions of older forms, as in cable television services, computer communication networks, or facsimile transmission (fax). As social scientists, we typically are not as concerned with technological innovations themselves as we are with how individuals, groups, or organizations change their patterns and capabilities for communication by uses of new media. Ultimately, our concern is more with the human and social impacts than the technology itself. Despite this avowed objective, those of us who do new media studies are often accused of not being sufficiently theoretical in our research. This is partly true, but in most cases there is good reason for it. New media technologies are changing so rapidly that just gaining a suitable level of description in research is sometimes a challenge; such description is a necessary precursor to moving on to levels of explanation, understanding, and prediction. On the other hand, as we are able to gain a "fix" on social aspects of new media applications, existing or modified theory can be of great advantage in generalizing about social uses and consequences. In this chapter, we illustrate this point with several different examples of theory and their applications to types and uses of new media. Theories discussed here include uses and gratifications, critical mass, and diffusion of innovations with some reference to media system dependency and social information theoretical perspectives.

USES AND GRATIFICATIONS: CABLE TELEVISION

The Basics of Uses and Gratifications

From the early 20th century when many researchers assumed media messages had uniform and direct effects on audiences, and on to the 1990s when researchers affirmed the tremendous variability in how audiences interact with the increasingly varied forms of messages, scholars have been occupied with characterizing the nature of the media interaction—the effects, the patterns of use, the process by which people make sense of messages. One of the best developed theoretical perspectives applied to studying this is the uses-and-gratifications tradition. Insofar as many newer communication technologies enhance opportunities for individuals to choose and tailor their media experiences, uses and gratifications perspectives have allowed us some insight into precisely how the "new" media differ from the "old" as far as audiences are concerned.

The uses-and-gratifications line of research espouses the idea that audience members are active in selecting and processing media content. Uses-and-gratifications approaches have in common the assumption that (a) audiences are active, (b) media use is goal directed, (c) media use fulfills a wide range of gratifications, and (d) the gratifications audiences report can be due to media content, the practice of exposure in and of itself, or the social situation in which media–audience interaction takes place (Palmgreen, Wenner, & Rosengren, 1985, p. 14). Other research traditions, including some in the "culturalist" school, make very similar assumptions and are in fact driven by latent "gratifications" or "uses" interests. Such related research on audiences is sometimes useful in that it often poses interesting variables overlooked by conventional uses-and-gratifications scholars. In Blumler and Katz's (1974) landmark collection of uses-and-gratifications, studies, a body of research addressed how audiences' media consumption patterns are related to the gratifications people report from various media. Gratifications reported by media researchers are various and encompass a range of categories, but the simplest set specifies just four *major* gratifications: Entertainment, personal relationships (companionship), personal identity, and surveillance. Later refinements of the approach acknowledge that audiences are fluid constituencies, occupying various "social positions" or roles at different times of day and in different settings. With these refinements in mind, recent uses-and-gratifications research has sought to better specify the nature of very specific audiences in order to better understand the linkage between social characteristics, context, media use, and gratifications.

General Applications to New Media

How do gratifications obtained from new media differ from those experienced via conventional media? New communications technologies generally offer users or audiences (a) more (and complex) choice in how they see or hear media content (e.g., cable television expands viewing options and possible sites for media consumption), (b) new opportunities for altering the message directly or upon replay (e.g., eliminating commercials from off-air taped television), (c) the ability to "time-shift" or reallocate time for certain media experiences, notably broadcast television and movie viewing, and (d) chances to interact with other audience members (computer conferences, telephone "chat" lines). Communication systems such as the VCR, cable television, and personal computers fundamentally expand the repertoire of media available to people, and in so doing fragment the "mass" audience into narrower viewer/user groups or cultures. The current research on cable television audiences, much of it undertaken from a uses-and-gratifications perspective, illustrates the range of social effects, and especially gratifications, one might observe with various communication technologies.

Applications to Cable Television Use

Early research on cable television focused largely on ascertaining why people subscribed to cable, and it was assumed that the answers to that question pointed to the gratifications people obtained from cable. Such studies relied exclusively on self-report measures. For example, work by Becker, Dunwoody, and Rafaell (1983); Jeffres (1978); McDermott and Medhurst (1984); Ducey, Krugman, and Eckrich (1983); Metzger (1983); and others explained subscription behavior by identifying peoples' interests in obtaining improved television reception (especially in more rural markets) and more variety in programming from cable television. These were the two leading reasons cited for subscribing. The desire for variety is sometimes associated with *specific* programming interests and hence with gratifications sought by the subscriber.

For example, some studies report that the "variety" cable subscribers are interested in obtaining amounts to an appetite for movies, sports, news, and religious programming; hence, one might infer that the gratifications associated with viewing cable television are entertainment (illustrated by interested in movies, sports), surveillance or information (illustrated by interested in news programming), and personal identity (illustrated by interested in religious programming).

Nevertheless, people express contradictory reasons for actually watching cable television. Simply put, people have different reasons at different times for doing what they do. Some of the investigations into television viewing styles and content preferences are illuminating on this point.

Zillmann and Bryant (1985), Rubin (1984), and Heeter and Baldwin (1988) examined relationships between reasons or motivations for television viewing and specific program choices. Zillmann and Bryant, for example, found that distressed individuals were most likely to watch soothing television programs lacking any jarring emotional content. Rubin distinguished between ritualized and instrumental television viewing in hypothesizing that there were two dominant styles of watching television; he positioned ritualized viewing as habitual and frequent television use in search of companionship or a way to pass time, whereas instrumental viewing is highly selective and purposeful. Building on such investigations, Heeter and Baldwin's study on cable television users reported that the additional program variety available through cable allowed certain viewing patterns to dominate. Given the program variety on cable television and, in particular, the opportunity to view certain channels that are consistently of one program type (all-music channels, all-news channels, all-weather channels, all-sports channels, etc.), cable affords ample opportunities for viewers to adopt specialized viewing patterns representing significant relationships to content types. For example, the increased presence on cable television of "browsing" low-involvement channels suggests an increase in opportunities for viewers to pass time with the television. There is ample anecdotal testimony that people use MTV much as they use radio, namely, for background music, a "ritualized" use category.

Addressing the realm of news (e.g., CNN) on cable, Heeter and Baldwin's (1988) analysis has unique implications concerning information content. They hypothesize that cable television may draw people away from news programming and toward entertainment, and that many cable users seem to be actively selective in their viewing. This is illustrated by the frequency with which they change channels during viewing sessions. To use Rubin's terms, cable television (and remote control devices) can facilitate instrumental viewing by maximizing choice and providing consistent, predictable fare on horizontally programmed channels (movie channels).

Other research on specific cable content and audiences has focused on the impacts of either news services such as CNN or music video channels such as MTV. Whereas numerous content analyses of MTV's fare have documented its range of sexual and violent music videos, studies of the news services such as CNN predictably have sought to assess the impact of cable services on presumably entrenched news viewing habits, and the social correlates of watching news. White (1988), for example, found that viewing local access services available on cable television was positively related to feelings of attachment to the community. Baldwin, Heeter, Anokwa, and Stanley (1988) found that cable subscribers paid little attention at all to networked cable news services (e.g., CNN), leading them to speculate that local news remains important even when national news alternatives are available. Such findings cannot comment on the attraction of a service like CNN on extraordinary "breaking news" occasions—CNN's coverage of the Gulf war, for example, attracted huge and dedicated audiences. It may be that cable channels function as "additions" to the normal complement of news available to subscribers from other sources, and may actually enhance attention to local news as a function of attention to *all* news.

Another category of research on cable television seeks to document the demographics of the cable subscriber compared to the nonsubscriber. That research yields a portrait of the typical cable subscriber as younger, middle class, having children, being more educated, and somewhat wealthier (Greenberg, Heeter, D'Alessio, & Sipes, 1988; Webster, 1983). In addition to offering information concerning the mesh of this technology with the social structure, such studies hint at the possibility of linking socioeconomic characteristics with viewing typologies. Although such research to date has not employed uses-and-gratifications approaches, it has led to notions about the uses to which subscribers put cable television. The attraction of additional children's programming available on cable to families with children provides an obvious example of such linkages. Current research, however, is unable to establish any stable relationship between subscriber status and particular viewing "styles." Simply interacting with one particular communication technology does not *automatically* denote marked gratifications shifts.

Finally, a discussion of cable television that neglected to note the way in which certain programming services have created national constituencies or audiences would be remiss. On a more macro level, it is clear that cable television has had broader social and cultural impacts that cannot be apprehended well by uses-and-gratifications perspectives. For example, when the Chicago-based superstation WGN attained broad distribution, Cubs fans proliferated throughout the country. "Fandom" was no longer limited to the immediate Chicago vicinity. Similarly, when a new music video ascends in popularity, fashion trends quickly incorporate the mode of dress represented in the video. So-called Madonna "wanna-bes" are a product of the interaction between audiences and specific programming fare, abetted by a willing fashion industry. This is an aspect of cable television's ability to narrowcast to highly targeted audiences that uses-and-gratifications researchers such as Lull (1985) are only beginning to recognize and investigate.

As media systems such as cable TV or personal computers create new, nongeographically based communities, the uses-and-gratifications approach can be helpful in exploring the relationship between technologies and people and in identifying how people negotiate their identity, their social position, and their emotional lives in an increasingly technologically mediated world.

CRITICAL MASS: ELECTRONIC MAIL AND MASS MEDIA

Meaning of "Critical Mass"

In studying new media technologies it is important to recognize that just as the technologies may have social impacts, a variety of social factors impact the diffusion and subsequent effects of these technologies. One factor of interest in current studies of new media is the concept of "critical mass." For physicists, a critical mass is the amount of radioactive material necessary to sustain a chain reaction. The term has been adopted by social scientists to refer to the number of individuals who must be involved in a social movement before it may "explode" into being (Oliver, Marwell, & Teixeira, 1985). Adoption of a new media technology is one such social phenomenon that offers an excellent example of the critical mass process. At a certain point, adoption of the technology begins to "take off" dramatically.

In examining this phenomenon, Markus (1987) developed a set of propositions relating to the critical mass for *interactive* communication technologies. First, she indicated that, within a community, adoption of a technology such as the telephone or electronic mail is an "all or nothing" proposition. If a critical mass is achieved, all individuals in the community will eventually adopt the technology. But, if the critical mass is not achieved, usage will drop because of the lack of reciprocity, and eventually no one will use the technology.

Other propositions relate to the resources of the individual and the community. Markus indicated that the fewer resources, that is, time, money, or skills, an individual is required to engage in using a technology, the greater the likelihood of achieving the critical mass leading to universal access. In discussing the distribution of resources throughout a community, she also indicated that greater heterogeneity of resources within a community, as well as early adoption by "high resource" individuals, will increase the likelihood of achieving a critical mass.

Application to E-Mail and Facsimile

In applying this concept of the critical mass to electronic mail, Rice, Grant, Schmitz, and Torobin (1990) oserved the relationship between an organization's communication network and the manner in which electronic mail was used by employees of the organization. After surveying all employees of the organization regarding the frequency of communication with each other member of the organization, network analysis was used to determine the underlying communication structure of the organization. Simple inspection of the patterns of adoption within these groups provides a clear indication of the process discussed by Markus (1987). The analysis indicated three distinct subgroups among the 36 employees included in the study. Within two of the three subgroups, all but two individuals were users of the electronic mail system, whereas no one in the third group adopted the technology. This analysis also reported a significant individual-level critical mass effect in which the combined adoption pattern of each person's communication partners, weighted by the frequency of communication, proved to be a significant predictor of whether an individual adopted the technology.

One of the best examples of the workings of critical mass in the new, interactive communication technologies is the facsimile or "fax" machine. The first facsimile machines were developed in the mid-1800s and were used for a century for transmitting pictures and maps over telephone lines. In the 1960s, standards were developed to ensure that machines made by different manufacturers could communicate with each other. But the technology did not become popular as a means of interorganizational communication until the mid 1980s, when enough organizations had adopted the technology. Suddenly, it seemed as if "everyone else" had a fax machine available. The interactive critical mass point had been reached and the technology was well on its way to universal adoption within business organizations. As the diffusion curve of the fax machine within the business community levels off, adoption of fax machines for residential use is beginning. The large number of fax machines already in use by businesses will contribute to the critical mass for residential fax machine use. An application of Markus' (1987) theory of critical mass suggests that fax machines may one day be as common as telephones in our homes. One social impact of this type of adoption suggests an important corollary of this critical mass theory, namely that people may be forced to adopt a communication technology, with all the benefits and drawbacks that go along with it, simply to maintain their current communication networks.

Application to Mass Media

The preceding discussion dealt exclusively with the critical mass for interactive communications technologies. For mass communication technologies, there are two different sets of critical mass concerns, relating first to the provision of the technology and second to the actual adoption of the technology. Grant (1990) explored a critical mass of organizational functions that must be served before an individual can adopt a mass communication technology. His analysis indicates that, before the first consumer adoption of a new mass medium such as HDTV can take place, a number of organizational functions must be provided. Production hardware use to develop the messages (software) must be manufactured and distributed. Software must then be manufactured and distributed, usually through a system that includes a sequence of national and local distribution. The reception hardware must also be manufactured and distribution, again through both national and local channels of distribution. Finally, after each of these functions is served, consumer adoption may begin. Grant's discussion indicates that technical standards, vertical integration, and compatibility with existing technologies are factors that aid in the achievement of this critical mass, termed the *diffusion threshold*.

The videocassette recorder (VCR) provides an excellent example of how the diffusion threshold works. Before the first consumer VCR purchase could be made, technical standards had to be developed and someone had to manufacture the VCRs. Then, these VCRs had to be distributed nationally (through wholesale operations) and locally (through retail stores). Because the first VCRs were manufactured by the same companies making television receivers, these companies could rely on their current national and local distribution systems to make the machines available to consumers. Early consumer VCR purchase was also dependent on the availability of software. Because VCRs could be used to "time-shift" (record programs off the air), software was already available and distributed nationally through television networks and locally through local television stations. Thus, because VCRs were compatible with the existing television distribution system, the "diffusion threshold" was reached more quickly. Once a large number of VCRs had been sold to consumers, a new software manufacturing and distribution system to produce prerecorded tapes was economically practical and video stores began appearing throughout the country.

Compared to most other mass media, initial adoption of the VCR was a relatively simple process. With many mass media, once the "diffusion threshold" is achieved, adoption of a mass media technology is still not guaranteed. In a capitalist society such as the United States, the fact that most mass media are advertiser supported provides a further barrier to the diffusion of a new mass medium. Because there are so many media channels for the dissemination of advertising messages, a new medium is at an extreme disadvantage. The medium must prove that it has an audience before earning substantial advertiser support, but, without income, the programming provided by the new medium is likely to be inferior to that provided by existing media. Although this relationship may, at first glance, appear to be a "chicken-and-egg" question, the answer is as simple as it is costly. A new mass medium must have the financial support to produce programming to attract an audience, and then the advertising dollars follow. The attainment of a large enough audience to sustain the medium through advertising revenues may be considered yet another element of critical mass.

The challenge of attaining this type of critical mass is complicated by the continuing proliferation of mass media channels. Neuman and Pool (1986) indicated that as the number of media channels and media messages increases, audience resistance to new media increases proportionately. Although they indicate that total media message consumption has increased moderately, the increase in the number of media messages targeted at each individual has increased much more dramatically. Rather than divide their time equally among the abundant media options, individuals are more likely to concentrate their efforts on the media outlets with which they have developed a relationship. The attainment of a critical mass for a new advertiser supported mass medium is therefore an extremely difficult proposition.

One example of this process is the adoption of FM radio. FM broadcasting was approved by the FCC in 1942 (with stereo broadcasting approved in 1961). However, for the next 30 years, the majority of the radio audience ignored this channel, even though it provided far superior sound quality to AM radio. But, as time passed, more and more people began listening to FM radio, and, eventually, advertisers began pumping money into FM radio stations and programmers started programming their FM stations to compete with the most popular AM radio stations. By 1979, FM audience share overtook AM radio's share and, today, FM radio stations garner the majority of the radio audience and radio advertising dollars (Smith, 1985).

DIFFUSION OF INNOVATIONS: TELEPHONE SERVICES

Overview of the Theory

Diffusion of innovations has long been a general theory of how new ideas or technologies are communicated, evaluated, adopted (or not), and reevaluated. The major source of information on this topic has been in the work of Everett Rogers and his colleagues (cf. Rogers, 1983, for an overview). The theory has been applied to everything from agricultural methods, to family planning, to adoption of personal computers. Moreover, Rogers and others (e.g., Williams, Rice, & Rogers, 1986, chapter 5) have devoted attention to its applications regarding adoption of new media.

Basically, the theory holds that the diffusion of innovations is a process through which ideas are communicated through various channels, over time, among people who belong to a given social system. Whereas uses-and-gratifications theory focuses mainly on how certain social and psychological needs may be fulfilled by media uses, diffusion theory encompasses a focus on communication channels, stages of awareness and decision making, criteria for decisions, characteristics of potential adopters, likely advantages of the adoption, complexity of what is being adopted, costs (relative and monetary), and who, if anyone, is promoting the adoption. Often "time" and "percent of adoption" are important outcome considerations as illustrated in the typical adoption curve shown in Fig. 16.1.

Some of the more process-oriented aspects of diffusion study include the differentiation of people by personality type, experiences, and education (to name a few characteristics) who may be characterized as "early adopters" as against slow adopters. Communication channels that carry the new information are often contrasted as public and mass oriented as against interpersonal. Studies have often revealed that public communication may often be the vehicle for communicating information that leads to the awareness of ideas, whereas interpersonal communication may be more crucial in the person's decision making. The diffusion process may be summarized in the following steps (with a focus on new media studies):

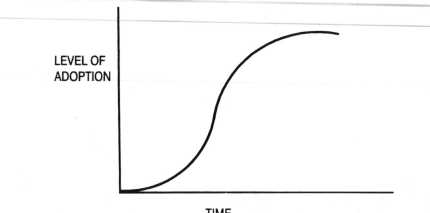

LEVEL OF
ADOPTION

TIME

FIG. 16.1. Classic diffusion curve.

1. *Knowledge.* The individual or group gains an awareness of something new, such as new computer software, cellular telephone service, or a personal computer in the home. However, the potential adopter has not yet formed an opinion about whether that idea would be valuable.

2. *Persuasion.* In this step the potential adopter makes attitudinal evaluations of the idea. Will the new E-mail system benefit this office? Will my family enjoy a compact disc machine? Can I use fax to advantage? These are not only evaluative opinions about the ideas, but also are personally associated with the individual or group. They form the necessary basis for whether the innovation is to be adopted.

3. *Decision.* This is the point at which the innovation is either adopted or rejected; the new idea is tried or avoided. Communication in the diffusion process typically propels the adopter toward a decision, so that the individual has to take action even if it is rejected. Communication does not stop after the decision is made, because the individual may continue to react and reevaluate the decision.

4. *Confirmation.* Further communication is used to evaluate the decision that was made and the consequences of the decision. Were the benefits of a new office computer network actually realized? Is office productivity improved? Am I less competitive because I did not make the adoption? In this last instance, there may be pressure to reverse a formerly negative decision.

Adoption of new media technologies has been of late a burgeoning subject for diffusion research. The practical question has been whether traditional models of the diffusion process apply to new media, for example, as in the adoption of VCRs, personal computers, facsimile machines, cellular telephones, and the like. A more theoretical question concerns whether the process itself may have some special social or psychological implications because of the nature of many new media. One example of this concern reflects the interactive quality of many new media (electronic mail, new telecommunications services) and even some older ones (e.g., the telephone). Adoption of the telephone, for example, was motivated not just by its availability to a single user, but also by how many other users could potentially be contacted on the network. (Having a telephone is hardly valuable if there is no one to call!) As we saw earlier in this chapter, the idea of "critical mass" has become important in theorizing about the adoption of new media, at least those media where a growing universe of users is involved.

There are also many other factors potentially relevant to the adoption of new media technologies and services. Next we explore examples reflecting telephone services (one category of innovation) and then ask ourselves how beneficial the theory of diffusion of innovations is for this topic.

Modified or Enhanced Telephone Services

The following example of the adoption of telephone services was a problem area that benefitted by interpretation relative to the theory of diffusion of innovations (drawn in part from Williams, Sawhney, & Brackenridge, 1990, and briefly reviewed in Williams, 1991). Over the years telephone companies (we will use United States examples here) have steadily sought to improve basic telephone services and, particularly since the divestiture of American Telephone and Telegraph in 1984, to introduce new services that would yield additional revenues. Typically in the business, "POTS" refers to the level of "plain old telephone service," and all enhancements build on this. An overview of such modifications and enhancements is given in Table 16.1.

The mostly "basic" service modifications, like getting private lines or "emergency" service like 911 calling, are not mainly an individual or group adopter phenomenon. Instead, they have been brought about more by the regulatory forces in telephony when public utility commissions, together with cooperating telephone companies, decide that services enhancements are worth the public investment. These are a part of so-called universal service, to which everyone is entitled. Still, however, a customer may have the option of deciding whether to stay on a party line, or pay a few more dollars for a private one. This, then, is more or less an "adoption" issue. The availability of "custom calling" and the newer "enhanced" services were initially a function of telephone switching technology. The coming of electronic switches in the 1960s

TABLE 16.1
Types of Enhanced Telephone Services

Variations on Basic Services

Private Line Service: Avoiding multiple customers sharing a single line ("party line").
Extra Lines: Adds more than one calling number for a residence; handy for children's phone use, special business, or fax line.
Alternative Long Distance: Gives you the choice of "1+" dialing access to the long-distance company of your choice.
Extended Area Service: Local calls can be made over a wider area than heretofore without paying toll charges.
Tone Dialing: Where dialing is by tones communicated to the switch rather than electronic pulses; allows for certain additional services.

Emergency Service

911 Emergency Calling: Rapid dial to access emergency services; in some area, address will automatically be displayed for service provider.

Custom Calling Services

Call Forwarding: Allows for transfer of incoming calls to any telephone that could be direct dialed without operator assistance.
Call Waiting: While you are talking, a special tone tells you another party is dialing in; you can put the first party on hold in order to answer the new call.
Three-Party Calling: Allows you to add third party to an existing conversation without operator assistance.
Speed Calling: Allows you to call frequently used numbers by dialing only one or two digits; often in groups of eight to 30 numbers.

Enhanced ("Class") Services

Caller ID: Allows you to see the number of an incoming call on a display unit.
Repeat Call: Automatically redials the last number you dialed.
Call Block: Allows you to block certain numbers from which you do not wish to receive calls.
Return Call: Automatically redials the last call you received whether you answered it or not.
Priority Call: Specifies certain important numbers to provide a distinctive ring.
Select Forward: Allows forwarding of multiple phone numbers to a new location.
Call Trace: Provides the telephone company with the number of the last call you received.

Additional Services

Fax at home
Linking computer with modem
Using a videotex service
Acquiring cellular mobile

made tone dialing and custom calling features available (e.g., call waiting) as an optional service, and digital switches support the newer enhanced services likes "caller identification." These are all optional services; that is, they require individual purchase and extra payment beyond basic service.

Typically in the telephone business before 1984, new services were introduced with a minimum of fanfare. The business was heavily regulated, meaning the Federal Communications Commission and state utility commissions controlled profits, so the motivation for aggressive marketing campaigns was limited. New services were announced as "trials," sometimes modestly advertised, and the public was left to adopt or reject. If customers picked up on the services, the services were retained; if not, they were dropped or their introduction elsewhere postponed. There was not much interest in the process of diffusion or the adoption behaviors of customers.

This pattern began to change after the intentional introduction of competition into the telephone business, a phenomenon that was growing in the 1970s with the introduction of competing long-distance services, and was unleashed as policy with the breakup of AT&T in 1984. This policy shift was initiated in part to encourage introduction of new services into the telephone business; some of these services would eventually become unregulated, meaning that they could become new profit centers for telephone companies.

Examining Customer Attitudes and Behavior

The move from regulation to competition in the telephone business has brought a much expanded interest in customer attitudes and behavior, and for this purpose some social theory has been useful. As introductions of new services move from being "take it or leave it" trials to marketing campaigns, it becomes important to understand the behaviors of potential adopters. One theory useful in this regard is uses and gratifications such as discussed earlier relative to cable television customers. Although there has been some progress in assessing gratifications associated with telephone use (see Pool, 1977, 1983; some studies reviewed in Williams, 1991), our focus for the present illustration will be on diffusion of innovations. The examples are drawn from several unpublished proprietary studies as well as a more recent study of rural Ohio telephone customers (Williams, Sawhney, & Brackenridge, 1990).

In the latter study, conducted in the summer of 1990, the United Telephone Company of Ohio was interested in rural customer attitudes and behaviors regarding residential services. First, it was clear that most of the residential customers in the study fell into one of three categories relative to service adoption. Briefly, these were as follows:

- POTS Residential. These are customers with no immediate need or interest in anything other than maintaining basic telephone service and costs at their present level.

- POTS-Plus Residential. These customers have typically purchased some extra or custom services related to family use, such as an extra line for children, or call waiting.
- Residential Doing Business. These customers bought extra lines for services because they were doing part or full-time business from their home.

Second, we can examine diffusion steps relative to these customer differences; for example:

1. *Knowledge.* The POTS residential customer had little interest in, or knowledge of, additional or enhanced services. An exception might be awareness of a discount long-distance service often offered to the customer via a telephone sales pitch, but promptly rejected. The POTS-Plus customer, may have a passive awareness of new services, having seen advertisements or read descriptions enclosed with their monthly phone bill. But he or she is not actively seeking this knowledge unless there is an immediate, pressing problem to be solved. By contrast, the Residential Doing Business customers are the most active knowledge seekers, presumably because they cannot be effective in doing their business without them.

2. *Persuasion.* The POTS Residential customer has already often built defenses against persuasion regarding new services, whereas the POTS-Plus customer might be alerted to a possible purchase if the connection is made with some existing problem (teenagers tying up the sole phone line, for example). Residential Doing Business customers seem more open to persuasion, because they are information seekers for anything that will benefit their occupation. They may be interested in a wide range of details, along with suggestions of business or personal productivity improvement.

3. *Decision.* The position to reject new services is mainly reinforced in the POTS customer when there is any attempt at persuasion. (Interviews with such customers often turn up anecdotes of rude telemarketers, or "hang up" reactions, all mostly negative.) As mentioned, POTS-Plus customers may be easily on the verge of a decision if they see a solution to a pressing problem. However, these customers may review their needs when moving into a new dwelling; enhanced phone services can "fit" into a wide range of new purchase decisions—for example, along with a new television set and cable service. Enhanced service decisions by the Residential Doing Business customer is like his or her other business decisions; if not solving a problem, they look for new cost-benefits, productivity, business opportunities, and the like.

4. Confirmation. Only Residential Doing Business customers seem interested in further communication regarding decisions they have made. They may seek reaffirmation of their business decision as a part of seeking new alternatives. On the other hand, POTS and POTS-Plus customers have no or little interest, respectively, in further communication or activity regarding the decisions they have made to adopt or reject.

Although the foregoing type of study surely offers no earth-shattering insights, it does serve several ends. First, from a theoretical standpoint, the growing innovations in telephone services, coupled with the move to competitive marketing in this business, provide a current context for reaffirming the utility of applying the diffusion of innovations paradigm. Second, the types of generalizations given above, if examined in more detail, form an excellent basis for planning differentiated marketing strategies for categories of residential customers.

FURTHER THEORETICAL VIEWS

Expanding the Level of Analysis

Although the foregoing sections illustrate how social scientific theories can usefully be applied in the study of new media, it is important to consider broader perspectives than "one theory-one medium" examples. Like the "critical mass" phenomenon discussed earlier, there are further, expanded levels of analysis to be considered. For example, we can consider at least two sets of structural variables in new media study and theory. The first concerns the network of relations among potential adopters and/or users to ascertain social information factors, adoption patterns, and boundaries of adopting communities. The second set of structural variables includes the external environment, including competition, general economic factors, interorganizational relations, regulatory factors, and policy factors, to name a few.

Additionally, the preceding discussion of critical mass factors illustrates that analyses of new media technologies can take place at multiple levels, from individual and group to organizational and system levels. Just as there are reciprocal impacts between a technology and society, factors at each level affect and are affected by each other level. In searching for a body of theory to apply to the study of new media technologies, some importance may be placed on a theoretical framework that operates at multiple levels of analysis. We close with two examples.

Media System Dependency Theory

One such theoretical framework is Media System Dependency Theory (Ball-Rokeach, 1985, 1988). This theory suggests that in order to understand media-related phenomena, it is important to analyze dependency relationships within and across levels of analysis. The theory states that the power of media is a function of the dependencies of individuals, groups, organizations, and systems on the scarce information resources controlled by the media. Thus, media content (and any related media effects) is a product of a variety of dependency relationships operating at multiple levels of analysis.

A good example of how these dependencies interact may be found in an analysis of the television system in the United States. To understand how television might be adopted by or have an effect on a specific individual, it is important to note that the medium is dependent on advertisers for revenue, the government for the right to broadcast, and the individual viewer for continuing to use the medium and provide a "product" for sale to advertisers. In turn, advertisers, the government, and individual viewers are each dependent on television in one form or another. Media system dependency theory states that because all of these dependency relationships affect each other, an analysis of the role of a medium in society should examine these dependency relationships across levels of analysis.

The theory explicitly addresses the relationship individuals have with the media (Ball-Rokeach, 1988; Ball-Rokeach, Rokeach, & Grube, 1984), indicating that, over time, individuals develop a dependency relationship with a medium to fulfill specific goals of play, orientation, and understanding. Although an individual's dependence on a specific medium is expected to be comparatively stable over time, Ball-Rokeach (1985) indicated that, in times of ambiguity or threat, dependency on mass media increases as individuals seek additional information to help them in their daily lives.

Media system dependency theory is one of many theories that provides insight into the complexity of new media technologies. By integrating this theory with others, such as the diffusion of innovations, social information processing, uses-and-gratifications notions, and critical mass theories, a more accurate picture of new media technologies may be possible than by simply using a single theory.

Social Information Processing Theory

How people choose among competing media introduces the subjectivity inherent in the evaluation of new media technologies. One especially illuminating perspective in this regard is the "Social Information Processing Model of Media Use" proposed by Fulk, Steinfield, Schmitz, and Power (1987). This model premises that, rather than engage in an objectivity rational process in which new media are evaluated based on their characteristics, individuals engage in a process in which the evaluations of others (social information) is crucial in choosing among competing media.

As applied by Fulk et al., the social information perspective suggests that the attitudes, statements, and behaviors of others are more important in media choice and evaluation than the inherent attributes recognized by the users. Fulk et al. indicated that the media choice process remains a rational one, but stated that the rationality is influenced by past statements and behavior as well as social norms rather than by a matching of media attributes with task requirements.

In their assessment of electronic mail, Rice et al. (1990) found moderate support for the role of social information processing variables in predicting the adoption, usage, and evaluations of the system. Schmitz and Fulk (1991) provided similar evidence for the role of social information in the evaluation of electronic messaging.

The above discussion of social information and critical mass provides some important directions for the study and understanding of new media technologies. First, and most important, it suggests the interaction between the technologies and the social environment. Just as the technologies may have social impacts, societal factors, in turn, impact the manner in which new technologies are adopted, used, and evaluated. Analysis of these technologies is further complicated by the fact that evaluations of these technologies are based on subjective social information. It is not enough to understand the features of a communication technology; the perception of those features (and the wide variety of factors influencing those perceptions) must be understood as well.

REFERENCES

Baldwin, R., Heeter, C., Anokwa, K., & Stanley, C. (1988). News viewing elaborated. In C. Heeter & B. Greenberg (Eds.), *Cableviewing* (pp. 179–190). Norwood, NJ: Ablex.

Ball-Rokeach, S. J. (1985). The origins of individual media system dependency: A sociological perspective. *Communication Research 12*(4), 485–510.

Ball-Rokeach, S. J. (1988). Media system dependency theory. In M. L. DeFleur & S. J. Ball Rokeach (Eds.), *Theories of mass communication* (pp. 297-327). New York: Longman.

Ball-Rokeach, S. J., Rokeach, M., & Grube, J. W. (1984). *The great American values test: Influencing behavior and belief through television.* New York: Free Press.

Becker, L., Dunwoody, S., & Rafaell, S. (1983). Cable's impact on use of other news media. *Journal of Broadcasting, 27,* 127-142.

Blumler, J., & Katz, E. (1974). *The uses of mass communications.* Beverly Hills, CA: Sage.

Ducey, R., Krugman, D., & Eckrich, D. (1983). Predicting market segments in the cable industry: The basic and pay subscribers. *Journal of Broadcasting, 27,* 155-161.

Fulk, J., Steinfield, C. W., Schmitz, J., & Power, J. G. (1987). A social information processing model of media use in organizations. *Communication Research, 14*(5), 529-552.

Grant, A. E. (1990, March). *The "pre-diffusion" of HDTV: Organizational factors and the diffusion threshold.* Paper presented to the annual convention of the Broadcast Education Association, Atlanta, GA.

Greenberg, B., Heeter, C., D'Alessio, D., & Sipes, S. (1988). Cable and noncable viewing style comparisons. In C. Heeter & B. Greenberg (Eds.), *Cableviewing* (pp. 207-225). Norwood, NJ: Ablex.

Heeter, C., & Baldwin, T. (1988). Channel types and viewing styles. In C. Heeter & B. Greenberg (Eds.), *Cableviewing* (pp. 167-176). Norwood, NJ: Ablex.

Jeffres, L. (1978). Cable TV and viewer selectivity. *Journal of Broadcasting, 22,* 176-177.

Lull, J. (1985). The naturalistic study of media use and youth culture. In K. Rosengren, L. Wenner, & P. Palmgreen (Eds.), *Media gratifications research: Current perspectives* (pp. 209-224). Beverly Hills, CA: Sage.

Markus, M. L. (1987). Toward a "critical mass" theory of interactive media: Universal access, interdependence and diffusion. *Communication Research, 14*(5), 491-511.

McDermott, S., & Medhurst, M. (1984, May). *Reasons for subscribing to cable television.* Paper presented to the International Communication Association conference, San Francisco.

Metzger, G. D. (1983). Cable television audiences: Learning from the past and the present. *Journal of Advertising Research, 23*(4), 41-47.

Neuman, W. R., & de Sola Pool, I. (1986). The flow of communications into the home. In S. J. Ball Rokeach & M. G. Cantor (Eds.), *Media, audience, and social structure* (pp. 71-86). Newbury Park, CA: Sage.

Oliver, P., Marwell, G., & Teixeira, R. (1985). A theory of critical mass: I. Interdependence, group heterogeneity, and the production of collective action. *American Journal of Sociology, 91*(3), 522-556.

Palmgreen, P., Wenner, L., & Rosengren, K. E. (1985). Uses and gratifications research: The past ten years. In K. Rosengren, L. Wenner, & P. Palmgreen (Eds.), *Media gratifications research: Current perspectives* (pp. 11-37). Beverly Hills, CA: Sage.

Pool, I. de Sola. (1977). *The social impact of the telephone.* Cambridge, MA: MIT Press.

Pool, I. de Sola. (1983). *Technologies of freedom.* Cambridge, MA: Belknap Press.

Rice, R. E., Grant, A. E., Schmitz, J., & Torobin, J. (1990). Individual and network influences on the adoption and perceived outcomes of electronic messaging. *Social Networks, 12,* 27-55.

Rogers, E. M. (1983). *Diffusion of innovations.* New York: Free Press.

Rubin, A. (1984). Ritualized and instrumental uses of television. *Journal of Communication, 34*(3), 67-77.

Schmitz, J., & Fulk, J. (1991). The role of organizational colleagues in media selection. *Communication Research, 18,* 487-523.

Smith, F. L. (1985). *Perspectives on radio and television: Telecommunication in the United States.* New York: Harper and Row.

Webster, J. (1983). The impact of cable and pay television on local station audiences. Report for the National Association of Broadcasters.

White, C. (1988). *Eye on the sparrow*. Unpublished doctoral dissertation, The University of Texas at Austin.

Williams, F. (1991). *The new telecommunications*. New York: Free Press.

Williams, F., Rice, R. E., & Rogers, E. M. (1986). *Research methods and the new media*. New York: Free Press.

Williams, F., Sawhney, H., & Brackenridge, E. (1990). *Rural telecommunications and development: A study of customer needs and applications at selected Ohio sites* (a study for the United Telephone Company of Ohio). Austin, TX: The University of Texas at Austin, Center for Research on Communication Technology and Society.

Zillmann, D., & Bryant, J. (1985). Pornography, sexual callousness and the trivilization of rape. *Journal of Communication, 34*(4), 10–21.

Author Index

A

Aaker, D. A., 327, 345, *357*
Abel, G. G., 259, *268*
Abelman, R., 250, 169, 427, 432
Abramson, P. R., 251, 256, *268*
Adams, S. M., 262, *270*
Adams, W. C., 134, *156*
Adhikarya, R., 283, 285, *385*
Adoni, H., 76, *86*, 425, 432
Advertising Research Foundation, 323, 355, *357*
Agahi, E., 203, *208*
Agres, S. J., 337, *357*
Aidman, A. J., 247, *271–272*
Aitken, P. P., 392, *410*
Ajzen, I., 114, *117–118*, 136, *157*, 357, *357*, 370, *385*
Alba, J. W., 106, 109, *117*
Albert, E., 401, *410*
Alcalay, R., 372, 377, 380, *385*
Alexander, A., 20, 24, 40, 426, *432–433*
Alexander, H. M., 392, *413*
Alexander, J., 405, *411*
Alfert, E., 227, 242

Alioto, J. T., 51, 54, *58*, 170, *204*
Allen, S. G., 134, 139–140, 147, 149, 151, *160*
Alpert, M. I., 330, *362*
Altheide, D. L., 133, *156*
Amor, D. L., 143, 147, 149, *156*, *159–160*
Anderson, C. A., 48, 50, 53, *58*
Anderson, D., 339–340, *358*
Anderson, J., 45, *58*
Anderson, J. A., 423, *432*
Anderson, K., 406, *415*
Anderson, R. L., 251q, 266, *270*
Andison, F., 44, *58*
Angelino, H., 230, *240*
Anning, N., 250, *269*
Anokawa, K., 467, *480*
Appel, V., 341, *363*
Arend, R. A., 445–446, *460*
Arkin, E. B., 404, *410*
Armstrong, C. B., 423, 429, 431, *432*
Armstrong, G. B., 302, *309*
Arterton, F. C., 139, *156*
Asp, K., 11–12, *15*
Asuncion, A. G., 109, *119*

483

Zaltman, G., 83, *90*
Zanna, M. P., 253, *271*
Zielske, H. A., 347–348, *363*
Ziemke, D., 224, 229, *241*
Ziemke, D. A., 143, *160*
Zill, N., 217, *245*
Zillmann, D., 71, *90*, 168, 187, 200,
  210–211, 215, 220–221, 223–229, *241*,
  243–245, 253–254, 259–260, 262–263,

266–267, 272, 326, 335, *363*, 399, *415*,
  424, 432, 441–457, *458–461*, 466, *482*
Zimbardo, P. G., 74, *90*
Zimmer, M. A., 350, *360*
Zimmerman, B. J., 66, 70, *89*
Zoglin, R., 215, *245*
Zucker, H. GF., 8, *16*
Zuckerman, D., 298–299, *314*
Zuckerman, M., 451, *461*

Subject Index